OBJECTIVE	CHAPTER
3.5 Configure files that are used to mount drives or partitions (e.g., fstab, mtab, SAMBA, nfs, syntax)	4
3.6 Implement DNS and describe how it works (e.g., edit /etc/hosts, edit /etc/host.conf, edit /etc/resolv.conf, nslookup, dig, host, named)	6
3.7 Configure a Network Interface Card (NIC) from ?	6
3.8 Configure Linux printing (e.g., CUPS, BSD LPD,	9
3.9 Apply basic printer permissions	9
3.10 Configure log files (e.g., syslog, remote logfile ?	8
3.11 Configure the X Window system	1
3.12 Set up environment variables (e.g., $PATH, $DISPLAY, $TERM, $PROMPT, $PS1)	2

Domain 4.0 Security

4.1 Configure security environment files (e.g., hosts.allow, sudoers, ftpusers, sshd_config)	3
4.2 Delete accounts while maintaining data stored in that user's home directory	3
4.3 Given security requirements, implement appropriate encryption configuration (e.g., blowfish 3DES, MD5)	3
4.4 Detect symptoms that indicate a machine's security has been compromised (e.g., review logfiles for irregularities or intrusion attempts)	7
4.5 Use appropriate access level for login (e.g., root level vs user level activities, su, sudo)	3
4.6 Set process and special permissions (e.g., SUID, GUID)	5
4.7 Identify different Linux Intrusion Detection Systems (IDS) (e.g., Snort, PortSentry)	7
4.8 Given security requirements, implement basic IP tables/chains (note: requires knowledge of common ports)	7
4.9 Implement security auditing for files and authentication	7
4.10 Identify whether a package or file has been corrupted / altered (e.g., checksum, Tripwire)	7
4.11 Given a set of security requirements, set password policies to match (complexity / aging / shadowed passwords) (e.g., convert to and from shadow passwords)	3

SYBEX

OBJECTIVE	CHAPTER
4.12 Identify security vulnerabilities within Linux services	7
4.13 Set up user-level security (i.e., limits on logins, memory usage and processes)	7

Domain 5.0 Documentation

5.1 Establish system performance baseline	8
5.2 Create written procedures for installation, configuration, security and management	8
5.3 Document installed configuration (e.g., installed packages, package options, TCP/IP assignment list, changes—configuration and maintenance)	8
5.4 Troubleshoot errors using systems logs (e.g., tail, head, grep)	8
5.5 Troubleshoot application errors using application logs (e.g., tail, head, grep)	8
5.6 Access system documentation and help files (e.g., man, info, readme, Web)	8

Domain 6.0 Hardware

6.1 Describe common hardware components and resources (e.g., connectors, IRQs, DMA, SCSI, memory addresses)	9
6.2 Diagnose hardware issues using Linux tools (e.g., /proc, disk utilities, ifconfig, /dev, knoppix, BBC, dmesg)	9
6.3 Identify and configure removable system hardware (e.g., PCMCIA, USB, IEEE1394)	9
6.4 Configure advanced power management and Advanced Configuration and Power Interface (ACPI)	9
6.5 Identify and configure mass storage devices and RAID (e.g., SCSI, ATAPI, tape, optical recordable)	4

Exam objectives are subject to change at any time without prior notice and at CompTIA's sole discretion. Please visit CompTIA's website (www.comptia.org/certification/index.htm) for the most current listing of exam objectives.

SYBEX

Linux+™
Study Guide
Third Edition

Roderick W. Smith

San Francisco • London

Publisher: Neil Edde
Acquisitions Editor: Jeff Kellum
Developmental Editor: Jeff Kellum
Production Editor: Rachel Gunn
Technical Editors: Elizabeth Zinkann, Michael Jang
Copyeditor: Liz Welch
Compositor: Craig J. Woods, Happenstance-Type-O-Rama
CD Coordinator: Dan Mummert
CD Technician: Kevin Ly
Proofreaders: Nancy Riddiough, Jim Brook
Indexer: Nancy Guenther
Book Designers: Judy Fung, Bill Gibson
Cover Designer: Archer Design
Cover Illustrator/Photographer: Photodisc and Victor Arre

SYBEX

To Our Valued Readers:

Thank you for looking to Sybex for your Linux+ exam prep needs. We at Sybex are proud of our reputation for providing certification candidates with the practical knowledge and skills needed to succeed in the highly competitive IT marketplace. Certification candidates have come to rely on Sybex for accurate and accessible instruction on today's crucial technologies.

Sybex serves as a member of CompTIA's Linux+ Advisory Committee, and just as CompTIA is committed to establishing measurable standards for certifying individuals who will support Linux systems, Sybex is committed to providing those individuals with the skills needed to meet those standards.

The author and editors have worked hard to ensure that the updated third edition of the Linux+ Study Guide you hold in your hands is comprehensive, in-depth, and pedagogically sound. We're confident that this book will exceed the demanding standards of the certification marketplace and help you, the Linux+ certification candidate, succeed in your endeavors.

As always, your feedback is important to us. Please send comments, questions, or suggestions to support@sybex.com. At Sybex we're continually striving to meet the needs of individuals preparing for certification exams.

Good luck in pursuit of your Linux+ certification!

Neil Edde
Publisher—Certification
Sybex, Inc.

This book is dedicated to all the open source programmers whose efforts have created Linux. Without their efforts, this book would not be possible.

Acknowledgments

A book doesn't just happen. At every point along the way from project conception to finished product, many people other than the author have their influence. Jeff Kellum, the Acquisitions Editor and Developmental Editor, helped guide the book's development, especially for the critical first few chapters. Rachel Gunn, as Production Editor, coordinated the work of the many others who contributed their thoughts to the book. Elizabeth Zinkann and Michael Jang, the Technical Editors, scrutinized the text for technical errors and made sure its coverage was complete. Also, my thanks go to Nancy Riddiough and Jim Brook, the proofreaders for this book; the Compositior at Happenstance Type-O-Rama; and to the entire CD team at Sybex for working together to produce the final product. I'd also like to thank Neil Salkind at Studio B; as my agent, he helped connect me with Sybex to write this book.

Contents at a Glance

Introduction   *xvii*

Assessment Test   *xxvi*

Chapter 1   Linux Installation   1

Chapter 2   Text-Mode Commands   73

Chapter 3   User Management   129

Chapter 4   Disk Management   179

Chapter 5   Package and Process Management   235

Chapter 6   Networking   305

Chapter 7   Security   369

Chapter 8   System Documentation   411

Chapter 9   Hardware   449

Glossary   511

Index   *541*

Contents

Introduction   *xvii*

Assessment Test   *xxvi*

Chapter   1   Linux Installation   1

Evaluating Computer Requirements   2
    Workstations   3
    Servers   3
    Dedicated Appliances   4
    Special Needs   4
Deciding What Hardware to Use   6
    A Rundown of PC Hardware   6
    CPU   8
    RAM   9
    Hard Disk Space   10
    Network Hardware   11
    Video Hardware   12
    Miscellaneous Hardware   13
Determining Software Needs   15
    A Rundown of Linux Distributions   15
    Common Workstation Programs   18
    Common Server Programs   21
    Useful Software on Any System   23
    Validating Software Requirements   25
Planning Disk Partitioning   26
    The PC Partitioning System   26
    Linux Partition Requirements   27
    Common Optional Partitions   28
    Linux Filesystem Options   30
    Partitioning Tools   32
Selecting an Installation Method   34
    Media Options   34
    Methods of Interaction during Installation   36
Installing Linux   38
Configuring Boot Loaders   39
    The Role of the Boot Loader   40
    Available Boot Loaders   41
Post-Installation X Configuration   50
    Selecting an X Server   50
    Configuring X   54

Summary   63
Exam Essentials   63
Commands in This Chapter   65
Review Questions   66
Answers to Review Questions   70

Chapter   2   Text-Mode Commands   73

Basic Command Shell Use   74
   Starting a Shell   74
   Viewing Files and Directories   75
   Launching Programs   76
   Using Shell Shortcuts   77
File Manipulation Commands   78
   Navigating the Linux Filesystem   79
   Manipulating Files   82
   Manipulating Directories   85
   Locating Files   86
   Examining Files' Contents   88
   Redirection and Pipes   90
File Permissions   91
   Account and Ownership Basics   91
   File Access Permissions   92
   Changing File Ownership and Permissions   97
   Setting Default Permissions   100
   Using ACLs   101
Editing Files with Vi   102
   Vi Modes   103
   Basic Text-Editing Procedures   103
   Saving Changes   106
Using *sed* and *awk*   106
Setting Environment Variables   108
   Where to Set Environment Variables   108
   The Meanings of Common Environment Variables   110
Basic Shell Scripting   112
   Beginning a Shell Script   113
   Using External Commands   113
   Using Variables   115
   Using Conditional Expressions   117
Summary   118
Exam Essentials   119
Commands in This Chapter   119
Review Questions   121
Answers to Review Questions   125

Chapter	**3**	**User Management**	**129**

Linux Multiuser Concepts   130
    User Accounts: The Core of a Multiuser System   130
    Groups: Linking Users Together for Productivity   135
    Mapping UIDs and GIDs to Users and Groups   136
    The Importance of Home Directories   138
Configuring User Accounts   139
    Adding Users   139
    Modifying User Accounts   141
    Deleting Accounts   148
Configuring Groups   149
    Adding Groups   149
    Modifying Group Information   149
    Deleting Groups   152
Common User and Group Strategies   152
    The User Private Group   153
    Project Groups   153
    Multiple Group Membership   154
Account Security   154
    Enforcing User Password Security   155
    Steps for Reducing the Risk of Compromised Passwords   157
    Disabling Unused Accounts   158
    Using Shadow Passwords   158
Controlling System Access   160
    Accessing Common Servers   160
    Controlling *root* Access   165
    Setting Filesystem Quotas   166
Summary   168
Exam Essentials   168
Review Questions   171
Answers to Review Questions   175

Chapter	**4**	**Disk Management**	**179**

Storage Hardware Identification   180
    Types of Storage Devices   180
    Linux Storage Hardware Configuration   182
Partition Management and Maintenance   184
    Using *fdisk* to Create Partitions   184
    Creating New Filesystems   186
    Using a Combined Tool   187
    Checking a Filesystem for Errors   189
    Adding Swap Space   190
Partition Control   194
    Identifying Partitions   194

Mounting and Unmounting Partitions 195
Using Network Filesystems 200
Using *df* 202
Defining Standard Filesystems 203
Using RAID 204
Writing to Optical Discs 208
Linux Optical Disc Tools 208
A Linux Optical Disc Example 210
Creating Cross-Platform Discs 212
Backing Up and Restoring a Computer 213
Common Backup Hardware 214
Common Backup Programs 216
Planning a Backup Schedule 222
Preparing for Disaster: Backup Recovery 223
Summary 225
Exam Essentials 225
Commands in This Chapter 226
Review Questions 228
Answers to Review Questions 232

Chapter   5   Package and Process Management   235

Package Concepts 236
File Collections 236
The Installed File Database 237
Rebuilding Packages 238
Installing and Removing Packages 240
RPM Packages 240
Debian Packages 247
Tarballs 254
Compiling Source Code 258
GUI Package Management Tools 262
Package Dependencies and Conflicts 265
Real and Imagined Package Dependency Problems 265
Workarounds to Package Dependency Problems 266
Startup Script Problems 269
Starting and Stopping Services 269
Starting and Stopping via SysV Scripts 269
Editing *inetd.conf* 273
Editing *xinetd.conf* or *xinetd.d* Files 275
Custom Startup Files 276
Setting the Runlevel 277
Understanding the Role of the Runlevel 277
Using *init* or *telinit* to Change the Runlevel 277
Permanently Changing the Runlevel 279

Running Jobs at Specific Times   280
    The Role of Cron   280
    Creating System Cron Jobs   280
    Creating User Cron Jobs   282
    Using *at*   282
Setting Process Permissions   283
    The Risks of SUID and SGID Programs   284
    When to Use SUID or SGID   284
    Finding SUID or SGID Programs   284
Managing Processes   285
    Examining Process Lists with *ps*   286
    Restricting Processes' CPU Use   291
    Killing Processes   292
    Foreground and Background Processes   293
Summary   294
Exam Essentials   295
Commands in This Chapter   296
Review Questions   297
Answers to Review Questions   301

Chapter   6   **Networking**   **305**

Understanding Networks   306
    Basic Functions of Network Hardware   306
    Types of Network Hardware   307
    Network Packets   309
    Network Protocol Stacks   309
Network Addressing   314
    Types of Network Addresses   314
    Resolving Hostnames   317
    Network Ports   318
Basic Network Configuration   319
    Network Hardware Configuration   319
    DHCP Configuration   320
    Static IP Address Configuration   321
    Using GUI Configuration Tools   323
    Initiating a PPP Connection   324
Network Server Configuration   329
    Super Server Configuration   329
    Delivering IP Addresses with DHCP   333
    Delivering Hostnames with DNS   335
    Delivering Files with Samba   336
    Delivering Files with NFS   338
    Setting Up a Remote Access Server   339
    Configuring Mail Servers   340
    Configuring Web Servers   344

Using Network Clients	346
Using X Programs Remotely	346
Using an E-Mail Client	347
Configuring Routing	350
Remote System Administration	351
Text-Mode Logins	351
GUI Logins	353
File Transfers	353
Remote Administration Protocols	354
Using NIS	355
Network Diagnostic Tools	357
Testing Basic Connectivity	357
Tracing a Route	358
Checking Network Status	359
Summary	359
Exam Essentials	360
Commands in This Chapter	361
Review Questions	362
Answers to Review Questions	366

Chapter 7	**Security**	**369**
	Sources of Security Vulnerability	370
	Physical Access Problems	371
	Stolen Passwords	371
	Local Program Bugs	371
	Server Bugs	372
	Denial-of-Service Attacks	373
	Encryption Issues	373
	The Human Element	374
	Physical Security	375
	What an Intruder Can Do with Physical Access	375
	Steps for Mitigating Damage from Physical Attacks	375
	Firewall Configuration	376
	Where a Firewall Fits in a Network	377
	Linux Firewall Software	378
	Common Server Ports	378
	Using *iptables*	381
	Super Server Security	387
	Controlling Access via TCP Wrappers	387
	Controlling Access via *xinetd*	388
	Intrusion Detection	389
	Symptoms of Intrusion	389
	Using Snort	390
	Using PortSentry	392

Using Tripwire	393
Using *chkrootkit*	394
Using Package Manager Checksums	394
Monitoring Log Files	395
Security Auditing	396
Checking for Open Ports	396
Reviewing Accounts	398
Verifying Installed Files and Packages	400
Imposing User Resource Limits	400
Summary	401
Exam Essentials	402
Review Questions	404
Answers to Review Questions	408

Chapter	**8**	**System Documentation**	**411**

Documenting System Configuration	412
Documenting the Installation	413
Maintaining an Administrator's Log	414
Backing Up Important Configuration Files	415
Documenting Official Policies and Procedures	416
Establishing Normal Performance Measures	418
Documenting CPU Load	418
Documenting Memory Load	420
Documenting Disk Use	420
Collecting System Statistics	421
Configuring Log Files	422
Understanding *syslogd*	423
Setting Logging Options	423
Rotating Log Files	425
Using a Remote Server for Log Files	428
Using Log Files	429
Which Log Files Are Important?	429
Using Log Files to Identify Problems	430
Tools to Help Scan Log Files	431
System Documentation and Help Resources	434
Using Man Pages	435
Using Info Pages	437
Using Miscellaneous Program Documentation	438
Using Internet-Based Help Resources	439
Summary	440
Exam Essentials	441
Commands in This Chapter	442
Review Questions	443
Answers to Review Questions	447

Chapter	**9**	**Hardware**	**449**
		Checking Hardware Configuration	450
		Checking Cabling	451
		Checking IRQ, DMA, and I/O Settings	453
		Checking ATA Devices	455
		Checking SCSI Devices	457
		Checking BIOS Settings	459
		Configuring Power Management	461
		Activating Kernel Support	461
		Using APM	462
		Using ACPI	462
		Configuring External Hardware Devices	463
		Configuring PCMCIA Devices	463
		Configuring USB Devices	464
		Configuring IEEE-1394 Devices	465
		Configuring Legacy External Devices	466
		Configuring Basic Printing	468
		The Linux Printing Architecture	468
		Understanding PostScript and Ghostscript	469
		Running a Printing System	471
		Configuring BSD LPD and LPRng	472
		Configuring CUPS	477
		Printing to Windows or Samba Printers	482
		Monitoring and Controlling the Print Queue	483
		Using Scanners in Linux	487
		Understanding Scanner Hardware	487
		Choosing and Using Linux Scanner Software	488
		Diagnosing Hardware Problems	489
		Core System Problems	489
		ATA Problems	491
		SCSI Problems	494
		Peripherals Problems	495
		Identifying Supported and Unsupported Hardware	498
		Using an Emergency Boot Disk	499
		Using *dmesg* for System Diagnosis	499
		Summary	500
		Exam Essentials	501
		Commands in This Chapter	502
		Review Questions	503
		Answers to Review Questions	507
		Glossary	**511**
		Index	*541*

Introduction

Why should you learn about Linux? It's a fast-growing operating system, and it is inexpensive and flexible. Linux is also a major player in the small and mid-sized server field, and it's an increasingly viable platform for workstation and desktop use as well. By understanding Linux, you'll increase your standing in the job market. Even if you already know the Windows or Mac Operating System and your employer uses these systems exclusively, understanding Linux will give you an edge when you are looking for a new job or if you are looking for a promotion. For instance, this knowledge will help you to make an informed decision about if and when you should deploy Linux.

The Computing Technology Industry Association (CompTIA) has developed its Linux+ exam as an introductory certification for people who want to enter careers involving Linux. The exam is meant to certify that an individual has the skills necessary to install, operate, and troubleshoot a Linux system and is familiar with Linux-specific concepts and basic hardware.

The purpose of this book is to help you pass the newly updated Linux+ exam (XK0-002). Because this exam covers basic Linux installation, management, configuration, security, documentation, and hardware interactions, those are the topics that are emphasized in this book. You'll learn enough to get a Linux system up and running and how to configure it for many common tasks. Even after you've taken and passed the Linux+ exam, this book should remain a useful reference.

 The original Linux+ exam was released in 2001, but in the fast-changing world of computers, updates became desirable within a few years. Thus, CompTIA released an updated version of the Linux+ exam in early 2005. This book covers this updated Linux+ exam, rather than the original Linux+ exam. The first and second editions of this book covered the original Linux+ exam.

What Is Linux?

Linux is a clone of the Unix OS that has been popular in academia and many business environments for years. Formerly used exclusively on large mainframes, Unix and Linux can now run on small computers—which are actually far more powerful than the mainframes of just a few years ago. Because of its mainframe heritage, Unix (and hence also Linux) scales well to perform today's demanding scientific, engineering, and network server tasks.

Linux consists of a kernel, which is the core control software, and many libraries and utilities that rely on the kernel to provide features with which users interact. The OS is available in many different distributions, which are bundlings of a specific kernel with specific support programs. These concepts are covered at greater length in Chapter 1.

Why Become Linux+ Certified?

Several good reasons to get your Linux+ certification exist. The CompTIA Candidates Information packet lists five major benefits:

Provides proof of professional achievement   Certifications are quickly becoming status symbols in the computer service industry. Organizations, including members of the computer service industry, are recognizing the benefits of certification, such as Linux+ or A+. Organizations are pushing for their members to become certified. Every day, more people are putting the CompTIA official certification logo on their business cards.

Increases your marketability   Linux+ certification makes individuals more marketable to potential employers. Also, Linux+ certified employees might receive a higher salary base because employers won't have to spend as much money on vendor-specific training.

Provides an opportunity for advancement   Most raises and advancements are based on performance. Linux+ certified employees work faster and more efficiently. The more productive employees are, the more money they will make for their company. And, of course, the more money they make for the company, the more valuable they will be to the company. So, if employees are Linux+ certified, their chances of getting promoted will be greater.

Fulfills training requirements   Each year, more and more major computer hardware vendors, including (but not limited to) IBM, Hewlett-Packard, and Novell, are recognizing CompTIA's certifications as prerequisites in their own respective certification programs. The use of outside certifications like Linux+ has the side benefit of reducing training costs for employers. Because more and more small companies are deploying the flexible and inexpensive OS we call Linux, the demand for experienced users is growing. CompTIA anticipates that the Linux+ exam, like the A+ exam, will find itself integrated into various certification programs as well.

Raises customer confidence   As the IT community, users, small business owners, and the like become more familiar with the Linux+ certified professional moniker, more of them will realize that the Linux+ professional is more qualified to work in their Linux environment than is a non-certified individual.

How to Become Linux+ Certified

The Linux+ certification is available to anyone who passes the test. You don't have to work for a particular company. It's not a secret society. It is, however, an elite group.

The exam is administered by Thomson Prometric and Pearson VUE. The exam can be taken at any Thomson Prometric or Pearson VUE testing center. If you pass, you will get a certificate in the mail from CompTIA saying that you have passed, and you will also receive a lapel pin and business cards. To find the Thomson Prometric testing center nearest you, call (800) 755-EXAM (755-3926). Contact (877) 551-PLUS (551-7587) for Pearson VUE information.

To register for the exam with Thomson Prometric, call at (800) 776-MICRO (776-4276) or register online at http://www.2test.com. To register with Pearson VUE, call (877) 551-PLUS (551-7587) or register online at http://www.vue.com/comptia/. However you do it, you'll be asked for your name, mailing address, phone number, employer, when and where you want to take the test (i.e., which testing center), and your credit card number (arrangement for payment must be made at the time of registration).

Who Should Buy This Book

Anybody who wants to pass the Linux+ exam may benefit from this book. If you're new to Linux, this book covers the material you will need to learn the OS from the beginning, and it continues to provide the knowledge you need up to a proficiency level sufficient to pass the Linux+ exam. You can pick up this book and learn from it even if you've never used Linux before, although you'll find it an easier read if you've at least casually used Linux for a few days. If you're already familiar with Linux, this book can serve as a review and as a refresher course for information with which you might not be completely familiar. In either case, reading this book will help you to pass the Linux+ exam.

This book is written with the assumption that you know at least a little bit about Linux (what it is, and possibly a few Linux commands). This book also assumes that you know some basics about computers in general, such as how to use a keyboard, how to insert a floppy disk into a floppy drive, and so on. Chances are you have used computers in a substantial way in the past—perhaps even Linux, as an ordinary user, or maybe you have used Windows or Mac OS. This book does *not* assume that you have extensive knowledge of Linux system administration, but if you've done some system administration, you can still use this book to fill in gaps in your knowledge.

How This Book Is Organized

This book consists of nine chapters plus supplementary information: a Glossary, this Introduction, and the Assessment Test after the Introduction. The chapters are organized as follows:

- Chapter 1, "Linux Installation," covers things you should consider before you install Linux on a computer, as well as the basics of Linux installation. This chapter explains Linux's hardware requirements, describes the various Linux distributions, and provides an overview of Linux installation.

- Chapter 2, "Text-Mode Commands," provides a grounding in using Linux at the command line. The chapter begins with a look at command shells generally and moves on to commands used to manipulate and edit files. The chapter also describes environment variables and introduces the basics of creating shell scripts, which can help automate otherwise tedious tasks.

- Chapter 3, "User Management," describes how to create and maintain user accounts; it also covers some basic user-related security issues. Because Linux is a clone of Unix, it includes extensive support for multiple users, and understanding Linux's model for user accounts is critical to many aspects of Linux's operation.

- Chapter 4, "Disk Management," covers Linux's approach to hard disks: partitions and the filesystems they contain. Specific topics include how to create and manage filesystems, how to create and use a RAID array, and how to back up and restore a computer.

- Chapter 5, "Package and Process Management," describes Linux's tools for maintaining software, both in the sense of software installed on the computer and in the sense of running software (that is, processes). This chapter covers common package management tools, procedures for compiling software from source code, and tools for keeping processes running properly.

- Chapter 6, "Networking," covers how to use Linux on a network. This chapter includes an overview of what a network is, including the popular TCP/IP networking tools on which the Internet is built. Several popular Linux network client programs are described, as is the subject of network diagnostics.

- Chapter 7, "Security," covers the important topic of keeping your system secure. Specific topics covered here include physical security, firewalls, super servers, intrusion detection, security auditing, and user-level security controls.

- Chapter 8, "System Documentation," covers three types of documentation: notes you should maintain on a system's configuration, log files the computer maintains, and sources of information about Linux that come with it or that you can find elsewhere.

- Chapter 9, "Hardware," covers various hardware topics. These include some basics about hardware devices, hardware troubleshooting, power management, and configuring printers. Some of these issues are the same as in other OSs, but Linux handles some hardware devices in fundamentally different ways than do many other OSs.

Each chapter begins with a list of the CompTIA Linux+ objectives that are covered in that chapter. (The book doesn't cover objectives in the same order as CompTIA lists them, so don't be alarmed when you notice gaps in the sequence.) At the end of each chapter, you'll find several elements you can use to help prepare for the exam:

Exam Essentials   This section summarizes important information that was covered in the chapter. You should be able to perform each of the tasks or convey the information requested.

Commands in This Chapter   Most chapters cover several Linux commands. You should be familiar with these commands before taking the exam. You might not need to know every option for every command, but you should know what the command does and be familiar with its major options. (Chapter 2 provides information on how to perform basic tasks in a Linux command shell.)

Review Questions   Each chapter concludes with 20 review questions. You should answer these questions and check your answer against the one provided after the questions. If you can't answer at least 80 percent of these questions correctly, go back and review the chapter, or at least those sections that seem to be giving you difficulty.

WARNING   The Review Questions, Assessment Test, and other testing elements included in this book are *not* derived from the CompTIA Linux+ exam questions, so don't memorize the answers to these questions and assume that doing this will enable you to pass the Linux+ exam. You should learn the underlying topic, as described in the text of the book. This will let you answer the questions provided with this book *and* pass the exam. Learning the underlying topic is also the approach that will serve you best in the workplace—the ultimate goal of a certification like Linux+.

To get the most out of this book, you should read each chapter from start to finish, then check your memory and understanding with the chapter-end elements. Even if you're already familiar with a topic, you should skim the chapter; Linux is complex enough that there are often multiple ways to accomplish a task, so you may learn something even if you're already competent in an area.

Bonus CD-ROM Contents

This book comes with a CD-ROM that contains several additional elements. Items available on the CD-ROM include the following:

Book contents as a PDF file   The entire book is available as a fully searchable PDF that runs on all Windows platforms.

Electronic "flashcards"   The CD-ROM includes 150 questions in "flashcard" format (a question followed by a single correct answer). You can use these to review your knowledge of the Linux+ exam objectives.

Sample tests   All of the questions in this book appear on the CD-ROM—both the 30-question Assessment Test at the end of this Introduction and the 180 questions that consist of the nine 20-question Review Question sections for each chapter. In addition, there are two 65-question Bonus Exams.

Conventions Used in This Book

This book uses certain typographic styles in order to help you quickly identify important information and to avoid confusion over the meaning of words such as on-screen prompts. In particular:

- *Italicized text* indicates key terms that are described at length for the first time in a chapter. (Italics are also used for emphasis.)

- A `monospaced font` indicates the contents of configuration files, messages displayed at a text-mode Linux shell prompt, filenames, text-mode command names, and Internet URLs.

- *`Italicized monospaced text`* indicates a variable—information that differs from one system or command run to another, such as the name of a client computer or a process ID number.

- **`Bold monospaced text`** is information that you're to type into the computer, usually at a Linux shell prompt. This text can also be italicized to indicate that you should substitute an appropriate value for your system. (When isolated on their own lines, commands are preceded by non-bold monospaced $ or # command prompts.)

In addition to these text conventions, which can apply to individual words or entire paragraphs, a few conventions highlight segments of text:

A Note indicates information that's useful or interesting, but that's somewhat peripheral to the main text. A Note might be relevant to a small number of networks, for instance, or it may refer to an outdated feature.

A Tip provides information that can save you time or frustration and that may not be entirely obvious. A Tip might describe how to get around a limitation, or how to use a feature to perform an unusual task.

 Warnings describe potential pitfalls or dangers. If you fail to heed a Warning, you may end up spending a lot of time recovering from a bug, or you may even end up restoring your entire system from scratch.

Sidebars

A Sidebar is like a Note but longer. The information in a Sidebar is useful, but it doesn't fit into the main flow of the text.

The Exam Objectives

Behind every computer industry exam you can be sure to find exam objectives—the broad topics in which exam developers want to ensure your competency. The official CompTIA objectives for the Linux+ exam are listed here. (They're also printed at the start of the chapters in which they're covered.)

 Exam objectives are subject to change at any time without prior notice and at CompTIA's sole discretion. Please visit the Linux+ Certification page of CompTIA's Web site (http://www.comptia.com/certification/linuxplus/index.htm) for the most current listing of exam objectives.

Domain 1.0 Installation

1.1   Identify all system hardware required (e.g., CPU, memory, drive space, scalability) and check compatibility with Linux Distribution

1.2   Determine appropriate method of installation based on environment (e.g., boot disk, CD-ROM, network (HTTP, FTP, NFS, SMB))

1.3   Install multimedia options (e.g, video, sound, codecs)

1.4   Identify purpose of Linux machine based on predetermined customer requirements (e.g., appliance, desktop system, database, mail server, web server, etc.)

1.5   Determine what software and services should be installed (e.g., client applications for workstation, server services for desired task)

1.6   Partition according to pre-installation plan using `fdisk` (e.g., `/boot`, `/usr`, `/var`, `/home`, Swap, RAID/volume, hotfix)

1.7   Configure file systems (e.g., (ext2) or (ext3) or REISER)

1.8   Configure a boot manager (e.g., LILO, ELILO, GRUB, multiple boot options)

1.9   Manage packages after installing the operating systems (e.g., install, uninstall, update) (e.g., RPM, `tar`, `gzip`)

1.10   Select appropriate networking configuration and protocols (e.g., `inetd`, `xinetd`, modems, Ethernet)

1.11   Select appropriate parameters for Linux installation (e.g., language, time zones, keyboard, mouse)

1.12   Configure peripherals as necessary (e.g., printer, scanner, modem)

Domain 2.0 Management

2.1   Manage local storage devices and file systems (e.g., `fsck`, `fdisk`, `mkfs`) using CLI commands

2.2   Mount and unmount varied filesystems (e.g., Samba, NFS) using CLI commands

2.3   Create files and directories and modify files using CLI commands

2.4   Execute content and directory searches using `find` and `grep`

2.5   Create linked files using CLI commands

2.6   Modify file and directory permissions and ownership (e.g., `chmod`, `chown`, sticky bit, octal permissions, `chgrp`) using CLI commands

2.7   Identify and modify default permissions for files and directories (e.g., umask) using CLI commands

2.8   Perform and verify backups and restores (`tar`, `cpio`, `jar`)

2.9   Access and write data to recordable media

2.10   Manage runlevels and system initialization from the CLI and configuration files (e.g., `/etc/inittab` and `init` command, `/etc/rc.d`, `rc.local`)

2.11   Identify, execute, manage and kill processes (e.g., `ps`, `kill`, `killall`, `bg`, `fg`, `jobs`, `nice`, `renice`, `rc`)

2.12   Differentiate core processes from non-critical services (e.g., PID, PPID, `init`, timer)

2.13   Repair packages and scripts (e.g., resolving dependencies, file repair)

2.14   Monitor and troubleshoot network activity (e.g., `ping`, `netstat`, `traceroute`)

2.15   Perform text manipulation (e.g., `sed`, `awk`, `vi`)

2.16   Manage print jobs and print queues (e.g., `lpd`, `lprm`, `lpq`)

2.17   Perform remote management (e.g., `rmon`, `ssh`)

2.18   Perform NIS-related domain management (`yppasswd`, `ypinit`, etc.)

2.19   Create, modify, and use basic shell scripts

2.20   Create, modify, and delete user and group accounts (e.g, `useradd`, `groupadd`, `/etc/passwd`, `chgrp`, `quota`, `chown`, `chmod`, `grpmod`) using CLI utilities

2.21   Manage mail queues (e.g., sendmail, postfix, `mail`, `mutt`) using CLI utilities

2.22   Schedule jobs to execute in the future using "`at`" and "`cron`" daemons

2.23   Redirect output (e.g., piping, redirection)

Domain 3.0 Configuration

3.1   Configure client network services and settings (e.g., settings for TCP/IP)

3.2   Configure basic server network services (e.g., DNS, DHCP, SAMBA, Apache)

3.3   Implement basic routing and subnetting (e.g., `/sbin/route`, `ip forward` statement)

3.4   Configure the system and perform basic makefile changes to support compiling applications and drivers

3.5   Configure files that are used to mount drives or partitions (e.g., `fstab`, `mtab`, SAMBA, nfs, syntax)

3.6   Implement DNS and describe how it works (e.g., edit `/etc/hosts`, edit `/etc/host.conf`, edit `/etc/resolv.conf`, `nslookup`, `dig`, `host`)

3.7   Configure a Network Interface Card (NIC) from a command line

3.8   Configure Linux printing (e.g., cups,SAMBA)

3.9   Apply basic printer permissions (e.g., `lpd.perm`)

3.10   Configure log files (e.g., syslog, remote logfile storage)

3.11   Configure terminal emulation for the X system (e.g., xterm, $TERMCAP)

3.12   Set up environment variables (e.g., $PATH, $DISPLAY, $TERM, $PROMPT, $PS1)

Domain 4.0 Security

4.1   Configure security environment files (e.g., `hosts.allow`, `sudoers`, `ftpusers`, `sshd_config`)

4.2   Delete accounts while maintaining data stored in that user's home directory

4.3   Given security requirements, implement appropriate encryption configuration (e.g., blowfish 3DES, MD5)

4.4   Detect symptoms that indicate a machine's security has been compromised (e.g., review logfiles for irregularities or intrusion attempts)

4.5   Use appropriate access level for login (e.g., `root` level vs. user level activities, `su`, `sudo`)

4.6   Set Daemon and process permissions (e.g., SUID, GUID)

4.7   Identify different Linux Intrusion Detection Systems (IDS) (e.g., Snort, PortSentry)

4.8   Given security requirements, implement basic IP tables/chains (note: requires knowledge of common ports)

4.9   Implement security auditing for files and authentication

4.10   Identify whether a package or file has been corrupted/altered (e.g., checksum, Tripwire)

4.11   Given a set of security requirements, set password policies to match (complexity /aging/shadowed passwords) (e.g., convert to and from shadow passwords)

4.12   Identify security vulnerabilities within Linux services

4.13   Set up user-level security (i.e., limits on logins, memory usage and processes)

Domain 5.0 Documentation

5.1   Establish system performance baseline

5.2   Create written procedures for installation, configuration, security and management

5.3   Document installed configuration (e.g., installed packages, package options, TCP/IP assignment list, changes, configuration, and maintenance)

5.4   Troubleshoot errors using systems logs (e.g., `tail`, `head`, `grep`)

5.5   Troubleshoot application errors using application logs (e.g., `tail`, `head`, `grep`)

5.6   Access system documentation and help files (e.g., man, info, readme, Web)

Domain 6.0 Hardware

6.1   Describe common hardware components and resources (e.g., connectors, IRQs, DMA, SCSI, memory addresses)

6.2   Diagnose hardware issues using Linux tools (e.g., `/proc`, disk utilities, `ifconfig`, /dev, knoppix, BBC, `dmesg`)

6.3   Identify and configure removable system hardware (e.g., PCMCIA, USB, IEEE1394)

6.4   Configure advanced power management and Advanced Configuration and Power Interface (ACPI)

6.5   Identify and configure mass storage devices and RAID (e.g., SCSI, ATAPI, tape, optical recordable)

Assessment Test

1. Where may LILO be installed?

    A. The MBR, a Linux partition's boot sector, or a floppy disk

    B. The MBR, a Linux partition's boot sector, or a Windows partition's boot sector

    C. A Linux partition's boot sector or a Windows partition's boot sector

    D. The MBR, a floppy disk, or a swap partition

2. Which of the following tools is it *most* important to have available on an emergency recovery disk?

    A. `fdformat`

    B. OpenOffice.org

    C. `mkfs`

    D. `traceroute`

3. Which of the following are power-management protocols? (Choose all that apply.)

    A. ACPI

    B. PPP

    C. SMTP

    D. APM

4. What does the `-t` parameter to `telinit` control?

    A. The time between a polite shutdown of unneeded servers (via `SIGTERM`) and a forceful shutdown (via `SIGKILL`)

    B. The time between issuing the `telinit` command and the time the runlevel change takes place

    C. The runlevel that's to be entered on completion of the command

    D. The message sent to users before the runlevel change is enacted

5. Which of the following programs might you want to remove on a system that's to function solely as a firewall? (Choose all that apply.)

    A. `init`

    B. The Telnet client

    C. The Linux kernel

    D. The Apache server

6. Which of the following is it wise to do when deleting an account with `userdel`?

    A. Ensure that the user's password isn't duplicated in `/etc/passwd` or `/etc/shadow`.

    B. Search the computer for stray files owned by the former user.

    C. Change permissions on system files to prevent the user from accessing them remotely.

    D. Delete the user's files with a utility that overwrites former file contents with random data.

7. An `ls -l` command reveals that the `loud` file has a permission string of `crw-rw----` and owner-ship by the user `root` and group `audio`. Which of the following is a true statement about this file?

   A. Only `root` and the account that created it may read or write the file.

   B. The file is a directory, as indicated by the leading `c`.

   C. Anybody in the `audio` group may read from and write to the file.

   D. The command `chmod 660 loud` will make it accessible to more users.

8. Which of the following is commonly found in `/etc/inetd.conf` entries for servers but not in the equivalent entries in `/etc/xinetd.conf` or a file in `/etc/xinetd.d`?

   A. A call to `tcpd`

   B. A specification of the protocol, such as `tcp`

   C. A specification of the user, such as `nobody`

   D. Arguments to be passed to the target server

9. Why might a script include a variable assignment like `CC="/usr/bin/gcc"`?

   A. To ensure that the script uses `gcc` rather than some other C compiler.

   B. Because some programs can't be called from scripts except when referred to by variables.

   C. The variable assignment allows the script to run the program even if it lacks execute permission.

   D. The variable can be easily changed or assigned different values, increasing the utility of the script.

10. Which of the following symptoms is more common in kernel bugs than in application problems?

   A. Programs consume an inordinate amount of CPU time.

   B. An error message containing the word `oops` appears in your log files.

   C. A program refuses to start and complains of a missing library file.

   D. The problem occurs for some users but not for others.

11. Which of the following are potential problems when using a partition resizing utility like `parted` or PartitionMagic? (Choose all that apply.)

   A. A power failure or crash during the resize operation could result in substantial data loss.

   B. Linux may not recognize a resized partition because resizers often change the partition ID code.

   C. No resizing programs exist for the most common Linux filesystems, ext2fs and ext3fs.

   D. If the resizer moves the Linux kernel and you boot using LILO, you'll need to reinstall LILO.

12. In which of the following circumstances is it *most* appropriate to run XFree86 3.3.6 over a 4.*x* version of the server?

   A. Never, since XFree86 4.0.*x* does everything 3.3.6 does, and better

   B. When you need support for multiple simultaneous monitors to display an oversized desktop

   C. When 3.3.6 includes a separate accelerated server for your card

   D. When 4.*x* provides unaccelerated support for your chipset but 3.3.6 provides acceleration

13. You want to set up a firewall on a Linux computer. Which of the following tools might you use to accomplish this task?

   A. Apache

   B. `iptables`

   C. `wall`

   D. TCP Wrappers

14. Which of the following is the intended purpose of the `rc.local` or `boot.local` startup script?

   A. It sets the system's time zone and language defaults.

   B. It holds startup commands created for its specific computer.

   C. It displays startup messages to aid in debugging.

   D. It verifies that all other startup scripts are operating correctly.

15. Which of the following is a protocol that can help automate configuration of SCSI devices?

   A. SCAM

   B. SMB

   C. ASPI

   D. ATAPI

16. Which of the following is an advantage of installing LILO in a primary Linux partition's boot sector?

   A. LILO can then boot a kernel from beyond the 1024-cylinder mark.

   B. LILO can then redirect the boot process to other OSs' boot sectors.

   C. The DOS or Windows FDISK utility can be used to reset LILO as the boot loader if the MBR is overwritten.

   D. LILO can work in conjunction with LOADLIN to boot multiple kernels.

17. Which of the following commands is *most* likely to stop a runaway process with PID 2939?

   A. `kill -s SIGHUP 2939`

   B. `kill -s SIGTERM 2939`

   C. `kill -s SIGKILL 2939`

   D. `kill -s SIGDIE 2939`

18. Which of the following is *not* one of the responsibilities of `lpd`?

   A. Maintaining the printer queues

   B. Accepting print jobs from remote systems

   C. Informing applications of a printer's capabilities

   D. Sending data to printers

19. Which of the following commands displays the contents of a tarball, including file sizes and time stamps?

   A. `tar xzf theprogram-1.2.3.tgz`

   B. `tar tzf theprogram-1.2.3.tgz`

   C. `tar tvzf theprogram-1.2.3.tgz`

   D. `tar x theprogram-1.2.3.tgz`

20. Which of the following does an Ethernet switch allow that a hub does not permit?

   A. 100Mbps operation

   B. Linking more than five computers

   C. Full-duplex operation

   D. Use with 10-Base5 cabling

21. How would you direct the output of the `uptime` command to a file called `uptime-stats.txt`?

   A. `echo uptime uptime-stats.txt`

   B. `uptime > uptime-stats.txt`

   C. `uptime | uptime-stats.txt`

   D. `uptime < uptime-stats.txt`

22. A workstation ordinarily runs with a load average of 0.25. Suddenly, its load average is 1.25. Which of the following might you suspect, given this information? (Choose all that apply.)

   A. The workstation's user may be running more programs or more CPU-intensive programs than usual.

   B. A process may have hung—locked itself in a loop consuming CPU time but doing no useful work.

   C. A process may have begun consuming an inordinate amount of memory.

   D. The CPU may be malfunctioning and require replacement.

23. Your manager tells you that all user passwords on the host must be moved from the /etc/ passwd file to the /etc/shadow file. Which command will allow you to accomplish this goal?

   A. `grpconv`

   B. `pwconv`

   C. `shadow`

   D. `hide`

24. The final step of your company's procedures for creating a new server requires you to store information on /dev/hda's partition table in a file named `documentation.txt`. Which of the following commands will allow you to accomplish this action?

   A. `df  /dev/hda > documentation.txt`

   B. `parted -l /dev/hda > documentation.txt`

   C. `fdisk -l /dev/hda > documentation.txt`

   D. `du  /dev/hda > documentation.txt`

25. You are configuring your company firewall and have been told that TCP and UDP data to port 53 must be allowed through. By default, what server uses this port?

A. NNTP

B. PortMapper

C. NetBIOS

D. BIND

26. You are logged in as a regular user when the need arises to start a report with higher permissions that you presently have. Which utility allows you to execute a single command as `root`?

A. `sgid`

B. `suid`

C. `su`

D. `sudo`

27. Which of the following daemons handles traditional logging from servers and other user-mode programs?

A. `init`

B. `sysklogd`

C. `kyslogd`

D. `syslogd`

28. You have been told to implement a packet filtering firewall on a new Linux server. The server is running a 2.6.*x* kernel. Which program is the preferred tool to implement this?

A. `ipchains`

B. Nmap

C. `iptables`

D. Tripwire

29. You are working on a legacy host that uses 3DES hashing for passwords. What is the maximum length a user may make a password on this system?

A. 6

B. 8

C. 10

D. 12

30. You have just used the `swapon` command to begin using newly initialized swap space. Which file must you edit in order to make your use of this swap file permanent?

A. `/etc/fstab`

B. `/etc/mount`

C. `/etc/swap`

D. `/etc/tab`

Answers to Assessment Test

1. A. LILO may reside in any of the locations listed in option A. If you install it in a FAT or NTFS partition (used by DOS or Windows), these partitions will be damaged, and if you install LILO in a swap partition that is then used, LILO will be wiped out. See Chapter 1 for more information.

2. C. Option C, mkfs, is a tool for creating a new filesystem, which is something you're likely to need to do in an emergency recovery situation. The first option, fdformat, does a low-level format on a floppy disk; OpenOffice.org is an office productivity suite; and traceroute helps diagnose network connectivity problems. You're unlikely to need to use any of these tools from an emergency disk. See Chapter 4 for more information.

3. A, D. The Advanced Configuration Power Interface (ACPI) and Advanced Power Management (APM) are power-management protocols. The Point-to-Point Protocol (PPP) forms TCP/IP network links over serial or telephone lines, and the Simple Mail Transfer Protocol (SMTP) handles e-mail exchanges. See Chapter 9 for more information.

4. A. When shutting down certain servers, telinit first tries asking them to shut themselves down by sending a SIGTERM signal. The server can then close open files and perform other necessary shutdown housekeeping. If the servers don't respond to this signal, telinit becomes more forceful and passes a SIGKILL signal, which is more likely to work but doesn't give the server a chance to shut itself down in an orderly fashion. The -t parameter specifies the time between these two signals. See Chapter 5 for more information.

5. B, D. You're unlikely to need to use a Telnet client on a firewall, but an intruder who breaks into the firewall could use it to access your internal systems. A firewall shouldn't run any servers that aren't absolutely required, and an Apache server is almost certainly not required. Option A, init, is the master process on a Linux system and cannot be removed without damaging the system. Likewise, the Linux kernel controls everything else; without it, the computer isn't a Linux computer at all. See Chapter 6 for more information.

6. B. Tracking down and removing or changing the permissions of a former user's files can prevent confusion or possibly even spurious accusations of wrongdoing in the future. Unless the user was involved in system cracking, there's no reason to think that the user's password will be duplicated in the password database. No system file's ownership or permissions should need changing when deleting a user. Although overwriting deleted files with random data may be useful in some high-security environments or with unusually sensitive data, it's not a necessary practice on most systems. See Chapter 3 for more information.

7. C. The second set of permission bits (rw-) indicates that the file's group (audio) may read from and write to the file. This permission string ensures that, if audio has more than one member, multiple users may access the file. The leading c indicates that the file is a character device file, not a directory. The command **chmod 660 loud** will not change the file's permissions; 660 is equivalent to rw-rw----. See Chapter 2 for more information.

8. A. The TCP Wrappers program, tcpd, includes security features that are largely provided directly by xinetd, so most systems that use xinetd don't call tcpd from xinetd. The other options appear in both types of files, although arguments for the server aren't required for either super server. See Chapter 5 for more information.

9.   D.   You can easily edit that line to change the program run by the $CC variable, or you can assign different values to the variable within a conditional in support of different system configurations. Specifying the program directly will as easily ensure that it's run. Any program that can be called from a variable can be called directly. Variable assignment doesn't allow the script to call programs for which the user lacks execute permission. See Chapter 2 for more information.

10.   B.   Kernel bugs often manifest themselves in the form of kernel oops messages, in which an error message including the word oops appears on the console and in log files. Although a program might conceivably trigger a kernel oops, the bug is fundamentally in the kernel. (Kernel oops messages also often indicate hardware problems.) See Chapter 9 for more information.

11.   A, D.   The biggest problem with resizers is the potential for data loss in the event of a crash or power failure during the resize operation. They also can render a system unbootable because of a moved kernel if you use LILO to boot Linux. This latter problem can be overcome by reinstalling LILO. Linux doesn't use partition ID codes except during installation, and resizing programs don't touch these codes. PartitionMagic and parted are two programs commonly used to resize ext2 and ext3 filesystems. See Chapter 1 for more information.

12.   D.   XFree86 4.*x* includes a new driver architecture, so some of 3.3.6's accelerated drivers haven't been ported to the new system. In such cases, using the old server can provide a snappier display. It's 4.*x* that provides support for multiple monitors. The presence of a separate accelerated driver in 3.3.6 does not necessarily mean that the 4.*x* support is slower. See Chapter 1 for more information.

13.   B.   Option B, iptables, is a tool for configuring the 2.4.*x* and 2.6.*x* Linux kernel's firewall features. (The ipfwadm and ipchains programs perform these tasks for the 2.0.*x* and 2.2.*x* kernels, respectively.) Apache is a Web server, and wall sends messages to all currently logged-on users. TCP Wrappers controls access to specific servers, but it isn't a firewall per se. See Chapter 1 for more information.

14.   B.   These scripts hold startup commands individualized for their host ("local") computer, as opposed to those that are provided with the distribution. In principle, these scripts *could* be used for any of the other listed purposes, but this isn't their usual function. See Chapter 5 for more information.

15.   A.   The SCSI Configured Automatically (SCAM) protocol, if supported by the host adapter and SCSI devices connected to it, auto-configures those devices. The Server Message Block (SMB) is a protocol used in Windows file sharing and implemented by Samba in Linux. The Advanced SCSI Programming Interface (ASPI) is a method common in DOS and Windows for programs that interface with SCSI devices. The Advanced Technology Attachment Packet Interface (ATAPI) is a protocol used by many EIDE devices. See Chapter 9 for more information.

16.   C.   When installed in the MBR, LILO is susceptible to being completely wiped out by other OSs' installation routines. Installing LILO in a primary Linux partition's boot sector eliminates this risk, making recovery easier. LILO's ability to boot from beyond the 1024-cylinder mark or to boot multiple OSs is identical no matter where it's installed. Likewise, LILO can boot multiple OSs without the use of LOADLIN no matter where LILO is installed. See Chapter 1 for more information.

17. C.   Many servers use SIGHUP as a code to reread their configuration files; this signal doesn't normally terminate the process. SIGTERM is a polite way to stop a process; it lets the process control its own shutdown, including closing open files. SIGKILL is a more forceful method of termination; it's more likely to work than SIGTERM, but open files won't be saved. There is no SIGDIE signal. See Chapter 5 for more information.

18. C.   The multifunction tool lpd accepts print jobs from local and remote systems, maintains print queues, and sends data to printers (both local and remote). It does *not*, however, feed back information on a printer to applications. (The newer CUPS printer utility suite does have this capability, but it's not implemented in the lpd utility.) See Chapter 9 for more information.

19. C.   Option A extracts files from the archive without displaying their names. Option B lists the files in the archive, but without the --verbose (v) option, it doesn't list file sizes or time stamps. Option D will cause tar to attempt to extract the named file from its standard tape device. See Chapter 5 for more information.

20. C.   Switches allow full-duplex operation and reduce the chance of collisions on a network relative to hubs. Both devices come in 100Mbps models and models supporting both fewer than and greater than five devices. Neither type of device normally supports 10-Base5 cabling; they're both intended for use with twisted-pair network cables. See Chapter 6 for more information.

21. B.   The output redirection operator is >, so option B sends the output of uptime to uptime-stats.txt. The echo command displays information on the screen, so option A simply causes uptime uptime-stats.txt to appear. Option C uses a pipe. If uptime-stats.txt were a program, it would process the output of uptime, but the result of this command will probably be a file not found or permission denied error. Option D uses an *input* redirection operator, so uptime receives the contents of uptime-stats.txt as its input. See Chapter 2 for more information.

22. A, B.   Sudden jumps in load average indicate that programs are making heavier demands on the CPU than is normal. This may be because of legitimate factors such as users running more programs or more demanding programs, or it could mean that a program has locked itself into an unproductive loop. Memory use isn't reflected in the load average. A malfunctioning CPU is likely to manifest itself in system crashes, not a change in the load average. See Chapter 5 for more information.

23. B.   The pwconv utility will move the user passwords from the /etc/passwd file to the more secure /etc/shadow file. The grpconv utility performs a similar action for group passwords, but not user passwords. There are no standard utilities named shadow or hide that will affect user passwords. See Chapter 3 for more information.

24. C.   The command **fdisk -1 /dev/hda > documentation.txt** will store information on /dev/hda's partition table in the file documentation.txt. The other utilities listed will not show the information about the partition table that you would want to record in this file. See Chapter 8 for more information.

25. D.   The Berkeley Internet Name Domain (BIND) server, which performs DNS name resolution, uses port 53 by default. NNTP (Network News Transfer Protocol) uses port 119, while PortMapper uses 111, and NetBIOS uses ports 137 through 139. See Chapter 7 for more information.

26. D.   The sudo utility allows you to execute a single command as root. The su utility allows you to become root (or another user) and then run any number of commands before exiting back to your normal account. The SGID and SUID bits are permission settings that can be applied to files, but are not utilities that can be executed. See Chapter 3 for more information.

27. D.   The sysklogd package actually contains two daemons: syslogd and klogd. The former handles traditional logging from servers and other user-mode programs, while the latter handles the logging of kernel messages. The init process keeps other services up and running but does not natively handle logging. See Chapter 8 for more information.

28. C.   The iptables program is the utility that manages firewalls on recent Linux kernels (from 2.4.*x* through at least 2.6.*x*). ipchains was used for earlier kernel versions. (Although 2.4.*x* and 2.6.*x* kernels *can* use ipchains if they're compiled with the appropriate support, iptables is definitely the *preferred* firewall program for these kernels.) Nmap is a program that looks for open ports, and Tripwire is a utility that scans a system for changes in critical system files. See Chapter 7 for more information.

29. B.   The maximum length for a password hash under 3DES (Triple Data Encryption Standard) is eight characters. See Chapter 3 for more information.

30. A.   The /etc/fstab file holds the file system table. To use the swap partition permanently, you must add an entry for it to this file. The other files are all fictitious. See Chapter 4 for more information.

Chapter

1

Linux Installation

THE FOLLOWING COMPTIA OBJECTIVES ARE COVERED IN THIS CHAPTER:

- ✓ 1.1 Identify all system hardware required (e.g., CPU, memory, drive space, scalability) and check compatibility with Linux Distribution.

- ✓ 1.2 Determine appropriate method of installation based on environment (e.g., boot disk, CD-ROM, network (HTTP, FTP, NFS, SMB)).

- ✓ 1.3 Install multimedia options (e.g., video, sound, codecs).

- ✓ 1.4 Identify purpose of Linux machine based on predetermined customer requirements (e.g., appliance, desktop system, database, mail server, web server, etc.).

- ✓ 1.5 Determine what software and services should be installed (e.g., client applications for workstation, server services for desired task).

- ✓ 1.6 Partition according to pre-installation plan using fdisk (e.g., /boot, /usr, /var, /home, Swap, RAID/volume, hotfix).

- ✓ 1.7 Configure file systems (e.g., (ext2) or (ext3) or REISER).

- ✓ 1.8 Configure a boot manager (e.g., LILO, ELILO, GRUB, multiple boot options).

- ✓ 1.11 Select appropriate parameters for Linux installation (e.g., language, time zones, keyboard, mouse).

- ✓ 3.11 Configure the X Window System

Sometimes you'll encounter a system that's already running Linux—say, if you're hired to administer systems that are already up and running, or if you buy a system with Linux preinstalled on it. Frequently, though, you must install Linux before you can begin using or administering it. This task isn't really any more difficult than installing most other OSs, but OS installation generally can be intimidating to those who've never done it. Linux also has its own installation quirks, which you should understand before proceeding. In addition, installation options can have an impact on how you use a system. That is, installation choices help determine how a Linux system is configured, such as what servers are available and how the network is configured. Although you can change these details later, getting them right when you first install Linux is generally preferable to modifying them afterward.

Understanding your computer's role is important in determining how you install an OS on it. Thus, this chapter begins with a look at the needs of various types of computers—workstations, servers, and more specialized types of computers. This chapter continues with information on the hardware and software needs of both Linux and of various Linux roles. Understanding these factors will help you plan a Linux installation. The first of the actual installation tasks is partitioning your disk, so this topic is up next. You must then plan how you're going to install Linux—that is, what source media to use and how to interact with the computer. The actual installation process is described in broad strokes next, although details do vary substantially from one distribution to another. Finally, this chapter looks at configuring the X Window System—Linux's GUI environment.

Evaluating Computer Requirements

If you're building or buying a new computer, one of the first steps you must take is to lay out the system's general hardware requirements—the amount of RAM, the approximate *central processing unit (CPU)* speed, the amount of disk space, and so on. These characteristics are determined in large part by the role or roles the computer will play. For instance, a workstation for a graphics designer will require a large monitor and good video card, but an Internet server needs neither. Once you've decided the general outline of the hardware requirements, you can evaluate your resource limitations (such as your budget) and arrive at more specific hardware selections—specific brands and models for the individual components or for a prebuilt computer.

Workstations

A *workstation* is a computer that is used primarily or exclusively from that computer's own *console* (the keyboard and monitor attached directly to the computer). Workstations are sometimes also referred to as *desktop computers*, although some people apply the latter term to somewhat lower-performance computers without network connections, reserving the term "workstation" for systems with network connections.

Because they're used by individuals, workstations typically require fairly good input/output devices—a large display (typically 17-inch or larger), a high-quality keyboard, and a good three-button mouse. (Linux, unlike Windows, uses all three buttons, so a two-button mouse is suboptimal.) Workstations also usually include audio hardware (a sound card, speakers, and sometimes a microphone) and high-capacity removable media drives (Zip or LS-120 drives, frequently CD-R or CD-RW burners, and often a DVD-ROM drive).

> *Cathode ray tube (CRT)* displays have been the traditional favorite for desktop use, but in 2003 *liquid crystal display (LCD)* monitor sales surpassed sales of CRT displays. LCD display sizes are measured slightly differently than are CRT display sizes, so an LCD monitor is equivalent to a CRT monitor one to two inches larger.

CPU speed, memory, and hard disk requirements vary from one application to another. A low-end workstation that's to be used for simple tasks such as word processing can get by with less of each of these values than is available on new computers today. A high-end workstation that will be used for video rendering, heavy-duty scientific simulations, or the like may need the fastest CPU, the most RAM, and the biggest hard disk available. Likewise, low-end workstations are likely to have less cutting-edge network hardware than are high-end workstations, and the differing hard disk requirements dictate less in the way of backup hardware for the low-end workstation.

Servers

The word *server* can mean one of two things: a program that responds to network requests from other computers, or the computer on which the server program runs. When designing a computer, the latter is the appropriate definition. Servers usually have little or no need for user-oriented features such as large monitors or sound cards. Most servers make heavy use of their hard disks, however, so large and high-performance disks are desirable in servers. For the same reason, *Small Computer System Interface (SCSI)* disks are preferred to *Advanced Technology Attachment (ATA)* disks, also known as *Enhanced Integrated Device Electronics (EIDE)* disks—SCSI disks tend to perform better, particularly when multiple disks are present on a single computer. (This issue is covered more later in this chapter, in the "Hard Disk Space" section.) Likewise, servers by definition rely on the network, and busy servers may need top-notch network cards, and perhaps special dedicated network connections outside the computer itself.

Small servers, such as those handling a few users in a small office, don't need much in the way of CPU speed or RAM, but larger servers demand more of these quantities, especially RAM. Linux automatically buffers disk accesses, meaning that Linux keeps recent disk accesses in memory, and reads more than it requested from disk. These practices mean that when subsequent requests come in, Linux can deliver them from memory, which is faster than going back to the disk to obtain the data. Thus, a server with lots of RAM can often outperform an otherwise similar server with only a modest amount of RAM.

It's important to realize that server needs fall along a continuum; a very low-demand Web site might not require a very powerful computer, but a very popular Web site might need an extraordinarily powerful system. Many other types of servers are also available, including Usenet news servers, database servers, time servers, and more. (News and database servers are particularly likely to require very large hard disks.)

Dedicated Appliances

Some Linux systems function as dedicated appliances—as routers, print servers for just one or two printers, the OS in small robots, and so on. In some cases, as when the computer functions as a small router, Linux can enable recycling of old hardware that's otherwise unusable. Dedicated applications like these often require little in the way of specialized hardware. Other times, the application demands very specialized hardware, such as custom motherboards or touch-panel input devices. Overall, it's difficult to make sweeping generalizations concerning the needs of dedicated appliances.

Increasingly, Linux is being used in dedicated commercial devices—hardware sold as gadgets to perform specific functions but that happens to run Linux. For instance, some Sharp Zaurus palmtop computers, a growing number of broadband routers, and the TiVo digital video recorder all run Linux. In most cases, these embedded Linux systems are intended to be used by people who aren't trained in Linux, so these systems tend to mask their Linux innards from the user. If you dig into them, though, they're much like other Linux systems at their core. Their hardware tends to be unique, though, and they may use unusual software components and lack software that's popular on workstations and servers.

 This book doesn't cover the unique aspects of embedded Linux.

Special Needs

Sometimes, the intended use of the computer requires specialized hardware of one variety or another. Common examples include the following:

Video input   If the computer must digitize video signals, such as those from a television broadcast or a videotape, you will need a video input board. The Linux kernel includes drivers for several such products, and a variety of programs are available to handle such inputs. The Video4Linux project (`http://www.exploits.org/v4l/`) supports these efforts.

⊕ **Real World Scenario**

Linux Thin Clients

One use of Linux that's interesting in certain environments is using Linux as a *thin client* OS—that is, an OS for a computer that runs just enough software to provide input/output functions for another computer. This can be handy if an office has several workers who need to use a computer for functions that are not, by and large, CPU-intensive. You can set up a single login server computer and provide the individual users with thin client computers with which they access the main server. This approach can save money by enabling you to reuse old computers as thin clients. It can also reduce administrative effort compared to giving every user a full workstation system.

Thin clients often boot using network boot protocols such as the *Preboot Execution Environment (PXE)*, which is a BIOS feature that enables booting from files stored on a *Trivial File Transfer Protocol (TFTP)* server. PXE essentially turns a network card and TFTP server into a boot device.

Of course, the TFTP server must hold suitable boot files—essentially, a miniature Linux distribution with thin client software. Examples of such software include PXES (`http://pxes.sourceforge.net`) and the Linux Terminal Server Project (LTSP; `http://www.ltsp.org`). Once configured, a Linux thin client can use Linux, Windows, or other OSs as servers, provided they're equipped with appropriate software.

Scientific data acquisition　Many scientific experiments require real-time data acquisition. This requires special timing capabilities, drivers for data acquisition hardware, and software. The Linux Lab Project (`http://www.llp.fu-berlin.de`) is a good starting point from which to locate appropriate information for such applications.

USB devices　The *Universal Serial Bus (USB)* is a multipurpose external hardware interface. It's a popular interface method for keyboards, mice, modems, scanners, digital cameras, printers, removable-media drives, and other devices. Linux added USB support in the 2.2.18 and later kernels. This support is good for many devices but weak or nonexistent for others. Check `http://www.linux-usb.org` to learn about support for specific devices. If you use an old distribution, it may lack USB support, but all current mainstream distributions provide good USB support.

IEEE-1394 devices　*IEEE-1394* (also known as FireWire or i.LINK) is a high-speed interface that's most commonly used for external hard disks and video input devices. As of the early 2.6.*x* kernel series, Linux's IEEE-1394 support is still weak, although some devices are supported, and the list of supported devices is growing. Check `http://www.linux1394.org` for details.

Deciding What Hardware to Use

Once you've decided on the approximate specifications for a computer and you've set a budget, you can begin deciding on details. If you possess the necessary knowledge, I recommend indicating manufacturer and model numbers for every component, along with one or two backups for each. You can then take this list to a store and compare it to the components included in particular systems, or you can deliver your list to a custom-build shop to obtain a quote. If you don't have enough in-depth knowledge of specific components, you can omit the make and model numbers for some components, such as the hard disk, CD-ROM drive, monitor, and possibly the motherboard. You should definitely research Linux compatibility with video cards, network cards, SCSI host adapters (if you decide to use SCSI components), and sound cards (if the computer is to be so equipped). These components can cause problems for Linux, so unless you buy from a shop that's experienced in building Linux systems, a little research now can save you a lot of aggravation later when you try to get a component working in Linux.

A Rundown of PC Hardware

Computers are built from several components that must interact with one another in highly controlled ways. If a single component misbehaves or if the interactions go awry, the computer as a whole will malfunction in subtle or obvious ways. Major components in computers include the following:

Motherboard   The *motherboard* (also sometimes called the mainboard) holds the CPU, RAM, and plug-in cards. It contains circuitry that "glues" all these components together. The motherboard determines what type of memory and CPU the computer can hold. It also includes the BIOS, which controls the boot process, and it usually has built-in support for hard disks, floppy disks, serial ports, and other common hardware.

CPU   The CPU is the computer's brain—it performs most of the computations that result in a system's ability to crunch numbers in a spreadsheet, lay out text in a word processor, transform PostScript to printer-specific formats for a print queue, and so on. To be sure, some computations are performed by other components, such as some video computations by a video card, but the CPU does the bulk of the computational work.

Memory   Computers hold various types of memory; the most common general classes of these are random access memory (RAM) and read-only memory (ROM). RAM is volatile storage; it can be easily changed and holds current computations. ROM is difficult or impossible to change, and holds static information. There are several varieties of each of these. Memory holds data, which can include Linux software and the data on which that software operates. Memory varies in access speed and capacity.

Disk storage   Disk storage, like memory, is used to retain data. Disk storage is slower than memory, but usually higher in capacity. In addition to the common hard disks, there are lower-capacity removable disks, CD-ROMs, and so on. Disks are controlled through ATA or SCSI circuitry on the motherboard or separate cards. As a general rule, Linux doesn't need specific drivers for disks, but Linux does need drivers for the controller.

Video hardware   Video hardware includes the video card and the monitor. The video card may or may not literally be a separate card; sometimes it's built into the motherboard. Linux's video support is provided in two ways: through drivers in the kernel that work with just about any video card, at least in text mode; and through drivers in X, Linux's GUI package, that work with most cards, but not absolutely all of them.

Input devices   The keyboard and mouse enable you to give commands to the computer. These devices are well standardized, although there are a few variants of each type. Linux provides standardized drivers for most common keyboards and mice (including trackballs and similar mouse alternatives).

Network devices   In most business settings, network hardware consists of an *Ethernet* card or a card for a similar type of computer network. Such networks link several computers together over a few tens or hundreds of feet, and they can interface to larger networks. Even many homes now use such a network. It's also possible to link computers via *modems*, which use telephone lines to create a low-speed network over potentially thousands of miles.

Audio hardware   Many workstations include audio hardware, which lets the system play back sounds and digitize sounds using microphones or other audio input devices. These aren't critical to basic system functioning, though; Linux will boot quite well without a sound card.

To understand how these components interact, consider Figure 1.1, which shows a simplified diagram of the relationship between various system components. Components are tied together with lines that correspond to traces on a circuit board, chips on a circuit board, and physical cables. These are known as *busses*, and they carry data between components. Some busses are contained within the motherboard, but others are not. Components on a single bus can often communicate directly with one another, but components on different busses require some form of mediation, such as from the CPU. (Although not shown in Figure 1.1, lines of communication exist between the memory and *Peripheral Component Interconnect (PCI)* busses that don't directly involve the CPU.) A lot of what a computer does is coordinate the transfer of data between components on different busses. For instance, to run a program, data must be transferred from a hard disk to memory, and from there to the CPU. The CPU then operates on data in memory, and may transfer some of it to the video card. Busses may vary in speed (generally measured in megahertz, MHz) and width (generally measured in bits). Faster and wider busses are better than slower and narrower ones. The most common busses that connect to plug-in cards are the PCI bus and the *Advanced Graphics Port (AGP)* bus. The former is used for SCSI host adapters, Ethernet cards, sound cards, and most other card types. It comes in 32- and 64-bit varieties, the latter being faster, although it's still rare. The AGP bus is used only by video cards. Older busses, such as the *Industry Standard Architecture (ISA)* bus, have been largely abandoned, but you may run into them on older computers. The term "bus" can also refer to communication lines within the CPU and between the CPU and components that can't be removed.

 Figure 1.1 is *very* simplified. For instance, the link between the CPU and RAM passes through the motherboard's chipset and various types of cache, as described briefly in the upcoming section, "RAM."

FIGURE 1.1   A computer is a collection of individual components that connect together in various ways.

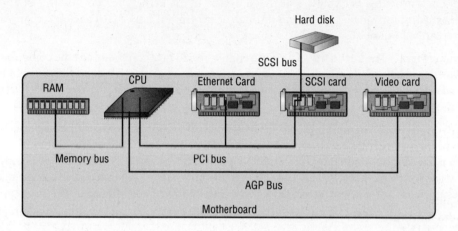

The next few sections examine several critical system components in more detail.

CPU

Linux was originally developed for Intel's popular 80x86 (or x86 for short) line of CPUs. In particular, a 386 was the original development platform. (Earlier CPUs in the line lack features required by Linux.) Linux also works on subsequent CPUs, including the 486, Pentium, Pentium MMX, Pentium Pro, Pentium II, Pentium III, Pentium 4, and Celeron.

In addition to working on Intel-brand CPUs, x86 versions of Linux work on competitors' x86-compatible chips. Today, the most important of these are the AMD Athlon and Duron lines. VIA also sells a line of CPUs originally developed by Cyrix and IDT, but these lag substantially behind the offerings from Intel and AMD in speed. Transmeta sells x86-compatible CPUs with low power requirements, and Linux runs well on these CPUs. A few other companies have sold x86-compatible CPUs in the past, but these companies have failed or been consumed by others.

As a general rule, Linux has no problems with CPUs from any of the x86 CPU manufacturers. When a new CPU is introduced, Linux distributions occasionally have problems booting and installing on it, but such problems are usually fixed quickly.

Traditional x86 systems use 32-bit internal registers, although Pentium systems and above have 64-bit links to memory. Some non-x86 systems use 64-bit internal registers, and both Intel and AMD have released 64-bit variants of the x86 architecture, which use 64-bit internal data busses and external address busses. The 64-bit variant of x86 is known as the *AMD64* or *x86-64* platform, and is available as the AMD Opteron, AMD Athlon-64, and some (but not all) Intel Xeon CPUs. (Intel uses the phrase "Extended Memory 64" to refer to the AMD64 architecture.) These CPUs can run both traditional 32-bit versions of Linux and 64-bit versions. When running a 64-bit version of Linux and applications compiled using a 64-bit compiler, you get a modest speed boost (about 10–30 percent). Most 32-bit binaries can run in an AMD64 environment, but a few don't.

Intel has also released another 64-bit *x*86 variant, known as IA-64. IA-64 CPUs are sold under the name Itanium, but this platform has not become popular. Most industry pundits predict that IA-64 will slowly fade away while AMD64 will take over the workstation and small server market.

In addition to *x*86 CPUs and their AMD64 and IA-64 derivatives, Linux runs on many unrelated CPUs, including the Apple/IBM/Motorola PowerPC (PPC), Compaq's (formerly DEC's) Alpha, and the SPARC CPU in Sun workstations. Linux is most mature on *x*86 hardware, and that hardware tends to be less expensive than hardware for other architectures; therefore, it's generally best to buy *x*86 hardware for Linux.

The best CPUs of some non-*x*86 lines sometimes perform slightly better than the best *x*86 CPUs, particularly in floating-point math, so you might favor alternative architectures for these reasons. You might also want to dual-boot between Linux and an OS that's available for some other architecture, such as Mac OS.

When comparing CPU performance, most people look at the chips' speeds in megahertz or gigahertz (GHz; 1GHz is 1,000MHz). This measure is useful when comparing CPUs of the same type; for instance, a 2.1GHz Celeron is slower than a 2.6GHz Celeron. Comparing across CPU models is trickier, though, because one model may be able to do more in a single CPU cycle than another can. When comparing different CPUs (for instance, Pentium 4 to Athlon), you should look at a measure such as MIPS (millions of instructions per second) or a benchmark test that's relevant to your intended application. (The Linux kernel uses a measure called BogoMIPS as a calibration loop when it boots, but this is *not* a valid measure of CPU performance; it's used only to calibrate some internal timing loops.) The best measure is how quickly the software *you* use runs on both CPUs.

CPUs plug into specific motherboards, which are the main (and sometimes the only) circuit board in a computer. The motherboard contains a *chipset*, which implements major functions such as an ATA controller, an interface between the CPU and memory, and an interface to the keyboard. Linux works with most motherboards, although on occasion, Linux doesn't support all of a motherboard's features. The key consideration in choosing a motherboard is that it is compatible with the CPU you buy—both its model and its speed. If you buy a preassembled system, this won't be a concern.

RAM

RAM comes in several forms, the most common of which in 2004 is the *dual inline memory module (DIMM)*. Older motherboards and some other components use the *single inline memory module (SIMM)* format, which comes in both 30-pin and 72-pin varieties. A few motherboards use *RDRAM inline memory modules (RIMMs)*, which physically resemble DIMMs but use a special type of RAM known as *RAMbus dynamic RAM (RDRAM)*. Laptops and some compact computers use a *Small Outline (SO) DIMM*, which is similar to a SIMM or DIMM but narrower. Motherboards host sockets for particular types of memory, so you must match your RAM purchases to your motherboard.

In addition to differences in physical interfaces, RAM varies in its electronic characteristics. RAM today is largely derived from *dynamic RAM (DRAM)*, which has spawned many improved variants, such as fast page mode (FPM) DRAM, extended data out (EDO) DRAM, synchronous DRAM (SDRAM), double data rate (DDR) SDRAM, and RDRAM. Most motherboards accept just one or two types of RAM, and with the exception of RDRAM and RIMMs, the physical format of the memory does not clearly indicate the RAM's electronic type. In 2004, most motherboards accept some combination of SDRAM, DDR SDRAM, or RDRAM, and possibly one or two lesser varieties. DDR SDRAM and RDRAM are the speed champions today.

RAM also varies in how well it copes with errors. Some memory modules incorporate a ninth bit (known as a parity bit) in each byte as an error-detection bit. This extra bit enables the motherboard's memory controller to detect, and often to correct, memory errors.

All of these characteristics apply to *main memory*, which, as you might imagine, is the main type of memory in a computer. Motherboards or CPUs also support another type of memory, though—*cache memory*. A computer has much less cache memory than main memory (typically about 1MB), but the cache memory is much faster. The system stores frequently used data in the cache, which results in a substantial performance increase.

Linux itself is unconcerned with these details. To Linux, memory is memory, and the OS doesn't particularly care about what physical or electronic form the memory takes or whether it supports any form of error detection or correction. All these details are handled by the motherboard, which is why it's so important that your memory match the motherboard's requirements.

When upgrading a computer's memory, try to buy from a retailer that has a memory cross-reference tool. Such a tool may be a Web-based form or a printed book. You look up or enter your motherboard or computer model and find a specific model of memory that's compatible with your computer. If such a tool is unavailable, check your motherboard's manual for detailed specifications about the types of memory it accepts, and use those specifications when shopping.

Hard Disk Space

The great divide in hard disks is between ATA and SCSI devices. Both of these busses come in a variety of speeds, ranging from less than 10 megabytes per second (MB/s) to 640MB/s, with higher speeds on the way. To achieve a given speed, both the hard disk and its interface must support the same speed. For instance, using an old 10MB/s Fast SCSI drive with an 80MB/s Ultra2 Wide SCSI host adapter will yield only 10MB/s speeds, not 80MB/s speeds.

It's important to distinguish between the speed of the *interface* and the speed of the *device*. Manufacturers typically emphasize the speed of the interface, but the mechanical device usually can't support these speeds. A hard disk might have an 80MB/s Ultra2 Wide SCSI interface but be capable of only 35MB/s sustained transfer rates. Manufacturers express the device's true maximum speed as an *internal transfer rate*, as opposed to the *external transfer rate* (of the interface). To further confuse matters, many manufacturers give the internal transfer rate in mega*bits* per second (Mbps), but the external rate in mega*bytes* per second (MB/s). If you fail to do the appropriate conversion (dividing or multiplying by 8), you'll erroneously believe that the interface is the bottleneck in data transfers to and from the device. Disks can transfer data at their external transfer rate only when they've previously stored data from the disk in their internal caches. For this reason, external speeds substantially higher than internal speeds can produce modest speed benefits, and disks with large caches are preferable to those with small caches.

As a general rule, SCSI devices are preferred in computers in which disk performance is important. This is because SCSI can support more devices per chain, SCSI handles multiple simultaneous transfers (from different devices) better than does ATA, and hard disk manufacturers tend to release their fastest and highest-capacity drives in SCSI format. These advantages are substantial, but for many situations, they're overwhelmed by one advantage of ATA: It's less expensive. As just mentioned, modern *x*86 motherboards ship with support for two ATA chains, so there's no need to buy an ATA controller. ATA hard disks are also typically less expensive than SCSI devices of the same capacity, although the ATA drives are often slower.

Both ATA and SCSI have traditionally been parallel busses, meaning that they consist of several data lines—enough to transfer an entire byte at once. Timing issues make it hard to boost the speed of a parallel interface past a certain point, though, so both ATA and SCSI are moving toward newer serial hardware interfaces. For ATA, the serial variant is known as *Serial ATA (SATA)*; for SCSI, it's *Serial Attached SCSI (SAS)*. In 2004, SATA is starting to become popular on new hardware, and SAS has yet to be released. The groups working on these standards are now merging them; the result may eventually be called SATA-2, but such devices don't yet exist. Other competing formats include IEEE-1394 and USB 2.0, both of which are popular for external hard drives.

Fortunately, Linux's support for both ATA and SCSI adapters is excellent. Most ATA controllers can be run in an old-style (and slow) mode using generic drivers, but faster speeds often require explicit driver support. Therefore, you may want to check on Linux's ATA drivers for your motherboard or ATA controller. There is no generic SCSI host adapter support, so you must have support for your specific SCSI host adapter. Serial variants require their own drivers, so check on Linux support before buying. Likewise, look into Linux drivers for IEEE-1394 or USB drives before buying one. Linux's IEEE-1394 and USB support makes these disks look like SCSI disks. (Some Linux SATA drivers also make them look like SCSI disks.)

Once you configure Linux to work with an ATA controller or a SCSI host adapter, you don't need to worry about support for specific models of disk. You can purchase hard disks and other storage devices on the basis of capacity, speed, and the reputation for quality of a manufacturer or model.

Network Hardware

Ethernet is the most common type of network today. There are several varieties of Ethernet, including 10Base-2 and 10Base-5 (which use thin and thick coaxial cabling, respectively); 10Base-T, 100Base-T, and 1000Base-T (which use twisted-pair cabling similar to telephone wires); and 1000Base-SX (which uses fiber-optic cabling). In any of these cases, the first number (10, 100, or 1000) represents the maximum speed of the network in Mbps. 1000Mbps Ethernet is often called gigabit Ethernet. Of these classes of Ethernet, 100Base-T is currently the most popular choice, although gigabit Ethernet is gaining in popularity.

Most 100Base-T network cards also support 10Base-T speeds. This fact can help you migrate a network from 10Base-T to 100Base-T; you can install dual-speed cards in new systems and eventually replace older 10Base-T hardware with dual-speed hardware to upgrade the entire network. Similarly, many 1000Base-T cards also support 100Base-T and even 10Base-T speeds.

Linux's support for Ethernet cards is, on the whole, excellent. Linux drivers are written for particular chipsets rather than specific models of network card. Therefore, the driver names often bear no resemblance to the name of the card you've bought, and you may use the same driver for boards purchased from different manufacturers. Fortunately, most distributions do a good job of auto-detecting the appropriate chipset during installation, so you probably won't have to deal with this issue if the card is installed when you install Linux.

Linux supports networking standards other than Ethernet, but these devices are less well supported overall. Linux includes support for some Token Ring, Fiber Distributed Data Interface (FDDI), LocalTalk, Fibre Channel, and wireless products, among others. If your existing network uses one of these technologies, you should carefully research Linux's support for specific network cards before buying one.

Most networking hardware outside the computer doesn't require Linux-specific drivers. Network cables, hubs, switches, routers, and so on are all OS-independent. They also generally work well with one another no matter what their brands, although brand-to-brand incompatibilities occasionally crop up.

One partial exception to the rule of needing no specific Linux support is in the case of network-capable printers. If you buy a printer with a network interface, you must still have appropriate Linux printer drivers to use the printer, as described in Chapter 9, "Hardware." Fortunately, network-capable printers usually understand PostScript, which is ideal from a Linux point of view.

Video Hardware

Linux works in text mode with just about any video card available for x86 systems. This means that you can log in, type commands, use text-based utilities, and so on. Such operation is probably adequate for a system intended to function as a server, so the selection of a video card for a server need not occupy too much of your time. Workstations, though, usually operate in GUI mode, which means they run the X Window System.

Unlike most other drivers, the drivers necessary to operate a video card in the bitmapped graphics modes used by X do not reside in the kernel; they're part of the X server. Therefore, you should research the compatibility of a video card with XFree86 (`http://www.xfree86.org`), X.org-X11 (`http://www.x.org`), or the Accelerated-X (`http://www.xig.com`) commercial X server. Because XFree86 or X.org-X11 ship with all major Linux distributions, it's best to use a board they support. (Prior to 2004, XFree86 was the preferred X server; but most distributions switched to X.org-X11 during 2004.) As a general rule of thumb, it's best to avoid the most recent video cards because drivers for XFree86 and X.org-X11 tend to lag a few months behind the release of the hardware. A few manufacturers do provide XFree86 and X.org-X11 drivers for their products, though, and Accelerated-X sometimes introduces drivers more rapidly than the open source developers do.

The Linux kernel includes a number of video drivers, known as frame buffer drivers. XFree86 and X.org-X11 include a driver to interface to these kernel-level drivers. This approach is particularly common outside the *x*86 world, but it usually produces poorer performance than using a native XFree86 driver.

Most video cards have at least 8MB of RAM, which is more than enough to handle a 1600 × 1200 display with a 32-bit color depth—a very high resolution and color depth. Cards with more memory than this typically use it in conjunction with 3D effects processors, which are useful in games and certain types of 3D rendering packages. 3D acceleration is still rare in Linux, and few Linux programs take advantage of these effects. If you need them, you should research 3D support carefully before settling on a product to buy.

Miscellaneous Hardware

Some hardware is so well standardized that there's no reason to give it much thought for Linux compatibility. The following are included in this category:

Cases   Cases vary in quality—check for rough edges, a good fit, and easy access. There's nothing OS-specific about them.

Floppy drives   Standard floppy drives are very standardized. A few variant technologies exist, though, such as LS-120 drives, which typically interface via the ATA port. These may need to be treated like hard disks in the `/etc/fstab` configuration file (described in Chapter 4, "Disk Management").

CD-ROM drives   Today, most CD-ROM drives use either the ATA or the SCSI interface, and the devices are very well standardized. (ATA drives use a software extension, known as the ATA Packet Interface, or ATAPI.) The main exceptions are drives that use USB or IEEE-1394 interfaces. Even DVD-ROM drives are well standardized. Recordable and rewriteable CDs (CD-R and CD-RW drives) and recordable DVD drives are also well standardized.

Tape drives   Most tape drives use a standard ATAPI or SCSI interface. These drives almost always respond to a standardized set of commands, and therefore don't require a special configuration in Linux. There are a few older floppy-interfaced drives that work with the Linux ftape drivers, which are part of the kernel. Some old parallel-interfaced drives can cause problems, and newer USB-interfaced drives are as yet rare and not well tested.

Keyboards   Standard PC keyboards are well supported by Linux and require no special configuration. Some keyboards include special keys that may not be recognized by Linux, though, such as volume-control keys or keys that launch specific applications. USB keyboards are also available. They are supported in 2.4.*x* and later kernels, but they aren't as well tested.

Mice   Most mice today use USB or PS/2 interfaces, but some older mice used RS-232 serial or various exotic interfaces. All are well supported, although USB support prior to the 2.4.*x* kernels was poor. Note that the tracking technology (conventional wheeled mouse, optical mouse, trackball, touchpad, and so on) is unimportant; it's only the interface protocols and the type of hardware interface that matter. Mice using USB or PS/2 hardware use the PS/2 protocol or a variant of it that supports wheels.

RS-232 serial and parallel ports   If you need to add extra RS-232 serial or parallel ports, you can do so with plug-in cards. These cards are fairly well standardized, so they'll seldom pose serious problems with Linux itself, although they can sometimes conflict with other hardware. USB-to-serial and USB-to-parallel adapters are also available and well supported in Linux.

Monitors   Monitors don't require drivers, although you may have to know certain features of a monitor to configure it in X. Specifically, you may need to know the monitor's maximum horizontal and vertical refresh rates (expressed in kHz and Hz, respectively). With XFree86 4.0 and later, and with any version of X.org-X11, the X server can sometimes obtain this information from the monitor. (X configuration is described in detail later in this chapter.)

Some other types of hardware require special consideration. These devices may require unusual drivers or configuration in Linux. Examples include the following:

USB devices   Check `http://www.linux-usb.org` for information on what USB devices are currently supported.

Internal modems   In years gone by, internal modems seldom caused problems in Linux, because they were essentially composed of ordinary modem hardware linked to an ordinary serial port, all on one card. Today, though, internal modems are more likely to be *software modems*—devices that rely on the CPU to do some of the modem's traditional chores. Such devices require special drivers, which sometimes don't exist for Linux. Check `http://www.linmodems.org` for information on what's supported and what's not.

Sound cards   Linux supports most sound cards. (Sound hardware is increasingly being integrated on the motherboard, but this fact is unimportant from a Linux software perspective.) The standard kernel includes two sets of sound drivers: the original Open Sound System (OSS) drivers and the new Advanced Linux Sound Architecture (ALSA) drivers. Commercial variants of the OSS drivers are also available from `http://www.4front-tech.com`. You can also check to see whether the sound card vendor provides drivers, which may be unique or work along with the kernel or ALSA core.

Video acquisition boards   Video acquisition hardware includes cameras (which typically interface via the parallel, USB, IEEE-1394, or RS-232 serial ports) and internal cards that accept television input signals. The Video4Linux project (`http://www.exploits.org/v4l/`; the l in v4l is a lowercase letter l, not a number 1.) is devoted to developing tools for such devices, and the standard kernel includes many of the requisite drivers—but be sure to check for supported hardware if this is important.

Aside from trivial components such as cables, you should be cautious about adding hardware to a Linux computer without checking its compatibility with Linux. It's easy to forget that computer hardware often requires drivers, and if nobody has written appropriate drivers for Linux, that hardware simply will not work. These drivers can also vary in quality, which partially explains why one device may work well while another works poorly.

Unreliable drivers can be a major cause of system instability. Most drivers have privileged access to the computer's hardware as well as to kernel data structures. As a result, a bug in a driver is unusually likely to crash the system or cause other major problems.

Determining Software Needs

When you plan a Linux installation, you must know what software you'll need on the system. This task begins with picking the Linux *distribution*, which is a collection of software along with installation routines that enable you to install everything from scratch. Once this is done, you must decide what types of programs you need. For each program class, you'll have to decide what particular package you want to run. For instance, if you want to configure a word processing workstation, you must decide if you want to use OpenOffice.org, KWord, AbiWord, LyX, or something else. Most of these packages come with most distributions of Linux, but sometimes you must obtain software from another source. In the case of downloadable software, if it doesn't accompany the distribution you use, you may want to download it before installing Linux. Depending on your available hardware, you can usually put a package on floppy disk, a high-capacity removable disk (like a Zip or LS-120 disk), or a CD-R to have it ready for installation once you've installed the main distribution. Doing this from Windows works just fine, if this is your first Linux installation.

A Rundown of Linux Distributions

Within the Linux world, several distributions exist. A distribution is a compilation of a Linux kernel, startup scripts, configuration files, and critical support software. Distributions also include some type of installation routine so that you can get a working Linux system. Any two distributions may use different versions of any or all of these components, which will produce distinctly different feels. Critical components, though, such as the kernel and certain support software, come from the same line in all distributions. For instance, one distribution might use the 2.6.8 Linux kernel and another might ship with 2.6.9, but they're both Linux kernels.

One important distinguishing characteristic of Linux distributions is which packaging methods they use. RPM Package Manager (RPM), Debian packages, and tarballs are the three most common package formats. The details of using these three package formats are covered in Chapter 5, "Package and Process Management."

Depending on your definition of "major," there are anywhere from two or three to over a dozen or more major Linux distributions. In addition, less popular and specialized distributions are available. Many Linux distributions are derived from either Debian or Red Hat. Some common Linux distributions include the following:

Conectiva Linux   This distribution is targeted at users in South and Central America, and is limited to running on *x*86 systems. You can learn more at `http://www.conectiva.com`.

Debian GNU/Linux   This distribution, headquartered at `http://www.debian.org`, is built by a nonprofit organization, rather than by a for-profit company, as are most other distributions. Debian eschews many of the GUI configuration tools used by most other distributions, and instead it aims to be a very stable and flexible distribution. For these reasons, it's well liked by open source hard-liners and those who like tinkering with the underlying text-based configuration files. Because it favors stability, Debian has a long release cycle and may not ship with the latest versions of many of its components. Debian is available on a very wide array of CPUs, including *x*86, IA-64, PowerPC, Alpha, SPARC, and 680*x*0.

Fedora Linux   This distribution is essentially the free version of Red Hat Linux. It's headquartered at `http://fedora.redhat.com`.

Gentoo Linux   Most distributions ship as collections of precompiled binary packages. To be sure, source code is available, but most distributions don't provide any simple means to recompile the entire distribution. Gentoo Linux is the exception to this rule. Although precompiled versions for *x*86, AMD64, PowerPC, and SPARC are available, much of the benefit of this distribution is that it supports recompiling everything with optimizations to suit your own hardware. (This feature is similar to the BSD ports system.) In theory, this ability should make a properly recompiled Gentoo faster than competing distributions. In practice, the effect is small, and the time spent recompiling everything can measure in the days. Like Debian, Gentoo is a noncommercial distribution. You can learn more about Gentoo at `http://www.gentoo.org`.

Libranet GNU/Linux   Debian has spawned a number of derivative distributions, and this is one of them. Libranet adds improved GUI system administration tools, but keeps many of Debian's core components and system administration defaults. Thus, you can easily install most Debian packages in Libranet. Libranet doesn't make its latest version available for free download; you must buy a CD-ROM or pay for a download. This distribution is headquartered at `http://www.libranet.com` and is available only for *x*86 CPUs.

Linspire   This distribution, which is a Debian derivative, lies at the fringes of Linux. It's designed as a replacement for Windows on the desktop (and was once called "Lindows" to emphasize this fact). The original Lindows plan was to make heavy use of WINE to enable the system to run Windows programs more-or-less seamlessly. This emphasis has been toned down, however, because Windows emulation is a very difficult task. Linspire is now included on some cut-rate retail PCs. Free downloads of Linspire are not available. You can learn more at `http://www.linspire.com`.

Lycoris   Like Linspire, Lycoris aims to be Linux for the desktop. Lycoris has never emphasized Windows compatibility, though, and it's an RPM-based distribution. The latest version is available only on CD-ROM from the company or preinstalled, although earlier versions can be downloaded from the Internet. The Lycoris home page is `http://www.lycoris.com`.

Mandrake Linux This distribution is a French-based offshoot of Red Hat Linux. Originally developed as a Red Hat with integrated K Desktop Environment (KDE), Mandrake has since developed more of its own personality, which includes a good GUI installer and some unusual choices in standard server software, such as Postfix rather than the more popular sendmail for a mail server. Its English Web page is `http://www.linux-mandrake.com/en/`. Mandrake is available for x86, AMD64, IA-64, SPARC, Alpha, and PowerPC CPUs.

Red Hat Linux Red Hat (`http://www.redhat.com`) is one of the oldest major distributions today, and one of the most influential. Red Hat developed the RPM format that's used by many other distributions, including some that aren't otherwise based on Red Hat. The distribution includes GUI installation and configuration tools that are unusually complete. Red Hat is or has been available on x86, AMD64, IA-64, SPARC, and Alpha CPUs, although the company has ceased SPARC development with version 6.2 and Alpha with 7.2. In late 2003, Red Hat split its distribution into Fedora Linux, which is freely available and developed by the community, and Red Hat Enterprise, which is an expensive product aimed at large businesses.

Slackware Linux Slackware is the oldest of the surviving Linux distributions. Like Debian, Slackware favors manual text-based configuration over GUI configuration tools, so it's often recommended for those who want the "Unix experience" without GUI "crutches." Slackware is the only major distribution to rely on tarballs for package management. You can read more at `http://www.slackware.com`. This distribution is available for x86, Alpha, and SPARC CPUs.

SuSE Linux The German company SuSE (`http://www.suse.com`; see also `http://www.novell.com`.) produces a distribution that's particularly popular in Europe. SuSE uses RPMs, but it's not otherwise based on Red Hat. Some SuSE packages use a DVD-ROM for software distribution, which is very helpful if your system has a DVD-ROM drive—SuSE ships with an unusually large number of packages, so juggling the half-dozen CD-ROMs can be awkward, compared to using a single higher-capacity DVD-ROM. This distribution includes GUI installation and configuration tools. Versions of SuSE for x86, AMD64, IA-64, PPC, and Alpha are all available. Novell purchased SuSE in early 2004, although SuSE remains headquartered in Germany.

TurboLinux This distribution (`http://www.turbolinux.com`) began as a Red Hat derivative, but recent versions have lost much of this heritage. This distribution includes unusually strong support for Asian languages, and is targeted at the server market. TurboLinux is available for x86 and AMD64 CPUs.

Xandros Linux Xandros (`http://www.xandros.com`) picked up an earlier and discontinued distribution from Corel, which based its distribution on Debian GNU/Linux. Xandros Linux adds a very user-friendly installation routine and GUI configuration tools. In implementing these features, though, Xandros has become less easily configured through traditional Linux command-line methods. This distribution is targeted at new Linux users who want to use the OS as a desktop OS to replace Windows. Xandros is an x86-only distribution.

Yellow Dog Linux This distribution is available exclusively for PPC systems, but is based on Red Hat. Yellow Dog (`http://www.yellowdoglinux.com`) uses its own unique installer, but once set up, it is quite similar to Red Hat.

When deciding on a Linux distribution, you'll find that some of these will fall out of the running for very basic reasons. For instance, there's no point in considering Yellow Dog for an *x*86 system, or Xandros for an Alpha CPU. The RPM and Debian package management systems are, on the whole, quite similar in overall features and capabilities, so if you're not already familiar with either, there's little reason to favor one over the other. (Chapter 3, "User Management," covers both systems in more detail.) Any of these distributions can be configured to do anything that another can do, with the exception of running on an unsupported CPU.

As a practical matter, you *do* need to decide between distributions. As a general rule, Lycoris, Mandrake, SuSE, and Xandros are probably the best suited as delivered to function as workstations, particularly for new Linux users. Debian and SuSE both ship with an unusually wide array of software (for SuSE, this is particularly true of the Professional package, which ships with a DVD-ROM and half a dozen CD-ROMs). Red Hat and its Fedora subdistribution are unusually popular, so finding support for them on newsgroups and the like is particularly easy. TurboLinux is specifically marketed for the server market, but others can fill that role just as easily. Some distributions come in variants that include additional software, such as secure servers, third-party partition managers, and so on.

If you have a fast Internet connection and a CD-R drive, and you want to experiment with several Linux distributions, check out the Linux ISO Web site at `http://www.linuxiso.org`. This site includes links to CD-R image files for most Linux distributions. You can also obtain distributions on no-frills CD-ROMs (with no manual and no support) for less than $10 from the likes of CheapBytes (`http://www.cheapbytes.com`) or Easy Linux CDs (`http://www.easylinuxcds.com`). Official boxed sets typically cost $20 to $100, or occasionally more for the most feature-packed versions. The boxed sets generally include printed manuals, support, and occasionally a commercial software product or two.

Common Workstation Programs

Workstations don't usually need much in the way of server software. Workstations may include such software to provide local services, though—for instance, Linux workstations usually include mail servers to handle mail for the administrator that is generated by automatic scripts and the like. The most important workstation programs are designed to help an individual get work done. Such software includes the X Window System, office tools, network clients, audio/visual programs, personal productivity tools, and scientific tools.

The X Window System

The X Window System (or X for short) is Linux's GUI environment. It's usually implemented through the X.org-X11 package, although prior to 2004, XFree86 usually did this job. Although Linux can be used without this GUI, most workstation users expect a GUI environment, and an increasing number of workstation programs require X in order to function.

X itself is a fairly spare environment, so it's frequently supplemented by additional tools, such as *window managers* (which provide borders and controls around windows) and *desktop environments* (which include a window manager and an assortment of utility programs to help make for a comfortable working environment). In particular, the K Desktop Environment

(KDE; `http://www.kde.org`) and the GNU Network Object Model Environment (GNOME; `http://www.gnome.org`) are two popular desktop environments for Linux. Most Linux distributions ship with both, but some install one or the other by default. Red Hat, for instance, favors GNOME, whereas SuSE favors KDE.

Office Tools

Office tools are the workhorses of computer use in offices; they are primarily made up of word processors, spreadsheets, and databases, but they may also contain various other applications, such as personal contact managers, calendar programs, and so on. Sun's (`http://www.sun.com`) StarOffice and its open source twin, OpenOffice.org (`http://www.openoffice.org`), are available in both Linux and Windows, and so they can be good choices in a mixed Linux/Windows environment.

 Corel used to make WordPerfect available for Linux, but it's been discontinued and is hard to find; however, if you need to exchange WordPerfect documents with others, it's worth tracking down a copy. You're more likely to have luck with WordPerfect 8. Although it requires old libc5 libraries, WordPerfect 8 is easier to install and use on modern Linux distributions than the more recent WordPerfect Office 2000, which relies on an obsolete version of WINE that's almost impossible to get working on modern distributions.

All of these products also include import/export filters for Microsoft Office documents, but as noted earlier, this approach is imperfect at best. (StarOffice is generally considered to have the best of these filters.) Both the GNOME (`http://www.gnome.org`) and KDE (`http://www.kde.org`) projects are building open source office suites.

Various singleton packages are also available. For instance, LyX (`http://www.lyx.org`), KWord (part of KDE), and AbiWord (`http://www.abisource.com`) are three popular What You See Is What You Get (WYSIWYG) Linux word processors. Markup languages like TeX and LaTeX (`http://www.latex-project.org`), in conjunction with editors like Emacs, can do much the same job. Gnumeric (`http://www.gnome.org/projects/gnumeric`) is a popular Linux spreadsheet. Ximian (`http://www.novell.com/linux/ximian.html`) produces an integrated mail reader/address book/calendar program called Evolution. Some of these tools are being integrated as part of the GNOME Office suite.

Network Clients

Users run network client programs to access network resources. Examples include Web browsers like Netscape (`http://www.netscape.com`), its open source twin Mozilla (`http://www.mozilla.org`), and Opera (`http://www.opera.com`); mail readers like Mutt (`http://www.mutt.org`) and KMail (part of KDE); and FTP clients like gFTP (`http://gftp.seul.org`). All major Linux distributions ship with a wide variety of network clients, but if you need a specific program, you should check whether it's included in your distribution. If it's not, track it down and install it. Most Linux network clients are open source, but a few aren't. Opera stands out in this respect.

For more information on network clients, refer to Chapter 6, "Networking."

Audio/Visual Programs

Audio/visual programs cover quite a wide range of products. Examples include graphics viewers and editors like XV (http://www.trilon.com/xv/) and the GIMP (http://www.gimp.org); ray tracing programs like POV-Ray (http://www.povray.org); MP3 players like the X Multimedia System (XMMS; http://www.xmms.org); multimedia players like XAnim (http://smurfland.cit .buffalo.edu/xanim/); audio/video editors like Cinelerra (http://heroines.sourceforge .net/cinelerra.php3) and Linux Video Studio (http://ronald.bitfreak.net); digital video recorder (DVR) software like MythTV (http://www.mythtv.org); and games like FreeCiv (http://www.freeciv.org) and Tux Racer (http://tuxracer.sourceforge.net). Some audio/visual programs are serious tools for work and are on a par with office utilities for some users. Somebody whose work involves graphics design, for instance, may need tools like the GIMP or POV-Ray. Other audio/visual programs fall more in the realm of entertainment, like games.

Linux's support for audio/visual programs has traditionally been weak. This has changed substantially since the mid-1990s, however, with the development of powerful programs like the GIMP and increasingly sophisticated multimedia players and editors. Even Linux games have come a long way, thanks in part to companies that specialize in porting other companies' games to Linux.

Personal Productivity Tools

Personal productivity tools are programs that individuals use to better their own lives. Examples include personal finance programs like GnuCash (http://www.gnucash.org) and slimmer versions of office programs (word processors for writing letters, for instance). As with audio/visual programs, personal productivity applications have traditionally been lacking in Linux, but that situation is improving. GnuCash, in particular, fills a niche that many users find important for personal use of Linux.

Personal productivity tools need not be restricted to the home, however. For instance, although big word processors like StarOffice and WordPerfect are very useful in some situations, many office users don't need anything nearly so powerful. Slimmer tools like Maxwell (http://sourceforge.net/projects/maxwellwp) suit some users' needs just fine. By forgoing the resource requirements of a larger package, a company may find that using such programs can help save it money by allowing its employees to use less powerful computers than might otherwise be required.

Scientific Programs

Unix systems have long been used in scientific research, and Linux has inherited a wealth of specialized and general scientific tools. These include data-plotting programs such as the GNU plotutils package (http://www.gnu.org/software/plotutils/plotutils.html) and

SciGraphica (`http://scigraphica.sourceforge.net`), data processing programs like Stata (`http://www.stata.com`), and many very specialized programs written for specific studies or purposes. Linux's software development tools (described shortly, in the section "Programming Tools") let you or your users write scientific programs, or compile those written by others.

Common Server Programs

A *server program* is one that provides some sort of service, usually to other systems via a network connection. Typically, a server runs in the background, unnoticed by the computer's users. In fact, many computers that run server programs don't have ordinary login users; instead, the computer's users are located at other systems, and they use the computer only for its servers. A Web server computer, for instance, may not have any local users aside from those who maintain the computer and its Web pages. Other servers include mail servers, remote login servers, file access servers, and miscellaneous servers.

 The term *server* is sometimes applied to an entire computer, as in "the Web server needs a bigger hard disk." Context is usually sufficient to distinguish this use from the use of the term in reference to a specific software product.

Web Servers

One very popular use of Linux is as a platform for running a Web server. This software uses the *Hypertext Transfer Protocol (HTTP)* to deliver files to users who request them with a Web client program, more commonly known as a Web browser. The most popular Web server for Linux by far is Apache (`http://httpd.apache.org`), which is an open source program included with Linux. Other Linux Web servers are available, however, including Zeus (`http://www.zeus.com`), Roxen (`http://www.roxen.com/products/webserver`), and `thttpd` (`http://www.acme.com/software/thttpd`). Zeus is a high-powered commercial Web server, Roxen is a high-powered open source Web server, and `thttpd` is a minimalist open source program suitable for small Web sites or those that don't need advanced features.

Some Linux distributions install Web servers even on workstations because the distributions use the Web servers to deliver help files to the local users. Such a configuration chews up resources, though, and can at least potentially be a security problem.

Mail Servers

Mail servers handle e-mail delivery. All major Linux distributions ship with a mail server, such as sendmail (`http://www.sendmail.org`), Exim (`http://www.exim.org`), or Postfix (`http://www.postfix.org`). These servers all handle the Simple Mail Transfer Protocol (SMTP), which is used to deliver mail between mail servers on the Internet at large, and can also be used as part of a local network's e-mail system. All major Linux distributions also ship with Post Office Protocol (POP) and Internet Message Access Protocol (IMAP) servers. These are used to deliver mail to end-user mail reader programs, which typically reside off the mail server. Most Linux SMTP, POP, and IMAP servers are open source, although commercial servers are available as well.

Disabling the SMTP server on a system that doesn't function as a mail server may seem like a good idea, but many Linux systems rely on this functionality to deliver important system status reports to the system administrator. Because of this, it's generally best to ensure that the mail server is configured in a secure way, which it normally is by default, and leave it running.

Remote Login Servers

A remote login server allows a user to log into the computer from a remote location. The traditional remote login protocol is Telnet, which is handled by a server called `telnetd` or `in.telnetd` in Linux. This server is open source and comes with all Linux distributions, although it's not always active by default.

Unfortunately, Telnet is an insecure protocol. Data passing between the Telnet client and server can be intercepted at points in-between the two, leading to compromised data. For this reason, it's best to disable the Telnet server on any Linux system and instead use a more secure protocol. Secure Telnet variants are available, but an alternative protocol, known as the *Secure Shell (SSH),* is more popular. SSH encrypts all data passing between two systems, making intercepted data useless. The most popular SSH implementation for Linux is the open source OpenSSH (`http://www.openssh.com`).

Telnet and SSH are basically text-based tools. SSH can be configured to tunnel X sessions through its connections, however. With this configuration, you can run X programs remotely. You can do the same by setting various parameters from a Telnet login, as described in Chapter 6. More direct GUI remote login tools (the X Display Manager [XDM], GNOME Display Manager [GDM], and K Display Manager [KDM]) are also available and come with all major distributions. Finally, the VNC package (`http://www.realvnc.com`) allows direct remote X logins as well. Most major Linux distributions ship with all of these servers.

File Access Servers

A file access server lets users read, write, and otherwise manipulate files and directories from a remote location. The traditional remote access protocol is the File Transfer Protocol (FTP), which is still in common use. Many local networks use *file-sharing protocols*, which allow programs on one computer to treat files on another system as if those files were local. Sun's Network Filesystem (NFS) is used for file sharing between Linux or Unix systems; the *Server Message Block (SMB)*, also known as the *Common Internet Filesystem (CIFS)*, is used to share files with DOS, Windows, and OS/2 systems; Novell's IPX/SPX (most strongly associated with the NetWare OS) is another PC file sharing protocol; and Apple's AppleShare is the protocol used for Macintosh file sharing. Linux supports all of these protocols—NFS with standard kernel tools and various NFS servers; SMB/CIFS with the Samba package; IPX/SPX with the `mars_nwe` and `lwared` packages; and AppleShare through Netatalk.

Most of these file-sharing servers have printer-sharing features as well, so you can provide network access to printers connected to Linux. NFS is an exception to this rule, but NFS's lack of printer sharing is offset by the fact that Linux's standard printing tools include this feature themselves.

Because of its excellent support for so many different file-sharing protocols, Linux makes an outstanding file- and printer-sharing platform in a cross-platform office. In an office that supports

Windows, Mac OS, OS/2, and Unix or Linux desktop systems, for instance, a single Linux computer can provide file- and printer-sharing services for all of these OSs, enabling users to move freely from one client platform to another or to collaborate with users of other platforms.

Miscellaneous Servers

The preceding sections cover many of the most popular server types, but that overview is far from complete. Many servers fall into less-used categories or simply defy categorization. Examples include:

- Proxy servers, such as Squid (`http://www.squid-cache.org`), which improve network performance or security by buffering Internet access attempts

- Dynamic Host Configuration Protocol (DHCP) servers, which keep track of network configurations and help automate the configuration of DHCP client systems

- Domain Name System (DNS) servers, such as BIND (also known as `named`), which convert between numeric IP addresses and hostnames

- Remote configuration tools like Webmin (`http://www.webmin.com`), which enable you to change a system's configuration from another computer

Most Linux distributions ship with a wide range of such servers, some of which are active by default and some of which aren't.

Although not a server per se, the `ipchains` and `iptables` tools are extremely useful when configuring a system as a firewall, or in protecting an individual workstation with firewall-like rules. These programs can block access to your system based on IP addresses or network ports (numbers associated with specific servers or runs of client programs). The `ipchains` tool fills this role with the 2.2.*x* kernel series, while `iptables` works with the 2.4.*x* and later kernels.

Useful Software on Any System

Whether a computer is to be used as a workstation or a server, certain classes of programs are extremely useful. These programs help users handle common user tasks and help administrators administer a system. Libraries are particularly important because they're the foundation on which most other programs are built.

Text Editors

A *text editor*, as you might imagine, is a program used to edit text. Most system administrators need to be familiar with Vi, which is a small and ubiquitous Unix and Linux text editor. (Chapter 3 includes an overview of Vi operation.) If you need to do emergency maintenance, there's a good chance your emergency tools will include Vi as the text editor, or a close relative, such as Vi Improved (VIM). A couple of other small text editors are jed and pico. These tools are designed to be similar to the popular Emacs program, which is an extremely large and flexible text editor.

Vi, jed, pico, and Emacs are all text-based programs, although some of them have at least some X extensions. In particular, XEmacs (`http://www.xemacs.org`) is an X-enhanced version of Emacs. Other text editors, such as Nedit (`http://www.nedit.org`), gEdit (part of

GNOME), and KEdit (part of KDE), are designed from the ground up as GUI text editors. Although you may prefer to use one of these in day-to-day operation, you *will* occasionally need to use a text-based editor, so you should familiarize yourself with at least one of them.

Programming Tools

Programming tools enable you to write programs for Linux. These tools can also be useful in getting Linux software you didn't write to run—some programs are distributed in a form that requires you to have programming tools available. Therefore, installing certain key programming tools on a Linux system is often necessary even if you don't know a thing about programming.

A *compiler* is a tool for converting a program's source code (its human-readable form, written by a programmer) into binary form (the machine-readable form, which users run). All major Linux distributions ship with a wide array of compilers, the most important of these being the GNU Compiler Collection (GCC). The Linux kernel is written mostly in C, as are many Linux programs, and GCC is best known for its C compiler. Some installations require other programming languages. If your users will be doing programming, ask them what tools they'll need. You'll have to install GCC, at a minimum, to compile most programs distributed as source code. Most programming languages are available with major Linux distributions, and the rest can be found in open source and, occasionally, commercial forms.

Some programming languages aren't compiled; they're interpreted. In an interpreted language, the computer translates from human-readable form to machine code on the fly. This reduces execution speed, but it can speed development since there's no need to explicitly compile the software. Many interpreted languages are known as *scripting languages*, because they're used to create simple programs known as scripts. Java, Python, and Perl are popular interpreted languages. The Bash and `tcsh` shells also provide scripting features, which are described in Chapter 2, "Text-Mode Commands." Some Linux or cross-platform programs are distributed in these forms, so installing them (particularly Perl and Python) may be necessary on many systems.

Many developers like to work with an integrated development environment (IDE). IDEs provide GUI front-ends to editors, compilers, linkers, debugging utilities, and other programming tools. Some software companies make money selling IDEs for Linux development, such as Metrowerks CodeWarrior (`http://www.metrowerks.com`). Other IDEs are open source projects, such as Code Crusader (`http://www.newplanetsoftware.com/jcc/`) and KDevelop (`http://www.kdevelop.org`). Chances are you won't need to install an IDE just to use software distributed in source code form; IDEs are most useful for active program development efforts.

WARNING   It's generally unwise to leave programming tools on a server system. If the system is ever compromised by crackers (those who break into computer systems), the programming tools can be turned against you to compile the cracker's own utilities. Nonetheless, compilers are useful in administering servers. Typically, you'll compile software on a system that's configured much like the server, and then you'll transfer the compiled software to the server system.

Libraries

A *library* isn't a program per se; rather, it's a collection of software routines that may be used by programs. Placing commonly used code in libraries saves both disk space and RAM. All Linux systems rely on a library known as the *C library (libc)* because it provides routines that are necessary for any C program to run in Linux. (The version of libc shipped with major distributions today is known as *glibc*.) Any but the most trivial Linux system will use a number of additional libraries as well. You must ensure that you install the appropriate libraries. If you fail to do so, your package system will probably tell you about the problem, expressed as a *failed dependency* (dependencies are described in more detail in Chapter 5).

Validating Software Requirements

Computer software is highly interdependent. Programs rely on others, which in turn rely on still others. This cycle ultimately leads to the Linux kernel—the "heart" of a Linux system. Even the kernel relies on other software—namely, the BIOS, which the kernel needs to start up. This web of dependencies and requirements sometimes poses a problem because you may need to install a dozen new programs in order to install a single package you want to use.

If a program comes with your Linux distribution, that program will most likely work well with that distribution. In some cases, you may need to install additional packages. Most distributions use package management systems that support dependency checking, as described in Chapter 5, so you'll be told what files or packages you're missing when you try to install a new program.

For programs that don't ship with a distribution—and even for those that do—you can usually find a list of requirements on the program's Web site or in its documentation. This requirement list may include several components:

Supported OSs   Most Linux software works on many Unix-like OSs. It's usually best to check that a package explicitly supports Linux. This is particularly true of binary-only packages, such as those that are common in the commercial world. A binary package for IRIX won't do you any good in Linux, for instance. Unix programs that come with source code can often be compiled without trouble on Linux, but the larger the program, the more likely you'll run into a snag if the author doesn't explicitly support Linux.

Supported distributions   Some packages' documentation refers to specific Linux distributions. As a general rule, what works on one distribution can be made to work on another. Sometimes the conversion process is trivial, but sometimes you'll need to wade through a tangled mess of unfulfilled dependencies to get a program working on a distribution its author doesn't explicitly support.

CPU requirements   Software that comes in source code form can usually be compiled on any type of CPU. Binary-only programs, though, usually work only on one CPU family, such as $x86$ or PowerPC. (One notable exception is the fact that most $x86$ programs can run on AMD64 CPUs.) This problem afflicts many commercial packages. Even some programs that come with source code don't compile properly on all CPUs, although this problem is rare.

Library requirements   The vast majority of programs rely on specific libraries, such as libc and GTK+. Check the requirements list and try to determine if the libraries are installed in your system. If your distribution uses the RPM or Debian package system, you can usually check for a library of the specified name.

 Chapter 5 describes software management, including RPM and Debian package utilities.

Development tools and libraries   If you intend to compile a program yourself, pay attention to any development tools or libraries the package uses. For instance, if a program is written in C++, you'll need a C++ compiler. Also, many libraries have matching development libraries. These include additional files needed to compile programs that use the libraries but that aren't needed merely to run such programs once compiled.

If your system seems to meet all the requirements specified by the program's author, try installing the package according to the provided instructions. If you have trouble, read any error messages you get when you try to install or run the program; these often contain clues. You may also want to check Chapter 5 for information on Linux packages.

Planning Disk Partitioning

Hard disks can be broken into logical chunks known as *partitions*. In Windows, partitions correspond to drive letters (C:, D:, and so on). In Linux, partitions are mounted at particular points in the Linux directory tree, so they're accessible as subdirectories. Before installing Linux, it's a good idea to give some thought to how you'll partition your hard disk. A poor initial partitioning scheme can become awkward because you'll run out of space in one partition when another has lots of available space or because the partition layout ties your hands in terms of achieving particular goals.

The PC Partitioning System

The original *x*86 partitioning scheme allowed for only four partitions. As hard disks increased in size and the need for more partitions became apparent, the original scheme was extended in a way that retained compatibility with the old scheme. The new scheme uses three partition types:

- *Primary partitions*, which are the same as the original partition types

- *Extended partitions*, which are a special type of primary partition that serves as a placeholder for the next type

- *Logical partitions*, which reside within an extended partition

For any one disk, you're limited to four primary partitions, or three primary partitions and one extended partition. Many OSs, such as DOS, Windows, and FreeBSD, *must* boot from primary partitions, and because of this, most hard disks include at least one primary partition. Linux, however, is not so limited, so you could boot Linux from a disk that contains no primary partitions, although in practice few people do this.

> The *x*86 partitioning scheme isn't the only one around. Linux includes support for many alternatives, but *x*86- and AMD64-based Linux systems generally use the PC partitioning scheme. Linux systems running on other architectures tend to use the partitioning systems native to those architectures. From an administrative point of view, these systems are almost always simpler than the PC system because there aren't any distinctions between primary, extended, and logical partitions.

A disk's primary partition layout is stored in a data structure known as the *partition table*, which exists on the first sector of the hard disk. This sector is known as the *master boot record (MBR)* because it also contains some of the first code to be run by the computer after the BIOS initializes. The locations of the logical partitions are stored within the extended partition, outside of the MBR. Although they are not a part of the MBR, these data are sometimes considered to be part of the partition table because they do define partition locations.

Linux Partition Requirements

To Linux, there's very little difference between the partition types. Linux numbers partitions on a disk, and the primary and extended partitions get the numbers from 1 to 4 (such as /dev/hda1 or /dev/sdc3), while logical partitions get numbers from 5 up. This is true even if there are fewer than four primary and extended partitions, so partitions might be numbered 1, 2, 4, 5, and 6 (omitting partition 3). Primary partition numbers are like fixed slots, so when a disk uses just 1–3 of these slots, any of the four numbers may go unused. Logical partitions, by contrast, are always numbered sequentially, without any missing numbers, so a system with precisely three logical partitions *must* number them 5, 6, and 7.

Some administrators use a primary Linux boot partition because a conventional *x*86 MBR can boot only from a primary partition. When the computer does so, it runs code in the boot sector of the boot partition. Typically, Linux places a special boot loader program in this location. The *Grand Unified Boot Loader (GRUB)* and the *Linux Loader (LILO)* are the two boot loaders most commonly found on *x*86 Linux systems. Alternatively, GRUB or LILO can reside directly in the MBR, which is more direct but leaves the boot loader more vulnerable to being wiped out should some other utility rewrite the MBR.

> Non-*x*86 distributions need boot loaders, too, but they're different from *x*86 boot loaders in various details. Sometimes a boot loader such as GRUB or LILO is ported or copied on non-*x*86 distributions. The IA-64 platform uses a boot loader called ELILO, for instance. Other times, a completely new boot loader is used, such as Yaboot for PowerPC systems.

At a bare minimum, Linux needs a single partition to install and boot. This partition is referred to as the *root partition*, or simply as /. This partition is so called because it holds the root directory, which lies at the "root" of the directory "tree"—all files on the system are identified relative to the root directory. The root partition also stores directories, such as /etc and /bin, that fall off the root directory and in which other files reside. Some of these directories can serve as *mount points*—directories to which Linux attaches other partitions. For instance, you might mount a partition on /home.

 One important directory in Linux is /root, which serves as the system administrator's home directory—the system administrator's default program settings and so on go here. The /root directory is not to be confused with the root (/) directory.

One partitioning strategy that's common on high-performance systems is a Redundant Array of Independent Disks (RAID). In a RAID configuration, partitions on separate physical hard disks are combined together to provide faster performance, greater reliability, or both. Some Linux distributions provide RAID options in their initial installation procedures, but others don't. RAID configuration is fairly advanced, and is covered in Chapter 4. If you're new to Linux, it's best to avoid RAID configurations on your first installation. After reading Chapter 4, you might try implementing a RAID configuration on subsequent installations.

Common Optional Partitions

In addition to the root partition, many system administrators like creating other partitions. Some advantages that come from splitting an installation into multiple partitions rather than leaving it as one monolithic root partition are:

Multiple disks   When you have two or more hard disks, you *must* create separate partitions— at least one for each disk. For instance, one disk might host the root directory and the second might hold /home. Also, removable disks (floppies, CD-ROMs, and so on) must be mounted as if they were separate partitions.

Better security options   By breaking important directories into separate partitions, you can apply different security options to different partitions. For instance, you might make /usr read-only, which reduces the chance of accidental or intentional corruption of important binary files.

Data overrun protection   Some errors or attacks can cause files to grow to huge sizes, which can potentially crash the system or cause serious problems. Splitting key directories into separate partitions guarantees that a runaway process in such a directory won't cause problems for processes that rely on the ability to create files in other directories. This makes it easier to recover from such difficulties. On the downside, splitting partitions up makes it more likely that a file will legitimately grow to a size that fills the partition.

Disk error protection   Disk partitions sometimes develop data errors, which are data structures that are corrupted, or a disk that has developed a physically bad sector. If your system consists of multiple partitions, such problems will more likely be isolated to one partition, which can make data recovery easier or more complete.

Backup   If your backup medium is substantially smaller than your hard disk, breaking up your disk into chunks that fit on a single medium can simplify your backup procedures.

Ideal filesystems   A *filesystem* is a set of low-level data structures that regulate how the computer allocates space on the disk for individual files, as well as what types of data are associated with files, such as file creation times and filenames. Sometimes, one filesystem works well for some purposes but not for others. You might therefore want to break the directory tree into separate partitions so that you can use multiple filesystems.

So, what directories are commonly split off into separate partitions? Table 1.1 summarizes some popular choices. Note that typical sizes for many of these partitions vary greatly depending on how the system is used. Therefore, it's impossible to make recommendations on partition size that will be universally acceptable.

    For more information, see Chapter 4.

TABLE 1.1   Common Partitions and Their Uses

Partition (mount point)	Typical size	Use
Swap (not mounted)	1.5–2 times system RAM size	Serves as an adjunct to system RAM; is slow, but enables the system to run more or larger programs. Described in more detail in Chapter 4.
/home	200MB–200GB	Holds users' data files. Isolating it on a separate partition preserves user data during a system upgrade. Size depends on number of users and their data storage needs.
/boot	5–50MB	Holds critical boot files. Creating as a separate partition allows for circumventing limitations of older BIOSs and boot loaders on hard disks over 8GB.
/usr	500MB–6GB	Holds most Linux program and data files; this is frequently the largest partition.
/usr/local	100MB–3GB	Holds Linux program and data files that are unique to this installation, particularly those that you compile yourself.
/opt	100MB–3GB	Holds Linux program and data files that are associated with third-party packages, especially commercial ones.

TABLE 1.1   Common Partitions and Their Uses *(continued)*

Partition (mount point)	Typical size	Use
/var	100MB–200GB	Holds miscellaneous files associated with the day-to-day functioning of a computer. These files are often transient in nature. Most often split off as a separate partition when the system functions as a server that uses the /var directory for server-related files like mail queues.
/tmp	100MB-20GB	Holds temporary files created by ordinary users.
/mnt	N/A	/mnt isn't itself a separate partition; rather, it or its subdirectories are used as mount points for removable media like floppies or CD-ROMs.
/media	N/A	Holds subdirectories that may be used as mount points for removable media, much like /mnt or its subdirectories.

Some directories—/etc, /bin, /sbin, /lib, and /dev—should *never* be placed on separate partitions. These directories host critical system configuration files or files without which a Linux system cannot function. For instance, /etc contains /etc/fstab, the file that specifies what partitions correspond to what directories, and /bin contains the mount utility that's used to mount partitions on directories.

The 2.4.*x* and later kernels include support for a dedicated /dev filesystem, which obviates the need for files in an actual /dev directory, so in some sense, /dev can reside on a separate filesystem, although not a separate partition.

Linux Filesystem Options

Linux supports many filesystems. Linux's standard filesystem for most of the 1990s was the *second extended filesystem (ext2 or ext2fs)*, which was the default filesystem for most distributions. Ext2fs supports all the features required by Linux (or by Unix-style OSs in general), and is well tested and robust.

Ext2fs has one major problem, though: If the computer is shut down improperly (because of a power outage, system crash, or the like), it can take several minutes for Linux to verify an ext2fs partition's integrity when the computer reboots. This delay is an annoyance at best, and it is a serious problem on mission-critical systems such as major servers. The solution is implemented in what's known as a *journaling filesystem*. Such a filesystem keeps a record of changes it's about to make in a special journal log file. Therefore, after an unexpected crash, the system

---

Real World Scenario

When to Create Multiple Partitions

One problem with splitting off lots of separate partitions, particularly for new administrators, is that it can be difficult to settle on appropriate partition sizes. As noted in Table 1.1, the appropriate size of various partitions can vary substantially from one system to another. For instance, a workstation is likely to need a fairly small /var partition (say, 100MB), but a mail or news server might need a /var partition that's gigabytes in size. Guessing wrong isn't fatal, but it is annoying. You'll need to resize your partitions (which is tedious and dangerous) or set up symbolic links between partitions so that subdirectories on one partition can be stored on other partitions.

For this reason, I generally recommend that new Linux administrators try simple partition layouts first. The root (/) partition is required, and swap is a very good idea. Beyond this, /boot can be very helpful on hard disks of more than 8GB with older distributions or BIOSs, but is seldom needed with computers or distributions sold since 2000. An appropriate size for /home is often relatively easy for new administrators to guess, so splitting it off generally makes sense. Beyond this, I recommend that new administrators proceed with caution.

As you gain more experience with Linux, you may want to break off other directories into their own partitions on subsequent installations, or when upgrading disk hardware. You can use the du command to learn how much space is used by files within any given directory.

---

can examine the log file to determine what areas of the disk might need to be checked. This design makes for very fast checks after a crash or power failure—a few seconds at most, typically. The four journaling filesystems for Linux are:

- The *third extended filesystem (ext3fs)*, which is derived from ext2fs and is the most popular journaling filesystem for Linux

- *ReiserFS* (`http://www.namesys.com`), which was added as a standard component to the 2.4.1 kernel

- The *Extent Filesystem*, or XFS (`http://linux-xfs.sgi.com/projects/xfs`), which was originally designed for Silicon Graphics' IRIX OS

- The *Journaled Filesystem*, or JFS (`http://oss.software.ibm.com/developerworks/opensource/jfs`), which IBM developed for its AIX and OS/2

Of these four, XFS and JFS are the most advanced, but ext3fs and ReiserFS are the most stable and popular. A derivative of the current ReiserFS, Reiser4, is under development.

The Linux swap partition doesn't use a filesystem per se. Linux does need to write some basic data structures to this partition in order to use it as swap space (as described in Chapter 4), but this isn't technically a filesystem because no files are stored within it.

Linux also supports many non-Linux filesystems, including:

- The File Allocation Table (FAT) filesystem used by DOS and Windows
- The New Technology Filesystem (NTFS) used by Windows NT/200*x*/XP
- The High-Performance Filesystem (HPFS) used by OS/2
- The Unix Filesystem (UFS; also known as the Fast Filesystem, or FFS) used by various versions of Unix
- The Hierarchical Filesystem (HFS) used by Mac OS
- ISO-9660 and Joliet filesystems used on CD-ROMs
- The Universal Disk Format (UDF), which is the up-and-coming successor to ISO-9660 for optical discs

Most of these filesystems are useful mainly in dual-boot configurations—for instance, to share files between Linux and Windows. Some—particularly FAT, ISO-9660, Joliet, and UDF—are useful for exchanging files between computers on removable media. As a general rule, these filesystems can't hold critical Linux files because they lack necessary filesystem features. There are exceptions, though—Linux sports extensions for cramming necessary information into FAT and HPFS partitions, UFS was designed for storing Unix filesystem features in the first place, and the Rock Ridge extensions add the necessary support to ISO-9660.

It's usually best to use a journaling filesystem for Linux partitions. As a general rule, any of the current crop of journaling filesystems works well, at least with recent (late 2.4.*x* or later) kernels. The best tested under Linux are ext3fs and ReiserFS. ReiserFS versions of 3.5 and earlier have a 2GB file-size limit, but this limit is raised to 16TB for ReiserFS 3.6 and later. XFS and JFS are both well tested under other OSs, but are not as well tested under Linux. XFS and ext3fs have the widest array of filesystem support tools, such as versions of `dump` and `restore` for creating and restoring backups. All of the journaling filesystems except for ReiserFS support a flexible security system known as access control lists (ACLs), which are particularly important if your system functions as a Samba server to Windows NT/200*x*/XP clients. All Linux distributions support ext2fs out of the box, and most released since 2001 support ReiserFS as well. Support for others is spottier, but increasing. Use non-Linux filesystems for data exchange with non-Linux systems.

Partitioning Tools

In order to create partitions, you use a partitioning tool. Dozens of such tools are available, but only a few are reasonable choices when you're installing a Linux system:

DOS's FDISK   Microsoft's DOS and Windows ship with a simple partitioning tool known as FDISK (for fixed disk). This program is inflexible and uses a crude text-based user interface, but it's readily available and can create partitions that Linux can use. (You'll probably have to modify the partition type codes using Linux tools in order to use DOS-created partitions, though.)

Linux's `fdisk`   Linux includes a partitioning tool that's named after the DOS program, but the Linux tool's name is entirely lowercase, whereas the DOS tool's name is usually written in uppercase. Linux's `fdisk` is much more flexible than DOS's `FDISK`, but it also uses a text-based user interface. If you have an existing Linux emergency disk, you can use it to create partitions for Linux before installing the OS.

Linux install-time tools   Most Linux installation utilities include partitioning tools. Sometimes the installers simply call `fdisk`, but other times they provide GUI tools that are much easier to use. If you're installing a Linux-only system, using the installer's tools is probably the best course of action.

PowerQuest's PartitionMagic   Symantec (`http://www.symantec.com`) makes an unusually flexible partitioning program known as PartitionMagic. This commercial program provides a GUI interface and can create partitions that are prepared with ext2fs, ext3fs, FAT, NTFS, or HPFS filesystems. (HPFS support is missing from the latest versions, though.) This makes it an excellent tool for configuring a disk for a multi-OS computer. PartitionMagic can also resize a partition without damaging its contents. The main program is Windows-based, but the package comes with a DOS version that can run from a floppy, so it's possible to use it on a system without Windows.

GNU Parted   GNU Parted (`http://www.gnu.org/software/parted/`) is an open source alternative to PartitionMagic. It can create, resize, and move various partition types, such as FAT, ext2fs, ext3fs, ReiserFS, and Linux swap. GNU Parted runs from Linux and provides a text-only user interface, though, which makes it intimidating and less than ideal for preparing a new disk for Linux installation. Nonetheless, you can prepare a Linux boot disk that runs Parted if you like.

QTParted   This program, headquartered at `http://qtparted.sourceforge.net`, provides a GUI front-end to GNU Parted. This GUI control system is similar to the one used by PartitionMagic, but QTParted runs in Linux and supports the filesystems that GNU Parted supports.

FIPS   The First Nondestructive Interactive Partition Splitting (FIPS) program comes with many Linux distributions. It's a fairly specialized partitioning tool that splits a single primary FAT partition into two partitions. It's designed to make room for Linux on computers that already have Windows installed—you run FIPS, delete the second (empty) partition that FIPS creates, and create Linux partitions in that empty space.

In theory, partitions created by any tool may be used in any OS, provided the tool uses the standard *x*86 partition table. In practice, though, OSs sometimes object to unusual features of partitions created by certain partitioning tools. Therefore, it's usually best to take one of two approaches to disk partitioning:

- Use a cross-platform partitioning tool like PartitionMagic. Such tools tend to create partitions that are inoffensive to all major OSs.
- Use each OS's partitioning tool to create that OS's partitions.

Selecting an Installation Method

After you've decided on a distribution, the first choice you must make when installing Linux is what installation method you intend to use. Two classes of options are available: the installation media and the method of interaction during installation. In both cases, some distributions offer more or different options than do others, so in truth, your preferences in these matters may influence your distribution choice. For instance, Debian GNU/Linux doesn't support GUI installations, so if you strongly desire this feature, you can't use Debian.

Media Options

Linux can be booted and installed from any of several different media—floppy disks, CD-ROMs, network connections, and so on. For both booting and installing files, different media offer different advantages and disadvantages.

The Boot Method

Linux installer programs run within Linux itself. This means that in order to install Linux, you must be able to boot a small Linux system, which is provided by the distribution maintainer. This system is useful only for installing Linux and sometimes for doing emergency maintenance. It typically fits on one or two floppy disks, or can boot from a bootable CD-ROM.

   Modern BIOSs include options for the selection of a boot medium. Typical choices include the floppy disk, CD-ROM drive, ATA hard disk, SCSI hard disk, and high-capacity removable-media drive (like a Zip or LS-120 disk). In addition, some network cards include BIOSs that enable a computer to boot from files stored on a server. In theory, any of these media can be used to boot a Linux installer. Additionally, some distributions provide a DOS or Windows program that can launch the installation from a working DOS or Windows system.

   Although many boot methods are possible, the three most common are as follows:

Floppy   Many boxed distributions come with one or more boot floppies. If you configure your BIOS to boot from floppy disks before any other working boot medium, you can insert the boot floppy and turn on the computer to start the installation process. Even if you download Linux or obtain it on a cut-rate CD-ROM without a boot floppy, you can create a boot floppy yourself from a file on the CD-ROM (often called `boot.img` or something similar), using a DOS program such as `RAWRITE`. Look for these files and instructions on how to use them on the installation CD-ROM. The floppy boot method may be necessary if you plan to install from a network server.

CD-ROM   Modern Linux distributions almost always come on CD-ROMs or DVD-ROMs that are themselves bootable. On a computer that's configured to boot from CD-ROM before other bootable media, you can insert the CD-ROM in the drive, then turn on the computer, and the boot program automatically starts up. If you download and burn a Linux CD-R image file, you don't need to take any special steps to make this CD-R bootable. Some older BIOSs don't support CD-ROM boots, in which case you should make boot floppies, as just described.

Existing OS bootstrap   Some distributions come with a DOS, Windows, or Mac OS program that shuts down that OS and boots up the Linux installer. These programs sometimes run automatically when you insert the Linux CD-ROM in the drive. Using them can be a good way to get started if you plan to install a dual-boot system, or if you plan to replace your current OS with Linux.

Ultimately, the boot method is unimportant, because the same installation programs run no matter what method you choose. Pick the boot method that's most convenient for your hardware and the form of installation medium you've chosen.

Installation Media

The installation medium is the physical form of the source of the Linux files. Linux is very flexible in its installation media. The most common choices are:

CD-ROM or DVD-ROM   If you buy Linux in a store or from an online retailer, chances are you'll get a CD-ROM. In fact, most distributions come on multiple CD-ROMs. Some companies, such as SuSE, have begun shipping a DVD-ROM with some of their packages. (DVD-ROMs can store much more data than can CD-ROMs, so a single DVD-ROM is equivalent to multiple CD-ROMs.) CD-ROM installations tend to be quick. Most distribution maintainers offer CD-ROM image files that you can burn to CD-Rs yourself. To find CD-R image files, check `http://www.linuxiso.org`, `http://linux.tucows.com/distributions_default.html`, `ftp://sunsite.unc.edu/pub/linux/distributions`, or your chosen distribution's Web or FTP site.

Network   If you have a fast network connection and don't want to be bothered with installation CD-ROMs, you can install many distributions via network connections. Download a boot floppy image, create a floppy disk from it, and boot the installer. Tell it you want to install via the network and point it to a public archive site for the distribution. This approach can also be useful if you've got a CD-ROM and a network but your target system doesn't have a CD-ROM drive. You can copy your installation CD-ROMs onto one computer on your network, configure that system to share the files, and use network installation tools to read the files over the network. The drawback to network installations is that they tend to be slower than installs from CD-ROMs. They require more information from the user, and so they can be more difficult for a new user to get working. They can also fail midway if a network connection goes down or a server stops responding. Network installations may use any of several protocols to transfer files, including FTP, HTTP (Web), SMB (Windows file sharing), and NFS (Unix/Linux file sharing). Precisely which protocols are supported varies from one distribution to another.

Hard disk   It's possible to put the Linux files on a DOS or Windows partition and install Linux in another partition using those files. This approach used to be somewhat common among hobbyists who would download the files but who didn't have a CD-R burner. It's less common today but is still occasionally useful. You might use it if your CD-ROM drive doesn't seem to work in Linux, for instance; you could copy the files from the CD-ROM to the hard disk and then install from there. Because Linux treats high-capacity removable-media drives as if they were hard disks, you could also store installation files on something like a Jaz or Orb drive, which might be convenient for installing Linux on multiple systems in some environments.

Floppy disks   Early Linux distributions came as floppy disk sets. With today's major distributions commonly exceeding 1GB compressed, floppy disks aren't a very appealing distribution medium. A few specialized distributions, however, are entirely floppy-based. Tom's Root/Boot disk (`http://www.toms.net/rb/`), for instance, is a single-floppy Linux distribution intended for emergency recovery use.

Monolithic files   It's possible to distribute an entire Linux system as a single file. One example along these lines is an image file of a demo Linux CD-ROM, which can boot directly from the CD-ROM drive and run Linux without installing it on the computer. Another example is the ZipSlack distribution, which is a stripped-down version of Slackware (`http://www.slackware.com`). This distribution uses extensions to the DOS or Windows File Allocation Table (FAT) filesystem so that you can store the distribution on an ordinary FAT partition or high-capacity removable-media drive, such as a Zip or LS-120 drive. Once this is done, you can boot ZipSlack using a floppy disk.

Not all distributions support all of these installation options. All mainstream distributions support installation from CD-ROM, and most support at least one form of network installation. Beyond this, you should check the documentation for the distribution.

Even if a system lacks a CD-ROM drive, you can temporarily install a drive from another computer in order to install Linux. This is usually not the most efficient course of action if the system has a network connection, but it can be handy for installing Linux in an isolated system.

Methods of Interaction during Installation

Most methods of Linux installation require you to make decisions during the process. You may need to tell the system how to partition your hard disk, what your network settings are, and so on. To handle such interactions, distribution maintainers have developed three methods of data entry: GUI-based, text-based, and scripted. The first two are most suitable for customized individual installations, while scripts are best used when you are configuring large numbers of nearly identical systems.

GUI Installations

As a general rule, Linux distributions are shifting toward GUI installer programs. These tools run the X GUI environment in a basic 640×480 (VGA) mode that works on most modern video cards. (Some installers can run at 800×600 or higher.) The system can then use familiar mouse-based point-and-click operations to obtain input from the user. Because the display is a bit-mapped graphics image, it's also possible to display graphical representations of information such as partition sizes. These displays can be very useful because people often find it easier to interpret graphs than the numbers that are more often used by text-based utilities.

GUI installations are most popular on CD-based installations. X and its related libraries are fairly large, so implementing an X-based installation over a network or floppy-based connection is tedious at best. Also, GUI installers don't work on all systems because some have unusual video hardware that's incompatible with the GUI installer. This problem is particularly acute with laptop computers, whose LCD screens sometimes don't work with the video modes used by GUI installers. If you're faced with such a situation, you may need to use a text-based installer.

Text-Based Installations

A few distributions (most notably Gentoo and Slackware) don't provide GUI tools, so you *must* use a text-based installer if you want to install one of these distributions. In principle, a text-based installation works just like a GUI one. Specifically, you must enter the same types of information—Linux partition information, TCP/IP network configuration options, package selections, and so on. Text-based tools require you to select options using your keyboard, though, and they can't display graphics that are nearly as sophisticated as can a GUI installer. Some text-based programs can produce crude progress bars and the like, though, and some use text-based menus in which you tab through options to select the one you want. A few even enable you to use the mouse to select options from textual menus.

Most Linux distributions offer a text-based installation option. Typically, an early screen gives you the choice of running a GUI or text-based install, or you can type a special command to switch into a text-based mode if the default is a GUI installer. Consult your distribution's documentation if you don't see an obvious way to start a text-based installer.

Scripted Installations

With an automatic scripted installation, you typically create a configuration file that includes the information you'd normally enter with the keyboard or mouse—partition sizes, networking options, packages to install, and so on. Early in the installation process, you tell the system to read the configuration file from a floppy disk or from the network. The system then proceeds with the installation without further intervention from you.

To create the configuration file, you must normally install Linux manually on one system. The installer gives you the option of saving the configuration file. When you install Linux on the next system, you use this file to create a system that's configured identically to the first.

Scripted installations work best when you need to install Linux on many identical or nearly identical computers. If the systems vary in important details like hard disk size or intended function (workstation, server, and so on), a scripted install won't give you the opportunity to change those details on the various systems, so you'll end up spending *more* time correcting matters after the installation than you'll save by using the scripting features. You can also save your configuration options so that you can quickly reinstall a distribution on a single computer, should the need arise.

If you have many nearly identical systems to install, invest time in getting the installation just right when you create a set of installation parameters. For instance, you might want to use a custom package selection option to fine-tune what packages are installed. You'll invest time in the initial installation, but you'll save time reconfiguring all the systems after they're installed.

Not all distributions include scripted installation options. Consult your distribution's documentation for details.

Installing Linux

The process of installing Linux varies from one distribution to another, so you may want to consult your distribution's documentation for details. Generally speaking, though, this process guides you through several stages in which you enter critical information about your system and its desired role:

Language options   Many Linux installers today support multiple languages, so you may need to select one.

Keyboard and mouse options   Keyboard options sometimes appear alongside language options, because keyboards vary with language. Even within a language, keyboard options can vary, such as 101-key versus 104-key keyboards. Mouse options are sometimes presented later in the installation process, along with X configuration, but sometimes this information is gathered early to support GUI installers. You must tell the system how the mouse is connected (via a USB port, PS/2 port, and so on) and what protocol the mouse uses (most today use the PS/2 protocol or a variant of that).

Partition creation   Most Linux installers give you the option of creating partitions for Linux. Sometimes the installer can automate this process, but this involves making assumptions about your system. Partition options were described earlier, in the section "Planning Disk Partitioning."

Network configuration   You can usually tell Linux about your network hardware and how it should be configured as you install the OS. This topic is described in more detail in Chapter 6. If you're uncertain of how to proceed, either select no networking support or consult your local network administrator. Ideally, you'll be able to select an option to use DHCP, which will automatically configure basic network settings, but not all networks support DHCP. You may also be able to select which network servers you want to run. I recommend taking a minimalist approach; don't run any server unless you know what it does and you know that you need it. Running servers unnecessarily can be a security risk.

Time and date options   Most installation procedures give you the ability to set the computer's time and date. One unusual feature of Linux is that it enables you to store the time in the hardware clock either in local time or in *Coordinated Universal Time (UTC),* which is essentially the same as *Greenwich Mean Time (GMT)*—the time in Greenwich, England, unadjusted for daylight saving. Linux, like Unix, uses UTC internally, so setting your hardware clock to UTC is preferable on a Linux-only system. If the computer dual-boots Linux and an OS, such as Windows, that assumes the hardware clock stores the local time, you may need to pick that option.

Package selection   One of the more tedious parts of some installations is picking software packages to be installed. Some distributions provide a few very high-level options, either by default or as part of a simplified process. On these distributions, you pick a package set such as "workstation" or "server," and the software installs whole clusters of packages. On other distributions, you pick packages individually. Most provide a middle ground in which you pick clusters of packages, and can sometimes fine-tune package sets.

X configuration   If the computer is to be used as a workstation, chances are you'll want to configure X. Most desktop-oriented distributions today make this very easy; they feature tools that can detect your video card make and model, your mouse, and perhaps even your optimal screen resolution. Other times, you'll need information on your hardware at hand to enter in the X configuration screens. Your monitor's horizontal and vertical refresh rates are particularly important. You may be able to enter these by selecting your monitor from a list, but you may need to enter the information manually from your monitor's manual. Thus, you should have this manual handy when you perform the installation.

Miscellaneous hardware detection   Distributions vary in precisely what hardware they detect and configure during installation. For instance, some enable you to configure a modem at system installation, but others don't. Other hardware that might or might not be detected includes the sound card, a second video card, and a printer.

Account creation   Almost all distributions require you to enter a `root` password as part of the installation process. This password should be unique and hard to guess. (Chapter 3 provides pointers on picking good passwords.) Some distributions also enable you to create one or more ordinary user accounts. Generally speaking, creating at least one such account is a good idea. Some distributions support configuring Linux to use a remote account database, such as one maintained by a Windows NT domain controller, a Network Information System (NIS) server, or a Lightweight Directory Access Protocol (LDAP) server. These systems can be very handy, but you shouldn't attempt to use one unless you know you should do so.

Boot loader configuration   Linux relies on a boot loader in order to boot, and boot loaders must be configured. Typically, you can select a few options from point-and-click menus, and these will work.

Most Linux installers provide text-mode or GUI menus that guide you through the process, as illustrated in Figure 1.2, which shows the package selection menu from a Fedora installation. Pick the appropriate package groups and click Next to move on to the next screen. Some text-based installers are less user-friendly, though. Gentoo requires you to enter text-mode commands at a command prompt, for instance. Gentoo makes up for this by providing very explicit installation instructions on its Web site, though.

However it's done, by the time you finish the process you should have a bootable Linux system. Follow the installer through to the end and, when prompted, reboot the computer as instructed. If all goes well, Linux will boot up.

Configuring Boot Loaders

The Linux kernel is at the heart of a Linux computer; in fact, technically speaking, the kernel *is* Linux—everything else is support programs. Because the kernel must run before Linux is completely booted, the kernel must be loaded into memory in a unique way. A program known as a *boot loader* handles this task. Several boot loaders are available, some of which can boot a Linux kernel directly, and others of which require help to do the job.

FIGURE 1.2   Most Linux installation tools provide options with at least minimal explanations to help guide you through the process.

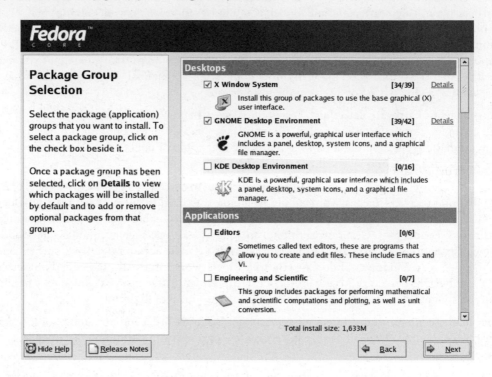

 This section describes boot loaders for *x*86 and AMD64 systems. If you're using Linux on another architecture, such as PowerPC (Macintosh) or Alpha, the available boot loaders will be different. Consult your distribution's documentation for details.

The Role of the Boot Loader

When it's first powered up, an *x*86 CPU checks a specific area of memory for code to execute. This code is the BIOS. You're probably familiar with the BIOS through your computer's BIOS setup screens, which enable you to configure features such as RAM timing and whether or not on-board ports are active. The BIOS also provides code that allows the computer to boot. The BIOS checks the first sector of your hard disk (or of your floppy disk, CD-ROM, or other disk devices, depending on the BIOS's capabilities and configuration) for a small boot loader program. This program normally resides on the MBR of a hard disk or the boot sector of a floppy disk. The MBR resides on the first sector of a hard disk and controls the boot process. A boot sector is the first sector of a floppy or of a hard disk partition and also controls the boot process. (In the case of a partition's boot sector, it's used after the MBR.)

In the case of a PC that runs nothing but Windows, the boot loader in the MBR is hard-coded to check for a secondary boot loader in the active primary partition. This secondary boot loader directly loads the Windows kernel. The approach in Linux is similar, but standard Linux boot loaders are somewhat more complex. LILO and GRUB are the most common Linux boot loaders. Both programs enable you to boot the Linux kernel or to redirect the boot process to another OS. (GRUB can directly boot several non-Linux OSs, as well.)

In some cases, a system uses multiple boot loaders. One resides in the MBR, and another resides in the boot sector of an individual disk partition. (OSs on different partitions can each have their own boot sector–based boot loaders.) In this configuration, the MBR-based boot loader is the *primary boot loader*, and the one in a partition's boot sector is a *secondary boot loader*. Some boot loaders work in only one of these positions. It's often possible for a secondary boot loader to redirect the boot process to a different partition, in which case that partition's boot loader becomes the tertiary boot loader, although the configuration is the same as for secondary status.

Available Boot Loaders

Many OSs ship with their own boot loaders, and others are available from third parties. Some of the most common boot loaders are:

LILO   This boot loader can directly boot a Linux kernel, and it can function as either a primary or a secondary boot loader. It may also be installed on a floppy disk, which is unusual for a boot loader. When used as a secondary boot loader, LILO should *only* be installed in a Linux partition; it will damage the contents of most non-Linux filesystems. Installing LILO in a swap partition is also inadvisable since it will be wiped out by swap activity. LILO can redirect the boot process to non-Linux partitions, and so it can be used to select Linux or Windows in a dual-boot system.

GRUB   This boot loader is on the way to becoming the standard Linux boot loader. GRUB was the first boot loader that could directly boot Linux from above the 1024th cylinder of a hard disk, which gained it some popularity. LILO has since achieved similar capabilities, though. GRUB can be installed in the same locations as LILO—a floppy disk, the MBR, or the boot sector of a Linux partition.

OS Loader   This is one name by which Windows NT/200*x*/XP's boot loader goes. Another is NTLDR. This is a secondary boot loader that cannot directly boot Linux, but it can boot a disk file that can contain LILO or GRUB, and hence boot Linux indirectly. It's common on some dual-boot installations.

System Commander   This boot loader, from V Communications (`http://www.v-com.com`), is the Cadillac of boot loaders, with some very advanced features. It cannot directly boot Linux, but like many others, it can direct the boot process to a Linux partition on which LILO or GRUB is installed.

LOADLIN   This is an unusual boot loader in that it's neither a primary nor a secondary boot loader. Rather, it's a DOS program that can be used to boot Linux after DOS has already loaded. It's particularly useful for emergency situations because it enables you to boot a Linux kernel using a DOS boot floppy, and you can also use it to pass kernel parameters to influence the booted system's behavior. LOADLIN comes with most Linux distributions, generally in a directory on the main installation CD-ROM.

After installing Linux, create a DOS boot floppy with LOADLIN and a copy of your Linux kernel. You can then use this boot floppy to boot Linux if LILO misbehaves or your kernel is accidentally overwritten.

Many additional third-party boot loaders are available, most of which, like System Commander, cannot directly boot a Linux kernel but can boot a partition on which LILO or GRUB is installed. For this reason, this chapter emphasizes configuring LILO and GRUB—these boot loaders can be used to boot Linux, whether they function as primary, secondary, or tertiary boot loaders. If you opt to use LILO or GRUB as a secondary boot loader, you'll need to consult the documentation for your primary boot loader to learn how to configure it.

On a Linux-only system, there's no need to deal with an advanced third-party boot loader; LILO or GRUB can function as a primary boot loader without trouble on such systems. Third-party boot loaders are most useful when you have two or more OSs installed, and particularly when LILO or GRUB has trouble redirecting the boot process to the other OSs, which is rare.

The usual configuration for LILO or GRUB is to place them in the MBR. Even in a Linux-only situation, however, it's sometimes desirable to place LILO or GRUB in the Linux boot partition. Used in this way, a standard DOS/Windows MBR will boot Linux *if* the Linux boot partition is a primary partition that's marked as active. This configuration can be particularly helpful in DOS/Linux or Windows/Linux dual-boot configurations because DOS and Windows tend to overwrite the MBR at installation. Therefore, putting LILO or GRUB in the Linux boot sector keeps it out of harm's way, and you can get LILO or GRUB working after installing or reinstalling DOS or Windows by using the DOS or Windows FDISK program and marking the Linux partition as active. If LILO or GRUB is on the MBR and is wiped out, you'll need to boot Linux in some other way, such as by using LOADLIN, and then rerun the lilo program to restore LILO to the MBR or rerun grub-install to restore GRUB to the MBR.

Configuring LILO

LILO is the traditional Linux boot loader, and some distributions still install it by default. Unlike most programs, LILO is really three things. First, it's a program you can run from within Linux, called lilo. This side of LILO is really an installer program; its job is to copy the boot loader code itself to the MBR, boot partition, or floppy disk. It's this boot loader that's the second side of LILO. LILO's third part is its configuration file, /etc/lilo.conf, which specifies the kernels and OSs LILO can boot. When you run the lilo utility, it modifies the code it copies to its ultimate destination to support the options you specify in this file.

An Overview of LILO Configuration

The /etc/lilo.conf file consists of lines with general configuration options, followed by one or more stanzas—groups of lines that define a single OS to be booted. For instance, Listing 1.1 shows a simple lilo.conf file that defines a system that can boot either Linux or Windows.

The 1024-Cylinder Limit

One bane of the PC world that reared its ugly head twice in the 1990s was the so-called *1024-cylinder limit*. This limit is derived from the fact that the *x*86 BIOS uses a three-number scheme for addressing hard disk sectors. Each sector is identified by a cylinder number, a head number, and a sector number, known collectively as the sector's *CHS address*. The problem is that each of these values is limited in size. The cylinder number, in particular, is allotted only 10 bits and so cannot exceed 2^{10}, or 1024, values. In conjunction with the limits for sectors and heads, this restricted addressable ATA hard disk size to precisely 504MB in the early 1990s.

When disks larger than 504MB became common, BIOSs were adjusted with *CHS translation* schemes, which allowed them to juggle numbers between cylinders, heads, and sectors. This increased the effective limit to just under 8GB. A similar scheme abandoned CHS addressing for BIOS-to-disk communications but retained it for BIOS-to-software communications. This was known as *linear block addressing (LBA)* mode.

These limits never affected Linux once it had booted, because Linux could handle more than 10-bit cylinder values, and it could access disks directly using LBA mode. The Linux boot process was limited, however, because LILO (this was pre-GRUB) relied on CHS addressing via the BIOS to boot the kernel. Therefore, the Linux kernel has traditionally had to reside below the 1024-cylinder mark.

Today, all new BIOSs include support for so-called *extended INT13* calls, which bypass the CHS addressing scheme. These BIOSs support booting an OS from past the 1024-cylinder mark on a hard disk, but only if the boot loader and OS support this feature. Recent versions of LILO and GRUB support extended INT13 calls, so new Linux distributions can be installed anywhere on a hard disk—if the BIOS supports this feature.

Listing 1.1: Sample `lilo.conf` File

```
boot=/dev/hda
prompt
delay=40
map=/boot/map
install=/boot/boot.b
default=linux
lba32
message=/boot/message
image=/boot/bzImage-2.6.10
        label=linux
        root=/dev/hda9
        append="mem=256M"
        read-only
```

```
other=/dev/hda3
        label=windows
        table=/dev/hda
```

Each line contains a command that defines some aspect of LILO's operation. The following entries describe some of the important general configuration options shown in Listing 1.1:

Boot device   The boot=/dev/hda option tells LILO that it will install itself to /dev/hda—the MBR of the first physical ATA disk. To install LILO as a secondary boot loader, put it in a Linux partition, such as /dev/hda9.

Prompt the user   The prompt option tells LILO to prompt the user. By default, LILO uses a simple text-mode prompt, such as lilo:. Many modern distributions include additional parameters that add menu-based and graphical prompts.

Boot delay   LILO boots a default OS after a configurable delay, expressed in tenths of a second. The delay=40 line sets the delay to 4 seconds.

Set default configuration   The default=linux option specifies the default OS or kernel to boot; it refers to the label line in the stanza in question. If this option is omitted, LILO uses the first stanza as the default.

Enable LBA mode   The lba32 option enables the ability to boot kernels located past the 1024th cylinder of the disk (about 8GB on most modern hard drives).

Other options are present, but you're not likely to need to change them unless you need to customize how LILO appears for users or enable advanced features.

Each stanza begins with its own line—image= for Linux kernels or other= for other OSs, such as DOS or Windows. Listing 1.1 shows all but the first line of each stanza indented, but this isn't required; it simply helps distinguish the stanzas from each other. Important options for specific stanzas include the following:

OS label   The label option sets the name by which an OS or kernel will be known. In the default LILO configuration, the user types this name at the lilo: prompt. If LILO is configured to use a menu, the name appears in that menu. Every stanza must have a label definition. Although Listing 1.1 shows labels named after the OSs in question, these labels are, in fact, arbitrary.

Linux root filesystem   The root option sets the root (/) filesystem for a Linux system. Once booted, the Linux kernel looks here for startup scripts, /etc/fstab (for the locations of other filesystems), and so on.

Kernel options   The append option line lets you pass parameters to the kernel. These parameters influence the way the kernel treats hardware. Listing 1.1 includes an append option that tells the kernel that the system has 256MB of RAM. (Linux usually detects this correctly, but some BIOSs throw Linux off.) You can also tell Linux what settings (IRQs and DMA channels) to use for hardware, if the drivers are built into the kernel.

Boot read-only   Linux normally starts up by booting the root filesystem in read-only mode, and later switches it to full read-write mode. The read-only option tells Linux to behave in this way; it's a standard part of a Linux boot stanza.

Partition table   The `table` option allows LILO to pass the location of the boot disk's partition table to a non-Linux OS. This is required for some OSs to boot. Its normal value is `/dev/hda` for ATA disks or `/dev/sda` for SCSI disks.

LILO is a complex program that has many additional options. Consult the `lilo.conf` man page for more information on these options.

It's important to realize that there are three aspects to LILO:

- The LILO configuration file, `/etc/lilo.conf`
- The installed boot loader, which resides in the MBR or boot sector
- The `lilo` program, which converts a `lilo.conf` file into an installed boot loader

After you've edited `/etc/lilo.conf`, you *must* type `lilo` as `root` to activate your changes. If you omit this step, your system will continue to use the old boot loader.

Adding a New Kernel to LILO

It's possible to configure LILO to boot either of two or more kernels using the same distribution. This can be very convenient when you want to test a new kernel. Rather than eliminate your old working configuration, you install a new kernel alongside the old one and create a new `lilo.conf` entry for the new kernel. The result is that you can select either the old kernel or the new one at boot time. If the new kernel doesn't work as expected, you can reboot and select the old kernel. This procedure allows you to avoid otherwise ugly situations should a new kernel not boot at all.

Assuming you don't need to change kernel `append` options or other features, one procedure for adding a new kernel to LILO is as follows:

1. Install the new kernel file, typically in `/boot`. Ensure that you *do not* overwrite the existing kernel file, though. If you compile your own kernel, remember to install the kernel modules (with `make modules_install`) as well.

2. Copy the stanza for the existing kernel file in `/etc/lilo.conf`. The result is two identical stanzas.

3. Modify the name (`label`) of one of the stanzas to reflect the new kernel name. You can use any arbitrary name you like, even a numeric one, such as `2610` for the 2.6.10 kernel.

4. Adjust the `image` line in the new kernel's stanza to point to the new kernel file.

5. If you want to make the new kernel the default, change the `default` line to point to the new kernel.

6. Save your `/etc/lilo.conf` changes.

7. Type `lilo` to install LILO in the MBR or boot partition's boot sector.

It's generally best to hold off on making the new kernel the default until you've tested it. If you make this change too early and then can't get around to fixing problems with the new kernel for a while, you might find yourself accidentally booting the bad kernel. This is normally a minor nuisance.

Once you've done this, you can reboot the computer to load the new kernel. Be sure to select the new kernel at the `lilo:` prompt, or you'll boot the old one. If everything works, you can go back to step 5 if you skipped it initially (remember to repeat steps 6 and 7 as well). If the new kernel doesn't work properly, you can reboot the computer and select the old kernel in LILO to boot it.

Adding a New OS to LILO

Adding a new OS to LILO works much as does adding a new Linux kernel. There are two basic conditions for doing this:

Multiple Linux OSs   You may want to install two or more Linux OSs on one computer—say, to have a small emergency system for disaster recovery or to be able to run and test multiple distributions on one computer. When doing this, the procedure is basically the same as that for adding a new kernel, except that you must also specify the correct root partition (with the `root` parameter). In many cases, you'll need to mount your alternate Linux's root partition within the first one's filesystem and point to the alternate system's kernel on this mount point. For instance, when installing an emergency boot system and configuring it from the main Linux system, you might mount the emergency installation's root filesystem at `/emerg`, so the `image` line might read `image=/emerg/boot/bzImage-2.4.22`.

Linux and another OS   LILO can boot most non-Linux OSs using the `other` line in `/etc/lilo.conf`, as shown in Listing 1.1. Model the entry for your non-Linux OS after this, pointing to the correct boot partition for the alternate OS.

In either case, once you've saved your changes, you must remember to type **lilo**. This action writes a new customized LILO to the MBR or Linux boot partition. If you fail to do this, you'll continue to use the old configuration the next time you boot.

 Real World Scenario

Naming Kernel Files

A good practice when adding a new kernel is to give it a name that includes its version number or other identifying information. For instance, Listing 1.1's kernel is called `bzImage-2.6.10`, identifying it as a 2.6.10 kernel. If you had such a kernel and wanted to try adding a new feature (say, XFS support), you might call this new kernel `bzImage2.6.10-xfs`. There are no hard-and-fast rules for such naming, so use whatever system you like. As a general rule, though, the base of the name begins with `vmlinux` (for a "raw" kernel file), `vmlinuz` (for a kernel compressed with `gzip`), `zImage` (another name for a kernel compressed with `gzip`), or `bzImage` (for a kernel compressed in a way that supports booting larger kernel images). Most distributions use `vmlinuz` for their kernels, but locally compiled kernels usually go by the `bzImage` name.

Configuring GRUB

Configuring GRUB is similar to configuring LILO in many respects, although there are several important differences. Like LILO, GRUB is a collection of several components, including the boot loader code proper, a configuration file, and a set of utilities for installing and manipulating the boot loader code. Unlike LILO, the boot loader code itself can read the configuration file, so there's no need to reinstall the boot loader code whenever you change your GRUB configuration. You can even place the configuration file on a non-Linux partition, which can be handy for quickly reconfiguring GRUB from another OS.

 GRUB wasn't developed exclusively for Linux. It can be installed from, and used to boot, a wide variety of OSs. Its home Web page is http://www.gnu.org/software/grub/.

An Overview of GRUB Configuration

The traditional location for the GRUB configuration file is /boot/grub/menu.1st. Fedora, Gentoo, and Red Hat, though, ship with a version of GRUB that uses /boot/grub/grub.conf as the configuration file. Whatever the name, the GRUB configuration file has the same basic form, as illustrated in Listing 1.2.

Listing 1.2: Sample menu.1st File

```
default=0
timeout=4
splashimage=(hd0,3)/grub/splash.xpm.gz
title Linux (2.6.10)
    root (hd0,3)
    kernel /bzImage-2.6.10 ro root=/dev/hda9 mem=256M
    boot
title Windows
    rootnoverify (hd0,1)
    chainloader +1
    boot
```

Because GRUB wasn't designed exclusively for Linux, it introduces a new way of referring to hard disks and their partitions. Rather than Linux device files, such as /dev/hda and /dev/hda9, GRUB uses strings of the form (hd*x,y*), where *x* is a disk number and *y* is a partition number. (The *y* and preceding comma may be omitted to refer to an entire disk or its MBR.) Both the *x* and the *y* are numbered starting from 0, which contrasts with Linux's numbering partitions starting with 1. Thus, Linux's /dev/hda9 is GRUB's (hd0,8). GRUB doesn't distinguish between ATA and SCSI disks; hd0 is the first disk recognized by the BIOS, hd1 is the second disk, and so on.

The first three lines of Listing 1.2 set global options:

Default OS   The `default=0` line tells GRUB to boot the first OS defined in the file by default. If this line read `default=1`, the default would be the second OS, and so on.

Timeout period   The `timeout=4` line sets the timeout before booting the default OS to 4 seconds. (Note that LILO uses tenths of a second, but GRUB uses full seconds.)

Splash image   The third line in Listing 1.2 sets a splash image—an image that's displayed as part of the boot process. Many Linux distributions ship a splash image with their GRUB files to make for a fancier boot loader menu, but you can omit this line if you like. This example uses a GRUB-style hard disk specification to point to the image file. In this case, it's the `grub/splash.xpm.gz` file on the fourth partition on the first disk (probably `/dev/hda4`). Depending on where this partition is mounted, that could be `/grub/splash.xpm.gz`, `/boot/grub/splash.xpm.gz`, or some other location.

The two OS definitions in Listing 1.2 both begin with the keyword `title`, which provides a label for the OS that's displayed by GRUB when it boots. Subsequent lines may be indented to help distinguish between the OS definitions, but this indentation is optional. Important features of OS definitions include:

Root partition   The `root` option identifies the GRUB root partition, which is the partition on which the GRUB configuration files reside. If you did *not* set aside a separate partition for `/boot` when you installed Linux, this line will identify the Linux root (/) partition, and subsequent file references will be relative to the Linux root partition. If you used a separate `/boot` partition, though, chances are the GRUB root partition will be the Linux `/boot` partition, and GRUB references to files in Linux's `/boot` directory will omit that directory name. Listing 1.2 identifies the GRUB root partition as (`hd0,3`), which is `/dev/hda4` on an ATA system.

WARNING   GRUB can read files from several filesystems, including ext2fs, ext3fs, ReiserFS, FAT, and FFS. You can use any of these filesystems as your GRUB root partition. If you want to use another filesystem, such as the JFS or XFS, as your Linux root partition, you should split off your GRUB root partition from the Linux root partition.

Linux kernel   The `kernel` option identifies a Linux kernel or a kernel for certain other Unix-like OSs, such as a GNU Hurd kernel. This reference is relative to the GRUB root partition, as defined by `root`. You can also pass kernel options on this line. (LILO uses separate lines for options.) Note that the `root` option passed to the Linux kernel identifies the Linux root partition using a Linux device filename, but the `root` option in the GRUB OS definition identifies the GRUB root partition. The two might be the same, but they might not be. In the case of Listing 1.2, they aren't the same—the GRUB root partition is (`hd0,3`), or `/dev/hda4`, whereas the Linux root partition is `/dev/hda9`. Chances are `/dev/hda4` is the Linux `/boot` partition. The `ro` option passed on the `kernel` line tells the kernel to mount the root partition in read-only mode initially, just as the `read-only` line does in `lilo.conf`.

Root partition without verification The `rootnoverify` option works just like the `root` option, except that it tells GRUB it shouldn't try to access files on the partition in question. It's most often found when booting non-Linux and non-Unix OSs, such as DOS or Windows.

Specify a chain loader The `chainloader +1` line in Listing 1.2 tells the system to load the first sector of the root partition and pass execution to it. This option is common when booting DOS, Windows, or other OSs that place boot loader code in their boot sectors.

Start the boot The `boot` line tells GRUB to actually boot the kernel or boot sector for the OS in this definition. In practice, it can often be omitted.

In order to boot, the GRUB boot loader code must reside in the MBR, the boot partition's boot sector, or a floppy disk. You can do this by using the `grub` utility:

```
# grub
grub> root (hd0,3)
grub> setup (hd0)
grub> quit
```

These commands set the GRUB root partition (the same as the one defined in your `menu.1st` or `grub.conf` file), install the boot loader code to the MBR of the hard disk (that is, to hd0), and exit from the utility. If you want to install the boot loader to a partition, you'd use **setup (hd0,3)** or some other partition identifier rather than **setup (hd0)**. The `grub-install` program provides a simplified method of performing these steps:

```
# grub-install (hd0)
```

This command installs GRUB to the MBR of the first disk. It should be able to locate the GRUB root partition automatically.

If you installed a distribution that uses GRUB by default, you shouldn't have to perform any of these steps; GRUB should already be installed and working. You might need to reinstall GRUB from an emergency boot system if it becomes corrupted, though, and you might want to replace the installed system if you learn of a serious GRUB bug. If you just want to add a new kernel or OS to your existing GRUB installation, you do *not* need to reinstall the boot loader code; you need only edit the `menu.1st` or `grub.conf` file.

Adding a New Kernel or OS to GRUB

You can add a new kernel or OS to GRUB much as you do for LILO—by copying an existing entry (or using one in Listing 1.2 as a model) and modifying it to suit your needs. When trying a new kernel, don't replace your old kernel; instead, add the new kernel to the /**boot** directory and add a description of the new kernel to the GRUB configuration file. Remember to change the `title` line so that you can tell your two kernels apart. When you reboot the computer, you should be able to select the new kernel or OS from the list; there's no need to reinstall the GRUB boot loader code using the `grub` or `grub-install` tool.

Post-Installation X Configuration

Once you've installed Linux, you may need to take additional steps to get it working at even a minimally acceptable level. The item that's most likely to cause problems is X configuration. You may find that you've installed Linux but that X doesn't work correctly. You might also want to modify your X configuration to work in a way that's more to your liking, such as running in a different resolution. You'll also need to change your X configuration if you replace your video card with an incompatible model. For all of these cases, Linux provides X configuration tools, or you can manually edit the X configuration file. The first task you may need to undertake is selecting an X server; only then can you move on to configuring it.

Selecting an X Server

X is a network-enabled GUI system. It consists of an *X server*, which displays information on its local monitor and sends back user input from a keyboard and mouse; and an *X client*, which is a program that relies on the X server for user interaction. Although these two programs frequently run on the same computer, they don't need to. Chapter 6 includes additional information on using X over a network. The rest of this chapter assumes you'll be running X programs on the same system that runs the X server, but you don't install X differently if you'll be running X programs remotely.

The X server includes the driver for your video card, as well as support for your mouse and keyboard. Therefore, it's important that you know something about your video card when you install and configure your X server.

Determining Your Video Card Chipset

To properly configure X for your system, you must know what video card chipset your system uses. Unfortunately, this information isn't always obvious from the video card's box or manual because many manufacturers use other companies' chipsets, and they don't always make the chipset manufacturer obvious. You have several ways of approaching this problem, including:

Auto-detection   Linux can often auto-detect the chipset, either during system installation or by running an X configuration tool after installation.

Video card documentation   Although some manufacturers attempt to hide the true identity of their products' chipsets, many do not. Because of this, it's worthwhile to check the product's documentation. This documentation might not use the word "chipset," though; it could use a phrase such as "powered by" or "based on."

Windows driver report   If the computer dual-boots to Windows, or if you've just bought a Windows system and intend to convert it to Linux, you can use the System tool in Windows to find out what driver (and thus, perhaps, what chipset) is installed. Double-click the System icon in the Windows Control Panel, then click the Hardware tab and the Device Manager button. (In Windows 9*x*/Me, click the Device Manager tab to achieve a similar effect.) Click the plus sign next to the Display Adapters item. This will produce a list of the video cards installed in the computer. (Normally, there'll be just one.) Double-click the entry for more information; this produces the Properties dialog box for the video card, as shown in Figure 1.3. The driver and manufacturer name may be that of the video card or of the chipset.

Visual inspection   You can examine your video card for signs of the chipset manufacturer. Most video cards are dominated by just one large chip. This chip may have markings identifying the manufacturer and model number, as shown in Figure 1.4. Normally, the first line or two of text contains the relevant information; the remaining lines specify the revision number, place of manufacture, and so on.

FIGURE 1.3   The Windows Properties dialog box for the video card may provide information on the video chipset manufacturer.

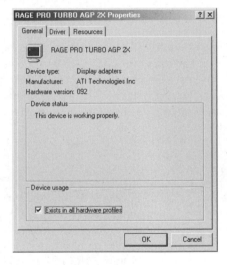

FIGURE 1.4   Markings on chips can help identify the chipset for X.

WARNING Increasingly, high-performance video card chipsets generate a great deal of heat, and for reliability, that heat must be dissipated by means of a heat sink— a finned metallic device that draws heat away from the chip so that it can be radiated into the surrounding air. Some boards also place a fan atop the heat sink. *Do not* attempt to remove a heat sink that's glued to a chip; doing so can damage the chip. Some manufacturers cover their chips with paper labels; these can be safely removed.

If you examine Figures 1.3 and 1.4, you'll see that they identify the chipset in the same way— as that of an ATI Rage Pro Turbo AGP. You won't always find consistency, however; sometimes a chipset may go by more than one name, or one identification method or another may reveal the board manufacturer's name rather than the chipset name. These situations need not be too troublesome, though; they just mean that you'll have to look for a driver under more than one name.

One point to keep in mind when identifying the video card chipset is that some manufacturers produce both video cards and the chipsets that go on them (ATI and Matrox both fall into this category). Other companies produce just one or the other; for instance, Trident produces chipsets, and ELSA produces video cards. Thus, if you find that the name you uncover matches your card manufacturer's name, that's not necessarily a sign that you've failed to turn up the correct chipset manufacturer.

X Server Options for Linux

All major Linux distributions ship with a free X server. In the past, a server known as XFree86 was common, but most distributions have switched to X.org-X11 instead, because of changes to the XFree86 licensing terms. These two servers are very similar, though; X.org-X11 6.7.0 was based on XFree86 4.3.99. You can learn more about XFree86 at `http://www.xfree86.org`, and X.org-X11 is headquartered at `http://www.x.org`. One particularly important subpage on the XFree86 site is `http://www.xfree86.org/current/Status.html`. This page hosts information about XFree86 compatibility with various chipsets, so it's a good place to go once you've discovered what chipset your board uses. You may find notes here on how to work around problems such as using an older or newer version of XFree86 than was shipped with your distribution.

Linux distributions from 2001 and before used XFree86 3.3.6 or earlier, but more recent distributions use XFree86 4.*x* or X.org-X11. Some major architectural modifications marked the change to XFree86 4.*x*, and some configuration files changed with this release. By the time X.org-X11 was forked off of the XFree86 project, XFree86 3.3 had become largely obsolete. Thus, I don't cover this old version of XFree86. If you encounter it or must use it because of poor support for an obscure video card in more recent X servers, though, you should be aware that some configuration options changed between XFree86 3.3.6 and 4.0.

Some video card and chipset manufacturers have made XFree86- and X.org-X11-compatible drivers available for their products. Thus, it's worth checking the Web sites maintained by your board and chipset manufacturers to see if drivers are available. This is definitely true if the main XFree86 or X.org-X11 release doesn't include appropriate drivers, and it may be true even if there are drivers—a few standard drivers are not accelerated, meaning that they don't support some of the video card's features for improving the speed of drawing or moving images. If the video card manufacturer has accelerated drivers but the main XFree86 or X.org-X11 distribution ships with unaccelerated drivers, you'll see a substantial improvement in video performance by installing the accelerated drivers.

XFree86 or X.org-X11 occasionally doesn't support a device at all. You have three choices in this case:

Use the frame buffer device.   The Linux kernel has some video drivers of its own. These can be accessed via the *frame buffer* XFree86 driver. For this to work, your kernel must include frame buffer support for your video chipset.

Use another X server.   As X.org-X11 and XFree86 diverge, they may develop different driver strengths and weaknesses, so you might want to check the other project for drivers. In addition, a company called Xi Graphics (`http://www.xig.com`) produces a commercial X server for Linux, known as Accelerated-X. This server occasionally works on hardware that's not supported by XFree86 or X.org-X11, or produces better speed.

Replace the hardware.   If you have a recalcitrant video card, the final option is to replace it. You may be able to swap with a Windows system that uses a different card, or you may need to buy a new card. Unfortunately, this isn't always an option; you can't replace the video card on a notebook computer, for instance.

Installing an X Server

Actually installing an X server is usually not very difficult; it's a matter of using your distribution's package management tools to install the software—much as you would any other software (described in Chapter 5). In most cases, this will be done during system installation, as described earlier in this chapter. You'll only have to manually install a server if you failed to install X during system installation or if you need to install a new server.

 X normally comes in several packages. Only one package contains the X server proper; others provide support libraries, fonts, utilities, and so on.

One server package supports all video chipsets. The name of this package varies from one distribution to another, but it's likely to be called `XFree86`, `XFree86-server`, `xserver-xfree86`, or something similar for XFree86; or `xorg-x11` or something similar for X.org-X11. You might install it using a command similar to the following in a distribution that uses RPMs:

```
# rpm -Uvh xorg-x11-6.8.0-2.i386.rpm
```

The result is the installation of a program called `Xorg`, which is usually stored in `/usr/X11R6/bin`. This program is a generic X server. It relies on separate driver modules, which are installed along with the main package in most cases. These driver modules probably reside in `/usr/X11R6/lib/modules/drivers`.

If you're using an X driver provided by a video card manufacturer, follow the manufacturer's directions for installing the driver. Chances are you'll be required to copy a driver file to the X drivers directory, although the driver may come as an RPM or Debian package that will do this automatically.

If your card isn't supported by XFree86 4.*x* or X.org-X11 but it is supported by XFree86 3.3.6, you'll need to install an old XFree86 3.3.6 X server. These come in files that typically include the name of the chipset, such as XFree86-S3-3.3.6-19.i386.rpm. This file provides an X server for various chipsets made by S3, some of which aren't supported in more recent versions of X. If you had one of these chipsets, you could install the 3.3.6 server file, which would install an X server called XF86_S3. Running this server program rather than the Xorg executable would let you use your video card. (The upcoming section "Choosing the Server or Driver" specifies how to have the system launch a particular X server program.)

Configuring X

XFree86 is configured through the XF86Config file, which is usually located in /etc or /etc/X11. For XFree86 4.*x*, this file is sometimes called XF86Config-4. X.org-X11 calls its configuration file xorg.conf; it's located in the same location and has the same format. (For simplicity, I refer to both files as xorg.conf from now on.) Accelerated X has its own configuration file, but its format differs from that described here for XFree86 and X.org-X11. Consult the Accelerated X documentation for configuration details.

When you configure X, you provide information on the input devices (the keyboard and mouse), the video card, and the monitor. Particularly important is information on the monitor's maximum horizontal and vertical refresh rates; if this information is wrong or missing, you might not get a display. This information can be obtained from the monitor's manual.

Methods of Configuring X

XFree86 can be configured via either of two methods: by using configuration tools and by configuring manually. Configuration tools are programs that prompt you for information or obtain it directly from the hardware and then write the xorg.conf file, which is a standard plain-text file like other Linux configuration files. Because this file is relatively complex, it's usually wise to begin with an automatic configuration, even if it's a flawed one. Manual configuration involves opening xorg.conf in a text editor and changing its settings using your own know-how. You can use this method to tweak a working configuration for better performance or to correct one that's not working at all. Either way, you may need to configure X, test it, reconfigure X, test it, and so on for several iterations until you find a configuration that works correctly.

The X Configure-and-Test Cycle

If your X configuration isn't working correctly, you need to be able to modify that configuration and then test it. Many Linux distributions configure the system to start X automatically; however, starting X automatically can make it difficult to test the X configuration. To a new Linux administrator, the only obvious way to test a new configuration is to reboot the computer.

A better solution is to kick the system into a mode in which X is *not* started automatically. On most distributions, this goal can be achieved by typing **telinit 3**. This action sets the computer to use runlevel 3, in which X normally doesn't run. Chapter 6 covers runlevels in more detail, but for now, know that setting the system to a runlevel of 3 normally shuts down the X session that launched automatically at system startup.

Debian and Gentoo don't use runlevels as a signal for whether or not to start X. With these distributions, you must shut down the GUI login server by typing **/etc/init.d/xdm stop**. (You may need to change xdm to gdm or kdm, depending on your configuration.)

Once the X session is shut down, you can log in using a text-mode login prompt and tweak your X settings manually, or you can use text-based X configuration programs, as described shortly. You can then type **startx** to start the X server again. If you get the desired results, quit from X and type **telinit 5 (/etc/init.d/xdm start** in Debian or Gentoo) to restore the system to its normal X login screen. If after typing **startx** you don't get the results you want, you can try modifying the system some more.

If X is working minimally but you want to modify it using X-based configuration tools, you can do so after typing **startx** to get a normal X session running. Alternatively, you can reconfigure the system before taking it out of the X-enabled runlevel.

Another approach to restarting X is to leave the system in its X-enabled runlevel and then kill the X server. The Ctrl+Alt+Backspace keystroke does this on many systems, or you can do it manually with the **kill** command, after finding the appropriate process ID with the **ps** command, as shown here:

```
# ps ax | grep X
1375 ?   S  6:32 /etc/X11/X -auth /etc/X11/xdm/authdir/
# kill 1375
```

This approach works better on systems that don't map the running of X to specific runlevels, such as Debian and its derivatives.

X Configuration Tools

Several utilities can help in X configuration, although not all distributions ship with all of them:

The X server   The XFree86 or Xorg server itself includes the capacity to query the hardware and produce a configuration file. To do so, type **XFree86 -configure** or **Xorg -configure** when no X server is running. The result should be a file called /root/XF86Config.new or /root/xorg.conf.new. This file might not produce optimal results, but it is at least a starting point for manual modifications.

Xconfigurator   A program called Xconfigurator can produce and modify the X configuration file format. Red Hat (Xconfigurator's developer) has abandoned this tool in favor of GUI utilities, though.

Distribution-specific tools   Many modern distributions ship with their own custom X configuration tools. These include Red Hat's (and Fedora's) Display Settings tool (accessible from the default desktop menu or by typing **system-config-xfree86** in an xterm) and SuSE's YaST and YaST2. These tools frequently resemble the distribution's install-time X configuration tools, which can vary substantially.

xf86cfg   This program is another that works only once X is already running. Its user interface (shown in Figure 1.5), like that of XF86Setup, enables you to jump around to configure different elements in whatever order you like. In xf86cfg, you right-click an icon and select the Configure option to configure the element, or you can select other options (Remove, Disable, and so on) to perform other actions.

Manually Editing the *xorg.conf* File

The xorg.conf file consists of a number of labeled sections, each of which begins with the keyword Section, followed by the section name in quotes, and ends with the keyword EndSection. Between these two lines are lines that define features relevant to the configuration of that feature. There may also be comments, which are lines that begin with hash marks (#). For instance, here's a section that defines where the computer can find certain critical files:

```
Section "Files"
    RgbPath    "/usr/X11R6/lib/X11/rgb"
    # Multiple FontPath entries are allowed
    FontPath  "/usr/X11R6/lib/X11/fonts/75dpi"
    FontPath  "/usr/X11R6/lib/X11/fonts/Type1"
EndSection
```

FIGURE 1.5   The xf86cfg program lets you configure X using point-and-click operations.

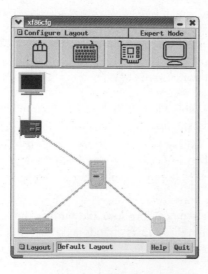

The pages that follow tell you what sections and critical options within these sections exist to modify X's operation. You should then be able to edit the xorg.conf file directly or use a configuration utility to do the job. (The configuration utilities tend to use terminology that's similar to that used in the configuration file, so figuring out what to change with a utility isn't difficult if you know for what option you're looking.)

If you have a working configuration, be sure to back up xorg.conf before modifying it. If you mistakenly delete or modify some critical line, you can easily end up with a system that won't start X at all, and without a backup or a perfect memory of what you changed, it can be difficult to restore even a partially functioning system.

Setting Miscellaneous Options

Some sections of the xorg.conf file relate to miscellaneous options or those that require just a handful of lines to set properly. (The big video sections often boast dozens of lines of configuration options.) Nonetheless, getting these settings right is important to a functioning X system.

Configuring Paths

The Files section hosts information on the locations of important files. The entries you're most likely to change relate to the locations of X's fonts. These are handled through the FontPath option line. Examples of the use of this line include the following:

```
FontPath   "/usr/share/fonts/Type1"
FontPath   "unix/:-1"
FontPath   "tcp/fontserver.example.com:7101"
```

The first of these lines indicates a directory in which fonts may be found. The second refers to a *font server* that runs locally, and is not accessible to other systems. The final line points to a font server that runs on another computer (*fontserver.example.com*) on port 7101. A font server is a program that delivers fonts to local or remote computers. Some Linux distributions use font servers for local font handling, and networks sometimes use them to reduce the effort of administering fonts. You don't need to use a font server if you don't want to, but if your distribution uses a local font server by default, you should leave its reference intact in xorg.conf. A single xorg.conf file can have multiple FontPath lines; X searches for fonts in each of the specified locations in order.

An important difference between XFree86 and X.org-X11 is in their default font directories. X.org-X11 uses subdirectories of /usr/share/fonts, whereas XFree86 uses subdirectories of /usr/X11R6/lib/X11/fonts.

Configuring the Keyboard

The Keyboard input device section defines the operation of the keyboard in XFree86. In most cases, there's little need to modify most xorg.conf keyboard settings, which typically look like this:

```
Section "InputDevice"
  Driver      "Keyboard"
  Identifier  "Keyboard[0]"
  Option      "MapName" "Generic keyboard [ pc101 ]"
  Option      "Protocol" "Standard"
  Option      "XkbLayout" "us"
  Option      "XkbModel" "pc101"
  Option      "XkbRules" "xfree86"
  Option      "AutoRepeat" 500 200
EndSection
```

One setting that you might want to change, however, is the AutoRepeat line. (This line may not even be present on a default installation, but you can add it if you like.) When you press and hold a key, the system begins repeating it, as if you were repeatedly pressing the key. This line controls the rate at which keys repeat when running X.

The first number on this line (500 in the preceding example) is the time in milliseconds (ms), thousandths of a second, before the system begins repeating a key, and the second number (200 in the preceding example) is the interval between repeats once they begin. For instance, in the preceding example, the system waits 500ms after the key is first pressed, and thereafter produces another character every 200ms (five per second) until you release the key.

 Users can override the default keyboard repeat rate by setting this option using a desktop environment's control utilities or various other programs.

In some cases, you might also want to adjust the XkbModel and XkbLayout lines. These lines set the keyboard model and layout. The model relates to the number of keys and their placement, and the layout determines what character each key produces. The layout is used to specify keyboards for different nationalities or languages, which often contain slightly different key selections.

Configuring the Mouse

A second InputDevice section defines the mouse. This section is typically quite short, as shown here:

```
Section "InputDevice"
    Identifier "Mouse1"
    Driver      "mouse"
    Option "Protocol"    "PS/2"
    Option "Device"       "/dev/psaux"
    Option "Emulate3Buttons"
    Option "Emulate3Timeout"    "50"
EndSection
```

Chances are you won't need to modify the `Identifier` or `Driver` options. The `Protocol` is the software protocol used by mice. It's often PS/2, but it may be something else (such as `Microsoft` or `Logitech`), particularly for older serial mice. Scroll mice frequently set `Protocol` to IMPS/2, which is the Microsoft IntelliMouse PS/2 protocol variant. The `Device` option points to the Linux device file with which the mouse is associated. This is sometimes `/dev/mouse`, which is a symbolic link to the real device file, such as `/dev/psaux` (for PS/2 mice), `/dev/usb/usbmouse` (for USB mice), or `/dev/ttyS0` or `/dev/ttyS1` (for serial mice). `Emulate3Buttons` tells X to treat simultaneous presses of the two buttons of a two-button mouse as if they were the third button, and `Emulate3Timeout` tells the system how close (in milliseconds) those two presses must be. If the system has a three-button mouse to begin with, these options should be commented out or deleted.

X programs frequently use the middle button; for instance, text editors use it for pasting text. Therefore, any Linux workstation should be equipped with a genuine three-button mouse rather than a two-button device. Scroll wheels on mice that are so equipped can usually function as a middle button, as well as handling wheel duty. Although the `Emulate3Buttons` option enables you to use a two-button mouse in Linux, doing so is awkward.

Setting Monitor Options

Some of the trickiest aspects of X configuration relate to the monitor options. You set these in the `Monitor` section, which has a tendency to be quite large, particularly in XFree86 3.3.6. A shortened `Monitor` section looks like this:

```
Section "Monitor"
    Identifier "Iiyama"
    ModelName  "VisionMaster Pro 450"
    HorizSync  27.0-115.0
    VertRefresh 50.0-160.0
    # My custom 1360x1024 mode
    Modeline "1360x1024" 197.8 \
             1360 1370 1480 1752 \
             1024 1031 1046 1072 -HSync -VSync
EndSection
```

The `Identifier` option is a free-form string that contains information that's used to identify a monitor in a later section. This later section links together various components of the configuration. `Identifier` can be just about anything you like. Likewise, the `ModelName` option also can be anything you like; it's used mainly for your own edification when reviewing the configuration file.

As you continue down the section, you'll see the `HorizSync` and `VertRefresh` lines, which are extremely critical; they define the range of horizontal and vertical refresh rates that the monitor can accept, in kilohertz (kHz) and hertz (Hz), respectively. Together, these values determine the maximum resolution and refresh rate of the monitor. Despite the name, the HorizSync item alone doesn't determine the maximum horizontal refresh rate. Rather, this value, the VertRefresh value, and the resolution determine the monitor's maximum refresh rate. X selects the maximum refresh rate that the monitor will support, given the resolution you specify in other sections. Some X configuration utilities show a list of monitor models or resolution and refresh rate combinations (such as "800 × 600 at 72 Hz") to obtain this information. This approach is often simpler to handle, but it's less precise than entering the exact horizontal and vertical sync values.

 Don't set random horizontal and vertical refresh rates; particularly on older hardware, setting these values too high can actually damage a monitor. (Modern monitors ignore signals presented at too high a refresh rate.)

To settle on a resolution, X looks through a series of *mode lines*, which are specified via the Modeline option. Computing mode lines is tricky, so I don't recommend you try it unless you're skilled in such matters. The mode lines define combinations of horizontal and vertical timing that can produce a given resolution and refresh rate. For instance, a particular mode line might define a 1024 × 768 display at a 90Hz refresh rate, and another might represent 1024 × 768 at 72Hz.

Some mode lines represent video modes that are outside the horizontal or vertical sync ranges of a monitor. X can compute these cases and discard the video modes that a monitor can't support. If asked to produce a given resolution, X searches all the mode lines that accomplish the job, discards those that the monitor can't handle, and uses the remaining mode line that creates the highest refresh rate at that resolution. (If no mode line supports the requested resolution, X drops down to another specified resolution, as described shortly, and tries again.)

As a result of this arrangement, you'll see a large number of Modeline entries in the XF86Config file for XFree86 3.3.*x*. Most end up going unused because they're for resolutions you don't use or because your monitor can't support them. You can delete these unused mode lines, but it's usually not worth the bother.

XFree86 4.*x* and X.org-X11 support a feature known as *Data Display Channel (DDC)*. This is a protocol that enables monitors to communicate their maximum horizontal and vertical refresh rates and appropriate mode lines to the computer. The XFree86 -configure or Xorg -configure command uses this information to generate mode lines, and on every start, the system can obtain horizontal and vertical refresh rates. The end result is that an XFree86 4.*x* or X.org-X11 system can have a substantially shorter Monitor section than is typical with XFree86 3.3.*x*.

Setting Video Card Options

Your monitor is usually the most important factor in determining your maximum refresh rate at any given resolution, but X sends data to the monitor only indirectly, through the video card. Because of this, it's important that you be able to configure this component correctly. An incorrect configuration of the video card is likely to result in an inability to start X.

Choosing the Server or Driver

XFree86 4.*x* and X.org-X11 use driver modules that are stored in separate files from the main X server executable. The server can't determine what module is required automatically, however. Instead, you must give it that information in the `xorg.conf` file. In particular, the driver module is set by a line in the `Device` section, which resembles the following:

```
Driver "ati"
```

This line sets the name of the driver. The drivers reside in the `/usr/X11R6/lib/modules/drivers/` directory. Most of the drivers' filenames end in `_drv.o`, and if you remove this portion, you're left with the driver name. For instance, `ati_drv.o` corresponds to the `ati` driver.

> The xf86cfg utility provides a large list of chipsets and specific video card models, so you can select the chipset or board from this list to have the utility configure this detail.

Setting Card-Specific Options

The `Device` section of the `xorg.conf` file sets various options related to specific X servers. A typical `Device` section resembles the following:

```
Section "Device"
    Identifier  "ATI Mach64"
    VendorName  "ATI"
    BoardName   "Xpert 98"
    Driver      "ati"
    VideoRam    8192
EndSection
```

The `Identifier` line provides a name that's used in the subsequent `Screen` section to identify this particular `Device` section. (`xorg.conf` files frequently host multiple `Device` sections—for instance, one for a bare-bones VGA driver and one for an accelerated driver.) The `VendorName` and `BoardName` lines provide information that's useful mainly to people reading the file.

The `VideoRam` line is unnecessary with many servers and drivers because the driver can detect the amount of RAM installed in the card. With some devices, however, you may need to specify the amount of RAM installed in the card, in kilobytes. For instance, the preceding example indicates a card with 8MB of RAM installed.

Many drivers support additional driver-specific options. They may enable support for features such as hardware cursors (special hardware that enables the card to handle mouse pointers more easily) or caches (using spare memory to speed up various operations). Consult the `xorg.conf` man page or other driver-specific documentation for details.

Setting Screen Options

The Screen section ties together the other sections. A short example is:

```
Section "Screen"
    Identifier "screen1"
    Device     "ATI Mach64"
    Monitor    "Iiyama"
    DefaultDepth 16
    Subsection "Display"
        Depth       8
        Modes       "1280x1024" "1024x768" "640x400"
    EndSubsection
    Subsection "Display"
        Depth       16
        Modes       "1024x768" "800x600" "640x480"
        Virtual     1280 1024
        ViewPort    0 0
    EndSubsection
EndSection
```

Several key points in this section should be emphasized:

- The Identifier specifies an overall configuration. A configuration file can hold multiple Screen sections, as described shortly.

- The Device and Monitor lines point to specific Device and Monitor sections, respectively.

- The DefaultDepth line specifies the number of bits per pixel to be used by default. For instance, the preceding example sets this value to 16, so a 16-bit color depth is used, resulting in 2^{16}, or 65,536, possible colors.

- Each Subsection defines a particular display type. They have associated color depths (specified by the Depth line) and a series of resolutions (specified by the Modes line). The system tries each resolution specified by the Modes line in turn, until it finds one that works. There are also various optional parameters, such as Virtual (which defines a virtual screen that can be larger than the one that's actually displayed) and ViewPort (a point within that virtual display at which the initial display is started).

One final section is required: the ServerLayout section. This section consists of lines that identify the default Screen section and link it to mouse and keyboard definitions. For instance, a typical configuration will include a ServerLayout section resembling the following:

```
Section "ServerLayout"
    Identifier   "layout1"
    Screen       "screen1"
    InputDevice "Mouse1" "CorePointer"
    InputDevice "Keyboard1" "CoreKeyboard"
EndSection
```

NOTE Although I describe the ServerLayout section last because it ties together all the other sections, it can appear earlier in the file—perhaps even first. The order of sections in the xorg.conf file is arbitrary.

Normally, an xorg.conf file will have just one ServerLayout section, but by passing the -layout parameter to the server program, you can tell the server to use a different ServerLayout section, if one is present. You might use this to start X using a different mouse, for instance—say, a USB mouse on a notebook rather than the built-in PS/2 touch pad.

Summary

Before installing Linux, you should take some time to plan the implementation. Although Linux works with a wide variety of hardware, you should consider this detail carefully, both to get a system with the features you need within your budget and to be sure that you don't have any components that are unsupported in Linux. Checking the hardware before you install Linux can also save you a great deal of aggravation, should some component be installed incorrectly or conflict with another device.

Planning your software configuration is also important. This begins with determining which Linux distribution to use, and continues with planning what software packages to install.

Actually installing Linux begins with planning the disk partitioning. Typically, you can perform the partitioning during the install process, but you should have an idea of how to proceed before you begin. You can then select installation media and perform the installation. Most distributions guide you through this process.

After installing Linux, you may need to attend to certain details. One of these is boot loader configuration. Although the installer usually gets this detail correct, particularly for single-OS systems, you may want to tweak the settings or add other OSs to the boot loader. You'll also need to understand this process when you install a new kernel down the road. Another common post-installation configuration detail is getting X working. Again, Linux distributions usually configure X correctly during installation, but you may need to tweak the settings or change them at a later date.

Exam Essentials

Describe the difference between a workstation and a server.   Individuals use workstations for productivity tasks; servers exchange data with other computers over a network.

Summarize some common workstation and server software.   Workstation software includes word processors, spreadsheets, mail readers, Web browsers, graphics editors, and other programs used by individuals on the local system. Server software includes Web servers, mail servers, file servers, time servers, news servers, login servers and other programs that are often accessed remotely.

Describe how CPU speed, available RAM, and hard disk characteristics influence performance. Faster CPUs result in faster computations, and thus faster speed in computationally intensive tasks, while plentiful RAM gives the computer room to perform computations on large data sets. Hard disks vary in capacity and speed, which affect your ability to store lots of data and your ability to rapidly access it.

Describe Linux's partitioning needs. Linux requires a single root partition, and may require a separate swap partition. Additional partitions, corresponding to directories such as /boot, /home, and /var, are desirable on some systems, but aren't usually required.

Summarize the concept of a Linux distribution. A distribution is a collection of software developed by diverse individuals and groups, bound by an installation routine. Linux distributions can differ in many details, but they all share the same heritage and the ability to run the same programs.

Summarize the x86 boot process. The CPU executes code stored on the BIOS, which redirects the CPU to load and execute a boot loader from the MBR. This boot loader may load the OS kernel or redirect the boot process to another boot loader, which in turn loads the kernel and starts the OS running.

Describe when it's most appropriate to use CD-ROM and network installations. CD-ROM installations are most convenient when installing to systems with poor network connectivity or when you have a CD-ROM and want to install quickly. Network installations are convenient when you are installing several systems simultaneously or when you don't have a Linux CD-ROM or a CD-ROM drive on the target system.

Ascertain what type of interaction is most appropriate during installation. GUI- and text-based installations are good for when you are installing a single system or when you are preparing a template for scripted installations with some distributions. Automatic scripted installations are convenient when you are installing nearly identical systems on multiple computers.

Describe why you might pick particular filesystems for Linux installation. Ext3fs is a popular choice, and generally a good one. ReiserFS, XFS, and JFS are also good choices on distributions that support them, but many don't. The older ext2fs can be a good choice for small partitions, but is better avoided for large partitions.

Determine what video chipset your system uses. Many manufacturers document the video card chipset in their manuals or on the product boxes. You can also check the Microsoft Windows System Control Panel or visually inspect the board, if the manufacturer did not make the information readily available.

Summarize how X determines the monitor's refresh rate. X uses the monitor's maximum horizontal and vertical refresh rates and a series of fixed mode lines, which define particular timings for various video resolutions. X picks the mode line that produces the highest refresh rate supported by the monitor at the specified resolution.

Commands in This Chapter

Command	Description
Xconfigurator	Text- or GUI-based XFree86 3.3.x and 4.0.x configuration program
Xorg	X.org-X11 server that can automatically produce its own configuration file
XFree86	XFree86 4.0.x server that can automatically produce its own configuration file
xf86cfg	GUI-based XFree86 4.0.x and X.org-X11 configuration program

Review Questions

1.   Which of the following are typical workstation tasks? (Choose all that apply.)

     A. Word processing

     B. Routing between networks

     C. Running a Web site

     D. Running scientific simulations

2.   A computer is to be used to capture 640 × 480 images of a room every 10 minutes and then store them for a day on hard disk. Which of the following components might you research before building such a computer?

     A. A 21-inch monitor for viewing the images

     B. A high-end SCSI disk to store the images quickly

     C. A 3D graphics card to render the image of the room

     D. USB support for a USB-interfaced camera

3.   Linux runs on many different types of CPUs. Which of the following measures is most useful when comparing the speed of CPUs from different families?

     A. The BogoMIPS measures reported by the kernel

     B. The CPU speeds in MHz

     C. The number of transistors in the CPUs

     D. How quickly each CPU runs your programs

4.   Which of the following is *not* an advantage of SCSI hard disks over ATA hard disks?

     A. SCSI supports more devices per IRQ.

     B. SCSI hard disks are less expensive than their ATA counterparts.

     C. SCSI allows multiple simultaneous transfers on a single chain.

     D. The highest-performance drives come in SCSI format.

5.   As a general rule, which of the following is most important in order for a video card to be used in a Linux business workstation?

     A. The card should be supported by the commercial Accelerated-X server.

     B. The card should have much more than 8MB of RAM for best speed.

     C. The card should be supported by XFree86.

     D. The card should be the most recent design to ensure continued usefulness in the future.

6. Why might you want to check the motherboard BIOS settings on a computer before installing Linux?

    A. The BIOS lets you configure the partition to be booted by default.

    B. You can use the BIOS to disable built-in hardware you plan not to use in Linux.

    C. The motherboard BIOS lets you set the IDs of SCSI devices.

    D. You can set the screen resolution using the motherboard BIOS.

7. You want to attach an old 10MB/s SCSI-2 scanner to a computer, but the only SCSI host adapter you have available is a 20MB/s UltraSCSI device. The system has no other SCSI devices. Which of the following is true?

    A. You can attach the scanner to the UltraSCSI host adapter; the two are compatible, although you may need an adapter cable.

    B. You must set an appropriate jumper on the UltraSCSI host adapter before it will communicate with the SCSI-2 scanner.

    C. You must buy a new SCSI-2 host adapter; SCSI devices aren't compatible across versions, so the UltraSCSI adapter won't work.

    D. You can attach the scanner to the UltraSCSI host adapter, but performance will be poor because of the incompatible protocols.

8. A new Linux administrator plans to create a system with separate /home, /usr/local, and /etc partitions. Which of the following best describes this configuration?

    A. The system won't boot because /etc contains configuration files necessary to mount non-root partitions.

    B. The system will boot, but /usr/local won't be available because mounted partitions must be mounted directly off their parent partition, not in a subdirectory.

    C. The system will boot only if the /home partition is on a separate physical disk from the /usr/local partition.

    D. The system will boot and operate correctly, provided each partition is large enough for its intended use.

9. Which of the following best summarizes the differences between DOS's FDISK and Linux's fdisk?

    A. Linux's fdisk is a simple clone of DOS's FDISK, but written to work from Linux rather than from DOS or Windows.

    B. The two are completely independent programs that accomplish similar goals, although Linux's fdisk is more flexible.

    C. DOS's FDISK uses GUI controls, whereas Linux's fdisk uses a command-line interface, but they have similar functionality.

    D. Despite their similar names, they're completely different tools—DOS's FDISK handles disk partitioning, whereas Linux's fdisk formats floppy disks.

10. In what ways do Linux distributions differ from one another? (Choose all that apply.)

    A. Package management systems

    B. Kernel development history

    C. Installation routines

    D. The ability to run popular Unix servers

11. Which of the following packages are *most* likely to be needed on a computer that functions as an office file server?

    A. Samba and Netatalk

    B. Apache and StarOffice

    C. Gnumeric and Postfix

    D. XV and BIND

12. What type of software is it most important to *remove* from a publicly accessible server?

    A. Unnecessary kernel modules

    B. Unused firewall software

    C. Uncompiled source code

    D. Software development tools

13. Which of the following best describes a typical Linux distribution's method of installation?

    A. The installation program is a small Linux system that boots from floppy, CD-ROM, or hard disk to install a larger system on the hard disk.

    B. The installation program is a set of DOS scripts that copies files to the hard disk, followed by a conversion program that turns the target partition into a Linux partition.

    C. The installation program boots only from a network boot server to enable installation from CD-ROM or network connections.

    D. The installation program runs under the Minix OS, which is small enough to fit on a floppy disk but can copy data to a Linux partition.

14. Which of the following is an advantage of a GUI installation over a text-based installation?

    A. GUI installers support more hardware than do their text-based counterparts.

    B. GUI installers can provide graphical representations of partition sizes, package browsers, and so on.

    C. GUI installers can work even on video cards that support only VGA graphics.

    D. GUI installers better test the system's hardware during the installation.

15. Which of the following tools may you use when creating partitions for Linux? (Choose all that apply.)

    A. Linux's `fdisk` from an emergency disk, run prior to the system installation

    B. PowerQuest's PartitionMagic or similar third-party utilities

    C. Distribution-specific install-time utility

    D. The DOS `FORMAT` utility, run prior to the system installation

16. What mount point should you associate with swap partitions?

  A. /

  B. /swap

  C. /boot

  D. None

17. Which of the following is the *most* useful information in locating an X driver for a video card?

  A. The interrupt used by the video card under Microsoft Windows

  B. Markings on the video card's main chip

  C. Whether the card uses the ISA, VLB, PCI, or AGP bus

  D. The name of the video card's manufacturer

18. When you configure an X server, you need to make changes to configuration files and then start or restart the X server. Which of the following can help streamline this process?

  A. Shut down X by switching to a runlevel in which X doesn't run automatically, then reconfigure it and use `startx` to test X startup.

  B. Shut down X by booting into single-user mode, then reconfigure X and use `telinit` to start X running again.

  C. Reconfigure X, then unplug the computer to avoid the lengthy shutdown process before restarting the system, and X along with it.

  D. Use the `startx` utility to check the X configuration file for errors before restarting the X server.

19. Which of the following summarizes the organization of the `xorg.conf` file?

  A. The file contains multiple sections, one for each screen. Each section includes subsections for individual components (keyboard, video card, and so on).

  B. Configuration options are entered in any order desired. Options relating to specific components (keyboard, video card, and so on) may be interspersed.

  C. The file begins with a summary of individual screens. Configuration options are preceded by a code word indicating the screen to which they apply.

  D. The file is broken into sections, one or more for each component (keyboard, video card, and so on). The end of the file has one or more sections that define how to combine the main sections.

20. In what section of `XF86Config` do you specify the resolution that you want to run?

  A. In the `Screen` section, subsection `Display`, using the `Modes` option

  B. In the `Monitor` section, using the `Modeline` option

  C. In the `Device` section, using the `Modeline` option

  D. In the `DefaultResolution` section, using the `Define` option

Answers to Review Questions

1. **A, D.** Workstations are used by individuals to perform productivity tasks, such as word processing, drafting, scientific simulations, and so on. Routing is a task that's performed by a router—typically a dedicated-appliance task. Web sites are run on servers.

2. **D.** Many digital cameras use USB interfaces, so Linux's support for USB, and for specific USB cameras, may be important for this application. (Some cameras use parallel-port, IEEE-1394, or specialized PCI card interfaces as well.) A 21-inch monitor is overkill for displaying 640 × 480 images, and a 3D graphics card isn't required, either. Likewise, a 10-minute pause between captures is slow enough that a high-end hard disk (SCSI or ATA) isn't necessary for speed reasons, although a large hard disk may be required if the images are to be retained for any length of time.

3. **D.** The ultimate measure of a CPU's speed is how quickly it runs *your* programs, so the best measure of CPU performance is the CPU's performance when running those programs. The BogoMIPS measure is almost meaningless; it's used to calibrate some internal kernel timing loops. CPU speed in MHz is also meaningless across CPU families, although it is useful *within* a family. Likewise, the number of transistors in a CPU is unimportant per se, although more sophisticated CPUs are often faster.

4. **B.** SCSI hard disks usually cost more than ATA drives of the same size, although the SCSI disks often perform better.

5. **C.** XFree86 comes with all full Linux distributions, so having XFree86 support is important to getting Linux working in GUI mode. Support in Accelerated-X and Metro-X can work around a lack of support in XFree86 or provide a few features not present in XFree86, but in most cases, XFree86 support is more important. More than 8MB of RAM is important if you want to use a card's 3D features, but few Linux programs use these today. The most recent designs are often incompatible with XFree86 because drivers have yet to be written.

6. **B.** Motherboards with built-in RS-232 serial, parallel, ATA, audio, and other devices generally allow you to disable these devices from the BIOS setup utility. The BIOS does *not* control the boot partition, although it *does* control the boot device (floppy, CD-ROM, hard disk, and so on). SCSI host adapters have their own BIOSs, with setup utilities that are separate from those of the motherboard BIOS. (They're usually accessed separately even when the SCSI adapter is built into the motherboard.) You set the screen resolution using X configuration tools, not the BIOS.

7. **A.** SCSI devices are compatible from one version of the SCSI protocols to another, with a few exceptions such as LVD SCSI devices. Several types of SCSI connectors are available, so a simple adapter may be required. No jumper settings should be needed to make the UltraSCSI adapter communicate with the SCSI-2 scanner. Performance will be at SCSI-2 levels, just as if you were using a SCSI-2 host adapter.

8. **A.** The /etc/fstab file contains the mapping of partitions to mount points, so /etc must be an ordinary directory on the root partition, not on a separate partition. Options B and C describe restrictions that don't exist. Option D would be correct if /etc were not a separate partition.

9. **B.** Although they have similar names and purposes, Linux's fdisk is not modeled after DOS's FDISK. DOS's FDISK does *not* have GUI controls. Linux's fdisk does *not* format floppy disks.

10. A, C. Different Linux distributions use different package management systems and installation routines. Although they may ship with slightly different kernel versions, they use fundamentally the same kernel. Likewise, they may ship with different server collections, but can run the same set of servers.

11. A. Samba is a file server for SMB/CIFS (Windows networking), while Netatalk is a file server for AppleShare (Mac OS networking). Apache is a Web server, and StarOffice is a workstation package. Gnumeric is a spreadsheet, and Postfix is a mail server. XV is a graphics package, and BIND is a name server. Any of these last six *might* be found on a file server computer, but none fills the file serving or any other necessary role, and so each is superfluous on a system that's strictly a file server.

12. D. System crackers can use compilers and other development tools to compile their own damaging software on your computer. Unnecessary kernel modules don't pose a threat. You may want to begin using unused firewall software, but removing it is unlikely to be necessary or helpful. Uncompiled source code may consume disk space, but it isn't a threat unless a compiler is available and the source code is for network penetration tools.

13. A. Most Linux distributions use installation programs written in Linux, not in DOS or Minix. The system usually boots from floppy or CD-ROM, although other boot media (such as hard disk or even network) are possible.

14. B. A bitmapped display, as used by a GUI installer, can be used to show graphical representations of the system's state that can't be done in a text-mode display. Text-based installers actually have an edge in hardware support because they can run on video cards that aren't supported by X.

15. A, B, C. You can usually define partitions using just about any tool that can create them, although with some tools (such as DOS's FDISK), you may need to change the partition type code using Linux tools. The DOS FORMAT utility is used to create a FAT filesystem, not define a partition.

16. D. Swap partitions aren't mounted in the way filesystems are, so they have no associated mount points.

17. B. Markings on the video card's main chip typically include a name or number for the chipset; this is what you need in order to locate an X driver for the card. The video card's manufacturer name might or might not be useful information. If it proves to be useful, you'd also need a model number. The interrupt used by the video card in Windows is irrelevant. The card's bus can narrow the range of possibilities, but it isn't extremely helpful.

18. A. On most Linux systems, some runlevels don't run X by default, so using one of them along with the startx program (which starts X running) can be an effective way to quickly test changes to an X configuration. The telinit program changes runlevels, which is a lengthy process compared to using startx. Unplugging the computer to avoid the shutdown process is self-defeating since you'll have to suffer through a long startup (if you use a non-journaling filesystem), and it can also result in data loss. The startx utility doesn't check the veracity of an X configuration file; it starts X running from a text-mode login.

19. D. The xorg.conf file design enables you to define variants or multiple components and easily combine or recombine them as necessary.

20. A. The `Modeline` option in the Monitor section defines *one* possible resolution, but there are usually several `Modeline` entries defining many resolutions. The `Modeline` option doesn't exist in the `Device` section, however, nor is that section where the resolution is set. There is no `DefaultResolution` section.

Chapter

2

Text-Mode Commands

THE FOLLOWING COMPTIA OBJECTIVES ARE COVERED IN THIS CHAPTER:

✓ **2.3 Create files and directories and modify files using CLI commands.**

✓ **2.4 Execute content and directory searches using** find **and** grep**.**

✓ **2.5 Create linked files using CLI commands.**

✓ **2.6 Modify file and directory permissions and ownership (e.g.,** chmod, chown, **sticky bit, octal permissions,** chgrp**) using CLI commands.**

✓ **2.7 Identify and modify default permissions for files and directories (e.g., umask) using CLI commands.**

✓ **2.15 Perform text manipulation (e.g.,** sed, awk, vi**).**

✓ **2.19 Create, modify, and use basic shell scripts.**

✓ **2.23 Redirect output (e.g., piping, redirection).**

✓ **3.12 Set up environment variables (e.g.,** $PATH, $DISPLAY, $TERM, $PROMPT, $PS1**).**

Linux can trace its intellectual heritage, if not its source code, to the Unix OS. Unix was developed before GUI environments were much more than pipe dreams. Thus, Unix (and hence Linux) provides a wide array of flexible text-mode commands. In fact, even many GUI tools are built atop the text-mode commands—the GUI tools simply translate mouse clicks into options passed to the text-mode tools, and display any output in a flashier way than the originals. In any event, because of Linux's strong text-mode heritage, Linux administrators, and even some nonadministrative Linux users, must understand how to use these text-mode tools. This chapter serves as an introduction to this topic.

The most fundamental text-mode tool is a command shell, which accepts typed commands from a user. Thus, this chapter begins with a look at shells. It then moves on to a look at many commands that are used to manipulate files in various ways—to display their contents, move them, and so on. One of the features of files is that they have access controls (that is, permissions), and understanding these permissions and the commands to manipulate them is critical for many Linux tasks, so this chapter covers this important topic. Linux also provides various tools for manipulating text files—both text-mode text editors and commands that can modify text files from the command line, so that topic is also covered in this chapter. Many commands rely on environment variables, which store small amounts of data that can be used by multiple commands, so knowing how to set environment variables can be important. Finally, this chapter looks at creating and using scripts, which help automate repetitive tasks.

Basic Command Shell Use

A *shell* is a program that allows you to interact with the computer by launching programs, manipulating files, and issuing commands. A shell is sometimes referred to as a *command-line interface (CLI)*. Shells aren't quite the same as the GUI desktop environments with which you may already be familiar, though; traditional Linux shells are text-mode tools. Even if you prefer to use a GUI environment, it's important that you understand basic shell use because the shell provides the user interface that's most consistent across distributions and other environments. You can also use text-based shells through text-mode network connections. Once you've started a shell, you can view and manipulate files and launch programs.

Starting a Shell

Linux supports many different shells, although precisely which ones might be installed varies from one distribution to another. The vast majority of Linux systems include bash, which is usually the default shell for new users. Another common shell is known as tcsh, and many others, such as zsh, csh, and ash, are also available. Most shells are similar in broad strokes, but some details differ.

There are many different ways to start a shell, most of which are at least partially automatic. The most common methods include the following:

Logging in at the text-mode console   If you log into the computer using a text-mode console, you'll be greeted by your default shell, as it is set in your user account information (see Chapter 3, "User Management").

Logging in remotely   Logging in remotely via Telnet, the Secure Shell (SSH; despite the name, SSH is not a shell in the sense described here, but it will start one automatically), or some other remote text-mode login tool will start a shell.

Starting an xterm   An xterm is a GUI program in which text-based programs can run. By default, xterms usually start your default shell unless told to do otherwise.

Explicitly launching a shell   You can start one shell from within another. This can be helpful if you find you need features of one shell but are running another. Type the new shell's name to start it.

When you start a shell, you'll see a *command prompt*. This is one or more characters that indicate the shell is waiting for input. Command prompts often (but not always) include your username, the computer's hostname, or the directory in which the shell is operating. For instance, a command prompt might resemble the following:

```
[rodsmith@nessus /mnt]$
```

Although not a universal convention (it can be set in a user's shell configuration files), the final character is often a dollar sign ($) for ordinary users or a hash mark (#) for root. This serves as a visual indication of superuser status; you should be cautious when entering commands in a root shell, because it's easy to damage the system from such a shell. (Chapter 3 describes root and its capabilities in more detail.)

This book includes command examples on separate lines. When the command is one that an ordinary user might issue, it's preceded by a $ prompt; when only root should be issuing the command, it's preceded by a # prompt. Because the username, computer name, and directory are usually unimportant, this information is omitted from the prompts printed in this book. The prompts are omitted from command examples within a paragraph of text.

Viewing Files and Directories

When you're using a shell, it's often necessary to see the files in a given directory. This task is accomplished with the ls command, which displays the contents of either the current directory or the directory you name after the command. (If you list a file, it shows only that filename.) This command is described in more detail later, in "The `ls` Command." In short, it's used like this:

```
$ ls /var
arpwatch   db    local   logcheck   opt        spool   www
cache      ftp   lock    mail       preserve   tmp     yp
catman     lib   log     nis        run        win4lin
```

To change to another directory, you should use the `cd` command. Type **cd** followed by the name of the directory to which you want to change, thus:

```
$ cd /tmp
```

You can specify the target directory name either in absolute form (starting with a / character), in which case the directory path is interpreted as being relative to the root directory; or in relative form (without the leading /), in which case it's relative to the current directory. (These rules also apply to specifying other filenames and directory names.)

Linux (and other Unix-like OSs) uses a slash (/) to separate elements of a directory. Windows uses a backslash (\) for this purpose, and Mac OS Classic uses a colon (:). (Mac OS X is Unix-based, though, and uses a slash, just like Linux.)

If you want to view the contents of a file, you can do so in many different ways. You can load it into a text editor, for instance. The `cat` command will copy the entire file to the screen, which is handy for short text files but not for long ones. Another possibility is to use either `more` or `less`. Both of these commands display a text file a page at a time, but `less` is the more sophisticated program. Both are described in greater detail later in this chapter, in the section "`more` and `less`."

Launching Programs

You can launch a program from a shell by typing its name. In fact, many shell "commands," including `ls` and `cat`, are actually external programs that the shell runs. Most of these standard commands reside in the `/bin` directory, but shells search all directories specified by the PATH environment variable (described in more detail later, in "Setting Environment Variables") for commands to run. If you type the name of a program that resides in any directory on the path, the shell runs that program. You can also pass *parameters* to a program—optional information that the program can use in a program-specific way. For instance, the names of the files to be manipulated are parameters to commands like `mv` and `rm`. Many programs accept parameters that are preceded by one or two dashes and a code, as in `-r` or `-t time`. Most parameters are case sensitive; in fact, many programs use upper- and lowercase versions of a parameter in different ways.

Most text-based programs take over the display (the text-mode login, Telnet session, xterm, or what have you). Many show little or no information before returning control to the shell, so you don't really notice this fact. Some programs, such as text-mode editors, truly control the display; they may clear all the information that has previously appeared and fill the display with their own information. Other programs may not clear the screen entirely, or even display their own information, but they may take a long time to operate. In some cases, you may want to retain control of your shell while the program does its thing in the background. To do this, follow the command with an ampersand (**&**). When you do this, the program you launch will still be attached to the display from which it was launched, but it shares that display with the shell. This works well for noninteractive programs but very poorly for interactive tools. For instance, suppose you have a program called `supercrunch` that performs some lengthy computation but requires no interaction from the user. You could launch it like this:

```
$ supercrunch &
```

If `supercrunch` produces text-based output, it will appear on the screen, but you'll still be able to use the shell for other purposes. If you've already launched a program and want to move it into the background, press Ctrl+Z. This suspends the currently running program and returns you to the shell. At this point, the program you've suspended will *not* be doing any work. This may be fine for a text editor you wanted to momentarily suspend, but if the program was performing computations that should continue, you must take additional steps to see that this happens. You can type **fg** to return to the suspended program, or **bg** to start it running again in the background. The latter is much like appending an ampersand to the command name when you launched it.

If you try to launch an X-based program, you must be running the shell in an xterm, or possibly in some other way that allows X programs to run, such as from another computer with its own X server and all appropriate environment variables set to permit remote X program operation, as described in Chapter 6, "Networking." If you try to launch an X program from a text-only login, you'll receive an error message along the lines of `Can't open display`.

Although X-based programs don't normally produce text output, they do take over the terminal from which they were launched. If you want to continue to use an xterm after launching an X-based program, follow its name with an ampersand (&), as just described.

Using Shell Shortcuts

Linux shells permit some important operational shortcuts. One of the most useful of these is the use of the Tab key for *filename completion*. Suppose you want to move a file that's called `shareholder-report-for-2004.txt`. You could type the entire filename, but that can become quite tedious. Most Linux shells, including the popular bash shell, support a feature in which hitting the Tab key completes an incomplete command or filename, as long as you've typed enough characters to uniquely define the file or command. For instance, suppose that `ls` reveals two files in a directory:

```
$ ls
share-price-in-2004.txt   shareholder-report-for-2004.txt
```

If you want to edit the second file with the Emacs editor (using the command name `emacs`), you could type **emacs shareh**, then press the Tab key. The shell will complete the filename, so your command line will include the entire name.

What happens when the characters you enter are *not* unique? In this case, the shell completes as much of the job as it can. For instance, if you type **emacs sh** and then press the Tab key, bash fills out the next three characters so that the command line reads **emacs share**. Some configurations also summarize the possible completions at this point. (For those that don't, pressing Tab again usually displays these completions.) If you then type either **h** or – and press Tab again, bash completes the filename.

Another shortcut is the use of the Up and Down arrow keys to scroll through previous commands. If you need to type two similar commands in a row, you can type one, then press the Up arrow key to retrieve the previous command. You can go back through several commands in this way, and if you overshoot, you can use the Down arrow key to retrieve more recent commands. Once you find the command you want, you can use the left arrow or Backspace keys to move back in the line to edit it (Backspace deletes characters, but the left arrow key doesn't). Pressing Ctrl+A moves the cursor to the start of the line, and Ctrl+E moves the cursor to the end of the line. Edit the line and press the Enter key to enter the new command.

These shortcuts, and other basic shell commands for that matter, are extremely helpful in working with packages and other files. You can perform many tasks with a file manager, of course, but text-based utilities were designed to be used from shells. Because package filenames are frequently very long, using filename completion can be particularly helpful with them.

Although not a shortcut in the same sense as using the Tab key, one particularly important tool is the Linux man page system. The `man` program (short for "manual") contains usage information on many Linux commands and files. Type **man** followed by the command name to learn more about the command, as in **man cd**. Linux man pages are usually written in a very succinct style; they aren't intended as complete documentation but rather as a reference aid. Some developers have ceased supporting man pages in favor of info pages, which you can view by typing **info** followed by the command or filename. Info pages support hierarchical documents; you can select a subtopic and press the Enter key to see information about it.

Both man pages and info pages are covered in more detail in Chapter 8, "System Documentation."

File Manipulation Commands

Linux provides traditional Unix commands to manipulate files. These commands can be classified into several categories: file system navigation, file manipulation, directory manipulation, file location, and file examination. A couple of closely related features are redirection and pipes, which let you redirect a program's input or output from or to a file or another program.

Navigating the Linux Filesystem

Moving about the Linux filesystem involves a few commands. It's also helpful to understand some features of common Linux shells that can help in this navigation. Some of these commands and features are similar to ones used in DOS and Windows. (This is no accident; DOS was partly modeled on Unix, and so it copied some Unix features that are now part of Linux.) Important tasks include taking directory listings, using wildcards, and manipulating the current directory.

The *ls* Command

To manipulate files, it's helpful to know what they are. This is the job of the `ls` command, whose name is short for "list." The `ls` command displays the names of files in a directory. Its syntax is simple:

```
ls [options] [files]
```

The command supports a huge number of options; consult the `ls` man page for details. The most useful options include the following:

Display all files   Normally, `ls` omits files whose names begin with a dot (`.`). These dot files are often configuration files that aren't usually of interest. Adding the `-a` or `--all` parameter displays dot files.

Color listing   The `--color` option produces a color-coded listing that differentiates directories, symbolic links, and so on by displaying them in different colors. This works at the Linux console, in xterm windows in X, and from some types of remote logins, but some remote login programs don't support color displays.

Display directory names   Normally, if you type a directory name as one of the *files*, `ls` displays the contents of that directory. The same thing happens if a directory name matches a wildcard (described in the next section, "Using Wildcards"). Adding the `-d` or `--directory` parameter changes this behavior to list only the directory name, which is sometimes preferable.

Long listing   The `ls` command normally displays filenames only. The `-l` parameter (a lowercase L, not a digit 1) produces a long listing that includes information such as the file's permission string (described later, in "File Permissions"), owner, group, size, and creation date.

Display file type   The `-p` or `--file-type` option appends an indicator code to the end of each name so you know what type of file it is. The meanings are as follows:

/	directory
@	symbolic link
=	socket
|	pipe

Recursive listing   The -R or --recursive option causes ls to display directory contents recursively. That is, if the target directory contains a subdirectory, ls displays both the files in the target directory *and* the files in its subdirectory. The result can be a huge listing if a directory has many subdirectories.

Both the *options* list and the *files* list are optional. If you omit the *files* list, ls displays the contents of the current directory. You may instead give one or more file or directory names, in which case ls displays information on those files or directories; for instance:

```
$ ls -p /usr /bin/ls
/bin/ls

/usr:
X11R6/    games/                 include/  man/     src/
bin/      i386-glibc20-linux/    lib/      merge@   tmp@
doc/      i486-linux-libc5/      libexec/  sbin/
etc/      i586-mandrake-linux/   local/    share/
```

This output shows both the /bin/ls program file and the contents of the /usr directory. The latter consists mainly of subdirectories, but it includes a couple of symbolic links, as well. By default, ls creates a listing that's sorted by filename, as shown in this example. Note, though, that uppercase letters (as in X11R6) always appear before lowercase letters (as in bin).

One of the most common ls options is -l, which creates a listing like this:

```
$ ls -l t*
-rwxr-xr-x  1 rodsmith users      111 Apr 13 13:48  test
-rw-r--r--  1 rodsmith users   176322 Dec 16 09:34  thttpd-2.20b-1.i686.rpm
-rw-r--r--  1 rodsmith users  1838045 Apr 24 18:52  tomsrtbt-1.7.269.tar.gz
-rw-r--r--  1 rodsmith users  3265021 Apr 22 23:46  tripwire-2.3.0-2mdk.i586.rpm
```

This output includes the permission strings, ownership, file sizes, and file creation dates in addition to the filenames. This example also illustrates the use of the * wildcard, which matches any string—thus, t* matches any filename that begins with t.

Using Wildcards

You can use *wildcards* with ls (and with many other commands as well). A wildcard is a symbol or set of symbols that stand in for other characters. Three classes of wildcards are common in Linux:

?   A question mark (?) stands in for a single character. For instance, b??k matches book, balk, buck, or any other four-letter filename that begins with b and ends with k.

*   An asterisk (*) matches any character or set of characters, including no character. For instance, b*k matches book, balk, and buck, just as does b??k. b*k also matches bk, bbk, and backtrack.

Bracketed values   Characters enclosed in square brackets ([]) normally match any character in the set. For instance, b[ao][lo]k matches balk and book, but not buck. It's also possible to specify a range of values; for instance, b[a-z]ck matches any back, buck, and other four-letter filenames of this form whose second character is a lowercase letter. This differs from b?ck— because Linux treats filenames in a case-sensitive way, b[a-z]ck doesn't match bAck, although b?ck does.

Wildcards are actually implemented in the shell and passed to the command you call. For instance, if you type **ls b??k**, and that wildcard matches the three files balk, book, and buck, the result is precisely as if you'd typed **ls balk book buck**.

The way wildcards are expanded can lead to some undesirable consequences. For instance, suppose you want to copy two files, specified via a wildcard, to another directory, but you forget to give the destination directory. The cp command (described shortly) will interpret the command as a request to copy one of the files over the other.

Finding and Changing the Current Directory

Linux command shells implement the concept of a current directory, a directory that's displayed by default if ls or some other command doesn't specify a directory. You can discover what your current directory is by typing **pwd**. This command's name stands for "print working directory," and it can be useful if you don't know in what directory you're currently operating.

You may specify either an *absolute directory name* or a *relative directory name* when giving a filename or directory name. The former indicates the directory name relative to the root directory. An absolute directory name uses a leading slash, as in /usr/local or /home. Relative directory names are specified relative to the current directory. They lack the leading slash. Relative directory names sometimes begin with a double dot (..). This is a code that stands for a directory's parent. For instance, if your current directory is /usr/local, .. refers to /usr. Similarly, a single dot (.) as a directory name refers to the current directory. As an example, if you're in /home/sally, the filename specifications document.sxw, ./document.sxw, and /home/sally/document.sxw all refer to the same file. The single dot can often be omitted, but including it is sometimes helpful when you're specifying commands. Without the dot, Linux tries searching your path, and if the dot isn't on the path and you aren't in a directory on the path, you won't be able to run programs in your current working directory.

Another important shortcut character is the tilde (~). This character is a stand-in for the user's home directory. For instance, ~/document.sxw refers to the document.sxw file within the user's home directory. This might be /home/sally/document.sxw for the user sally, for instance.

To change to another directory, use the cd command. Unlike most commands, cd is built into the shell (bash, tcsh, or what have you). Its name stands for "change directory," and it alters the current directory to whatever you specify. Type the command followed by your target directory, as in

```
$ cd somedir
```

You may use either absolute or relative directory names with the cd command—or with other commands that take filenames or directory names as input.

Manipulating Files

A few file-manipulation commands are extremely important to everyday file operations. These commands enable you to copy, move, rename, and delete files.

The *cp* Command

The cp command copies a file. Its basic syntax is as follows:

```
cp [options] source destination
```

The *source* is normally one or more files, and the *destination* may be a file (when the source is a single file) or a directory (when the source is one or more files). When copying to a directory, cp preserves the original filename; otherwise, it gives the new file the filename indicated by *destination*. The command supports a large number of options; consult its man page for more information. Some of the more useful options enable you to modify the command's operation in helpful ways:

Force overwrite   The -f or --force option forces the system to overwrite any existing files without prompting.

Interactive mode   The -i or --interactive option causes cp to ask you before overwriting any existing files.

Preserve ownership and permissions   Normally, a copied file is owned by the user who issues the cp command and uses that account's default permissions. The -p or --preserve option preserves ownership and permissions, if possible.

Recursive copy   If you use the -R or --recursive option and specify a directory as the *source*, the entire directory, including its subdirectories, will be copied. Although -r also performs a recursive copy, its behavior with files other than ordinary files and directories is unspecified. Most cp implementation use -r as a synonym for -R, but this behavior isn't guaranteed.

Update copy   The -u or --update option tells cp to copy the file only if the original is newer than the target, or if the target doesn't exist.

This list of cp options is incomplete, but covers the most useful options. Consult the cp man page for information on additional cp options.

As an example, the following command copies the /etc/fstab configuration file to a backup location in /root, but only if the original /etc/fstab is newer than the existing backup:

```
# cp -u /etc/fstab /root/fstab-backup
```

The *mv* Command

The mv command (short for "move") is commonly used both to move files and directories from one location to another and to rename them. Linux doesn't distinguish between these two types of operations, although many users do. The syntax of mv is similar to that of cp:

mv [*options*] *source destination*

The command takes many of the same *options* as cp does. From the earlier list, --preserve and --recursive don't apply to mv, but the others do.

To move one or more files or directories, specify the files as the *source* and specify a directory or (optionally for a single file move) a filename for the *destination*:

```
$ mv document.sxw important/purchases/
```

This command copies the document.sxw file into the important/purchases subdirectory. If the copy occurs on one low-level filesystem, Linux does the job by rewriting directory entries; the file's data don't need to be read and rewritten. This makes mv fast. When the target directory is on another partition or disk, though, Linux must read the original file, rewrite it to the new location, and delete the original. This slows down mv. Also, mv can move entire directories within a filesystem, but not between filesystems.

> The preceding example used a trailing slash (/) on the destination directory. This practice can help avoid problems caused by typos. For instance, if the destination directory were mistyped as important/purchase (missing the final s), mv would move document.sxw into the important directory under the filename purchase. Adding the trailing slash makes it explicit that you intend to move the file into a subdirectory. If it doesn't exist, mv complains, so you're not left with mysterious misnamed files. You can also use the Tab key to avoid problems. When you press Tab in many Linux shells, such as bash, the shell tries to complete the filename automatically, reducing the risk of a typo.

Renaming a file with mv works much like moving a file, except that the source and destination filenames are in the same directory, as shown here:

```
$ mv document.sxw washer-order.sxw
```

This renames document.sxw to washer-order.sxw in the same directory. You can combine these two forms as well:

```
$ mv document.sxw important/purchases/washer-order.sxw
```

This command simultaneously moves and renames the file.

The *rm* Command

To delete a file, use the rm command, whose name is short for "remove." Its syntax is simple:

rm [*options*] *files*

The rm command accepts many of the same *options* as cp or mv. Of those described with cp, --preserve and --update do not apply to rm, but all the others do. With rm, -r is synonymous with -R.

> By default, Linux doesn't provide any sort of "trash-can" functionality for its rm command; once you've deleted a file with rm, it's gone and cannot be recovered without retrieving it from a backup or performing low-level disk maintenance. Therefore, you should be cautious when using rm, particularly when you're logged on as root. This is particularly true when you're using the -R option— rm -R / will destroy an entire Linux installation! Many Linux GUI file managers do implement trash-can functionality so that you can easily recover files moved to the trash (assuming you haven't emptied the trash), so you may want to use a file manager for removing files.

The *ln* Command

The ln command creates *hard links* and *soft links* (aka *symbolic links*). Its syntax is similar to that of cp:

ln [*options*] *source link*

The *source* is the original file, while the *link* is the name of the link you want to create. This command supports options that have several effects:

Remove target files   The -f option causes ln to remove any existing links or files that have the target *link* name.

Create directory hard links   Ordinarily, you can't create hard links to directories. The root user can do so, though, by passing the -d, -F, or --directory option to ln. (Symbolic links to directories are not a problem. This distinction is described shortly.)

Create a symbolic link   The ln command creates hard links by default. To create a symbolic link, pass the -s or --symbolic option to the command.

A few other options exist to perform more obscure tasks; consult the ln man page for details. The default type of link created by ln, hard links, are produced by creating two directory entries that point to the same file. Both filenames are equally valid and prominent; neither is a "truer" filename than the other, except that one was created first (when creating the file) and the other was created second. To delete the file, you must delete both hard links to the file. Because of the way hard links are created, they can only exist on one low-level filesystem; you can't create a hard link from, say, your root (/) filesystem to a separate filesystem you've mounted on it, such as your /home filesystem (if it's on a separate partition). The underlying filesystem must support hard links. All Linux native filesystems support this feature, but some non-Linux filesystems don't.

Symbolic links, by contrast, are special file types. The symbolic link is a separate file whose contents point to the linked-to file. Linux knows to access the linked-to file whenever you try to access the symbolic link, though, so in most respects accessing a symbolic link works just like accessing the original file. Because symbolic links are basically files that contain filenames, they can point across low-level filesystems—you can point from the root (/) filesystem to a file on a separate /home filesystem, for instance. The lookup process for accessing the original file from the link consumes a tiny bit of time, so symbolic link access is slower than hard link access—but not by enough that you'd notice in any but very bizarre conditions or artificial tests. Long directory listings show the linked-to file:

```
$ ls -l alink.sxw
lrwxrwxrwx  1 rodsmith users 8 Dec  2 15:31 alink.sxw -> test.sxw
```

Manipulating Directories

Files normally reside in directories. Even normal users frequently create, delete, and otherwise manipulate directories. Some of the preceding commands can be used with directories—you can move or rename directories with mv, for instance. The rm command won't delete a directory unless used in conjunction with the -R parameter. Linux provides additional commands for manipulating directories.

The *mkdir* Command

The mkdir command creates a directory. This command's official syntax is as follows:

```
mkdir [options] directory-names
```

In most cases, mkdir is used without *options*, but a few are supported:

Set mode   The -m *mode* or --mode=*mode* option causes the new directory to have the specified permission mode, expressed as an octal number. (The upcoming section, "File Permissions," describes permission modes.)

Create parent directories   Normally, if you specify the creation of a directory within another directory that doesn't exist, mkdir responds with a No such file or directory error and doesn't create the directory. If you include the -p or --parents option, though, mkdir creates the necessary parent directory.

The *rmdir* Command

The rmdir command is the opposite of mkdir; it destroys a directory. Its syntax is similar:

```
rmdir [options] directory-names
```

Like mkdir, rmdir supports few options, the most important of which handle these tasks:

Ignore failures on nonempty directories   Normally, if a directory contains files or other directories, rmdir won't delete it and returns an error message. With the --ignore-fail-on-non-empty option, rmdir still won't delete the directory, but it doesn't return an error message.

Delete tree   The -p or --parents option causes rmdir to delete an entire directory tree. For instance, typing **rmdir -p one/two/three** causes rmdir to delete one/two/three, then one/two, and finally one, provided no other files or directories are present.

When you're deleting an entire directory tree filled with files, rm -R is a better choice than rmdir because rm -R deletes files within the specified directory but rmdir doesn't.

Locating Files

You use file-location commands to locate a file on your computer. Most frequently, these commands help you locate a file by name, or sometimes by other criteria, such as modification date. These commands can search a directory tree (including root, which scans the entire system) for a file matching the specified criteria in any subdirectory.

The *find* Command

The find utility implements a brute-force approach to finding files. This program finds files by searching through the specified directory tree, checking filenames, file creation dates, and so on to locate the files that match the specified criteria. Because of this method of operation, find tends to be slow, but it's very flexible and is very likely to succeed, assuming the file for which you're searching exists. The find syntax is as follows:

```
find [path...] [expression...]
```

You can specify one or more paths in which find should operate; the program will restrict its operations to these paths. The *expression* is a way of specifying what you want to find. The find man page includes information on these expressions, but some of the more common enable you to search by various common criteria:

Search by filename   You can search for a filename using the -name *pattern* expression. Doing so finds files that match the specified *pattern*. If *pattern* is an ordinary filename, find matches that name exactly. You can use wildcards if you enclose *pattern* in quotes, and find will locate files that match the wildcard filename.

Search by permission mode   If you need to find files that have certain permissions, you can do so by using the -perm *mode* expression. The *mode* may be expressed either symbolically or in octal form. If you precede *mode* with a +, find locates files in which *any* of the specified permission bits are set. If you precede *mode* with a -, find locates files in which *all* the specified permission bits are set.

Search by file size   You can search for a file of a given size with the -size *n* expression. Normally, *n* is specified in 512-byte blocks, but you can modify this by trailing the value with a letter code, such as c for bytes or k for kilobytes.

Search by group ID   The -gid *GID* expression searches for files whose group ID (GID) is set to *GID*.

Search by user ID   The -uid *UID* expression searches for files owned by the user whose user ID (UID) is *UID*.

Restrict search depth If you want to search a directory and, perhaps, some limited number of subdirectories, you can use the -maxdepth *levels* expression to limit the search.

There are many variant and additional options; find is a very powerful command. As an example of its use, consider the task of finding all C source code files, which normally have names that end in .c, in all users' home directories. If these home directories reside in /home, you might issue the following command:

```
# find /home -name "*.c"
```

The result will be a listing of all the files that match the search criteria.

> Ordinary users may use find, but it doesn't overcome Linux's file permission features. If you lack permission to list a directory's contents, find will return that directory name and the error message Permission denied.

The *locate* Command

The locate utility works much like find if you want to find a file by name, but it differs in two important ways:

- The locate tool is far less sophisticated in its search options. You normally use it to search only on filenames, and the program returns all files that contain the specified string. For instance, when searching for rpm, locate will return other programs, like gnorpm and rpm2cpio.

- The locate program works from a database that it maintains. Most distributions include a cron job that calls locate with options that cause it to update its database periodically, such as once a night or once a week. (You can also use the updatedb command to do this task at any time.) For this reason, locate may not find recent files, or it may return the names of files that no longer exist. If the database update utilities omit certain directories, files in them won't be returned by a locate query.

Because locate works from a database, it's typically much faster than find, particularly on system-wide searches. It's likely to return many false alarms, though, especially if you want to find a file with a short name. To use it, type **locate** *search-string*, where *search-string* is the string that appears in the filename.

> Some Linux distributions use slocate rather than locate. The slocate program includes security features to prevent users from seeing the names of files in directories they should not be able to access. On most systems that use slocate, the locate command is a link to slocate, so locate implements slocate's security features. A few distributions, including SuSE, don't install either locate or slocate by default.

The *whereis* Command

The whereis program searches for files in a restricted set of locations, such as standard binary file directories, library directories, and man page directories. This tool does *not* search user directories or many other locations that are easily searched by find or locate. The whereis utility is a quick way to find program executables and related files like documentation or configuration files.

The whereis program returns filenames that begin with whatever you type as a search criterion, even if those files contain extensions. This feature often turns up configuration files in /etc, man pages, and similar files. To use the program, type the name of the program you want to locate. For instance, the following command locates ls:

```
$ whereis ls
ls: /bin/ls /usr/share/man/man1/ls.1.bz2
```

The result shows both the ls executable (/bin/ls) and the ls man page. The whereis program accepts several parameters that modify its behavior in various ways. These are detailed in the program's man page.

Examining Files' Contents

Locating files by name, owner, or other surface characteristics is very convenient, but sometimes you need to locate files based on their contents, or quickly examine files without loading them into a text editor. Naturally, Linux provides tools to perform these tasks.

The *grep* Command

The grep command is extremely useful. It searches for files that contain a specified string and returns the name of the file and (if it's a text file) a line of context for that string. The basic grep syntax is as follows:

```
grep [options] pattern [files]
```

Like find, grep supports a large number of options. Some of the more common options enable you to modify the way grep searches files:

Count matching lines   Instead of displaying context lines, grep displays the number of lines that match the specified pattern if you use the -c or --count option.

Specify a pattern input file   The -f *file* or --file=*file* option takes pattern input from the specified file, rather than from the command line.

Ignore case   You can perform a case-insensitive search, rather than the default case-sensitive search, by using the -i or --ignore-case option.

Search recursively   The -r or --recursive option searches in the specified directory and all subdirectories, rather than simply the specified directory.

The *pattern* is a *regular expression*, which can be a complex specification that can match many different strings. Alphabetic and numeric characters are interpreted in a literal way in a regular expression, but some others have special meaning. For instance, if you enclose a series of letters or numbers in square braces ([]), the system matches any one of those characters. Suppose you want to locate all the files in /etc that contain the strings tty1 or tty2. You could enter the following command:

```
# grep tty[12] /etc/*
```

You can use grep in conjunction with commands that produce a lot of output in order to sift through that output for the material that's important to you. (Several examples throughout this book use this technique.) Suppose you want to find the process ID (PID) of a running xterm. You can use a pipe (described shortly, in the section "Redirection and Pipes") to send the result of a ps command (described in Chapter 5, "Package and Process Management") through grep, thus:

```
# ps ax | grep xterm
```

The result is a list of all running processes called xterm, along with their PIDs. You can even do this in series, using grep to further restrict the output on some other criterion, which can be useful if the initial pass still produces too much output.

The *cat* Command

The cat program has nothing to do with feline pets. Rather, it's short for the word "concatenate," and it's a tool for combining files, one after the other, and sending them to *standard output* (that is, your screen, xterm, or remote login session). One common use for cat is to forgo the multifile aspect of the command and display a single file. For instance, the following command displays the contents of /etc/fstab:

```
$ cat /etc/fstab
```

This can be a good way to quickly view a short file. It's much less effective for large files, though, because the top of the file will scroll off the top of the display. For very long files, it may also take a long time to scroll through the entire file.

Another use of cat is to quickly combine two files into one. This is best achieved in conjunction with the redirection operator (>), which is described shortly. For instance, suppose you want to combine /etc/fstab with /etc/fstab-addition. You might issue the following command:

```
# cat /etc/fstab fstab-addition > fstab-plus
```

You could then examine the resulting file, fstab-plus. If fstab-addition contains a new entry you wanted to add to /etc/fstab, copying fstab-plus over the old /etc/fstab will accomplish the job. In fact, cat can even serve as a quick-and-dirty way to create a text file:

```
$ cat - > text.txt
```

The – character from which cat is reading is a shorthand for *standard input*—normally your keyboard. Anything you type after this point will be entered into text.txt, until you press Ctrl+D. This keystroke terminates the cat program, at which point text.txt will contain your desired text. This can be a particularly useful trick if you're using an extremely spare emergency system and need to quickly create a short configuration file.

The *more* and *less* Commands

A program that's used in many OSs to allow users to view information in a controlled way is known as more. Typing **more *filename*** results in a screen-by-screen display of *filename*'s contents. You can press the Enter key to move down one line of text, or the spacebar to move forward by one screen. When you're done, press the Q key to exit. This can be a convenient way to view configuration or other text files.

Although more is useful, the original program has many limitations. For instance, there's no way to page *backward* through a file or search for text within the file. These needs spawned a better version of more, which is known as less in a twist of humor. In addition to paging forward, less enables you to type in various keystrokes to do other things. Some of these are modeled after the keystrokes used in the Emacs editor, such as Ctrl+V to move forward by a screen and Esc-V to move backward by a screen. You can also search for text by typing **/** followed by the search pattern. Typing **q** exits from less. You can learn more from the less man page.

Most Linux systems use less to display man pages, so you can practice the less commands while viewing the less man page.

The *tail* Command

Sometimes, you want to view the last few lines of a file but not the beginning of the file. For instance, you might want to check a log file to see if an action you've just performed has created an entry. Because programs log actions at the ends of log files, a way to quickly check the end of the file is convenient. This was the purpose for which tail was written. It displays the last 10 lines of a file (or if you include the –n *num* parameter, the last *num* lines). For instance, to view the last 20 lines of /var/log/messages, you could type the following command:

```
# tail -n 20 /var/log/messages
```

Redirection and Pipes

Several of the preceding examples have used *redirection* and *pipes* (a.k.a. *pipelines*). These are mechanisms that you can use to redirect the input to a process or the output from a process. Redirection passes input to or from a file, and a pipe enables you to tie two or more programs together so that one uses the output of another as input.

Normally, the standard output of a program goes to the display you used to launch it. The output redirection operator, >, changes this, sending standard output to a file that you specify.

For instance, suppose you want to capture the output of `ifconfig` in a file called `iface.txt`. You could use the following command to do this:

```
$ ifconfig > iface.txt
```

This operator wipes out the current `iface.txt` file, if it exists. If you want to append information rather than overwrite it, you can use the >> operator instead of >.

You can replace standard input by using the input redirection operator, <. This is most useful when you must routinely provide the same information to a program time after time. You can create a file with that information and pass it to the program with the input redirection operator, thus:

```
$ superscript < script-input.txt
```

To have one program take another's output as input, you use a pipe, which is represented by a vertical bar (|). An earlier example illustrated this process: The output of `ps` may contain too much information to be quickly parsed, so you can pass its output through `grep` to locate just the information you want, thus:

```
# ps ax | grep xterm
```

This command searches for the string `xterm` in the `ps` output, and displays all the lines that match. The output of `ps` goes into `grep`, and `grep`'s output appears on your screen. (You could use another pipe or redirect `grep`'s output, if you prefer.)

File Permissions

Linux uses a set of *file permissions*, or the file's *mode*, to determine how a file may be accessed. File permissions are at the heart of Linux's local security configuration, as described further in Chapter 3. To use these features, though, you must understand how Linux treats file permissions, and what tools the OS provides for permission manipulation.

Account and Ownership Basics

Chapter 3 describes Linux accounts in detail; however, file permissions interact with accounts, so before proceeding, you should understand the basics of Linux accounts. A Linux account is a set of data structures that programs and the kernel treat in a particular way in order to control access to the system. An account includes an alphanumeric username, a user ID (UID) number, a group ID (GID) number, information on the user's default shell, and so on. When you log into a Linux computer, you provide a username and Linux thereafter associates all actions you perform with the account that matches the username you provided. File permissions enable you to specify what accounts may access your files, as well as what files and programs you may access as a given user.

In addition to accounts, Linux supports groups, which are collections of accounts. The system administrator defines a set of users who belong to a specific group. In addition to being owned by a particular user, each file is associated with a specific group, and permissions to the file may be defined for that group. This feature can be used to define different sets of users, such as people who are working together on a specific project, in order to give them access to project-related files while keeping other users from accessing those files.

File Access Permissions

File access permissions in Linux involve several components, which combine to determine who may access a file and in what way. These components also help you determine precisely what a file is—an ordinary data file, a program file, a subdirectory, or something else. You must understand this setup if you want to manipulate file permissions.

File Access Components

There are three components to Linux's file permission handling:

Username (or UID)   A username (or UID, as it's stored in this form) is associated with each file on the computer. This is frequently referred to as the *file owner*.

Group (or GID)   Every file is associated with a particular GID, which links the file to a group. This is sometimes referred to as the *group owner*. Normally, the group of a file is one of the groups to which the file's owner belongs, but root may change the file's group to one unassociated with the file's owner.

File access permissions   The file access permissions (or file permissions or mode for short) are a code that represents who may access the file, relative to the file's owner, the file's group, and all other users.

You can see all three elements by using the ls -l command on a file, as shown here:

```
$ ls -l /usr/sbin/lsof
-rwxr-xr-x  1 root    kmem  84124 Oct  3 02:37  /usr/sbin/lsof
```

The output of this command has several components, each with a specific meaning:

Permission string   The first component, -rwxr-xr-x, is the permission string. Along with the user and group names, it's what determines who may access a file. As displayed by ls -l, the permission string is a series of codes, which are described in more detail in the upcoming section "Interpreting File Access Codes." Sometimes the first character of this string is omitted, particularly when describing ordinary files, but it's always present in an ls -l listing.

Number of hard links   Internally, Linux uses a data structure known as an *inode* to keep track of the file, and multiple filenames may point to the same inode. The number 1 in the preceding example output means that just one filename points to this file; it has no hard links. Larger numbers indicate that hard links exist—for instance, 3 means that the file may be referred to by three different filenames.

Soft links are *not* referenced in the linked-to file's directory listing.

Owner   The next field, `root` in this example, is the owner of the file. In the case of long user-names, the username may be truncated.

Group   The example file belongs to the `kmem` group. Many system files belong to the `root` owner and `root` group; for this example, I picked a file that belongs to a different group.

File size   The next field, `84124` in the preceding example, is the size of the file in bytes.

Creation time   The next field contains the file creation date and time (`Oct 3 02:37` in this example). If the file is older than a year, you'll see the year rather than the creation time, although the time is still stored with the file.

Filename   The final field is the name of the file. Because the `ls` command in the preceding example specified a complete path to the file, the complete path appears in the output. If the command had been issued without that path but from the `/usr/sbin` directory, `lsof` would appear alone.

Although information such as the number of hard links and file-creation date may be useful on occasion, it's not critical for determining file access rights. For this, you need the file's owner, group, and file access permission string.

Linux Filesystem Data Structures

Linux filesystems store several types of data. Most of the space is consumed by file data—the contents of word processing documents, spreadsheets, program executable files, and so on. In order to give you access to file data, though, the system also uses directories, which are lists of filenames. (In fact, directories are stored as ordinary files with special file attributes set.)

In order to link between a directory entry and a file, Linux filesystems use an inode. This is a special filesystem data structure that holds assorted data about the file, including a pointer to the location of the data on the disk, the file's mode, the UID, the GID, and so on. The directory entry points to the inode, which in turn points to the file data proper.

Filesystems also have free space bitmaps, which let the OS know which sectors on a disk have and have not been used. When storing a new file or expanding an existing one, Linux checks the free space bitmap to see where free space is available.

Not all filesystems use actual inodes. For instance, the File Allocation Table (FAT) filesystem used by DOS and Windows doesn't use inodes; instead, it places the information that's in Linux filesystems' inodes in the directory and in the free space bitmap. When Linux uses such a filesystem, it creates virtual inodes from the actual FAT data structures.

Interpreting File Access Codes

The file access control string is 10 characters in length. The first character has special meaning—it's the *file type code*. The type code determines how Linux will interpret the file—as ordinary data, a directory, or a special file type. Table 2.1 summarizes Linux type codes.

TABLE 2.1   Linux File Type Codes

Code	Meaning
-	Normal data file; may be text, an executable program, graphics, compressed data, or just about any other type of data.
d	Directory; disk directories are files just like any others, but they contain filenames and pointers to disk inodes.
l	Symbolic link; the file contains the name of another file or directory. When Linux accesses the symbolic link, it tries to read the linked-to file.
p	Named pipe; a pipe enables two running Linux programs to communicate with each other. One opens the pipe for reading, and the other opens it for writing, enabling data to be transferred between the programs.
s	Socket; a socket is similar to a named pipe, but it permits network and bidirectional links.
b	Block device; a file that corresponds to a hardware device to and from which data is transferred in blocks of more than one byte. Disk devices (hard disks, floppies, CD-ROMs, and so on) are common block devices.
c	Character device; a file that corresponds to a hardware device to and from which data is transferred in units of one byte. Examples include parallel and RS-232 serial port devices.

The remaining nine characters of the permission string (rwxr-xr-x in the example in the earlier section "File Access Components") are broken up into three groups of three characters. The first group controls the file owner's access to the file, the second controls the group's access to the file, and the third controls all other users' access to the file (often referred to as world permissions).

In each of these three cases, the permission string determines the presence or absence of each of three types of access: read, write, and execute. Read and write permissions are fairly self-explanatory, at least for ordinary files. If the execute permission is present, it means that the file may be run as a program. (Of course, this doesn't turn a nonprogram file into a program; it only means that a user may run a program if it is a program. Setting the execute bit on a nonprogram file will probably cause no real harm, but it could be confusing.) The absence of the permission is denoted by a hyphen (-) in the permission string. The presence of the permission is indicated by a letter—r for read, w for write, or x for execute.

Thus, the example permission string of rwxr-xr-x means that the file's owner, members of the file's group, and all other users can read and execute the file. Only the file's owner has write permission to the file. You can easily exclude those who don't belong to the file's group, or even all but the file's owner, by changing the permission string, as described in "Changing File Ownership and Permissions" a bit later in this chapter.

Individual permissions, such as execute access for the file's owner, are often referred to as *permission bits*. This is because Linux encodes this information in binary form. Because it is binary, the permission information can be expressed as a single 9-bit number. This number is usually expressed in octal (base 8) form because a base-8 number is 3 bits in length, which means that the base-8 representation of a permission string is 3 digits long, one digit for each of the owner, group, and world permissions. The read, write, and execute permissions each correspond to one of these bits. The result is that you can determine owner, group, or world permissions by adding base-8 numbers: 1 for execute permission, 2 for write permission, and 4 for read permission.

Table 2.2 shows some examples of common permissions and their meanings. This table is necessarily incomplete, though; with 9 permission bits, the total number of possible permissions is 2^9, or 512. Most of those possibilities are peculiar, and you're not likely to encounter or create them except by accident.

TABLE 2.2   Example Permissions and Their Likely Uses

Permission string	Octal code	Meaning
rwxrwxrwx	777	Read, write, and execute permissions for all users.
rwxr-xr-x	755	Read and execute permission for all users. The file's owner also has write permission.
rwxr-x---	750	Read and execute permission for the owner and group. The file's owner also has write permission. Users who are not the file's owner or members of the group have no access to the file.
rwx------	700	Read, write, and execute permissions for the file's owner only; all others have no access.
rw-rw-rw-	666	Read and write permissions for all users. No execute permissions to anybody.
rw-rw-r--	664	Read and write permissions to the owner and group. Read-only permission to all others.
rw-rw----	660	Read and write permissions to the owner and group. No world permissions.
rw-r--r--	644	Read and write permissions to the owner. Read-only permission to all others.

TABLE 2.2   Example Permissions and Their Likely Uses *(continued)*

Permission string	Octal code	Meaning
rw-r-----	640	Read and write permissions to the owner, and read-only permission to the group. No permission to others.
rw-------	600	Read and write permissions to the owner. No permission to anybody else.
r--------	400	Read permission to the owner. No permission to anybody else.

Execute permission makes sense for ordinary files, but it's meaningless for most other file types, such as device files. Directories, though, make use of the execute bit in another way. When a directory's execute bit is set, that means that the directory's contents may be searched. This is a highly desirable characteristic for directories, so you'll almost never find a directory on which the execute bit is *not* set in conjunction with the read bit.

Directories can be confusing with respect to write permission. Recall that directories are files that are interpreted in a special way. As such, if a user can write to a directory, that user can create, delete, or rename files in the directory, even if the user isn't the owner of those files and does not have permission to write to those files. The *sticky bit* (described shortly) can alter this behavior.

Symbolic links are unusual with respect to permissions. This file type always has 777 (rwxrwxrwx) permissions, thus granting all users full access to the file. This access applies only to the link file itself, however, not to the linked-to file. In other words, all users can read the contents of the link to discover the name of the file to which it points, but the permissions on the linked-to file determine its file access. Attempting to change the permissions on a symbolic link affects the linked-to file.

Many of the permission rules do not apply to root. The superuser can read or write any file on the computer—even files that grant access to nobody (that is, those that have 000 permissions). The superuser still needs an execute bit to be set to run a program file, but the superuser has the power to change the permissions on any file, so this limitation isn't very substantial. Some files may be inaccessible to root but only because of an underlying restriction—for instance, even root can't access a hard disk that's not installed in the computer.

A few special permission options are also supported, and they may be indicated by changes to the permission string:

Set user ID (SUID)   The *set user ID (SUID)* option is used in conjunction with executable files, and it tells Linux to run the program with the permissions of whoever owns the file, rather than with the permissions of the user who runs the program. For instance, if a file is owned by root and has its SUID bit set, the program runs with root privileges and can therefore read any file on the computer. Some servers and other system programs run in this way, which is often called SUID root. SUID programs are indicated by an s in the owner's execute bit position of the permission string, as in rwsr-xr-x. (As described in Chapter 5, SUID programs can pose a security risk.)

Set group ID (SGID)   The *set group ID (SGID)* option is similar to the SUID option, but it sets the group of the running program to the group of the file. It's indicated by an s in the group execute bit position of the permission string, as in rwxr-sr-x.

Sticky bit   The sticky bit has changed meaning during the course of Unix history. In modern Linux implementations (and most modern versions of Unix), it's used to protect files from being deleted by those who don't own the files. When this bit is present on a directory, the directory's files can be deleted only by their owners, the directory's owner, or root. The sticky bit is indicated by a t in the world execute bit position, as in rwxr-xr-t.

Changing File Ownership and Permissions

Changing who can read, write, or execute a file can be done using several programs, depending on the desired effect. Specifically, chown changes a file's owner, and optionally, its group; chgrp changes the file's group; and chmod changes the permissions string.

Ownership Modification

To begin, chown's syntax is as follows:

chown [*options*] [*newowner*][:*newgroup*] *filename*...

The variables *newowner* and *newgroup* are, of course, the new owner and group of the file. One or both are required. If both are included, there must be no space between them, only a single colon (:). For instance, the following command gives ownership of the file report.tex to sally, and sets the file's group to project2:

```
# chown sally:project2 report.tex
```

Old versions of chown used a period (.) instead of a colon. Current versions (through at least 5.2.1) still accept periods in this role, but they may complain about your use of an unfashionably old syntax.

The chown command supports a number of options, such as --dereference (which changes the referent of a symbolic link) and --recursive (which changes all the files within a directory and all its subdirectories). The latter is probably the most useful option for chown.

The chgrp command is similar to chown, except that it doesn't change or alter the file's owner—it works only on the group. The group name is *not* preceded by a period. For instance, to change the group of report.tex to project2, you could issue the following command:

```
# chgrp project2 report.tex
```

The chgrp command takes the same options as chown does. One caveat to the use of both commands is that even the owner of a file may not be able to change the ownership or group of a file. The owner may change the group of a file to any group to which the file's owner belongs, but not to other groups. Normally, only root may change the owner of a file.

Permissions Modification

You can modify a file's permissions using the chmod command. This command may be issued in many different ways to achieve the same effect. Its basic syntax is as follows:

chmod [*options*] [*mode*[,*mode*...]] *filename*...

The chmod options are similar to those of chown and chgrp. In particular, --recursive (or -R) will change all the files within a directory tree.

Most of the complexity of chmod comes in the specification of the file's mode. There are two basic forms in which you can specify the mode: as an octal number or as a symbolic mode, which is a set of codes related to the string representation of the permissions.

The octal representation of the mode is the same as that described earlier and summarized in Table 2.2. For instance, to change permissions on report.tex to rw-r--r--, you could issue the following command:

chmod 644 report.tex

In addition, it's possible to precede the three digits for the owner, group, and world permissions with another digit that sets special permissions. Three bits are supported (hence values between 0 and 7): adding 4 sets the set user ID (SUID) bit; adding 2 sets the set group ID (SGID) bit; and adding 1 sets the sticky bit. If you omit the first digit (as in the preceding example), Linux clears all three bits. Using four digits causes the first to be interpreted as the special permissions code. For instance, suppose you've created a script called bigprogram in a text editor. You want to set both SUID and SGID bits (6); to make the script readable, writeable, and executable by the owner (7); to make it readable and executable by the group (5); and to make it completely inaccessible to all others (0). The following commands illustrate how to do this; note the difference in the mode string before and after executing the chmod command:

```
$ ls -l bigprogram
-rw-r--r--    1 rodsmith users    10323 Oct 31 18:58 bigprogram
$ chmod 6750 bigprogram
$ ls -l bigprogram
-rwsr-s---    1 rodsmith users    10323 Oct 31 18:58 bigprogram
```

A symbolic mode, by contrast, consists of three components: a code indicating the permission set you want to modify (the owner, the group, and so on); a symbol indicating whether you want to add, delete, or set the mode equal to the stated value; and a code specifying what the permission should be. Table 2.3 summarizes all these codes. Note that these codes are all case sensitive.

To use symbolic permission settings, you combine one or more of the codes from the first column of Table 2.3 with one symbol from the third column and one or more codes from the fifth column. You can combine multiple settings by separating them by commas. Table 2.4 provides some examples of chmod using symbolic permission settings.

TABLE 2.3   Codes Used in Symbolic Modes

Permission set code	Meaning	Change type code	Meaning	Permission to modify code	Meaning
u	owner	+	add	r	read
g	group	–	remove	w	write
o	world	=	set equal to	x	execute
a	all			X	execute only if file is directory or already has execute permission
				s	SUID or SGID
				t	sticky bit
				u	existing owner's permissions
				g	existing group permissions
				o	existing world permissions

TABLE 2.4   Examples of Symbolic Permissions with *chmod*

Command	Initial Permissions	End Permissions
chmod a+x bigprogram	rw-r--r--	rwxr-xr-x
chmod ug=rw report.tex	r--------	rw-rw----
chmod o-rwx bigprogram	rwxrwxr-x	rwxrwx---
chmod g=u report.tex	rw-r--r--	rw-rw-r--
chmod g-w,o-rw report.tex	rw-rw-rw-	rw-r-----

As a general rule, symbolic permissions are most useful when you want to make a simple change (such as adding execute or write permissions to one or more class of users), or when you want to make similar changes to many files without affecting their other permissions (for instance, adding write permissions without affecting execute permissions). Octal permissions are most useful when you want to set some specific absolute permission, such as rw-r--r-- (644). In any event, a system administrator should be familiar with both methods of setting permissions.

A file's owner and root are the only users who may adjust a file's permissions. Even if other users have write access to a directory in which a file resides and write access to the file itself, they may not change the file's permissions (but they may modify or even delete the file). To understand why this is so, you need to know that the file permissions are stored as part of the file's inode, which isn't part of the directory entry. Read/write access to the directory entry, or even the file itself, doesn't give a user the right to change the inode structures (except indirectly—for instance, if a write changes the file's size or a file deletion eliminates the need for the inode).

Setting Default Permissions

When a user creates a file, that file has default ownership and permissions. The default owner is, understandably, the user who created the file. The default group is the user's primary group. The default permissions, however, are configurable. These are defined by the *user mask (umask)*, which is set by the umask command. This command takes as input an octal value that represents the bits to be removed from 777 permissions for directories, or from 666 permissions for files, when creating a new file or directory. Table 2.5 summarizes the effect of several possible umask values.

TABLE 2.5   Sample Umask Values and Their Effects

Umask	Created Files	Created Directories
000	666 (rw-rw-rw-)	777 (rwxrwxrwx)
002	664 (rw-rw-r--)	775 (rwxrwxr-x)
022	644 (rw-r--r--)	755 (rwxr-xr-x)
027	640 (rw-r-----)	750 (rwxr-x---)
077	600 (rw-------)	700 (rwx------)
277	400 (r--------)	500 (r-x------)

Note that the umask isn't a simple subtraction from the values of 777 or 666; it's a bit-wise removal. Any bit that's set in the umask is removed from the final permission for new files, but if the execute bit isn't set (as in ordinary files), its specification in the umask doesn't do any harm. For instance, consider the 7 values in several entries of Table 2.5's Umask column. This corresponds to a binary value of 111. An ordinary file might have rw- (110) permissions, but applying the umask's 7 (111) eliminates 1 values but doesn't touch 0 values, thus producing a 000 (binary) value—that is, --- permissions, expressed symbolically.

Ordinary users can enter the umask command to change the permissions on new files they create. The superuser can also modify the default setting for all users by modifying a system configuration file. Typically, /etc/profile contains one or more umask commands. Setting the umask in /etc/profile might or might not actually have an effect, because it can be overridden at other points, such as a user's own configuration files. Nonetheless, setting the umask in /etc/profile or other system files can be a useful procedure if you want to change the default system policy. Most Linux distributions use a default umask of 002 or 022.

To find what the current umask is, type **umask** alone, without any parameters. Typing **umask -S** produces the umask expressed symbolically, rather than in octal form. You may also specify a umask in this way when you want to change it, but in this case, you specify the bits that you *do* want set. For instance, **umask u=rwx,g=rx,o=rx** is equivalent to **umask 022**.

Using ACLs

The Unix file permission system used by Linux was designed long ago. As frequently happens, real-world needs highlight limitations in early designs, and this is true of Unix permissions. For instance, using Unix permissions to provide fine-grained access control on a user-by-user basis is difficult or impossible. That is, if you want to enable the users amy, david, theo, and lola to read a file, but no other users, you must create a group that holds just those four users and no others, assign group ownership of the file to that group, and set group and world permissions appropriately. If you want only amy, david, and lola to be able to read another file, you must repeat this process, creating *another* group. What's more, because only root can ordinarily create groups, users have little control over these matters.

A more flexible approach is to use *access control lists (ACLs)*. These are permissions that can be assigned on a user-by-user basis. For instance, you can create ACLs enabling amy, david, and lola to access a file without creating or modifying any groups. In Linux, ACLs can provide separate read, write, and execute access; they are effectively an extension of the normal Unix-style permissions.

One major problem with ACLs is that they're not yet universally supported. The filesystem you use must support ACLs. As of the 2.6.8.1 kernel, ext2fs, ext3fs, JFS, and XFS all support ACLs, but ReiserFS doesn't. (ACL support is being added to ReiserFS, but it's not yet part of the mainstream kernel.) ACL support is optional with all of these filesystems; it must be enabled when the kernel is compiled, and this isn't always done.

Assuming your Linux filesystem supports ACLs, both root and ordinary users may create ACLs using the setfacl command:

```
setfacl [options] [{-m | -x} acl_spec] [{-M | -X} acl_file] file
```

The −m and −M parameters set an ACL, while the −x and −X parameters remove an ACL. The uppercase variants take an ACL out of a file, whereas the lowercase variants require you to enter the ACL on the command line. The ACL format itself takes this form:

scope:*ID*:*perms*

In this case, scope is the type of entity to which the ACL applies—typically u or user for a user, but g or group for a group is also possible, as is o or others to set a world ACL. The *ID* is a UID, GID, username, or group name. (This component is omitted if you use a *scope* of other.) The *perms* field specifies the permissions, either in octal form (as a single digit from 0 to 7) or in symbolic form (for instance, rw- or r-x).

As an example, consider a user who wants to create an ACL to enable another user (theo) to be able to read a file:

```
$ setfacl -m user:theo:r-- dinosaur.txt
```

Once this command is issued, theo can read the dinosaur.txt file, even if the file's ordinary Unix permissions would not permit this access. Because ordinary users may create and modify ACLs on their own files, the system administrator need not be bothered to create new groups. Users can only create and modify ACLs on files they own, though, much as they can only modify the Unix permissions on their own files.

If you want to see the ACLs on a file, you can use the getfacl command:

```
$ getfacl dinosaur.txt
# file: dinosaur.txt
# owner: amy
# group: users
user::rw-
user:theo:rw-
group::---
mask::rw-
other::---
```

Many Linux systems still have no need for ACLs; Unix-style permissions are adequate for many purposes. As ACL support works its way into more filesystems, though, and as more Linux tools are written to take full advantage of ACLs, they're likely to become more important.

Editing Files with Vi

Vi was the first full-screen text editor written for Unix. It's designed to be small and simple. Vi is small enough to fit on tiny, floppy-based emergency boot systems. For this reason alone, Vi is worth learning; you may need to use it in an emergency recovery situation. Vi is, however, a bit strange, particularly if you're used to GUI text editors. To use Vi, you should first understand the three modes in which it operates. Once you understand those modes, you can begin learning about the text-editing procedures Vi implements. This section also examines how to save files and exit from Vi.

> Most Linux distributions actually ship with a variant of Vi known as Vim, or "Vi Improved." As the name implies, Vim supports more features than the original Vi does. The information presented here applies to both Vi and Vim. Most distributions that ship with Vim support launching it by typing **vi**, as if it were the original Vi.

Vi Modes

At any given moment, Vi is running in one of three modes:

Command mode   This mode accepts commands, which are usually entered as single letters. For instance, i and a both enter edit mode, although in somewhat different ways, as described shortly, and o opens a line below the current one.

Ex mode   To manipulate files (including saving your current file and running outside programs), you use ex mode. You enter ex mode from command mode by typing a colon (:), typically directly followed by the name of the ex mode command you want to use. After you run the ex mode command, Vi returns automatically to command mode.

Edit mode   You enter text in edit mode. Most keystrokes result in text appearing on the screen. One important exception is the Esc key, which exits from edit mode back to command mode.

> If you're not sure what mode Vi is in, press the Esc key. This will return you to command mode, from which you can reenter edit mode, if necessary.

Basic Text-Editing Procedures

As a method of learning Vi, consider the task of editing /etc/lilo.conf to add a new kernel. Listing 2.1 shows the original lilo.conf file used in this example. If you want to follow along, enter it using a text editor with which you're already familiar, and save it to a file on your disk.

Listing 2.1: Sample /etc/lilo.conf File

```
boot=/dev/sda
map=/boot/map
install=/boot/boot.b
prompt
default=linux
timeout=50
```

```
image=/boot/vmlinuz
        label=linux
        root=/dev/sda6
        read-only
```

WARNING   Don't try editing your *real* /etc/lilo.conf file as a learning exercise; a mistake could render your system unbootable the next time you type lilo. You might put your test lilo.conf file in your home directory for this exercise.

The first step to using Vi is to launch it and have it load the file. In this example, type **vi lilo.conf** while in the directory holding the file. The result should resemble Figure 2.1, which shows Vi running in an xterm window. The tildes (~) down the left side of the display indicate the end of the file. The bottom line shows the status of the last command—an implicit file load command because you specified a filename when launching the program.

FIGURE 2.1   The last line of a Vi display is a status line that shows messages from the program.

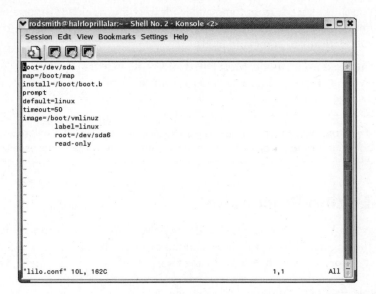

Adding a new entry to lilo.conf involves duplicating the lines beginning with the image= line and modifying the duplicates. Therefore, the first editing task is to duplicate these four lines. To do this, follow these steps:

1. Move the cursor to the beginning of the image= line by using the Down arrow key; you should see the cursor resting on the i.

2. You must now "yank" four lines of text. This term is used much as "copy" is used in most text editors—you copy the text to a buffer from which you can later paste it back into the

file. To yank text, you use the yy command, preceded by the number of lines you want to yank. Thus, type **4yy** (*do not* press the Enter key, though). Vi responds with the message 4 lines yanked on its bottom status line. The dd command works much like yy, but it deletes the lines as well as copying them to a buffer.

3. Move the cursor to the last line of the file by using the arrow keys.

4. Type **p** (again, without pressing the Enter key). Vi pastes the contents of the buffer starting on the line after the cursor. The file should now have two identical image= stanzas. The cursor should be resting at the start of the second one. If you want to paste the text into the document starting on the line *before* the cursor, use an uppercase P command.

Now that you've duplicated the necessary lines, you must modify one copy to point to your new kernel. To do so, follow these steps:

1. Move the cursor to the v in vmlinuz on the second image= line. You're about to begin customizing this second stanza.

2. Up until now, you've operated Vi in command mode. There are several commands that you can use to enter edit mode. At this point, the most appropriate is R, which enters edit mode so that it is configured for text replacement rather than insertion. If you prefer insert mode, you could use i or a (the latter advances the cursor one space, which is sometimes useful at the end of a line). For the purposes of these instructions, type **R** to enter edit mode. You should see -- REPLACE -- appear in the status line.

3. Type the name of a new Linux kernel. For the purposes of this example, let's say you've called it bzImage-2.6.13, so that's what you'd type. This entry should replace vmlinuz.

4. Use the arrow keys to move the cursor to the start of linux on the next line. You must replace this label so that your new entry has its own label.

5. Type a new label, such as **mykernel**. This label should replace the existing linux label.

6. Exit from edit mode by pressing the Esc key.

7. Save the file and quit by typing **:wq**. This is actually an ex mode command, as described shortly.

Many additional commands are available that you might want to use in some situations. Here are some of the highlights:

Case changes   Suppose you need to change the case of a word in a file. Instead of entering edit mode and retyping the word, you can use the tilde (~) key in command mode to change the case. Position the cursor on the first character you want to change and press ~ repeatedly until the task is done.

Undo   To undo any change, type **u** in command mode.

Searches   To search forward for text in a file, type **/** in command mode, followed immediately by the text you want to locate. Typing **?** will search backward rather than forward.

Global replacement   To replace all occurrences of one string by another, type **:%s/*original*/ *replacement***, where *original* is the original string and *replacement* is its replacement. Change % to a starting line number, comma, and ending line number to perform this change on just a small range of lines.

There's a great deal more depth to Vi than is presented here; the editor is quite capable, and some Linux users are very attached to it. Entire books have been written about Vi. Consult one of these, or a Vi Web page like http://www.vim.org, for more information.

Saving Changes

To save changes to a file, type :**w** from command mode. This enters ex mode and runs the w ex-mode command, which writes the file using whatever filename you specified when you launched Vi. Related commands enable other functions:

Edit new file   The :e command edits a new file. For instance, :**e /etc/inittab** loads /etc/ inittab for editing. Vi won't load a new file unless the existing one has been saved since its last change or unless you follow :e with an exclamation mark (!).

Include existing file   The :r command includes the contents of an old file in an existing one.

Quit   Use the :q command to quit from the program. As with :e, this command won't work unless changes have been saved or you append an exclamation mark to the command.

You can combine ex commands such as these to perform multiple actions in sequence. For instance, typing :**wq** writes changes and then quits from Vi.

Using *sed* and *awk*

A pair of tools that are often used together are sed and awk. The command name sed stands for "stream editor;" it's a text editor that uses command-line commands rather than GUI operations or even Vi-style interactive commands to edit a file. The awk command name is based on the names of its creators (Alfred J. Aho, Peter J. Weinberger, and Brian W. Kernighan). It's a scripting language that's built around pattern matching. Thus, you can use awk to control sed, making changes to files based on pattern matches in other files.

Most Linux distributions ship with GNU awk, or gawk. Although there are a few differences between gawk and other awk implementations, for the most part they're the same. Most Linux distributions create a symbolic link called awk that points to the gawk binary. The syntax for gawk follows one of two patterns:

```
gawk [options] -f program-file [files]
gawk [options] program-text [files]
```

In the first case, you pass an awk program in a separate file (the *program-file*); in the second case, you pass the awk program (the *program-text*) on the same command line as the call to awk itself. Typically, this program is enclosed in single quote marks ('). For instance, the following command renames all the .txt files in a directory to end in .txt.old:

```
$ ls --color=none *.txt | awk '{print "mv "$0" "$0".vs"}' | /bin/bash
```

This command comes in three parts, tied together via pipes. The first uses ls to obtain a list of all the .txt files in the current directory. (The obscure --color=none option is required to suppress formatting associated with color outputs on many systems.) The second part is the actual call to awk, which includes a short program that creates a command based around mv and the $0 variable, which stands in for each filename generated by the ls command. The awk script uses its own print command to generate mv commands as output. The final part of this line, a call to /bin/bash, forces bash to process the output of the awk script.

The sed command more directly modifies the contents of files. Its syntax, like awk's, can take one of two forms:

```
sed [options] -f script-file [input-file]
sed [options] script-text [input-file]
```

In either case, the *input-file* is the name of the file you want to modify. (Modifications are actually temporary unless you save them in some way, as illustrated shortly.) The script (*script-text* or the contents of *script-file*) is the set of commands you want sed to perform. When passing a script directly on the command line, the *script-text* is typically enclosed in single quote marks. Table 2.6 summarizes a few sed commands that can be used in its scripts.

TABLE 2.6   Common sed Commands

Command	Meaning
=	Display the current line number
a*text*	Append *text* to the file
i*text*	Insert text into the file
r *filename*	Append text from filename into the file
s/*regexp*/ *replacement*	Replace text that matches the regular expression (*regexp*) with *replacement*

> Table 2.6 is incomplete; sed (like awk) is quite complex, and this section merely introduces this tool.

In operation, sed looks something like this:

```
$ sed 's/2004/2005/' cal-2004.txt > cal-2005.txt
```

This command processes the input file, cal-2004.txt, using sed's s command to replace every occurrence of 2004 with 2005. By default, sed sends its output to standard output, so this example uses redirection to send the output to `cal-2005.txt`. The idea in this example is to quickly convert a file created for the year 2004 so that it can be used in 2005. If you don't specify an input filename, `sed` works from standard input, so it can accept the output of another command as its input.

Although they're conceptually simple, both `sed` and `awk` are very complex tools; even a modest summary of their capabilities would fill a chapter. You can consult their man pages for basic information, but to fully understand these tools, you may want to consult a book on the subject, such as Dale Dougherty and Arnold Robbins' *sed & awk, 2nd Edition* (O'Reilly, 1997).

Setting Environment Variables

People exist in certain environments—office buildings, homes, streets, forests, airplanes, and so on. These environments provide us with, among other things, certain information. For instance, we can tell by reading a street sign that we're at the intersection of State and Main streets, or that there's an old mill a short distance away. Just as we humans live in an environment, so do the programs we run on computers.

The features that are salient to people, though, aren't the same as the ones that are important to computer programs. Computer programs must be concerned with issues such as the amount of free disk space or the availability of memory. Linux also provides programs with a set of supplementary information known as *environment variables*. Like street signs, environment variables convey information about the resources available to the program. Therefore, understanding how to set and use environment variables is important for both system administrators and users.

Programs query environment variables to learn about the state of the computer as a whole, or what resources are available. These variables contain information such as the location of the user's home directory, the computer's Internet hostname, and the name of the command shell that's in use. Individual programs may also use program-specific environment variables to tell them where their configuration files are located, how to display information, or how to use other program-specific options. As a general rule, though, environment variables provide information that's useful to multiple programs. Program specific information is more often found in program configuration files.

Where to Set Environment Variables

If you're using the bash shell, you can set an environment variable from a command prompt for a specific login by typing the variable name followed by an equal sign (=) and the variable's value, then typing **export** and the variable name on the next line. For instance, you could type the following:

```
$ NNTPSERVER=news.abigisp.com
$ export NNTPSERVER
```

The first line sets the environment variable in your shell, and the second makes it available to programs you launch from the shell. You can shorten this syntax to a single line by typing **export** at the start of the first line:

```
$ export NNTPSERVER=news.abigisp.com
```

The former syntax is sometimes preferable when setting multiple environment variables because you can type each variable on a line and then use a single `export` command to make them all available. This can make shorter line lengths than you would get if you tried to export multiple variables along with their values on a single line. For instance, you could type the following:

```
$ NNTPSERVER=news.abigisp.com
$ YACLPATH=/usr/src/yacl
$ export NNTPSERVER,YACLPATH
```

This syntax is the same as that used for setting environment variables in /etc/profile. This system-wide configuration file is called from a bash shell script, which means it contains commands that could be typed at a command prompt.

 When setting environment variables in a shell script such as /etc/profile, you should ignore the command prompts ($) shown in these examples.

Users of the tcsh shell don't use /etc/profile for setting environment variables, and in fact, the syntax just described doesn't work for this shell. For tcsh, the appropriate command to set an environment variable is setenv. It's used much like export in its single-line form, but without an equal sign:

```
$ setenv NNTPSERVER news.abigisp.com
```

Instead of using /etc/profile, tcsh uses the /etc/csh.cshrc and /etc/csh.login files for its system-wide configuration. Therefore, if your system has both bash and tcsh users, you'll need to modify both files, using the appropriate syntax for each file.

The preceding examples assigned values to environment variables. In other contexts, though, the environment variable is preceded by a dollar sign ($). You can use this notation to refer to an environment variable when setting another. For instance, in bash, the following command adds :/opt/bin to the existing PATH environment variable:

```
$ export PATH=$PATH:/opt/bin
```

This syntax is somewhat more complicated for tcsh. In this shell, you must add quotes around the new value and use curly braces around the PATH variable reference:

```
$ setenv PATH "${PATH}:/opt/bin"
```

In addition to the system-wide files, individual users may set environment variables by editing their local configuration files: .bashrc for bash, and .tcshrc, .cshrc, or .login for tcsh (tcsh tries each of these files in turn until it finds one that exists).

The Meanings of Common Environment Variables

You may encounter many common environment variables on your system. You can find out how environment variables are configured by typing **env**. This command is used to run a program with a changed set of environment variables, but when it is typed alone, it returns all the environment variables that are currently set, in a format similar to that of bash environment variable assignments:

NNTPSERVER=news.abigisp.com

Of course, the variables you see and their values will be unique to your system and even your account—that's the whole point of environment variables. Table 2.7 summarizes variables you may see in this output.

TABLE 2.7   Common Environment Variables and Their Meanings

Variable Name	Explanation
USER	This is your current username. It's a variable that's maintained by the system.
SHELL	This variable holds the path to the current command shell.
PWD	This is the present working directory. This environment variable is maintained by the system. Programs may use it to search for files when you don't provide a complete pathname.
HOSTNAME	This is the current TCP/IP hostname of the computer.
PATH	This is an unusually important environment variable. It sets the *path* for a session, which is a colon-delimited list of directories in which Linux searches for executable programs when you type a program name. For instance, if PATH is /bin:/usr/bin and you type **ls**, Linux looks for an executable program called ls in /bin and then in /usr/bin. If the command you type isn't on the path, Linux responds with a command not found error. The PATH variable is typically built up in several configuration files, such as /etc/profile and the .bashrc file in the user's home directory.
HOME	This variable points to your home directory. Some programs use it to help them look for configuration files or as a default location in which to store files.
LD_LIBRARY_PATH	A few programs use this environment variable to indicate directories in which library files may be found. It works much like PATH.

TABLE 2.7   Common Environment Variables and Their Meanings *(continued)*

Variable Name	Explanation
PS1	This is the default prompt in bash. It generally includes variables of its own, such as \u (for the username), \h (for the hostname), and \W (for the current working directory). This value is frequently set in /etc/profile, but it is often overridden by users.
NNTPSERVER	Some Usenet news reader programs use this environment variable to specify the name of the news server system. This value might be set in /etc/profile or in the user's configuration files.
TERM	This variable is the name of the current terminal type. To move a text-mode cursor and display text effects for programs like text-mode editors, Linux has to know what commands the terminal supports. The TERM environment variable specifies the terminal in use, which is combined with information from additional files to provide terminal-specific code information. TERM is normally set automatically at login, but in some cases you may need to change it.
DISPLAY	This variable identifies the display used by X. It's usually :0.0, which means the first (numbered from 0) display on the current computer. When you use X in a networked environment, though, this value may be preceded by the name of the computer at which you're sitting, as in machine4.threeroomco.com:0.0. This value is set automatically when you log in, but you may change it if necessary. You can run multiple X sessions on one computer, in which case each one gets a different DISPLAY number—for instance, :0.0 for the first session and :1.0 for the second.
EDITOR	Some programs launch the program pointed to by this environment variable when they need to call a text editor for you to use. Thus, changing this variable to your favorite editor can help you work in Linux. It's best to set this variable to a text-mode editor, though; GUI editors might cause problems if they're called from a program that was launched from a text-mode login.

WARNING   The PATH variable often includes the current directory indicator (.) so that programs in the current directory can be run. This practice poses a security risk, though, because a miscreant could create a program with the name of some other program (such as ls) and trick another user into running it by simply leaving it in a directory the victim frequents. Even the root user may be victimized in this way. For this reason, it's best to omit the current directory from the PATH variable, especially for the superuser. If it's really needed for ordinary users, put it at the *end* of the path.

Any given system is likely to have several other environment variables set, but these are fairly esoteric or relate to specific programs. If a program's documentation says that it needs certain environment variables set, you can set them system-wide in /etc/profile or some other suitable file, or you can set them in user configuration files, as you deem appropriate.

Although you can see the entire environment by typing **env**, this output can be long enough to be intimidating. If you just want to know the value of one variable, you can use the echo command, which echoes what you type to the screen. If you pass it a variable name preceded by a dollar sign ($), echo returns the value of the variable. For instance:

```
$ echo $PS1
[\u@\h \W]\$
```

This command reveals that the PS1 environment variable is set to [\u@\h \W]\$, which in turn produces a bash prompt like [david@penguin homes]$.

Basic Shell Scripting

You'll do much of your work on a Linux system by typing commands at a shell prompt. As you use Linux, though, you're likely to find some of these tasks to be quite repetitive. If you need to add a hundred new users to the system, for instance, typing **useradd** a hundred times can be tedious. Fortunately, Linux includes a way to cut through the tedium: *shell scripts*. These are simple programs written in an interpreted computer language that's embedded in the Linux shell you use to type commands.

Most Linux systems use the bash shell by default, so shell scripts are often written in the bash shell scripting language, but the tcsh and other shell scripting languages are quite similar. In fact, it's not uncommon to see shell scripts that run in any common Linux shell. You're not restricted to running shell scripts written in your default shell, however; the first line of a shell script identifies the shell that should be used to run it.

Many Linux startup scripts, including SysV startup scripts, are in fact shell scripts. Therefore, understanding shell scripting is necessary if you want to modify a Linux startup script.

Like any programming task, shell scripting can be quite complex. Consequently, this chapter barely scratches the surface of what can be accomplished through shell scripting. Consult a book on the topic, such as *Learning the Bash Shell, 2nd Edition*, by Cameron Newham and Bill Rosenblatt (O'Reilly, 1998), for more information.

To use a shell script, you must first know how to start one. Once you start one, you'll find that one of the easiest tasks to do is to call external commands. More advanced tasks include using variables and using conditional expressions.

Beginning a Shell Script

Shell scripts are plain-text files, so you create them in text editors. A shell script begins with a line that identifies the shell that's used to run it, such as the following:

```
#!/bin/sh
```

The first two characters are a special code that tells the Linux kernel that this is a script and to use the rest of the line as a pathname to the program that's to interpret the script. Shell scripting languages use a hash mark (#) as a comment character, so the script utility itself ignores this line, although the kernel doesn't. On most systems, /bin/sh is a symbolic link that points to /bin/bash, but it could point to some other shell. Specifying the script as using /bin/sh guarantees that any Linux system will have a shell program to run the script, but if the script uses any features specific to a particular shell, you should specify that shell instead—for instance, use /bin/bash or /bin/tcsh instead of /bin/sh.

When you're done writing the shell script, you should modify it so that it's executable. You do this with the chmod command, as described earlier, in "Permissions Modification." Specifically, you use the +x option to add execute permissions, probably in conjunction with a to add these permissions for all users. For instance, to make a file called my-script executable, you'd issue the following command:

```
$ chmod a+x my-script
```

You'll then be able to execute the script by typing its name, possibly preceded by ./ to tell Linux to search in the current directory for the script. If you fail to make the script executable, you can still run the script by running the shell program followed by the script name (as in **bash my-script**), but it's generally better to make the script executable. If the script is one you run regularly, you may want to move it to a location on your path, such as /usr/local/bin. When you do that, you won't have to type the complete path or move to the script's directory to execute it; you can just type **my-script**.

Using External Commands

One of the most basic features of shell scripts is the ability to run external commands. Almost all the commands you type in a shell prompt are in fact external commands—they're programs located in /bin, /usr/bin, and other directories on your path. You can run such programs by including their names in the script. You can also specify parameters to such programs in a script. For instance, suppose you want to start a script that launches two xterms and the KMail mail reader program. Listing 2.2 presents a shell script that accomplishes this goal.

Listing 2.2: A Simple Script That Launches Three Programs

```
#!/bin/bash
/usr/bin/xterm &
/usr/bin/xterm &
/usr/bin/kmail &
```

Aside from the first line that identifies it as a script, the script looks just like the commands you might type to accomplish the task manually, except for one fact: The script lists the complete paths to each program. This is usually not strictly necessary, but listing the complete path ensures that the script will find the programs even if the PATH environment variable changes. Also, each program-launch line in Listing 2.2 ends in an ampersand (&). This character tells the shell to go on to the next line without waiting for the first to finish. If you omit the ampersands in Listing 2.2, the effect will be that the first xterm will open, but the second won't open until the first is closed. Likewise, KMail won't start until the second xterm is stopped.

Although launching several programs from one script can save time in startup scripts and some other situations, scripts are also frequently used to run a series of programs that manipulate data in some way. Such scripts typically do *not* include the ampersands at the ends of the commands, because one command must run after another or may even rely on output from the first. A comprehensive list of such commands is impossible because you can run any program you can install in Linux as a command—even another script. A few commands that are commonly used in scripts include the following:

Normal file manipulation commands   The file manipulation commands described earlier in this chapter, such as ls, mv, cp, and rm, are often used in scripts. You can use these commands to help automate repetitive file maintenance tasks.

grep   This command is described earlier in this chapter, in the section "grep." It locates files that contain specific strings.

find   Where grep searches for patterns within the contents of files, find does so based on filenames, ownership, and similar characteristics. This command is described earlier in this chapter, in the section "find."

cut   This command extracts text from fields in a file. It's frequently used to extract variable information from a file whose contents are highly patterned. To use it, you pass it one or more options that control what it cuts followed by one or more filenames. For instance, users' home directories appear in the sixth colon-delimited field of the /etc/passwd file. You could therefore type **cut -f 6 -d ":" /etc/passwd** to extract this information.

sed   This program is described briefly earlier, in "Using sed and awk." It provides many of the capabilities of a conventional text editor but via commands that can be typed at a command prompt or entered in a script.

echo   Sometimes a script must provide a message to the user; echo is the tool to accomplish this goal. You can pass various options to echo or just a string to be shown to the user. For instance, **echo "Press the Enter key"** causes a script to display the specified string.

Many of these commands are extremely complex, and completely describing them is beyond the scope of this chapter. You can consult these commands' man pages for more information.

Even if you have a full grasp of how to use some key external commands, simply executing commands you might type at a command prompt is of limited utility. Many administrative tasks require you to modify what you type at a command, or even what commands you enter, depending on information from other commands. For this reason, scripting languages include additional features to help you make your scripts useful.

Using Variables

Variables can help you expand the utility of scripts. A variable is a placeholder in a script for a value that will be determined when the script runs. Variables' values can be passed as parameters to scripts, generated internally to the scripts, or extracted from the script's environment.

Variables that are passed to the script are frequently called parameters. They're represented by a dollar sign ($) followed by a number from 0 up—$0 stands for the name of the script, $1 is the first parameter to the script, $2 is the second parameter, and so on. To understand how this might be useful, consider the task of adding a user. As described in Chapter 3, creating an account for a new user typically involves running at least two commands—useradd and passwd. You might also need to run additional site-specific commands, such as commands that create unusual user-owned directories aside from the user's home directory.

As an example of how a script with a parameter variable can help in such situations, consider Listing 2.3. This script creates an account and changes the account's password (you'll be prompted to enter the password when you run the script). It creates a directory in the /shared directory tree corresponding to the account, and it sets a symbolic link to that directory from the new user's home directory. It also adjusts ownership and permissions in a way that may be useful, depending on your system's ownership and permissions policies.

Listing 2.3: A Script That Reduces Account-Creation Tedium

```
#!/bin/sh
useradd -m $1
passwd $1
mkdir -p /shared/$1
chown $1.users /shared/$1
chmod 775 /shared/$1
ln -s /shared/$1 /home/$1/shared
chown $1.users /home/$1/shared
```

If you use Listing 2.3, you need type only three things: the script name with the desired username, and the password (twice). For instance, if the script is called mkuser, you might use it like this:

```
# mkuser ajones
Changing password for user ajones
New password:
Retype new password:
passwd: all authentication tokens updated successfully
```

Most of the scripts' programs operate silently unless they encounter problems, so the interaction (including typing the passwords, which don't echo to the screen) is a result of just the `passwd` command. In effect, Listing 2.3's script replaces seven lines of commands with one. Every one of those lines uses the username, so by using this script, you also reduce the chance of an error.

Another type of variable is assigned within scripts themselves—for instance, they can be set from the output of a command. These variables are also identified by leading dollar signs, but they're typically given names that at least begin with a letter, such as $Addr or $Name. (When assigning values to variables, the dollar sign is omitted, as illustrated shortly.) You can then use these variables in conjunction with normal commands as if they were command parameters, but the value of the variable is passed to the command.

For instance, consider Listing 2.4, which implements simple firewall rules using the `ipchains` utility. This script uses two variables. The first is $ip, which is extracted from the output of `ifconfig` using `grep` and `cut` commands. (The trailing backslash on the second line of the script indicates that the following line is a continuation of the preceding line.) When assigning a value to a variable from the output of a command, that command should be enclosed in back-quote characters (`` ` ``), which appear on the same key as the tilde (~) on most keyboards. These are *not* ordinary single quotes, which appear on the same key as the regular quote character (") on most keyboards. The second variable, $ipchains, simply points to the `ipchains` program. It could as easily be omitted, with subsequent uses of $ipchains replaced by the full path to the program. Variables like this are sometimes used to make it easier to modify the script in the future. For instance, if you move the `ipchains` program, you need only modify one line of the script. They can also be used in conjunction with conditionals to ensure that the script works on more systems—for instance, if `ipchains` were called something else on some systems.

Listing 2.4: Script Demonstrating Assignment and Use of Variables

```
#!/bin/sh
ip=`ifconfig eth0 | grep inet | cut -f 2 -d ":" | \
    cut -f 1 -d " "`
ipchains="/sbin/ipchains"
echo "Restricting access to $ip"
$ipchains -A input -p tcp -s 0/0 -d $ip 25 -j REJECT
$ipchains -A input -p tcp -s 0/0 -d $ip 80 -j REJECT
```

Listing 2.4 is a poor firewall. It blocks only two ports and omits many other features useful in a firewall. It is, however, an accessible demonstration of the use of variables in a script.

Scripts like Listing 2.4, which obtain information from running one or more commands, are useful in configuring features that rely on system-specific information or information that varies with time. You might use a similar approach to obtain the current hostname (using the hostname command), the current time (using date), the total time the computer's been running (using uptime), free disk space (using df), and so on. When combined with conditional expressions (described shortly), variables become even more powerful because then your script can perform one action when one condition is met, and another in some other case. For instance, a script that installs software could check free disk space and abort the installation if there's not enough disk space available.

One special type of variable was mentioned earlier in this chapter: environment variables, described in "Setting Environment Variables." Environment variables are assigned and accessed just like shell script variables. The difference is that the script or command that sets an environment variable uses the export command (in bash) to make the value of the variable accessible to programs launched from the shell or shell script that made the assignment. Environment variables are most often set in shell startup scripts, but the scripts you use can access them. For instance, if your script calls X programs, it might check for the presence of a valid $DISPLAY environment variable and abort if it finds that this variable isn't set. By convention, environment variable names are all uppercase, whereas nonenvironment shell script variables are all lowercase or mixed case.

Using Conditional Expressions

Scripting languages support several types of *conditional expressions*. These enable a script to perform one of several actions contingent on some condition—typically the value of a variable. One common command that uses conditional expressions is if, which allows the system to take one of two actions depending on whether some condition is true. The if keyword's conditional expression appears in brackets after the if keyword and can take many forms. For instance, -f *file* is true if *file* exists and is a regular file; -s *file* is true if *file* exists and has a size greater than 0; and *string1* = *string2* is true if the two strings have the same values.

To better understand the use of conditionals, consider the following code fragment:

```
if [ -s /tmp/tempstuff ]
   then
       echo "/tmp/tempstuff found; aborting!"
       exit
fi
```

This fragment causes the script to exit if the file /tmp/tempstuff is present. The then keyword marks the beginning of a series of lines that execute only if the conditional is true, and fi (if backwards) marks the end of the if block. (Some other multiline conditionals, such as case, use the opening keyword reversed to mark the end of the block; other multiline code blocks, such as those marked out by while, begin with the do keyword and end with the done keyword.) Such code might be useful if the script creates and then later deletes this file, since its presence indicates that a previous run of the script didn't succeed.

Conditional expressions are sometimes used in *loops*, as well. Loops are structures that tell the script to perform the same task repeatedly until some condition is met (or until some condition is no longer met). For instance, Listing 2.5 shows a loop that plays all the .wav audio files in a directory.

Listing 2.5: A Script That Executes a Command on Every Matching File in a Directory

```
#!/bin/bash
for d in `ls *.wav` ;
   do play $d ;
done
```

The for loop as used here executes once for every item in the list generated by ls *.wav. Each of those items (filenames) is assigned in turn to the $d variable and so is passed to the play command.

Summary

Linux has strong historical ties to text-mode commands, and in fact Linux systems can be administered entirely from a text-mode login. Furthermore, even GUI tools in Linux are often front-ends to text-mode commands. For these reasons, familiarity with text-mode Linux tools is important for any Linux system administrator, and even for some users.

Text-mode use begins with an understanding of text-mode shells, such as bash and tcsh. Shells accept text-mode commands and display their results, so knowing how to use a shell is necessary for effective use of a Linux system.

Once you've mastered shell basics, you can move on to basic file manipulation commands. These commands support navigating through Linux directories, moving and copying files, manipulating directories, locating files, and examining files. Using redirection and pipes with such commands is also a useful skill to posses. Beyond basic file manipulation commands lies commands to actually edit files, such as the Vi editor and sed stream editor. Vi is particularly important for system administration because it's a popular editor for inclusion on emergency Linux systems.

Environment variables represent another key in text-mode Linux use. They can be set on a system-wide basis to control certain aspects of a user's Linux experience, such as the default prompt. Users can adjust their environment variables by typing appropriate commands or by editing their personal startup files.

Many system administration tasks involve repetitive actions. For this reason, most administrators learn to write at least basic shell scripts, which can combine many commands in one, frequently using variables and conditional expressions to improve the flexibility of the scripts.

Exam Essentials

Summarize how redirection operators and pipes can be useful.   Redirection operators send a program's output to a file or send a file's contents to a program as input, enabling you to save a diagnostic tool's output for later perusal or give consistent input to a program. Pipes enable you to link together multiple programs, giving you more flexible and powerful multicommand tools.

Describe how files are moved and renamed in Linux.   The mv command performs both of these tasks. When used on a single low-level filesystem, it changes disk pointers so that a file's location or name is changed, without altering or copying the file's data. When used across low-level filesystems, mv must copy the data, though.

Explain how directories are created and deleted in Linux.   The mkdir command creates directories. Empty directories can be deleted with rmdir, or directory trees (including any files they contain) can be deleted with rm, by passing it the -r parameter.

Describe the differences between hard and symbolic links.   Hard links are multiple directory entries that point to a single file. Symbolic links are special files that point to other files by filename.

Summarize the Linux ownership and permissions system.   Files are owned by an individual account, and are also associated with one group. Permission bits enable the file's owner to control separately the read, write, and execute access for the file's owner, members of the file's group, and all other users.

Summarize Vi's three editing modes.   You enter text using the edit mode, which supports text entry and deletion. The command and ex modes are used to perform more complex commands or run outside programs to operate on the text entered or changed in edit mode.

Describe when you might use find versus grep.   The find command locates files based on surface features—the filename, file creation date, owner, and so on. The grep command reads the file's contents and enables you to search for files based on those contents.

Summarize the purpose of environment variables.   Environment variables provide information that should be invariant across programs, such as the user's name and the path to be searched for program files.

Describe how a shell script can be useful.   A shell script combines several commands, possibly including conditional expressions, variables, and other programming features to make the script respond dynamically to a system. Therefore, a shell script can reduce administrative effort by performing a series of repetitive tasks at one command.

Commands in This Chapter

Command	Description
ls	Displays the contents of a directory or information on a file

Command	Description
pwd	Displays the present working directory
cd	Changes the present working directory
cp	Copies one or more files or directories
mv	Moves or renames one or more files or directories
Command	**Description**
rm	Deletes one or more files or directories
ln	Creates a hard or symbolic link
mkdir	Creates a directory
rmdir	Deletes a directory
chown	Changes a file's owner
chgrp	Changes a file's group
chmod	Changes a file's permissions (mode)
umask	Changes the current umask; alters the permissions on files created by a process
export	Makes an environment variable available from the bash shell
setenv	Sets an environment variable in tcsh and related shells
env	Displays the current environment variables, or temporarily changes them
find	Locates files that match any of many search criteria, such as name, owner, and permissions
locate	Locates files in a system-wide database based on name
whereis	Locates files in common binary, documentation, and configuration directories
grep	Locates files that include a specified search string
cat	Concatenates multiple files; often used to display a complete file on the screen
sed	Edits files from the command line; may be called in a script
awk	Scripting language that provides complex pattern-matching facilities

Review Questions

1. Which of the following will add `/usr/local/bigprog/bin` to the end of the PATH environment variable, if placed in `/etc/profile`?

    A. `export PATH=/usr/local/bigprog/bin`

    B. `setenv PATH=$PATH:/usr/local/bigprog/bin`

    C. `export PATH=$PATH:/usr/local/bigprog/bin`

    D. `setenv PATH "${PATH}:/usr/local/bigprog/bin"`

2. Who may set default environment variables for an ordinary user?

    A. Either `root` or the user, with the user's settings taking precedence

    B. Either `root` or the user, with `root`'s settings taking precedence

    C. `root` only

    D. The user only

3. Where is the best location for the current directory indicator (`.`) to reside in `root`'s PATH environment variable?

    A. Before all other directories.

    B. After all other directories.

    C. Nowhere; it shouldn't be in `root`'s path.

    D. Wherever is convenient.

4. After using a text editor to create a shell script, what step should you take before trying to use the script?

    A. Set one or more executable bits using `chmod`.

    B. Copy the script to the `/usr/bin/scripts` directory.

    C. Compile the script by typing **bash *scriptname***, where *scriptname* is the script's name.

    D. Run a virus checker on the script to be sure it contains no viruses.

5. Describe the effect of the following short script, `cp1`, if it's called as `cp1 big.c big.cc`:

    ```
    #!/bin/sh
    cp $2 $1
    ```

    A. It has the same effect as the `cp` command—copying the contents of `big.c` to `big.cc`.

    B. It compiles the C program `big.c` and calls the result `big.cc`.

    C. It copies the contents of `big.cc` to `big.c`, eliminating the old `big.c`.

    D. It converts the C program `big.c` into a C++ program called `big.cc`.

6. What is the purpose of conditional expressions in shell scripts?

A. They prevent scripts from executing if license conditions aren't met.

B. They display information on the script's computer environment.

C. They enable the script to take different actions in response to variable data.

D. They enable scripts to learn in a manner reminiscent of Pavlovian conditioning.

7. Which of the following procedures normally launches a shell? (Choose all that apply.)

A. Starting an xterm window.

B. Typing **shell** at a command prompt.

C. Logging in using SSH.

D. You can't; the shell is started automatically at boot time.

8. What key does the bash shell use to complete filenames based on the first few characters?

A. End

B. Tab

C. Enter

D. Insert

9. What command would you type to change the ownership of `somefile.txt` from `ralph` to `tony`?

A. `chown ralph:tony somefile.txt`

B. `chmod somefile.txt tony`

C. `chown somefile.txt tony`

D. `chown tony somefile.txt`

10. Which of the following umask values will result in files with `rw-r-----` permissions?

A. 640

B. 210

C. 022

D. 027

11. You want to discover the sizes of several dot files in a directory. Which of the following commands might you use to do this?

A. `ls -la`

B. `ls -p`

C. `ls -R`

D. `ls -d`

12. You want to move a file from your hard disk to a floppy disk. Which of the following is true?

    A. You'll have to use the `--preserve` option to `mv` to keep ownership and permissions set correctly.

    B. The `mv` command will adjust filesystem pointers without physically rewriting data if the floppy uses the same filesystem type as the hard disk partition.

    C. You must use the same filesystem type on both media to preserve ownership and permissions.

    D. The `mv` command will delete the file on the hard disk after copying it to the floppy.

13. You type `mkdir one/two/three` and receive an error message that reads, in part, `No such file or directory`. What can you do to overcome this problem? (Choose all that apply.)

    A. Add the `--parents` parameter to the `mkdir` command.

    B. Issue three separate `mkdir` commands: `mkdir one`, then `mkdir one/two`, then `mkdir one/two/three`.

    C. Type `touch /bin/mkdir` to be sure the `mkdir` program file exists.

    D. Type `rmdir one` to clear away the interfering base of the desired new directory tree.

14. Which mode in Vi would you use to type text?

    A. Ex mode

    B. Command mode

    C. Type mode

    D. Edit mode

15. How would you remove two lines of text from a file using Vi?

    A. In command mode, position the cursor on the first line and type **2dd**.

    B. In command mode, position the cursor on the last line and type **2yy**.

    C. In edit mode, position the cursor at the start of the first line, hold the shift key down while pressing the Down arrow key twice, and hit the Delete key on the keyboard.

    D. In edit mode, position the cursor at the start of the first line and press Ctrl+K twice.

16. Which of the following file-location commands is likely to take the *most* time to find a file that might be located anywhere on the computer?

    A. `find`

    B. `locate`

    C. `whereis`

    D. They're all equal in speed.

17. Which of the following commands is an improved version of `more`?

    A. `grep`

    B. `tail`

    C. `cat`

    D. `less`

18. Which of the following commands will change all occurrences of dog in the file animals.txt to mutt in the screen display?

   A. sed -s "dog" "mutt" animals.txt

   B. grep -s "dog||mutt" animals.txt

   C. sed 's/dog/mutt/' animals.txt

   D. cat animals.txt | grep -c "dog" "mutt"

19. Which of the following commands will change the group associated with the modes.tex file to marketing?

   A. chgrp modes.tex marketing

   B. chgrp marketing modes.tex

   C. group modes.tex marketing

   D. newgrp modes.tex marketing

20. Which of the following commands will print lines from the file world.txt that contain matches to changes and changed?

   A. grep change[ds] world.txt

   B. sed change[d-s] world.txt

   C. find "change'd|s'" world.txt

   D. search world.txt changes changed

Answers to Review Questions

1. C. Option A sets the path to contain *only* the /usr/local/bigprog/bin directory, rather than *adding* that directory to the existing path. Options B and D use the tcsh syntax for setting the path, and option B uses it incorrectly (/etc/profile is used for setting environment variables in bash, not tcsh).

2. A. The root user may set environment variables in /etc/profile or other system-wide configuration files, and users may set their own environment variables in .bashrc or other user-level configuration files, or by typing them in manually. Because the user's settings come later, they override system defaults, if in conflict.

3. C. The current directory indicator is particularly dangerous in root's PATH environment variable because it can be used by unscrupulous local users to trick root into running programs of the unscrupulous user's design.

4. A. Scripts, like binary programs, normally have at least one executable bit set, although they can be run in certain ways without this feature. There is no standard /usr/bin/scripts directory, and scripts can reside in any directory. Scripts are interpreted programs, which means they don't need to be compiled. Typing **bash *scriptname*** will run the script. Viruses are extremely rare in Linux, and because you just created the script, the only ways it could possibly contain a virus would be if your system was already infected or if you wrote it as a virus.

5. C. The cp command is the only one called in the script, and that command copies files. Because the script passes the arguments ($1 and $2) to cp in reverse order, their effect is reversed—where cp copies its first argument to the second name, the cp1 script copies the second argument to the name of the first. The cp command has nothing to do with compiling C or C++ programs, so neither does the script.

6. C. Conditional expressions return a "true" or "false" response, enabling the script to execute one set of instructions or another, or to terminate or continue a loop.

7. A, C. Shells are started automatically when you log in or start xterm windows unless you configure your account strangely or specify another program to run when you launch an xterm. Typing **shell** won't start a shell, because no standard shell is called shell. (Typing the shell name will do the job, though.) Shells aren't normally started when the computer boots; you must first log in.

8. B. When you press the Tab key when you are typing a command or filename, bash checks to see if the characters you've typed so far are enough to uniquely identify the command or filename. If they are, bash completes the command or filename, saving you keystrokes.

9. D. Typing **chown ralph:tony somefile.txt** sets the owner of the file to ralph and the group to tony. The chmod command is used to change file permissions, not ownership. Option C reverses the order of the filename and the owner. Answer D uses the correct command and options.

10. D. Option D, 027, removes write permissions for the group and all world permissions. (Files normally don't have execute permissions set, but explicitly removing write permissions when removing read permissions ensures reasonable behavior for directories.) Option A, 640, is the octal equivalent of the desired rw-r----- permissions, but the umask sets the bits that are to be *removed* from permissions, not those that are to be set. Option B, 210, would remove write permission for the owner, but it would not remove write permission for the group, which is incorrect. This would also leave all world permissions open. Finally, option C, 022, would not remove world read permission.

11. A. The -1 parameter produces a long listing, including file sizes. The -a parameter produces a listing of all files in a directory, including the dot files. Combining the two produces the desired information (along with information on other files).

12. D. When moving from one partition or disk to another, mv must necessarily read and copy the file, then delete the original if that copy was successful. If both filesystems support ownership and permissions, they'll be preserved; mv doesn't need an explicit --preserve option to do this, and this preservation does not rely on having exactly the same filesystem types. Although mv doesn't physically rewrite data when moving within a single low-level filesystem, this approach cannot work when you are copying to a separate low-level filesystem (such as from a hard disk to a floppy disk); if the data isn't written to the new location, it won't be accessible should the disk be inserted in another computer.

13. A, B. If you try to create a directory inside a directory that doesn't exist, mkdir responds with a No such file or directory error. The --parents parameter tells mkdir to automatically create all necessary parent directories in such situations. You can also manually do this by creating each necessary directory separately. (It's possible that mkdir one wouldn't be necessary in this example, if the directory one already exists. No harm will come from trying to create a directory that already exists, although mkdir will return a File exists error.)

14. D. Edit mode is used for entering text. Ex mode is used for file operations (including loading, saving, and running external programs). Command mode is used for entering commands of various sorts. There is no "type mode" in Vi.

15. A. In Vi, dd is the command-mode command that deletes lines. Preceding this command by a number deletes that number of lines. While yy works similarly, it copies ("yanks") text rather than deleting it. Option C works in many more modern text editors, but not in Vi. Option D works in Emacs and similar text editors, but not in Vi.

16. A. The find utility operates by searching all files in a directory tree, and so it is likely to take a long time to search all a computer's directories. The locate program uses a precompiled database, and whereis searches a limited set of directories, so these commands will take less time.

17. D. The less program, like more, displays a text file a page at a time. The less utility also includes the ability to page backward in the text file, search its contents, and more.

18. C. The sed utility can be used to "stream" text, and change one value to another. In this case, the s option is used to replace dog with mutt. The syntax in option A is incorrect, while choices B and D are incorrect since grep does not include the functionality needed to make the changes.

19. B. The chgrp utility is used to change the group associated with a file, just as chown is used to change the owner associated with the file. The correct syntax requires the first parameter given be the name of the group to be associated with the file, followed by the name of the file. There is no group utility and newgrp does not perform this function.

20. A. The grep utility is used to find matching text within a file and print those line. It accepts regular expressions, which allow for the placing of the two characters you are looking for within brackets. The syntax for sed and find would not perform the needed task, and there is no standard Linux utility named search.

Chapter

3

User Management

THE FOLLOWING COMPTIA OBJECTIVES ARE COVERED IN THIS CHAPTER:

✓ **1.13 Assign users, groups, passwords, and permissions based on company's security policy.**

✓ **2.20 Create, modify, and delete user and group accounts (e.g,** useradd, groupadd, /etc/passwd, chgrp, quota, chown, chmod, grpmod) **using CLI utilities.**

✓ **4.1 Configure security environment files (e.g.,** hosts.allow, sudoers, ftpusers, sshd_config).

✓ **4.2 Delete accounts while maintaining data stored in that user's home directory.**

✓ **4.3 Given security requirements, implement appropriate encryption configuration (e.g., blowfish 3DES, MD5).**

✓ **4.5 Use appropriate access level for login (e.g.,** root **level vs user level activities,** su, sudo).

✓ **4.11 Given a set of security requirements, set password policies to match (complexity / aging / shadowed passwords) (e.g., convert to and from shadow passwords).**

Traditional PC OSs, such as DOS and early versions of Windows, are basically single-user OSs. Although it's certainly possible for two or more people to use computers running these OSs, the OSs themselves provide no mechanisms to help keep users from reading or even damaging one another's files. Linux, on the other hand, is modeled after Unix, which was designed as a multi-user OS. In Linux and Unix, the OS provides tools designed to help keep users from harming one another's files. The same mechanisms are used to provide security and to keep users from damaging the OS as a whole. For these reasons, Linux system administrators must understand how the OS handles users and what tools are available to help you manage the users on your own system.

This chapter covers several specific user management topics, starting with an overview of basic multiuser concepts. Next up is information on configuring users and groups of users, as well as common strategies you can employ in managing users and groups. Because Linux's account system is a pillar in its security system, this chapter describes policies you can use in account management to improve security, focusing on good password practices. This chapter concludes with a look at access control—using accounts, encryption, and server-specific options to limit access to the computer by particular users or computers.

Linux Multiuser Concepts

Before dealing with the nitty-gritty details of administering user accounts on a Linux system, you should understand the underlying concepts, including a few implementation details. Knowing this information will help you plan an effective account structure or expand an existing one to meet new needs. This information may also be critically important when you're moving accounts from one computer to another, adding a new hard disk, or performing other types of system maintenance.

User Accounts: The Core of a Multiuser System

Linux user accounts are basically the same as user accounts in other Unix-like OSs. They allow several people to use the same system, either at different times or at the same time, without interfering with one another. A single user can even have several simultaneous logins active, which is sometimes convenient. It's important to understand what user accounts allow you to do with a system, and also how users are identified.

Accounts in a Multiuser System

Technically, a user is a person, whereas an account is a set of data structures and permissions associated with that user. Frequently, though, the term *user* is used as if it were synonymous with *account*, as in "you must delete this user." Don't take such language literally—delete the account, not the user.

Several important features have been associated with Linux accounts, including the following:

Username   The *username* is the name by which the account is known to humans, such as ellen. The characteristics of Linux usernames are described in more detail shortly, in "Linux Usernames."

Login privileges   An account enables an individual to log into a Linux computer. Depending on the system's configuration, this could be a login at the console (that is, the keyboard and monitor that are directly connected to the computer) or remotely (via serial line, modem, or network). When an individual logs in, that person may use some or all of the programs and resources available on the computer. Some other resources, like files delivered by a Web server, don't require a login.

Password protection   Linux accounts are protected by a password. A person attempting to log in must provide both a username and a password. The username is generally public knowledge, but the password is secret. Some forms of login bypass the password protection, usually by deferring to authentication performed by another computer.

Permissions   Every account has permission to run certain programs and access certain files. These permissions are controlled on a file-by-file basis, as described in Chapter 2, "Text-Mode Commands."

Home directory   Every account has a home directory associated with it. This is a directory in which the user can store data files. Typically, each user has his or her own home directory, although it's possible to configure a system so that two or more users share a home directory. It's also possible, but seldom useful, to specify a home directory to which a user cannot write. (You might use such a configuration if a user should be able to run programs that don't generate their own data but should not be able to store files on the computer.)

User and group IDs   Computers operate on numbers, not words—the words we see on computer screens are encoded as numbers internally. Linux associates two numbers with each account. The first is the *user ID (UID)*, which is mapped to a specific username. The second is the *group ID (GID)*, which is mapped to a specific group of users. Both these processes are described further in the section "Mapping UIDs and GIDs to Users and Groups."

Default shell   When using a Linux computer at a text-based login (say, at the console without the X Window System running, or via a text-based network protocol like Telnet), Linux presents users with a program known as a shell. The shell accepts commands, such as ls and cd, and enables the user to run additional programs. Several shells are available for Linux and can be set on an account-by-account basis.

Chapter 2 describes the use of shells in more detail.

Program-specific files   Some programs generate files that are associated with a particular user, in or out of that user's home directory. Many programs create configuration files in the user's home directory, for instance. Another important example is the mail spool, in which a Linux system stores incoming e-mail messages for a user. Assuming the basic mail software is installed, creating a user account is usually necessary and sufficient for a user to receive mail, although exceptions to this rule exist, particularly with some mail server packages.

Some of these features are defined in one or two critical system configuration files: /etc/passwd and /etc/shadow. The /etc/passwd file is the traditional repository for critical account information, including the username, UID number, GID number, password, home directory location, and default shell specification. Creating or modifying an account is mostly a matter of modifying this one file. There are enough additional details, though, that most administrators use special tools to perform these tasks, as described in the section "Configuring User Accounts."

Unfortunately, the needs of the system dictate that /etc/passwd be readable by all users. This fact makes the placement of password information in /etc/passwd—even in encrypted form—a risky proposition. For this reason, most Linux distributions since the late 1990s ship with *shadow password* support. In this system, users' passwords are stored in a separate file, /etc/shadow. This file cannot be read by most users, making it more difficult for a miscreant with an account on the computer to break into other users' accounts.

Accounts in a Multitasking System

Linux is both a multiuser and a multitasking system. Linux's multiuser nature allows multiple people to use one computer without causing problems for one another. Linux's multitasking ability allows multiple programs to run at one time. Although single-user multitasking OSs are available, combining the two has many advantages, particularly in a networked environment. Specifically, several people can be logged onto a Linux computer at one time, and they can run the same or different programs simultaneously. For instance, Sally can run the Emacs editor while Sam and Ellen both run the Mozilla Web browser and George runs a C compiler.

Although it's possible to use a single account for multiple simultaneous logins, using multiple accounts can be helpful, particularly when multiple individuals are involved. Each account can be configured with its owner's preferences in mind, and therefore, simultaneous logins can present different defaults for things like the placement of icons on a desktop environment or the command shell to be used. Furthermore, if a user changes a default value, that change will not affect other users currently logged on to the system. If the system were a single-user computer that allowed multiple logins, changes to system defaults could adversely affect other users or be undone when other users logged out.

Of course, Linux's multitasking ability doesn't mean that the computer can support an unlimited number of simultaneous users. Some activities, such as George's C program compilation, are likely to consume a great deal of RAM, CPU time, or disk I/O. If many users try to run such resource-intensive programs simultaneously, all the users will see a performance decrease. Just how many simultaneous users a Linux computer can support depends on many factors, including the types of programs they're likely to run and how much of critical system resources (RAM, CPU speed, network speed, disk speed, and disk capacity) the system has. If the applications used aren't very resource intensive, a single modern computer can support dozens or hundreds of simultaneous users, but if the programs are hogs of one or more resources, one user per computer may seem like too many.

Simultaneous use of one computer by multiple users generally requires some form of network connectivity, although it can also be handled through terminals connected to serial ports. Typically, remote login protocols like Telnet or the Secure Shell (SSH) support text-mode logins. Linux's GUI environment, the X Window System (or X for short), is network-enabled, and so it permits remote use of GUI programs. Alternatively, the VNC program (`http://www.realvnc.com`) supports similar connectivity.

Linux supports multiple simultaneous logins through its standard console via a feature known as *virtual terminals (VTs)*. From a text-mode login, hitting the Alt key along with a function key from 1 to 6 typically switches to a different virtual screen, and you can log into as many of these as you like. You can even run multiple X sessions at different resolutions by issuing appropriate parameters to `startx`. Ordinarily, the first X session runs on VT 7. When switching out of a VT that's running X, you must add Ctrl to the key sequence—for instance, you must press Ctrl+Alt+F1 to switch from X to the first text-mode VT. You can run a second X session by logging into a text VT and issuing the following command:

```
$ startx -- :1 vt8
```

This command will run X in VT 8. You can switch back and forth between it and the first X session by pressing Ctrl+Alt+F7 and Ctrl+Alt+F8.

Of course, this VT capability is most useful for a single-user workstation—two people can't make practical use of the same keyboard at the same time. Nonetheless, it's still useful if you as an administrator want to run Linux under multiple accounts or X configurations, or if you want to easily switch between multiple text-based programs without running X.

The Superuser Account

One particularly important account on all Linux systems is that of the *superuser*. The superuser is also referred to as the administrator. The account used by the superuser is normally known as `root`.

Whenever you perform system administration tasks on a Linux computer, you'll do so as `root`. You can do this in any of several ways:

Direct administrative login   You can log into the computer as `root`. Thereafter, any action you perform will be done as the superuser. This can be a very dangerous way to use the system, so it's best to do so only for brief periods. Most systems contain restrictions on `root` logins, so they can only be done from the console. This helps prevent outsiders from gaining access to a system over a network by using a stolen password.

Switching identities after login   The `su` program lets you temporarily acquire superuser privileges or take on any other user's identity. Type **su** and press the Enter key after logging on as an ordinary user, and the system will prompt you for the `root` password. If you type that password correctly, subsequent commands will be executed as root. Type **exit** to return to your normal user privileges. To take on a non-root user's privileges, add that user's name, as in **su george**, to take on the george account's role. If you're already root, you can take on another user's identity without that user's password; su doesn't ask root for a password. This can be useful when you're debugging problems that may be related to a particular user's configuration.

Running an individual program as the superuser   Once configured, the sudo command allows you to execute a single command as root. This limits the danger of running as root, and so it can be a good way to run the programs that you most frequently run as root. The /etc/sudoers file contains a list of users who may use sudo, and the commands they may run in this way. You can edit this file with the visudo command, which invokes the Vi editor (as described in Chapter 2) in such a way that it helps you get the format of the configuration file right. To use sudo, you type this command followed by the command you want to execute, as in **sudo fdisk /dev/hda** to edit the partition table on /dev/hda without using su or some other method of acquiring root privileges.

SUID root files   As described in the section "Interpreting File Access Codes" in Chapter 2, it's possible to set a file to execute as if run by root even when it's run by another user. This feature must be set on a program-by-program basis.

Program prompts   Some configuration tools prompt you for the root password and then run themselves as root. This setup is most common with the GUI configuration tools that ship with many Linux distributions.

The Danger of *root* Power

The root account is special because it bypasses normal security features. Specifically, the superuser may read, write, or delete any file on the computer, no matter who owns that file or whether the owner has granted other users read or write access to it. This sort of power is dangerous not just because of the ability to invade other users' privacy, but because it allows root to do serious damage to the OS. For instance, suppose you want to delete a directory and its contents. You might issue the following command to do so:

```
# rm -r /home/george/olddir
```

This command deletes the /home/george/olddir directory and all its files and subdirectories. Unfortunately, a single typo can create a much more destructive command:

```
# rm -r / home/george/olddir
```

Note the stray space between / and home/george/olddir. This typo causes the computer to delete all files in the / directory—that is, all files on the computer, not just the files in home/george/olddir. This is the sort of power that you should grant yourself only when you absolutely need it.

Linux Usernames

Linux is fairly flexible about its usernames. Most versions of Linux support usernames consisting of any combination of upper- and lowercase letters, numbers, and many punctuation symbols, including periods and spaces. Some punctuation symbols, however, such as spaces, cause problems for certain Linux utilities, so it's generally best to avoid using punctuation in Linux usernames. Underscores (_) and periods (.) are relatively unlikely to cause problems and so are occasionally used. Also, usernames must begin with a letter, so a username such as 45u is invalid, although u45 is fine. Although usernames may consist of up to 32 characters, many utilities truncate usernames longer than 8 characters or so in their displays, so many administrators try to limit username length to 8 characters.

Linux treats usernames in a case-sensitive way. Therefore, a single computer can support both ellen and Ellen as separate users. This practice can lead to a great deal of confusion, however, so it's best to avoid creating accounts whose usernames differ only in case. In fact, the traditional practice is to use entirely lowercase letters in Linux usernames, such as sally, sam, ellen, and george. Usernames don't need to be based on first names, of course—you could use sam_jones, s.jones, sjones, jones, jones17, or u238, to name just a few possibilities. Most sites develop a standard method of creating usernames, such as using the first initial and the last name. Creating and following such a standard practice can help you locate an account that belongs to a particular individual. If your computer has many users, though, you may find a naming convention produces duplicates, particularly if your standard uses initials to shorten usernames. You may therefore be forced to deviate from the standard or incorporate numbers to distinguish between all the Davids or Smiths of the world.

Groups: Linking Users Together for Productivity

Linux uses *groups* as a means of organizing users. In many ways, groups parallel users. Groups are similar to users in several ways:

- Groups are defined in a single file, /etc/group, which has a structure similar to that of /etc/passwd.
- Groups have names similar to usernames.
- Group names are tied to group IDs (GIDs).

Groups are *not* accounts, however. Rather, groups are a means of organizing collections of accounts, largely as a security measure. As described in Chapter 2, every file on a Linux system is associated with a specific group, and various permissions can be assigned to members of that group. For instance, group members (such as faculty at a university) might be allowed to read a file, but others (such as students) might be disallowed such access. Because Linux provides access to most hardware devices (such as serial ports and tape backup units) through files, this same mechanism can be used to control access to hardware.

Every group has anywhere from no members to as many members as there are users on the computer. Group membership is controlled through the /etc/group file. This file contains a list of groups and the members belonging to each group. The details of this file's contents are described in the section "Configuring Groups."

In addition to membership defined in /etc/group, each user has a default or primary group. The user's primary group is set in the user's configuration in /etc/passwd. When users log onto the computer, their group membership is set to their primary groups. When users create files or launch programs, those files and running programs are associated with a single group—the current group membership. A user can still access files belonging to other groups, as long as the user belongs to that group and the group access permissions allow the access. To run programs or create files with other than the primary group membership, however, the user must run the newgrp command to switch current group membership. For instance, to change to the project2 group, you might type the following:

```
$ newgrp project2
```

If the user typing this command is listed as a member of the project2 group in /etc/group, the user's current group membership will change. Thereafter, files created by that user will be associated with the project2 group. Alternatively, users can change the group associated with an existing file by using the chgrp or chown command, as described in Chapter 2.

This group structure enables you to design a security system that permits different collections of users to easily work on the same files while simultaneously keeping other users of the same computer from prying into files they should not be able to access. In a simple case, you might create groups for different projects, classes, or workgroups, with each user restricted to one of these groups. A user who needs access to multiple groups could be a member of each of these groups—for instance, a student who takes two classes could belong to the groups associated with each class, or a supervisor might belong to all the supervised groups. The section "Common User and Group Strategies" describes the approaches taken by various Linux distributions by default, and it then explains how you can expand and use these strategies to suit your own needs.

Mapping UIDs and GIDs to Users and Groups

As mentioned earlier, Linux defines users and groups by numbers (UIDs and GIDs, respectively). Internally, Linux tracks users and groups by these numbers, not by name. For instance, the user sam might be tied to UID 523, and ellen might be UID 609. Similarly, the group project1 might be GID 512, and project2 might be GID 523. For the most part, these details take care of themselves—you use names, and Linux uses /etc/passwd or /etc/group to locate the number associated with the name. You may occasionally need to know how Linux assigns numbers when you tell it to do something, though. This is particularly true when you are troubleshooting or if you have cause to manually edit /etc/passwd or /etc/group.

Linux distributions reserve the first hundred user and group IDs (0–99) for system use. The most important of these is 0, which corresponds to root (both the user and the group). Subsequent low numbers are used by accounts and groups that are associated with specific Linux utilities and functions. For instance, UID 2 and GID 2 are generally the daemon account and group, respectively, which are used by various servers; and UID 8 and GID 12 are usually the mail account and group, which can be used by mail-related servers and utilities. Not all account and group numbers from 0 to 99 are in use; there are usually only one or two dozen accounts and a dozen or so groups used in this way. You can check your /etc/passwd and /etc/group files to determine which user and group IDs are so used.

Aside from UID 0 and GID 0, UID and GID numbers aren't fully standardized. For instance, although UID 2 and GID 2 map to the daemon account and daemon group on Red Hat and SuSE, on Debian UID 2 and GID 2 map to the `bin` account and `bin` group; the daemon account and group correspond to UID 1 and GID 1. If you need to refer to a particular user or group, use the name rather than the number.

Beyond 100, user and group IDs are available for use by ordinary users and groups. Many distributions, however, reserve up to 500 or even 1000 for special purposes. Frequently, therefore, the first normal user account is assigned a UID of 500 or 1000. When you create additional accounts, the system typically locates the next-highest unused number, so the second user you create is UID 501, the third is 502, and so on. When you remove an account, that account's ID number may be reused, but the automatic account-creation tools typically don't do so if subsequent numbers are in use, leaving a gap in the sequence. This gap causes no harm unless you have so many users that you run out of ID numbers. (The limit is 65,536 users with the 2.2.*x* kernels and over 4.2 billion with the 2.4.*x* and later kernels, including `root` and other system accounts. The limit can be set lower in configuration files or because of limits in support programs.) In fact, reusing an ID number can cause problems if you don't clear away the old user's files—the new user will become the owner of the old user's files, which can lead to confusion.

Typically, GID 100 is `users`—the default group for some distributions. (See "Common User and Group Strategies" later in this chapter.) On any but a very small system with few users, you'll probably want to create your own groups. Because different distributions have different default ways of assigning users to groups, it's best that you familiarize yourself with your distribution's way of doing this, and plan your own group-creation policies with this in mind. For instance, you might want to create your own groups within certain ranges of IDs to avoid conflicts with the distribution's default user- and group-creation processes.

It's possible to create multiple usernames that use the same UID, or multiple group names that use the same GID. In some sense, these are different accounts or groups; they have different entries in `/etc/passwd` or `/etc/group`, so they can have different home directories, different passwords, and so on. Because these users or groups share IDs with other users or groups, though, they're treated identically in terms of file permissions. Unless you have a compelling reason to do so, you should avoid creating multiple users or groups that share an ID.

Intruders sometimes create accounts with UID 0 to give themselves root privileges on the systems they invade. *Any* account with a UID of 0 is effectively the root account, with all the power of the superuser. If you spot a suspicious account in your /etc/passwd file with a UID of 0, your system has probably been compromised.

Real World Scenario

Coordinating UIDs and GIDs across Systems

If you maintain several Linux computers and want to set up Network Filesystem (NFS) file sharing, one problem that can arise is keeping UIDs and GIDs synchronized across systems. Because all Linux filesystems, including NFS, track numeric IDs rather than the names that humans use, mismatched UIDs and GIDs can cause one person's files to appear to be owned by another person on an NFS mount. For instance, suppose that two computers each have two users, ellen and george. On one computer, ellen has UID 500 and george has UID 501, but these numbers are reversed on the other. As a consequence, when one computer mounts the other's files via NFS, the UID values will indicate that ellen owns files that are really owned by george, and vice versa.

One solution to this problem is to keep UIDs and GIDs consistent across computers. This isn't too difficult with a handful of small systems with few users, but it becomes tedious with larger or more systems. Some versions of the Linux NFS clients and servers also support various mapping options, such as using a static map file or using a user ID mapping server run on the client system. Unfortunately, these options are no longer being actively supported. Another option is to use a centralized login database, such as one maintained via the Network Information System (NIS), to coordinate accounts on multiple computers.

The Importance of Home Directories

A user's *home directory* is a directory on the disk that's usually intended for one user alone. On Linux systems, the standard placement of home directories is in the /home directory tree, with each user's home directory named after the user's account name. For instance, the home directory for the sally account would be /home/sally. This naming and placement is only a convention, though—it's not a requirement. The /etc/passwd file contains the location of each user's home directory, so you can modify this location by editing that file. You can also specify an alternative location when you create an account (as described shortly in the section "Adding Users"), or use the usermod utility to change it after the fact.

Typically, a user's home directory belongs to that user only. Therefore, it's created with fairly restrictive permissions, particularly for writing to the directory. The exact permissions used by default vary from one distribution to another, so you should check yours to see how it's done. If you want to create more stringent (or more lax) permissions, you'll have to do so yourself after creating an account, or you'll need to create your own account-creation scripts to automate the process.

You can create separate directories for shared projects, if you like. For instance, you might want to have a directory in which group members can store files that belong to the group as a whole, or in which group members may exchange files. Linux distributions don't create such directories automatically when creating groups, so you'll have to attend to this task yourself, as well as decide where to store them. (Somewhere in /home is a logical choice, but it is up to you.)

One problem that's commonly faced by Linux system administrators is the depletion of available disk space. The /home directory frequently resides on a separate partition, and sometimes an entirely separate physical hard disk, from other Linux files. This arrangement can make the system more secure because it helps to isolate the data—filesystem corruption on one partition need not affect data on another. It also limits room for expansion, however. If your users begin creating very large files, or if the number of users you must support grows and causes your initial estimates of required /home disk space to be exceeded, you'll need to take action to correct this matter. For instance, you might move home directories to some other partition; enlarge the home partition with a tool like resize2fs, GNU Parted (http://www.gnu.org/software/parted/), or PartitionMagic (http://www.powerquest.com); or add a new hard disk to store some or all of the user home directories.

Configuring User Accounts

How frequently you'll do user maintenance depends on the nature of the system you administer. Some systems, such as small personal workstations, will need changes very rarely. Others, such as large systems in environments in which users are constantly coming and going, may require daily maintenance. The latter situation would seem to require more knowledge of user account configuration tools, but even in a seldom-changing system, it's useful to know how to do these things so that you can do them quickly and correctly when you do need to add, modify, or delete user accounts.

Adding Users

Adding users can be accomplished through the useradd utility. (This program is called adduser on some distributions.) Its basic syntax is as follows:

```
useradd [-c comment] [-d home-dir] [-e expire-date] [-f inactive-days]
➥[-g initial-group] [-G group[,...]]  [-m [-k skeleton-dir] | -M]
➥[-p password] [-s shell]  [-u UID [-o]] [-r] [-n] username
```

Some of these parameters modify settings that are valid only when the system uses shadow passwords. This is the standard configuration for most distributions today.

In its simplest form, you may type just **useradd** *username*, where *username* is the username you want to create. The rest of the parameters are used to modify the default values for the system, which are stored in the file /etc/login.defs.

The parameters for the useradd command modify the program's operation in various ways:

Add a comment   The -c *comment* parameter passes the comment field for the user. Some administrators store public information like a user's office or telephone number in this field. Others store just the user's real name, or no information at all.

Home directory   You specify the account's home directory with the -h *home-dir* parameter. This defaults to /home/*username* on most systems.

Account expiration date   Set the date on which the account will be disabled, expressed in the form *YYYY-MM-DD*, with the -e *expire-date* option. (Many systems will accept alternative forms, such as *MM-DD-YYYY*, or a single value representing the number of days since January 1, 1970, as well.) The default is for an account that does not expire. This option is most useful in environments in which user accounts are inherently time-limited, such as accounts for students taking particular classes or temporary employees.

Inactive days   The -f *inactive-days* parameter sets the number of days after a password expires after which the account becomes completely disabled. A value of -1 disables this feature, and is the default.

Default group   You set the name or GID of the user's default group with the -g *default-group* option. The default for this value varies from one distribution to another, as described later, in "Common User and Group Strategies."

Additional groups   The -G *group[, ...]* parameter sets the names or GIDs of one or more groups to which the user belongs. These groups need not be the default group, and more than one may be specified by separating them with commas.

Home directory options   The system automatically creates the user's home directory if -m is specified. Normally, default configuration files are copied from /etc/skel, but you may specify another template directory with the -k *skeleton-dir* option. Many distributions use -m as the default when running useradd.

Do not create a home directory   The -M option forces the system to *not* automatically create a home directory, even if /etc/login.defs specifies that this action is the default.

Encrypted password specification   The -p *encrypted-password* parameter passes the *pre-encrypted* password for the user to the system. The *encrypted-password* value will be added, *unchanged*, to the /etc/passwd or /etc/shadow file. This means that if you type an unencrypted password, it won't work as you probably expected. In practice, this parameter is most useful in scripts, which can encrypt a password (using crypt) and then send the encrypted result through useradd. The default value disables the account, so you must run passwd to change the user's password.

Default shell   Set the name of the user's default login shell with the -s *shell* option. On most systems, this defaults to /bin/bash, but Linux supports many alternatives, such as /bin/tcsh and /bin/zsh.

Specify a UID   The -u *UID* parameter creates an account with the specified user ID value (*UID*). This value must be a positive integer, and it is normally above 500 for user accounts. System accounts typically have numbers below 100. The -o option allows the number to be reused so that two usernames are associated with a single UID.

System account creation   The -r parameter specifies the creation of a system account—an account with a value lower than UID_MIN, as defined in /etc/login.defs. (This is normally 100, 500, or 1000.) useradd also doesn't create a home directory for system accounts.

No user group   In some distributions, such as Red Hat, the system creates a group with the same name as the specified username. The -n parameter disables this behavior.

Suppose you've added a new hard disk in which some users' home directories are located and mounted it as /home2. You want to create an account for a user named Sally in this directory and make the new user a member of the project1 and project4 groups, with default membership in project4. The user has also requested tcsh as her default shell. You might use the following commands to accomplish this goal:

```
# useradd -d /home2/sally -g project4 -G project1,project4  -s /bin/tcsh sally
# passwd sally
Changing password for user sally
New UNIX password:
Retype new UNIX password:
passwd: all authentication tokens updated successfully
```

 The passwd command asks for the password twice, but it does not echo what you type. This prevents somebody who sees your screen from reading the password off it. passwd is described in more detail in the next section.

Modifying User Accounts

User accounts may be modified in many ways: You can directly edit critical files such as /etc/passwd, modify user-specific configuration files in the account's home directory, or use system utilities like those used to create accounts. You usually modify an existing user's account at the user's request or to implement some new policy or system change, such as moving home directories to a new hard disk. Sometimes, though, you must modify an account immediately after its creation, in order to customize it in ways that aren't easily handled through the account-creation tools or because you realize you forgot a parameter to useradd.

Setting a Password

Although useradd provides the -p parameter to set a password, this tool is not very useful when directly adding a user because it requires a pre-encrypted password. Therefore, it's usually easiest to create an account in disabled form (by not using -p with useradd) and set the password after creating the account. This can be done with the passwd command, which has the following syntax:

```
passwd [-k] [-l] [-u [-f]] [-d] [-S] [username]
```

The parameters to this command enable you to modify its behavior:

Update expired accounts   The -k parameter indicates that the system should update an expired account.

Lock accounts   The -1 parameter locks an account by prefixing the encrypted password with an exclamation mark (!). The result is that the user can no longer log into the account, but the files are still available and the change can be easily undone.

Unlock accounts   The -u parameter unlocks an account by removing a leading exclamation mark. useradd creates accounts that are locked and have no password, so using this command on a fresh account would result in an account with no password. Normally, passwd doesn't allow this—it returns an error if you attempt it. Adding -f forces passwd to turn the account into one with no password.

Create password-less accounts   The -d parameter removes the password from an account, rendering it password-less.

Display account information   The -S option displays information on the password for an account—whether or not it's set and what type of encryption it uses.

Ordinary users may use passwd to change their passwords, but many passwd parameters may only be used by root. Specifically, -1, -u, -f, -d, and -S are all off-limits to ordinary users. Similarly, only root may specify a username to passwd. When ordinary users run the program, they should omit their usernames, and passwd will change the password for the user who ran the program. As a security measure, passwd asks for a user's old password before changing the password when an ordinary user runs the program. This precaution is *not* taken when root runs the program so that the superuser may change a user's password without knowing the original password. Since the administrator normally doesn't know the user's password, this is necessary.

Linux passwords may consist of letters, numbers, and punctuation. Linux distinguishes between upper- and lowercase letters in passwords, which means you can use mixed-case passwords to improve security.

The section "Account Security" later in this chapter includes additional information on selecting good passwords.

Using *usermod*

The usermod program closely parallels useradd in its features and parameters. This utility changes an existing account instead of creating a new one, however. The major differences between useradd and usermod are as follows:

- usermod allows the addition of a -m parameter when used with -d. The -d parameter alone changes the user's home directory, but it does not move any files. Adding -m causes usermod to move the user's files to the new location.

- `usermod` supports a `-l` parameter, which changes the user's login name to the specified value. For instance, typing **`usermod sally -l sjones`** changes the username from `sally` to `sjones`.

- You may lock or unlock a user's password with the `-L` and `-U` options, respectively. This duplicates functionality provided by `passwd`.

The `usermod` program changes the contents of `/etc/passwd` or `/etc/shadow`, depending on the option used. If `-m` is used, `usermod` also moves the user's files, as already noted.

WARNING   Changing an account's characteristics while the owner is logged in can have undesirable consequences. This is particularly true of the `-d -m` combination, which can cause the files a user was working on to move. Most other changes, such as changes to the account's default shell, simply don't take effect until the user has logged out and back in again.

If you change the account's UID, this action does *not* change the UIDs stored with a user's files. Because of this, the user may lose access to these files. You can manually update the UIDs on all files by using the `chown` command (see the section "Ownership Modification" in Chapter 2). Specifically, a command like the following, issued after changing the UID on the account `sally`, will restore proper ownership on the files in `sally`'s home directory:

```
# chown -R sally /home/sally
```

This action does *not* change the ownership of files that aren't in `sally`'s home directory. If you believe such files exist, you may need to track them down with the `find` command, as you'll see in the upcoming section "Deleting Accounts." Also, this command blindly changes ownership of *all* files in the `/home/sally` directory. This is probably desirable, but it's conceivable that some files in that directory *should* be owned by somebody else—say, because `sally` and another user are collaborating on a project.

When using the `-G` option to add a user to new groups, be aware that any groups *not* listed will be removed. The `gpasswd` command, described in the upcoming section, "Using `gpasswd`," provides a way to add a user to one or more specific groups without affecting existing group memberships, and so it is generally preferable for this purpose.

Using *chage*

The `chage` command allows you to modify account settings relating to account expiration. It's possible to configure Linux accounts so that they automatically expire if either of two conditions is true:

- The password hasn't been changed in a specified period of time.

- The system date is past a predetermined time.

The first option is generally used to enforce password changes—say, to get users to change their passwords once a month. The second option is useful when an account should exist for a specific limited period of time, such as until the end of an academic semester or until a temporary employee leaves. These settings are controlled through the chage utility, which has the following syntax:

```
chage [-1] [-m mindays] [-M maxdays] [-d lastday]  [-I inactivedays]
➥[-E expiredate] [-W warndays] username
```

The program's parameters modify the command's actions:

Display information   The -1 option causes chage to display account expiration and password aging information for a particular user.

Set minimum time between password changes   The -m *mindays* parameter sets the minimum number of days between password changes. 0 indicates that a user can change a password multiple times in a day; 1 means that a user can change a password once a day; 2 means that a user may change a password once every two days; and so on.

Set maximum time between password changes   The -M *maxdays* parameter sets the maximum number of days that may pass between password changes. For instance, 30 would require a password change approximately once a month.

 If the user changes a password before the deadline, the counter is reset from the password change date.

Set last password change date   The -d *lastday* parameter sets the last day a password was changed. This value is normally maintained automatically by Linux, but you can use this parameter to artificially alter the password change count. For instance, you could use this to set the last changed date to force a password change in some period of time you determine. *lastday* is expressed in the format *YYYY/MM/DD*, or as the number of days since January 1, 1970.

Maximum inactive days   The -I *inactivedays* parameter sets the number of days between password expiration and account disablement. An expired account may not be used or may force the user to change the password immediately upon logging in, depending on the distribution. A disabled account is completely disabled, however.

Set expiration date   You can set an absolute expiration date with the -E *expiredate* option. For instance, you might use **-E 2006/05/21** to have an account expire on May 21, 2006. The date may also be expressed as the number of days since January 1, 1970. A value of -1 represents no expiration date.

Set number of warning days   The -W *warndays* option sets the number of days before account expiration that the system will warn the user of the impending expiration. It's generally a good idea to use this feature to alert users of their situation, particularly if you make heavy use of password change expirations.

The chage command can normally only be used by root. The one exception to this rule is if the -1 option is used; this feature allows ordinary users to check their account expiration information.

Directly Modifying Account Configuration Files

User configuration files can be modified directly. /etc/passwd and /etc/shadow control most aspects of an account's basic features, but many files within a user's home directory control user-specific configuration; for instance, .bashrc can be used to set user-specific bash shell features. This latter class of configuration files is far too broad to cover here, but /etc/passwd and /etc/shadow are not. Both files consist of a set of lines, one line per account. Each line begins with a username and continues with a set of fields, delimited by colons (:). Many of these items may be modified with usermod or passwd. A typical /etc/passwd entry resembles the following:

sally:x:529:100:Sally Jones:/home/sally:/bin/bash

Each field has a specific meaning, as follows:

Username   The first field in each /etc/passwd line is the username (sally in this example).

Password   The second field has traditionally been reserved for the password. Most Linux systems, however, use a shadow password system in which the password is stored in /etc/shadow. The x in the example's password field is an indication that shadow passwords are in use. In a system that does not use shadow passwords, an encrypted password will appear here instead.

UID   Following the password is the account's user ID (529 in this example).

Primary GID   The default login group ID is next in the /etc/passwd line for an account. The example uses a primary GID of 100.

Comment   The comment field may have different contents on different systems. In the preceding example, it's the user's full name. Some systems place additional information here, in a comma-separated list. Such information might include the user's telephone number, office number, title, and so on.

Home directory   The user's home directory is next up in the list.

Default shell   The default shell is the final item on each line in /etc/passwd. This is normally /bin/bash, /bin/tcsh, or some other common command shell. It's possible to use something unusual here, though. For instance, many systems include a shutdown account with /bin/shutdown as the shell. If you log into this account, the computer immediately shuts down. You can create user accounts with a shell of /bin/false, which prevents users from logging in as ordinary users but leaves other utilities intact. Users can still receive mail and retrieve it via a remote mail retrieval protocol like POP or IMAP, for instance. A variant on this scheme uses /bin/passwd so that users may change their passwords remotely but not actually log in using a command shell.

You can directly modify any of these fields, although in a shadow password system, you probably do *not* want to modify the password field; you should make password-related changes via passwd so that they can be properly encrypted and stored in /etc/shadow. As with changes initiated via usermod, it's best to change /etc/passwd directly only when the user in question isn't logged in, to prevent a change from disrupting an ongoing session.

Like /etc/passwd, /etc/shadow may be edited directly. An example /etc/shadow line resembles the following:

```
sally:E/moFkeT5UnTQ:12269:0:-1:7:-1:-1:
```

Most of these fields correspond to options set with the chage utility, although some are set with passwd, useradd, or usermod. The meaning of each colon-delimited field of this line is as follows:

Username   Each line begins with the username. Note that the UID is *not* used in /etc/shadow; the username links entries in this file to those in /etc/passwd.

Password   The password is stored in encrypted form, so it bears no obvious resemblance to the actual password. An asterisk (*) or exclamation mark (!) denotes an account with no password (that is, the account doesn't accept logins—it's locked). This is common for accounts used by the system itself.

> If you've forgotten the root password for a system, you can boot with an emergency recovery system and copy the contents of a password field for an account whose password you do remember. You can then boot normally, log in as root, and change the password. In a real pinch, you can delete the contents of the password field, which results in a root account with *no* password (that is, none is required to log in). Be *sure* to *immediately* change the root password after rebooting if you do this, though!

Last password change   The next field (12269 in this example) is the date of the last password change. This date is stored as the number of days since January 1, 1970.

Days until change allowed   The next field (0 in this example) is the number of days before a password change is allowed.

Days before change required   This field is the number of days after the last password change before another password change is required.

Days warning before password expiration   If your system is configured to expire passwords, you may set it to warn the user when an expiration date is approaching. A value of 7, as in the preceding example, is typical.

Days between expiration and deactivation   Linux allows for a gap between the expiration of an account and its complete deactivation. An expired account either cannot be used or requires that the user change the password immediately after logging in. In either case, its password remains intact. A deactivated account's password is erased, and the account cannot be used until it's reactivated by the system administrator.

Expiration date   This field shows the date on which the account will be expired. As with the last password change date, the date is expressed as the number of days since January 1, 1970.

Special flag   This field is reserved for future use and is normally not used or contains a meaningless value. This field is empty in the preceding example.

For fields relating to day counts, values of –1 or 99999 typically indicate that the relevant feature has been disabled. The /etc/shadow values are generally best left to modification through
the usermod or chage commands because they can be tricky to set manually—for instance, it's
easy to forget a leap year or the like when computing a date as the number of days since
January 1, 1970. Similarly, because of its encrypted nature, the password field cannot be edited
effectively except through passwd or similar utilities. (You could cut and paste a value from a
compatible file or use crypt yourself, but it's usually easier to use passwd. Copying encrypted
passwords from other systems is also somewhat risky because it means that the users will have
the same passwords on both systems, and this fact will be obvious to anybody who's acquired
both encrypted password lists.)

Real World Scenario

Network Account Databases

Many networks employ network account databases. Such systems include the Network Information System (NIS), an update to this system called NIS+, the Lightweight Directory Access
Protocol (LDAP), Kerberos realms, Windows NT 4.0 domains, and Active Directory (AD)
domains. All of these systems move account database management onto a single centralized
computer (often with one or more backup systems). The advantage of this approach to account
maintenance is that users and administrators need not deal with maintaining accounts independently on multiple computers. A single account database can handle accounts on dozens
(or even hundreds or thousands) of different computers, greatly simplifying day-to-day administrative tasks and simplifying users' lives. Using such a system, though, means that most user
accounts won't appear in /etc/passwd and /etc/shadow, and groups may not appear in /etc/
group. (These files will still hold information on local system accounts and groups, though.)

Linux can participate in these systems, naturally. In fact, some distributions provide options to
enable such support at OS installation time. Typically, you must know the name or IP address of
the server that hosts the network account database, and you must know what protocol that system uses. You may also need a password or some other protocol-specific information, and the
server may need to be configured to accept accesses from the Linux system you're configuring.

Activating use of such network account databases after installing Linux is a complex topic. It
involves installing appropriate software, modifying the /etc/nsswitch.conf file, and modifying the Pluggable Authentication Module (PAM) configuration files in /etc/pam.d. Such systems often alter the behavior of tools such as passwd and usermod in subtle or not-so-subtle
ways. If you need to use such a system, you'll have to consult documentation specific to the
service you intend to use. Chapter 6, "Networking," covers a few basics for NIS. My upcoming
book, *Linux in a Windows World* (O'Reilly, 2005), covers this topic for Windows NT 4.0
domains, LDAP, and Kerberos.

> /etc/shadow is normally stored with very restrictive permissions, such as rw-------, with ownership by root. This fact is critical to the shadow password system's utility since it keeps non-root users from reading the file and obtaining the password list, even in an encrypted form. Therefore, if you manually modify /etc/shadow, be sure it has the correct permissions when you're done.

Deleting Accounts

On the surface, deleting user accounts is easy. You may use the userdel command to do the job of removing a user's entries from /etc/passwd and, if the system uses shadow passwords, /etc/shadow. The userdel command takes just one parameter: -r. This parameter causes the system to remove all files from the user's home directory, as well as the home directory itself. Thus, removing a user account such as sally is easily accomplished with the following command:

```
# userdel -r sally
```

You may omit the -r parameter if you want to preserve the user's files. There is one potential complication, however: Users may create files *outside* their home directories. For instance, many programs use the /tmp directory as "scratch space," so user files often wind up there. These files will be deleted automatically after a certain period, but you may have other directories in which users might store files. To locate all such files, you can use the find command with its -uid parameter. For instance, if sally had been UID 529, you might use the following command to locate all her files:

```
# find / -uid 529
```

The result will be a list of files owned by UID 529 (formerly sally). You can then go through this list and decide what to do with the files—change their ownership to somebody else, delete them, back them up to floppy, or what have you. It's wise to do *something* with these files, though, or else they may be assigned ownership to another user if Sally's UID is reused. This could become awkward if the files exceed the new user's disk quota or if they contain information that the new user should not have—such a person might mistakenly be accused of indiscretions or even crimes.

A few servers—most notably Samba—may keep their own list of users. If you run such a server, it's best to remove the user's listing from that server's user list when you remove the user's main account. In the case of Samba, this is normally done by manually editing the smbpasswd file (usually located in /etc, /etc/samba or /etc/samba.d) and deleting the line corresponding to the user in question or using the smbpasswd command and its -x option, as in **smbpasswd -x sally** to delete the sally account from Samba's database.

Configuring Groups

Linux provides group configuration tools that parallel those for user accounts in many ways. Groups are not accounts, however, so many features of these tools differ. Likewise, you can create or modify groups by directly editing the configuration files in question. Their layout is similar to that for account control files, but the details differ.

Adding Groups

Linux provides the `groupadd` command to add a new group. This utility is similar to `useradd` but has fewer options. The `groupadd` syntax is shown here:

```
groupadd [-g GID [-o]] [-r] [-f] groupname
```

The parameters to this command enable you to adjust its operation:

Specify a GID   You can provide a specific GID with the `-g GID` parameter. If you omit this parameter, `groupadd` uses the next available GID. Normally, the GID you specify must be unused by other groups, but the `-o` parameter overrides this behavior, allowing you to create multiple groups that share one GID.

Create a sub-500 GID   The `-r` parameter instructs `groupadd` to create a group with a GID of less than 500. Not all distributions support this option; it was added by Red Hat and has been used on some related distributions. Red Hat uses GIDs of 500 and above for user private groups (as described shortly, in the section "The User Private Group"), hence the `-r` parameter.

Force creation   Normally, if you try to create a group that already exists, `groupadd` returns an error message. The `-f` parameter suppresses that error message. Not all versions of `groupadd` support this parameter.

In most cases, you'll create groups without specifying any parameters except for the group name itself, thus:

```
# groupadd project3
```

This command creates the `project3` group, giving it whatever GID the system finds convenient—usually the highest existing GID plus 1. Once you've done this, you can add users to the group, as described in the next section. When you add new users, you can add them directly to the new group with the `-g` and `-G` parameters to `useradd`, described earlier.

Modifying Group Information

Group information, like user account information, may be modified either using utility programs or by directly editing the underlying configuration file, `/etc/group`. As with creation, there are fewer options for modifying groups than for modifying accounts, and the utilities and configuration files are similar. In fact, `usermod` is one of the tools that's used to modify groups.

Using *groupmod* and *usermod*

The groupmod command modifies an existing group's settings. Its syntax is shown here:

groupmod [-g *GID* [-o]] [-n *newgroupname*] *oldgroupname*

The options to this command modify its operation:

Specify a GID Specify the new group ID using the -g *GID* option. groupmod returns an error if you specify a new group ID that's already in use, unless you include the -o parameter, in which case you can create two groups that share a single GID.

Specify a group name Specify a new group name with the -n *newgroupname* option.

One of the most common group manipulations you'll perform, however, is not handled through groupmod; it's done with usermod. Specifically, usermod allows you to add a user to a group with its -G parameter. For instance, the following command sets sally to be a member of the users, project1, and project4 groups, and it removes her from all other groups:

```
# usermod -G users,project1,project4 sally
```

Be sure to list all the user's current groups in addition to any groups to which you want to add the user. Omitting any of the user's current groups will remove the user from those groups. You can discover the groups to which a user currently belongs with the groups command, as in **groups sally**. To avoid accidentally omitting a group, many system administrators prefer to modify the /etc/group file in a text editor, or use gpasswd. Both options allow you to add users to groups without specifying a user's existing group memberships.

Using *gpasswd*

The gpasswd command is the group equivalent to passwd. The gpasswd command also enables you to modify other group features and to assign *group administrators*—users who may perform some group-related administrative functions for their groups. The basic syntax for this command is:

gpasswd [-a *user*] [-d *user*] [-R] [-r] [-A *user*[,...]] [-M *user*[,...]]
↪*group*

The options for this command modify its actions:

Add a user The -a *user* option adds the specified user to the specified group.

Delete a user The -d *user* option deletes the specified user from the specified group.

Disallow newgrp additions The -R option configures the group to not allow anybody to become a member through newgrp.

Remove password The -r option removes the password from a group.

Add group administrators The root user may use the -A *user*[,...] parameter to specify group administrators. Group administrators may add and remove members from a group and change the group password. Using this parameter completely overwrites the list of administrators, so if you want to add an administrator to an existing set of group administrators, you must specify *all* of their usernames.

Add users The -M *user*[,...] option works like -A, but it also adds the specified user(s) to the list of group members.

If entered without any parameters except a group name, gpasswd changes the password for the group. Group passwords enable you to control temporary membership in a group, as granted by newgrp. Ordinarily, members of a group may use newgrp to change their current group membership (affecting the group of files they create). If a password is set, even those who aren't members of a group may become temporary group members; newgrp prompts for a password that, if entered correctly, gives the user temporary group membership.

Unfortunately, some of these features are not implemented correctly in all distributions. In particular, password entry by non-group members sometimes does *not* give group membership—the system responds with an access denied error message. The -R option also sometimes doesn't work correctly—group members whose primary group membership is with another group may still use newgrp to set their primary group membership.

Directly Modifying Group Configuration Files

Group information is stored primarily in the /etc/group file. Like account configuration files, the /etc/group file is organized as a set of lines, one line per group. A typical line in this file resembles the following:

```
project1:x:501:sally,sam,ellen,george
```

Each field is separated from the others by a colon. The meanings of the four fields are as follows:

Group name The first field (project1 in the preceding example) is the name of the group.

Password The second field (x in the preceding example) is the group password. Distributions that use shadow passwords typically place an x in this field; others place the encrypted password directly in this field.

GID The group ID number (in this example's case, 501) goes in this field.

User list The final field is a comma-separated list of group members.

Users may also be members of a group based on their own /etc/passwd file primary group specification. For instance, if user george had project1 listed as his primary group, he need not be listed in the project1 line in /etc/group. If user george uses newgrp to change to another group, though, he won't be able to change back to project1 unless he's listed in the project1 line in /etc/group.

Systems with shadow passwords also use another file, /etc/gshadow, to store shadow password information on groups. This file stores the shadow password and information on group administrators, as described earlier, in "Using gpasswd."

If you configure Linux to use a network account database, the /etc/group file will be present and may define groups important for the system's basic operation. As with /etc/passwd and /etc/shadow, though, important user groups are likely to be defined only on the network account server, not in /etc/group.

Deleting Groups

Deleting groups is done via the groupdel command, which takes a single parameter: a group name. For instance, **groupdel project3** removes the project3 group. You can also delete a group by editing the /etc/group file (and /etc/gshadow, if present) and removing the relevant line for the group. It's generally better to use groupdel, though, because groupdel checks to see if the group is any user's primary group. If it is, groupdel refuses to remove the group; you must change the user's primary group or delete the user account first.

As with deleting users, deleting groups can leave "orphaned" files on the computer. You can locate them with the find command, which is described in more detail in Chapter 2. For instance, if the deleted group had used a GID of 503, you can find all the files on the computer with that GID by using the following command:

```
# find / -gid 503
```

Once you've found any files with the deleted group's ownership, you must decide what to do with them. In some cases, leaving them alone won't cause any immediate problems, but if the GID is ever reused, it could lead to confusion and even security breaches. Therefore, it's usually best to delete the files or assign them other group ownership using the chown or chgrp command.

Common User and Group Strategies

Linux's tools for handling users and groups can be quite powerful, but until you have some experience using them in a practical working environment, it's not always easy to see how best to use them. This is also one area of system configuration that can't be preconfigured by distribution maintainers in a way that's very helpful. After all, user accounts and groups are necessarily local features—your system's users and groups will almost certainly be different from those of a system across town. Nonetheless, Linux distributions need to have some sort of default scheme for handling users and groups—what UIDs and GIDs to assign, and what groups to use for newly created users by default. Two such schemes are in common use, and each can be expanded in ways that may be useful to your system.

The strategies described here can be further modified by employing access control lists (ACLs), as described in Chapter 2. These have the effect of giving individual users fine-grained control over who may access their files.

The User Private Group

The *user private group* scheme is used by Red Hat Linux and some of its derivative distributions, such as Fedora and Mandrake. This scheme creates an initial one-to-one mapping of users and groups. In this system, whenever a user account is created, a matching group is created, usually of the same name. This matching group has one member—its corresponding user. For instance, when you create the account `sally`, a group called `sally` is also created. The account `sally`'s primary group is the group `sally`. When used without modification, the user private group strategy effectively eliminates groups as a factor in Linux security—because each group has just one member, group permissions on files become unimportant.

It's possible to modify group membership to control file access, however. For instance, if you want the user `george` to be able to read `sally`'s files, you can add `george` to the `sally` group and set the `sally` user's umask to provide group read access to new files created by the user `sally`. Indeed, if you make all users group administrators of their own groups, users may control who has access to their own files by using `gpasswd` themselves. Overall, this approach provides considerable flexibility, particularly when users are sophisticated enough to handle `gpasswd`. Giving users such power may run counter to your system's security needs, though. Even when security policy dictates against making users group administrators, a user private group strategy can make sense if you need to fine-tune file access on a user-by-user basis. This approach can also provide asymmetrical file access. For instance, `george` may be able to read `sally`'s files (at least, those with appropriate group permissions), but `sally` might not have access to `george`'s files (unless `george` sets the world read bit on his files).

Project Groups

A second approach to group configuration is to create separate groups for specific purposes or projects. Therefore, I refer to this as the project group approach. Consider an example of a company that's engaged in producing three different products. Most employees work on just one product, and for security reasons, you don't want users working on one product to have access to information relating to the other two products. In such an environment, a Linux system may be well served by having three main user groups, one for each product. Most users will be members of precisely one group. If you configure the system with a umask that denies world access, those who don't belong to a specific product's group won't be able to read files relating to that product. You can set read or read/write group permission to allow group members to easily exchange files. (Individual users may use `chmod` to customize permissions on particular files and directories, of course.) If a user needs access to files associated with multiple products, you can assign that user to as many groups as necessary to accommodate the need. For instance, a supervisor might have access to all three groups.

The project group approach tends to work well when a system's users can be easily broken down into discrete groups whose members must collaborate closely. It can also work well when users need not (and even should not) have ready access to each other's files, as with students taking the same class. In such a case, you would set the umask to block group access to users' files. The logical grouping of users can still be helpful to you as an administrator, however, because you can track users according to their group—you can easily find all files owned by users taking a particular class, for instance. (Keep in mind that this tracking ability breaks down when users are members of multiple groups.)

Many Linux distributions default to using a type of project group approach. The default primary group for new users on such systems is typically called users. You can, and in most cases should, create additional groups to handle all your projects. You can leave the users group intact but not use it, rename it to the first project group name, or use users as an overarching group for when you want to give access to a file to most ordinary users, but perhaps not everyone (such as guest users on an FTP server).

Multiple Group Membership

On any system but a very simple one, it's likely that at least some users will be members of multiple groups. This means that these users will be able to do the following things:

- Read files belonging to any of the user's groups, provided that the file has group read permission.

- Write to existing files belonging to any of the user's groups, provided that the file has group write permission.

- Run programs belonging to any of the user's groups, provided that the file has group execute permission.

- Change the group ownership of any of the user's own files to any of the groups to which the user belongs.

- Use newgrp to make any of the groups to which the user belongs the user's primary group. Files created thereafter will have the selected group as the group owner.

Multiple group membership is extremely important when using user private groups, as described earlier—without this, it's impossible to fine-tune access to users' files. Even in a project group configuration, though, multiple group membership is critical for users who need access to multiple groups' files.

You may find yourself creating a group membership scheme that's some combination of these two, or one that's unique unto itself. For instance, you might create multiple overlapping subgroups in order to fine-tune access control. It might be common in such a situation for users to belong to multiple groups. Part of the problem with such configurations is in teaching users to properly use the newgrp and chgrp commands—many less technically savvy users prefer to simply create files and not worry about such details.

Account Security

Creating, maintaining, and removing user accounts are obviously important activities on a Linux system. One particularly essential account maintenance task (or set of tasks) is maintaining account security. Crackers sometimes attack a system through vulnerable user accounts. Once access to a normal account is achieved, bugs or lax internal security can be exploited to allow the attacker to acquire `root` access, or the account can be used to attack other systems. Therefore, it's vital that you attend to this matter, and periodically review your configuration to see that it remains secure.

> The popular media uses the term *hacker* to refer to computer miscreants. This term has an older meaning, however—somebody who enjoys programming or doing other technically challenging work on computers but not in an illegal or destructive sense. Many Linux programmers consider themselves hackers in this positive sense. Thus, I use the term *cracker* to refer to those who break into computers.

Enforcing User Password Security

As a general rule, people tend to be lazy when it comes to security. In computer terms, this means that users tend to pick passwords that are easy to guess, and they change them infrequently. Both these conditions make a cracker's life easier, particularly if the cracker knows the victim. Fortunately, Linux includes tools to help make your users select good passwords and change them regularly.

Common (and therefore poor) passwords include those based on the names of family members, friends, and pets; favorite books, movies, television shows, or the characters in any of these; telephone numbers, street addresses, or Social Security numbers; or other meaningful personal information. Any single word that's found in a dictionary (in *any* language) is a poor choice for a password. The best possible passwords are random collections of letters, digits, and punctuation. Unfortunately, such passwords are difficult to remember. A reasonable compromise is to build a password in two steps: First, choose a base that's easy to remember but difficult to guess. Second, modify that base in ways that increase the difficulty of guessing the password.

One approach to building a base is to use two *unrelated* words, such as "bun" and "pen." You can then merge these two words (`bunpen`). Another approach, and one that's arguably better than the first, is to use the first letters of a phrase that's meaningful to the user. For instance, the first letters of "yesterday I went to the dentist" become `yiwttd`. In both cases, the base should not be a word in any language. As a general rule, the longer the password the better. Older versions of Linux had password length limits of eight characters, but those limits have been lifted by the use of the MD5 password hash, which is the standard on modern Linux distributions. Many Linux systems require passwords to be at least four to six characters in length; the `passwd` utility won't accept anything shorter than the distribution's minimum.

With the base in hand, it's time to modify it to create a password. The user should apply at least a couple of several possible modifications:

Adding numbers or punctuation   The single most important modification is to insert random numbers or punctuation in the base. This step might yield, for instance, `bu3npe&n` or `y#i9wttd`. As a general rule, add at least two symbols or numbers.

Mixing case   Linux uses case-sensitive passwords, so jumbling the case of letters can improve security. Applying this rule might produce Bu3nPE&n and y#i9WttD, for instance.

Order reversal   A change that's very weak by itself but that can add somewhat to security when used in conjunction with the others is to reverse the order of some or all letters. You might apply this to just one word of a two-word base. This could yield nu3BPE&n and DttW9i#y, for instance.

Your best tool for getting users to pick good passwords is to educate them. Tell them that passwords can be guessed by malicious individuals who know them, or even who target them and look up personal information in telephone books, on Web pages, and so on. Tell them that, although Linux encrypts its passwords internally, programs exist that feed entire dictionaries through Linux's password encryption algorithms for comparison to encrypted passwords. If a match is found, the cracker has found the password. Therefore, using a password that's not in a dictionary, and that isn't a simple variant of a dictionary word, improves security substantially. Tell your users that their accounts might be used as a first step toward compromising the entire computer, or as a launching point for attacks on other computers. Explain to your users that they should *never* reveal their passwords to others, even people claiming to be system administrators—this is a common scam, but real system administrators don't need users' passwords. You should also warn them not to use the same password on multiple systems because doing so quickly turns a compromised account on one system into a compromised account on all the systems. Telling your users these things will help them understand the reasons for your concern, and it is likely to help motivate at least some of them to pick good passwords.

If your users are unconcerned after being told these things (and in any large installation, some will be), you'll have to rely on the checks possible in passwd. Most distributions' implementations of this utility require a minimum password length (typically four to six characters). They also usually check the password against a dictionary, thus weeding out some of the absolute worst passwords. Some require that a password contain at least one or two digits or punctuation.

WARNING   Password-cracking programs, such as Crack (http://www.crypticide.org/ users/alecm/), are easy to obtain. You might consider running such programs on your own encrypted password database to spot poor passwords, and in fact, this is a good policy in many cases. It's also grounds for dismissal in many organizations, and can even result in criminal charges being brought, at least if done without authorization. If you want to weed out bad passwords in this way, discuss the matter with your superiors and obtain written permission from a person with the authority to grant it before proceeding. Take extreme care with the files involved, too; it's probably best to crack the passwords on a computer with *no* network connections.

Another password security issue is password changes. Frequently changing passwords minimizes the window of opportunity for crackers to do damage; if a cracker obtains a password but it changes before the cracker can use it (or before the cracker can do further damage using the compromised account), the password change has averted disaster. As described earlier in this chapter, you can configure accounts to require periodic password changes. When so configured, an account will stop accepting logins after a time if the password isn't changed periodically. (You can configure the system to warn users when this time is approaching.) This is a very good option to enable on sensitive systems or those with many users. Don't set the expire time too low, though—if users have to change their passwords too frequently, they'll probably just switch between a couple of passwords, or pick poor ones. Precisely what "too low" a password change time is depends on the environment. For most systems, 1–4 months is probably a reasonable change time, but for some it might be longer or shorter.

Steps for Reducing the Risk of Compromised Passwords

Passwords can end up in crackers' hands in various ways, and you must take steps to minimize these risks. Steps you can take to improve your system's security include the following:

Use strong passwords.   Users should employ good passwords, as just described. This practice won't eliminate all risk, though.

Change passwords frequently.   As just mentioned, doing this can minimize the chance of damage due to a compromised password.

Use shadow passwords.   If a cracker who's broken into your system through an ordinary user account can read the password file, or if one of your regular users is a cracker who has access to the password file, that individual can run any of several password-cracking programs on the file. For this reason, you should use shadow passwords stored in /etc/shadow whenever possible. Most Linux distributions use shadow passwords by default. If yours doesn't, consult the upcoming section, "Using Shadow Passwords," for information on enabling this feature.

Keep passwords secret.   You should remind your users not to reveal their passwords to others. Such trust is sometimes misplaced, and sometimes even a well-intentioned password recipient might slip up and let the password fall into the wrong hands. This can happen by writing the password down, storing it in electronic form, or sending it by e-mail or other electronic means. Indeed, users shouldn't e-mail their own passwords even to themselves, because e-mail can be intercepted.

Use secure remote login protocols.   Certain remote login protocols are inherently insecure; all data traverse the network in an unencrypted form. Intervening computers can be configured to snatch passwords from such sessions. Because of this, it's best to disable Telnet, FTP, and other protocols that use cleartext passwords, in favor of protocols that encrypt passwords, such as Secure Shell (SSH). Chapter 6 describes these protocols in more detail.

Be alert to shoulder surfing.   If your users log in using public terminals, as is common on college campuses, in Internet cafes, and the like, it's possible that others will be able to watch them type their passwords (a practice sometimes called "shoulder surfing"). Users should be alert to this possibility and minimize such logins if possible.

Some of these steps are things you can do, such as replacing insecure remote login protocols with encrypted ones. Others are things your users must do. Once again, this illustrates the importance of user education, particularly on systems with many users.

Disabling Unused Accounts

Linux computers sometimes accumulate unused accounts. This occurs when employees leave a company, when students graduate, and so on. You should be diligent about disabling such accounts because they can easily be abused, either by the individual who's left your organization or by others who discover the password through any of the means already described. As covered in detail earlier in this chapter, you do this with the `userdel` command.

If the individual has had legitimate access to the `root` account, you must carefully consider how to proceed. If you have no reason to suspect the individual of wrongdoing, changing the `root` password and deleting the user's regular account are probably sufficient. If the individual might have sabotaged the computer, though, you'll have a hard time checking for every possible type of damage, particularly if the individual was a competent administrator. In such situations, you're better off backing up user data and reinstalling from scratch, just as you should if your system is compromised by an outsider.

Many Linux distributions create a number of specialized accounts that are normally not used for conventional user logins. These may include `daemon`, `lp`, `shutdown`, `mail`, `news`, `uucp`, `games`, `nobody`, and others. Some of these accounts have necessary functions. For instance, `daemon` is used by some servers, `lp` is associated with Linux's printing system, and `nobody` is used by various programs that don't need high-privilege access to the system. Other accounts are likely to be unused on many systems. For instance, `games` is used by some games, and so it isn't of much use on most servers or true productivity workstations. You may be able to delete some of these unused specialty accounts, but if you do so, you should definitely record details on the accounts' configurations so that you can restore them if you run into problems because the account wasn't quite as unnecessary as it first seemed.

Using Shadow Passwords

Most Linux distributions use shadow passwords by default, and for the most part, this chapter is written with the assumption that this feature is active. In addition to providing extra security by moving hashed passwords out of the world-readable `/etc/passwd` file and into the more secure `/etc/shadow` file, shadow passwords add extra account information. (The earlier section, "Directly Modifying Account Configuration Files," describes the `/etc/shadow` file's contents in detail.)

If you happen to be using a system that hasn't enabled shadow passwords but you want to add that support, you can do so. Specifically, the `pwconv` and `grpconv` programs do this job for `/etc/passwd` and `/etc/group`, respectively. These programs take no parameters; simply type their names to create `/etc/shadow` and `/etc/gshadow` files that hold the passwords and related account control information, based on the contents of the unprotected files. You can run these programs even if most accounts already use shadow passwords; when used in this way, any accounts that do not yet use shadow passwords are converted, and those that already exist are left untouched. This feature can be handy when duplicating accounts from one system on another—you can cut and paste `/etc/passwd` entries from an old system that doesn't use shadow passwords and then type **pwconv** to create appropriate shadow password entries.

The pwconv and grpconv utilities can loop forever or otherwise misbehave if their source files are malformed. You may want to check the format of these files with pwck and grpck. These programs look for errors such as an incorrect number of fields, missing home directories, and duplicate names, and report any problems to you.

Although converting a system so that it no longer uses shadow passwords is generally inadvisable, you can do so with the pwunconv and grpunconv commands, which merge the contents from the shadow files back into /etc/passwd and /etc/group, respectively. In practice, you're most likely to need to do this if you must move Linux account information over to a computer that doesn't support shadow passwords. If you do this, you may want to first back up the /etc/passwd and /etc/shadow (or /etc/group and /etc/gshadow) files. You can then copy the backups back to /etc when you're done, reversing the process. This procedure will preserve some shadow information, such as account expiration data, that will be lost in the conversion process.

One of the advantages of shadow passwords is that the Linux shadow password system enables use of more advanced password hashes. The earliest Linux systems used a *Triple Data Encryption Standard (3DES)* hash. This hash, although good not too many years ago, is outdated by today's standards. Most Linux distributions today use the *Message Digest 5 (MD5)* hash instead. Linux's password tools support passwords longer than eight characters for MD5 hashes, but not for 3DES hashes. You can tell which one your distribution uses by examining the password field in /etc/shadow (or /etc/passwd, if you're not using shadow passwords). MD5 passwords begin with the string 1; 3DES passwords don't.

You can't convert existing 3DES passwords to MD5, or vice versa, except by reconfiguring your system to use the new password and then having users re-enter their passwords. You can, though, tell Linux to use one tool or the other for new passwords. To do so, edit the /etc/pam.d/passwd file. This file controls the PAM module for the passwd utility—that is, it controls how passwd does its work. Locate a line that looks something like this:

```
password    required    pam_unix.so    nullok use_authtok
```

The line may look somewhat different on your system, but the key points are that it begins with the string password and references the pam_unix.so library file. Some distributions, such as Fedora and Gentoo, place this line in the /etc/pam.d/system-auth file rather than in /etc/pam.d/passwd.

To configure Linux to encode new passwords using MD5, add md5 to the list of parameters after pam_unix.so. To switch to 3DES, remove any reference to md5 in this parameter list.

If you can't find a line that looks like this one in /etc/pam.d/passwd, look for it in /etc/pam.d/system-auth. This file serves as a stand-in for several other configuration files in some distributions, so making the change there may do the job.

Additional encryption and hashing functions exist, such as *MD4* and *blowfish*. These are not commonly used in Linux password databases, but they may be used in network account database systems, in encrypted data transfer tools such as the Secure Shell (SSH), and elsewhere.

Controlling System Access

One of the many uses of accounts is as a tool to control access to a computer—that is, to allow `sally` to log in remotely, but not `sam`, much less a cracker from halfway around the world. Precisely how such tasks may be accomplished varies from one server program to another—some provide better access controls than others, and each server has its own methods of handling the matter. The `root` account is often handled in a unique way with respect to access control, and for good reason—`root` is powerful enough that you may want to restrict its access to local logins, in order to minimize the chance of abuse by a distant cracker. Another access-control measure of a sort is the use of filesystem quotas, which are limits to the disk space that an individual account may use.

Accessing Common Servers

Several common server programs provide some means to limit access by username, often via PAM. Others don't provide this facility, but do provide a way to limit access by computer hostname or IP address. Servers you're particularly likely to want to limit in these ways include login servers and various types of file-access servers (such as FTP, NFS, and Samba).

Many of the access methods described here rely on servers. Running these servers, and configuring them more generally, are described in Chapter 6.

Controlling Access via PAM

Most servers that provide access to particular users employ PAM to do the bulk of the work of authenticating users and authorizing access. Thus, you can use PAM configurations to control access to the computer. This is done either through the `/etc/pam.d/system-auth` file or the file corresponding to the server in `/etc/pam.d`. (The `/etc/pam.d/system-auth` file is a generic PAM configuration file that's used by PAM configurations that refer to the `pam_stack.so` module. Some distributions, such as Fedora, use this mechanism. Others, such as SuSE, do not.) Individual server files are usually named after the server, such as `/etc/pam.d/ftp`, but some important login servers use the `/etc/pam.d/login` control file.

Access control is handled by a PAM module called `pam_access.so`. It's called as part of a series of `account` calls in a PAM configuration, thus:

```
account     requisite    pam_time.so
account     required     pam_access.so
account     required     pam_unix.so
```

The `pam_access.so` module might or might not be referred to in your default file. If it's not present, add a line like the one above that calls this module. You can call it using either the `requisite` or `required` keyword.

 You can add an `accessfile=filename` parameter after `pam_access.so` to pass a specific configuration file to the module. (The default configuration file is `/etc/security/access.conf`.) This can be useful if you want to limit access in different ways for different servers—place the call to `pam_access.so` in the server's own PAM configuration rather than in `/etc/pam.d/system-auth` and create unique configuration files for each server.

Once this line is present, you can use the `/etc/security/access.conf` file (or another file you specify) to control who may access the login server. This file contains comment lines (denoted by hash marks, #) and configuration lines that consist of three colon-delimited fields:

```
[+|-] : user(s) : source(s)
```

The first of these fields is a code to specify whether access is granted (+) or denied (-).

The second field specifies a user or group of users. It may be a single username, a space-delimited set of usernames, one or more group names, a *user@hostname* specification, or the keyword ALL (which matches all users).

The final field specifies the source of the login attempt. It may be a hostname, a domain name (which begins with a dot, as in `.pangaea.edu` for the `pangaea.edu` domain), numeric IP or network addresses, teletype (tty) names, the ALL keyword (to match any source), or the LOCAL keyword (to match any name that lacks a dot).

The final two fields both support the EXCEPT keyword, which enables you to set up a rule with a limited number of exceptions. For instance, `ALL EXCEPT sam` in the second field applies the rule to all users except for `sam`.

As an example, consider these `/etc/security/access.conf` entries:

```
-:sally harry:.pangaea.edu
+:ALL EXCEPT sam:ALL
-:ALL:ALL
```

The PAM system searches the `/etc/security/access.conf` file for the first entry to match the user who's trying to access the system and grants or denies access based on that entry. If no entry matches an access attempt, access is granted. Thus, for best security, the file should end with a line that denies all access (as in the `-:ALL:ALL` line in this example). This example includes other lines that apply to more specific situations. The first line denies access to the users sally and harry when they're attempting to access the computer from the pangaea.edu domain—perhaps this domain isn't trusted for the type of work these users do. The second line grants all users access to the system *except* for sam; this user is denied access to the computer from any location. Note that the order of these two lines is important; if the first two lines were reversed, the first one (the second in the preceding example) would grant access to sally and harry when they're attempting to log in from pangaea.edu, rendering the second line (the first in the preceding example) ineffective.

Controlling Login Access

Remote login access is usually provided by a Telnet or SSH server. These servers provide remote text-mode access, enabling users to run Bash or other shells and text-mode programs. SSH also supports tunneling X connections, so if the user's computer runs an X server, the user can run X programs hosted on the login server computer.

Unfortunately, Telnet provides only very limited security options. The server uses the login program to process user logins, so user-by-user login restrictions are those provided by login. You can adjust PAM's login configuration, as just described, to employ the pam_access.so module to restrict remote login access.

Telnet servers are usually called from a super server (inetd or xinetd), so you can use these servers' features (or the features of programs they call, such as TCP Wrappers) to restrict access to Telnet on the basis of the calling systems' IP addresses. These options are described in Chapter 7.

SSH servers don't normally use login to control the login process. These servers may employ PAM, though, so you can configure PAM to limit who may log in via SSH. To do so, you would edit either the /etc/pam.d/system-auth file or an SSH-specific PAM configuration file (usually /etc/pam.d/sshd) to do the job. SSH servers can usually be configured to not use PAM, though, so if you try this configuration and can't seem to get it to work, check the /etc/ssh/sshd_config file. (Don't confuse this file with the ssh_config file, which controls the SSH client rather than the SSH server.) Look for the UsePAM option and set it to yes:

```
UsePAM yes
```

In addition to these controls, other options can limit root access to these login servers, as described later, in "Controlling root Access."

Controlling FTP Access

Most FTP servers use PAM to authenticate user access. Thus, you can use the methods described earlier, in "Controlling Access via PAM," to limit access to FTP on a user-by-user basis. You may need to adjust the /etc/pam.d/system-auth file or a file for your FTP server in particular, depending on your system configuration. (The server-specific file varies depending on the particular FTP server in use, but it usually contains the string ftp in its name, so look for that.)

Instead of or in addition to PAM, some FTP servers use a file called /etc/ftpusers to limit who may access the computer. This file contains a list of users who may *not* access the FTP server. Typically, it includes root and various other system accounts, but you can add ordinary users to the list, if you like. You cannot use this file to restrict access based on the remote system, though, unlike the PAM-based restrictions.

The presence of an `/etc/ftpusers` file doesn't mean that the file is actually in use. This file could be a relic from an earlier FTP server installed on the system, or the FTP server might be configured to not use the file. Before you rely on this file, you should test it by adding an ordinary username to the file and then attempting to access your FTP server using that username. If you succeed, try restarting the FTP server and test it again. If you can still access the FTP server, consult its documentation to learn how to get it to use `/etc/ftpusers` or use the PAM tools described earlier to limit access.

Controlling NFS Access

The Network File System (NFS) is a popular file server for Linux and Unix systems. NFS provides user-level access controls in the sense that it passes UID and GID information stored on the server to the client. The client is then responsible for enforcing access restrictions based on this information. The sidebar earlier in this chapter, "Coordinating UIDs and GIDs across Systems," describes one problem with this system: If UIDs and GIDs on two systems don't match, files owned by one user will appear to be owned by another user. Another problem is that if a client system is compromised, or if an untrusted client connects to the server, security on the shared files becomes nil.

For this reason, NFS security focuses on limiting access to trusted clients. This is done by specifying the computers that may mount NFS exports. This setting is part of the basic NFS configuration, controlled in the `/etc/exports` file. Chapter 6 describes this file in more detail. In brief, you list directories you want to share, one per line. Each line contains a list of IP addresses or hostnames that are allowed to mount the share, along with options that apply to them in parentheses. For instance, you might share a directory with two clients:

```
/opt client1(rw),client2(ro)
```

The `rw` and `ro` options stand for read/write and read-only access, respectively. Thus, `client1` can both read and write to files on the exported directory, whereas `client2` may only read files. Within these restrictions, the clients control access to files using their own account databases and the file modes stored on the server.

Controlling Samba Access

Samba is a server package for the Server Message Block/Common Internet File System (SMB/CIFS) protocol suite, which is most commonly used for file sharing among Windows computers. Samba attempts to emulate the behavior of a Windows computer as much as possible, and to that end, Samba uses accounts and passwords as a basic means of access control. Samba also integrates with the Linux account and permissions system, however. This interaction can be complex at times.

When a user accesses files via Samba, the server uses the username and password provided by the client to control access. Ordinarily, access is granted to files as if the user had logged in using some other means, and if the user creates new files, they'll be owned by the user whose name was given when logging on.

In most cases, Samba does not use PAM for authentication, so the PAM controls described earlier, in "Controlling Access via PAM," won't work with Samba. (An exception to this rule is if you enable use of cleartext passwords, but this requires reconfiguring all Windows versions released since the mid-1990s.) Instead, Samba uses its own account database, in which it stores password hashes in a form that SMB/CIFS clients can use. Samba does provide several controls similar to those available via PAM, which you can set in Samba's `smb.conf` configuration file (which is usually stored in `/etc/samba`):

Granting or restricting write access   The `read only = Yes` parameter sets a share to be read-only. (The `writeable = No` and `write ok = No` parameters have an identical effect.) You can also control read/write access on a per-user basis. The `write list` parameter enables you to specify users who may write to an otherwise read-only share, while `read list` specifies users who may only read files on a share that's otherwise read/write.

Valid and invalid users   You can grant or deny access to specific users with the `valid users` and `invalid users` parameters, respectively. For instance, `valid users = sam sally harry ellen` tells Samba to give only those four users access to a share; anybody else is denied access.

Forcing users and groups   The `force user` and `force group` settings enable you to set a username or group name that Samba will use for file accesses. For instance, if you set `force user = sam`, all file accesses to the share will be done as if `sam` had been the one who logged on.

Guest accesses   The `guest ok = Yes` parameter, if set, enables guest accesses to a share, in which a username and password are not required. Linux still needs to use a local account for the accesses, though; the global `guest account` parameter sets the account that's used. For instance, if you set `guest account = sam`, guest accesses are done as if by `sam`.

Unix extensions support   Samba supports extensions to the SMB/CIFS protocol designed to provide UID, GID, and file mode information, among other things, to clients. Enable this support by setting `unix extensions = Yes` (which is the default in Samba 3.0 and later). This feature adds Unix-style ownership and permissions atop the access controls used natively by SMB/CIFS. In order to do any good, the client must also support the Unix extensions. In Linux, this support is present in the `cifs` filesystem driver, but not in the older `smbfs` driver.

In addition to these tools, you can take advantage of Samba's separate account database to control access by user. For instance, if you want to deny the user `sam` access to the Samba server, you can simply avoid creating an entry for `sam` in the Samba account database. On most systems, this database is stored as `/etc/samba/smbpasswd`, and it uses a one-account-per-line format that's similar in principle to the `/etc/passwd` file. If an account for a user exists in this file but you don't want the user to have further access via Samba, you can delete the line from the `smbpasswd` file manually or use the `smbpasswd` utility and its `-x` or `-d` option. The `-x` option completely removes an entry, but `-d` merely disables it. For instance, typing **`smbpasswd -x sam`** deletes the `sam` account's entry from the `smbpasswd` file.

Samba is an extremely complex server. Chapter 6 describes the basics of setting it up, but completely describing this server's configuration is well beyond the scope of this book. Consult a book such as my *Linux Samba Server Administration* (Sybex, 2001) or my *Definitive Guide to Samba 3* (Apress, 2004) for more information on this topic.

Controlling *root* Access

The root account is unusually powerful, so a compromise of that account is far more serious than a compromise of an ordinary account. Furthermore, in many cases root should not be accessing a computer over a network, at least not in certain ways. For instance, a standard Telnet server doesn't encrypt its traffic, so its use for root access exposes the root password on the network wires—or over radio waves, if you're using wireless networking. What's more, the data transferred by root may be unusually sensitive. For instance, you might edit /etc/shadow as root, thus exposing the data in that file, if you edit it via a Telnet link.

For these reasons, many servers and login protocols provide extra tools to help control root access to the system. Frequently, these tools simply deny all access to direct root logins. Administrators can still log in using a normal account and then use su, sudo, or similar tools to perform administrative tasks. This approach, however, requires two passwords, which means that a miscreant is less likely to be able to get in than if direct root logins were accepted.

The default configuration for most Linux distributions is to deny direct root logins via Telnet (or any other remote login server that uses the login program). Thus, you shouldn't need to change anything to keep this server from accepting root logins. If you do, the key lies in the /etc/securetty file. This file holds a list of terminals from which root is permitted to log in. It normally contains a list of local device filenames, one per line, minus the leading /dev directory indicator. If this list is incomplete, you may not be able to log in as root from the console. Adding appropriate specifications, such as tty1 through tty6 and vc/1 through vc/6, should fix the problem. If you want to use a directly connected "dumb" RS-232 serial terminal, you can add its device filename, such as ttyS0. (You'll also need to enable this terminal for normal logins by adding it to the /etc/inittab file.)

WARNING Even if you log in using Telnet via a normal user account, using su and performing administrative functions can be risky. The password you type after you type **su** will be passed over the network in an unencrypted form, as will all the data you type or see on your screen. Remote text-mode administration is best done via SSH or some other encrypted protocol.

Most default SSH configurations allow root to log in directly. Although SSH's encryption makes this practice much safer than the equivalent when using Telnet, you can gain the added benefit of requiring two passwords by disabling direct root logins via SSH. To do so, you must edit the server's /etc/ssh/sshd_config file (not to be confused with ssh_config, which controls the SSH client). Look for the PermitRootLogin line and set it to no:

```
PermitRootLogin no
```

You may want to consult the documentation for other servers you run, as well. Some, including remote administration tools such as the Samba Web Administration Tool (SWAT), require root access to do more than display basic information and perhaps change user passwords. Others, such as the main Samba servers themselves, should ordinarily not give root access—they simply aren't designed for administrative functions, and root may be able to do things with the server that you'd rather not be done. For the most part, remote root access should be limited to SSH (ideally *after* a regular user login) or to tools that are explicitly designed to support root access for administrative purposes.

Setting Filesystem Quotas

Just one or two users of a multiuser system can cause serious problems for others by consuming too much disk space. If a single user creates huge files (say, multimedia recordings), those files can prevent other users from creating their own files. To help manage this situation, Linux supports *disk quotas*—limits enforced by the OS on how many files or how much disk space a single user may consume. The Linux quota system supports both quotas for individual users and for Linux groups.

Quotas require both support in the kernel for the filesystem being used and various user-space utilities. As of the early 2.6.x kernels, the ext2fs, ext3fs, and ReiserFS filesystems support quotas, but you must explicitly enable support via the Quota Support kernel option in the filesystem area when recompiling your kernel. Many distributions ship with this support precompiled, so recompiling your kernel may not be necessary, but you should be aware of this option if you do recompile your kernel.

Two general quota support systems are available for Linux. The first was used through the 2.4.x kernels and is referred to as the quota v1 support. The second was added with the 2.6.x kernel series and is referred to as the quota v2 system. This description applies to the latter system, but the former works in a similar way.

Outside of the kernel, you need support tools to use quotas. For the quota v2 system, this package is usually called quota, and it installs a number of utilities, configuration files, SysV startup scripts, and so on.

You can install the support software from source code, if you like; however, this job is handled most easily using a package for your distribution. This description assumes that you install the software in this way. If you don't, you may need to create SysV or local startup scripts to initialize the quota support when you boot your computer. The Quota Mini-HOWTO, at http://en.tldp.org/HOWTO/Quota.html, provides details of how to do this.

You must modify your /etc/fstab entries for any partitions on which you want to use the quota support. In particular, you must add the usrquota filesystem mount option to employ user quotas, and the grpquota option to use group quotas. Entries that are so configured resemble the following:

```
/dev/hdc5  /home  ext3  usrquota,grpquota  1  1
```

This line activates both user and group quota support for the /dev/hdc5 partition, which is mounted at /home. Of course, you can add other options if you like.

The format of the /etc/fstab file is described in more detail in Chapter 4.

Depending on your distribution, you may need to configure the quota package's SysV startup scripts to run when the system boots. Chapter 5 describes SysV startup script management in detail. Typically, you'll type a command such as **chkconfig quota on**; however, you should check on the SysV scripts installed by your distribution's quota package. Some distributions require use of commands other than chkconfig to do this task, as well, as described in Chapter 5.

After installing software and making configuration file changes, you must activate the systems. The simplest way to do this is to reboot the computer, and this step is necessary if you had to recompile your kernel to add quota support directly into the kernel. If you didn't do this, though, you should be able to get by with less disruptive measures: using modprobe to install the kernel module, if necessary; running the SysV startup script for the quota tools; and remounting the filesystems on which you intend to use quotas by typing **mount -o remount /*mount-point***, where /*mount-point* is the mount point in question.

At this point, quota support should be fully active on your computer, but the quotas themselves are not set. You can set the quotas by using edquota, which starts the Vi editor (described in Chapter 2) on a temporary configuration file (/etc/quotatab) that controls quotas for the user you specify. When you exit from the utility, edquota uses the temporary configuration file to write the quota information to low-level disk data structures that control the kernel's quota mechanisms. For instance, you might type **edquota sally** to edit sally's quotas. The contents of the editor will show the current quota information:

```
Quotas for user sally:
/dev/hdc5: blocks in use: 3209, limits (soft = 5000, hard = 6500)
          inodes in use: 403, limits (soft = 1000, hard = 1500)
```

The temporary configuration file provides information on both the number of disk blocks in use and the number of inodes in use. (Each file or symbolic link consumes a single inode, so the inode limits are effectively limits on the number of files a user may own. Disk blocks vary in size depending on the filesystem and filesystem creation options, but they typically range from 512 bytes to 8KB.) Changing the use information has no effect, but you can alter the soft and hard limits for both blocks and inodes. The hard limit is the maximum number of blocks or inodes that the user may consume; the kernel will not permit a user to surpass these limits. Soft limits are somewhat less stringent; users may temporarily exceed soft limit values, but when they do so, the system issues warnings. Soft limits also interact with a grace period; if the soft quota limit is exceeded for longer than the grace period, the kernel begins treating it like a hard limit and refuses to allow the user to create more files. You can set the grace period by using edquota with its -t option, as in **edquota -t**. Grace periods are set on a per-filesystem basis, rather than a per-user basis.

A couple more quota-related commands are useful. The first is quotacheck, which verifies and updates quota information on quota-enabled disks. This command is normally run as part of the quota package's SysV startup script, but you may want to run it periodically (say, once a week) as a cron job. (Chapter 5 describes cron jobs.) Although theoretically not necessary if everything works correctly, quotacheck ensures that quota accounting doesn't become inaccurate. The second useful auxiliary quota command is repquota, which summarizes the quota information on the filesystem you specify, or on all filesystems if you pass it the -a option. This tool can be very helpful in keeping track of disk usage.

Summary

Linux's accounts and its security model are inextricably intertwined. A single Linux system can support many users, who can be tied together in groups. Users can create files that they own and that have permissions that define which other users may access the files and in what ways. To manage these users, you'll use a handful of commands, such as `useradd`, `groupadd`, `userdel`, `usermod`, and `passwd`. These commands enable you to manage your user accounts to suit your system's needs.

Managing account security is critically important. You must educate your users about the importance of good passwords, and about proper procedures for safeguarding their passwords. Most importantly, users should know to *never* divulge their passwords to others. They should also be alert to suspicious activities that might indicate shoulder surfing or other methods crackers employ to obtain passwords. As a system administrator, you can disable or delete unused accounts and manage shadow passwords.

Controlling access to a computer is an important part of security and user management. You can employ PAM to restrict access to PAM-mediated servers and login tools on a user-by-user basis. Many programs also provide their own tools to accomplish these goals. Some servers provide special options to disable or limit `root` access to the computer, and you should often take advantage of such options.

Exam Essentials

Describe why accounts are important on a Linux system. Accounts enable several users to work on a computer with minimal risk that they'll damage or (if you so desire) read one another's files. Accounts also enable you to control normal users' access to critical system resources, limiting the risk of damage to the Linux installation as a whole.

Summarize important files in controlling access to Linux. The `/etc/passwd` and `/etc/shadow` files contain information on Linux accounts. Files in `/etc/pam.d` control PAM, including defining how PAM authenticates users. Individual programs and servers often have their own security files, such as `/etc/sudoers` to control `sudo`, `/etc/ftpusers` to control who may access an FTP server, and `/etc/ssh/sshd_config` to control the SSH server.

Describe the characteristics of a good password. Good passwords resemble random strings of letters, numbers, and punctuation. To make them memorable to the account holder, they can be generated by starting from a base built on a personally relevant acronym or a pair of unrelated words, then modified by adding letters and punctuation, mixing the case of letters, and reversing some sequences in the password.

Explain the importance of shadow passwords. The shadow password system stores password hashes in a file that can be read only by `root`, thus reducing the risk that a cracker can read the file and use a password-cracking program to discover users' passwords.

Describe the role of PAM in restricting user access.   PAM is a modular authentication system for Linux that enables you to change the way Linux authenticates users. You can add PAM modules to your configuration that can deny any specified user access to the computer based on the user's location or other characteristics, even if the user enters a valid password.

Summarize Linux password hashes.   Linux has traditionally used 3DES, but modern distributions invariably use the MD5 hash instead. Other password hashes are possible, and are sometimes used with network authentication tools.

Describe methods of deleting user accounts.   Accounts can be deleted by deleting the appropriate entries in /etc/passwd and /etc/shadow or by using utilities such as userdel. You might also need to delete user files (userdel can optionally do at least part of this job) and delete or change references to the user in other configuration files, such as /etc/samba/smbpasswd.

Summarize why using root access is dangerous.   Every time the root password is entered is a chance for it to be discovered, so overuse of the root account increases the odds that your computer will be compromised. Commands can also contain typos or other errors, and when this happens as root, the consequences can be far more damaging than is the case when an ordinary user mistypes a command.

Commands in This Chapter

Command	Description
su	Changes a user's login account. Often used to acquire superuser privileges after a normal user login.
sudo	Executes a single command with alternative permission. Often used to run administrative programs as root.
newgrp	Changes a user's login group.
useradd	Creates a new user account.
usermod	Modifies settings for an existing user account.
chage	Changes account expiration (aging) information.
userdel	Deletes an existing user account.
passwd	Changes an account's password.
groups	Displays the groups to which a user belongs.
groupadd	Adds a new group.
groupmod	Modifies settings for an existing group.
groupdel	Deletes an existing group.

gpasswd   Changes a group password; adds and deletes users from a group.

pwconv   Converts conventional (unshadowed) /etc/passwd file entries into shadow
               password format.

pwunconv   Converts shadow passwords into conventional (unshadowed) /etc/
               password entries.

grpconv   Converts conventional (unshadowed) /etc/group file entries into
               shadowed format.

grpunconv   Converts shadow group entries into conventional (unshadowed) /etc/
               group format.

edquota   Edits disk quota information.

quotacheck   Checks quota information on disk and writes corrections, as necessary.

repquota   Displays disk quota summary information.

Review Questions

1. Which of the following are legal Linux usernames? (Choose all that apply.)

   A. `larrythemoose`

   B. `4sale`

   C. `PamJones`

   D. `Samuel_Bernard_Delaney_the_Fourth`

2. Why are groups important to the Linux user administration and security models?

   A. They can be used to provide a set of users with access to files, without giving *all* users access to the files.

   B. They allow you to set a single login password for all users within a defined group.

   C. Users may assign file ownership to a group, thereby hiding their own creation of the file.

   D. By deleting a group, you can quickly remove the accounts for all users in the group.

3. Which of the following actions allow one to perform administrative tasks? (Choose all that apply.)

   A. Logging in as an ordinary user and using the `chgrp` command to acquire superuser privileges

   B. Logging in at the console with the username `root`

   C. Logging in as an ordinary user and using the `su` command to acquire superuser privileges

   D. Logging in when nobody else is using the system, thus using it as a single-user computer

4. What command would you type to change the ownership of `somefile.txt` from `ralph` to `tony`?

   A. `chown ralph.tony somefile.txt`

   B. `chmod somefile.txt tony`

   C. `chown somefile.txt tony`

   D. `chown tony somefile.txt`

5. Which of the following is true of Linux passwords?

   A. They are changed with the `password` utility.

   B. They may consist only of lowercase letters and numbers.

   C. They must be changed once a month.

   D. They may be changed by the user who owns an account or by `root`.

6. Which of the following commands configures the `laura` account to expire on January 1, 2005?

   A. `chage -I 2005-01-01 laura`

   B. `usermod -e 2005-01-01 laura`

   C. `usermod -e 2005 laura`

   D. `chage -E 2005/01/01 laura`

7. Which of the following does `groupadd` allow you to create?

   A. One group at a time

   B. An arbitrary number of groups with one call to the program

   C. Only user private groups

   D. Passwords for groups

8. Which of the following is true of the `groupdel` command? (Choose all that apply.)

   A. It won't remove a group if that group is any user's default group.

   B. It won't remove a group if the system contains any files belonging to that group.

   C. It removes references to the named group in `/etc/group` and `/etc/gshadow`.

   D. It won't remove a group if it contains any members.

9. Which of the following describes the user private group strategy?

   A. It is a requirement of the Red Hat and Mandrake distributions.

   B. It cannot be used with Debian GNU/Linux.

   C. It lets users define groups independently of the system administrator.

   D. It creates one group per user of the system.

10. Which of the following is true when a user belongs to the `project1` and `project2` groups?

   A. The user must type **newgrp project2** to read files belonging to `project2` group members.

   B. If group read permissions are granted, any file created by the user will automatically be readable to both `project1` and `project2` group members.

   C. The user may use the `newgrp` command to change the default group associated with files the user subsequently creates.

   D. The user's group association (`project1` or `project2`) just after login is assigned randomly.

11. How should you engage users in helping to secure your computer's passwords?

   A. Educate them about the importance of security, the means of choosing good passwords, and the ways crackers can obtain passwords.

   B. Give some of your users copies of the encrypted database file as backup in case a cracker breaks in and corrupts the original.

   C. Enforce password change rules but don't tell users how crackers obtain passwords since you could be educating a future cracker.

   D. Instruct your users to e-mail copies of their passwords to themselves on other systems so that they're readily available in case of an emergency.

12. Which of the following accounts is the most likely prospect for deletion on a mail server?

   A. `daemon`

   B. `games`

   C. `mail`

   D. `nobody`

13. While looking at the /etc/passwd file, you notice that an x appears in the second field for every user. What does this indicate?

   A. All passwords are set to expire

   B. Passwords do not expire

   C. Passwords are not required on the system

   D. Passwords are stored in the shadow file

14. Which of the following utilities is used to convert conventional passwords to shadow passwords?

   A. skel

   B. shadow

   C. pwconv

   D. crypt

15. Which of the following commands can be used to summarize the quota information on all filesystems?

   A. repquota

   B. repquota -a

   C. quotacheck

   D. quotacheck -a

16. Which of the following commands converts shadow group entries into the conventional (unshadowed) format?

   A. grpunconv

   B. grpconv

   C. convert

   D. unconvert

17. You have recently been assigned administration of an older Linux server using 3DES password encryption. You want to send an e-mail to users encouraging them to change their passwords. How long can their passwords be?

   A. Eight characters

   B. Fifteen characters

   C. Thirty-two characters

   D. Unlimited

18. You are trying to explain to management why developers should use Linux to debug their applications. Which feature of Linux supports multiple simultaneous logins through the standard console and could be useful in application development?

   A. Multitasking

   B. Multithreading

   C. Virtual terminals

   D. Concurrency

19. Which of the following commands can be used to delete a user named `kristin` and remove all files from the user's home directory, as well as the home directory itself?

A. `userdel kristin`

B. `userdel -r kristin`

C. `userdel -a kristin`

D. `deluser -a kristin`

20. You have just installed a new server that uses Pluggable Authentication Modules (PAM). Access control is handled by which of the following PAM modules?

A. `pam_security.conf`

B. `pam_access.so`

C. `pam_securty.access`

D. `security_access.pam`

Answers to Review Questions

1. A, C. A Linux username must contain fewer than 32 characters and start with a letter, and it may consist of letters, numbers, and certain symbols. Options A and C both meet these criteria. (Option C uses mixed upper- and lowercase characters, which is legal but discouraged.) Option B begins with a number, which is invalid. Option D is longer than 32 characters.

2. A. Groups provide a good method of file-access control. Although they may have passwords, these are *not* account login passwords; those passwords are set on a per-account basis. Files do have associated groups, but these are *in addition* to individual file ownership, and so they cannot be used to mask the file's owner. Deleting a group *does not* delete all the accounts associated with the group.

3. B, C. Direct login as `root` and using `su` to acquire `root` privileges from an ordinary login both allow a user to administer a system. The `chgrp` command is used to change group ownership of a file, not to acquire administrative privileges. Although Linux does support a single-user emergency rescue mode, this mode isn't invoked simply by having only one user logged on.

4. D. Typing **chown ralph.tony somefile.txt** sets the owner of the file to `ralph` and the group to `tony`. The `chmod` command is used to change file permissions, not ownership. Option C reverses the order of the filename and the owner.

5. D. Both the superuser and the account owner may change an account's password. The utility for doing this is called `passwd`, not `password`. Although an individual user might use just lowercase letters and numbers for a password, Linux also supports uppercase letters and punctuation. The system administrator may enforce once-a-month password changes, but such changes aren't required by Linux per se.

6. D. Either `chage -E` or `usermod -e` may be used for this task, followed by a date expressed in *YYYY/ MM/DD* format. Options A and B use dashes (-) instead of slashes (/) in the date format, and option A uses the wrong parameter (`-I`) as well. Option C is actually a legal command, but it specifies a date 2005 days after January 1, 1970—in other words, in mid-1975.

7. A. The `groupadd` command creates one group per call to the program. Such a group *may* be a user private group, but need not be. Group passwords are created with `gpasswd`, not `groupadd`.

8. A, C. The `groupdel` command modifies the group configuration files, but it checks the user configuration files to be sure that it doesn't "orphan" any users first. The group may contain members, though, as long as none list the group as their primary group. The `groupdel` command performs no search for files belonging to the group, but it's a good idea for you to do this manually after removing the group.

9. D. Although Red Hat and Mandrake use the user private group strategy by default, you can design and use another strategy yourself. Likewise, you *may* use the user private group strategy with any Linux distribution, even if it doesn't use this strategy by default. Ordinary users can't create groups by themselves, although if they're group administrators in a user private group system, they may add other users to their own existing groups.

10. C. The `newgrp` command changes the user's active group membership, which determines the group associated with any files the user creates. This command is *not* required to give the user access to files with other group associations, if the user is a member of the other group and the file has appropriate group access permissions. Files have exactly one group association, so a user who belongs to multiple groups must specify to which group any created files belong. This is handled at login by setting a default or primary group recorded with the user's other account defaults in `/etc/passwd`.

11. A. Education helps users to understand the reasons to be concerned, which can motivate conformance with password procedures. Cracking procedures are common knowledge, so withholding general information won't keep that information out of the hands of those who want it. Copying password files and sending unencrypted passwords through e-mail are both invitations to disaster; encrypted files can be cracked, and e-mail can be intercepted.

12. B. One or both of `daemon` and `mail` might be required by the mail server or other system software, so these are poor prospects for removal. Likewise, `nobody` is used by a variety of processes that need only low-privilege access rights. The `games` account is most frequently used by games for high-score files and the like, and so is most likely unused on a mail server.

13. D. When an `x` appears for entries in the second field of the `passwd` file, it indicates that the passwords are stored elsewhere—in the `/etc/shadow` file. Expiration information is stored in `/etc/shadow`, not `/etc/passwd`. An account that does not require a password for login has an empty password field in `/etc/passwd` or `/etc/shadow`.

14. C. The `pwconv` utility is used to convert conventional passwords to shadow passwords (the opposite of this action is performed by `pwunconv`). `skel` is a file, not a utility, that holds a "skeleton" of settings to be applied to newly created users. The shadow file (`/etc/shadow`) is where the passwords are stored, but it is not a utility. `crypt` is a utility that hashes data; it can be used to encrypt passwords, but doesn't convert conventional to shadow passwords or vice-versa.

15. B. The `repquota utility is used to` summarize the quota information on the filesystem. When used with the −a option, it will show this information for all filesystems. The `quotacheck` utility checks quota information on a disk and writes corrections.

16. A. The `grpunconv` utility converts shadow group entries into conventional (unshadowed) format in the `/etc/group` file. The opposite of this utility is `grpconv`. `convert` and `unconvert` are not utilities for working with group entries.

17. A. Linux's password tools support passwords longer than eight characters for MD5 hashes, but not for 3DES hashes. 3DES hashes are limited to passwords of eight characters or less.

18. C. Linux supports multiple simultaneous logins through its standard console through the use of *virtual terminals (VTs)*. From a text-mode login, pressing the Alt key along with a function key from 1 to 6 typically switches to a different virtual screen. Multitasking allows the machine to do more than one task at a time, while multithreading simply means that more than one thread can be executed at a time. Concurrency is not a common term used other than describing how many different users can log on at one time.

19. B. While the `userdel` utility removes the user, the −r parameter causes the system to remove all files from the user's home directory, as well as the home directory itself. There is no −a option for the `userdel` utility, and there is no standard utility in Linux named `deluser`.

20. B. Access control in PAM is controlled by the `pam_access.so` module. The other options listed are not standard modules in PAM.

Chapter

4

Disk Management

THE FOLLOWING COMPTIA OBJECTIVES ARE COVERED IN THIS CHAPTER:

- ✓ **2.1 Manage local storage devices and filesystems (e.g.,** `fsck`, `fdisk`, `mkfs`**) using CLI commands**

- ✓ **2.2 Mount and unmount varied filesystems (e.g., Samba, NFS) using CLI commands**

- ✓ **2.8 Perform and verify backups and restores** (`tar`, `cpio`)

- ✓ **2.9 Access and write data to recordable media (e.g., CDRW, hard drive, NVRAM)**

- ✓ **3.5 Configure files that are used to mount drives or partitions (e.g.,** `fstab`, `mtab`, **Samba,** `nfs`, **syntax)**

- ✓ **6.5 Identify and configure mass storage devices and RAID (e.g., SCSI, ATAPI, tape, optical recordable)**

Most computers' actions are tied very closely to their disk partitions and the files they contain. Web servers must be able to deliver Web files stored on disk, workstations must be able to run applications and store data on disk, and so on. Therefore, it's important that you be able to manage these files and the filesystems that contain them when you work with a Linux computer. Much of this chapter is devoted to this topic, starting with a look at the underlying hardware and Linux's interfaces to it, moving on to partition management and then looking at the Linux filesystem layout and backups.

The term "filesystem" has two meanings. First, it may refer to an organized collection of files, stored in some specific set of directories. For instance, certain filesystem standards for Linux specify in what directories certain types of files reside. Second, "filesystem" may refer to the low-level data structures used to organize files on a hard disk partition or removable disk. Several different filesystems of this second variety exist, such as ext3fs, ReiserFS, and FAT. This chapter covers both types of filesystems; which meaning is intended is usually clear from the context. When it isn't, I clarify by using terms such as "directory structure" or "directory tree" for the first type or "low-level filesystem" for the second variety.

Storage Hardware Identification

Before delving into the details of how Linux manages partitions and files, you should understand some of the basics of storage devices. Several types of storage device exist, and specific types have characteristics that can influence how Linux interacts with them. Understanding how Linux interacts with the hardware (device filenames, for instance) is also critically important.

Chapter 9, "Hardware," describes low-level hardware concerns in more detail, including configuration checks and troubleshooting for disk devices.

Types of Storage Devices

History has seen a progression of storage devices, from clay tablets to the latest recordable Digital Versatile Discs (DVDs). We seldom completely abandon a storage technology, although we may shift our emphasis to new devices. For instance, engravings in clay today aren't often used to record financial transactions, but they are still used in school art projects. Computer technology mirrors these effects, but in a more limited way. Early digital computers used punched cards and paper tape, then moved to magnetic tape, flexible disks, fixed disks, and so on. Today, many storage devices are in common use on small computers:

Hard disks   The most important form of storage for most desktop and server computers is the hard disk. This device consists of one or more spinning platters with magnetic coatings and a read/write head that accesses the data stored on the disk. Hard disks use *Advanced Technology Attachment (ATA)* and *Small Computer System Interface (SCSI)* interfaces, which are explained in more detail shortly, in "Linux Storage Hardware Configuration." Hard disks have high capacity and are reasonably fast and inexpensive, which means they're the ideal storage tool for the OS itself and for most user data files.

Removable magnetic disks   Removable magnetic disks are much like hard disks, but they can be easily removed from a computer. Also, most removable magnetic disk technologies provide much lower storage capacities than do hard disks. These range from under 1MB for some of the smaller floppy disks to a few gigabytes for some of the higher-capacity units. Common types of removable disks include floppies, Zip disks, LS-120 disks, Jaz disks, and Orb disks, but many other variants exist. One form, the magneto-optical disk, shares some characteristics with recordable optical disks, but in practice works much more like removable magnetic disks. In most respects, these disks can be treated like small hard disks—you can create filesystems on them, store files using the same commands, and so on. Their removability alters a few details of their configuration, though.

Optical media   Optical media include the Compact Disc Read-Only Memory (CD-ROM), CD Recordable (CD-R), CD Re-Writable (CD-RW), DVD, and various recordable DVD variants. These media all use entirely optical methods for storing and reading data. In practice, although they can be read much like removable magnetic disks, optical media require special tools to be written, as described later in the section "Writing to Optical Discs." In fact, not all optical media are recordable—CD-ROMs and DVDs are not recordable. Some media, including CD-Rs and some recordable DVD formats, can be written just once; data cannot be changed, once written.

Magnetic tape   Magnetic tape has long been an important storage medium for computers, and it remains an important medium for backups. It has speed, cost, and access limitations that make it impractical for day-to-day storage of ordinary files, however. You'll learn more about its uses in the section "Backing Up and Restoring a Computer."

Removable solid-state storage   In recent years, solid-state storage devices have grown in popularity. Examples include the Compact Flash (CF) card and memory sticks. These devices can interface with computers much like hard disks or removable magnetic disks, and can be treated much like these devices from a software perspective. They differ in their underlying technologies, though; rather than store data on magnetized spinning disks, solid-state storage devices use non-volatile electronic storage, similar in some ways to ordinary RAM. These technologies are expensive and low in capacity compared to most other removable media, but they have the advantage of compact size and durability, which make them ideal for use in various portable digital devices, such as digital cameras and personal digital assistants (PDAs). Thus, Linux support for these devices is most important for Linux used as an embedded OS on such devices and to enable a Linux desktop or laptop system to extract data from the media used by such devices.

NVRAM   *Nonvolatile RAM (NVRAM)* is a way of storing small amounts of data in chips. Although NVRAM is conceptually similar to removable solid state storage, it's used in computers to store small amounts of fixed data, such as BIOS options. NVRAM is generally not removable from the computer, and is quite limited in size. Linux provides the means to read and write NVRAM. Typically, this requires use of specialized data access tools.

Each of these classes of storage device has its own unique place on a Linux system. For a typical laptop, desktop, or server, the hard disk plays the most important role in day-to-day operations, although one or more removable magnetic disks and optical devices may be important as well. Aside from tapes and NVRAM, all of these devices are most commonly accessed with the help of a low-level filesystem, although the filesystems that are most useful vary from one device to another. (Chapter 1 describes Linux filesystem options in more detail.)

Linux Storage Hardware Configuration

To use a storage device, programs must be able to access it. In most cases, this is done through a low-level filesystem, which is then mounted to a directory—that is, the directory serves as a way to access the files and directories on the filesystem.

The upcoming section, "Mounting and Unmounting Partitions," describes how to mount filesystems.

In other cases, you must know the device filename that corresponds to the device. By reading from or writing to this device file, you may access data stored on the hardware. In fact, device filenames are important even for mounted filesystems, because you tell Linux what partition to mount by using a device filename.

The most common type of disk device today is the ATA hard disk. Such disks are identified by a device filename of the form /dev/hd*x*, where *x* is a letter from a onward. Specifically, the master disk on the first disk controller is /dev/hda, the slave disk on that controller is /dev/hdb, the master disk on the second controller is /dev/hdc, and so on. Device letters can be skipped, depending on how disks are configured. For instance, if you have two hard disks, both masters on their chains, they might be known as /dev/hda and /dev/hdc, with /dev/hdb unused.

SCSI devices are identified in a similar way, but their device filenames take the form /dev/sd*x*. Unlike ATA devices, SCSI disk devices are assigned letters sequentially, beginning with a; thus, a system with two SCSI disks will identify them as /dev/sda and /dev/sdb, even if they have noncontiguous SCSI ID numbers.

The latest variant on ATA, *serial ATA (SATA)*, may be treated either as ATA or as SCSI, depending on the Linux drivers you use. Some SATA controllers are supported by Linux ATA drivers, others are supported by Linux SCSI drivers, and some have both types of drivers, enabling you to choose which driver type to use. (Which is best depends on the specific drivers.) Thus, you might treat an SATA device like a conventional ATA device or like a SCSI device, depending on your kernel configuration. Similarly, removable media drives that use the Universal Serial Bus (USB), IEEE-1394, or other external interfaces are identified as either ATA or (more commonly) SCSI devices.

Both ATA and SCSI hard disks are commonly broken into partitions. These are identified by numbers after the hardware identifier. For instance, /dev/hda3 identifies a specific partition on /dev/hda, and /dev/sdb5 identifies a partition on /dev/sdb. On $x86$ hardware, partitions are numbered starting with 1, and partitions 1–4 are *primary partitions*. These partitions are defined using very old data structures, which support a maximum of four partitions. To work around this limitation, a special type of primary partition, known as an *extended partition*, can be used to define additional partitions, known as *logical partitions*. Partitions 5 and up are logical partitions.

The actual order of partitions on a disk need not correspond to their partition numbers. For instance, /dev/hda3 might appear before /dev/hda2. Likewise, gaps may appear in the primary partition sequence—a disk might have /dev/hda1 and /dev/hda3 but not /dev/hda2 or /dev/hda4.

Most removable magnetic media and solid-state storage devices use hard disk device files. These devices look almost exactly like hard disks from Linux's point of view. One important exception is floppy disks—at least, those that interface via a conventional motherboard floppy disk controller. Typically, the first floppy disk is /dev/fd0 and the second (if it's present) is /dev/fd1. Most distributions also provide assorted specialized files, such as /dev/fd0u1440, which enable you to force the OS to access the device at a given capacity. This can be particularly useful when you're performing a low-level disk format with the fdformat utility, which prepares a floppy disk for use. (You must also create a filesystem on the disk, using mkfs or a similar utility, as described later in "Creating New Filesystems.")

Hard disks are almost always partitioned before use. This is also true of some types of removable magnetic media, such as Zip disks, which use conventional ATA or SCSI disk device files to access the hardware. Other removable magnetic media, such as magneto-optical disks and floppy disks, are conventionally not partitioned. This is just a convention, at least for devices that use hard disk device files. (No device filenames for accessing partitioned floppy disks exist.)

Optical media are unusual because their access devices vary depending on the device interface. ATA devices are accessed just like hard disks. For instance, an ATA CD-RW drive that's configured as the slave device on the first disk controller will be accessed as /dev/hdb, just as if it were a hard disk. SCSI optical drives, though, are identified with filenames of the form /dev/scd$x$, where x is a number from 0 up. Thus, /dev/scd0 is typically your SCSI optical device. Linux kernels provide SCSI emulation support, which enables you to access an ATA optical drive as if it were a SCSI model. With 2.4.x and earlier kernels, this was necessary to use recordable optical devices; however, with the 2.6.x kernels, Linux supports writing to these media using the ATA drivers, and this is the preferred approach. The bottom line is that an ATA optical disc *might* look like a SCSI one, depending on your kernel configuration. Most distributions set up a symbolic link from /dev/cdrom to your primary optical media device, so you may be able to use this filename when specifying your disc. Optical discs are not conventionally partitioned.

Magnetic tape devices are identified using a pair of device files, whose names differ from ATA to SCSI. For an ATA tape device, /dev/ht$x$ and /dev/nht$x$, where x is a number from 0 up, identify the tape device. The /dev/ht$x$ file, when accessed, causes the tape to automatically rewind after every operation; the /dev/nhtx file, by contrast, is nonrewinding, which can be handy if you want to store multiple backups on a single tape. The SCSI device filenames take a similar form: /dev/stx and /dev/nstx. Because few systems have multiple tape devices, chances are you'll only see the 0-numbered ones, such as /dev/st0 and /dev/nst0. Typically, tape devices are accessed like ordinary files—you pass their filenames to backup programs as if they were disk files.

NVRAM is accessed through the /dev/nvram file. This file contains very precisely structured data, so you should *not* try to access it directly. Instead, you can use a utility, such as NVRAM Wakeup (http://sourceforge.net/projects/nvram-wakeup/) or tpb (http://www.nongnu.org/tpb/). These programs provide specialized functionality to read or write some or all of the NVRAM data.

Never attempt to write a filesystem to /dev/nvram or otherwise write to it without the help of a program designed to do so. Even using such a program designed for a CPU or BIOS other than the one you're using could render your system *unbootable*!

Partition Management and Maintenance

As just described, Linux systems store their data on disk partitions. Most partitions hold low-level filesystems. Creating partitions and preparing them to hold data are critically important tasks in using disks. To create partitions on a new disk, you use a tool called fdisk. You then create a new low-level filesystem on the partition using mkfs. Alternatively, you can use other tools to do the jobs of one or both of these programs. Sometimes filesystems develop errors, in which case checking their integrity with fsck is critically important.

Some partitions hold *swap space* rather than filesystems. Swap space can function as a stand-in for RAM when the system runs out of physical memory. Having adequate swap space is important for overall system functioning, and being able to manage it will help your system work well.

Using *fdisk* to Create Partitions

Linux's native tool for partition creation is known as fdisk, which stands for "fixed disk." This utility is named after a DOS tool, which I refer to in this book in uppercase letters (FDISK) to differentiate it from Linux's fdisk; although the tools perform similar tasks, they're very different in operation. Most other OSs include their own disk partitioning software as well.

Linux on non-*x*86 systems may not use a tool called fdisk. For instance, PowerPC versions of Linux use a tool called pdisk. (Further complicating matters, some PowerPC Linux distributions call their pdisk programs fdisk.) Some important operational details differ between platforms, so if you're using a non-*x*86 system, consult the documentation for your distribution and its disk-partitioning tool.

Linux's fdisk is a text-based tool that requires you to type one-letter commands. You can obtain a list of commands by typing **?** or **m** at the fdisk prompt. The most important fdisk commands are listed in Table 4.1.

TABLE 4.1   fdisk Commands

Command	Description
d	Deletes a partition.
n	Creates a new partition.
p	Displays (prints) the partition layout.
q	Quits without saving changes.
t	Changes a partition's type code.
w	Writes (saves) changes and quits.

To start fdisk, type its name followed by the Linux device filename associated with your disk device, as in **fdisk /dev/hdb**. When you first start fdisk, the program displays its prompt. It's often helpful to type **p** at this prompt to see the current partition layout, as shown in Figure 4.1. This will help you verify that you're operating on the correct disk, if you have more than one hard disk. It will also show you the device IDs of the existing disk partitions.

FIGURE 4.1   As a text-based program, fdisk can be run in text mode or in an xterm, as shown here.

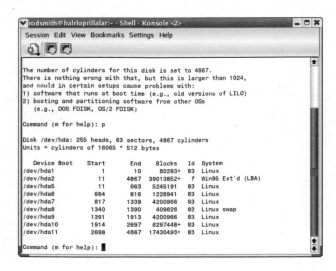

The fdisk program identifies the extended partition, if it's present, in the System column of its output, as shown in Figure 4.1; these partitions may be labeled as Extended or Win95 Ext'd (LBA); Linux treats both types identically. Primary and logical partitions are not explicitly identified as such; you must use the partition number, as described earlier in "Linux Storage Hardware Configuration," to identify the partition type.

You can use the commands outlined in Table 4.1 to alter a disk's partition layout, but be aware that your changes are potentially destructive. Deleting partitions will make their data inaccessible. Some commands require you to enter additional information, such as partition numbers or sizes for new partitions. For instance, the following sequence illustrates the commands associated with adding a new logical partition that's 2GB in size:

```
Command (m for help): n
Command action
   l   logical (5 or over)
   p   primary partition (1-4)
l
First cylinder (519-784, default 519): 519
Last cylinder or +size or +sizeM or +sizeK (519-784, default 784): +2G
```

You can enter the partition size in terms of cylinder numbers or as a size in bytes, kilobytes, megabytes, or gigabytes (which isn't mentioned in the prompt but does work). When you've made your changes, type w to write them to disk and exit. If you make a mistake, type q immediately; doing this will exit from fdisk without committing changes to disk.

Creating New Filesystems

Just creating partitions isn't enough to make them useful in Linux. To make them useful, you must create a filesystem on the partition (a task that's also sometimes called "formatting" a partition). Linux uses the mkfs program to accomplish this task. This tool has the following syntax:

```
mkfs [-V] [-t fstype] [options] device [blocks]
```

mkfs is actually just a front-end to tools that do the real work for specific filesystems, such as mke2fs (also known as mkfs.ext2). You can call these tools directly if you prefer, although their syntax may vary from that of mkfs.

The mkfs parameters can be used to perform several tasks:

Generate verbose output   The -V option causes mkfs to generate verbose output, displaying additional information on the filesystem-creation process.

Setting the filesystem type   You specify the filesystem type with the -t fstype option. Common values for fstype include ext2 (for ext2fs), ext3 (for ext3fs), reiserfs (for ReiserFS), xfs (for XFS), jfs (for JFS), msdos (for FAT), and minix (for Minix). Some other options are available as well.

Options   You can pass filesystem-specific options to the utility. Most underlying filesystem creation tools support -c (to perform a low-level disk check to be sure the hardware is sound) and -v (to perform a verbose creation; note that this option is lowercase, unlike the main mkfs parameter to produce verbose output).

Device filename   The *device* is the name of the device on which you want to create the filesystem, such as /dev/sda5 or /dev/fd0. You should *not* normally specify an entire hard disk here (such as /dev/sda or /dev/hdb). One exception might be if it's a removable disk, but even these are often partitioned.

Filesystem size   The *blocks* parameter sets the size of the filesystem in blocks (usually 1024 bytes in size). You don't normally need to specify this value, since mkfs can determine the filesystem size from the size of the partition.

Depending on the size and speed of the disk device, the filesystem-creation process is likely to take anywhere from a second or less to a minute or two. If you specify a filesystem check (which is often a good idea, particularly on brand-new or very old disks), this process can take several minutes, or possibly over an hour. Once it's done, you should be able to mount the filesystem and use it to store files.

The filesystem-creation process is inherently destructive. If you accidentally create a filesystem in error, it will be impossible to recover files from the old filesystem unless you're very knowledgeable about filesystem data structures, or you can pay somebody with such knowledge. Recovery costs are apt to be very high.

As noted earlier, mkfs is just a front-end to other utilities, which are sometimes called directly instead. For instance, you might call the mkreiserfs utility to prepare a ReiserFS partition, mkfs.ext3 to prepare an ext3fs partition, or mkdosfs to prepare a FAT partition or floppy disk. Check the /sbin directory for files whose names begin with mkfs to see what other filesystem-specific mkfs tools exist on your system.

The presence of a filesystem-creation tool on your computer doesn't necessarily mean that you'll be able to read and write the filesystem on your computer. Mounting a filesystem requires appropriate kernel support, which can be compiled and installed independently of the filesystem's mkfs.*fstype* tool.

Using a Combined Tool

The Linux fdisk and mkfs tools, although reliable, are sometimes restricting. They can also be intimidating to new users. Several alternatives exist, many of which are dynamic partition resizing tools. These programs can change the size of an existing partition without destroying its data. Some of these tools work only for specific filesystems, such as resize2fs for ext2fs and ext3fs, and resize_reiserfs for ReiserFS. The GNU Parted program (http://www.gnu.org/software/parted/) is another option. This program supports resizing several partition types, including FAT, ext2fs, ext3fs, and ReiserFS. A GUI variant of this program is QTParted (http://qtparted.sourceforge.net), which provides a GUI interface on various partitioning operations, as shown in Figure 4.2. QTParted can also call external programs, including one that enables it to resize Windows NT/200*x*/XP NTFS partitions. One of the major problems with most of these tools is that they cannot resize partitions that are currently mounted, which of course makes it hard to modify your working Linux system.

 You may want an easy-to-use partitioning tool for resizing Linux partitions that are normally mounted or for resizing FAT or NTFS partitions on computers on which Linux is not yet installed. Using QTParted from a full-featured Linux emergency boot system is one way to accomplish this goal. Another approach is to use a DOS-based tool from a DOS boot floppy.

Another option for resizing partitions is to use the commercial PartitionMagic from Symantec (http://www.symantec.com). This program comes in DOS and Windows versions, including a DOS boot floppy so that you can run it from a floppy disk on a Linux-only system. PartitionMagic provides a GUI interface similar to that of QTParted. In fact, QTParted's interface is modeled after that of PartitionMagic, which is the older program. PartitionMagic's maturity means that it's a very stable and well-tested program, although it's not infallible.

You might have to adjust your /etc/fstab entries and reinstall your boot loader after performing a partition resize operation. Backing up your data before performing such an operation is also wise. Nonetheless, dynamic partition resizers can greatly simplify reconfiguring swap files.

FIGURE 4.2   The QTParted program provides a GUI for filesystem resizing operations.

Number	Partition	Type	Status	Size	Used space	Start	End
01	/dev/hda1	fat16		917.74MB	570.27MB	0.03MB	917.78MB
02	/dev/hda2	unknow		4.57GB	N/A	917.78MB	5.46GB
03	/dev/hda3	ntfs		1.27GB	599.04MB	5.46GB	6.73GB
04	/dev/hda4	extended	Active	49.16GB	N/A	6.73GB	55.90GB
05	/dev/hda5	ext2	Active	31.35MB	18.45MB	6.73GB	6.76GB
06	/dev/hda6	ext2	Active	23.50MB	2.47MB	6.76GB	6.79GB
07	/dev/hda7	ntfs		2.46GB	573.92MB	6.79GB	9.25GB
08	/dev/hda8	unknow	Active	2.02GB	N/A	9.25GB	11.27GB
09	/dev/hda9	reiserfs	Active	14.65GB	7.31GB	11.27GB	25.92GB
10	/dev/hda10	unknow	Active	21.99GB	18.44GB	25.92GB	47.92GB
11	/dev/hda11	ext3	Active	5.01GB	4.25GB	47.92GB	52.93GB
12	/dev/hda12	linux-swap	Active	556.91MB	0.00MB	52.93GB	53.47GB
13	/dev/hda13	ext3	Active	2.43GB	1.79GB	53.47GB	55.90GB

qtparted v0.4.0

File Operations Disks Device Options Help

The following drives have been detected:

Device
Disks
/dev/hda
/dev/hdb

Drive Info

Device:	/dev/hda
Model:	WDC WD600AB-32BVA0
Capacity (Mb):	57241.9
Length sectors:	117231408
Status:	busy.

hda2   hda9 (7.31GB)   hda10 (18.44GB)

QTParted :) | by Zanac (c) 2002-2003

Checking a Filesystem for Errors

Creating partitions and filesystems are tasks you're likely to perform every once in a while—say, when adding a new hard disk or making major changes to an installation. Another task is much more common: checking a filesystem for errors. Bugs, power failures, and mechanical problems can all cause the data structures on a filesystem to become corrupted. The results are sometimes subtle, but if they are left unchecked, they can cause severe data loss. For this reason, Linux includes tools for verifying a filesystem's integrity, and for correcting any problems that might exist. The main tool you'll use for this purpose is called fsck. Like mkfs, fsck is actually a front-end to other tools, such as e2fsck (aka fsck.ext2 and fsck.ext3). The syntax for fsck is as follows:

```
fsck  [-sACVRTNP] [-t fstype] [--] [fsck-options]  filesystems
```

The more common parameters to this command enable you to perform useful actions:

Check all files   The -A option causes fsck to check all the filesystems marked to be checked in /etc/fstab. This option is normally used in system startup scripts.

Progress indication   The -C option displays a text-mode progress indicator of the check process. Most filesystem check programs don't support this feature, but e2fsck does.

Verbose output   The -V option produces verbose output of the check process.

No action   The -N option tells fsck to display what it would normally do, without actually doing it.

Set the filesystem type   Normally, fsck determines the filesystem type automatically. You can force the type with the -t fstype flag, though. If used in conjunction with -A, this causes the system to check only the specified filesystem types, even if others are marked to be checked. If fstype is prefixed with no, then all filesystems *except* the specified type are checked.

Filesystem-specific options   Filesystem check programs for specific filesystems often have their own options. The fsck command passes options it doesn't understand, or those that follow a double dash (--), to the underlying check program. Common options include -a or -p (perform an automatic check), -r (perform an interactive check), and -f (force a full filesystem check even if the filesystem initially appears to be clean).

Filesystem list   The final parameter is usually the name of the filesystem or filesystems being checked, such as /dev/sda6.

Normally, you run fsck with only the filesystem name, as in fsck /dev/sda6. You can add options as needed, however. Check the fsck man page for less common options.

WARNING   Run fsck *only* on filesystems that are not currently mounted or that are mounted in read-only mode. Changes written to disk during normal read/write operations can confuse fsck and result in filesystem corruption.

Linux runs `fsck` automatically at startup on partitions that are marked for this in `/etc/fstab`, as described later in the section "Defining Standard Filesystems." The normal behavior of `e2fsck` causes it to perform just a quick cursory examination of a partition if it's been unmounted cleanly. The result is that the Linux boot process isn't delayed because of a filesystem check unless the system wasn't shut down properly. A couple of exceptions to this rule exist, however: `e2fsck` forces a check if the disk has gone longer than a certain amount of time without checks (normally six months), or if the filesystem has been mounted more than a certain number of times since the last check (normally 20). Therefore, you will occasionally see automatic filesystem checks of ext2fs and ext3fs partitions even if the system was shut down correctly.

A new generation of filesystems, exemplified by ext3fs, ReiserFS, JFS, and XFS, does away with filesystem checks at system startup even if the system was not shut down correctly. These journaling filesystems keep a log of pending operations on the disk so that in the event of a power failure or system crash, the log can be checked and its operations replayed or undone to keep the filesystem in good shape. This action is automatic when mounting such a filesystem. Nonetheless, these filesystems still require check programs to correct problems introduced by undetected write failures, bugs, hardware problems, and the like. If you encounter odd behavior with a journaling filesystem, you might consider unmounting it and performing a filesystem check—but be sure to read the documentation first. Some Linux distributions do odd things with some journaling filesystem check programs. Most notably, Mandrake uses a symbolic link from `/sbin/fsck.reiserfs` to `/bin/true`. This configuration speeds system boot times should ReiserFS partitions be marked for automatic checks, but it can be confusing if you need to manually check the filesystem. If this is the case, run `/sbin/reiserfsck` to do the job.

Adding Swap Space

Linux enables you to run programs that consume more memory than you have RAM in your system. It does this through the use of swap space, which is disk space that Linux treats as an extension of RAM. When your RAM fills with programs and their data, Linux moves some of this information to its swap space, freeing actual RAM for other uses. This feature, which is common on modern operating systems, is very convenient when your users run an unusually large number of programs. If you rely on this feature too much, however, performance suffers because disk accesses are far slower than are RAM accesses. It's also important that you have adequate swap space on your system. If the computer runs out of swap space, programs may begin to behave erratically.

Evaluating Swap Space Use

An invaluable tool in checking your system's memory use is `free`. This program displays information on your computer's total memory use. Typically, you just type **free** to use it, but it does support various options that can fine-tune its output. Consult its man page for more information.

Listing 4.1 shows a sample output from `free` on a system with 256MB of RAM. (The total memory reported is less than 256MB because of memory consumed by the kernel and inefficiencies in the x86 architecture.)

Listing 4.1: Sample Output from *free*

```
$ free
          total    used    free  shared  buffers  cached
Mem:     256452  251600    4852       0    10360  130192
-/+ buffers/cache: 111048  145404
Swap:    515100    1332  513768
```

The Mem line shows the total RAM used by programs, data, buffers, and caches. (All of these values are in kilobytes by default.) Unless you need information on memory used by buffers or caches, this line isn't too useful. The next line, `-/+ buffers/cache`, shows the total RAM used *without* considering buffers and caches. This line can be very informative in evaluating your system's overall RAM requirements, and hence in determining when it makes sense to add RAM. Specifically, if the used column routinely shows values that approach your total installed RAM (or alternatively, if the free column routinely approaches 0), then it's time to add RAM. This information isn't terribly helpful in planning your swap space use, though.

The final line shows swap space use. In the case of Listing 4.1, a total of 515,100KB of swap space is available. Of that, 1,332KB is in use, leaving 513,768KB free. Given the small amount of swap space used, it seems that the system depicted in Listing 4.1 has plenty of swap space, at least assuming this usage is typical.

 Real World Scenario

When to Add Swap, When to Add RAM

Swap space exists because hard disks are less expensive than RAM, on a per-megabyte basis. With the price of both falling, however, it's often wise to forgo expanding your swap space in favor of adding extra RAM. RAM is faster than swap space, so all other things being equal, RAM is better.

A general rule of thumb derived from the days of Unix mainframes is that swap space should be 1.5–2 times as large as physical RAM. For instance, a system with 512MB of RAM should have 768–1024MB of swap space. With 2.2.*x* kernels, it's often more helpful to look at this as a *maximum* for swap space. If your swap space use regularly exceeds 1.5–2 times your RAM size, your overall system performance will very likely be severely degraded. Adding RAM to such a system will almost certainly improve its performance. It won't hurt to have extra swap space, though, aside from the fact that this reduces the disk space available for programs and data files. The 2.4.*x* kernels have changed how swap space is managed, so 2.4.*x* and later kernels use more swap space than 2.2.*x* kernels do when they are running the same programs. For this reason, you should ensure that a system using a 2.4.*x* or later kernel has at least twice as much swap space as physical RAM.

Adding a Swap File

One method of adding swap space is to create a *swap file*. This is an ordinary disk file that's configured to be used by Linux as swap space. To add a swap file, follow these steps:

1. Create an empty file of the appropriate size. You can do this by copying bytes from /dev/zero (a device file that returns bytes containing the value 0) using the dd utility. The dd program takes parameters of bs (block size, in bytes) and count (the number of blocks to copy); the total file size is the product of these two values. You specify the input file with if and the output file with of. For instance, the following command creates a file called /swap.swp that's 134,217,728 bytes (128MB) in size:

   ```
   # dd if=/dev/zero of=/swap.swp bs=1024 count=131072
   ```

2. Use the mkswap command to initialize the swap file for use. This command writes data structures to the file to enable Linux to swap memory to disk, but mkswap does *not* activate the swap file. For instance, the following command does this job:

   ```
   # mkswap /swap.swp
   ```

Swap space can reside on most Linux filesystem types, but may *not* reside on *Network Filesystem (NFS)* mounts. If you try creating a swap file and the swapon command in step 3 doesn't work, this could be the problem. Most Linux hard disk filesystem drivers, including Linux-native drivers and even the vfat driver, can support swap space. These are the filesystems you're most likely to want to use for this purpose.

3. Use the swapon command to begin using the newly initialized swap space:

   ```
   # swapon /swap.swp
   ```

If you use free before and after performing these steps, you should see the total swap space count increase, reflecting the addition of the new swap space. If you want to make your use of this swap file permanent, you must add an entry to /etc/fstab (described later in the section "Defining Standard Filesystems"). This entry should resemble the following:

```
/swap.swp    swap    swap    defaults    0 0
```

One key point is to list the complete path to the swap file in the first column, including the leading /. Once this entry is added, the system will use the swap file after you reboot. If you want to use all of the swap spaces defined in /etc/fstab, type **swapon -a**; this command causes Linux to read /etc/fstab and activate all the swap partitions defined there.

To deactivate use of swap space, use the swapoff command, thus:

```
# swapoff /swap.swp
```

This command may take some time to execute if the swap file has been used much because the system takes time to read data from the disk for storage in memory or in other swap areas.

To disable all swapping, type **swapoff -a**; this command deactivates all swap spaces—both those listed in /etc/fstab and those you've added manually. The swapon and swapoff commands are actually the same program on most systems; this program does different things depending on the name you use to call it.

Adding swap space in the form of a swap file can be a convenient way to add swap space quickly; however, this approach does have certain problems. Most importantly, if you create a large swap file on a partition that's already been heavily used, it's likely that the swap file will be *fragmented*—that is, that the file's contents will be spread across multiple groups of sectors on the disk. Fragmentation of disk files slows performance, and this can be a major problem in a swap file. The ability to quickly add a temporary swap file makes this method appealing in many cases, though. Indeed, the difficulty of repartitioning, as described shortly, makes adjusting swap partitions a task you may not want to undertake unless you're already planning to perform other partition maintenance.

Adding a Swap Partition

Traditionally, Unix and Linux have used *swap partitions* for swap space. These are entire disk partitions devoted to swap space. In fact, some distributions won't install unless you create at least one swap partition. Therefore, chances are good you already have such a partition configured.

If you want to install multiple Linux distributions on one computer, they may share a single swap partition.

What if your existing swap partition is too small, though? The easiest approach in this case is usually to create a supplementary swap file, as described earlier. Another approach is to create a new swap partition. This procedure works best if you're adding a hard disk or want to repartition the disk for some other reason. In this case, you'll be adjusting your partition layout anyway, so you might as well take the opportunity to add new swap space. The basic procedure for doing this is as follows:

1. Clear space for the swap partition. This can be done by deleting existing partitions, by shrinking existing partitions, or by using a previously unused hard disk.

2. Create a new partition and give it a type code of 0x82 ("Linux swap"). Many OSs (but not Linux) use type codes to help them identify their partitions. Type codes 0x82 and 0x83 stand for Linux swap and filesystem partitions, respectively. The main reason to use these codes is to keep other OSs from damaging the Linux partitions.

Solaris for *x*86 uses the 0x82 partition type code for its own filesystem partitions. This fact can lead to confusion and even damage to Solaris filesystem data if you mistakenly believe that a 0x82 partition is a Linux swap partition when in fact it's a Solaris data partition. You may also need to temporarily change the type of a Linux swap partition if you want to install Solaris on the computer.

3. When you're done partitioning or repartitioning, use mkswap to prepare the swap partition to be swap space. This operation works just like using mkswap on a file, except that you apply it to a partition, thus:

```
# mkswap /dev/sdc6
```

4. Once the swap space has been prepared for use, you can add it manually using the swapon command described above, but you'll need to specify the swap partition's device rather than a swap file. For instance, you might use the following command to access a swap partition on /dev/sdc6:

```
# swapon /dev/sdc6
```

5. To use the swap partition permanently, add an entry for it to /etc/fstab, as described earlier in reference to swap files.

This procedure glosses over several critically important details concerning partition management. For one thing, when you modify an existing disk's partitions, you may need to adjust the device filenames for Linux filesystems in /etc/fstab. You'll have to do this either from an emergency boot or *before* you make the changes to the disk. It is at least as important, if you delete any existing partitions, to back up their contents before you delete the partition, even if you intend to re-create the partition with a smaller size. You may also need to reinstall the LILO or GRUB boot loader if you modify your boot partition. In any event, this procedure will require the use of a disk partitioning tool such as Linux's fdisk or a partition-resizing tool such as GNU Parted.

Partition Control

One of a system administrator's tasks is to manage disk partitions. This task begins with identifying partitions, but the core task is mounting and unmounting partitions and filesystems stored on removable media. If you want to make your changes permanent, you must modify a file called /etc/fstab. On a high-performance system, you might also want to link two or more disks together to improve performance or reliability.

Identifying Partitions

Linux identifies partitions using device files whose names are based on those for the low-level hardware devices, as described earlier, in "Linux Storage Hardware Configuration." If you installed Linux on the system, chances are you told it what partitions to use. If you don't remember what Linux called your partitions at system installation, you can use the fdisk program to find out. Pass it the -1 parameter (that's a lowercase L, not a number 1) and the name of a disk device (such as /dev/hdb or /dev/sda) to obtain a listing of the partitions on that disk, as in:

```
# fdisk -1 /dev/hdb
```

```
Disk /dev/hdb: 255 heads, 63 sectors, 1216 cylinders
Units = cylinders of 16065 * 512 bytes

   Device Boot  Start   End  Blocks   Id  System
/dev/hdb1             257  1216  7711200    5  Extended
/dev/hdb2               1   192  1542208+  fb  Unknown
/dev/hdb3             193   256   514080   17  Hidden HPFS/ NTFS
/dev/hdb5             257   516  2088418+   6  FAT16
/dev/hdb6     *       517   668  1220908+   7  HPFS/NTFS
/dev/hdb7             669  1216  4401778+  83  Linux
```

This output shows the device name associated with each partition, the start and end cylinder numbers, the number of 1024-byte blocks in each partition, each partition's hexadecimal (base 16) ID code, and the partition or OS type associated with that code.

Linux ignores the partition ID code except during installation and to identify extended partitions, but some other OSs use it to determine which partitions they should try to mount. Therefore, it's important that you set any Linux partition's ID code to 0x83. (Linux swap partitions use 0x82.)

If Linux boots, you can also use the df utility (described later in "Using df") to identify the partitions your system is using. This tool won't identify partitions that aren't mounted, though, including swap partitions and partitions you simply aren't using (such as those for non-Linux OSs, unless they're currently mounted).

Mounting and Unmounting Partitions

Linux provides the mount command to *mount* a filesystem to a *mount point*—that is, to make the filesystem available as files and directories in the specified mount point (which is an ordinary directory). The umount command reverses this process. (Yes, umount is spelled correctly; it's missing the first n.) In practice, using these commands is usually not too difficult, but they support a large number of options.

Syntax and Parameters for *mount*

The syntax for mount is as follows:

```
mount [-alrsvw] [-t fstype] [-o options] [device]  [mountpoint]
```

Common parameters for mount support a number of features:

Mount all filesystems   The -a parameter causes mount to mount all the filesystems listed in the /etc/fstab file, which specifies the most-used partitions and devices. The upcoming section, "Defining Standard Filesystems," describes this file's format.

Mount read-only   The -r parameter causes Linux to mount the filesystem read-only, even if it's normally a read/write filesystem.

Verbose output   As with many commands, -v produces verbose output—the program provides comments on operations as they occur.

Mount Read/write   The -w parameter causes Linux to attempt to mount the filesystem for both read and write operations. This is the default for most filesystems, but some experimental drivers default to read-only operation.

Filesystem type specification   Use the -t *fstype* parameter to specify the filesystem type. Common filesystem types are ext2 (for ext2fs), ext3 (for ext3fs), reiserfs (for ReiserFS), jfs (for JFS), xfs (for XFS), vfat (for FAT with VFAT long filenames), msdos (for FAT using only short DOS filenames), iso9660 (for CD-ROM filesystems), nfs (for NFS network mounts), smbfs (for SMB/CIFS network shares), and cifs (a newer driver for SMB/CIFS network shares). Linux supports many others. If this parameter is omitted, Linux will attempt to auto-detect the filesystem type.

Additional options   You can add many options using the -o parameter. Many of these are filesystem specific.

Linux requires support in the kernel or as a kernel module to mount a filesystem of a given type. If this support is missing, Linux will refuse to mount the filesystem in question.

Device   The *device* is the device filename associated with the partition or disk device, such as /dev/hda4, /dev/fd0, or /dev/cdrom. This parameter is usually required, but it may be omitted under some circumstances, as described shortly.

Mount point   The *mountpoint* is the directory to which the device's contents should be attached. As with *device*, it's usually required, but it may be omitted under some circumstances.

The preceding list of mount parameters isn't comprehensive; consult the mount man page for some of the more obscure options. The most common applications of mount use few parameters, because Linux generally does a good job of detecting the filesystem type, and the default parameters work reasonably well. For instance, consider this example:

```
# mount /dev/sdb7 /mnt/shared
```

This command mounts the contents of /dev/sdb7 on /mnt/shared, auto-detecting the filesystem type and using the default options. Ordinarily, only root may issue a mount command; however, if /etc/fstab specifies the user, users, or owner option, an ordinary user may mount a filesystem using a simplified syntax in which only the device *or* mount point is specified, but not both. For instance, a user might type **mount /mnt/cdrom** to mount a CD-ROM, if /etc/fstab specifies /mnt/cdrom as its mount point and uses the user, users, or owner option.

Many Linux distributions ship with auto-mounter support, which causes the OS to automatically mount removable media when they're inserted. In GUI environments, a file browser may also open on the inserted disk. In order to eject the disk, the user will need to unmount the filesystem by using umount, as described shortly, or by selecting an option in the desktop environment.

When Linux mounts a filesystem, it ordinarily records this fact in /etc/mtab. This file has a format similar to that of /etc/fstab and is stored in /etc, but it's not a configuration file that you should edit. You might examine this file to determine what filesystems are mounted, though. (The df command, described in more detail in the section "Using df," is another way to learn what filesystems are mounted.)

Options for *mount*

When you do need to use special parameters, it's usually to add filesystem-specific options. Table 4.2 summarizes the most important filesystem options. Some of these are meaningful only in the /etc/fstab file.

TABLE 4.2   Important Filesystem Options for the *mount* Command

Option	Supported Filesystems	Description
defaults	All	Uses the default options for this filesystem. It's used primarily in the /etc/fstab file to ensure that there's an options column in the file.
loop	All	Uses the loopback device for this mount. Allows you to mount a file as if it were a disk partition. For instance, mount -t vfat -o loop image.img /mnt/image mounts the file image.img as if it were a disk.
auto or noauto	All	Mounts or does not mount the filesystem at boot time or when root issues the mount -a command. The default is auto, but noauto is appropriate for removable media. Used in /etc/fstab.
user or nouser	All	Allows or disallows ordinary users to mount the filesystem. The default is nouser, but user is often appropriate for removable media. Used in /etc/fstab. When included in this file, user allows users to type **mount /*mountpoint***, where /*mountpoint* is the assigned mount point, to mount a disk. Only the user who mounted the filesystem may unmount it.
users	All	Similar to user, except that any user may unmount a filesystem once it's been mounted.

TABLE 4.2   Important Filesystem Options for the *mount* Command *(continued)*

Option	Supported Filesystems	Description
owner	All	Similar to user, except that the user must own the device file. Some distributions, such as Red Hat, assign ownership of some device files (such as /dev/fd0, for the floppy disk) to the console user, so this can be a helpful option.
remount	All	Changes one or more mount options without explicitly unmounting a partition. To use this option, you issue a mount command on an already-mounted filesystem, but with remount along with any options you want to change. Can be used to enable or disable write access to a partition, for example.
ro	All	Specifies a read-only mount of the filesystem. This is the default for filesystems that include no write access and for some with particularly unreliable write support.
rw	All read/write filesystems	Specifies a read/write mount of the filesystem. This is the default for most read/write filesystems.
uid=*value*	Most filesystems that don't support Unix-style permissions, such as vfat, hpfs, ntfs, and hfs	Sets the owner of all files. For instance, uid=500 sets the owner to whoever has Linux user ID 500. (Check Linux user IDs in the /etc/passwd file.)
gid=*value*	Most filesystems that don't support Unix-style permissions, such as vfat, hpfs, ntfs, and hfs	Works like uid=*value*, but sets the group of all files on the filesystem. You can find group IDs in the /etc/group file.
umask=*value*	Most filesystems that don't support Unix-style permissions, such as vfat, hpfs, ntfs, and hfs	Sets the umask for the permissions on files. *value* is interpreted in binary as bits to be removed from permissions on files. For instance, umask=027 yields permissions of 750, or –rwxr-x---. Used in conjunction with uid=*value* and gid=*value*, this option lets you control who can access files on FAT, HPFS, and many other foreign filesystems.
conv=*code*	Most filesystems used on Microsoft and Apple OSs: msdos, umsdos, vfat, hpfs, hfs	If *code* is b or binary, Linux doesn't modify the files' contents. If *code* is t or text, Linux auto-converts files between Linux-style and DOS- or Macintosh-style end-of-line characters. If *code* is a or auto, Linux applies the conversion unless the file is a known binary file format. It's usually best to leave this at its default value of binary because file conversions can cause serious problems for some applications and file types.

TABLE 4.2   Important Filesystem Options for the *mount* Command *(continued)*

Option	Supported Filesystems	Description
norock	iso9660	Disables Rock Ridge extensions for ISO-9660 CD-ROMs.
nojoliet	iso9660	Disables Joliet extensions for ISO-9660 CD-ROMs.

Some filesystems support additional options that aren't described here. The mount man page covers some of these, but you may need to look to the filesystem's documentation for some filesystems and options. This documentation may appear in /usr/src/linux/Documentation/filesystems or /usr/src/linux/fs/*fsname*, where *fsname* is the name of the filesystem.

Using *umount*

The umount command is simpler than mount. The basic umount syntax is as follows:

umount [-afnrv] [-t *fstype*] [*device | mountpoint*]

Most of these parameters have similar meanings to their meanings in mount, but some differences deserve mention:

Unmount all   Rather than unmount partitions listed in /etc/fstab, the -a option causes the system to attempt to unmount all the partitions listed in /etc/mtab, the file that holds information on mounted filesystems. On a normally running system, this operation is likely to succeed only partly because it won't be able to unmount some key filesystems, such as the root partition.

Force unmount   You can tell Linux to force an unmount operation that might otherwise fail with the -f option. This feature is sometimes helpful when unmounting NFS mounts shared by servers that have become unreachable.

Fallback to read-only   The -r option tells umount that if it can't unmount a filesystem, it should attempt to remount it in read-only mode.

Unmount partitions of a specific filesystem type   The -t *fstype* option tells the system to unmount only partitions of the specified type. You can list multiple filesystem types by separating them with commas.

The device and mount point   You need to specify only the *device* or only the *mountpoint*, not both.

As with mount, normal users cannot ordinarily use umount. The exception is if the partition or device is listed in /etc/fstab and specifies the user, users, or owner option, in which case normal users can unmount the device. (In the case of user, only the user who mounted the partition may unmount it; and in the case of owner, the user issuing the command must also own the device file, as with mount.) These options are most useful for removable-media devices.

Be cautious when removing floppy disks. Linux caches accesses to floppies, which means that data may not be written to the disk until some time after a write command. Because of this, it's possible to corrupt a floppy by ejecting the disk, even when the drive isn't active. You must *always* issue a umount command before ejecting a mounted floppy disk. This isn't an issue for most non-floppy removable media because Linux can lock their eject mechanisms, preventing this sort of problem. Another way to write the cache to disk is to use the sync command, but because this command does *not* fully unmount a filesystem, it's not really a substitute for umount.

Using Network Filesystems

Although they aren't local disk partitions, network filesystems can be mounted using the same commands used to mount local disk partitions and removable disks. They do possess certain unique features, though. Two network filesystems are most common in Linux: NFS, which is commonly used among Unix and Unix-like operating systems, and the Server Message Block /Common Internet File System (SMB/CIFS), which is most strongly associated with Windows systems, although the Samba server for Linux can also deliver SMB/CIFS shares.

Chapter 6 briefly describes configuring NFS and Samba servers in Linux. This chapter covers the client side.

Accessing SMB/CIFS Shares

Microsoft Windows uses SMB/CIFS for file and printer sharing. Using this protocol, it's possible to configure one Windows system to share a hard disk or directory with other computers. The client systems can mount the shared disk or directory as if it were a local drive. Printers can be shared in a similar manner. This type of configuration is very useful because it allows for easy file exchange between co-workers and because a network administrator can install software once on the file server rather than multiple times on each computer, saving disk space and administrative effort.

Linux includes tools that provide the ability to interact with Windows systems that use SMB/CIFS. The main package for this is called Samba, and it comes with all major Linux distributions. Samba includes two major client programs: smbclient and smbmount. The smbclient program provides an FTP-like access to remote shares, but smbmount actually mounts the share in the Linux directory tree. The standard Linux mount command can also mount SMB/CIFS shares.

To use smbmount, type **smbmount //server/share /mount/point**, where *server* and *share* are the name of the server and the share you want to access, respectively, and */mount/point* is the local mount point you want to use. You'll be asked to provide a password. (By default, smbmount passes your login name as your username.) You can then use standard Linux file-access commands on the share. When you're done, you can use smbumount to unmount the share.

One drawback to smbmount is that it assigns Linux ownership of all files on the remote server to the user who ran the command, unless you use the -o uid=*UID* option, which sets ownership to the user whose user ID is *UID*. You might also need to use the -o username=*name* option, to set the username used to access the shares.

> For ordinary users to run smbmount and smbumount, the smbmnt and smbumount programs must have their SUID bits set, which allows ordinary users to run programs with root privileges. (smbmnt is a helper program to smbmount.) If this isn't the case when Samba is installed, type **chmod a+s /usr/bin/smbmnt /usr/bin/ smbumount** as root. Thereafter, ordinary users will be able to use these programs, but they'll need to own the mount points they use.

Another way to mount SMB/CIFS shares is via the standard Linux mount command. This requires you to pass a filesystem type of either smbfs or cifs with the -t parameter, along with the server and share name rather than a local Linux device filename:

```
# mount -t smbfs //apollo/hschmidt /mnt/al7
```

The smbfs filesystem type code is older than cifs, and provides better-tested but somewhat more limiting features. Most notably, cifs adds support for Unix-specific extensions to SMB/CIFS. These extensions enable cifs to provide limited support for ownership, permissions, symbolic links, and other Linux-style filesystem information. These features are only important when the server supports them, though. Windows servers do not do so, although Samba does. Thus, using cifs may make sense when mounting shares from a Samba server. On the other hand, some older clients, such as Windows 9*x*/Me, lack support for the protocols required by the cifs driver. Therefore, if you want to mount shares from such systems, you *must* use smbfs rather than cifs.

Accessing NFS Shares

Like SMB/CIFS, Sun's NFS is a file sharing protocol, but it was designed with the needs of Unix systems in mind. NFS includes Unix features, like support for owners, groups, and permission strings that aren't supported by SMB/CIFS. Because Linux conforms closely to the Unix model, NFS is the preferred method for file sharing between Linux systems.

In Linux, client access to NFS exports is tightly integrated into normal Linux file-access utilities. Specifically, you use the mount command to mount the NFS exports, and you can then access files stored on the NFS server as if they were ordinary files. To do so, you provide mount with a server hostname or IP address and a path to the directory on the server you want to access, rather than a device filename. For instance, you might issue commands like the following:

```
# mount apollo:/home/hschmidt /mnt/al7
# ls -l /mnt/al7
total 152
-rwxr-xr-x 1 rodsmith users  152576 Mar 29 13:01 drrock.wpd
drwxr-xr-x 1 rodsmith users     512 Apr  2  2000 geology
# cp /mnt/al7/drrock.wpd ./
# umount /mnt/al7
```

It's important to note that you aren't required to enter a password when you access NFS exports. An NFS server allows a specified set of clients to access the exported directories in a more-or-less unrestricted manner; the server relies on the client's security policies to prevent abuses.

Using *df*

If you need information on disk space used on an entire partition, the df command does the job. This command summarizes total, used, and available disk space. You can provide options to df to vary the data it produces:

Produce more intelligible output   Normally, df provides output in 1024-byte blocks. The --human-readable (or -h) option makes it provide listings in labeled units of kilobytes (k), megabytes (M), or gigabytes (G) instead.

Summarize inodes   By default, df displays disk space used, but the --inodes (or -i) option causes df to display information on the consumption of inodes. These are data structures used on Linux filesystems that hold file information. Some filesystems, such as ext2fs, have a fixed number of inodes when formatted. Others, such as FAT and ReiserFS, don't, so this information is spurious or meaningless with these filesystems.

Display local filesystems only   The --local (or -l) option causes df to ignore network filesystems.

Display type code   The --print-type (or -T) option causes df to display the filesystem type code along with other information.

You can type **df** alone or in combination with options to obtain information on your system's mounted partitions. If you want information on just one partition, you can add either the device on which it resides or any file or directory on the filesystem to restrict df's output to that one partition. In action, df works like this:

```
# df -hT
Filesystem     Type  Size  Used Avail Use% Mounted on
/dev/hda9      ext2  2.0G  1.8G   96M  95% /
/dev/hdb5      vfat  2.0G  1.4G  564M  72% /mnt/windows
speaker:/home   nfs  4.5G  2.2G  2.3G  49% /mnt/speaker/home
/dev/hdb7  reiserfs  4.2G  1.9G  2.3G  45% /home
```

The df command is extremely useful in discovering how much free space is available on a disk and how well distributed across partitions your files are.

Linux's ext2 filesystem normally reserves about 5 percent of its available space for root. The intent is that if users come close to filling the disk, there'll be enough space for the system administrator to log in and perform basic maintenance to correct problems. If a critical filesystem were to fill completely, root might not be able to log in.

Defining Standard Filesystems

The /etc/fstab file controls how Linux provides access to disk partitions and removable media devices. Linux supports a unified directory structure in which every disk device (partition or removable disk) is mounted at a particular point in the directory tree. For instance, you might access a floppy disk at /mnt/floppy. The root of this tree is accessed from /. Directories off this root may be other partitions or disks, or they may be ordinary directories. For instance, /etc should be on the same partition as /, but many other directories, such as /home, may correspond to separate partitions. The /etc/fstab file describes how these filesystems are laid out. (The filename fstab is an abbreviation for "filesystem table.")

The /etc/fstab file consists of a series of lines, each of which contains six fields that are separated by one or more spaces or tabs. A line that begins with a hash mark (#) is a comment, and is ignored. Listing 4.2 shows a sample /etc/fstab file.

Listing 4.2: Sample /etc/fstab File

```
#device         mount point   filesystem options            dump fsck
/dev/hda1       /             ext3       defaults              1 1
LABEL=/home     /home         reiserfs   defaults              0 0
/dev/hdb5       /windows      vfat       uid=500,umask=0 0 0
/dev/hdc        /mnt/cdrom    iso9660    user,noauto           0 0
/dev/fd0        /mnt/floppy   auto       user,noauto           0 0
server:/home    /other/home   nfs        user,exec             0 0
//winsrv/shr    /other/win    smbfs      user,credentials=/etc/creds 0 0
/dev/hda4       swap          swap       defaults              0 0
```

The meaning of each field in this file is as follows:

Device   The first column specifies the mount device. These are usually device filenames that reference hard disks, floppy drives, and so on. Some distributions, such as Red Hat, have taken to specifying partitions by their labels, as in the LABEL=/home entry in Listing 4.2. When Linux encounters such an entry, it tries to find the partition whose filesystem has the specified name and mount it. This practice can help reduce problems if partition numbers change, but many filesystems lack these labels. It's also possible to list a network drive, as in server:/home, which is the /home export on the computer called server.

Mount point   The second column specifies the *mount point*; in the unified Linux filesystem, this is where the partition or disk will be mounted. This should usually be an empty directory in another filesystem. The root (/) filesystem is an exception. So is swap space, which is indicated by an entry of swap.

Filesystem type   The filesystem type code is the same as the type code used to mount a filesystem with the mount command. You can use just about any filesystem type code you can use directly with the mount command. A filesystem type code of auto lets the kernel auto-detect the filesystem type, which can be a convenient option for removable media devices. Auto-detection doesn't work with all filesystems, though.

Mount options Most filesystems support several mount options, which modify how the kernel treats the filesystem. You may specify multiple mount options, separated by commas. For instance, `uid=500,umask=0` for `/windows` in Listing 4.2 sets the user ID (owner) of all files to 500 and sets the umask to 0. (Chapter 3 includes a description of the meaning of the user ID and umask.) Table 4.2 summarizes the most common mount options. Type **man mount** or consult filesystem-specific documentation to learn more.

dump operation The next-to-last field contains a 1 if the `dump` utility should back up a partition, or a 0 if it should not. If you never use the `dump` backup program, this option is essentially meaningless. (The `dump` program is a common backup tool, but it's by no means the only one. Backup and restore operations are covered in more detail later in this chapter, in "Backing Up and Restoring a Computer.")

Filesystem check order At boot time, Linux uses the `fsck` program to check filesystem integrity. The final column specifies the order in which this check occurs. A 0 means that `fsck` should *not* check a filesystem. Higher numbers represent the check order. The root partition should have a value of 1, and all others that should be checked should have a value of 2. Some filesystems, such as ReiserFS, should not be automatically checked, and so should have values of 0.

If you add a new hard disk or have to repartition the one you've got, you'll probably need to modify `/etc/fstab`. You might also need to edit it to alter some of its options. For instance, setting the user ID or umask on Windows partitions mounted in Linux may be necessary to let ordinary users write to the partition.

The `credentials` option for the `/other/win` mount point in Listing 4.2 deserves greater elaboration. Ordinarily, most SMB/CIFS shares require a username and password as a means of access control. Although you can use the `username=`*name* and `password=`*pass* options to `smbfs` or `cifs`, these options are undesirable, particularly in `/etc/fstab`, because they leave the password vulnerable to discovery—anybody who can read `/etc/fstab` can read the password. The `credentials=`*file* option provides an alternative—you can use it to point Linux at a file that holds the username and password. This file has labeled lines:

```
username=hschmidt
password=yiW7t9Td
```

Of course, the file you specify (`/etc/creds` in Listing 4.2) must be well protected—it must be readable only to `root`, and perhaps to the user whose share it describes.

Using RAID

Two problems with traditional disk subsystems plague high-performance computers such as midsized and large servers:

Reliability Although modern hard disks are reliable enough for most uses, the consequences of disk failure on truly mission-critical systems can be catastrophic. If the reliability of disk storage can be improved, it should be.

Speed Systems that transfer large amounts of data often run into the speed limitations of modern hard disks.

Both of these problems can be overcome, or at least minimized, by using a technology known as *redundant array of independent disks (RAID)*. Several different forms of RAID exist, and using them requires additional Linux configuration.

Forms of RAID

RAID uses multiple disks and special drivers or controllers. Linux supports several varieties of RAID, each with its own features and priorities:

Linear (append)   This approach is very simple: It enables you to combine partitions from multiple disks into a single large virtual partition. It's more useful for creating partitions larger than your individual disks support than for anything else; it provides no reliability or speed benefits. Total capacity is identical to using the drives in a conventional configuration.

RAID 0 (striping)   This approach is similar to linear mode, but it interleaves data intended for each physical disk—that is, the combined logical partition consists of small strips from each component disk. The result is improved performance, because disk accesses are spread across multiple physical disks. Reliability is not improved, however, and could actually be degraded compared to using a single larger disk, because a failure of *any* disk in the array will cause data loss. Total capacity is identical to using the drives in a conventional configuration.

RAID 1 (mirroring)   A RAID 1 array uses one disk to exactly duplicate the data on another disk—when you write data to the first disk, the data is actually written to both disks. This provides redundancy that can protect against drive failures, but it slows performance, at least when it's implemented in the OS. (Some hardware RAID controllers can perform this task without a performance hit, though.) Total capacity is the same as having a single drive—the extra drives provide improved reliability, not capacity per se.

RAID 4/5   This RAID variant combines the features of RAID 0 and RAID 1: It spreads data across multiple disks and provides redundancy. RAID 4/5 does this by using parity bits, which can be used to regenerate data should a single drive stop functioning. RAID 4 stores the parity bits on a single drive, whereas RAID 5 stores them on all the drives. In either event, a set of N identical drives provides a capacity equal to $N-1$ drives.

RAID 6   The latest twist in the RAID world is RAID 6, which works much like RAID 5 but provides protection for failure of *two* drives, rather than the one that can be handled by RAID 4/5. To do this, RAID 6 requires an extra drive—that is, a set of N drives provides the capacity of $N-2$ drives. As of the early 2.6.*x* kernels, RAID 6 is considered experimental, which means it could contain bugs that could cause serious problems.

RAID versions of 1 and above support *hot standby*—a feature that enables an extra drive to be automatically activated and used should one of the main drives fail. This feature requires adding one more drive to the array, above and beyond the requirements described above.

Designing a RAID Array

RAID configuration requires that you decide how to combine multiple partitions to best effect. In theory, you can combine just about any partitions; however, some techniques will help you get the most from your RAID array:

Ensure your computer is adequate.   Old computers may lack the internal data-processing capacity to make effective use of a RAID array of modern disks. This is particularly true of 486 and earlier computers that lack the Peripheral Component Interconnect (PCI) bus. Ideally, the disk controller circuitry should be built into the motherboard's chipset, which can improve its throughput.

Place disks on different controllers.   For best performance, use different disk controllers or host adapters for your disks. This advice is less important for SCSI than for ATA; ATA support for multiple simultaneous transfers on a single controller is very limited, so you shouldn't attempt to combine the master and slave devices on one cable into a single RAID array.

Use hardware RAID.   Some disk controllers support hardware RAID. These devices can provide superior performance, particularly for RAID 1 and above. Unfortunately, identifying these controllers can be tricky—many claim to support RAID, but they really provide a few minimal hooks and Windows drivers. Such devices present no advantages in Linux over conventional controllers. If you use a hardware RAID controller, consult its documentation, and the documentation for its Linux drivers, for information on its use; the upcoming section, "Linux RAID Configuration," does *not* apply to such controllers.

Use disks of similar performance.   You should use disks that are as similar as possible in performance and capacity—ideally, all the disks in an array should be the same model. If performance varies wildly between disks, you'd probably be better off simply using the faster drive than trying to use a RAID array, at least if your goal is improved disk performance.

Use identically sized partitions.   Linux's RAID configuration combines partitions together. This works best when the partitions are as close as possible in size. If you try to combine partitions of different sizes, the "extra" space in the larger partition will be wasted.

Configuring the system to boot using RAID.   Unless you use a hardware RAID controller, your computer's BIOS won't understand your RAID configuration. Because the BIOS must read the kernel, you must either place your kernel on a non-RAID partition or use RAID 1 for your kernel's partition (which enables you to refer to an underlying Linux partition in your boot loader). If you want a wholly RAID computer, you can create a separate /boot partition as RAID 1 and use RAID 0 or RAID 5 for your remaining partitions.

You can mix-and-match RAID types on a single Linux RAID array, and even use some non-RAID partitions. (In the latter case, you must either create identically sized non-RAID partitions on all the array's disks or use disks of unequal size, filling the extra space in the larger disks with non-RAID partitions.)

Linux RAID Configuration

To use RAID, you must compile support into your kernel. This support is provided by default by most distributions, but if you need to activate it, look in the Device Drivers ➢ Multi-Device Support (RAID and LVM) section of the kernel.

In addition to kernel support, use of RAID requires one of two software packages: `raidtools` or `mdadm`. Both tools ship with most distributions. The tools differ in their approaches: `raidtools` uses a configuration file, `/etc/raidtab`, to define RAID arrays, whereas `mdadm` is a command-line program in which you can create RAID arrays interactively. This section emphasizes the use of `raidtools`. Whichever program you use, you should use `fdisk` (described earlier, in "Using `fdisk` to Create Partitions") to convert the partitions' type codes to `fd`, using the `t` command in `fdisk`. This type code identifies Linux RAID partitions. Upon boot, Linux will search these partitions for RAID information and should combine them together.

To actually define your RAID configuration using `raidtools`, you use a file called `/etc/raidtab`. A simple RAID 1 configuration looks like this:

```
raiddev /dev/md0
      raid-level            1
      nr-raid-disks         2
      persistent-superblock 1
      nr-spare-disks        1
      device          /dev/sda1
      raid-disk             0
      device          /dev/sdb1
      raid-disk             1
      device          /dev/sdc1
      spare-disk            0
```

This configuration creates a RAID 1 (`raid-level`) device that will subsequently be accessed as `/dev/md0` (`raiddev`). This configuration uses two disks (`nr-raid-disks`) and enables a persistent superblock, which is how Linux stores its RAID information within each RAID partition. The `nr-spare-disks` line defines the number of hot standby disks that are held in reserve—if another disk fails, a spare disk may be automatically called up by the RAID tools as a replacement. (Note that the spare disks, if used, are *not* counted among the RAID disks on the `nr-raid-disks` line.) The following pairs of lines define the partitions that are to be used in the RAID array. The main disks are identified by their conventional device filenames (`device`) and given numbers starting with 0 (`device`). If a spare disk is used, it's identified and numbered using the `spare-disk` directive as well.

A RAID 5 configuration looks much the same, but adds a few lines:

```
raiddev /dev/md1
      raid-level              5
      nr-raid-disks           3
      nr-spare-disks          0
      persistent-superblock   1
      parity-algorithm    left-symmetric
      chunk-size             32
      device            /dev/sda2
      raid-disk               0
      device            /dev/sdb2
      raid-disk               1
      device            /dev/sdc2
      raid-disk               2
```

The first main addition to this configuration is the `parity-algorithm`, which sets how the parity bits should be computed. Possible options are `left-symmetric`, `right-symmetric`, `left-asymmetric`, and `right-asymmetric`. The first of these options usually provides the best performance. The `chunk-size` option sets the size of the stripes used in the array, in kilobytes. This value must be a power of 2. Typical values range from 4 to 128. The best value depends on your hardware, so if you must have the best performance, you'll have to experiment; otherwise, a value of 32 is not unreasonable.

Once you've created your `/etc/raidtab` file, you must initialize the system by using `mkraid`, which takes one or more RAID device filenames as options:

```
# mkraid /dev/md0 /dev/md1
```

This command reads `/etc/raidtab` and initializes the specified devices using the settings in that file. If `mkraid` detects data on the partitions, it may complain; to force it to proceed without complaint, include the `-f` option. Once this is done, you can treat these devices as if they were ordinary disk partitions, creating filesystems and storing files on them. You can even refer to them in `/etc/fstab` to mount them automatically when the system boots.

The `mkraid` command destroys all data on the partitions in question. You should run it only on *new* RAID arrays, and you should double- and triple-check your `/etc/raidtab` file to be sure you haven't inadvertently specified non-RAID disks for inclusion in an array.

Writing to Optical Discs

Optical media are an extremely popular means of exchanging moderately large files. Most CD-R and CD-RW media hold 700MB of files (older discs held 650MB), while recordable DVD formats have capacities of several gigabytes. Plain write-once CD-R discs cost 50 cents or less and are likely to remain readable for several decades, given proper storage, so they're an excellent low-cost archival medium. You can't simply mount an optical disc and write files to it as you would a floppy disk, though; you must create a complete filesystem and then copy (or "burn") that filesystem to the disc. This process requires using two tools, `mkisofs` and `cdrecord`; or variants of or front-ends to these tools.

Linux Optical Disc Tools

The Linux optical disc creation process involves three steps:

1. Collect source files. You must first collect source files in one location, typically a single subdirectory of your home directory.

2. Create a filesystem. You point a filesystem-creation program, `mkisofs`, at your source directory. This program generates an ISO-9660 filesystem in an image file. Alternatively, you can create another filesystem in an appropriately sized partition or image file and copy

files to that partition or image file. This latter approach can be used to create ext2fs, FAT, or other types of optical discs, but there's seldom any advantage to doing this.

This section describes *creating* CD-Rs. To *read* a CD-R, you can treat it like a CD-ROM and mount it using a standard removable-media mount point, as described earlier in "Partition Control."

If you install an OS to a partition that's less than 700MB in size, you can back it up by burning the partition directly to CD-R. The result is a CD-R that uses the OS's native filesystem. You can restore the backup by using dd, assuming the target partition is exactly the same size as the original. You can do the same with recordable DVDs, but they can support larger partitions.

3. Burn the disc. You use an optical disc burning program, such as `cdrecord`, to copy the image file to the optical device.

Recent Linux distributions provide both `mkisofs` and `cdrecord` in a single package called `cdrtools`.

The traditional three-step approach to optical disc creation is a bit on the tedious side. One way to minimize this tedium is to use GUI front-ends to `mkisofs` and `cdrecord`. These GUI tools provide a point-and-click interface, eliminating the need to remember obscure command-line parameters. Popular GUI Linux optical disc creation tools include:

X-CD-Roast   This program, headquartered at `http://www.xcdroast.org`, was one of the first GUI front-ends to `mkisofs` and `cdrecord`, although the latest versions are substantially improved over earlier versions.

ECLiPt Roaster   This program, which is also known as ERoaster, is part of the ECLiPt project (`http://eclipt.uni-klu.ac.at`), which aims to support various Linux tools and protocols, frequently through the use of GUI front-ends.

GNOME Toaster   This program, which is also known as GToaster, is tightly integrated with GNOME, although it can be used from other environments. Check `http://gnometoaster` `.rulez.org` for more information on this package.

K3B   This program, based at `http://k3b.sourceforge.net`, is a front-end that uses Qt (the KDE toolkit). It's the default optical disc tool for some distributions.

All of these programs work in similar ways, although the details differ. X-CD-Roast must first be run by `root` before ordinary users can use it. Other programs may require setting the SUID bit on the `cdrecord` executable, and ensuring it's owned by `root`, if ordinary users are to use them. In order to work, a GUI front-end must be able to detect your optical drive or be told what it is. On one of my test systems, X-CD-Roast, ECLiPt, and K3B had no problem with this task, but GNOME Toaster failed to detect a CD-R drive. The moral: If one tool doesn't work, try another.

All of these optical disc tools provide a dizzying array of options. For the most part, the default options work quite well, although you will need to provide information to identify your drive and burn speed, as described in the next section. Some mkisofs options can also be important in generating image files that can be read on a wide variety of OSs, as described later in "Creating Cross-Platform Discs."

A Linux Optical Disc Example

If you're unfamiliar with Linux optical disc creation, the gentlest introduction is usually to try a GUI tool. Here's how to do the job using X-CD-Roast:

1. Start the program by typing **xcdroast** in an xterm window or by selecting the program from a desktop environment menu.

> The first time you start X-CD-Roast, it may inform you that you lack sufficient privileges. If so, start the program as root, click Setup, click the Users tab, and ensure that Allow All is selected in the Access by Users area (alternatively, add specific users who should be given write privileges to the list). Click Change Non-root Configuration and confirm that you want to enable non-root mode. After you quit, ordinary users should be able to run X-CD-Roast.

2. Click the Create CD button in the main window.

3. Click the Master Tracks button. The result is the X-CD-Roast track-mastering window, shown in Figure 4.3.

FIGURE 4.3 X-CD-Roast provides GUI tools for specifying what files to include on an optical disc.

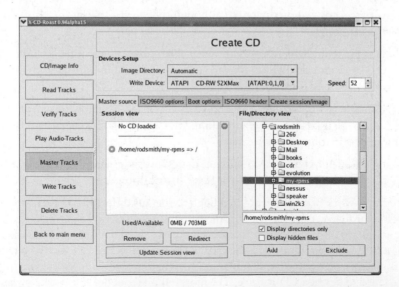

4. Add files and directories to the file list. Do this by selecting the files or directories you want to add in the File/Directory View pane and clicking Add. X-CD-Roast will ask what part of the path to the files or directories you want to keep. Make a selection and click OK. Your selection will appear in the Session View pane.

5. Click the Create Session/Image tab, which brings up the display shown in Figure 4.4. Check in the New Session Size field in the Session Information area to be sure you haven't exceeded the capacity of your media. If you have, go back and remove files.

FIGURE 4.4   Other CD-R creation options are available on additional program tabs.

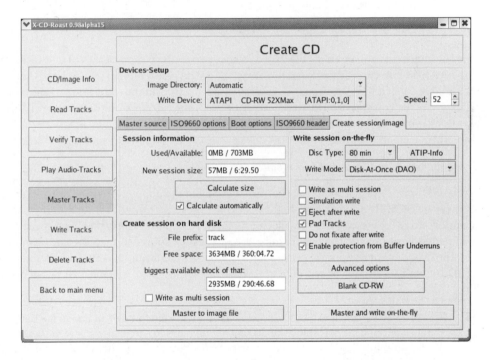

6. Click the ISO-9660 Options tab in the main window. This action displays a large number of options you can set. The defaults are usually fine, but you should be sure that both the Joliet Extension (for Windows) and Rock Ridge (Anonymous) options are selected. You may also want to check the options on the ISO-9660 Header tab, in which you can set a volume title and similar information.

7. From the Create Session/Image tab (see Figure 4.4), click the Master and Write On-the-Fly button. The program displays a dialog box asking for confirmation that you're ready to continue. If you haven't already inserted a blank disc in your drive, do so, and then click OK. The program displays a progress dialog box summarizing the burn operation.

X-CD-Roast presents many additional options, of course. For instance, you can create a bootable disc by using the Boot Options tab (shown in Figures 4.3 and 4.4), selecting the

El Torito (for *x*86) or Sparc (for Sun workstations) option, and entering the path to a bootable floppy disk image in the Boot Image field. You can create audio CD-Rs by placing .wav or other supported audio files in the temporary storage directory (specified from the setup area's HD Settings tab, typically /tmp). Click Write Tracks and use the Layout Tracks tab to select which audio files you want to burn and in what order. You can also burn an existing image file in much the same way—copy the file to the temporary storage directory and tell X-CD-Roast to copy it using the Write Tracks option.

Despite their wide range of options, X-CD-Roast and other GUI tools aren't always the best way to create an optical disc. Sometimes, the command-line tools are the solution. To create an image file, you use the mkisofs command:

```
$ mkisofs -J -r -V "volume name" -o ../image.iso ./
```

This command creates an image file called *image.iso* in the parent of the current directory, placing files from the current working directory (./) in the resultant image file. The -J and -r options enable Joliet and Rock Ridge extensions, respectively, and the -V option sets the volume name to whatever you specify. Dozens of other options and variants on these are available; check the mkisofs man page for details.

Once you've created an image file, you can burn it with a command such as the following:

```
$ cdrecord dev=0,4,0 speed=2 ../image.iso
```

In this example, dev=0,4,0 option specifies that SCSI host adapter 0 is used, burning to the CD-R drive on SCSI ID 4, with logical unit (LUN) 0. Alternatively, with a 2.6.*x* kernel and an ATA optical drive, you can specify the device filename, as in dev=/dev/hdd. The speed is set using the speed option, and the final parameter specifies the source of the file to be burned. As with mkisofs, cdrecord supports many additional options; consult its man page for details. If the SUID bit isn't set on this program, with ownership set to root, you must run it as root.

 You can use the loopback option to verify the contents of an image file before burning it. For instance, typing **mount -t iso9660 -o loop** *image.iso* **/mnt/cdrom** mounts the *image.iso* file to */mnt/cdrom*. You can then check that all the files that should be present are present. You must be root to use this option, or you must have created an appropriate /etc/fstab entry.

Creating Cross-Platform Discs

You may want to create a disc that works on many different OSs. If so, you may want to use a wide range of filesystems and filesystem extensions. Such discs contain just one copy of each file; the filesystems are written in such a way that they all point their unique directory structures at the same files. Thus, the extra space required by such a multiplatform disc is minimal. Features you may want to use on such a disc include:

Follow symbolic links　　The -f option to mkisofs causes the tool to read the files that symbolic links point to and include them on the CD-R, rather than to write symbolic links as such using

Rock Ridge extensions. Following symbolic links can increase the disk space used on a CD-R, but this option is required if you want symbolic links to produce reasonable results on systems that don't understand Rock Ridge, such as Windows.

Long ISO-9660 filenames   Normally, `mkisofs` creates only short filenames for the base ISO-9660 filesystem. Long filenames are stored in Rock Ridge, Joliet, or other filesystem extensions. You can increase the raw ISO-9660 name length to 31 characters with the `-l` (that's a lowercase L) option. This option yields a disc with some files that may not be readable on MS-DOS, but some OSs may display the full filenames when they otherwise wouldn't.

Joliet support   The `-J` option to `mkisofs`, as noted earlier, creates an image with Joliet extensions. These extensions do *not* interfere with reading the disc from OSs that don't understand Joliet.

Rock Ridge support   The `-R` and `-r` options both add Rock Ridge extensions. The `-R` option adds the extensions, but it doesn't change ownership or permissions on files. Using `-r` works the same, except that it changes ownership of all files to **root**, gives all users access to the files, and removes write permissions. These features are usually desirable on a disc that's to be used on any but the original author's computer.

UDF support   You can add support for the Universal Disk Format (UDF) filesystem by including the `-udf` option. UDF is the "up and coming" optical disc filesystem, and is the likely successor to ISO-9660. It's not yet universally supported, though, and in most cases ISO-9660 with Joliet or Rock Ridge support added is quite adequate. As of `cdrtools` 2.0.1, UDF support is considered experimental, and the generated filesystem doesn't support all UDF features.

HFS support   To create a disc that includes Mac OS HFS support, add the `-hfs` option. When you insert the resulting disc into a Macintosh, the computer will read the HFS filenames. A slew of options are related to this one. These options include `-map` *mapping-file* (to point `mkisofs` at a file to map filename extensions to HFS file and creator types), `--netatalk` (to include file and creator types stored on directories used by a Netatalk server), and `-probe` (which tells `mkisofs` to try to determine the creator and type codes by examining the files' contents).

Translation table   You can pass the `-T` option to have `mkisofs` create a file called TRANS.TBL (or something else you specify with the `-table-name` option). This file contains the mapping of long (Rock Ridge) filenames to short (ISO-9660) filenames. This file can be useful if the disc will be read on a DOS system or something else that doesn't understand your long filename extensions.

Because `mkisofs` supports so many filesystems and options, it can be an excellent way to create a disc that's maximally accessible on as many platforms as possible. For instance, you can add all the filesystem options and have a disc that will be readable, complete with long filenames, on Linux, other Unix-like OSs, Windows, and Mac OS. Few other optical disc programs can make this claim.

Backing Up and Restoring a Computer

Many things can go wrong on a computer that might cause it to lose data. Hard disks can fail, you might accidentally enter some extremely destructive command, a cracker might break into your system, or a user might accidentally delete a file, to name just a few possibilities. To protect against such problems, it's important that you maintain good backups of the computer. To do this, select appropriate backup hardware, choose a backup program, and implement backups on a regular schedule. You should also have a plan in place to recover some or all of your data should the need arise.

Common Backup Hardware

Just about any device that can store computer data and read it back can be used as a backup medium. The best backup devices are inexpensive, fast, high in capacity, and reliable. They don't usually need to be *random-access* devices, though. Random-access devices are capable of quickly accessing any piece of data. Hard disks, floppy disks, and CD-ROMs are all random-access devices. These devices contrast with *sequential-access* devices, which must read through all intervening data before accessing the sought-after component. Tapes are the most common sequential-access devices. Table 4.3 summarizes critical information about the most common types of backup device. For some, such as tape, there are higher-capacity (and more expensive) devices for network backups.

TABLE 4.3 Vital Statistics for Common Backup Devices

Device	Cost of Drive	Cost of Media	Uncompressed Capacity	Speed	Access Type
Tape	$200–$4000	$0.50–$4.00/ GB	10–160GB	1–15MB/s	Sequential
Hard disks	$100 (for removable mounting kit)	$1.50/GB (including mounting frame)	60–200GB	15–50MB/s	Random
Removable disks	$75–$2000	$15.00–$100.00/GB	40MB–9.1GB	1–12MB/s	Random
Optical	$50–$4000	$0.50–$5.00/ GB	650MB–9.4GB	1–6MB/s	Random

Numbers are approximate as of late 2004. Prices on all storage media have historically fallen rapidly, and capacities have risen. Costs are likely to be lower, and capacities higher, in the future.

The types of devices that appear in Table 4.3 are those most often used for backing up Linux systems. The pros and cons of using specific devices are:

Tapes   Tape drives have historically been the most popular choice for backing up entire computers. Their sequential-access nature is a hindrance for some applications, but it isn't a problem for routine backups. The biggest problem with tapes is that they're less reliable than some backup media, although reliability varies substantially from one type of tape to another, and the best are reasonably reliable.

Hard disks   It's possible to use hard disks for backup purposes. If your computer is equipped with a kit that enables a drive to be quickly removed from a computer, you can swap hard disks in and out, and move them off-site for storage, if desired. Without such a kit, however, hard drives are susceptible to theft or damage along with the computer they're meant to back up.

Removable disks   Removable disks range from 40MB PocketZip drives to Orb, magneto-optical, and other disks that exceed 2GB in capacity. (Although floppies can in theory be used for backup, their limited capacity and slow speed means they aren't practical for anything but backing up small data files.) The high cost per gigabyte and low capacities of these drives makes them suitable for personal backup of data files, but not of entire systems.

Optical   Optical media are extremely reliable and therefore well suited to long-term archival storage. (Most estimates suggest that CD-Rs, for instance, will last 10–100 years, although some recent studies suggest these estimates may be optimistic.) Some optical media are large enough to back up entire small systems, but for really large jobs, the higher capacity of tapes is desirable. The need to use special tools, such as `cdrecord`, to write to optical devices can complicate backup plans, but this isn't an insurmountable hurdle.

In the past, the best backup devices for entire computers and networks have been tapes. The low cost and high capacity of tapes made them well suited to performing multiple backups of entire computers. In recent years, though, hard disks have plummeted in price, making removable hard disks more appealing than tapes for many applications. It's sometimes desirable to supplement tape or removable hard disk backups with optical backups (typically to 700MB CD-R or CD-RW drives, although recordable DVD media are becoming increasingly affordable and common). CD-R backups are particularly helpful for small client systems, on which an entire installation may fit in 700MB, especially when compression is applied. Because a CD-R can be read in an ordinary CD-ROM drive, it's possible to use a networked backup server to create backups of clients' basic installations and, in an emergency situation, recover the data using an emergency Linux boot floppy, the CD-R, and the computer's ordinary hardware. A tape backup would require dedicated tape hardware on each client, an easily transportable tape drive, or network connections to restore the basic boot system.

If you restrict computers' main installation partitions to about 1–1.4GB, those entire partitions will most likely fit, when compressed, on standard 700MB CD-Rs. This can simplify backup and recovery efforts.

It's generally wise to keep multiple backups and to store some of them away from the computers they're meant to protect. Such off-site storage protects your data in case of fire, vandalism, or other major physical traumas. Keeping several backups makes it more likely you'll be able to recover something, even if it's an older backup, should your most recent backup medium fail.

If you decide to use a tape drive, your choices aren't over. Several competing tape formats are in common use. These include Travan, which dominates the low end of the spectrum; digital audio tape (DAT), which is generally considered a step up; digital linear tape (DLT) and Super DLT, which are well respected for use on servers and networks; 8mm, which is similar to DAT but has higher capacities; and Advanced Intelligent Tape (AIT), which is a high-end tape medium. Each of these competes at least partially with some of the others. Travan drives tend to be quite inexpensive (typically $200–$500), but the media are pricey. The other formats feature more costly drives ($500–$4000 for a single drive), but the media cost less. Maximum capacities vary, ranging from under 1GB for obsolete forms of Travan to 20GB for top-of-the-line Travan to 160GB for the largest Super DLT drives. Overall, Travan is a good solution for low-end workstations; DAT is best used on high-end workstations, small servers, and small networks; and the other formats are all good for high-end workstations, servers, and networks.

If you decide to use hard disks in removable mounts as a backup medium, you'll need ordinary internal drives and mounting hardware. The hardware comes in two parts: a mounting bay that fits in the computer and a frame in which you mount the hard drive. To use the system, you slide the frame with hard drive into the mounting bay. You can get by with one of each component, but it's best to buy one frame for each hard drive, which effectively raises the media cost (the frame accounts for roughly 50 cents of the $1.50/GB media cost for hard drives in Table 4.3). From a Linux software point of view, removable hard disk systems work like regular hard disks or other removable disk systems, like Zip disks. Most of these systems use ATA disks, which you'll access as /dev/hdb, /dev/hdc, or some other ATA device identifier. The disks are likely to be partitioned, and the partitions are likely to hold ordinary Linux filesystems.

Common Backup Programs

Linux supports several backup programs. Some are tools designed to back up individual files, directories, or computers. Others build on these simpler tools to provide network backup facilities. Basic backup programs include tar (described in Chapter 5), dump, and cpio. ARKEIA (http://www.arkeia.com) and BRU (http://www.bru.com) are two commercial backup packages that provide explicit network support and GUI front-ends. AMANDA (http://www.amanda.org) is a network-capable scripting package that helps tar or dump perform a backup of an entire network. When dealing with tapes, the mt program is useful for controlling the tape hardware. This section provides a look at cpio and mt as an example of a way to back up a Linux system.

The *cpio* Utility

The cpio program is one of several tools that can be used to back up a computer. It operates on the principle of creating an archive file. That file can be stored on disk, much like a tar archive or RPM package, or it can be directed straight to your tape device. This can be a convenient way to back up the computer, because it requires no intermediate storage. To restore data, you use cpio to read directly from the tape device file.

 The tar program can be used to create backups in much the same way as cpio, although the precise options you use differ. Chapter 5 covers tar in more detail, so consult it in addition to the following description if you want to use tar for backups.

The cpio utility has three operating modes:

Copy-out mode   This mode, activated by use of the -o or --create option, creates an archive and copies files into it.

Copy-in mode   You activate copy-in mode by using the -i or --extract option. This mode extracts data from an existing archive. If you provide a filename or a pattern to match, cpio will extract only the files whose names match the pattern you provide.

Copy-pass mode   This mode is activated by the -p or --pass-through option. It combines the copy-out and copy-in modes, enabling you to copy a directory tree from one location to another.

The copy-out and copy-in modes are named confusingly.

In addition to the options used to select the mode, cpio accepts many other options, the most important of which are summarized in Table 4.4. To back up a computer, you'll combine the --create (or -o) option with one or more of the options in Table 4.4; to restore data, you'll do the same, but use --extract (or -i). In either case, cpio acts on filenames that you type at the console. In practice, you'll probably use the redirection operator (<) to pass a filename list to the program.

TABLE 4.4   Options for use with cpio

Option	Abbreviation	Description
--reset-access-time	-a	Resets the access time after reading a file, so that it doesn't appear to have been read.
--append	-A	Appends data to an existing archive.
--pattern-file=*filename*	-E *filename*	Uses the contents of *filename* as a list of files to be extracted in copy-in mode.
--file=*filename*	-F *filename*	Uses *filename* as the cpio archive file; if this parameter is omitted, cpio uses standard input or output.
--format=*format*	-H *format*	Uses a specified format for the archive file. Common values for *format* include bin (the default, an old binary format), crc (a newer binary format with a checksum), and tar (the format used by tar).
N/A	-I *filename*	Uses the specified *filename* instead of standard input. (Unlike -F, this option does not redirect output data.)

TABLE 4.4   Options for use with cpio *(continued)*

Option	Abbreviation	Description
--no-absolute-filenames	N/A	In copy-in mode, extracts files relative to the current directory, even if filenames in the archive contain full directory paths.
N/A	-O *filename*	Uses the specified *filename* instead of standard output. (Unlike -F, this option does not redirect input data.)
--list	-t	Displays a table of contents for the input.
--unconditional	-u	Replaces all files, without first asking for verification.
--verbose	-v	Displays filenames as they're added to or extracted from the archive. When used with -t, displays additional listing information (similar to ls -l).

Using *cpio* or *tar* to Back Up a Computer

The cpio and tar commands are generally considered the lowest common denominator backup programs. Tapes created with cpio or tar can be read on non-Linux systems—something that's often not true of dump archives, whose format is tied to specific filesystems. For this reason, dump must explicitly support whatever filesystem you intend to back up. In early 2005, dump supports Linux's ext2fs and ext3fs, and an XFS-specific dump variant is also available, but versions that support other filesystems, such as ReiserFS and JFS, are not yet available.

On the downside, cpio and tar have a compression problem: These programs don't compress data themselves. To do this, these programs rely on an external program, such as gzip or bzip2, to compress an entire cpio or tar archive. The problem with this approach is that if an error occurs while restoring the compressed archive, all the data from that error onward will be lost. This makes compressed cpio or tar archives risky for backup. Fortunately, most tape drives support compression in their hardware, and these use more robust compression algorithms. Therefore, if your tape drive supports compression, you should *not* compress a cpio or tar backup. Let the tape drive do that job, and if there's a read error at restore, you'll probably lose just one or two files. If your tape drive doesn't include built-in compression features, you should either not compress your backups or use another utility, most of which don't suffer from this problem.

To back up a computer with cpio, a command like the following will do the job:

```
# find / | cpio -oF /dev/st0
```

Because `cpio` expects a list of files on standard input, this command uses the `find` command and a pipe to feed this information to `cpio`. The `-o` option then tells `cpio` to create an archive, and `-F` specifies where it should be created—in this case, it uses `/dev/st0` to create the archive on the tape device.

Both the `find` command and pipes were described in more detail in Chapter 2.

This command, though, has some negative effects. Most notably, it backs up everything, including the contents of the `/proc` filesystem and any mounted removable disks that might be present. You can use the `-xdev` option to `find` to have that program omit mounted directories from its search, but this means you'll have to explicitly list each partition you want to have backed up. For instance, you might use a command like the following to back up the `/home`, root (`/`), `/boot`, and `/var` partitions:

```
# find /home / /boot /var -xdev | cpio -oF /dev/st0
```

This command lists directories in a particular order. Because tape is a sequential-access medium, the system will restore items in the order in which they were backed up. Therefore, for the fastest partial restores, list the filesystems that you most expect to have to restore first. In this example, `/home` is listed first because users sometimes delete files accidentally. Backing up `/home` first, therefore, results in quicker restoration of such files.

Depending on the filesystem you use, you may see a string of `truncating inode number` messages. This happens when you use an old `cpio` format with a filesystem that uses inode numbers greater than 65,536. To overcome this problem, specify another format, such as `crc`, using `-H`.

The procedure for backing up with `tar` is similar; however, `tar` doesn't need a list of files piped to it; you provide a list of files or directories on the command line:

```
# tar cvlpf /dev/st0 /home / /boot /var
```

Ordinarily, `tar` descends the directory tree; the `--one-file-system` (`l`) option prevents this, much like the `-xdev` option to `find`.

For more information on the operation of tar, consult Chapter 5.

After creating a backup with `tar`, you may want to use the `tar --diff` (also known as `--compare`, or d) command to verify the backup you've just written against the files on disk. Alternatively, you can include the `--verify` (W) qualifier to have this done automatically. Verifying your backup doesn't guarantee it will be readable when you need it, but it should at least catch major errors caused by severely degraded tapes. On the other hand, the verification will almost certainly return a few spurious errors because of files whose contents have legitimately changed between being written and being compared. This may be true of log files, for instance.

 Real World Scenario

Backing Up Using Optical Media

Optical media require special backup procedures. Normally, cdrecord accepts input from a program like mkisofs, which creates an ISO-9660 filesystem—the type of filesystem that's most often found on CD-ROMs.

One option for backing up to optical discs is to use mkisofs and then cdrecord to copy files to the disc. If you copy files "raw" in this way, though, you'll lose some information, such as write permission bits. You'll have better luck if you create a cpio or tar file on disk, much as you would when you back up to tape. You would then use mkisofs to place that archive in an ISO-9660 filesystem, and then you would burn the ISO-9660 image file to the optical disc. The result will be a CD-R that you can mount and that will contain an archive you can read with cpio or tar.

A somewhat more direct option is to create an archive file and burn it directly to the optical disc using cdrecord, bypassing mkisofs. Such a disc won't be mountable in the usual way, but you can access the archive directly by using the CD-ROM device file. On restoration, this works much like a tape restore, except that you specify the CD-ROM device filename (such as /dev/cdrom) instead of the tape device filename (such as /dev/st0).

Using *mt* to Control a Tape Drive

In cpio and tar terminology, each backup is a file. This file is likely to contain many files from the original system, but like an RPM or Debian package file, the archive file is a single entity. Sometimes an archive file is far smaller than the tape on which it's placed. If you want to store more than one archive file on a tape, you can do so by using the nonrewinding tape device filename. For instance, the following commands accomplish the same goal as the ones shown in the previous section, but in a somewhat different manner, and with subtly different results:

```
# tar cvlpf /dev/nst0 /home
# tar cvlpf /dev/nst0 /
# tar cvlpf /dev/nst0 /boot
# tar cvlpf /dev/nst0 /var
```

After you issue these commands, the tape will contain four tar files, one for each of the four directories. To access each file after writing them, you need to use a special utility called mt. This program moves forward and backward among tape files and otherwise controls tape features. Its syntax is as follows:

`mt -f device operation [count] [arguments]`

The *device* parameter is the tape device filename. The `mt` utility supports many operations, including the following:

`fsf`   Moves forward *count* files.

`bsf`   Moves backward *count* files.

`eod or seod`   Moves to the end of data on the tape.

`rewind`   Rewinds the tape.

`offline or rewoffl`   Rewinds and unloads the tape. (Unloading is meaningless on some drives but ejects the tape on others.)

`retension`   Rewinds the tape, winds it to the end, and then rewinds it again. This action improves reliability with some types of tape, particularly if the tape has been sitting unused for several months.

`erase`   Erases the tape. (This command usually doesn't actually erase the data; it just marks the tape as being empty.)

`status`   Displays information on the tape drive.

`load`   Loads a tape into the drive. Unnecessary with many drives.

`compression`   Enables or disables compression by passing an argument of 1 or 0, respectively.

`datcompression`   Also enables and disables compression.

The compression and datcompression operations aren't identical; sometimes a tape drive works with one but not the other.

For instance, suppose you created a backup on a SCSI tape, but now you want to create another backup on the same tape without eliminating the first backup. You could issue the following commands to accomplish this task:

```
# mt -f /dev/nst0 rewind
# mt -f /dev/nst0 fsf 1
# tar cvlpf /dev/nst0 /directory/to/back/up
# mt -f /dev/nst0 offline
```

These commands rewind the tape, space past the first file, create a new backup, and then unload the tape. Such commands are particularly useful when performing incremental backups, as described shortly.

Planning a Backup Schedule

Regular computer backup is important, but precisely *how* regularly is a matter that varies from one system to another. If a computer's contents almost never change (as might be true of a dedicated router or a workstation whose user files reside on a file server), backups once a month or even less often might be in order. For critical file servers, once a day is not too often. You'll have to decide for yourself just how frequently your systems require backup. Take into consideration factors such as how often the data change, the importance of the data, the cost of recovering the data without a current backup, and the cost of making a backup. Costs may be measured in money, your own time, users' lost productivity, and perhaps lost sales.

Even the most zealous backup advocate must admit that creating a full backup of a big system on a regular basis can be a tedious chore. A backup can easily take several hours, depending on backup size and hardware speed. For this reason, most backup packages, including `tar`, support *incremental backups*. You can create these using the `--listed-incremental` `file` qualifier to `tar`, as shown in this example:

```
# tar cvplf /dev/st0 --listed-incremental /root/inc / /home
```

This command stores a list of the files that have been backed up (along with identifying information to help `tar` determine when the files have changed) in `/root/inc`. The next time the same command is issued, `tar` will not back up files that have already been backed up; it will only back up new files. Thus, you can create a schedule in which you do a full backup of the entire computer only occasionally—say, once a week or once a month. You'd do this by deleting the increment file and running a backup as usual. On intervening weeks or days, you can perform an incremental backup, in which only new and changed files are backed up. These incremental backups will take comparatively little time.

With `cpio`, the key to incremental backups is in the list of files fed to the program. You can perform an incremental backup by using `find` options to locate only new files or files that have changed since the last backup. For instance, the `-newer` `file` option to `find` causes that program to return only files that have been modified more recently than `file`. Thus, you could create a file (perhaps a log of your backup activity) during each backup and use it as a way of determining what files have been modified since the last backup.

You can use incremental backups in conjunction with `mt` to store multiple incremental backups on one tape. Typically, you'll have two tapes for a backup set: one for a full backup and one for intervening incremental backups. Suppose you do a full backup on Monday. On Tuesday, you'd insert the incremental tape and perform the first incremental backup. On Wednesday, you'd insert this tape and type `mt -f /dev/nst0 fsf 1` to skip past Tuesday's incremental backup, and then perform another incremental backup. On Thursday, you'd type `mt -f /dev/nst0 fsf 2`, and so on.

Performing incremental backups has a couple of drawbacks. One is that they complicate restoration. Suppose you do a full backup on Monday and incremental backups every other day. If a system fails on Friday, you'll need to restore the full backup and several incremental backups. Second, after restoring an incremental backup, your system will contain files that you'd deleted since the full backup. If files have short life spans on a computer, this can result in a lot of "dead" files being restored when the time comes to do so.

Despite these problems, incremental backups can be an extremely useful tool for helping make backups manageable. They can also reduce wear and tear on tapes and tape drives, and they can minimize the time it takes to restore files if you know that the files you need to restore were backed up on an incremental tape.

Whether you perform incremental backups or nothing but complete backups, you should maintain multiple backups. Murphy's Law guarantees that your backup will fail when you need it most, so having a backup for your backup (even if it's from a week or a month earlier) can help immensely. A typical backup plan includes a rotating set of backup tapes. For instance, you might have two tapes per week—one for a full backup on one day and one to hold several incremental backups. Eight tapes will then hold backups for four weeks.

Preparing for Disaster: Backup Recovery

Creating backups is advisable, but doing this isn't enough. You must also have some way to restore backups in case of disaster. This task involves two aspects: partial restores and emergency recovery.

Partial restores involve recovering just a few noncritical files. For instance, users might come to you and ask you to restore files from their home directories. You can do so fairly easily by using the --extract (x) tar command, as in:

```
# cd /
# tar xvlpf /dev/st0 home/username/filename
```

This sequence involves changing to the root directory and issuing a relative path to the file or directory that must be restored. This is required because tar normally strips away the leading / in files it backs up, so the files are recorded in the archive as relative filenames. If you try to restore a file with an absolute filename, it won't work.

When you're using cpio, the procedure is similar, but you use the --extract (-i) option, along with other options to feed the name of the archive, and perhaps do other things:

```
# cd /
# cpio -ivF /dev/st0 home/username/filename
```

This cpio command uses -F to have cpio retrieve data from the specified file (/dev/st0) rather than from standard input. Alternatively, you could use redirection to do the job, as in cpio -iv < /dev/st0 home/username/filename.

Whether you're using `tar` or `cpio`, you'll need to know the exact name of the file or directory you want to restore in order to do this. If you don't know the exact filename, you may need to use the `--list` (`t`) command to `cpio` or `tar` to examine the entire contents of the tape, or at least everything until you see the file you want to restore.

 If you use incremental backups, you can use the incremental file list to locate the filename you want to restore.

A much more serious problem is that of recovering a system that's badly damaged. If your hard disk has crashed or your system has been invaded by crackers, you must restore the entire system from scratch, without the benefit of your normal installation. You can take any of several approaches to this problem, including the following:

Distribution's installation disk   Most Linux distributions' installation disks have some sort of emergency recovery system. These may come as separate boot floppy images or as options to type during the boot process. In any event, these images are typically small but functional Linux systems with a handful of vital tools, such as `fdisk`, `mkfs`, `Vi`, and `tar`. Check your distribution's documentation or boot its boot media and study its options to learn more.

CD-based Linux system   Several Linux systems are now available that boot from CD-ROM. One example is Knoppix (`http://www.knoppix.com`); another is a demo version of SuSE (`http://www.suse.com`; but the site is being transitioned to Novell's site, `http://www.novell.com`). Both of these systems can be used to help recover or restore a corrupted Linux installation.

Emergency system on removable disk   You can create your own emergency system on a removable disk. If you have a moderately high-capacity removable disk, like a Zip or LS-120 disk, you can create a moderately comfortable Linux system on this disk. The ZipSlack distribution (a variant of Slackware, `http://www.slackware.com`) is particularly handy for this purpose because it's designed to fit on a 100MB Zip disk. You can use this even if your regular installation is of another version of Linux.

Emergency recovery partition   If you plan ahead, you might create a small emergency installation of your preferred distribution alongside the regular installation. You should *not* mount this system in `/etc/fstab`. This system can be useful for recovering from some problems, like software filesystem corruption, but it's not useful for others, like a total hard disk failure.

Partial reinstallation   You can reinstall a minimal Linux system, and then use it to recover your original installation. This approach is much like the emergency recovery partition approach, but it takes more time at disaster recovery. On the other hand, it will work even if your hard disk is completely destroyed.

Whatever approach you choose to use, you should test it before you need it. Learn at least the basics of the tools available in any system you plan to use. If you use unusual backup tools (such as commercial backup software), be sure to copy those tools to your emergency system or have them available on a separate floppy disk. If you'll need to recover clients via network links, test those setups as well.

You may not be able to *completely* test your emergency restore tools. Ideally, you should boot the tools, restore a system, and test that the system works. This may be possible if you have spare hardware on which to experiment, but if you lack this luxury, you may have to make do with performing a test restore of a few files and testing an emergency boot procedure—say, using LOADLIN (a DOS-based boot loader that can boot a Linux system when LILO or GRUB isn't installed or working). Note that a freshly restored system will not be bootable; you'll need a kernel on a DOS boot floppy and LOADLIN, or some other emergency boot system, to boot the first time. You can then reinstall LILO or GRUB to restore the system's ability to boot from the hard disk.

Summary

Linux uses a unified filesystem, which means it doesn't use drive letters as Windows does. Instead, partitions are mounted within a single directory structure, starting at the root (/) partition. You can create filesystems on partitions or removable disks, mount them, store files on them, and back them up individually or across partitions. You can mount partitions temporarily or create entries in /etc/fstab to make changes permanent, as you see fit. You might also want to create a RAID array, which can improve speed, reliability, or both.

Optical media can be very convenient, but they require special tools to be accessed. The mkisofs program creates a filesystem for such media, while cdrecord stores the filesystem on disk. GUI front-ends to these tools, such as X-CD-Roast, can simplify creation of optical discs.

Backup is critically important for most computers, but backup is also often neglected. Traditionally, tapes have been used to back up computers, but the cost of hard disks has dropped so much that removable disks are now a viable alternative for many installations. Typically, systems are backed up using tools designed for this purpose, such as tar, cpio, or BRU. Such programs can write directly to tape devices, or they can be used to create archive files on removable disks. You can also create an archive file that's subsequently stored on an optical disc using cdrecord.

Exam Essentials

Summarize how Linux's filesystem (that is, its directory tree) is structured.   Linux's directory tree begins with the root (/) directory, which holds mostly other directories. Specific directories may hold specific types of information, such as user files in /home and configuration files in /etc. Some of these subdirectories and their subdirectories may in fact be separate partitions, which helps isolate data in the event of filesystem corruption.

Explain the operation of the mount command.   In its basic form, mount takes a device filename and directory and ties the two together so that files on the device may be accessed in the specified directory. A number of parameters and options can modify its function or how it treats the filesystem that it mounts.

Identify when swap space needs to be increased.   The output of the free command shows how much memory Linux is using—both RAM and swap space. When the amount of used swap space approaches available swap space, it's necessary to increase swap space or RAM.

Describe the purpose of a RAID array.   A RAID array may be used to increase disk speed, disk reliability, or both. The array uses multiple disks to work around individual disk speed limitations or to store duplicate copies of (or checksums for) data.

Explain how Linux knows what partitions to mount when it boots.   Linux looks to the /etc/fstab file for information on the filesystems it should mount automatically (and perhaps some that it shouldn't mount automatically, but that should be available for users to mount manually).

Know how to create a new filesystem on a disk or partition.   The mkfs program creates new filesystems on removable media drives or hard disk partitions. This program is actually a front-end to programs that do the actual work, such as mke2fs (aka mkfs.ext2 and mkfs.ext3) for ext2fs and ext3fs.

Describe how to check a filesystem for errors.   The fsck program checks a filesystem's internal consistency. Like mkfs, it's a front-end to filesystem-specific programs, such as e2fsck (aka fsck.ext2 and fsck.ext3) for ext2fs and ext3fs.

Describe how Linux writes to optical media.   Linux uses the mkisofs program to create an ISO-9660 filesystem (and optionally other common optical disc filesystems), which is then burned to the disc by cdrecord. These programs may be piped together, and common GUI front-ends can help in this process by providing a friendlier user interface.

Summarize backup hardware options.   Backup hardware includes tapes, dedicated hard disks, removable disks, and optical media. Tapes have been the most common type of backup hardware in the past, but each of the others has its place for particular backup types, and hard disks have dropped in price enough to make them appealing as an everyday backup medium.

Commands in This Chapter

Command	Description
free	Displays information on total system memory use.
mount	Mounts a partition or device to a specified location in the Linux directory tree.
umount	Removes a partition or device from its location in the Linux directory tree.
df	Displays disk usage information for one or all mounted partitions or devices.
smbmount	Mounts an SMB/CIFS share in the Linux directory tree.
smbumount	Unmounts an SMB/CIFS share from the Linux directory tree.

Command	Description
fdisk	Modifies partitions on an *x*86 computer.
mkfs	Creates a filesystem.
mkswap	Prepares a file or partition to be used as swap space.
swapon	Activates use of swap space.
swapoff	Deactivates use of swap space.
mkisofs	Creates an ISO-9660 filesystem.
cdrecord	Writes a file (typically containing a filesystem created by mkisofs) to an optical disc.
mkraid	Initializes partitions as part of a RAID array, using information in /etc/raidtab.
mdadm	An alternative to mkraid for managing RAID devices.
cpio	Common archive creation tool; often used in backup operations
tar	Common archive creation tool; often used in backup operations
mt	Tape control program; used to move the tape forward and backward, rewind it, set hardware options, and so on.

Review Questions

1. Typing **fdisk -l /dev/hda** on an *x*86 Linux computer produces a listing of four partitions: /dev/hda1, /dev/hda2, /dev/hda5, and /dev/hda6. Which of the following is true?

   A. The disk contains two primary partitions and two extended partitions.

   B. Either /dev/hda1 or /dev/hda2 is an extended partition.

   C. The partition table is corrupted; there should be a /dev/hda3 and a /dev/hda4 before /dev/hda5.

   D. If you add a /dev/hda3 with fdisk, /dev/hda5 will become /dev/hda6, and /dev/hda6 will become /dev/hda7.

2. Which of the following pieces of information can df *not* report?

   A. How long the filesystem has been mounted

   B. The number of inodes used on an ext3fs partition

   C. The filesystem type of a partition

   D. The percentage of available disk space used on a partition

3. Which of the following commands backs up the /home directory to an ATAPI tape drive?

   A. tar cvlpf /home /dev/st0

   B. tar cvlpf /home /dev/ht0

   C. tar cvf /dev/st0 /home

   D. tar cvf /dev/ht0 /home

4. What is wrong with the following commands, which are intended to record an incremental backup on a tape that already holds one incremental backup?

   ```
   # mt -f /dev/st0 fsf 1
   # tar cvlpf /dev/st0 --listed-incremental /root/inc /home
   ```

   A. The mt command should terminate in 2, rather than 1, to skip to the second position on the tape.

   B. When backing up /home, the incremental file must reside in /home, not in /root.

   C. The device filename should be a nonrewinding name (such as /dev/nst0), not a rewinding name (/dev/st0).

   D. The incremental backup must include the root (/) directory; it cannot include only /home.

5. You run Linux's fdisk and modify your partition layout. Before exiting from the program, though, you realize that you've been working on the wrong disk. What can you do to correct this problem?

   A. Nothing; the damage is done, so you'll have to recover data from a backup.

   B. Type **w** to exit from fdisk without saving changes to disk.

   C. Type **q** to exit from fdisk without saving changes to disk.

   D. Type **u** repeatedly to undo the operations you've made in error.

6. What does the following command accomplish?

```
# mkfs -V -t ext2 /dev/sda4
```

   A. It sets the partition table type code for `/dev/sda4` to `ext2`.

   B. It converts a FAT partition into an ext2fs partition without damaging the partition's existing files.

   C. It creates a new ext2 filesystem on `/dev/sda4`, overwriting any existing filesystem and data.

   D. Nothing; the `-V` option isn't valid, and so it causes `mkfs` to abort its operation.

7. You want to allow Linux users running StarOffice to directly edit files stored on a Windows 2000 SMB/CIFS file server. Which of the following would you use to enable this?

   A. Linux's standard NFS file sharing support

   B. An FTP server running on the Windows system

   C. The Linux `smbclient` program

   D. The Linux `smbmount` program

8. What is wrong with the following `/etc/fstab` file entry? (Choose all that apply.)

```
/dev/hda8  nfs  default  0 0
```

   A. The entry is missing a mount-point specification.

   B. All `/etc/fstab` fields should be separated by commas.

   C. The `default` option may only be used with ext2 filesystems.

   D. `/dev/hda8` is a disk partition, but `nfs` indicates a network filesystem.

9. Where may a swap file be located?

   A. Only on the root (/) Linux filesystem

   B. On local read/write Linux filesystems

   C. On NFS or ext2 filesystems

   D. On any partition with more than 512MB of free disk space

10. In which of the following situations would it be *most* reasonable to create a new swap partition?

   A. Your heavily used server is nearly out of swap space and needs no routine maintenance.

   B. A workstation user has been using memory-hungry programs that exceed memory capacity and needs a quick fix.

   C. You're adding a new hard disk to a multiuser system and expect several new users in the next month or so.

   D. A system has been experiencing slow performance because of excessive swapping.

11. Which type of hard disk device is the most common in use today?

   A. SCSI

   B. ATA

   C. SATA

   D. Zip

12. Which of the following is a GUI tool that supports resizing several filesystems, including FAT, ext2fs, and ReiserFS?

A. QTParted

B. Parted

C. Part

D. Trap

13. Which of the following options is used with `fsck` to force it to use a particular filesystem type?

A. `-A`

B. `-N`

C. `-t`

D. `-C`

14. Which of the following utilities would create the following display?

```
              total      used    free  shared  buffers  cached
Mem:         256452    251600    4852       0    10360  130192
-/+ buffers/cache: 111048  145404
Swap:        515100      1332  513768
```

A. mt

B. df

C. swapon

D. free

15. What will be the result of the `root` user running the following command?

`# mount /dev/sdc5 /home2`

A. The contents of /home2 will be mounted on /dev/sdc5 with the default filesystem used and a prompt for options will appear.

B. The contents of /home2 will be mounted on /dev/sdc5 with the filesystem type auto-detected and default options used.

C. The contents of /dev/sdc5 will be mounted on /home2 with the filesystem type auto-detected and default options used.

D. The contents of /dev/sdc5 will be mounted on /home2 with the default filesystem used and a prompt for options will appear.

16. As an administrator, you want to increase the security on a Linux SMB/CIFS client system. You want to accomplish this by storing the authorization information in its own file, rather than in /etc/fstab. When this is done, what /etc/fstab mount option must you use to point to the file?

A. certs=

B. securefile=

C. authorization=

D. credentials=

17. A new server is arriving at the end of the week. It will have four 40GB hard drives installed and configured in a RAID 5 array with no hot standby spare drives. How much data can be stored within this array?

    A. 160GB

    B. 120GB

    C. 80GB

    D. 40GB

18. You have been told by your manager that the server being moved from the test lab to production must have the two drives within it mirrored. What level of RAID is used for mirroring?

    A. RAID 6

    B. RAID 5

    C. RAID 1

    D. RAID 0

19. You need to restore some files that were accidentally deleted. Which of the following commands can be used to list the contents of an archive stored on a SCSI tape?

    A. `cpio -itv > /dev/st0`

    B. `cpio -otv > /dev/st0`

    C. `cpio -otv < /dev/st0`

    D. `cpio -itv < /dev/st0`

20. You arrive at work on Monday morning to find that the server has crashed. All indications point to the crash as occurring after midnight on Monday morning. Scripts automatically do a full backup of the server every Friday night and an incremental backup all other nights. Which tapes do you need to restore the data on a new server? (Choose all that apply.)

    A. Thursday's tape

    B. Friday's tape

    C. Saturday's tape

    D. Sunday's tape

Answers to Review Questions

1. B. Logical partitions are numbered from 5 and up, and they reside inside an extended partition with a number between 1 and 4. Therefore, one of the first two partitions must be an extended partition that houses partitions 5 and 6. Because logical partitions are numbered starting at 5, their numbers won't change if /dev/hda3 is subsequently added. The disk holds one primary, one extended, and two logical partitions.

2. A. A default use of df reports the percentage of disk space used. The number of inodes and file-system types can both be obtained by passing parameters to df. This utility does *not* report how long a filesystem has been mounted.

3. D. The device filename for an ATAPI tape drive is /dev/ht0; /dev/st0 refers to a SCSI tape drive. The target device or filename must follow the --file (f) qualifier; the first two options try to back up the contents of the tape device to the /home file.

4. C. The /dev/st0 device (and /dev/ht0, for that matter) rewinds after every operation. Therefore, the first command as given will wind past the first incremental backup, and then immediately rewind. The second command will therefore overwrite the first incremental backup.

5. C. Linux's fdisk doesn't write changes to disk until you exit from the program by typing **w**. Typing **q** exits without writing those changes, so typing **q** in this situation will avert disaster. Typing **w** would be precisely the wrong thing to do. Typing **u** would do nothing useful since it's not an undo command.

6. C. The mkfs command creates a new filesystem, overwriting any existing data and therefore making existing files inaccessible. This command does not set the partition type code in the partition table. The -V option is valid; it causes mkfs to be more verbose in reporting its activities. The -t ext2 option tells mkfs to create an ext2 filesystem.

7. D. The smbmount program enables you to mount a remote SMB/CIFS share as if it were a local disk. Linux's NFS support would work if the Windows system were running an NFS server, but the question specifies that it's using SMB/CIFS, not NFS. An FTP server on the Windows system would enable file transfers, but not direct file access. The same would be true for the Linux smbclient program.

8. A, D. A mount directory must be specified between the device entry (/dev/hda8) and the file-system type code (nfs). The nfs filesystem type code may only be used with an NFS export specification of the form *server:/export* as the device specification. Fields in /etc/fstab are separated by spaces or tabs, not commas (but commas are used between individual options if several options are specified in the options column). The default option may be used with *any* filesystem type.

9. B. A swap file may be located on local read/write filesystems. This includes, but is not limited to, the root filesystem. Swap space may *not* exist on NFS mounts (which are very slow compared to local disk partitions in any event). The amount of free disk space on the partition is irrelevant, as long as it's sufficient to support the swap file size.

10. C. It's easy to create a swap partition when adding a new disk, and in option C, the new user load might increase the need for memory and swap space, so adding a new swap partition is prudent. In options A and B, adding a swap partition would require downtime while juggling the partitions, and so it would disrupt use of the system. Adding a swap file makes more sense in those cases. In option D, adding swap space won't speed performance much (unless it's on a faster disk than the current swap space); a memory upgrade is in order to reduce reliance on swap space.

11. B. The most common type of disk device today is the ATA hard disk. SCSI drives are widely used, but are surpassed in popularity by ATA. The latest variant on ATA, *serial ATA (SATA)*, may be treated either as ATA or as SCSI, depending on the Linux drivers you use. Zip drives are popular, but for removable media and not as hard disks.

12. A. QTParted is a GUI variant of the GNU Parted program. This program supports resizing several partition types, including FAT, ext2fs, ext3fs, and ReiserFS. Parted is not a GUI tool and the other options are not valid.

13. C. The −t option is used to tell `fsck` what filesystem to use. Normally, `fsck` determines the filesystem type automatically. The −A option causes `fsck` to check all the filesystems marked to be checked in `/etc/fstab`. The −N option tells `fsck` to take no action and to display what it would normally do, without actually doing it. The −C option displays a text-mode progress indicator of the check process.

14. D. The `free` utility would create the display shown. The `mt` command controls a tape device and does not produce output like this. The `df` utility is used to see the amount of free disk space, not memory use. The `swapon` utility enables swap space, but does not produce a summary like this one.

15. C. The command given will cause the contents of `/dev/sdc5` to be mounted on `/home2` with the filesystem type auto-detected and default options used.

16. D. Ordinarily, most SMB/CIFS require a username and password as a means of access control. The `credentials=file` mount option can be used to point Linux at a file that holds the username and sensitive password information.

17. B. In a RAID 5 array, the amount of data that can be stored is equal to the number of disks minus 1, since that amount of space will be used for holding parity information. (Hot standby spare drives further reduce available storage space, if used.) In this case, there are a total of 4 drives. Subtracting one means the amount of data space available is equal to 3 times the 40GB, or a total of 120GB.

18. C. In a RAID 1 array, the disks are mirrored. RAID 5 is an implementation of disk striping with parity, while RAID 0 is disk striping without parity. RAID 6 is an experimental implementation of striping with parity that can survive the failure of two disks at a time.

19. D. With the `cpio` utility, the -i option is used to read in from an external source—in this case coming in (<) from `/dev/st0`. The -tv options are used to show the files on the tape and provide a listing of what is there.

20. Answers: B, C, D. In order to restore the data, you must restore the most recent full backup—which was done on Friday night. After the full restore, you must restore the incremental backups in the order in which they were done. In this case, two incremenatals (Saturday's and Sunday's) were done after the full backup and they must be restored as well.

Chapter

5

Package and Process Management

THE FOLLOWING COMPTIA OBJECTIVES ARE COVERED IN THIS CHAPTER:

- ✓ **1.9 Manage packages after installing the operating systems (e.g., install, uninstall, update) (e.g., RPM,** tar, gzip**)**

- ✓ **2.10 Manage runlevels and system initialization from the CLI and configuration files (e.g.,** /etc/inittab **and** init **command,** /etc/rc.d, rc.local**)**

- ✓ **2.11 Identify, execute, manage and kill processes (e.g.,** ps, kill, killall, bg, fg, jobs, nice, renice, rc**)**

- ✓ **2.12 Differentiate core processes from non-critical services (e.g., PID, PPID,** init**, timer)**

- ✓ **2.13 Repair packages and scripts (e.g., resolving dependencies, file repair)**

- ✓ **2.22 Schedule jobs to execute in the future using "**at**" and "**cron**" daemons**

- ✓ **3.4 Configure the system and perform basic makefile changes to support compiling applications and drivers**

- ✓ **4.6 Set process and special permissions (e.g., SUID, GUID)**

Managing installed software involves a wide variety of tasks, many of which are specific to particular types of software or even individual packages. Other chapters cover some specific examples, such as installing the OS as a whole (covered in Chapter 1, "Installation") or network client and server configuration (Chapter 6, "Networking"). This chapter covers the mechanics of package installation in general, using any of three common packaging schemes. This chapter also covers the basics of handling packages once they're installed and running—that is, managing running programs. This includes running programs as specific users, terminating errant programs, running programs at particular times, and managing programs that should always be running.

Package Concepts

Any OS is defined largely by the files it installs on the computer. In the case of Linux, these files include the Linux kernel; critical utilities stored in directories like /bin, /sbin, /usr/bin, and /usr/sbin; and configuration files stored in /etc. How those files came to reside in their locations is irrelevant to the identity of the computer as a Linux box, but this detail is critically important to the day-to-day duties of a system administrator. When an updated version of a program is released, it's extremely helpful to be able to track down the installed version of the program, determine just what version the installed program is, and update all the necessary files. A failure to do all of this can leave a system with two copies of a program or its support files, which can result in confusion. It's also important that when you install a new program you avoid accidentally overwriting files that belong to another program.

To help you keep track of installed programs, documentation, and so on, various package maintenance utilities have emerged. Some of these, such as the *RPM Package Manager (RPM)* and *Debian package tools*, are tightly woven into various Linux distributions, thus providing a centralized mechanism for program updates.

File Collections

Most programs today consist of several files. Many programs come with one or more documentation files, configuration files, and support programs. For this reason, it's long been common practice, on all platforms, to bundle related files together in one carrier file. This carrier file typically uses compression to save disk space and download time, and it may include information on the placement of specific files once they're extracted and installed on the computer.

Linux package file formats all provide these useful features. A package file may contain a single program file or dozens (even hundreds or thousands) of files. A complete Linux distribution, in turn, consists of hundreds of package files, all designed to coexist and even work together to provide the features associated with Linux.

In addition to providing a common carrier mechanism for package transport, the RPM and Debian package systems provide a means of recording additional information about the package. This information includes a version number, a build number, the name of the package maintainer, the date and time of the package's last compilation, the hostname of the computer that built the package, one or more descriptions of the package, and a few other miscellaneous pieces of information. Typically, you can access all of this information either before or after installing a package on the computer, which can be quite helpful—you can read the package description to determine whether it's really what you want to install, before you do so.

The Installed File Database

One of the problems with a simple file-collection mechanism is that there's no way to track what files you've installed, what files are associated with other files, and so on. It's easy for a system using such a simple package mechanism to fall into chaos or collect stray files. A partial solution to these problems is to maintain a centralized database of installed files, known as the *installed file database*, *package database*, or similar terms. Both the RPM and Debian systems provide this feature. With RPM, the database is stored in the /var/lib/rpm directory; for Debian packages, the database is in /var/lib/dpkg. These directories actually contain several files, each of which tracks a different type of information. Tarballs don't support a package database, although it's possible to have special programs track tarball installations, as Slackware does.

 Tarballs are file collections created by the tar utility program. Although they lack some of the features of RPM and Debian packages, they're more universally compatible, and they're easier to create than RPM or Debian packages.

Most people don't need to understand the details of how the installed file database works; this information is most useful to those who write the tools or need to recover a seriously corrupted system. What is important are the features that the database provides to a Linux system, which include those listed here:

Package information The supplementary information associated with a package—build date, description, version number, and so on—is copied from the package file to the installed file database when you install the package. This allows you to retrieve this information even if you delete the original package file.

File information The database includes information on all of the files installed on the computer via the package system. This information includes the name of the package to which the file belongs so that you can track a file back to its owner. There's also a checksum value and information on file ownership and permissions, which make it possible to detect when a file has been altered—assuming the database hasn't been tampered with. This file information does *not* extend to any files users create or even to nonstandard configuration files for some packages. Standard configuration files are typically tracked, however.

Dependencies   A *dependency* is a reliance of one package on another. For instance, many programs rely on libc. Packages include information on the files or packages on which they depend. This feature allows the package management system to detect these dependencies and prevent installation of a package if its dependencies are unmet. The system can also block the removal of a package if others depend on it.

Provision information   Some packages provide features that are used by other packages. For instance, a mail client may rely on a mail server, and various mail servers exist for Linux. In this case, a simple file or package dependency can't be used because more than one mail server can be used to fulfill the client's requirements. Nonetheless, this feature is essentially a type of dependency.

Whenever you install, remove, or modify a package through a package management system, that system updates its database to reflect the changes you've made. You can then query the database about your installed packages, and the system can use the database when you subsequently modify your installation. In this way, the system can head off trouble—for instance, it can warn you and abort installation of a package if that package contains files that would overwrite files belonging to another package.

The package database does not include information on files or packages installed in any way but through the package management system. For this reason, it's best not to mix different types of packages. Although it's possible to install both RPM and Debian package management systems on one computer, their databases remain separate, thus cutting the benefits of conflict tracking, dependencies, and so on. For instance, you might install an important library in Debian format, but RPM packages that rely on that library won't know the library is installed, and so they will not install unless you provide an override switch. Further, you may not be warned that other programs require the library when you remove or upgrade it, so you might inadvertently break the RPM packages.

Some programs are distributed only in tarball form. In such cases, you can attempt to build an RPM or Debian package from the tarball or install from the tarball without the benefit of a package management system. Although the latter option has the drawbacks just outlined, it's often simpler than trying to create an RPM or Debian package. If you install only a few such programs, chances are you won't have too much trouble, especially if you keep good records on what you're installing from tarballs. Typically, programs you compile from source code go in the /usr/local directory tree, which isn't used by most RPM or Debian packages. This fact helps keep the two program types isolated, further reducing the chance of trouble.

Rebuilding Packages

One of the features of package systems is that they allow you to either install a *binary package* (sometimes referred to as a precompiled package) or recompile a *source package* on your own system. The former approach is usually simpler and less time-consuming, but the latter approach has its advantages, too. Specifically, it's possible to customize a program when you recompile it from source code. This can include both changes to the program source code and compile-time customizations (such as compiling a package on an unusual architecture). Recompilation is possible both with the sophisticated RPM and Debian systems and with simpler tarballs—in fact, the primary means of source code distribution is usually as a tarball.

If you find a tarball for a package that is not available in other forms, you have two basic choices: You can compile or install the software as per the instructions in the tarball, which bypasses your RPM or Debian database if your distribution uses one, or you can create an RPM or Debian package from the original tarball and install the resulting binary package. The former approach is usually simpler when you want to install the package on just one system, despite the drawback of losing package database information. The latter approach is superior if you need to install the package on many similar systems, but it takes more effort—you must create special files to control the creation of a final RPM or Debian package, and then use special commands to create that package.

The upcoming section, "Compiling Source Code," covers the basics of compiling programs from source code. Creating binary RPMs and Debian packages from source code tarballs, though, is beyond the scope of this book. Consult the documentation for the package system for more information. In particular, the RPM HOWTO (`http://tldp.org/HOWTO/RPM-HOWTO`) contains this information for RPM. The book *Red Hat RPM Guide*, by Eric Foster-Johnson (Wiley, 2003) may also be useful for those who need to delve deeply into the RPM system.

Source code is available in formats other than tarballs. Today, many program authors take the time to create *source RPMs*, which are source code packages meant to be processed by the RPM tools. Debian uses a control file, a patch file, and an original source code tarball as an equivalent to a source RPM. These files are most commonly found on sites catering specifically to Debian-based systems. A source RPM is easy to compile into a binary RPM for any given computer; all you need to do is call the `rpm` or `rpmbuild` program (depending on your RPM package version) with the `--rebuild` argument and the name of the source package. (Sometimes additional arguments are needed, as when you are cross-compiling for one platform on another.) This recompilation may take anywhere from a few seconds to several minutes, or conceivably hours for large packages on slow computers. The result is one or more binary RPMs in the `/usr/src/redhat/RPMS/i386` directory or someplace similar (`redhat` may be something else on non-Red Hat distributions, and `i386` may be something else on non-*x*86 platforms or on distributions that optimize for Pentium or later CPUs).

However you do it, recompiling programs from source code has several advantages and disadvantages compared to using a ready-made binary package. One of the primary advantages is that you can control various compilation options, and you can even modify the source code to fix bugs or customize the program for your particular needs. Making such changes is much easier when you start with a tarball than when you start with an RPM or Debian source package, however. Another advantage is that you can compile a program for an unusual distribution. You might not be able to find a package of a particular program for Alpha or PowerPC architectures, for instance, but if a source package is available, you can compile it yourself. Similarly, if you compile a package yourself, you can work around some library incompatibilities you might encounter with prebuilt binaries, particularly if the binaries were created on a distribution other than the one you use.

The primary drawback to compiling your own packages is that it takes time. This problem is exacerbated if you need to install additional development libraries, compilers, or other tools in order to make a package compile. (Many programs need particular utilities to compile but not to run.) Sometimes a source package needs certain versions of other programs to compile, but you may have an incompatible version, making compilation impossible until you change the version you've got. New Linux users also often have troubles with recompiling because of unfamiliarity with the procedures.

The Gentoo Linux distribution was designed to enable users to recompile the entire distribution relatively easily. This process takes many hours (sometimes well over a day), though.

Installing and Removing Packages

The three most common package formats in Linux are RPM packages, Debian packages, and tarballs (files collected together using the `tar` program). Of these three, tarballs are the most primitive, but they are also the most widely supported. Most distributions use RPMs or Debian packages as the basis for most installed files. Therefore, it's important to understand how to use at least one of these two formats for most distributions, as well as tarballs. Compiling from source code has its own challenges and is covered briefly as well.

RPM Packages

The most popular package manager in the Linux world is RPM. In fact, RPM is available on non-Linux platforms, although it sees less use outside the Linux world. The RPM system provides all the basic tools described in the earlier section, "Package Concepts," such as a package database that allows for checking conflicts and ownership of particular files.

RPM Distributions and Conventions

RPM was developed by Red Hat for its own distribution. Red Hat released the software under the General Public License (GPL), so others have been free to use it in their own distributions. In fact, this is precisely what has happened. Some distributions, such as Mandrake, Linux-PPC, and Yellow Dog, are based on Red Hat, and so they use RPMs as well as many other parts of the Red Hat distribution. Others, such as SuSE and Conectiva, borrow less from the Red Hat template, but they do use RPMs. Of course, all Linux distributions share many common components, so even those that weren't originally based on Red Hat are very similar to it in many ways other than just their use of RPM packages. On the other hand, distributions that were originally based on Red Hat have diverged from it over time. As a result, the group of RPM-using distributions shows substantial variability, but all of them are still Linux distributions that provide the same basic tools, such as the Linux kernel, common shells, an X server, and so on.

 Red Hat has splintered into two distributions: Fedora is the downloadable version favored by home users, students, and businesses on a tight budget. The *Red Hat* name is now reserved for the for-pay version of the distribution.

RPM is a cross-platform tool. As noted earlier, some non-Linux Unix systems can use RPM, although most don't use it as their primary package distribution system. RPM supports any CPU architecture. In fact, Red Hat Linux is or has been available for at least five CPUs: x86, AMD64, IA-64, Alpha, and SPARC. Among the distributions mentioned earlier, LinuxPPC and Yellow Dog are PowerPC distributions (they run on Apple PowerMacs and some non-Apple systems), and SuSE is available on x86, AMD64, PowerPC, and Alpha systems. For the most part, source RPMs are transportable across architectures—you can use the same source RPM to build packages for x86, AMD64, PowerPC, Alpha, SPARC, or any other platform you like. Some programs are actually composed of architecture-independent scripts, and so they need no recompilation. There are also documentation and configuration packages that work on any CPU.

The convention for naming RPM packages is as follows:

packagename-a.b.c-x.arch.rpm

Each of the filename components has a specific meaning:

packagename   This is the name of the package, such as samba for the Samba file and print server.

a.b.c   This is the package version number, such as 2.2.7a. The version number doesn't have to be three period-separated numbers, but that's the most common form. The program author assigns the version number.

x   The number following the version number is the *build number* (also known as the *release number*). This number represents minor changes made by the package maintainer, not by the program author. These changes may represent altered startup scripts or configuration files, changed file locations, added documentation, or patches appended to the original program to fix bugs or to make the program more compatible with the target Linux distribution. Some distribution maintainers add a letter code to the build number to distinguish their packages from those of others. Note that these numbers are *not* comparable across package maintainers— George's build number 5 of a package is *not* necessarily an improvement on Susan's build number 4 of the same package.

arch   The final component preceding the .rpm extension is a code for the package's architecture. The i386 architecture code is the most common one; it represents a file compiled for any x86 CPU from the 80386 onward. Some packages include optimizations for Pentiums or above (i586 or i686), and non-x86 binary packages use codes for their CPUs, such as ppc for PowerPC CPUs. Scripts, documentation, and other CPU-independent packages generally use the noarch architecture code. The main exception to this rule is source RPMs, which use the src architecture code.

For instance, the SuSE Linux 9.1 distribution ships with a Samba package called `samba-3.0.4-1.27.i586.rpm`, indicating that this is build 1.27 of Samba 3.0.4, compiled with Pentium optimizations. These naming conventions are just that, though—conventions. It's possible to rename a package however you like, and it will still install and work. The information in the filename is retained within the package. This fact can be useful if you're ever forced to transfer RPMs using a medium that doesn't allow for long filenames. In fact, early versions of SuSE eschewed long filenames, preferring short filenames such as `samba.rpm`.

In an ideal world, any RPM package will install and run on any RPM-based distribution that uses an appropriate CPU type. Unfortunately, compatibility issues can crop up from time to time. These include:

- Distributions may use different versions of the RPM utilities, as described shortly, in "Upgrades to RPM." This problem can completely prevent an RPM from one distribution from being used on another.

- An RPM package designed for one distribution may have dependencies that are unmet in another distribution. A package may require a newer version of a library than is present on the distribution you're using, for instance. This problem can usually be overcome by installing or upgrading the depended-on package, but sometimes this causes problems because the upgrade may break other packages. By rebuilding the package you want to install from a source RPM, you can often work around these problems, but sometimes the underlying source code also needs the upgraded libraries.

- An RPM package may be built to depend on a package of a particular name, such as `samba-client` depending on `samba-common`, but if the distribution you're using has named the package differently, the `rpm` utility will object. You can override this objection by using the `--nodeps` switch, but sometimes the package won't work once installed. Rebuilding from a source RPM may or may not fix this problem.

- Even when a dependency appears to be met, different distributions may include slightly different files in their packages. For this reason, a package meant for one distribution may not run correctly when installed on another distribution. Sometimes installing an additional package will fix this problem.

- Some programs include distribution-specific scripts or configuration files. This problem is particularly acute for servers, which may include startup scripts that go in `/etc/rc.d/init.d` or elsewhere. Overcoming this problem usually requires that you remove the offending script after installing the RPM and either start the server in some other way or write a new startup script, perhaps modeled after one that came with some other server for your distribution.

Despite this list of caveats, mixing and matching RPMs from different distributions usually works reasonably well for most programs, particularly if the distributions are closely related or you rebuild from a source RPM. If you have trouble with an RPM, though, you may do well to try to find an equivalent package that was built with your distribution in mind.

Upgrades to RPM

The earliest versions of RPM were quite primitive by today's standards; for instance, they did not support dependencies. Over time, though, improvements have been made. This fact occasionally causes problems when Red Hat releases a new version of RPM. For instance, Red Hat 7.0 introduced version 4 of the RPM utilities, but version 4 RPM files cannot be installed with most earlier versions of RPM. This led to frustration on the part of many people who used RPM-based distributions in late 2000 because they couldn't use Red Hat 7.0 RPMs on their systems. (RPM 4.3.*x* is current in late 2004.)

It's usually possible to overcome such problems by installing a newer version of RPM and upgrading the RPM database. Unfortunately, there's a chicken-and-egg problem, because without the new version of RPM, it's impossible to install the updated version of RPM. Red Hat and many other RPM-based distribution providers frequently do make a version of the next-generation version of RPM available for older systems. In the case of the switch to RPM 4.0 with Red Hat 7.0, Red Hat has made this upgrade available in its Red Hat 6.2 updates area, for instance. After installing such an upgrade, be sure to type **rpm --rebuilddb** to have the system rebuild your RPM database to conform to the new program's expectations. If you fail to do this, you may be unable to install new programs or access information on old ones.

The *rpm* Command Set

The main RPM utility program is known as rpm. Use this program to install or upgrade a package at the shell prompt. The rpm command has the following syntax:

```
rpm [operation][options] [package-files|package-names]
```

Table 5.1 summarizes the most common rpm operations, and Table 5.2 summarizes the most important options. Be aware, however, that rpm is a very complex tool, so this listing is necessarily incomplete. Tables 5.1 and 5.2 do include information on the most common rpm features, however. For information on operations and options more obscure than those listed in Tables 5.1 and 5.2, see the rpm man pages. Many of rpm's less-used features are devoted to the creation of RPM packages by software developers.

TABLE 5.1   Common *rpm* Operations

Operation	Description
-i	Installs a package; system must *not* contain a package of the same name
-U	Installs a new package or upgrades an existing one
-F or --freshen	Upgrades a package only if an earlier version already exists
-q	Queries a package—finds if a package is installed, what files it contains, and so on

TABLE 5.1   Common *rpm* Operations *(continued)*

Operation	Description
-V or -y or --verify	Verifies a package—checks that its files are present and unchanged since installation
-e	Uninstalls a package
-b	Builds a binary package, given source code and configuration files; moved to the rpmbuild program with RPM version 4.2
--rebuild	Builds a binary package, given a source RPM file; moved to the rpmbuild program with RPM version 4.2
--rebuilddb	Rebuilds the RPM database to fix errors

TABLE 5.2   Common *rpm* Options

Option	Used with Operations	Description
--root *dir*	Any	Modifies the Linux system having a root directory located at *dir*. This option can be used to maintain one Linux installation discrete from another one (say, during OS installation or emergency maintenance).
--force	-i, -U, -F	Forces installation of a package even when it means overwriting existing files or packages.
-h or --hash	-i, -U, -F	Displays a series of hash marks (#) to indicate the progress of the operation.
-v	-i, -U, -F	Used in conjunction with the -h option to produce a uniform number of hash marks for each package.
--nodeps	-i, -U, -F, -e	Performs no dependency checks. Installs or removes the package even if it relies on a package or file that's not present or is required by a package that's not being uninstalled.
--test	-i, -U, -F	Checks for dependencies, conflicts, and other problems without actually installing the package.

TABLE 5.2   Common *rpm* Options *(continued)*

Option	Used with Operations	Description
--prefix *path*	-i, -U, -F	Sets the installation directory to *path* (works only for some packages).
-a or --all	-q, -V	Queries or verifies all packages.
-f *file* or --file *file*	-q, -V	Queries or verifies the package that owns *file*.
-p *package-file*	-q	Queries the uninstalled RPM *package-file*.
-i	-q	Displays package information, including the package maintainer, a short description, and so on.
-R or --requires	-q	Displays the packages and files on which this one depends.
-l or --list	-q	Displays the files contained in the package.

To use rpm, you combine one operation with one or more options. In most cases, you include one or more package names or package filenames as well. (A package filename is a complete filename, but a package name is a shortened version. For instance, a package filename might be samba-3.0.4-1.27.i586.rpm, while the matching package name is samba.) You can either issue the rpm command once for each package, or you can list multiple packages, separated by spaces, on the command line. The latter is often preferable when you're installing or removing several packages, some of which depend on others in the group. Issuing separate commands in this situation requires that you install the depended-on package first or remove it last, whereas issuing a single command allows you to list the packages on the command line in any order.

Some operations require that you give a package filename, and others require a package name. In particular, -i, -U, -F, and the rebuild operations require package filenames; -q, -V, and -e normally take a package name, although the -p option can modify a query (-q) operation to work on a package filename.

When installing or upgrading a package, the -U operation is generally the most useful because it allows you to install the package without manually uninstalling the old one. This one-step operation is particularly helpful when packages contain many dependencies because rpm detects these and can perform the operation should the new package fulfill the dependencies provided by the old one.

WARNING   When upgrading your kernel, install the new one with the -i option rather than -U. This ensures that you'll still have the old kernel to boot, in case the new one gives you troubles.

To use rpm to install or upgrade a package, issue a command similar to the following:

```
# rpm -Uvh samba-3.0.4-1.27.i586.rpm
```

You could also use **rpm -ivh** in place of **rpm -Uvh** if you don't already have a samba package installed.

It's possible to distribute the same program under different names. In this situation, upgrading may fail, or it may produce a duplicate installation, which can yield bizarre program-specific malfunctions. Red Hat has described a formal system for package naming to avoid such problems, but they still occur occasionally. Therefore, it's best to upgrade a package using a subsequent release provided by the same individual or organization that provided the original.

Verify that the package is installed with the **rpm -qi** command, which displays information such as when and on what computer the binary package was built. Listing 5.1 demonstrates this command. (rpm -qi also displays an extended plain-English summary of what the package is, which has been omitted from Listing 5.1.)

Listing 5.1: RPM Query Output

```
$ rpm -qi samba
Name        : samba                    Relocations: (not relocatable)
Version     : 3.0.4                         Vendor: SuSE Linux AG,
➥Nuernberg, Germany
Release     : 1.27                      Build Date: Wed 21 Jul 2004
➥06:01:40 AM EDT
Install date: Fri 27 Aug 2004 09:33:14 PM EDT  Build Host: gambey.suse.de
Group       : Productivity/Networking/Samba  Source RPM:
➥samba-3.0.4-1.27.src.rpm
Size        : 15251557                     License: GPL
Signature   : DSA/SHA1, Wed 21 Jul 2004 06:04:27 AM EDT, Key ID
➥a84edae89c800aca
Packager    : http://www.suse.de/feedback
URL         : http://www.samba.org/
Summary     : A SMB/ CIFS File Server
```

RPM Compared to Other Package Formats

RPM is a very flexible package management system. In most respects, it's comparable to Debian's package manager, and it offers many more features than tarballs do. When compared to Debian packages, the greatest strength of RPMs is probably their ubiquity. Many software packages are available in RPM form from their developers and/or from distribution maintainers.

Distribution packagers frequently modify the original programs in order to make them integrate more smoothly into the distribution as a whole. For instance, distribution-specific startup scripts may be added, program binaries may be relocated from default /usr/local subdirectories, and program source code may be patched to fix bugs or add features. Although these changes can be useful, you may not want them, particularly if you're using a program on another distribution.

The fact that there are so many RPM-based distributions can also be a boon. You may be able to use an RPM intended for one distribution on another, although as noted earlier, this isn't certain. In fact, this advantage can turn into a drawback if you try to mix and match too much—you can wind up with a mishmash of conflicting packages that can be very difficult to disentangle.

The RPMFind Web site, http://rpmfind.net, is an extremely useful resource when you want to find an RPM of a specific program. Another site with similar characteristics is Fresh RPMs, http://www.freshrpms.net. These sites include links to RPMs built by programs' authors, specific distributions' RPMs, and those built by third parties.

Compared to tarballs, RPMs offer much more sophisticated package management tools. This can be important when you're upgrading or removing packages and also for verifying the integrity of installed packages. On the other hand, although RPMs are very common in the Linux world, they're less common on other platforms. Therefore, you're more likely to find tarballs of generic Unix source code, and tarballs are preferred if you've written a program that you intend to distribute for other platforms.

Debian Packages

In their overall features, Debian packages are similar to RPMs, but the details of operation for each differ, and Debian packages are used on different distributions than are RPMs. Because each system uses its own database format, RPMs and Debian packages aren't interchangeable without converting formats.

As the name implies, Debian packages originated with the Debian distribution. Since that time, the format has been adopted by several other distributions, including Libranet and Xandros. Such distributions are derived from the original Debian, which means that packages from the original Debian are likely to work well on other Debian-based systems. Although Debian doesn't emphasize flashy GUI installation or configuration tools, its derivatives—particularly Xandros—add GUI configuration tools to the base Debian system, which makes these distributions more appealing to Linux novices. The original Debian favors a system that's as bug-free as possible, and it tries to adhere strictly to open source software principles rather than invest effort in GUI configuration tools. The original Debian is unusual in that it's maintained by volunteers who are motivated by the desire to build a product they want to use, rather than by a company that is motivated by profits.

Like RPM, the Debian package format is neutral with respect to both OS and CPU type. Debian packages are extremely rare outside Linux, although efforts are under way to create a Debian distribution that uses the GNU Hurd kernel rather than the Linux kernel. Such a distribution would not be Linux, but would closely resemble Debian GNU/Linux in operation and configuration.

The original Debian distribution has been ported to many different CPUs, including $x86$, IA-64, PowerPC, Alpha, 680x0, MIPS, and SPARC. The original architecture was $x86$, and subsequent ports exist at varying levels of maturity. Derivative distributions generally work only on $x86$ systems, but this could change in the future.

Debian packages follow a naming convention similar to those for RPMs, but Debian packages sometimes omit codes in the filename to specify a package's architecture, particularly on $x86$ packages. When these codes are present, they may differ from RPM conventions. For instance, a filename ending in i386.deb indicates an $x86$ binary, **powerpc.deb** is a PowerPC binary, and **all.deb** indicates a CPU-independent package, such as documentation or scripts. As with RPM files, this file-naming convention is only that—a convention. You can rename a file as you see fit, either to include or omit the processor code. There is no code for Debian source packages because, as described in the upcoming section, "Debian Packages Compared to Other Package Formats," Debian source packages actually consist of several separate files.

The *dpkg* Command Set

Debian packages are incompatible with RPM packages, but the basic principles of operation are the same across both package types. Like RPMs, Debian packages include dependency information, and the Debian package utilities maintain a database of installed packages, files, and so on. You use the dpkg command to install a Debian package. This command's syntax is similar to that of rpm:

```
dpkg [options][action] [package-files|package-name]
```

The *action* is the action to be taken; common actions are summarized in Table 5.3. The options (Table 5.4) modify the behavior of the action, much like the options to rpm.

TABLE 5.3 *dpkg* Primary Actions

Action	Description
-i or --install	Installs a package
--configure	Reconfigures an installed package: runs the post-installation script to set site-specific options
-r or --remove	Removes a package, but leaves configuration files intact
-P or --purge	Removes a package, including configuration files
-p or --print-avail	Displays information about an installed package
-I or --info	Displays information about an uninstalled package file

TABLE 5.3   *dpkg* Primary Actions *(continued)*

Action	Description
-l *pattern* or --list *pattern*	Lists all installed packages whose names match *pattern*
-L or --listfiles	Lists the installed files associated with a package
-S *pattern* or --search *pattern*	Locates the package(s) that own the file(s) specified by *pattern*
-C or --audit	Searches for partially installed packages and suggests what to do with them

TABLE 5.4   Options for Fine-Tuning *dpkg* Actions

Option	Used with Actions	Description
--root=*dir*	All	Modifies the Linux system using a root directory located at *dir*. Can be used to maintain one Linux installation discrete from another one, say during OS installation or emergency maintenance.
-B or --auto-deconfigure	-r	Disables packages that rely on one that is being removed.
--force-*things*	Assorted	Forces specific actions to be taken. Consult the dpkg man page for details of *things* this option does.
--ignore-depends=*package*	-i, -r	Ignores dependency information for the specified package.
--no-act	-i, -r	Checks for dependencies, conflicts, and other problems without actually installing or removing the package.
--recursive	-i	Installs all packages that match the package name wildcard in the specified directory and all subdirectories.
-G	-i	Doesn't install the package if a newer version of the same package is already installed.
-E or --skip-same-version	-i	Doesn't install the package if the same version of the package is already installed.

As with rpm, dpkg expects a package name in some cases and a package filename in others. Specifically, --install (-i) and --info (-I) both require the package filename, but the other commands take the shorter package name.

As an example, consider the following command, which installs the samba-common_ 2.2.3a-12.3_i386.deb package:

 # dpkg -i samba-common_2.2.3a-12.3_i386.deb

If you're upgrading a package, you may need to remove an old package before installing the new one. To do this, use the -r option to dpkg, as in

 # dpkg -r samba

To find information on an installed package, use the -p parameter to dpkg, as shown in Listing 5.2. This listing omits an extended English description of what the package does.

Listing 5.2: *dpkg* Package Information Query Output

```
$ dpkg -p samba-common
Package: samba-common
Priority: optional
Section: net
Installed-Size: 5156
Maintainer: Eloy A. Paris <peloy@debian.org>
Architecture: powerpc
Source: samba
Version: 2.2.3a-12.3
Replaces: samba (<= 2.0.5a-2)
Depends: debconf, libpam-modules, libc6 (>= 2.2.4-4), libcupsys2
➥(>= 1.1.13-1), libpam0g (>= 0.72-1)
Filename: pool/updates/main/s/samba/samba-common_2.2.3a-12_powerpc.deb
Size: 1036524
MD5sum: e4b852940d6bdce313cb3e7b668e2c21
```

Debian-based systems often use a somewhat higher-level utility called dselect to handle package installation and removal. The dselect utility provides a text-mode list of installed packages and packages available from a specified source (such as a CD-ROM drive or an FTP site), and it allows you to select which packages you want to install and remove. This interface can be very useful when you want to install several packages, but dpkg is often more convenient when manipulating just one or two packages. Because dpkg can take package filenames as input, it's also the preferred method of installing a package that you download from an unusual source or create yourself.

Using *apt-get*

Another option for Debian package management is the Advanced Package Tool (APT) utilities, and particularly apt-get. This tool enables you to perform easy upgrades of packages, especially if you have a fast Internet connection. Debian-based systems include a file, /etc/apt/sources.list, that specifies locations from which important packages can be obtained. If you installed the OS from a CD-ROM drive, this file will initially list directories on the installation CD-ROM in which packages can be found. There are also likely to be a few lines near the top, commented out with hash marks (#), indicating directories on an FTP or Web site from which you can obtain updated packages. (These lines may be uncommented if you did a network install initially.)

Although APT is most strongly associated with Debian systems, a port to RPM-based systems is also available. Check http://apt4rpm.sourceforge.net for information on this port.

Don't add a site to /etc/apt/sources.list unless you're sure it can be trusted. The apt-get utility does automatic and semiautomatic upgrades, so if you add a network source to sources.list and that source contains unreliable programs or programs with security holes, your system will become vulnerable after upgrading via apt-get.

The apt-get utility works by obtaining information on available packages from the sources listed in /etc/apt/sources.list and then using that information to upgrade or install packages. The syntax is similar to that of dpkg:

apt-get [*options*][*command*] [*package-names*]

Table 5.5 lists the apt-get commands, and Table 5.6 lists the most commonly used options. In most cases, you won't actually use *any* options with apt-get, just a single command and possibly one or more package names. One particularly common use of this utility is to keep your system up to date with any new packages. The following two commands will accomplish this goal, if /etc/apt/sources.list includes pointers to up-to-date file archive FTP sites:

apt-get update
apt-get dist-upgrade

TABLE 5.5   *apt-get* Commands

Command	Description
update	Obtains updated information on packages available from the installation sources listed in /etc/apt/sources.list.
upgrade	Upgrades all installed packages to the newest versions available, based on locally stored information on available packages.
dselect-upgrade	Performs any changes in package status (installation, removal, etc.) left undone after running dselect.

TABLE 5.5 *apt-get* Commands *(continued)*

Command	Description
dist-upgrade	Similar to upgrade, but performs "smart" conflict resolution to avoid upgrading a package if that would break a dependency.
install	Installs a package by package name (not by package filename), obtaining the package from the source that contains the most up-to-date version.
remove	Removes a specified package by package name.
source	Retrieves the newest available source package file by package filename, using information on available packages and installation archives listed in /etc/apt/sources.list.
check	Checks the package database for consistency and broken package installations.
clean	Performs housekeeping to help clear out information on retrieved files from the Debian package database. If you don't use dselect for package management, run this from time to time in order to save disk space.
autoclean	Similar to clean, but only removes information on packages that can no longer be downloaded.

TABLE 5.6 Most Useful *apt-get* Options

Option	Used with Commands	Description
-d or --download-only	upgrade, dselect-upgrade, install, source	Downloads package files but does not install them.
-f or --fix-broken	install, remove	Attempts to fix a system on which dependencies are unsatisfied.
-m, --ignore-missing, or --fix-missing	upgrade, dselect-upgrade, install, remove, source	Ignores all package files that can't be retrieved (because of network errors, missing files, or the like).
-q or --quiet	All	Omits some progress indicator information. May be doubled (for instance, -qq) to produce still less progress information.
-s, --simulate, --just-print, --dry-run, --recon, or --no-act	All	Performs a simulation of the action without actually modifying, installing, or removing files.

TABLE 5.6   Most Useful *apt-get* Options *(continued)*

Option	Used with Commands	Description
-y, --yes, or --assume-yes	All	Produces a "yes" response to any yes/no prompt in installation scripts.
-b, --compile, or --build	source	Compiles a source package after retrieving it.
--no-upgrade	install	Causes apt-get to *not* upgrade a package if an older version is already installed.

If you use apt-get to automatically upgrade all packages on your system, you are effectively giving control of your system to the distribution maintainer. Although Debian or other distribution maintainers are unlikely to try to break into your computer in this way, an automatic update with minimal supervision on your part could easily break something on your system, particularly if you've obtained packages from unusual sources in the past.

Debian Packages Compared to Other Package Formats

The overall functionality of Debian packages is similar to that of RPMs, although there are differences. Debian source packages are not actually single files; they're groups of files—the original source tarball, a patch file that's used to modify the source code (including a file that controls the building of a Debian package), and a .dsc file that contains a digital "signature" to help verify the authenticity of the collection. The Debian package tools can combine these and compile the package to create a Debian binary package. This structure makes Debian source packages slightly less convenient to transport because you must move at least two files (the tarball and patch file; the .dsc file is optional) rather than just one. Debian source packages also support just one patch file, whereas RPM source packages may contain multiple patch files. Although you can certainly combine multiple patch files into one, doing so makes it less clear where a patch comes from, thus making it harder to back out of any given change.

These source package differences are mostly of interest to software developers, however. As a system administrator or end user, you need not normally be concerned with them, unless you must recompile a package from a source form—and even then, the differences between the formats need not be overwhelming. The exact commands and features used by each system differ, but they accomplish similar overall goals.

Because all distributions that use Debian packages are derived from Debian, these distributions tend to be more compatible with one another (in terms of their packages) than RPM-based distributions are. In particular, Debian has defined details of its system startup scripts and many other features to help Debian packages install and run on any Debian-based system. This helps Debian-based systems avoid the sorts of incompatibilities in startup scripts that can cause problems using one distribution's RPMs on another one. Of course, some future distribution could violate Debian's guidelines for these matters, so this advantage isn't guaranteed to hold over time.

As a practical matter, it can be harder to locate Debian packages than RPM packages for some more exotic programs. Nonetheless, Debian maintains a good collection at http:// www.debian.org/distrib/packages, and some program authors make Debian packages available as well. If you can find an RPM but not a Debian package, you may be able to convert the RPM to Debian format using a program called alien. If all else fails, you can use a tarball, but you'll lose the advantages of the Debian package database.

Tarballs

All distributions can use tarballs—files collected together with the tar utility and typically compressed with compress, gzip, or bzip2. Like RPM and Debian packages, tarballs may contain source code, binary files, or architecture-independent files such as documentation or fonts. These files lack dependency information, however, and tar maintains no database of installed files. Therefore, it's harder to remove programs installed via tarballs than it is to remove RPM or Debian packages. Slackware, though, maintains a database of files installed via Slackware's tarballs and the Slackware pkgtool utility.

The Role of *tar* and Tarballs

A multipurpose tool, tar was originally created for archiving files to tape—the name stands for "tape archiver." Because Unix (and hence Linux) treats hardware devices as files, a tape-archiving program like tar can be used to create archives as files on disk. These files can then be compressed, copied to floppy disk or other removable media, sent over a network, and so on.

In the Linux world, tarballs fill a role that's similar to that of zip files in the DOS and Windows worlds. There are differences, however. Zip utilities (including the zip and unzip commands in Linux) compress files and then add them to the archive. By contrast, tar does not directly support compression, so to compress files, the resulting archive is compressed with a second utility, such as gzip, bzip2, or compress. The gzip and bzip2 programs are the most popular on Linux systems, although compress is still used on some older Unix systems. (The gzip utility can uncompress old compress archives.) The resulting file may have two extensions (such as .tar.gz or .tar.bz2), or that dual extension may be combined into a single, three-character extension (.tgz or .tbz) for easy storage on filesystems (like DOS's FAT) that don't support longer or multiple extensions. (The older compress archives used an uppercase Z extension, so these tarballs have .tar.Z extensions.)

Both RPM and Debian packages are similar to tarballs internally. RPM uses a compressed cpio archive (similar to a compressed tar archive) to store its files, and custom file components aside from the cpio archive to store RPM-specific information. Debian packages use tarballs for file storage and a control file, merged together into one file using the ar utility. (This is an archiving utility similar to tar in overall principles.)

Considered as a package distribution mechanism, tarballs are used primarily by the Slackware distribution, which is the oldest of the major Linux distributions still in common use. Slackware eschews flashy configuration tools in favor of a bare-bones approach. In this respect, Slackware resembles Debian, but Slackware uses custom extensions to `tar` as a way of tracking package installations. As noted earlier, Debian also uses source tarballs as part of its source package management system, but most administrators don't need to be concerned with this detail.

Although most other distributions don't rely on tarballs, they can be used with any distribution. Tarballs are particularly likely to be useful when you're faced with the task of compiling a program from source code, and especially if you must modify that source code for your system. If you like, you can go to the effort of creating appropriate control files and turn a source tarball into an RPM or Debian package, but if you only need to use a program on a single computer, it's usually not worth the effort to do this.

Source code in tarball form usually comes with installation instructions. These will probably tell you to edit one or two configuration files, run a configuration command, and run two or three commands to build binary files from the source code and install them on your system. Details vary substantially from one package to another, though, so check the instructions.

Binary tarballs contain precompiled programs. Sometimes the tarball contains the program files in a form that allows you to expand the tarball directly into a target directory. For instance, you could change to the `/usr/local` directory and uncompress the tarball to have the program files dropped directly into `/usr/local/bin`, `/usr/local/man`, and so on. Other times you may need to uncompress the tarball in a temporary directory and then run an installation utility to install the software.

If you're unsure of how to proceed with a tarball installation, extract it into a temporary directory and look for instructions. Sometimes you'll find separate installation instructions on the program's Web site or on the FTP site from which you obtained the software.

The *tar* Command Set

The `tar` program is a complex package with many options. Most of what you'll do with the utility, however, can be covered with a few common commands. Table 5.7 lists the primary `tar` commands, and Table 5.8 lists the qualifiers for these commands that modify what the command does. Whenever you run `tar`, you use exactly one command and you usually use at least one qualifier.

TABLE 5.7   *tar* Commands

Command	Abbreviation	Description
--create	c	Creates an archive
--concatenate	A	Appends tar files to an archive

TABLE 5.7   *tar* Commands *(continued)*

Command	Abbreviation	Description
--append	r	Appends non-tar files to an archive
--update	u	Appends files that are newer than those in an archive
--diff or --compare	d	Compares an archive to files on disk
--list	t	Lists archive contents
--extract or --get	x	Extracts files from an archive

TABLE 5.8   *tar* Qualifiers

Command	Abbreviation	Description
--directory *dir*	C	Changes to directory *dir* before performing operations
--file [*host:*]*file*	f	Uses file called *file* on computer called *host* as the archive file
--listed-incremental *file*	g	Performs incremental backup or restore, using *file* as a list of previously archived files
--one-file-system	l	Backs up or restores only one filesystem (partition)
--multi-volume	M	Creates or extracts a multitape archive
--tape-length *N*	L	Changes tapes after *N* kilobytes
--same-permissions	p	Preserves all protection information
--absolute-paths	P	Retains the leading / on filenames
--verbose	v	Lists all files read or extracted; when used with --list, displays file sizes, ownership, and time stamps
--verify	W	Verifies the archive after writing it
--exclude *file*	(none)	Excludes *file* from the archive

TABLE 5.8   *tar* Qualifiers *(continued)*

Command	Abbreviation	Description
--exclude-from *file*	X	Excludes files listed in *file* from the archive
--gzip or --ungzip	z	Processes archive through gzip
--bzip2	j (some older versions used I or y)	Processes archive through bzip2

Of the commands listed in Table 5.7, the most commonly used are --create, --extract, and --list. The most useful qualifiers from Table 5.8 are --file, --listed-incremental, --one-file-system, --same-permissions, --gzip, --bzip2, and --verbose. (--bzip2 is a fairly recent addition, so it may not work if you're using an older version of tar.) If you fail to specify a filename with the --file qualifier, tar will attempt to use a default device, which is often (but not always) a tape device file.

A typical tar command to extract files from a tarball looks like this:

```
# tar --extract --verbose --gunzip --file  samba-3.0.4.tar.gz
```

This command can be expressed somewhat more succinctly using command abbreviations:

```
# tar xvzf samba-3.0.4.tar.gz
```

In either form, this tar command extracts files from samba-3.0.4.tar.gz to the current directory. Most tarballs include entire directory trees, so this command results in one or more directories being created, if they don't already exist, as well as files within the directories.

Before extracting a tarball, use the --list command to find out what files and directories it contains. This information can help you locate the files stored in the tarball. In addition, it can help you spot problems before they would occur in case a tarball does *not* contain a neat directory structure, but instead contains files that would all be dropped in the current directory.

Tarballs Compared to Other Package Formats

Although all Linux distributions ship with tar, gzip, and usually bzip2, few use these tools as a means of distributing packages that are part of the OS. The reason is that tar lacks any means of maintaining a package database. Although it's possible to create a set of tarballs that together contain a complete Linux distribution, and it's even possible to write installation scripts to install appropriate subsets of tarballs, maintaining such a system poses certain challenges. Without dependency information or information on what files belong to what packages, it can become difficult to remove packages or even install new ones that may depend on other packages. If you install a new mail reader, for instance, it might crash or fail to start because it depends on a library you don't have or on a newer version of a library that you do have. Experienced system administrators can sometimes diagnose such problems without too much trouble, but these difficulties frequently stump new administrators. Slackware overcomes these problems by including dependency files in its tarballs and using a special tool, `pkgtool`, to install packages.

One feature of `tar` that you may find valuable is that the program can be used to easily create packages, as well as extract files from them. You can use this feature to move data files, documentation, or programs you've written or built yourself. Of course, you can also create RPM or Debian packages, but this process is more complex, and the usual method of doing this requires that you provide a tarball of the source code to begin with. It's easiest to create a tarball of all the files in a single directory:

```
# tar cvzf my-stuff.tgz my-stuff-dir
```

A similar command can be used to back up a directory or even an entire computer to tape. Instead of providing a tarball filename, though, you specify the name of a tape device file, such as `/dev/st0` for the first SCSI tape unit. This topic is described further in Chapter 4.

Whether or not you create your own tarballs or your distribution uses tarballs for its packages, you should be familiar with `tar` because of the common nature of tarballs as a source code distribution mechanism and because of `tar`'s utility as a tape backup tool. (You may choose to use other tools for tape backup, but `tar` is the lowest-common-denominator choice for this task.)

Compiling Source Code

Linux's open source nature means that source code is available for most or all of the programs you run. This fact is a curiosity to some users, but it's extremely valuable to others. For instance, you might be able to fix a minor bug or change a default value by modifying the source code and recompiling it. Other times, you may be forced to compile a program from source code—say, if it's an obscure program that's not available in binary form for your computer's CPU.

Some distributions—most notably Gentoo—emphasize locally compiled programs. The idea is that compiling programs locally enables you to set compiler optimizations, add or omit optional libraries, and so on. Such changes can, at least in theory, result in improved system performance. In practice, though, the time involved in compiling everything yourself is likely to be too great to make any minor program efficiency improvements worthwhile. The knowledge required to set good optimization options is also quite substantial. Although Gentoo is a good distribution in other ways, its compile-it-yourself approach isn't a big plus for new Linux users.

Procedures for Compiling and Installing Source Code

Source code can be compiled either as part of a source package for your package format (such as a source RPM) or from an original tarball provided by the program author. In either case, you should see to several prerequisites before compiling a program:

Appropriate compilers   Source code requires one or more compilers and related programs. Most commonly, the GNU Compiler Collection (GCC) is needed, but sometimes programs are written in more exotic languages. The package's documentation should detail these requirements. GCC is installed by default on many Linux systems, but if it's not installed on yours, check your distribution's installation media. Some programs are written in interpreted, rather than compiled, languages. These require you to have an appropriate interpreter package, such as Perl or Python, rather than a compiler.

make   Most compiled programs use a utility called make to direct the compilation process. As with GCC, make is usually installed by default on Linux systems, but you may want to double-check this detail.

Support libraries and header files   All Linux programs rely on one or more *libraries*, which provide support functions used by many different programs. Before you can compile a program, your system must have all the libraries upon which it relies. What's more, compiling a program requires that you have a set of *header files*, which are files that tell a program how to call library functions. On most distributions, the header files are installed separately from the libraries themselves. Typically, the header file package name is similar to that for the library, but includes a term such as dev or devel in the package name. The documentation for the program you're compiling should detail the libraries it requires, but if you're installing from a source tarball, the documentation may not tell you the precise package name you'd install for your distribution; you may need to hunt a bit and perhaps guess.

System resources   Compiling a program takes disk space, CPU time, and RAM. For most programs, the resources required aren't huge by modern standards, but you may want to check, particularly when compiling large programs. Disk space can become an issue with big packages, and the CPU time consumed might interfere with other uses of the system. For this reason, you may want to compile programs at off times, if the computer is normally used for other tasks.

When compiling a source RPM, you pass the --rebuild option to rpm or rpmbuild, depending on your RPM version, as briefly described earlier, in "Rebuilding Packages." With luck, the process will complete without errors. If it doesn't, you face the daunting task of troubleshooting the problem. Most frequently, the issue is a missing development library package (that is, library headers) or development tool. Scrolling back over the output of the build process should yield a clue, such as a comment that a library wasn't present on your system.

Compiling a package from a source tarball cannot be easily summarized in a simple procedure, because the procedure varies from one package to another. After uncompressing the package, you should search for a file called README, README.INSTALL, README.CONFIGURE, or something similar. This file should describe the configuration and installation process. Frequently, the source package includes a script called configure, which you execute to have the package auto-detect your computer's installed libraries and configure itself appropriately.

You may be able to pass options to this script to further customize it—say, to add or remove support for a particular protocol or feature. Read the documentation to learn about such options, because they're highly package-specific.

Some packages are poorly documented. In such cases, reading the configure script itself in a text editor may give you some idea about the options it accepts.

Some programs have no `configure` script, but provide similar functionality through some other means. The Linux kernel itself is one such program—you type **make config**, **make menuconfig**, or **make xconfig** to configure it using text-mode, menu-based text-mode, or GUI tools, respectively. This process is tedious. The upcoming section, "Special Procedures for the Kernel and Drivers," touches on this topic.

Some programs (particularly small ones) don't use configuration scripts. To change their options, you must typically edit a file called `Makefile` or `makefile`. Precisely what you might want to change in this file is highly package-specific, so consult its documentation for details.

You can compile most programs by typing **make** in their source directories. This process can take anywhere from a few seconds to several hours, depending on the package's size and the speed of your computer.

As with compiling a source RPM, compiling source from a source tarball can fail. This can occur either when configuring the package (via a `configure` script or any other method) or during the actual compilation stage. Diagnosing and fixing such problems requires troubleshooting. Typically, the process fails with an error message shortly before the point at which it stopped. This message should provide you with a clue, but it could be cryptic. If you see many lines of errors, scroll up until you find the first one. This is typically the real problem; subsequent errors occur because of the first error and are not themselves diagnostic.

Once you get the package to compile, you must install it. Most packages today include a way to do this by typing a simple command—typically **./install** or **make install**. This command installs all the package components in their default directories (or whatever directories you've specified as part of the configuration process). This process does *not*, though, use your distribution's package management system. If you subsequently install the same package via your distribution's package system, you'll probably end up with two copies of the program. This can cause confusion, because depending on features such as the order of directories in your PATH environment variable, either version might be launched. Some packages include a way to uninstall a program to avoid such problems, or simply to remove the package if you decide you don't want it. Typically, this is done by typing **./uninstall** or **make uninstall** in the package directory.

Special Procedures for the Kernel and Drivers

Kernel compilation is particularly important because the kernel holds most Linux hardware drivers and influences all other aspects of the system. Linux distributions normally ship with kernels that work reasonably well. However, if you want to optimize the system's functioning, one way to do so is to recompile the kernel. In broad strokes, the procedure for doing so is as follows:

1. Obtain kernel source code from `http::://www.kernel.org` or some other trusted source.

2. Extract the kernel source code using `tar`. Typically, it resides in a subdirectory of `/usr/src` named after the kernel version, such as `linux-2.6.9` for Linux 2.6.9.

3. Create a symbolic link called `/usr/src/linux` that points to the directory in which the kernel resides.

4. Change into the `/usr/src/linux` directory.

5. Configure the kernel by typing **make config**, **make menuconfig**, or **make xconfig**. This procedure will present you with a huge number of options. Covering them all here is impossible. You'll need to know a lot about your hardware to select the correct options. If in doubt, compile the option as a module, if possible—that will make it available if it's needed but won't increase the size of the main kernel file. It's best if your kernel contains drivers for your hard disk controller, so be sure to include the appropriate driver.

6. Exit from the configuration utility.

7. Type **make** to build the new kernel. This process is likely to take several minutes and possibly over an hour.

8. With 2.4.*x* or earlier kernels, type **make modules**. This command builds the kernel modules (the parts of the kernel it loads from independent files). This action is handled automatically in step 7 with 2.6.*x* kernels.

9. As `root`, type **make modules_install** to install the kernel modules.

10. As `root`, copy the main kernel file to /boot. The file is stored as `bzImage` in the `arch/i386/boot` subdirectory of the main kernel directory for *x*86 systems—change `i386` to an appropriate architecture code for other CPUs. I recommend adding the version number to the kernel name, as in **cp arch/i386/boot/bzImage /boot/bzImage-2.6.9**.

11. Add the kernel to your boot loader configuration, as described in Chapter 1. *Do not* replace a working boot loader configuration; *add* the new kernel to your boot loader. This way, you can fall back on your working configuration if there's a problem with the new kernel.

12. Reboot the computer to use the new kernel.

Most modern distributions rely on a RAM disk to deliver certain drivers to the kernel. These drivers are needed for reading the hard disk, and providing them on a RAM disk enables the boot loader to read the modules for the main kernel file. When you recompile a kernel yourself, it's usually easier to compile the modules into the main kernel file rather than compile them yourselves and add them to a RAM disk. If you just want to add a single driver to an existing RAM disk or create a new one, though, you can do so with the `mkinitrd` command. One common use of this command is to add a driver you've compiled yourself or obtained in some other way (such as in precompiled module form from a hardware manufacturer). You can do so with the `-m` option, which takes a list of modules you want to add:

```
# mkinitrd -m newmodule.o
```

This command adds the `newmodule.o` module to the current RAM disk. This approach can be simpler than recompiling the kernel if you have a prebuilt kernel module for your system; but if you're recompiling your kernel to get the new module, you might as well add the driver into the main kernel file rather than build it as a module.

> You do *not* need to reconfigure the RAM disk for most kernel drivers, just for drivers that are needed to read files off of the hard disk. Once the kernel has all the drivers it needs to read your hard disk, it can read additional modules from the hard disk itself.

GUI Package Management Tools

The text-mode utilities that underlie all Linux package management systems are very flexible, but they can be intimidating to new administrators. For this reason, several GUI administrative tools also exist. These programs typically serve as front ends to the text-based programs described earlier—that is, they call the text-mode programs and interpret the results in a GUI window. Many distributions ship with their own unique GUI package management tools, and it's impossible to cover them all here. Therefore, this section outlines just one: the Package Management tool that ships with Fedora and Red Hat. Others are similar to this one.

> If you're using a Debian-based system, a utility similar to Package Management is the Storm Package Manager, which was developed for the now-defunct Storm Linux, but it can be used on Debian or other Debian-based systems, and actually ships with Debian.

The Package Management program (see Figure 5.1) ships with Red Hat Linux and is Red Hat's primary GUI interface to the RPM utilities. Package Management supports basic package installation, removal, upgrading, and maintenance functions. It lacks interfaces to some of the more advanced RPM features, such as the tools used to build binary RPMs from source RPMs or to create your own RPM packages. To start it, type **system-config-packages** in a command prompt window such as an xterm or select System Settings ➤ Add/Remove Applications from the Red Hat desktop menu.

The Package Management tool collects packages into groups, such as the X Window System, GNOME Desktop, KDE (K Desktop Environment), and Editors groups, as shown in Figure 5.1. Some package management tools use groups that are encoded in the packages themselves, but the trend in most recent distributions has been to ignore the group information stored in packages.

You can install all the packages in a group by selecting the checkmark next to the group description. This can be a convenient way to install a lot of programs, but you'll often end up installing a lot of unnecessary programs. Instead, you can click the Details button next to a package group to bring up a list of individual packages, as shown in Figure 5.2. This list collects packages in two groups: Standard Packages, which are typically required, and Extra Packages, which are optional. You can expand or collapse these lists by clicking the triangle next to the Standard Packages or Extra Packages lines. Select or deselect individual packages by placing or removing a checkmark in the box next to the package names. When you're done with a package area, click Close.

FIGURE 5.1   The Package Management program provides a point-and-click interface to package management on Fedora and Red Hat systems.

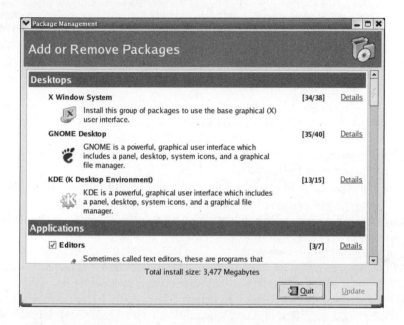

FIGURE 5.2   The Package Details window enables you to fine-tune the packages selected in a given package category.

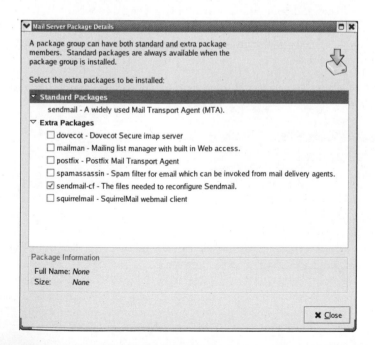

The Package Management tool separates its package group and package listings into two windows, but this isn't true of all package management utilities. Some use a single pane similar to the package group listing of GNOME RPM, but individual packages are included in this list, sometimes using expandable categories similar to the Standard Packages and Extra Packages items in the Red Hat Package Management Package Details window.

When you finish selecting packages to install or uninstall, click the Update button in the main Package Management window. The system will display a progress dialog box as it computes dependencies, and then it presents a dialog box summarizing your changes. Click Continue to install and uninstall packages, as you specified. The system may ask you to insert specific CD-ROMs, and it will display the Updating System dialog box, shown in Figure 5.3.

The Package Management tool can be a convenient way to add software distributed with Fedora or Red Hat; it knows what packages come on the installation media and so can present a complete list in its GUI. Unfortunately, it doesn't know about other packages you might want to add from other sources. For that, you'll need to rely on the text-based tools or locate another GUI package management tool, such as the old GNOME RPM, which shipped with older versions of Red Hat. Also, Red Hat Package Management doesn't know about programs you've already installed from other sources, so you can't use it to remove such packages.

Most modern distributions include tools to help you keep your system up to date in an automated or semiautomated way. Red Hat uses one called Update Agent. SuSE bundles this functionality in its YaST and YaST2 tools. For Debian, it's APT that does this. Most of these tools are GUI utilities, although APT is an exception to this rule. How these tools function differs greatly from one OS to another, but the basic principles are the same: The software checks an online database of packages and compares the available packages to what you have installed. If your packages are too old, the system updates your system to the latest software. This process can be helpful in averting security problems, but it can also cause problems if the new packages break something on your system.

FIGURE 5.3   The Updating System dialog box informs you of the status of your software updates.

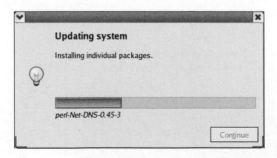

Package Dependencies and Conflicts

Although package installation often proceeds smoothly, there are times when it doesn't. The usual sources of problems relate to unsatisfied dependencies or conflicts between packages. The RPM and Debian package management systems are intended to help you locate and resolve such problems, but on occasion (particularly when mixing packages from different vendors), they can actually cause problems. In either event, it pays to recognize these errors and know how to resolve them.

Although dependency and conflict problems are often described in terms of RPM or Debian package requirements, they also occur with tarballs. These more primitive packages lack the means to automatically detect these problems, although some systems, such as Slackware, add dependency checking to their tarballs.

Real and Imagined Package Dependency Problems

Package dependencies and conflicts can arise for a variety of reasons, including the following:

Missing libraries or support programs   One of the most common dependency problems is caused by a missing support package. For instance, all K Desktop Environment (KDE) programs rely on Qt, a widget set on which these programs are built. If Qt isn't installed, you won't be able to install any KDE packages using RPMs or Debian packages. Libraries—support code that can be used by many different programs as if it were part of the program itself—are particularly common sources of problems in this respect.

Incompatible libraries or support programs   Even if a library or support program is installed on your system, it may be the wrong version. For instance, if a program requires Qt 3.2, the presence of Qt 2.2 won't do much good. Fortunately, Linux library naming conventions enable you to install multiple versions of a library, in case you have programs with competing requirements.

Duplicate files or features   Conflicts arise when one package includes files that are already installed and that belong to another package. Occasionally, broad features can conflict as well, as in two Web server packages. Feature conflicts are usually accompanied by name conflicts. Conflicts are most common when mixing packages intended for different distributions because distributions may split files up across packages in different ways.

Mismatched names   RPM and Debian package management systems give names to their packages. These names don't always match across distributions. For this reason, if one package checks for another package by name, the first package may not install on another distribution, even if the appropriate package is installed, because that target package has a different name.

Some of these problems are very real and serious. Missing libraries, for instance, must be installed. (Sometimes, though, a seemingly missing library isn't quite as missing as it seems, as described in the upcoming section, "Forcing the Installation.") Others, like mismatched package names, are artifacts of the packaging system. Unfortunately, it's not always easy to tell into which category a conflict fits. When using a package management system, you may be able to use the error message returned by the package system, along with your own experience with and knowledge of specific packages, to make a judgment. For instance, if RPM reports that you're missing a slew of libraries with which you're unfamiliar, you'll probably have to track down at least one package—unless you know you've installed the libraries in some other way, in which case you may want to force the installation.

When installing tarballs, and sometimes when compiling a program from source code, you won't get any error messages during installation; you'll only see problems when you try to run the program. These messages may relay an inability to locate a library or run a file, or they may simply cause the program to crash or otherwise misbehave. Conflicts can be particularly insidious with tarballs because you won't be warned about conflicts, so installing a package can break an existing one, and you might not notice the damage for some time. You can use the `--keep-old-files` qualifier to keep `tar` from overwriting existing files, though.

Workarounds to Package Dependency Problems

When you encounter a package dependency or conflict, what can you do about it? There are several approaches to these problems. Some of these approaches work well in some situations but not others, so you should review the possibilities carefully. The options include forcing the installation, modifying your system to meet the dependency, rebuilding the problem package from source code, and finding another version of the problem package.

Forcing the Installation

One approach is to ignore the issue. Although this sounds risky, in some cases involving failed RPM or Debian dependencies, it's appropriate. For instance, if the dependency is on a package that you installed by compiling the source code yourself, you can safely ignore the dependency. When using rpm, you can tell the program to ignore failed dependencies by using the --nodeps parameter, thus:

```
# rpm -i apackage.rpm --nodeps
```

You can force installation over some other errors, such as conflicts with existing packages, by using the --force parameter:

```
# rpm -i apackage.rpm --force
```

WARNING   Do *not* use --nodeps or --force as a matter of course. Ignoring the dependency checks can lead you into trouble, so you should use these options only when you need to do so. In the case of conflicts, the error messages you get when you first try to install without --force will tell you which packages' files you'll be replacing, so be sure you back them up or are prepared to reinstall the package in case of trouble.

If you're using dpkg, you can use the --ignore-depend=*package*, --force-depends, and --force-conflicts parameters to overcome dependency and conflict problems in Debian-based systems. Because there's less deviation in package names and requirements among Debian-based systems, though, these options are less often needed on such systems.

Upgrading or Replacing the Depended-On Package

Officially, the proper way to overcome a package dependency problem is to install, upgrade, or replace the depended-on package. If a program requires, say, Qt 3.3 or greater, you should upgrade an older version (such as 3.2) to 3.3. To perform such an upgrade, you'll need to track down and install the appropriate package. This usually isn't too difficult if the new package you want comes from a Linux distribution; the appropriate depended-on package should come with the same distribution.

One problem with this approach is that packages intended for different distributions sometimes have differing requirements. If you run Distribution A and install a package that was built for Distribution B, the package will express dependencies in terms of Distribution B's files and versions. The appropriate versions may not be available in a form intended for Distribution A, and by installing Distribution B's versions, you can sometimes cause conflicts with other Distribution A packages. Even if you install the upgraded package and it works, you could run into problems in the future when it comes time to install some other program or upgrade the distribution as a whole—the upgrade installer might not recognize Distribution B's package or might not be able to upgrade to its own newer version.

Rebuilding the Problem Package

Some dependencies result from the libraries and other support utilities installed on the computer that compiled the package, not from requirements in the underlying source code. If the software is recompiled on a system that has different packages, the dependencies will change. Therefore, rebuilding a package from source code can overcome at least some dependencies.

If you use an RPM-based system, the command to rebuild a package is straightforward: You call `rpm` or `rpmbuild` with the name of the source package and use `--rebuild`, as follows:

```
# rpmbuild --rebuild packagename-version.src.rpm
```

Of course, to do this you must have the source RPM for the package. This can usually be obtained from the same location as the binary RPM. When you execute this command, `rpm` extracts the source code and executes whatever commands are required to build a new package—or sometimes several new packages. (One source RPM can build multiple binary RPMs.) The compilation process can take anywhere from a few seconds to several hours, depending on the size of the package and the speed of your computer. The result should be one or more new binary RPMs in `/usr/src/distname/RPMS/arch`, where `distname` is a distribution-specific name (such as `redhat` on Red Hat or `packages` on SuSE) and `arch` is your CPU architecture (such as `i386` or `i586` for *x*86 or `ppc` for PowerPC). You can move these RPMs to any convenient location and install them just like any others.

Source packages are also available for Debian systems, but aside from sites devoted to Debian and related distributions, Debian source packages are rare. The sites that do have these packages provide them in forms that typically install easily on appropriate Debian or related systems. For this reason, it's less likely that you'll rebuild a Debian package from source.

You can also recompile a package from a source tarball. This process is described earlier, in "Compiling Source Code." This section also describes some of the potential pitfalls with compiling source code, whether from a tarball or using a source RPM.

Locating Another Version of the Problem Package

Frequently, the simplest way to fix a dependency problem or package conflict is to use a different version of the package you want to install. This could be a newer or older official version (4.2.3 rather than 4.4.7, say), or it might be the same official version but built for your distribution rather than for another distribution. Sites like RPM Find (`http://www.rpmfind.net`) or Debian's package listing (`http://www.debian.org/distrib/packages`) can be very useful in tracking down alternative versions of a package. Your own distribution's Web or FTP site can also be a good place to locate packages as well.

If the package you're trying to install requires newer libraries than you've got, and you don't want to upgrade those libraries, an older version of the package may work with your existing libraries.

The main problem with locating another version of the package is that sometimes you really need the version that's not installing correctly. It might have features that you need, or it might fix important bugs. On occasion, other versions might not be available, or you might be unable to locate another version of the package in your preferred package format.

Startup Script Problems

One particularly common problem when trying to install servers from one distribution in another is in getting SysV startup scripts working. Although most major Linux distributions use SysV startup scripts, these scripts are not always transportable across distributions. Different distributions frequently implement support routines in unique ways, so these scripts may be incompatible. The result is that the server you installed may not start up, even if the links to the startup scripts are correct, as described later, in "Starting and Stopping Services." Possible workarounds include modifying the startup script that came with the server, building a new script based on another one from your distribution, and starting the server through a local startup script like /etc/rc.d/rc.local or /etc/rc.d/boot.local.

Startup script problems affect only servers and other programs that are started automatically when the computer boots; they don't affect typical user applications or libraries.

Starting and Stopping Services

Once you've installed a package, you must be able to run it. For user programs, this task is accomplished by typing the program's filename at a command prompt or launching it via an icon or menu in a desktop environment or window manager. Other programs, though, are run automatically by Linux itself, typically when the system boots. Some such programs handle routine local services, such as text-based login prompts. Others are servers that make the computer available to remote systems. Several means exist to start and stop such services, including SysV startup scripts, super servers (inetd or xinetd), and local startup scripts.

Linux normally runs any given server using just one of the methods described here, and most distributions provide a single default method of launching a server. This fact is particularly important for SysV startup scripts and xinetd, because both of these methods rely on the presence of configuration files that won't be present if the package maintainer intended that the server be run in some other way.

Starting and Stopping via SysV Scripts

When Linux starts, it enters one of several *runlevels*, each of which corresponds to a specific set of running services. Runlevel 0 shuts down the computer, runlevel 1 configures it to run in a single-user maintenance mode, and runlevel 6 reboots the system. On most Linux systems, runlevel 3 corresponds to a multiuser text-mode boot, and runlevel 5 adds X to the mix (for a GUI login prompt). Slackware uses 3 and 4 for these functions, though. By default, Debian attempts to start X in all its runlevels. In any event, one or two runlevels are unused by default. You can start and stop services controlled through SysV startup scripts either temporarily by running the scripts manually or permanently by setting appropriate links to have the system start or stop the service when it reboots.

The section "Setting the Runlevel," later in this chapter, covers temporarily or permanently switching runlevels.

The Gentoo distribution uses named runlevels rather than numbered runlevels. This configuration can be handy if you want to define many runlevels and switch to them by name—say, for using a laptop on any of several networks.

Temporarily Starting or Stopping a Service

SysV startup scripts reside in particular directories—normally /etc/rc.d/init.d or /etc/init.d. You may run one of these scripts, followed by an option like start, stop, or restart, to affect the server's run status. (Some startup scripts support additional options, like status. Type the script name without any parameters to see a list of its options.) For instance, the following command starts the Samba server on a Mandrake 10.0 system:

```
# /etc/rc.d/init.d/smb start
```

You'll usually see some indication that the server is starting up. If the script responds with a FAILED message, it typically means that something about the configuration is incorrect, or the server may already be running. You should keep a few things in mind when manually starting or stopping a service in this way:

- The name of the startup script is usually related to the package in question, but it's not fully standardized. For instance, some Samba server packages call their startup scripts smb, but others use samba. A few startup scripts perform fairly complex operations and start several programs. For instance, many distributions include a network or networking script that initializes many network functions.

- SysV startup scripts are designed for specific distributions, and may not work if you install a package on another distribution. For instance, a Red Hat SysV startup script is unlikely to work properly on a SuSE system.

- Startup scripts occasionally appear to work, when in fact the service doesn't operate correctly. You can often find clues to failure in the /var/log/messages file (type tail /var/log/messages to see the last few entries).

- One way to reinitialize a server so that it rereads its configuration files is to use the restart startup script command. Some server packages provide a reload command that makes the server reload its configuration file without shutting down, which is preferable to using restart if users are currently using the server. Some startup scripts don't include a restart or reload command, though. With these, you may need to manually issue the stop command followed by the start command when you change configuration options. Some servers provide commands you can issue directly to have them reread their configuration options without explicitly restarting them as well; consult the server's documentation for details.

Temporarily starting or stopping a service is useful when you need to adjust a configuration, or when you first install a server. It's almost always possible to reconfigure a running Linux system without rebooting it by reconfiguring and restarting its services.

Permanently Starting or Stopping a Service

If you want to permanently change the mix of services your system runs, you may need to adjust which SysV startup scripts the computer runs. As described earlier, Linux determines which services to run by using the runlevel. In addition to the /etc/rc.d/init.d or /etc/init.d directory in which the SysV startup scripts reside, Linux systems host several directories that contain symbolic links to these scripts. These directories are typically named /etc/rc.d/rc*n*.d or /etc/ rc*n*.d, where *n* is a runlevel number. For instance, /etc/rc.d/rc3.d is the directory associated with runlevel 3. Gentoo uses named subdirectories of /etc/runlevels to define its runlevels— for instance, /etc/runlevels/default defines the default runlevel, which the system enters when it boots.

In most distributions, the links in these directories use filenames of the form K*nnservice* or S*nnservice*, where *nn* is a two-digit number and *service* is the name of a service. When the computer enters a given runlevel, it executes the K* and S* scripts in the associated directory. The system passes the start command to the scripts that begin with S, and it sends the stop command to the scripts that begin with K. Thus, the key to controlling the starting and stopping of services is in the naming of the files in these SysV script directories—if you rename a script that starts with S so that it starts with K, it will stop running the next time the system enters the affected runlevel.

The numbers that come after the S and K codes control the order in which various services are started and stopped. The system executes these scripts from the lowest-numbered to the highest-numbered. This factor can be quite important. For instance, you'll normally want to start servers like Samba or Apache *after* basic networking is brought up.

Gentoo is an exception to this rule. Its SysV startup script links are not named in any special way. Instead, the Gentoo startup scripts incorporate dependency information, enabling them to start the services on which they rely. This design greatly simplifies SysV administration on Gentoo systems.

Various tools exist to help you adjust what services run in various runlevels. Not all distributions include all these tools, though. Some of the tools for adjusting services are:

chkconfig   This command-line utility is most common on Red Hat and related distributions; some don't include it. Pass it the --list parameter to see a summary of services and whether or not they're enabled in each runlevel. You can add or delete a service in a given runlevel by using the --level parameter, as in **chkconfig --level 5 smb on**, which enables Samba in runlevel 5. (Pass it off rather than on to disable a service.)

rc-update   This tool is Gentoo's equivalent of chkconfig. To add a script to a runlevel, type **rc-update add *script runlevels***, where *script* is the name of the SysV startup script and *runlevels* is one or more runlevel names. Replace add with del to remove a script from a runlevel. For instance, typing **rc-update add samba default** adds the samba startup script to the default runlevel, causing Samba to run when the system boots.

ntsysv   This is a text-mode utility that, like chkconfig, is most common on Red Hat and related distributions. It presents a menu of services run at the runlevel specified with the --level parameter. You can enable or disable a service by moving the cursor to the runlevel and pressing the spacebar.

ksysv   Figure 5.4 shows this GUI utility. It allows you to enable or disable services in any runlevel from 1 through 6. Locate and select the service in the Start or Stop section of the given runlevel, right-click the entry, and then select Cut from the pop-up menu. This removes its start or stop entry. You can then drag the service from the Available Services list to the runlevel's Start or Stop list. The system will create an entry in that runlevel and give it a sequence number based on the location to which you dropped it.

Distribution-specific tools   Many distributions' general system administration tools, such as Red Hat's Service Configuration tool and SuSE's YaST, provide the means to start and stop SysV services in specific runlevels. Details vary from one distribution to another, so consult your distribution's documentation to learn more.

FIGURE 5.4   The ksysv program provides a GUI interface to runlevel service management.

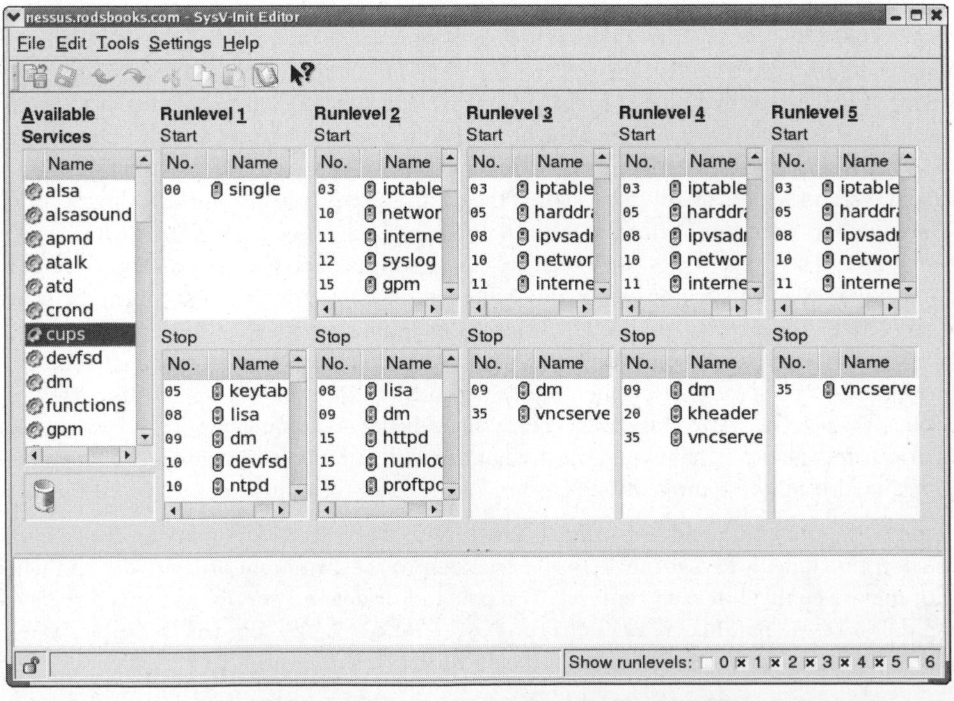

Once you've modified a service's SysV startup script listings, that service will run (or not run, if you've disabled it) the next time you restart the computer or change runlevels, as described in the upcoming section "Setting the Runlevel." Setting the startup script runlevel information, however, does not immediately run or shut down a service. For that, you'll need to manually enable or disable the service, as described earlier.

One additional method of permanently disabling a service deserves mention: removing it completely from the computer. You can use a package management system, or you can track down the program's binary files and delete them, to ensure that a service never runs. This is certainly the best way to accomplish the task if the computer never needs to run a program, because it saves on disk space and makes it impossible to misconfigure the computer to run an unwanted server—at least, short of reinstalling the server.

Editing *inetd.conf*

One of the problems with running servers through SysV startup scripts is that the running servers constantly consume memory, even if they're not used much. This is one of the primary motivating factors behind *super servers*, which are servers that listen for network connections intended for any of several other servers. When the super server detects such a connection, it launches the appropriate conventional server. Prior to that time, the conventional server was not running, and so it did not consume any memory. The drawback to this arrangement is that it may take some time for the conventional server to start up, particularly if it's a large one like Samba or Apache. This can result in delays in initiating connections. Nonetheless, this approach is common for many smaller and infrequently used servers. Two super servers are common on Linux: inetd, which is described here, and xinetd, which is described in the next section.

Be sure you edit the appropriate configuration file! Administrators used to one tool are often confused when they work on a system that uses the other super server. The administrator may edit the wrong configuration file and find that changes have no effect. Ideally, a system won't have a configuration file for an uninstalled super server, but sometimes these do exist, particularly when a distribution has been upgraded to a new version that changes the super server.

You control servers that launch via inetd through the /etc/inetd.conf file. This file consists of a series of lines, one for each server. A typical line resembles the following:

```
ftp stream tcp nowait root /usr/sbin/tcpd /usr/sbin/in.ftpd -l
```

This and several subsequent examples refer to in.ftpd, an FTP server that was once quite popular but that's being replaced on many systems by other FTP servers. Some of these servers cannot be run from a super server, so using another server might not work in all of these cases.

Each line consists of several fields separated by one or more spaces. The meanings of these fields are:

Service name   The first field (`ftp` in the preceding example) is the name of the service as it appears in the `/etc/services` file.

Socket type   The socket type entry tells the system what type of connection to expect—a reliable two-way connection (`stream`), a less reliable connection with less overhead (`dgram`), a low-level connection to the network (`raw`), or various others. The differences between these types are highly technical; your main concern in editing this entry should be to correctly type the value specified by the server's documentation.

Protocol   This is the type of TCP/IP protocol used, usually `tcp` or `udp`.

Wait/Nowait   For `dgram` socket types, this entry specifies whether the server connects to its client and frees the socket (`nowait`) or processes all its packets and then times out (`wait`). Servers that use other socket types should specify `nowait` in this field.

User   This is the username used to run the server. The `root` and `nobody` users are common choices, but others are possible as well.

Server name   This is the filename of the server. In the preceding example, the server is specified as `/usr/sbin/tcpd`, which is the TCP Wrappers binary. This program provides some security checks, enabling you to restrict access to a server based on the origin and other factors. Chapter 7, "Security," covers TCP Wrappers in more detail.

Parameters   Everything after the server name consists of parameters that are passed to the server. If you use TCP Wrappers, you pass the name of the true target server (such as `/usr/sbin/in.ftpd`) in this field, along with its parameters.

The hash mark (#) is a comment symbol for `/etc/inetd.conf`. Therefore, if a server is running via `inetd` and you want to disable it, you can place a hash mark at the start of the line. If you want to add a server to `inetd.conf`, you'll need to create an entry for it. Most servers that can be run from `inetd` include sample entries in their documentation. Many distributions ship with `inetd.conf` files that include entries for common servers as well, although many of them are commented out; remove the hash mark at the start of the line to activate the server.

After modifying `inetd.conf`, you must restart the `inetd` super server itself. This super server normally runs as a standard SysV server, so you can restart it by typing something similar to the following:

```
# /etc/rc.d/init.d/inetd restart
```

Alternatively, you can tell `inetd` to reload its configuration by passing the SysV startup script the `reload` parameter rather than `restart`. The `restart` option shuts down the server and then starts it again. When you use `reload`, the server never stops running; it just rereads the configuration file and implements any changes. As a practical matter, the two are quite similar. Using `restart` is more likely to correctly implement changes, but it's also more likely to disrupt existing connections.

It's generally wise to disable as many servers as possible in `inetd.conf` (or the `xinetd` configuration files, if you use `xinetd`). As a general rule, if you don't understand what a server does, disable it. This will improve the security of your system by eliminating potentially buggy or misconfigured servers from the equation.

Editing *xinetd.conf* or *xinetd.d* Files

The `xinetd` (pronounced "zi-net-dee") program is an extended super server. It provides the functionality of `inetd`, plus security options that are similar to those of TCP Wrappers. Distributions have been slowly shifting from `inetd` to `xinetd`, although some still use `inetd` by default or at least provide it as an option. If you like, you can replace `inetd` with `xinetd` on any distribution.

The `/etc/xinetd.conf` file controls `xinetd`. Typically, though, this file contains only global default options and a directive to include files stored in `/etc/xinetd.d`. Each server that should run via `xinetd` then installs a file in `/etc/xinetd.d` with its own configuration options.

Whether the entry for a service goes in `/etc/xinetd.conf` or a file in `/etc/xinetd.d`, it contains information similar to that in the `inetd.conf` file. The `xinetd` configuration file spreads the information across multiple lines and labels it more explicitly. Listing 5.3 shows an example that's equivalent to the earlier `inetd.conf` entry. This entry provides precisely the same information as the `inetd.conf` entry except that it doesn't include a reference to `/usr/sbin/tcpd`, the TCP Wrappers binary. Because `xinetd` includes similar functionality, it's generally not used with TCP Wrappers.

Chapter 7 covers `xinetd` security features.

Listing 5.3: Sample `xinetd` Configuration Entry

```
service ftp
{
        socket_type     = stream
        protocol        = tcp
        wait            = no
        user            = root
        server          = /usr/sbin/in.ftpd
        server_args     = -l
}
```

One additional `xinetd.conf` parameter is important: `disable`. If you include the line `disable = yes` in a service definition, `xinetd` ignores the entry. Many servers install startup files in /etc/xinetd.d that have this option set by default; you must edit the file and change the entry to read disable = no to enable the server. You can also disable a set of servers by listing their names in the defaults section of the main xinetd.conf file on a line called disabled, as in disabled = ftp shell.

As with inetd, after you make changes to xinetd's configuration, you must restart the super server. You do this by typing a command similar to the one used to restart inetd. As with that command, you can use either reload or restart, with similar effects. For instance:

```
# /etc/rc.d/init.d/xinetd restart
```

Custom Startup Files

Occasionally it's desirable to start a server through some means other than a SysV script or super server. This is most frequently the case when you've compiled a server yourself or installed it from a package file intended for a distribution other than the one you're using, and when you don't want to run it through a super server for performance reasons. In such cases, the program may not come with a SysV startup script, or the provided SysV script may not work correctly on your system.

Many Linux distributions include a startup script that runs after the other SysV startup scripts. This script is generally called /etc/rc.d/rc.local, /etc/rc.d/boot.local, or something similar. You can launch a server from this script by entering the command you would use to launch the server manually, as described in the server's documentation. For instance, you might include the following line to launch an FTP server:

```
/usr/sbin/in.ftpd -l -D
```

Some programs must have an ampersand (&) added to the end of the line to have them execute in the background. If you fail to add this, subsequent lines in the startup script may not run.

One thing to keep in mind when running a server via the local startup script is that this method provides no means to shut down a server, as you can do by passing the stop parameter to a SysV startup script. If you want to stop such a server, you'll need to use the Linux kill or killall command, possibly after locating the server's process ID number via ps. For instance, take a look at the following:

```
# ps ax | grep ftp
 6382 ?        S      0:00 in.ftpd -l -a
# kill 6382
```

NOTE | The ps and kill commands are covered in more detail shortly, in the section "Managing Processes." The grep command and the pipe (|) are covered in Chapter 2, "Text-Mode Commands."

Rather than provide a single custom local startup script, Debian and its derivatives provide a directory, /etc/rc.boot, in which you can add your own startup scripts. This approach enables you to create separate scripts for each program you want to start up, or you can create a single script to do them all, as you would with other distributions. Call your script whatever you like within /etc/rc.boot; the /etc/init.d/rcS startup script runs all the scripts in /etc/rc.boot, no matter what they're called.

Setting the Runlevel

One way to change the services a system offers en masse is to change the computer's runlevel. As with individual services, you can change the runlevel either temporarily or permanently. Both can be useful. Temporary changes are useful in testing changes to a system, and permanent changes are useful in creating a system that boots with the desired services running.

Understanding the Role of the Runlevel

As described earlier in this chapter, Linux enters a specific runlevel when it boots in order to run some predetermined subset of the programs installed on the computer. For instance, you might want to have two configurations for a computer: one that provides all the computer's usual array of network servers, and another that provides a more limited set, which you use when performing maintenance on the computer. By defining appropriate runlevels and switching between them, you can easily enable or disable a large number of servers.

On most Linux systems, the runlevel also controls whether or not the computer provides a GUI or text-mode login prompt. The former is the preferable default state for most workstations, but the latter is better for many servers or in cases when the X configuration is suspect.

Using *init* or *telinit* to Change the Runlevel

The init program is critical to Linux's boot process because it reads the /etc/inittab file that controls the boot process and implements the settings found in that file. Among other things, init sets the system's initial runlevel.

Once the computer has booted, you can use the telinit program to alter the runlevel. (In practice, calling init directly also usually works because telinit is usually just a symbolic link to init.) When using telinit, the syntax is as follows:

```
telinit [-t time] runlevel
```

You can discover what runlevel your computer is in with the runlevel command. This command displays the previous and current runlevels as output.

In most cases, *runlevel* is the runlevel to which you want the system to change. There are, however, a few special codes you can pass as well. Most importantly, S or s brings the system into a single-user mode; and Q or q tells the system to reexamine the /etc/inittab file and implement any changes in that file.

It's possible to misconfigure X so that it doesn't start. If you do this and your system is set to start X automatically, with some distributions, one consequence is that the system will try to start X, fail, try again, fail, and so on ad infinitum. If the computer has network connections, one way to stop this cycle is to log in remotely and change the runlevel to one that doesn't start X. This will stop the annoying screen flickering that results as X tries to start and fails. You can then correct the problem from the remote login or from the console, test X, and restore the default runlevel.

When switching runlevels, init must sometimes kill processes. It does so "politely" at first by sending a SIGTERM signal, which is a way to ask a program to manage its own shutdown. If that doesn't work, though, init becomes imperious and sends a SIGKILL signal, which is more likely to work but can be more disruptive because the program may leave temporary files lying about and be unable to save changes to open files. The -t *time* parameter tells telinit how long to wait between sending these two signals to a process. The default is 5 seconds, which is normally plenty of time.

One special case of runlevel change happens when you are shutting down the computer. Runlevel 0 shuts down the computer and halts it—depending on kernel options and hardware capabilities, this may shut off power to the computer, or it may simply place the computer in a state from which it's safe to turn off system power. Runlevel 6 reboots the computer. You can enter these runlevels using telinit, but it's better to use a separate command called **shutdown** to accomplish this task because it offers additional options. The syntax for this command is as follows:

shutdown [-t *sec*] [-arkhcfF] *time* [*warning-message*]

The meanings of the parameters are as follows:

-t *sec*   This is the delay, in seconds, between **shutdown** telling processes to stop via SIGTERM and SIGKILL. The default is 5 seconds. This gives programs the chance to shut down cleanly (closing open files, for instance).

-a   The /etc/inittab file contains an invocation of **shutdown** that's called whenever the Ctrl+Alt+Del keystroke is pressed. This allows anybody with physical access to the computer to restart it. If this is undesirable, add the -a parameter, and the system will check the /etc/shutdown.allow file for a list of users authorized to shut down the system. Only if one of those users is logged in at the console will **shutdown** proceed.

-r   This parameter causes a reboot after a shutdown. Essentially, it invokes a change to runlevel 6.

-k   This parameter "fakes" a shutdown—it sends a shutdown warning message to users, but it doesn't shut down the computer.

-h   This parameter causes the system to halt after a shutdown. Essentially, it invokes a change to runlevel 0.

-c   If you initiate a shutdown some time in the future but then change your mind, issuing `shutdown` again with this parameter cancels it.

-f   This option causes the system to skip its disk check (`fsck`) when it reboots.

-F   This option forces a disk check (`fsck`) when it reboots.

time   Shutdowns may be scheduled with this parameter, which can take many different formats. One common value is `now`, which causes an immediate shutdown. You can also specify a time in 24-hour *hh:mm* format, as in `13:15` for a shutdown at 1:15 p.m. A *time* in the format *+m* causes a shutdown in *m* minutes.

warning-message   When many people use a system for remote logins, it's generally a good idea to give these users advance warning of a shutdown. You can include a message explaining why the system is going down or how long you expect it to be down.

On a single-user system, `shutdown -h now` and `shutdown -r now` are perfectly reasonable uses of `shutdown`. When the system has many users, you might be better off scheduling a shutdown for 5, 10, or more minutes in the future and giving information on the expected downtime, as in the following:

```
# shutdown -h +10 "adding new hard disk; up again in 30 minutes"
```

A few distributions include commands called `halt` and `reboot` that are equivalent to `shutdown -h now` and `shutdown -r now`, respectively.

Permanently Changing the Runlevel

You can permanently change the computer's runlevel by editing the `/etc/inittab` file. This file contains a line like the following:

```
id:3:initdefault:
```

This example shows a system configured for runlevel 3. To modify it, you'd change the 3 to whatever value is appropriate. After making this change, you can cause the system to switch immediately to the new runlevel by running `telinit`, as described in the previous section. Typing **telinit Q** will cause the system to read your changes directly, or you can use the runlevel in place of Q.

Do not set the default runlevel to 0 or 6 since this will cause the system to shut down or reboot as soon as it boots.

Running Jobs at Specific Times

Some system maintenance tasks should be performed at regular intervals and are highly automated. For instance, the /tmp directory (which holds temporary files created by many users) tends to collect useless data files. Linux provides a means of scheduling tasks to run at specified times to handle such issues. This tool is the cron program, which runs what are known as *cron jobs*. A related tool is at, which enables you to run a command on a one-time basis at a specified point in the future, as opposed to doing so on a regular basis, as cron does.

The Role of Cron

Cron is a *daemon*, which means that it runs continuously, looking for events that cause it to spring into action. Unlike most daemons, which are network servers, cron responds to temporal events. Specifically, it "wakes up" once a minute, examines configuration files in the /var/spool/cron and /etc/cron.d directories and the /etc/crontab file, and executes commands specified by these configuration files if the time matches the time listed in the files.

There are two types of cron jobs: *system cron jobs* and *user cron jobs*. System cron jobs are run as root and perform system-wide maintenance tasks. By default, most Linux distributions include system cron jobs that clean out old files from /tmp, perform *log rotation* (renaming log files and deleting old ones so that they don't grow to fill the disk), and so on. You can add to this repertoire, as described shortly. Ordinary users can create user cron jobs, which might run some user program on a regular basis. You can also create a user cron job as root, which might be handy if you need to perform some task at a time not supported by the system cron jobs, which are scheduled rather rigidly.

One of the critical points to remember about cron jobs is that they run unsupervised. Therefore, you shouldn't call any program in a cron job if that program requires user input. For instance, you wouldn't run a text editor in a cron job. You might, however, run a script that automatically manipulates text files, such as log files.

Creating System Cron Jobs

The /etc/crontab file controls system cron jobs. This file normally begins with several lines that set environment variables, such as PATH and MAILTO (the former sets the path, and the latter is the address to which programs' output is mailed). The file then contains several lines that resemble the following:

```
02 4 * * * root run-parts /etc/cron.daily
```

This line begins with five fields that specify the time. The fields are, in order, the minute (0–59), the hour (0–23), the day of the month (1–31), the month (1–12), and the day of the week (0–7; both 0 and 7 correspond to Sunday). For the month and day of the week values, you can use the first three letters of the name rather than a number, if you like.

In all cases, you can specify multiple values in several ways:

- An asterisk (*) matches all possible values.

- A list separated by commas (such as 0,6,12,18) matches any of the specified values.

- Two values separated by a dash (-) indicate a range, inclusive of the end points. For instance, 9-17 in the hour field specifies a time of from 9:00 a.m. to 5:00 p.m.

- A slash, when used in conjunction with some other multivalue option, specifies stepped values—a range in which some members are skipped. For instance, */10 in the minute field indicates a job that's run every 10 minutes.

After the first five fields, /etc/crontab entries continue with the account name to be used when executing the program (root in the preceding example) and the command to be run (run-parts /etc/cron.daily in this example). The default /etc/crontab entries generally use run-parts, cronloop, or a similar utility that runs any executable scripts within a directory. Thus, the preceding example runs all the scripts in /etc/cron.daily at 4:02 a.m. every day. Most distributions include monthly, daily, weekly, and hourly system cron jobs, each corresponding to scripts in a directory called /etc/cron.*interval*, where *interval* is a word associated with the run frequency. Others place these scripts in /etc/cron.d/*interval* directories.

The exact times chosen for system cron jobs to execute vary from one distribution to another. Normally, though, daily and longer-interval cron jobs run early in the morning—between midnight and 6:00 a.m. Check your /etc/ crontab file to determine when your system cron jobs run.

To create a new system cron job, you may create a script to perform the task you want performed (as described in Chapter 2) and copy that script to the appropriate /etc/cron.*interval* directory. When the runtime next rolls around, cron will run the script.

Before submitting a script as a cron job, test it thoroughly. This is particularly important if the cron job will run when you're not around. You don't want a bug in your cron job script to cause problems by filling the hard disk with useless files or producing thousands of e-mail messages when you're not present to quickly correct the problem.

If you need to run a cron job at a time or interval that's not supported by the standard /etc/ crontab, you can either modify that file to change or add the cron job runtime, or create a user cron job, as described shortly. If you choose to modify the system cron job facility, model your changes after an existing entry, changing the times and script storage directory as required.

System cron job storage directories should be owned by root, and only root should be able to write to them. If ordinary users can write to a system cron directory, unscrupulous users could write scripts to give themselves superuser privileges and place them in the system cron directory. The next time cron runs those scripts, the users will have full administrative access to the system.

Creating User Cron Jobs

To create a user cron job, you use the crontab utility, not to be confused with the /etc/crontab configuration file. The syntax for crontab is as follows:

```
crontab [-u user] [-l | -e | -r] [file]
```

If given without the -u *user* parameter, crontab modifies the cron job associated with the current user. (User cron jobs are often called crontabs, but with the word already used in reference to the system-wide configuration file and the utility itself, this usage can be perplexing.) The crontab utility can become confused by the use of su to change the current user identity, though, so if you use this command, it's safest to also use -u *user*, even when you are modifying your own cron job.

If you want to work directly on a cron job, use one of the -l, -e, or -r options. The -l option causes crontab to display the current cron job; -r removes the current cron job; and -e opens an editor so that you can edit the current cron job. (Vi is the default editor, but you can change this by setting the VISUAL or EDITOR environment variables, as described in Chapter 2.)

Alternatively, you can create a cron job configuration file and pass the filename to crontab using the *file* parameter. For instance, **crontab -u tbaker my-cron** causes crontab to use my-cron for tbaker's cron jobs.

Whether you create the cron job and submit it via the *file* parameter or edit it via -e, the format of the cron file is similar to that described earlier. You can set environment variables by using the form *VARIABLE=value*, or you can specify a command preceded by five numbers or wildcards to indicate when the job is to run. In a user cron job, however, you do *not* specify the username used to execute the job, as you do with system cron jobs. That information is derived from the owner of the cron job. Listing 5.4 shows a sample cron job file. This file runs two programs at different intervals: The fetchmail program runs every 30 minutes (on the hour and half hour), and clean-adouble runs on Mondays at 2:00 a.m. Both programs are specified via complete paths, but you could include a PATH environment variable and omit the complete path specifications.

Listing 5.4: A Sample User Cron Job File

```
SHELL=/bin/bash
MAILTO=tbaker
HOME=/home/tbaker
0,30 * * * * /usr/bin/fetchmail -s
0 2 * * mon /usr/local/bin/clean-adouble $HOME
```

Using *at*

Sometimes cron is overkill. You might simply want to run a single command at a specific point in the future on a onetime basis, rather than on an ongoing basis. For this task, Linux provides another command: at. In ordinary use, this command takes a single option (although options to fine-tune its behavior are also available): a time. This time can take any of several forms:

Time of day   You can specify the time of day as *HH:MM*, optionally followed by AM or PM if you use a 12-hour format. If the specified time has already passed, the operation is scheduled for the next occurrence of that time—that is, for the next day.

noon, midnight, or teatime   These three keywords stand for what you'd expect (teatime is 4:00 p.m.).

Day specification   To schedule an at job more than 24 hours in advance, you must add a day specification after the time of day specification. This can be done in numeric form, using the formats *MMDDYY*, *MM/DD/YY*, or *DD.MM.YY*. Alternatively you can specify the date as *month-name day* or *month-name day year*.

now + *count time-units*   You can specify a time using the keyword now, a plus sign (+), and a time period, as in now + 2 hours to run a job in two hours.

When you run at and give it a time specification, the program responds with its own prompt, at>, which you can treat much like your normal bash or other command shell prompt. When you're done typing commands, press Ctrl+D to terminate input. Alternatively, you can pass a file with commands by using the -f parameter to at, as in **at -f commands.txt noon** to use the contents of commands.txt as the commands you want to run at noon.

The at command has several support tools. The most important of these is atd, the at daemon. This program must be running for at to do its work. If it's not, check for its presence using ps, as described shortly, in "Examining Process Lists with ps." If it's not running, look for a SysV startup script and ensure it's enabled, as described earlier, in "Starting and Stopping via SysV Scripts."

Other at support programs include atq, which lists pending at jobs; atrm, which removes an at job from the queue; and batch, which works much like at but executes jobs when the system load level drops below 0.8.

Setting Process Permissions

Most Linux programs run with the permissions of the user who executed them. For instance, if jane runs a program, that program can read precisely the same files that jane can read. A few programs, though, need additional privileges. For instance, su, which allows one user to take on another's identity, requires root privileges to do this identity switching. Such programs use the set user ID (SUID) bit to have the program run with the privileges of the program file's owner. That is, the SUID bit alters the *effective user ID*. The set group ID (SGID) bit works in a similar manner, but it sets the group with which the process is associated. Although these features are useful and even occasionally necessary, they're also at least potential security risks, so you should be sure that as few programs use these features as possible.

The Risks of SUID and SGID Programs

There are two major potential risks with SUID and SGID programs:

- If the program allows users to do something potentially dangerous, ordinary users might abuse the program. For instance, Linux's fdisk program can modify a disk's partitions, potentially leading to a completely destroyed system if abused. Even comparatively innocuous programs like cp could be abused if set to be SUID root—if so configured, any user could copy any file on the computer, which is clearly undesirable in the case of sensitive files like /etc/shadow. For these reasons, neither fdisk nor cp is normally installed as an SUID program.

- Bugs in SUID and SGID programs can cause damage with greater than normal privileges. If some random program contains a bug that causes it to try to recursively remove all files on the computer, and if an ordinary user encounters this bug, Linux's filesystem security features will minimize the damage. If this program were SUID root, though, the entire system would be wiped out.

For these reasons, only programs that absolutely require SUID or SGID status should be so configured. Typically, these are programs that ordinary users might reasonably be expected to use and that require privileged access to the system. The programmers who write such programs take great pains to ensure they're bug free. The root user may set *any* program's SUID or SGID bit, though.

When to Use SUID or SGID

SUID and SGID are necessary when a program needs to perform privileged operations but may also legitimately be run by ordinary users. Some common programs that meet this description include passwd, gpasswd, crontab, su, sudo, mount, umount, and ping. This list is not complete, however.

You can remove the SUID bits on some of these programs, but that may mean that ordinary users won't be able to use them. Sometimes this may be acceptable—for instance, you might not want ordinary users to be able to mount and unmount filesystems. Other times, ordinary users really do need access to these facilities. The su utility is the best way for you to acquire root privileges in many cases, for instance; and ordinary users should be able to change their passwords with passwd.

Some programs have SUID or SGID bits set, but they aren't SUID or SGID root. These programs may need special privilege to access hardware device files or the like, but they don't need full root privilege to do so. For instance, some older distributions configured their xterm programs in this way. Such configurations are much less dangerous than SUID root programs because these special users typically don't have unusual privileges except to a handful of device or configuration files.

Finding SUID or SGID Programs

You can use the find command to locate files with their SUID or SGID bits set. Specifically, you need to use the -perm parameter to this command, and specify the s permission code in the user or group. For instance, the following command locates all SUID or SGID files on a computer:

```
# find / -perm +ug+s
```

You may want to run this command and study the results for your system. If you're uncertain about whether a program should have its SUID or SGID bit set, check its man page and try to verify the integrity of its package using RPM, if your system uses RPM. For instance, type **rpm -V packagename**. This will turn up changes to the permissions of files in *packagename*, including changes to SUID or SGID bits. Of course, it's conceivable that a program might have had its SUID or SGID bit set inappropriately even in the original package file.

 Real World Scenario

Controlling Daemon Process Permissions

Servers are run in various ways, as described earlier. Some of these allow you to set the effective user IDs of the server processes. For instance, both inetd and xinetd allow you to specify the user under whose name the server runs. Sometimes a server needs to run with root permissions, but other times that's not necessary. You should consult a server's documentation to learn what its requirements are.

Some servers let you adjust their process ownership through configuration files. For instance, Apache lets you adjust the username used on most of its processes with the User option in its httpd.conf file. (In the case of Apache, one process still runs as root, but it spawns children that run with the ownership you specify.)

Managing Processes

Unfortunately, programs don't always behave themselves. For instance, a program might stop responding, or it may consume an inordinate amount of CPU time. In these cases, you can rein in their appetites or terminate them outright. The first step to doing this, though, is knowing how to find out what programs are running on the computer.

Before proceeding, it's important that you understand a bit of terminology. In Linux, a *process* is more or less synonymous with a running program. Because Linux is a multiuser, multitasking OS, it's possible for one program to be running as more than one process at a time. For instance, suppose that tbaker and smccoy both use Vi to edit text files. The computer will have two Vi processes running at once. Indeed, a single user can do this. It's also possible for a single program to create (or *fork*) subprocesses. For instance, Vi can launch a spell-checker program. In fact, this is what happens when you launch a program from a shell—the shell forks the program you're launching. When one process forks another, the original process is known as the *parent process*, and the forked process is known as the *child process*. This parent/child relationship produces a tree-like hierarchy that ultimately leads back to init, the first process. Figure 5.5 shows a simplified example. In Figure 5.5, init forks the login processes, which in turn fork bash processes, which fork additional processes. (It's actually slightly more complex than this; init doesn't directly fork login but instead does this by using another process, such as getty.) This can continue for an arbitrary number of layers, although many programs aren't able to fork others.

FIGURE 5.5 Linux processes have parents, leading back to init, the first program the Linux kernel runs.

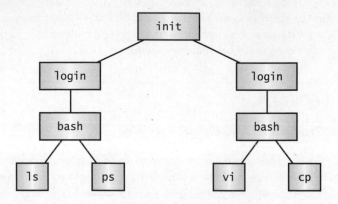

Examining Process Lists with *ps*

One of the most important tools in process management is ps. This program displays processes' status (hence the name, ps). It sports many useful options, and it's useful in monitoring what's happening on a system. This can be particularly critical when the computer isn't working as it should be—for instance, if it's unusually slow. The ps program supports an unusual number of options, but just a few of them will take you a long way. Likewise, interpreting ps output can be tricky because so many options modify what's available. Some ps-like programs, most notably top, also deserve some attention.

Useful *ps* Options

The official syntax for ps is fairly simple:

```
ps [options]
```

This simplicity of form hides considerable complexity because ps supports three different *types* of options, as well as many options within each type. The three types of options are as follows:

Unix98 options   These single-character options may be grouped together and are preceded by a single dash (-).

BSD options   These single-character options may be grouped together and must *not* be preceded by a dash.

GNU long options   These multi-character options are not grouped together. They're preceded by two dashes (--).

Options that may be grouped together may be clustered without spaces between them. For instance, rather than typing **ps -a -f**, you can type **ps -af**. The reason for so much complexity is that the ps utility has historically varied a lot from one Unix OS to another. The version of ps that ships with major Linux distributions attempts to implement most features from all these different ps versions, so it supports many different personalities. In fact, you can change some of its default behaviors by setting the PS_PERSONALITY environment variable to posix, old, linux, bsd, sun, digital, or various others. (Chapter 2 describes how to set environment variables.) The rest of this section describes the default ps behavior on most Linux systems.

Some of the more useful ps features include the following:

Display help   The --help option presents a summary of some of the more common ps options.

Display all processes   By default, ps displays only processes that were run from its own terminal (xterm, text-mode login, or remote login). The -A and -e options cause it to display all the processes on the system, and x displays all processes owned by the user who gives the command. The x option also increases the amount of information that's displayed about each process.

Display one user's processes   You can display processes owned by a given user with the -u *user*, U *user*, or --User *user* options. The *user* variable may be a username or a user ID.

Display extra information   The -f, -l, j, l, u, and v options all expand the information provided in the ps output. Most ps output formats include one line per process, but ps can display enough information that it's impossible to fit it all on one 80-character line. Therefore, these options provide various mixes of information.

Display process hierarchy   The -H, -f, and --forest options group processes and use indentation to show the hierarchy of relationships between processes. These options are useful if you're trying to trace the parentage of a process.

Display wide output   The ps command output can be more than 80 columns wide. Normally, ps truncates its output so that it will fit on your screen or xterm. The -w and w options tell ps not to do this, which can be useful if you direct the output to a file, as **in ps w > ps.txt**. You can then examine the output file in a text editor that supports wide lines.

You can combine these ps options in many ways to produce the output you want. You'll probably need to experiment to learn which options produce the desired results because each of these options modifies the output in some way. Even those that would seem to influence just the selection of processes to list sometimes modify the information that's provided about each process.

Interpreting *ps* Output

Listings 5.5 and 5.6 show a couple of examples of ps in action. Listing 5.5 shows **ps -u rodsmith --forest**, and Listing 5.6 shows **ps u U rodsmith**.

Listing 5.5: Output of *ps -u rodsmith --forest*

```
$ ps -u rodsmith --forest
  PID TTY          TIME CMD
 2451 pts/3     00:00:00 bash
 2551 pts/3     00:00:00 ps
 2496 ?         00:00:00 kvt
 2498 pts/1     00:00:00 bash
```

```
 2505 pts/1    00:00:00  \_ nedit
 2506 ?        00:00:00      \_ csh
 2544 ?        00:00:00          \_ xeyes
19221 ?        00:00:01 dfm
```

Listing 5.6: Output of *ps u U rodsmith*

```
$ ps u U rodsmith
USER        PID %CPU %MEM   VSZ  RSS TTY    STAT START   TIME COMMAND
rodsmith  19221  0.0  1.5  4484 1984 ?      S    May07   0:01 dfm
rodsmith   2451  0.0  0.8  1856 1048 pts/3  S    16:13   0:00 -bash
rodsmith   2496  0.2  3.2  6232 4124 ?      S    16:17   0:00 /opt/kd
rodsmith   2498  0.0  0.8  1860 1044 pts/1  S    16:17   0:00 bash
rodsmith   2505  0.1  2.6  4784 3332 pts/1  S    16:17   0:00 nedit
rodsmith   2506  0.0  0.7  2124 1012 ?      S    16:17   0:00 /bin/cs
rodsmith   2544  0.0  1.0  2576 1360 ?      S    16:17   0:00 xeyes
rodsmith   2556  0.0  0.7  2588  916 pts/3  R    16:18   0:00 ps u U
```

The output produced by ps normally begins with a heading line, which displays the meaning of each column. Important information that might be displayed (and labeled) includes the following:

Username   The name of the user who runs the programs. Listings 5.5 and 5.6 restricted this output to one user to limit the size of the listings.

Process ID   The process ID (PID) is a number that's associated with the process. This item is particularly important because you need it to modify or kill the process, as described later in this chapter.

Parent process ID   The parent process ID (PPID) identifies the process's parent. (Neither Listing 5.5 nor Listing 5.6 shows the PPID, though.)

TTY   The teletype (TTY) is a code used to identify a terminal. As illustrated by Listings 5.5 and 5.6, not all processes have TTY numbers—X programs and daemons, for instance, do not. Text-mode programs do have these numbers, though, which point to a console, xterm, or remote login session.

CPU time   The TIME and %CPU headings are two measures of CPU time used. The first indicates the total amount of CPU time consumed, and the second represents the percentage of CPU time the process is using when ps executes. Both can help you spot runaway processes—those that are consuming too much CPU time. Unfortunately, just what constitutes "too much" varies from one program to another, so it's impossible to give a simple rule to help you spot a runaway process.

CPU priority   As described shortly, in "Restricting Processes' CPU Use," it's possible to give different processes different priorities for CPU time. The NI column, if present (it's not in the preceding examples) lists these priority codes. The default value is 0. Positive values represent *reduced* priority, while negative values represent *increased* priority.

Memory use   Various headings indicate memory use—for instance, RSS is resident set size (the memory used by the program and its data) and %MEM is the percentage of memory the program is using. Some output formats also include a SHARE column, which is memory that's shared with other processes (such as shared libraries). As with CPU use measures, these columns can help point you to the sources of difficulties, but because legitimate memory needs of programs vary so much, it's impossible to give a simple criterion for when a problem exists.

Command   The final column in most listings is the command used to launch the process. This is truncated in Listing 5.6 because this format lists the complete command, but so much other information appears that the complete command won't usually fit on one line. (This is where the wide-column options can come in handy.)

As you can see, a lot of information can be gleaned from a ps listing—or perhaps that should be the plural *listings*, because no one format includes all of the available information. For the most part, the PID, username, and command are the most important pieces of information. In some cases, though, you may need specific other components. If your system's memory or CPU use has skyrocketed, for instance, you'll want to pay attention to the memory or CPU use columns.

It's often necessary to find specific processes. You might want to find the PID associated with a particular command in order to kill it, for instance. This information can be gleaned by piping the ps output through grep, as in **ps ax | grep bash** to find all the instances of bash. (Both grep and pipes are covered in more detail in Chapter 2.)

Although you may need a wide screen or xterm to view the output, you may find **ps -A --forest** to be a helpful command in learning about your system. Processes that don't fall off others were either started directly by init or have had their parents killed, and so they have been "adopted" by init. Most of these processes are fairly important—they're servers, login tools, and so on. Processes that hang off several others in this tree view, such as xeyes and nedit in Listing 5.5, are mostly user programs launched from shells.

top: A Dynamic *ps* Variant

If you want to know how much CPU time various processes are consuming relative to one another, or if you simply want to quickly discover which processes are consuming the most CPU time, a tool called top is the one for the job. The top tool is a text-mode program, but of course it can be run in an xterm, as shown in Figure 5.6, and there are also GUI variants, like kpm and gnome-system-monitor. By default, top sorts its entries by CPU use, and it updates its display every few seconds. This makes it a very good tool for spotting runaway processes on an otherwise lightly loaded system—those processes almost always appear in the first position or two, and they consume an inordinate amount of CPU time. By looking at Figure 5.6, you might think that setiathome is such a process, but in fact, it's legitimately consuming a lot of CPU time. You'll need to be familiar with the purposes and normal habits of programs running on *your* system in order to make such determinations; the legitimate needs of different programs vary so much that it's impossible to give a simple rule for judging when a process is consuming too much CPU time.

FIGURE 5.6 The top command shows system summary information and information on the most CPU-intensive processes on a computer.

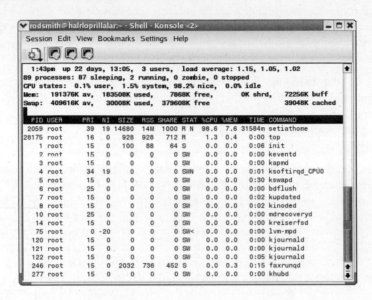

Like many Linux commands, top accepts several options. The most useful of these options are:

-d *delay* This specifies the delay between updates, which is normally 5 seconds.

-p *pid* If you want to monitor specific processes, you can list them using this option. You'll need the PIDs, which you can obtain with ps, as described earlier. You can specify up to 20 PIDs by using this option multiple times, once for each PID.

-n *iter* You can tell top to display a certain number of updates (*iter*) and then quit. (Normally, top continues updating until you terminate the program.)

-b This specifies batch mode, in which top doesn't use the normal screen update commands. You might use this to log CPU use of targeted programs to a file, for instance.

You can do more with top than watch it update its display. When it's running, you can enter any of several single-letter commands, some of which prompt you for additional information. These commands include the following:

h or ? These keystrokes display help information.

k You can kill a process with this command. The top program will ask for a PID number, and if it's able to kill it, it will do so. (The upcoming section "Killing Processes" describes other ways to kill processes.)

q This option quits from top.

r You can change a process's priority with this command. You'll have to enter the PID number and a new priority value—a positive value will decrease its priority and a negative value will increase its priority, assuming it has the default 0 priority to begin with. Only `root` may increase a process's priority. The `renice` command (described shortly, in "Restricting Processes' CPU Use") is another way to accomplish this task.

s   This command changes the display's update rate, which you'll be asked to enter (in seconds).

P   This sets the display to sort by CPU usage, which is the default.

M   You can change the display to sort by memory usage with this command.

More commands are available in `top` (both command-line options and interactive commands) than can be summarized here; consult the `top` man page for more information.

One of the pieces of information provided by `top` is the *load average*, which is a measure of the demand for CPU time by applications. In Figure 5.6, you'll see three load-average estimates on the top line; these correspond to the current load average and two previous measures. A system on which no programs are demanding CPU time will have a load average of 0. A system with one program running CPU-intensive tasks will have a load average of 1. Higher load averages reflect programs competing for available CPU time. You can also find the current load average via the `uptime` command, which displays the load average along with information on how long the computer has been running. The load average can be useful in detecting runaway processes. For instance, if a system normally has a load average of 0.5 but it suddenly gets stuck at a load average of 2.5, there may be a couple of CPU-hogging processes that have *hung*—that is, become unresponsive. Hung processes sometimes needlessly consume a lot of CPU time. You can use `top` to locate these processes and, if necessary, kill them.

Restricting Processes' CPU Use

There may be times when you'll want to prioritize your programs' CPU use. For instance, you might be running a program that's very CPU-intensive but that will take a long time to finish its work, and you don't want that program to interfere with others that are of a more interactive nature. Alternatively, on a heavily loaded computer, you might have a job that's more important than others that are running, so you might want to give it a priority boost. In either case, the usual method of accomplishing this goal is through the `nice` and `renice` commands. You can use `nice` to launch a program with a specified priority, or use `renice` to alter the priority of a running program.

You can assign a priority to `nice` in any of three ways: by specifying the priority preceded by a dash (this works well for positive priorities, but makes them look like negative priorities); by specifying the priority after a `-n` parameter; or by specifying the priority after an `--adjustment=` parameter. In all cases, these parameters are followed by the name of the program you want to run:

```
nice [argument] [command [command-arguments]]
```

For instance, the following three commands are all equivalent:

```
$ nice -12 number-crunch data.txt
$ nice -n 12 number-crunch data.txt
$ nice --adjustment=12 number-crunch data.txt
```

All three of these commands run the `number-crunch` program at priority 12 and pass it the `data.txt` file. If you omit the adjustment value, `nice` uses 10 as a default. The range of possible values is –20 to 19, with negative values having the highest priority. Only `root` may launch a program with increased priority (that is, give a negative priority value), but any user may use `nice` to launch a program with low priority. The default priority for a program run without `nice` is 0.

If you've found that a running process is consuming too much CPU time or is being swamped by other programs and so should be given more CPU time, you can use the `renice` program to alter its priority without disrupting the program's operation. The syntax for `renice` is as follows:

```
renice priority [[-p] pids] [[-g] pgrps] [[-u] users]
```

You must specify the *priority*, which takes the same values as with `nice`. In addition, you must specify one or more PIDs (*pids*), one or more group IDs (*pgrps*), or one or more usernames (*users*). In the latter two cases, `renice` changes the priority of all programs that match the specified criterion—but only `root` may use `renice` in this way. Also, only `root` may increase a process's priority. If you give a numeric value without a -p, -g, or -u option, `renice` assumes the value is a PID. You may mix and match these methods of specification. For instance, you might enter the following command:

```
# renice 7 16580 -u pdavison tbaker
```

This command sets the priority to 7 for PID 16580 and for all processes owned by `pdavison` and `tbaker`.

Killing Processes

Sometimes reducing a process's priority isn't a strong enough action. A program may have become totally unresponsive, or you might want to terminate a process that shouldn't be running at all. In these cases, the `kill` command is the tool to use. This program sends a *signal* (a method that Linux uses to communicate with processes) to a process. The signal is usually sent by the kernel, the user, or the program itself to terminate the process. Linux supports many numbered signals, each of which is associated with a specific name. You can see them all by typing `kill -l`. If you don't use -l, the syntax for `kill` is as follows:

```
kill -s signal pid
```

 Although Linux includes a `kill` program, many shells, including bash and csh, include built-in `kill` equivalents that work in much the same way as the external program. If you want to be sure you're using the external program, type its complete path, as in `/bin/kill`.

The -s *signal* parameter sends the specified signal to the process. You can specify the signal using either a number (such as 9) or a name (such as SIGKILL). The signals you're most likely to use are 1 (SIGHUP, which causes many daemons to reread their configuration files), 9 (SIGKILL, which causes the process to exit without performing routine shutdown tasks), and 15 (SIGTERM, which causes the process to exit but allows it to close open files and so on). If you don't specify a signal, the default is 15 (SIGTERM). You can also use the shortened form *-signal*. If you do this and use a signal name, you should omit the SIG portion of the name—for instance, use KILL rather than SIGKILL. The *pid* option is, of course, the PID for the process you want to kill. You can obtain this number from ps or top.

> The kill program will only kill processes owned by the user who runs kill. The exception is if that user is root; the superuser may kill any user's processes.

A variant on kill is killall, which has the following form:

```
killall [options] [--] name [...]
```

This command kills a process based on its name rather than its PID number. For instance, **killall vi** kills all the running processes called **vi**. You may specify a signal in the shortened form (*-signal*) or by preceding the signal number with -s or --signal. As with kill, the default is 15 (SIGTERM). One potentially important option to killall is -i, which causes it to ask for confirmation before sending the signal to each process. You might use it like this:

```
$ killall -i vi
Kill vi(13211) ? (y/n) y
Kill vi(13217) ? (y/n) n
```

In this example, two instances of the Vi editor were running but only one should have been killed. As a general rule, if you run killall as **root**, you should use the -i parameter; if you don't, it's all too likely that you'll kill processes that you should not, particularly if the computer is being used by many people at once.

> Some versions of Unix provide a killall command that works very differently from Linux's killall. This alternate killall kills all the processes started by the user who runs the command. This is a potentially much more destructive command, so if you ever find yourself on a non-Linux system, *do not* use killall until you've discovered what that system's killall does, say by reading the killall man page.

Foreground and Background Processes

Less extreme process management tools enable you to control whether a process is running in the foreground or the background—that is, whether or not it's monopolizing the use of the terminal from which it was launched. Normally, when you launch a program it takes over the terminal, preventing you from doing other work in that terminal. (Some programs, though, release the terminal. This is most common for servers and some GUI programs.)

If a program is running but you decide you want to use that terminal for something else, pressing Ctrl+Z normally pauses the program and gives you control of the terminal. (An important point is that this procedure pauses the program, so if it's performing real work, that work stops!) This can be handy if, say, you're running a text editor in a text-mode login and you want to check a filename so you can mention it in the file you're editing. You'd press Ctrl+Z and type **ls** to get the file listing. To get back to the text editor, you'd then type **fg**, which restores the text editor to the foreground of your terminal. If you've suspended several processes, you'd add a job number, as in **fg 2** to restore job 2. You can obtain a list of jobs associated with a terminal by typing **jobs**, which displays the jobs and their job numbers.

> Job numbers are not the same as PIDs. PIDs are used by the kernel to track processes, and many utilities, such as ps, top, and kill, report PIDs or use them. Job numbers are linked to the terminal from which the process was launched and are used by fewer programs. Don't try to use a PID in place of a job number, or vice versa.

A variant on **fg** is **bg**. Where **fg** restores a job to the foreground, **bg** restores a job to running status, but in the background. You might use this command if the process you're running is performing a CPU-intensive task that requires no human interaction but you want to use the terminal in the meantime. Another use of **bg** is in a GUI environment—after launching a GUI program from an xterm or similar window, that shell is tied up servicing the GUI program, which probably doesn't really need the shell. Pressing Ctrl+Z in the xterm window will enable you to type shell commands again, but the GUI program will be frozen. To unfreeze the GUI program, type **bg** in the shell, which enables the GUI program to run in the background while the shell continues to process your commands.

An alternative to launching a program, using Ctrl+Z, and typing **bg** is to append an ampersand (&) to the command when launching the program. For instance, rather than edit a file with the NEdit GUI editor by typing **nedit myfile.txt**, you could type **nedit myfile.txt &**. This command launches the **nedit** program in the background from the start, leaving you able to control your xterm window for other tasks.

Summary

One of your primary duties as a system administrator is to manage the packages installed on a computer. To do this, you must often remove unused programs, install new ones, and upgrade existing packages. You may also need to verify the integrity of installed programs or track down what libraries or other programs another one uses. In all these tasks, the RPM and Debian package management systems can be extremely helpful. These systems track installed files and dependencies, giving you access to information that's not otherwise available. On occasion, though, you may need to use the simpler tarballs—particularly if you use a tarball-based distribution like Slackware. Sometimes you can convert between package formats using alien or other package conversion tools.

Once a package is installed, you must be able to use it. For program packages, this means running the programs installed. Although this task is fairly straightforward for interactive user programs such as editors and shells, running servers and other behind-the-scenes system tools requires a less obvious approach. These programs are typically run via SysV startup scripts, local startup scripts, super servers, or time-sensitive program running tools.

For all program types, managing running programs is an important task. For that, tools such as ps, top, nice, and kill are vital. These programs enable you to monitor running processes, control their priorities, and even terminate misbehaving programs.

Exam Essentials

Identify critical features of RPM and Debian package formats.   RPM and Debian packages store all files for a given package in a single file that also includes information on what other packages the software depends on. These systems maintain a database of installed packages and their associated files and dependencies.

Describe the process of installing an RPM or Debian package.   Use the rpm program to install an RPM package, or use dpkg or apt-get to install a Debian package. These programs install, upgrade, or remove all files associated with a package and maintain the associated databases.

Summarize methods of working around package dependency problems.   Dependency problems can be overcome by forcing an installation, upgrading or installing the depended-on package, recompiling the package, or installing another version of the target package. Which approach is best depends on the specifics of the system involved.

Describe how to install a program from a source code tarball.   Compiling a program from source code depends greatly on the program in question. Most provide a configuration script called configure or a configure target in the Makefile. Once that's run, you type **make** to build the package and then install it with an install script or an install target in the Makefile.

Evaluate the need for SUID or SGID programs.   Some programs, such as su and passwd, must have enhanced privileges in order to operate. Most programs, though, do not require these privileges and so should not have their SUID or SGID bits set.

Describe the SysV startup procedure.   The init process reads the /etc/inittab file, which controls programs that run when changing from one runlevel to another. Scripts in directories corresponding to each runlevel start and stop services when the runlevel changes.

Explain the differences between SysV startup scripts and super servers for running servers. SysV startup scripts start servers running on a computer at startup or when changing runlevels so that the servers are always running and can respond quickly to requests, but servers run in this way consume RAM at all times. Super servers run the target servers only in response to requests from clients, thus reducing the memory burden for infrequently used servers but at the cost of slower responses to incoming requests.

Describe the function of the runlevel.   Sometimes you may want to run a Linux system with a different set of services than you run at other times. The runlevel lets you define several sets of services and switch quickly between them.

Know how to create a cron job. You create a system cron job by placing a script in an appropriate directory, such as /etc/cron.daily. You can create a user cron job by using the crontab command, which enables you to edit a script or pass one to the utility for appropriate handling.

Understand how to limit the CPU time used by a process. You can launch a program with nice, or use renice to alter its priority in obtaining CPU time. If a process is truly out of control, you can terminate it with the kill command.

Commands in This Chapter

The following list contains a summary of all of the commands used in this chapter:

Command	Description
rpm	Installs, removes, updates, queries, or verifies packages on an RPM-based Linux distribution.
dpkg	Installs, removes, updates, queries, or verifies packages on a Debian-based Linux distribution.
apt-get	Installs, removes, or updates packages on a Debian-based Linux distribution; can automatically retrieve packages from a remote site.
tar	Adds to, deletes from, or displays the contents of a tarball.
system-config-packages	GUI front end to the rpm utility.
init	Sets the initial runlevel of the computer.
telinit	Changes the runlevel of the computer. (In reality, it's a symbolic link to init.)
shutdown	Shuts down (halts) or restarts the computer.
crontab	Creates a user cron job.
ps	Displays process status information.
top	Dynamic variant of ps; shows most CPU-hungry programs and updates the display periodically.
nice	Runs a program with a specified priority.
renice	Changes a running program's priority.
kill	Terminates a process based on its PID.
killall	Terminates a process based on its name.

Review Questions

1. You are installing a small program on your server and need to change a number of options. You cannot find a specific configuration script for the program. In this case, what file should you edit?

    A. `configfile`

    B. `change`

    C. `make`

    D. `makefile`

2. Which of the following is *not* an advantage of a source package over a binary package?

    A. A single source package can be used on multiple CPU architectures.

    B. By recompiling a source package, you can sometimes work around library incompatibilities.

    C. You can modify the code in a source package, altering the behavior of a program.

    D. Source packages can be installed more quickly than binary packages can.

3. Which is true of using both RPM and Debian package management systems on one computer?

    A. It's generally inadvisable because the two systems don't share installed file database information.

    B. It's impossible because their installed file databases conflict with one another.

    C. It causes no problems if you install important libraries once in each format.

    D. It's a common practice on Red Hat and Debian systems.

4. Which of the following statements is true about binary RPM packages that are built for a particular distribution?

    A. They can often be used on another RPM-based distribution for the same CPU architecture, but this isn't guaranteed.

    B. They may be used in another RPM-based distribution only when you set the `--convert-distrib` parameter to `rpm`.

    C. They may be used in another RPM-based distribution only after you convert the package with `alien`.

    D. They can be recompiled for an RPM-based distribution running on another type of CPU.

5. Which is true of source RPM packages?

    A. They consist of three files: an original source tarball, a patch file of changes, and a PGP signature indicating the authenticity of the package.

    B. They require programming knowledge to rebuild.

    C. They can sometimes be used to work around dependency problems with a binary package.

    D. They are necessary to compile software for RPM-based distributions.

6. Which of the following do RPM filenames conventionally include?

    A. Single-letter codes indicating Red Hat-certified build sites

    B. Build date information

    C. Version number and CPU architecture information

    D. The initials of the package's maintainer

7. To use dpkg to remove a package called theprogram, including its configuration files, which of the following commands would you issue?

    A. dpkg -P theprogram

    B. dpkg -p theprogram

    C. dpkg -r theprogram

    D. dpkg -r theprogram-1.2.3-4.deb

8. Which of the following describes a difference between apt-get and dpkg?

    A. apt-get provides a GUI interface to Debian package management; dpkg does not.

    B. apt-get can install tarballs in addition to Debian packages; dpkg cannot.

    C. apt-get can automatically retrieve and update programs from Internet sites; dpkg cannot.

    D. apt-get is provided only with the original Debian distribution, but dpkg comes with Debian and its derivatives.

9. Which of the following is true of an attempt to use a Debian package from one distribution on another Debian-derived distribution?

    A. It's unlikely to work because of library incompatibilities and divergent package-naming conventions.

    B. It's guaranteed to work because of Debian's strong package definition and enforcement of standards for startup scripts and file locations.

    C. It will work only when the distributions are built for different CPUs or when the alien package is already installed on the target system.

    D. It's likely to work because of the close relationship of Debian-based distributions, assuming the two distributions are for the same CPU architecture.

10. The tar program may be used to complete which of the following tasks? (Choose all that apply.)

    A. Install RPM and Debian packages.

    B. Install software from binary tarballs.

    C. Back up a computer to tape.

    D. Create source code archive files.

11. The `tar` program provides a much easier _____ process than RPM and Debian package tools do.

    A. Dependency tracking

    B. Source code compilation

    C. File ownership setting

    D. Package creation

12. Which of the following are risks of SUID and SGID programs? (Choose all that apply.)

    A. The program files are large and thus may cause a disk to run out of space.

    B. Bugs in the programs may cause more damage than they would in ordinary programs.

    C. Users may be able to abuse a program's features, thus doing more damage than would otherwise be possible.

    D. Because the programs require password entry, running them over an insecure network link runs the risk of password interception.

13. To alter a Linux system's default runlevel, what would you do?

    A. Issue the `telinit` *x* command, where *x* is the desired runlevel.

    B. Edit /etc/modules.conf and enter the runlevel as an option to the `runlevel` module.

    C. Issue the `telinit Q` command to have the system query you for a new runlevel.

    D. Edit /etc/inittab and enter the correct runlevel in the `initdefault` line.

14. A Linux system keeps its SysV startup scripts in the /etc/init.d directory. Which of the following commands will temporarily stop the ProFTPd server on that computer, if it's started from these startup scripts?

    A. `/etc/init.d/proftpd stop`

    B. `sysvstop /etc/init.d/proftpd`

    C. `sysvstop proftpd`

    D. `/etc/init.d/proftpd stop5m`

15. A new Linux system administrator edits /etc/inetd.conf to add a server. After making this change, the administrator tests the new server, but a remote system can't access the new server. Why might this be? (Choose all that apply.)

    A. The administrator may have forgotten to restart `inetd`.

    B. The system might be using `xinetd` rather than `inetd`.

    C. The administrator may have forgotten to edit the /etc/rc.d/init.d script for the new server.

    D. The administrator may have forgotten to start the new server manually for the first time.

16. You've installed a server by compiling it from source code. The source code included no SysV startup script, and you don't want to run it from a super server, so you start it in a local startup script (/etc/rc.d/rc.local). You need to temporarily shut down the server. How might you do this?

A. Type **/etc/rc.d/rc.local stop**.

B. Edit the startup script to remove the server and rerun the script.

C. Remove the server's entry from /etc/inetd.conf and type **/etc/rc.d/init.d/inetd restart**.

D. Find the server's process ID number (*pid*) with ps and then type **kill *pid***.

17. Which of the following commands switches a running system into runlevel 3?

A. `telnet 3`

B. `runlevel 3`

C. `telinit 3`

D. `switch-runlevel 3`

18. What does the following command, when typed by a system administrator at noon, accomplish?

`# shutdown -r 01:00 "Up again soon."`

A. Reboots the computer at 1:00 p.m. (in 1 hour) and displays the message Up again soon as a warning to users

B. Shuts down (halts) the computer at 1:00 p.m. (in 1 hour) and displays the message Up again soon as a warning to users

C. Shuts down (halts) the computer at 1:00 a.m. (in 13 hours) and displays the message Up again soon as a warning to users

D. Reboots the computer at 1:00 a.m. (in 13 hours) and displays the message Up again soon as a warning to users

19. Which of the following tasks is likely to be handled by a cron job? (Choose all that apply.)

A. Starting an important server when the computer boots

B. Finding and deleting old temporary files

C. Scripting supervised account creation

D. Monitoring the status of servers and e-mailing a report to the superuser

20. Which of the following lines, if used in a user cron job, will run /usr/local/bin/cleanup twice a day?

A. `15 7,19 * * * tbaker /usr/local/bin/cleanup`

B. `15 7,19 * * * /usr/local/bin/cleanup`

C. `15 */2 * * * tbaker /usr/local/bin/cleanup`

D. `15 */2 * * * /usr/local/bin/cleanup`

Answers to Review Questions

1. D. Some programs (particularly small ones) don't use configuration scripts. To change their options, you must typically edit a file called `Makefile` or `makefile`.

2. D. Because they must be compiled prior to installation, source packages require *more* time to install than binary packages do.

3. A. Package management systems don't share information, but neither do their databases actively conflict. Installing the same libraries using both systems would almost guarantee that the files served by both systems would conflict with one another. Actively using both RPM and Debian packages isn't common on any distribution, although it's possible with all of them.

4. A. RPMs are usually portable across distributions, but occasionally they contain incompatibilities. There is no `--convert-distrib` parameter to `rpm`, nor is `alien` used to convert from RPM format to RPM format. Binary packages can't be rebuilt for another CPU architecture, but source packages may be rebuilt for any supported architecture, provided the source code doesn't rely on any CPU-specific features.

5. C. Some dependencies result from dynamically linking binaries to libraries at compile time, and so they can be overcome by recompiling the software from a source RPM. Option A describes Debian source packages, not RPM packages. Recompiling a source RPM requires only issuing an appropriate command, although you must also have appropriate compilers and libraries installed. Source tarballs can also be used to compile software for RPM systems, although this results in none of RPM's advantages.

6. C. The package version number (as well as an RPM build number) and CPU architecture code (or `src` for source code or `noarch` for architecture-independent files) are included in most RPM package filenames. Red Hat does not provide certification for RPM maintainers. Build dates and package maintainers' names are stored in the RPM, but not in the filename. (Some distributions include a code for the distribution name in the RPM filename, but this is not a universal practice.)

7. A. An uppercase `-P` invokes the purge operation, which completely removes a package and its configuration files. The lowercase `-p` causes `dpkg` to print information on the package's contents. The `-r` parameter removes a package but leaves configuration files behind. The final variant (option D) also specifies a complete filename, which isn't used for removing a package—you should specify only the shorter package name.

8. C. You can specify Debian package archive sites in `/etc/apt/sources.list`, and then you can type **apt-get update** and **apt-get upgrade** to quickly update a Debian system to the latest packages. GUI package management tools for Debian and related distributions exist, but they aren't `apt-get`. The `alien` program can convert an RPM file and install the converted package on a Debian system; `dpkg` and `apt-get` both come with all Debian-based distributions.

9. D. Systems that use Debian are based on the same core OS, and so they share most components, making package transplants likely—but not certain—to succeed. Library incompatibilities *could* cause problems but aren't likely to, especially if you use recent packages and distributions. Although Debian has clearly defined key file locations, startup scripts, and so on, these can't guarantee success. Binary packages built for *different* CPUs are almost guaranteed *not* to work, although scripts or other non-binary packages most likely will work across CPU types.

10. B, C, D. The `tar` program can do all these things except for directly installing RPM or Debian packages, although it could be used to do that after you convert the package with `alien`.

11. D. The `tar --create` command creates an archive from any specified directory; RPM and Debian package creation tools are more complex than this. The `tar` utility provides no dependency-tracking mechanisms at all, making you do that work. Although `tar` can be used to distribute source code, it's not used in compiling it per se. All the package tools discussed in this chapter automatically set file ownership appropriately.

12. B, C. SUID and SGID programs run with effective permissions other than those of the person who runs the program—frequently as `root`. Therefore, bugs or abuses perpetrated by the user may do more damage than could be done if the programs were not SUID or SGID. These programs don't consume more disk space than otherwise identical ordinary programs. Although some SUID and SGID programs ask for passwords (such as `passwd` and `su`), this isn't true of all such programs (such as `mount` and `ping`).

13. D. The `/etc/inittab` file controls the default runlevel. Although `telinit` can be used to *temporarily* change the runlevel, this change will not be permanent. The command `telinit Q` tells the system to reread `/etc/inittab`, so it could be used to implement a changed default after you've edited the file, but it will have no effect before editing this file. The `/etc/modules.conf` file has nothing to do with runlevels, and there is no standard `runlevel` module.

14. A. There is no standard `sysvstop` command, so options B and C can't be correct. Option D uses a parameter (`stop5m`) that's not standard, and so it won't stop the server. Option A stops the server, which can be manually restarted later or which will restart automatically when the system is rebooted, if it's configured to do so.

15. A, B. After editing `/etc/inetd.conf`, inetd should be restarted, typically by typing **/etc/rc.d/init.d/inetd restart** or something similar. An unused `/etc/inetd.conf` file can sometimes lure administrators used to configuring this file into editing it rather than configuring xinetd on systems that run this alternative super server. Running or editing the target server's startup script is unnecessary in this scenario because the server is started from the super server; it's not run directly.

16. D. Killing the server with `kill` will stop a running server. Local startup scripts don't accept `start` and `stop` parameters like those used by SysV startup scripts. Rerunning the startup script, even after editing it to remove references to the target server, won't kill running processes. `inetd` is a super server, and since the server in question isn't being run from a super server, restarting `inetd` won't kill the target server.

17. C. The `telinit` command changes runlevels. Option A, `telnet`, is Linux's Telnet client for initiating remote logins. Option B, `runlevel`, displays the current and previous runlevel, but doesn't change the runlevel. There is no `switch-runlevel` command (option D).

18. D. The reboot time, when specified in *hh:mm* form, is given as a 24-hour clock time, so 01:00 corresponds to 1:00 a.m. The -r parameter specifies a reboot, not a halt. (-h specifies a halt.)

19. B, D. Cron is a good tool for performing tasks that can be done in an unsupervised manner, like deleting old temporary files or checking to see that servers are running correctly. Tasks that require interaction, like creating accounts, are not good candidates for cron jobs, which must execute unsupervised. Although a cron job could restart a crashed server, it's not normally used to start a server when the system boots; that's done through SysV startup scripts or a super server.

20. B. User cron jobs don't include a username specification (tbaker in options A and C). The */2 specification for the hour in options C and D causes the job to execute every other hour; the 7,19 specification in options A and B causes it to execute twice a day, on the 7th and 19th hours (in conjunction with the 15 minute specification, that means at 7:15 a.m. and 7:15 p.m.).

Chapter

6

Networking

THE FOLLOWING COMPTIA OBJECTIVES ARE COVERED IN THIS CHAPTER:

- ✓ **1.10 Select appropriate networking configuration and protocols (e.g.,** `inetd`, `xinetd`, **modems, Ethernet).**

- ✓ **2.14 Monitor and troubleshoot network activity (e.g.,** `ping`, `netstat`, `traceroute`**).**

- ✓ **2.17 Perform remote management (e.g., rmon,** `ssh`**).**

- ✓ **2.18 Perform NIS-related domain management (e.g.,** `yppasswd`, `ypinit`, **etc.).**

- ✓ **2.21 Manage mail queues (e.g., sendmail,** `postfix`, `mail`, `mutt`**) using CLI utilities.**

- ✓ **3.1 Configure client network services and settings (e.g., settings for TCP/IP).**

- ✓ **3.2 Configure basic server network services (e.g., DNS, DHCP, SAMBA, Apache).**

- ✓ **3.3 Implement basic routing and subnetting (e.g,** `/sbin/` `route`, **ip forward statement).**

- ✓ **3.6 Implement DNS and describe how it works (e.g., edit** `/etc/hosts`, **edit** `/etc/host.conf`, **edit** `/etc/resolv.conf`, `nslookup`, `dig`, `host`, `named`**).**

- ✓ **3.7 Configure a Network Interface Card (NIC) from a command line.**

Networking is a complex topic that's touched on in several chapters of this book. This chapter provides an introduction to basic Transmission Control Protocol/Internet Protocol (TCP/IP) network configuration and proceeds with an overview of many of the network client and server functions a Linux system can fulfill. This chapter also includes information on administering a Linux computer from a distance by using networking protocols. For more information on network clients and servers, you'll need to consult other books or documentation.

When considered broadly, networking is a way for computers to communicate with one another. Just as with human-to-human communication, though, computer communication can be used to accomplish many different goals. These goals are associated with one or more networking protocols. For instance, e-mail transfer uses certain protocols, which are different from the protocols used in file sharing. This chapter is devoted largely to these protocols and the basics of configuring them.

Understanding Networks

In the last two decades of the 20th century, networks grew dramatically. Both local networks and larger networks exploded in importance as increasingly sophisticated network applications were written. To understand these applications, it's useful to know something about network hardware and the most common network protocols. Both of these things influence what a network can do.

Basic Functions of Network Hardware

Network hardware is designed to enable two or more computers to communicate with one another. As described shortly, this hardware can take a variety of forms. Most network hardware comes as a card you plug into a computer, although some devices are external and interface through an ordinary port like a USB port and other network "cards" are built into computer motherboards. Many networks rely on wires or cables to transmit data between machines as electrical impulses, but network protocols that use radio waves or even light to do the job are growing rapidly in popularity.

Sometimes the line between network hardware and peripheral interface ports can be blurry. For instance, a parallel port is normally not considered a network port, but when it is used with the Parallel Line Interface Protocol (PLIP; http://tldp.org/HOWTO/PLIP.html), the parallel port becomes a network device. More commonly, a USB or RS-232 serial port can become a network interface when used with the *Point-to-Point Protocol (PPP)*, as described in the upcoming section, "Initiating a PPP Connection."

At its core, network hardware is hardware that facilitates the transfer of data between computers. Hardware that's most often used for networking includes features that help this transfer in various ways. For instance, such hardware may include ways to address data intended for specific remote computers, as described later in the section "Hardware Addresses." When basically non-network hardware is pressed into service as a network medium, the lack of such features may limit the utility of the hardware or require extra software to make up for the lack. If extra software is required, you're unlikely to notice the deficiencies as a user or system administrator because the protocol drivers handle the work, which makes them harder to configure and more prone to sluggishness or other problems.

Types of Network Hardware

Aside from traditionally non-network ports like USB, RS-232 serial, and parallel ports, Linux supports several types of common network hardware:

Ethernet   Ethernet is the most common type of network hardware on local networks today. It comes in several varieties ranging from the old 10Base-2 and 10Base-5 (which use coaxial cabling similar to cable TV cable) to 10Base-T and 100Base-T (which use twisted-pair cabling that resembles telephone wire, but with broader connectors, hence the "-T") to the cutting-edge 1000Base-T and 1000Base-SX (also known as *gigabit Ethernet*, using twisted-pair or optical cables, respectively). In all these cases, the number preceding the "Base" (short for "baseband," a type of transmission medium) indicates the technology's maximum speed in megabits per second (Mbps). Plans are under way to develop another tenfold speed increase. Of the versions in use in early 2005, 100Base-T is the most common for new installations, but gigabit Ethernet is becoming more common as its price drops. Linux includes excellent Ethernet support, including drivers for almost every Ethernet card on the market.

Token Ring   At one time an important competitor to Ethernet, IBM's *Token Ring* technology is rapidly falling behind. The most common type of Token Ring clocks in at just 16Mbps, although 100Mbps varieties are available. Just as important, Token Ring is costlier than Ethernet and has less in the way of hardware support. For instance, fewer printers support direct connection to Token Ring networks than to Ethernet networks. Linux includes support for several Token Ring cards, so if you need to connect Linux to an existing Token Ring network, you can do so.

FDDI   *Fiber Distributed Data Interface (FDDI)* is a networking technology that's comparable to 100Base-T Ethernet in speed. FDDI uses fiber-optic cables, but a variant known as CDDI works over copper cables similar to those of 100Base-T. Both technologies are supported by the Linux FDDI drivers.

HIPPI   *High-Performance Parallel Interface (HIPPI)* provides 800Mbps or 1600Mbps speeds. It's most commonly used to link computer clusters or supercomputers over dozens or hundreds of meters. Linux includes limited HIPPI support.

LocalTalk   *LocalTalk* is a network hardware protocol developed by Apple for its Macintosh line. It's slow by today's standards (2Mbps), and Apple no longer includes LocalTalk connectors on modern Macintoshes. Nonetheless, there were a few *x*86 LocalTalk boards produced, and Linux supports some of these. Therefore, if you need to connect an *x*86 Linux system to a

LocalTalk network, you can do so—if you can find a LocalTalk board on the used market. (Ironically, the PowerPC port of Linux doesn't support the LocalTalk hardware that comes standard on older Macintoshes.)

Fibre Channel   *Fibre Channel* supports both optical and copper media, with speeds of between 133Mbps and 1062Mbps. The potential reach of a Fibre Channel network is unusually broad—up to 10 kilometers. Linux support for Fibre Channel is relatively new and incomplete, but it does exist.

Wireless protocols   Several wireless networking standards are becoming popular, particularly in small offices, homes, and public areas. These protocols vary in speed and range. The most popular of these standards is 802.11b (also known as Wi-Fi), which supports operation at up to 11Mbps. Other standards, such as 802.11a and 802.11g, provide faster speeds. This area is evolving rapidly, so you should be particularly careful about checking on Linux driver availability for any wireless networking products you buy.

If you're putting together a new network for a typical office, chances are that 100Base-T or gigabit Ethernet is the best choice. Wireless products are a good choice if running new cabling is a hassle and speed isn't vitally important, or if you want to provide a network that enables roaming use of notebook computers. If you need to connect to an existing network, you should find out what type of hardware it uses. If necessary, consult with your local network administrator to find out what type of network card you require.

Some computers ship with network hardware preinstalled. This is true of all modern Macintoshes and many *x*86 PCs, especially those sold as office workstations and servers. This hardware is almost always Ethernet.

In addition to the network cards you place in your computers, you need network hardware outside of the computer. With the exception of wireless networks, you'll need some form of network cabling that's unique to your hardware type. (For 100Base-T Ethernet, get cabling that meets at least Category 5, or Cat-5, specifications.) Many network types, including twisted-pair Ethernet, require the use of a central device known as a *hub* or *switch*. You plug every computer on a local network into this central device, as shown in Figure 6.1. The hub or switch then passes data between the computers.

As a general rule, switches are superior to hubs. Hubs mirror all traffic to all computers, whereas switches are smart enough to send packets only to the intended destination. The result is that switches let two pairs of computers engage in full-speed data transfers with each other; with a hub, these two transfers would interfere with each other. Switches also allow *full-duplex* transmission, in which both parties can send data at the same time (like two people talking on a telephone). Hubs permit only *half-duplex* transmission, in which the two computers must take turns (like two people using walkie-talkies).

A hub or switch is located centrally in a logical sense, but it doesn't have to be so located geographically. An approximately central location may help simplify wiring, but when you decide where to put the device, take into account the layout of your computers, your rooms, and available conduits between rooms.

FIGURE 6.1   Many networks link computers together via a central device known as a hub or switch.

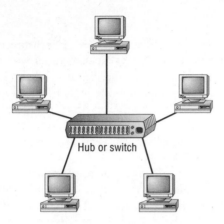

Hub or switch

Network Packets

Modern networks operate on discrete chunks of data known as *packets*. Suppose you want to send a 100KB file from one computer to another. Rather than send the file in one burst of data, you break it down into smaller chunks. You might send 100 packets of 1KB each, for instance. This way, if there's an error sending one packet, you can re-send just that one packet rather than the entire file. (Many network protocols include error-detection procedures.)

Typically, each packet includes an *envelope* (which includes the sender address, the recipient address, and other housekeeping information) and a *payload* (which is the data intended for transmission). When the recipient system receives packets, it must hold onto them and reassemble them in the correct order to re-create the complete data stream. It's not uncommon for packets to be delayed or even lost in transmission, so error-recovery procedures are critical for protocols that handle large transfers. Some types of error recovery are handled transparently by the networking hardware.

There are several types of packets, and they can be stored within each other. For instance, Ethernet includes its own packet type (known as a *frame*), and the packets generated by networking protocols that run atop Ethernet, such as those described in the next section, "Network Protocol Stacks," are stored within Ethernet frames. All told, a data transfer can involve several layers of wrapping and unwrapping data. With each layer, packets from the layer above may be merged or split up.

Network Protocol Stacks

The packing and unpacking of network data is frequently described in terms of a *protocol stack*. Knowing how the pieces of such a stack fit together can help you understand networking as a whole, including the various network protocols used by Linux. Therefore, this section presents this information; it starts with a description of protocol stacks in general and moves on to the TCP/IP stack and alternatives to it.

What Is a Protocol Stack?

It's possible to think of network data at various levels of abstractness. For instance, at one level, a network carries data packets for a specific network type (such as Ethernet), which are addressed to specific computers on a local network. Such a description, while useful for understanding a local network, isn't very useful for understanding higher-level network protocols, such as those that handle e-mail transfers. These high-level protocols are typically described in terms of commands sent back and forth between computers, frequently without reference to packets. The addresses used at different levels also vary, as explained in the upcoming section "Types of Network Addresses."

A protocol stack is a set of software that converts and encapsulates data between layers of abstraction. For instance, the stack can take the commands of e-mail transfer protocols, and the e-mail messages that are transferred, and package them into packets. Another layer of the stack can take these packets and repackage them into Ethernet frames. There are several layers to any protocol stack, and they interact in highly specified ways. It's often possible to swap out one component for another at any given layer. For instance, at the top of each stack is a program that uses the stack, such as an e-mail client. You can switch from one e-mail client to another without too much difficulty; both rest atop the same stack. Likewise, if you change a network card, you have to change the driver for that card, which constitutes a layer very low in the stack. Applications above that driver can remain the same.

Each computer in a transaction requires a compatible protocol stack. When they communicate, the computers pass data down their respective stacks, and then send data to the partner system, which passes the data up its stack. Each layer on the receiving system sees the data as packaged by its counterpart on the sending computer.

The OSI Model

The interactions of a protocol stack should become clearer with an example. A common model used for describing protocol stacks generically is the *Open System Interconnection (OSI) model*, illustrated in Figure 6.2. This model breaks networking tasks down into seven layers, from the Application layer (in which users' clients and the servers to which they connect run) to the Physical layer (which consists of network hardware like Ethernet cards). Each layer in between these does some task related to the packaging of data for transport or its unpacking.

Each component layer of the sending system is equivalent to a layer on the receiving system, but these layers need not be absolutely identical. For instance, you can have different models of network card at the Physical layer, or you can even use entirely different network hardware types, such as Ethernet and Token Ring, if some intervening system translates between them. The computers may run different OSs entirely and hence use different—but logically equivalent—protocol stacks. What's important is that the stacks operate in compatible ways.

FIGURE 6.2   Information travels "down" and "up" protocol stacks, being checked and packed at each step of the way.

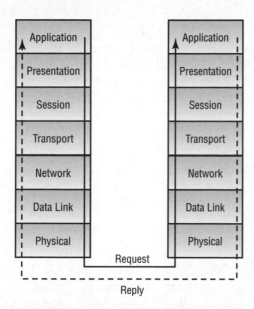

The TCP/IP Protocol Stack

The OSI model describes an idealized protocol stack; its features can be implemented in many different ways. One of the most common implementations is the *Transmission Control Protocol/ Internet Protocol (TCP/IP)* stack. The TCP/IP stack is usually described in slightly different terms than the OSI stack is. Specifically, the TCP/IP stack is generally described using just four layers (Application, Transport, Internet, and Link), as opposed to OSI's seven (shown in Figure 6.2). The principles are the same for both models; the differences are just a matter of how the terms are applied and precisely how the stacks are implemented.

TCP/IP has several important features that make it a popular network protocol and the one on which the Internet is based. These characteristics include the following:

Routable   TCP/IP was designed so that computers configured in a particular manner could route packets between two networks. These computers (known as *gateways* or *routers*) make the Internet possible. A small network links to another one via a router, which links to another, and so on. Such a collection of networks is known as an *internet* (without capitalization). The *Internet* (capitalized) is a particularly large globe-spanning internet.

Flexible naming system   TCP/IP supports two types of names, one based on numbers and one based on text. The current numeric system supports approximately 4 billion addresses, and the textual system supports multiple levels of names. Both features support large and complex network structures.

Multiple connection types   TCP/IP supports several types of connection, including the Transmission Control Protocol (TCP) after which the stack is named, the User Datagram Protocol (UDP), and the Internet Control Message Protocol (ICMP). These connection protocols support differing levels of complexity and error correction.

Standards-based   The TCP/IP stack and many of the protocols that use it are described by documents maintained by the Internet Engineering Task Force (IETF; `http://www.ietf.org`), an international standards organization. IETF protocols are nonproprietary, so they may be implemented by anybody who cares to examine and put to use the IETF standards documents, which are known as *Requests for Comments (RFCs)*.

This combination has made TCP/IP a formidable protocol stack. It's been implemented in a large array of OSs, ranging from DOS to Linux. A huge number of network tools are built atop TCP/IP, including everything related to the Internet—Web browsers, e-mail clients, and so on. A few networking programs, though, either don't use TCP/IP or use it only optionally. Other protocol stacks remain popular in certain environments, and you should be aware of them and how they interact and compete with TCP/IP.

Alternatives to TCP/IP

TCP/IP was initially developed using Unix, but today it is supported by many other platforms. Some of these other OSs have their own protocol stacks. Most of these have also been implemented on other OSs, including Linux. These TCP/IP alternatives don't support as many networking applications, though, and they're generally limited to use on much smaller networks than TCP/IP supports. Nonetheless, you may encounter these protocol stacks in some environments. They include:

NetBEUI   IBM and Microsoft have been the driving forces behind *NetBEUI*, which is a nonroutable protocol stack that was developed for local networks of DOS and, later, OS/2 and Windows systems. NetBEUI is closely associated with *NetBIOS*, on which Microsoft's file-sharing protocols are built. For this reason, many Windows networks make extensive use of NetBEUI. It's also possible to use NetBIOS over TCP/IP, and this is the approach that Linux's Samba file server package uses to interconnect with Windows clients. Linux doesn't include a NetBEUI stack of its own, although Procom Technologies (`http://www.procom.com`) has developed one that is not part of the regular Linux kernel. Chances are you won't need to use this stack because Samba works well over TCP/IP, and Samba is the only Linux package that might use a NetBEUI stack.

IPX/SPX   The *Internet Packet Exchange (IPX)* and *Sequenced Packet Exchange (SPX)* protocols constitute a protocol stack that's similar in broad strokes to TCP/IP or NetBEUI. IPX/SPX was the core of Novell's networking tools through NetWare 5.0, although later versions use TCP/IP by default. Novell's networking software competes for file and printer sharing in DOS and Windows networks against NetBEUI and its associated tools. IPX/SPX support is included in the Linux kernel, although it might not be compiled by default in all kernels. File- and printer-sharing packages are also available that use the IPX/SPX stack. IPX/SPX are routable, but aren't as amenable to creation of globe-spanning internetworks as is TCP/IP.

AppleTalk   Apple developed the *AppleTalk* stack for use with its LocalTalk network hardware. Its main use is with the AppleShare file-sharing protocols. Although initially tied to LocalTalk, AppleTalk can now be used over Ethernet (a combination that's sometimes called EtherTalk). The Linux kernel includes support for AppleTalk, but this may not be compiled in all kernels. The Linux package that supports AppleTalk and AppleShare is Netatalk. Netatalk supports not just the old AppleTalk, but AppleShare IP, which uses TCP/IP as the protocol stack for file sharing. Mac OS X doesn't rely on AppleTalk nearly as much as its predecessors did; thus AppleTalk is less important for modern Macintosh-dominated networks than it once was. Nonetheless, this support is still occasionally handy. For the best functionality on a Macintosh network, you need both TCP/IP and AppleTalk support in Linux.

These alternatives to TCP/IP are all used on local networks, not on the Internet at large, which is a TCP/IP-based network. All of these alternatives are limited in ways that restrict their expansion. For instance, they lack the capacity to handle more than a couple of levels in their machine names. That is, as described in the upcoming section "Hostnames," TCP/IP supports a hierarchical name structure that reduces the chance of conflicts in names, enabling every computer connected to the Internet to have a unique name. The naming schemes of these alternative stacks are much simpler, making it extremely impractical to maintain a worldwide naming system.

Different protocol stacks are incompatible in the sense that they aren't completely interchangeable—for instance, you can't run an FTP client using AppleTalk. (A few protocols, like those used for Windows file sharing, can bind to multiple protocol stacks, though.) In another sense, these protocol stacks are *not* incompatible. Specifically, you can run multiple protocol stacks on one network or one computer. Many local networks today run two, three, or more protocol stacks. For instance, an office with both Macintoshes and Windows systems might run TCP/IP, NetBEUI, and AppleTalk.

The Coming of IPv6

Another alternative protocol stack is actually an extension of TCP/IP. The current version of the IP portion of TCP/IP is 4. A major upgrade to this is in the works, however, and it goes by the name *IPv6*, for IP version 6. IPv6 adds several features and improvements to TCP/IP, including standard support for more secure connections and support for many more addresses. Check `http://playground.sun.com/pub/ipng/html/ipng-main.html` for detailed information on IPv6.

Although the 4 billion addresses allowed by TCP/IP sounds like plenty, those addresses have not been allocated as efficiently as possible. Therefore, as the Internet has expanded, the number of truly available addresses has been shrinking at a rapid rate. IPv6 raises the number of addresses to 2^{128}, or 3.4×10^{38}. This is enough to give every square millimeter of land surface on Earth 2.2×10^{18} addresses.

IPv6 is starting to emerge as a real networking force in many parts of the world. The United States, though, is lagging behind on IPv6 deployment. The Linux kernel includes IPv6 support, so you can use it if you need to. Chances are that by the time the average office will need IPv6, it will be standard. Configuring a system for IPv6 is somewhat different from configuring it for IPv4, which is what this chapter describes.

Network Addressing

In order for one computer to communicate with another over a network, the computers need to have some way to refer to each other. The basic mechanism for doing this is provided by a network address, which can take several different forms, depending on the type of network hardware, protocol stack, and so on. Large and routed networks pose additional challenges to network addressing, and TCP/IP provides answers to these challenges. Finally, to address a specific program on a remote computer, TCP/IP uses a *port number*, which identifies a specific running program, something like the way a telephone extension number identifies an individual in a large company. This section describes all these methods of addressing.

Types of Network Addresses

Consider an Ethernet network. When an Ethernet frame leaves one computer, it is normally addressed to another Ethernet card. This addressing is done using low-level Ethernet features, independent of the protocol stack in question. Recall, however, that the Internet is composed of many different networks that use many different low-level hardware components. A user might have a dial-up telephone connection (through a serial port) but connect to one server that uses Ethernet and another that uses Token Ring. Each of these devices uses a different type of low-level network address. TCP/IP requires something more to integrate across different types of network hardware. In total, three types of addresses are important when you are trying to understand network addressing: network hardware addresses, numeric IP addresses, and text-based hostnames.

Hardware Addresses

At the lowest level of the OSI model is the Physical layer, which corresponds to network hardware. One of the characteristics of dedicated network hardware such as Ethernet or Token Ring cards is that they have unique *hardware addresses,* also known as *Media Access Control (MAC) addresses*, programmed into them. In the case of Ethernet, these addresses are 6 bytes in length, and they're generally expressed as hexadecimal (base 16) numbers separated by colons. You can discover the hardware address for an Ethernet card by using the `ifconfig` command. Type **`ifconfig eth`**n, where n is the number of the interface (0 for the first card, 1 for the second, and so on). You'll see several lines of output, including one like the following:

```
eth0      Link encap:Ethernet  HWaddr 00:A0:CC:24:BA:02
```

This line tells you that the device is an Ethernet card and that its hardware address is 00:A0:CC:24:BA:02. What use is this, though? Certain low-level network utilities and hardware use the hardware address. For instance, network switches use it to direct data packets. The switch learns that a particular address is connected to a particular wire, and so it sends data directed at that address *only* over the associated wire. The Dynamic Host Configuration Protocol (DHCP), which is described in the upcoming section, "DHCP Configuration," is a means of automating the configuration of specific computers. It has an option that uses the hardware address to consistently assign the same IP address to a given computer. In addition, advanced network diagnostic tools are available that let you examine packets that come from or are directed to specific hardware addresses.

For the most part, though, you don't need to be aware of a computer's hardware address. You don't enter it in most utilities or programs. It's important for what it does in general.

IP Addresses

Earlier, I said that TCP/IP, at least in its IPv4 incarnation, supports about 4 billion addresses. This figure is based on the size of the *IP address* used in TCP/IP: 4 bytes (32 bits). Specifically, $2^{32} = 4,294,967,296$. Not all of these addresses are usable; some are overhead associated with network definitions, and some are reserved.

The 4-byte IP address and 6-byte Ethernet address are mathematically unrelated. Instead, the TCP/IP stack converts between the two using the *Address Resolution Protocol (ARP)*. This protocol enables a computer to send a *broadcast* query—a message that goes out to all the computers on the local network. This query asks the computer with a given IP address to identify itself. When a reply comes in, it includes the hardware address, so the TCP/IP stack can direct traffic for a given IP address to the target computer's hardware address.

> The procedure for computers that aren't on the local network is more complex. For such computers, a router must be involved. Local computers send packets destined to distant addresses to routers, which send the packets on to other routers or to their destination systems.

IP addresses are usually expressed as four base-10 numbers (0–255) separated by periods, as in 192.168.29.39. If your Linux system's protocol stack is already up and running, you can discover its IP address by using `ifconfig`, as described earlier. The output includes a line like the following, which identifies the IP address (`inet addr`):

```
inet addr:192.168.29.39   Bcast:192.168.29.255    Mask:255.255.255.0
```

Although not obvious from the IP address alone, this address is broken down into two components: a network address and a computer address. The network address identifies a block of IP addresses that are used by one physical network, and the computer address identifies one computer within that network. The reason for this breakdown is to make the job of routers easier—rather than record how to direct packets destined for each of the 4 billion IP addresses, routers can be programmed to direct traffic based on packets' network addresses, which is a much simpler job.

The *network mask* (also known as the *subnet mask* or *netmask*) is a number that identifies the portion of the IP address that's a network address and the part that's a computer address. It's helpful to think of this in binary (base 2) because the netmask uses binary 1 values to represent the network portion of an address and binary 0 values to represent the computer address. The network portion ordinarily leads the computer portion. Expressed in base 10, these addresses usually consist of 255 or 0 values, 255 being a network byte and 0 being a computer byte. If a byte is part network and part computer address, it will have some other value. Another way of expressing a netmask is as a single number representing the number of network bits in the address. This number usually follows the IP address and a slash. For instance, 192.168.29.39/24 is equivalent to 192.168.29.39 with a netmask of 255.255.255.0—the last number shows the network portion to be three solid 8-bit bytes, hence 24 bits.

IP addresses and netmasks are extremely important for network configuration. If your network doesn't use DHCP or a similar protocol to assign IP addresses automatically, you must configure your system's IP address manually. A mistake in this configuration can cause a complete failure of networking or more subtle errors, such as an inability to communicate with just some computers.

Non-TCP/IP stacks have their own addressing methods. NetBEUI uses machine names; it has no separate numeric addressing method. AppleTalk uses two 16-bit numbers. These addressing schemes are independent from IP addresses.

Hostnames

Computers work with numbers, so it's not surprising that TCP/IP uses numbers as computer addresses. People, though, work better with names. For this reason, TCP/IP includes a way to link names for computers (known as *hostnames*) to IP addresses. In fact, there are *several* ways to do this, some of which are described in the next section, "Resolving Hostnames."

As with IP addresses, hostnames are composed of two parts: *machine names* and *domain names*. The former refers to a specific computer and the latter to a collection of computers. Domain names are not equivalent to the network portion of an IP address, though; they're completely independent concepts. Domain names are registered for use by an individual or organization, which may assign machine names within the domain and link those machine names to any arbitrary IP address desired. Nonetheless, there is frequently some correspondence between domains and network addresses because an individual or organization that controls a domain is also likely to want a block of IP addresses for the computers in that domain.

Internet domains are structured hierarchically. At the top of the hierarchy are the top-level domains (TLDs), such as .com, .edu, and .uk. These TLD names appear at the *end* of an Internet address. Some correspond to nations (such as .uk and .us, for the United Kingdom and the United States, respectively), but others correspond to particular types of entities (such as .com and .edu, which stand for commercial and educational organizations, respectively). Within each TLD are various domains that identify specific organizations, such as sybex.com for Sybex or loc.gov for the Library of Congress. These organizations may optionally break their domains into *subdomains*, such as cis.upenn.edu for the Computer and Information Science department at the University of Pennsylvania. Even subdomains may be further subdivided into their own subdomains; this structure can continue for many levels, but usually doesn't. Domains and subdomains include specific computers, such as www.sybex.com, Sybex's Web server.

When you configure your Linux computer, you may need to know its hostname. This will be assigned by your network administrator and will be a machine within your organization's domain. If your computer isn't part of an organizational network (say, if it's a system that doesn't connect to the Internet at all, or if it connects only via a dial-up account), you'll have to make up a hostname. Alternatively, you can register a domain name, even if you don't use it for running your own servers. Check `http://www.icann.org/registrars/`accredited-list.html for pointers to accredited domain registrars. Most registrars charge between $10 and $15 per year for domain registration. If your network uses DHCP, it may or may not assign your system a hostname automatically.

> If you make up a hostname, choose an invalid TLD, such as `.invalid`. This will guarantee that you don't accidentally give your computer a name that legitimately belongs to somebody else. Such a name conflict could prevent you from contacting that system, and it could cause other problems as well, such as misdirected e-mail.

Resolving Hostnames

The *Domain Name System (DNS)* is a distributed database of computers that convert between IP addresses and hostnames. Every domain must maintain at least two DNS servers that can either provide the names for every computer within the domain or redirect a DNS query to another DNS server that can better handle the request. Therefore, looking up a hostname involves querying a series of DNS servers, each of which redirects the search until the server that's responsible for the hostname is found. In practice, this process is hidden from you because most organizations maintain DNS servers that do all the dirty work of chatting with other DNS servers. You need only point your computer to your organization's DNS servers. This detail may be handled through DHCP, or it may be information you need to configure manually, as described later in the section "Basic Network Configuration."

Sometimes, you need to look up DNS information manually. You might do this if you know the IP address of a server through non-DNS means and suspect your DNS configuration is delivering the wrong address, or to check whether a DNS server is working at all. Several programs can be helpful in performing such checks:

nslookup   This program performs DNS lookups (on individual computers, by default) and returns the results. It also sports an interactive mode in which you can perform a series of queries. This program is officially deprecated, meaning that it's no longer being maintained and will eventually be dropped from its parent package (`bind-utils` or `bind-tools` on most distributions). Thus, you should get in the habit of using `host` or `dig` instead of `nslookup`.

host   This program serves as a replacement for the simpler uses of `nslookup`, but it lacks an interactive mode, and of course many details of its operation differ. In the simplest case, you can type **host *target.name***, where *target.name* is the hostname or IP address you want to look up. You can add various options that tweak its basic operation; consult the `host` man page for details.

dig   This program performs more complex DNS lookups than `host`. Although you can use it to find the IP address for a single hostname (or a hostname for a single IP address), it's more flexible than `host`.

Sometimes DNS is overkill. For instance, you might just need to resolve a handful of host-names. This might be because you're configuring a small private network that's not connected to the Internet at large, or because you want to set up a few names for local (or even remote) computers that aren't in the global DNS database. For such situations, /etc/hosts may be just what you need. This file holds mappings of IP addresses to hostnames, on a one-line-per-mapping basis. Each mapping includes at least one name, and sometimes more:

```
127.0.0.1     localhost
192.168.7.23  apollo.luna.edu  apollo
```

In this example, the name localhost is associated with the 127.0.0.1 address and the names apollo.luna.edu and apollo are tied to 192.168.7.23. The first of these linkages is standard; it should exist in any /etc/hosts file. The second linkage is an example that you can modify as you see fit. The first name is a full hostname, including the domain portion; subsequent names on the line are aliases—typically the hostname without its full domain specification.

Once you've set up an /etc/hosts file, you can refer to computers listed in the file by name, whether or not those names are recognized by the DNS servers the computer uses. One major drawback to /etc/hosts is that it's a purely local file; setting a mapping in one computer's /etc/hosts file only affects name lookups performed by that computer. Thus, to do good on an entire network, you must modify the /etc/hosts files on all of the computers on the network.

Linux normally performs lookups in /etc/hosts before it uses DNS. You can, however, modify this behavior by editing the /etc/nsswitch.conf file and editing the hosts line, which lists the order of the files and dns options, which stand for /etc/hosts and DNS, respectively. Very old programs that use libc4 or libc5 rather than glibc look to the /etc/host.conf file and its order line instead of nsswitch.conf. Change the order of the hosts and bind items in this file to match the order of the files and dns items in /etc/nsswitch.conf.

Network Ports

Contacting a specific computer is important, but one additional type of addressing is still left: The sender must have an address for a specific program on the remote system. For instance, suppose you're using a Web browser. The Web server computer may be running more servers than just a Web server—it might also be running an e-mail server or an FTP server, to name just two of many possibilities. Another number beyond the IP address enables you to direct traffic to a specific program. This number is a network port number, and every program that accesses a TCP/IP network does so through one or more ports.

When they start up, servers tie themselves to specific ports, which by convention are associated with specific server programs. For instance, port 25 is associated with e-mail servers, and port 80 is used by Web servers. Thus, a client can direct its request to a specific port and expect to contact an appropriate server. The client's own port number isn't fixed; it's assigned by the OS. Because the client initiates a transfer, it can include its own port number in the connection request, so clients don't need fixed port numbers. Assigning client port numbers dynamically also enables one computer to easily run several instances of a single client because they won't compete for access to a single port.

Fortunately, for basic functioning, you need to do nothing to configure ports on a Linux system. You may have to deal with this issue if you run unusual servers, though, because you may need to configure the system to link the servers to the correct ports.

Basic Network Configuration

Now that you know something about how networking functions, the question arises: How do you implement networking in Linux? Most Linux distributions provide you with the means to configure a network connection during system installation, as mentioned in Chapter 1, "Linux Installation." Therefore, chances are good that networking already functions on your system. In case it doesn't, though, this section summarizes what you must do to get the job done. Actual configuration can be done using either the automatic DHCP tool or static IP addresses. Linux's underlying network configuration mechanisms rely on startup scripts and their configuration files, but you may be able to use GUI tools to do the job instead. Chapter 8, "System Documentation," includes a few additional network troubleshooting tips, so if you have problems, you may want to consult that chapter.

Clients and Servers

One important distinction is the one between clients and servers. A *client* is a program that initiates a network connection to exchange data. A server listens for such connections and responds to them. For instance, a Web browser, such as Mozilla or Opera, is a client program. You launch the program and direct it to a Web page, which means that the Web browser sends a request to the Web server at the specified address. The Web server sends back data in reply to the request. Clients can also send data, however, as when you enter information in a Web form and click a Submit or Send button.

The terms "client" and "server" can also be applied to entire computers that operate mostly in one or the other role. Thus, a phrase such as "Web server" is somewhat ambiguous—it can refer either to the Web server program or to the computer that runs that program. When this distinction is important and unclear from context, I clarify it (for instance, by referring to "the Web server program").

Network Hardware Configuration

The most fundamental part of network configuration is getting the network hardware up and running. In most cases, this task is fairly automatic—most distributions ship with system startup scripts that auto-detect the network card and load the correct driver module. If you recompile your kernel, building the correct driver into the main kernel file will also ensure that it's loaded at system startup.

If your network hardware isn't correctly detected, though, subsequent configuration (as described in the upcoming sections, "DHCP Configuration" and "Static IP Address Configuration") won't work. To correct this problem, you must load your network hardware driver. You can do this with the modprobe command:

```
# modprobe tulip
```

You must know the name of your network hardware's kernel module, though (tulip in this example). This name may not be immediately obvious, because it varies greatly depending on your hardware, and the name is usually based on the chipset used in the network card, rather than on the name of the network card or its manufacturer. Try doing a Web search to locate the correct driver. For instance, search on Linux GigaEth driver to locate the driver name for a card sold under the (fictitious) GigaEth name. If the computer dual-boots to another OS or if you use the same card in a computer that runs another OS, you might also find some clues by examining its configuration.

Once Linux has recognized the network hardware, you should be able to continue with network configuration, as described in the next couple of sections. To make Linux recognize your hardware at every boot, though, you may need to add the modprobe command to a startup script. This task can be tricky; most distributions use very convoluted startup scripts. These scripts *should* already be detecting and loading the network driver. If they don't, the best approach may be to recompile the kernel and build the driver into the main kernel file. Alternatively, you can try adding a call to modprobe to an appropriate network startup script; however, placing this call in a good location can be a difficult task.

Laptop computers can be tricky to configure because their network hardware is frequently inserted and removed from the computer after it's booted. Chapter 9 briefly describes these devices and the Card Services tools that help manage them. If you can't seem to get networking functioning correctly when you insert a PCMCIA network adapter in an already-running laptop, consult that section, and any documentation your distribution provides on PCMCIA devices.

DHCP Configuration

One of the easiest ways to configure a computer to use a TCP/IP network is to use the *Dynamic Host Configuration Protocol (DHCP)*, which enables one computer on a network to manage the settings for many other computers. It works like this: When a computer running a DHCP client boots up, it sends a broadcast in search of a DHCP server. The server replies (using nothing but the client's hardware address) with the configuration information the client needs to allow it to communicate with other computers on the network—most importantly the client's IP address and netmask and the network's gateway and DNS server addresses. The DHCP server may also give the client a hostname. The client then configures itself with these parameters. The IP address is not assigned permanently; it's referred to as a *DHCP lease*, and if it's not renewed, the DHCP server may give the lease to another computer. Therefore, from time to time, the client checks back with the DHCP server to renew its lease.

Three DHCP clients are in common use on Linux: pump, dhclient, and dhcpcd (not to be confused with the DHCP server, dhcpd). Some Linux distributions ship with just one of these, but others ship with two or even all three. All distributions have a default DHCP client, though—the one that's installed when you tell the system you want to use DHCP at system installation time. Those that ship with multiple DHCP clients typically enable you to swap out one for another simply by removing the old package and installing the new one.

Ideally, the DHCP client runs at system bootup. This is usually handled either by a SysV startup file, as described in Chapter 5, "Package and Process Management," or as part of the main network configuration startup file (typically a SysV startup file called `network` or `networking`). The system often uses a line in a configuration file to determine whether to run a DHCP client. For instance, Red Hat Linux sets this option in a file called `/etc/sysconfig/network-scripts/ifcfg-eth0` (this filename may differ if you use something other than a single Ethernet interface). The line in question looks like this:

```
BOOTPROTO=dhcp
```

If the `BOOTPROTO` variable is set to something else, changing it as shown here will configure the system to use DHCP. It's usually easier to use a GUI configuration tool to set this option, however, as described in the upcoming section "Using GUI Configuration Tools."

Static IP Address Configuration

If a network lacks a DHCP server, you must provide basic network configuration options manually. You can set these options using interactive commands, as described shortly, but to set them in the long term, you adjust a configuration file such as `/etc/sysconfig/network-scripts/ifcfg-eth0`. Listing 6.1 shows a typical `ifcfg-eth0` file, configured to use a static IP address. (Note that this file's exact location and name may vary from one distribution to another.)

Listing 6.1: A Sample Network Configuration File

```
DEVICE=eth0
BOOTPROTO=static
IPADDR=192.168.29.39
NETMASK=255.255.255.0
NETWORK=192.168.29.0
BROADCAST=192.168.29.255
GATEWAY=192.168.29.1
ONBOOT=yes
```

Several specific items are required, or at least helpful, for static IP address configuration:

IP address   You can set the IP address manually via the `ifconfig` command (described in more detail shortly), or via the `IPADDR` item in the configuration file.

Network mask   The netmask can be set manually via the `ifconfig` command or via the `NETMASK` item in a configuration file.

Gateway address   You can manually set the gateway via the `route` command. To set it permanently, you need to adjust a configuration file, which may be the same configuration file that holds other options or another file, such as /etc/sysconfig/network/routes. In either case, the option is likely to be called GATEWAY. The gateway isn't necessary on a system that isn't connected to a wider network—that is, if the system works *only* on a local network that contains no routers.

DNS settings   In order for Linux to use DNS to translate between IP addresses and hostnames, you must specify at least one DNS server in the /etc/resolv.conf file. Precede the IP address of the DNS server by the keyword nameserver, as in nameserver 192.168.29.1. You can include up to three nameserver lines in this file. Adjusting this file is all you need to do to set the name server addresses; you don't have to do anything else to make the setting permanent.

The network configuration script may hold additional options, but most of these are related to others. For instance, Listing 6.1 has an option specifying the interface name (DEVICE=eth0), another that tells the computer to assign a static IP address (BOOTPROTO=static), and a third to bring up the interface when the computer boots (ONBOOT=yes). The NETWORK and BROADCAST items in Listing 6.1 are derived from the IPADDR and NETMASK items, but you can change them if you understand the consequences.

If you aren't sure what to enter for the basic networking values (the IP address, network mask, gateway address, and DNS server addresses), you should consult your network administrator. *Do not* enter random values or values you make up that are similar to those used by other systems on your network. Doing so is unlikely to work at all, and it could conceivably cause a great deal of trouble—say, if you mistakenly use an IP address that's reserved for another computer.

As just mentioned, the ifconfig program is critically important for setting both the IP address and netmask. This program can also display current settings. Basic use of ifconfig to bring up a network interface resembles the following:

ifconfig *interface* up *addr* netmask *mask*

For instance, the following command brings up eth0 (the first Ethernet card) using the address 192.168.29.39 and the netmask 255.255.255.0:

 # ifconfig eth0 up 192.168.29.39 netmask 255.255.255.0

This command links the specified IP address to the card so that the computer will respond to the address and claim to be that address when sending data. It doesn't, though, set up a route for traffic beyond your current network. For that, you need to use the route command:

 # route add default gw 192.168.29.1

Substitute your own gateway address for 192.168.29.1. (Routing and the route command are described in more detail shortly, in "Configuring Routing.") Both ifconfig and route can display information on the current network configuration. For ifconfig, omit up and everything that follows; for route, omit add and everything that follows. For instance, to view interface configuration, you might issue the following command:

 # ifconfig eth0
eth0 Link encap:Ethernet   HWaddr 00:A0:CC:24:BA:02

```
      inet addr:192.168.29.39  Bcast:192.168.29.255   Mask:255.255.255.0
      UP BROADCAST RUNNING MULTICAST  MTU:1500  Metric:1
      RX packets:10469 errors:0 dropped:0 overruns:0 frame:0
      TX packets:8557 errors:0 dropped:0 overruns:0 carrier:0
      collisions:0 txqueuelen:100
      RX bytes:1017326 (993.4 Kb)  TX bytes:1084384 (1.0 Mb)
      Interrupt:10 Base address:0xc800
```

When configured properly, `ifconfig` should show a hardware address (HWaddr), an IP address (`inet addr`), and additional statistics. There should be few or no errors, dropped packets, or overruns for both received (RX) and transmitted (TX) packets. Ideally, few (if any) collisions should occur, but some are unavoidable if your network uses a hub rather than a switch. If collisions total more than a few percent of the total transmitted and received packets, you may want to consider replacing a hub with a switch. To use `route` for diagnostic purposes, you might try the following:

```
# route
Kernel IP routing table
Destination Gateway       Genmask       Flags Metric Ref  Use Iface
192.168.29.0 *            255.255.255.0 U     0      0      0 eth0
127.0.0.0   *             255.0.0.0     U     0      0      0 lo
default     192.168.29.1 0.0.0.0        UG    0      0      0 eth0
```

This shows that data destined for 192.168.29.0 (that is, any computer with an IP address between 192.168.29.1 and 192.168.29.254) goes directly over `eth0`. The 127.0.0.0 network is a special interface that "loops back" to the originating computer. Linux uses this for some internal networking purposes. The last line shows the *default route*—everything that doesn't match any other entry in the routing table. This line specifies the default route's gateway system as 192.168.29.1. If it's missing or misconfigured, some or all traffic destined for external networks, such as the Internet, won't make it beyond your local network segment.

As with DHCP configuration, it's almost always easier to use a GUI configuration tool to set up static IP addresses, at least for new administrators. The exact locations of the configuration files differ from one distribution to another, so the examples listed earlier may not apply to your system.

Using GUI Configuration Tools

Most distributions include their own GUI configuration tools for network interfaces. For instance, Fedora and Red Hat ship with a custom GUI tool called Network Configuration and a text-mode tool called `netconfig`, and SuSE has a text-mode and GUI tool called YaST. The details of operating these programs differ, but the GUI configuration tool provides a means to enter the information described earlier.

Figure 6.3 shows the Fedora Network Configuration tool, which you can use by typing **system-config-network** or by selecting the System Settings ➢ Network menu item from the default Red Hat desktop menu. Figure 6.3 shows both the main window (Network

Configuration) and the one in which you can set the most basic settings for an individual device (Ethernet Device). To see the latter window, you must highlight a device (only one is available in Figure 6.3's Network Configuration window) and click Edit. You can then enter your static IP address or, as in Figure 6.3, click the Automatically Obtain IP Address Settings With button to use DHCP. (Alternatively, you can choose the older BootP protocol or configure a dial-up configuration with this tool.) Additional options, including those to set the route and DNS features, are available from other tabs on these two dialog boxes.

FIGURE 6.3   GUI network configuration tools provide fields in which you enter basic networking parameters.

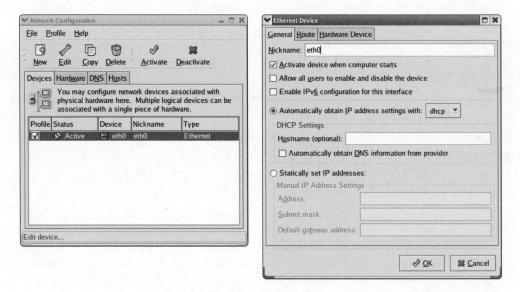

The precise details of how to configure a Linux system using GUI tools differ from one distribution to another. For instance, SuSE's YaST doesn't lay out its options in precisely the same way as Fedora's Network Configuration tool shown in Figure 6.3. The basic principles are the same, though; you must choose whether to use static IP address assignment or an automatic system such as DHCP, and enter a number of key options, depending on what configuration method you choose.

Initiating a PPP Connection

A conventional telephone modem is the low end of network connectivity. This device turns the public telephone network into a computer networking medium, linking precisely two points together. In its simplest form, a modem can be used to initiate a text-mode connection using a *terminal program*—a program that enables remote text-based logins but nothing else. Today, though, a modem is more often used in conjunction with PPP. PPP establishes a TCP/IP link between the two computers, so you can use any of the many TCP/IP-based tools, such as those described later in this chapter, in the section "Using Network Clients." Most PPP accounts, though, are designed to be used for brief periods at a time, not continuously. Modem connections are also much slower than most other types of network connection. Therefore, running servers on PPP-connected systems is usually inadvisable because most servers require always-on Internet connections, and many need more speed than a PPP link can provide. Some Internet service providers (ISPs) do offer full-time PPP links, though.

To initiate a PPP connection, you must have PPP software installed on your Linux system. The most important PPP package is known as pppd, for "PPP daemon." This utility can both initiate PPP links and respond to attempts to initiate them. This section describes the former. You can also use GUI interfaces to pppd, which can simplify PPP setup for those unfamiliar with the text-based tools.

A variant of PPP, PPP Over Ethernet (PPPoE), is used by some Digital Subscriber Line (DSL) broadband providers. Although PPPoE configuration is theoretically similar to what's described here, distribution-specific Linux network configuration tools often provide explicit PPPoE options to help out with this task.

Using Text-Based PPP Utilities

In Linux, a PPP connection usually requires an entry in a file called /etc/ppp/pap-secrets or /etc/ppp/chap-secrets. Both files use the same format. They provide information that's passed between the PPP client and server for authentication, using the Password Authentication Protocol (PAP) or Challenge-Handshake Authentication Protocol (CHAP). Because PPP was designed for use over public dial-up telephone lines, the caller must normally present a username and password to the other system; PAP and CHAP are merely protocols for doing this in a standard way. The format of lines in the secrets files is as follows:

username server password IP_address

The *username* and *password* values are your username and password, respectively, on the remote PPP system. Enter the values obtained from your ISP. The *server* value is the name of the system to which you're connecting. Normally, it's an asterisk (*), signifying that pppd will connect to any computer. *IP_address* is the IP address that pppd expects to get. This will normally be blank, meaning that the system will accept any IP address.

Connecting from the command line requires modifying certain connection scripts. These are called ppp-on, ppp-on-dialer, and ppp-off. The first two start a connection, and the third breaks it. These scripts are often stored in a documentation directory, such as /usr/share/doc/ppp-2.4.2/scripts. Copy them to a convenient binary directory that's on your path, such as /usr/local/bin. You must then modify them with information relevant to your ISP:

- In ppp-on, locate the lines that begin TELEPHONE=, ACCOUNT=, and PASSWORD=, and modify them so that they're appropriate for your ISP and account. (The ACCOUNT and PASSWORD variables should contain dummy values if you use PAP or CHAP, as is almost always the case.)

- Check that the DIALER_SCRIPT variable in ppp-on points to the correct location of ppp-on-dialer. The default location is /etc/ppp.

- Check the call to pppd in the last lines of ppp-on. Most of the parameters to this call are quite cryptic, but you should at least be able to confirm that it's using the correct modem device filename and speed. RS-232 serial modems generally use /dev/ttyS0 or /dev/ttyS1 as the filename. 115200 is an appropriate speed in most cases, but the default is 38400.

- Check the ppp-on-dialer script. This script includes a "chat" sequence—a series of strings the program expects to see from the modem or remote system in one column, and a series of responses in another column. You may need to log on using a terminal program like Seyon or minicom and then capture to disk the prompts your ISP uses to ask for your username and password; you'll then need to modify the last two lines of the script in order to make it work. Alternatively, you may have to comment out the last two lines by preceding them with hash marks (#) and remove the backslash (\) from the CONNECT line if your ISP uses PAP or CHAP.

The chat program expects a single line; its input is only formatted in columns in ppp-on-dialer for the convenience of humans. The backslashes ending most lines signify line continuations so that chat interprets multiple input lines as a single line. Only the final line should lack a backslash.

When you're done making these changes, type **ppp-on** (preceding it with a complete path, if necessary) as root to test the connection. If all goes well, your system should dial the modem, link up, and give you Internet access. If this fails to occur, check the last few lines of /var/log/messages with a command such as **tail -n 20 /var/log/messages**. You should see some sort of error messages, which may help you to diagnose the problem. To terminate a connection, type **ppp-off**.

Using a GUI Dialer

Many people prefer to use GUI dialing utilities to control PPP connections. Many such programs are available. One that comes with most Linux systems is the KDE PPP (KPPP) dialer, which is part of the KDE system. You can use KPPP even from other environments, though, or you can use another GUI PPP dialer. Most PPP dialers offer similar features and functionality.

Figure 6.4 shows the main KPPP window. You can launch it by typing **kppp** in a terminal window or by selecting it from the main KDE menu (its location varies, but it's often in a submenu called Network, Internet, or something similar). Once it's configured, you need only select your ISP's name from the Connect To list, enter your username (in the Login ID field) and password, and click Connect to begin a connection. This button changes to enable you to disconnect once a connection is initiated.

FIGURE 6.4   GUI dialers enable you to select from among several ISPs or dial-up numbers and connect by clicking a button.

To configure KPPP, follow these steps:

1. Click Configure. This action produces the KPPP Configuration window shown in Figure 6.5. This window controls basic KPPP features and enables you to modify specific accounts.

FIGURE 6.5   The KPPP Configuration window controls accounts and overall KPPP settings.

2. Click New to create a new account. The system displays a dialog box asking if you want to use a wizard or set up using dialog boxes. The wizard doesn't support U.S. ISPs, so if you're in the United States, you'll need to use the dialog box option. KPPP then displays the New Account dialog box (Figure 6.6).

FIGURE 6.6   The KPPP New Account dialog box lets you enter critical account-specific information.

3. Type an identifying name in the Connection Name field. This name exists so you can identify the configuration, so use whatever you like here.

4. Click Add, type in your ISP's phone number, and click OK. Repeat this step if your ISP provides multiple local access numbers.

5. Select the form of authentication used by your ISP. (PAP is the most common, followed by CHAP and scripted logins. The PAP/CHAP option tries to auto-detect which system your ISP uses.)

6. Click OK in the New Account dialog box to close it.

7. In the KPPP Configuration window, check the settings on the Device and Modem tabs. You may need to adjust some of these, like the Modem Device and Connection Speed.

8. Click OK in the KPPP Configuration window.

When you make a connection the first time, click Show Log Window in the main KPPP window (Figure 6.4). This produces a window that shows the interactions between your system and your ISP's, which can be helpful in case things don't go as you expect.

Network Server Configuration

Linux frequently functions as a network server platform—that is, Linux's primary role is to run one or more programs that listen to network requests and respond to them. This chapter covers the basics of several common server programs and protocols, including super servers, DHCP servers, DNS servers, time servers, file-sharing tools, mail servers, and Web servers.

> Most of these servers are very complex, and entire books have been written about them. This chapter can only scratch the surface of configuring, running, and using these servers. If you need more information, consult appropriate server-specific documentation.

Super Server Configuration

A *super server* is an unusual type of server. Instead of handling one network protocol itself, a super server functions as an intermediary for other servers, as described next in "The Role of a Super Server." The end result is increased flexibility, but not all servers need or work well with super servers. In Linux, two super servers are in common use: `inetd` and `xinetd`. Most systems run only one of these super servers, which play similar roles but do things differently from one another.

The Role of a Super Server

Super servers sit between calling client systems and some or all of the individual server programs they're attempting to access, as shown in Figure 6.7. As illustrated by this figure, though, super servers often do not manage *all* of the individual server programs run on a particular computer—some server programs don't work well via a super server, and so manage their own connections.

A single super server can manage connections from multiple client computers, just as most server programs can. A single client computer can connect to multiple servers on a single server system, with or without a super server intermediary. From the point of view of the client computer, the super server effectively does not exist; it looks just like the target server program that it manages. In fact, the super server does minimal direct "talking" to the client; it listens for the initial connection and, once that connection has been detected and passes certain preliminary tests, passes it on to the target server program.

What, then, does a super server do? That is, why use one? Super servers offer several advantages over letting target servers listen for their connections directly:

Reduced overhead   Every program that a computer runs consumes resources, such as memory and CPU time. By running a super server, that overhead can be minimized, particularly for memory—a single super server can stand in for several target servers. This advantage is greatest for seldom-used servers, though; if a server is used frequently, it will be running most of the time whether or not a super server mediates access.

FIGURE 6.7 Super servers manage connections between clients and individual server programs.

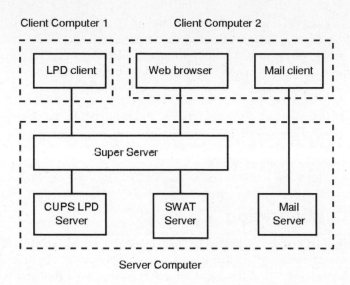

Unified configuration Super servers can help simplify configuration by providing a single control point for multiple servers. You can go through the super server configuration file to enable or disable all the servers it manages. This advantage is limited, though, because many servers do *not* use super servers. That is, you can't assume that a server isn't running just because it's not listed in the super server configuration file.

Access control Super servers can provide unified security features. For instance, they can restrict access to the servers based on time of day, calling IP address, and so on. The `inetd` super server does this with the help of another package, TCP Wrappers; `xinetd` implements these controls itself.

Of course, super servers aren't without their drawbacks. The most important of these is that servers launched via super servers typically respond slightly more slowly than do servers that run directly. The cause is simple: The super server must launch the server program every time it's accessed, and this process takes time. This effect is greatest for large servers; it can be trivial for small servers. Another problem with super servers is that they can't manage every server program; some have requirements that super servers can't handle. For instance, a server might need to maintain information in memory between accesses, and if the super server launches a new instance for every access, this maintenance won't work.

In practice, you'll need to consult a server program's documentation to learn whether to launch it directly or via a super server. Some programs can be launched in either way, but most work best in one way or another. Most Linux distributions provide server packages with appropriate startup scripts to enable a server to launch in the correct way, although you may need to edit these scripts, particularly for servers that are handled by super servers.

Configuring *inetd*

Linux distributions have been slowly shifting from inetd to xinetd. Nonetheless, you may still find inetd in use on some systems. Type **ps ax | grep inetd** to see which super server is running on your system—the output should include a line with either the inetd or the xinetd command. Some systems run neither super server, though.

You control servers that launch via inetd through the /etc/inetd.conf file. This file consists of a series of lines, one for each server. A typical line resembles the following:

```
ftp stream tcp nowait root /usr/sbin/tcpd /usr/sbin/in.ftpd -l
```

NOTE   This and several subsequent examples refer to in.ftpd, an FTP server that was once quite popular but that's being replaced on many systems by other FTP servers. Some of these servers cannot be run from a super server, so using another server might not work in all of these cases.

Each line consists of several fields separated by one or more spaces. The meanings of these fields are:

Service name   The first field (ftp in the preceding example) is the name of the service as it appears in the /etc/services file.

Socket type   The socket type entry tells the system what type of connection to expect—a reliable two-way connection (stream), a less reliable connection with less overhead (dgram), a low-level connection to the network (raw), or various others. The differences between these types are highly technical; your main concern in editing this entry should be to correctly type the value specified by the server's documentation.

Protocol   This is the type of TCP/IP protocol used, usually tcp or udp.

Wait/no wait   For dgram socket types, this entry specifies whether the server connects to its client and frees the socket (nowait) or processes all its packets and then times out (wait). Servers that use other socket types should specify nowait in this field.

User   This is the username used to run the server. The root and nobody users are common choices, but others are possible as well.

Server name   This is the filename of the server. In the preceding example, the server is specified as /usr/sbin/tcpd, which is the TCP Wrappers binary. This program provides some security checks, enabling you to restrict access to a server based on the origin and other factors. Chapter 7, "Security," covers TCP Wrappers in more detail.

Parameters   Everything after the server name consists of parameters that are passed to the server. If you use TCP Wrappers, you pass the name of the true target server (such as /usr/sbin/in.ftpd) in this field, along with its parameters.

The hash mark (#) is a comment symbol for /etc/inetd.conf. Therefore, if a server is running via inetd and you want to disable it, you can place a hash mark at the start of the line. If you want to add a server to `inetd.conf`, you'll need to create an entry for it. Most servers that can be run from `inetd` include sample entries in their documentation. Many distributions ship with `inetd.conf` files that include entries for common servers as well, although many of them are commented out; remove the hash mark at the start of the line to activate the server.

After modifying `inetd.conf`, you must restart the `inetd` super server itself. This super server normally runs as a standard SysV server, so you can restart it by typing something similar to the following:

```
# /etc/rc.d/init.d/inetd restart
```

Alternatively, you can tell `inetd` to reload its configuration by passing the SysV startup script the `reload` parameter rather than `restart`. The `restart` option shuts down the server and then starts it again. When you use `reload`, the server never stops running; it just rereads the configuration file and implements any changes. As a practical matter, the two are quite similar. Using `restart` is more likely to correctly implement changes, but it's also more likely to disrupt existing connections.

It's generally wise to disable as many servers as possible in `inetd.conf` (or the `xinetd` configuration files, if you use `xinetd`). As a general rule, if you don't understand what a server does, disable it. This will improve the security of your system by eliminating potentially buggy or misconfigured servers from the equation.

Configuring *xinetd*

The `xinetd` program is an extended super server. It provides the functionality of `inetd`, plus security options that are similar to those of TCP Wrappers. Modern versions of Fedora, Mandrake, Red Hat, SuSE, and a few other distributions use `xinetd` by default. Other distributions may use it in the future. If you like, you can replace `inetd` with `xinetd` on any distribution.

The `/etc/xinetd.conf` file controls `xinetd`. On distributions that use `xinetd` by default, though, this file contains only global default options and a directive to include files stored in `/etc/xinetd.d`. Each server that should run via `xinetd` then installs a file in `/etc/xinetd.d` with its own configuration options.

Whether the entry for a service goes in `/etc/xinetd.conf` or a file in `/etc/xinetd.d`, it contains information similar to that in the `inetd.conf` file. The `xinetd` configuration file, though, spreads the information across multiple lines and labels it more explicitly. Listing 6.2 shows an example that's equivalent to the earlier `inetd.conf` entry. This entry provides precisely the same information as the `inetd.conf` entry except that it doesn't include a reference to `/usr/sbin/tcpd`, the TCP Wrappers binary. Because `xinetd` includes similar functionality, it's generally not used with TCP Wrappers.

Chapter 7 covers `xinetd` security features.

Listing 6.2: Sample `xinetd` Configuration Entry

```
service ftp
{
        socket_type     = stream
        protocol        = tcp
        wait            = no
        user            = root
        server          = /usr/sbin/in.ftpd
        server_args     = -l
}
```

One additional `xinetd.conf` parameter is important: `disable`. If you include the line `disable = yes` in a service definition, `xinetd` ignores the entry. Some servers install startup files in `/etc/xinetd.d` that have this option set by default; you must edit the file and change the entry to read `disable = no` to enable the server. You can also disable a set of servers by listing their names in the `defaults` section of the main `xinetd.conf` file on a line called `disabled`, as in `disabled = ftp shell`.

As with `inetd`, after you make changes to `xinetd`'s configuration, you must restart the super server. You do this by typing a command similar to the one used to restart `inetd`. As with that command, you can use either `reload` or `restart`, with similar effects:

 # /etc/rc.d/init.d/xinetd restart

Delivering IP Addresses with DHCP

The earlier section "DHCP Configuration" described how to configure a computer to use an existing DHCP server to obtain its IP address. Linux can function as that DHCP server, though. If you want Linux to do this, you must first install the DHCP server package, which is usually called `dhcp-server` or `dhcp`. This package normally includes a SysV startup script, such as `/etc/init.d/dhcpd`, which launches the server at system startup time. The server program itself is called `dhcpd`, and is normally located in `/usr/sbin`.

WARNING   The DHCP server program (dhcpd) has a name that's very similar to one of the three common Linux DHCP clients (dhcpcd). This similarity can be confusing; it's easy to install the wrong package or waste time trying to get the wrong daemon running.

The main DHCP server configuration file is `/etc/dhcpd.conf`. Listing 6.3 shows a sample of this file, which can serve as a starting point for a basic configuration. The file consists of two main parts: a series of global options and a `subnet` declaration that sets options for a particular subnet the DHCP server handles. (In a complex network, a single DHCP server might have multiple network interfaces, each with its own `subnet` declaration in `dhcpd.conf`.)

Listing 6.3: Sample DHCP Server Configuration

```
default-lease-time 86400;
max-lease-time 172800;
option subnet-mask 255.255.255.0;
option domain-name-servers 192.168.1.3, 10.128.60.8;
option domain-name "rodsbooks.com";
option netbios-name-servers 192.168.1.3;
option netbios-node-type 8;
get-lease-hostnames true;
use-host-decl-names true;
ddns-update-style none;

subnet 192.168.1.0 netmask 255.255.255.0 {
    range 192.168.1.50 192.168.1.175;
    option routers 192.168.1.1;
}
```

Most of the options in Listing 6.3 set features that are self-explanatory or that you shouldn't need to change. Features you're most likely to want to adjust are:

Lease times   The `default-lease-time` and `max-lease-time` options set the default and maximum DHCP lease times in seconds. For testing purposes, lease times of just a few minutes (perhaps 100–500 seconds) are reasonable. For a working network, lease times of several hours to several days (5,000–1,000,000 seconds) are more reasonable.

Network mask   The `option subnet-mask` line sets the network mask delivered to clients.

Name servers   You can point clients to one or more name servers with the `option domain-name-servers` line. (As in Listing 6.3, multiple servers should be separated by commas.)

Domain name   You can set the domain name with the `option domain-name` line. Clients might or might not use this information.

NetBIOS options   You can provide several NetBIOS options to Windows systems with various options that include the string `netbios` in their name. Listing 6.3 points Windows systems to a NetBIOS name server and sets the NetBIOS node type. The values in Listing 6.3 are reasonable for most networks, although you must change the IP address of the NetBIOS name server for your network. If you don't know what your NetBIOS name server's IP address is, you should omit these lines.

Subnet declaration   The `subnet` line begins the definition of a subnet the server is to handle. This begins with a specification of the subnet range, in the form of a network address (`192.168.1.0`), the `netmask` keyword, and a network mask (`255.255.255.0`). The network mask often matches the one specified with the `option subnet-mask` line, but it doesn't have to. An open curly brace (`{`) then begins the subnet declaration itself, in which you set options that apply only to this subnet. The subnet declaration ends with a close curly brace (`}`)

IP address assignments   You tell the DHCP server what IP addresses to manage on the range line, which includes two IP addresses. The server assigns addresses within that range to any client that asks for one. Note that this range should *not* include the IP address used by the DHCP server itself or any other computer to which you assign a static IP address.

Routers   The `option routers` line sets the IP address of the router for this subnet.

Most lines in `dhcpd.conf` end in semicolons (`;`). The exceptions are lines that denote the start or end of a block of lines, such as the first and last lines in a `subnet` declaration.

The Linux DHCP server is very flexible and supports many options not described here. For more information, consult the `dhcpd.conf` man page or a book on DHCP, such as Ralph Droms and Ted Lemon's *The DHCP Handbook, 2nd Edition* (Sams, 2002).

Delivering Hostnames with DNS

Just as Linux uses a DNS server to resolve hostnames to IP addresses (and vice versa), Linux can run a DNS server program for the benefit of other systems. The most common Linux DNS package is the Berkeley Internet Name Domain (BIND), which installs a server under the filename `named`. This server is typically started through a SysV startup script of the same name—like a DHCP server, a DNS server works best when it can run continuously to cache the names it serves, so DNS servers aren't typically run from super servers.

The main BIND configuration file is `/etc/named.conf`. This file controls overall server operation, including global options (in a section that begins with the keyword `options`) and one or more `zone` sections that point to files that describe the domains the server manages. Managing a DNS domain is beyond the scope of this book, but you may want to configure BIND as a *forwarding-only DNS server*—that is, as a server that merely forwards DNS lookups to another computer. This configuration can improve DNS lookup times because your local DNS server can cache the names most frequently looked up by users on your local network, eliminating the need for your systems to consult an outside DNS server. A forwarding-only DNS configuration is enabled in the `options` section of `named.conf`:

```
options {
        directory "/var/named";
        forwarders {
                10.9.16.30;
                10.13.16.30;
                };
        listen-on{
                192.168.1.1;
                172.24.21.1;
        };
        forward only;
};
```

The key sections of this definition are the `forwarders` lines and the `forward only` line. The `forwarders` definition specifies the DNS servers to which BIND should forward the lookup requests it receives. This example specifies two outside systems; BIND will try each of them in turn, stopping when it receives a reply. The `forward only` line tells BIND that it should *only* function as a forwarding server; that is, it won't attempt to do lookups itself. If you change this line to `forward first`, then BIND will attempt to get an answer from the systems specified in the forwarders area, but if they don't answer, BIND will attempt to perform a *full recursive DNS lookup*. In this process, BIND contacts the *root DNS servers*, which know which systems handle the TLDs. These systems know which servers handle individual domain names, and so on. BIND queries each of these systems in turn. Full recursive lookups can take some time by computer standards (perhaps a couple of seconds), and the faster the network connection, the faster this happens. Thus, leaving this task to a server that's closer to the Internet at large than your own system is generally a good idea. Performing a full recursive lookup also requires that your system have an accurate root zone record. This is normally installed along with BIND and is referenced by the `zone "."` section of `named.conf`, but if the root servers ever change (as they do from time to time), your existing configuration might not work. For these reasons, `forward only` is usually the safer configuration.

This example also has a `listen-on` section, which tells BIND on which IP addresses it should listen. This option is most useful on server computers that have multiple network interfaces; you can have BIND respond to queries from some interfaces but not others.

DNS in general, and BIND in particular, are very complex. As already noted, this description completely ignores an important part of DNS and BIND configuration—setting up your own domain. If you need to do this, or perform other tasks with BIND, you should consult more complete documentation, such as Paul Albitz and Cricket Liu's *DNS and BIND, 4th Edition* (O'Reilly, 2001).

Delivering Files with Samba

The Samba server suite (`http://www.samba.org`) shares Linux files and printers with Windows computers. This package implements the *Server Message Block/Common Internet File System (SMB/CIFS)* protocol suite. It's controlled through a master configuration file, `smb.conf`, which is usually stored in `/etc/samba`. The Samba suite actually consists of two major servers, `smbd` and `nmbd`, along with several auxiliary programs and servers. It's started via one or more SysV startup scripts. Typically, either one script called `samba` or something similar starts both `smbd` and `nmbd`, or these servers have independent SysV startup scripts named after themselves.

Non-Windows computers, including Linux, can function as Samba clients. Chapter 4, "Disk Management," describes using Linux as an SMB/CIFS client.

The main `smb.conf` file consists of several sections, each of which begins with a keyword in square brackets. The first of these is the `[global]` section, which sets global options. Subsequent sections define file or printer *shares*—named resources on the SMB/CIFS server that can be accessed to share files or printers. Each of these sections is named with a share name; for instance, [common] defines a share called COMMON. Within each section, Samba parameters look like this:

parameter = value

The *parameter* is a keyword, such as security or netbios name. It's essentially a variable name that's set to the *value* specified. This *value* may be numeric (such as a time in seconds), a filename, a hostname, a Boolean (Yes or No; True or False; 1 or 0), or some other type of value. The intent is that the smb.conf file's meaning be fairly self-explanatory, at least if you know the server's basic features. Unfortunately, there are so many features that you might not understand everything, much less be able to generate new entries, unless you're an expert. Most default smb.conf files include extensive comments to help you with this process, or you can consult the smb.conf man page, which is unusually complete.

Two parameters in the [global] section are particularly important: workgroup and encrypt passwords. The workgroup parameter sets the name of the NetBIOS workgroup or domain. The default value is usually WORKGROUP, but most networks have their own workgroup name, so you should adjust this parameter appropriately. If you don't, clients may have trouble finding the Samba server using their network browsers. The encrypt passwords parameter is a Boolean that determines whether Samba uses its own encrypted password database or requires unencrypted passwords that it authenticates using the standard Linux password database. The default value is No for Samba 2.*x*, but Yes for Samba 3.0 and later. In most cases, encrypt passwords = Yes is the most appropriate choice, because all versions of Windows since the mid-1990s require the use of encrypted passwords by default.

Unfortunately, using encrypted passwords means that you must maintain a Samba-specific password database. The reason is that the encrypted password exchange tools of SMB/CIFS are incompatible with the methods Linux uses to store passwords in /etc/shadow. To create and maintain an encrypted password database, you can use the smbpasswd utility, which stores data in the /etc/samba/smbpasswd file. (This file sometimes resides elsewhere, particularly if you compile Samba yourself.) To add a user to this file, pass it the -a parameter and the username:

smbpasswd -a john

This command creates an entry in /etc/samba/smbpasswd for john, provided that the local Linux user john already exists. (The smbpasswd program will only create entries for users who already have standard Linux accounts.) When you type this command, you'll be prompted twice for a password, much as when you use the Linux passwd command to change a password. In fact, you can then use smbpasswd to change Samba passwords for existing users.

The first time you use the smbpasswd command, it will complain about the lack of an /etc/samba/smbpasswd file. This complaint looks like an error message, but the utility creates the file, so nothing is wrong or needs your attention.

To actually share files, you must create file share definitions. These can be as simple as a share name in square brackets in the smb.conf file:

[sample]

This line creates a share called SAMPLE. If no other lines are present until the end of the file or the next share definition, the share is read-only and provides access to the /tmp directory. To make the share useful, chances are you'll want to change at least some of these defaults:

```
[sample]
   comment = Sample Samba Share
   path = /home/samba/sample
   read only = No
```

This example sets three parameters. The comment line sets a comment string that's associated with the share and that appears in many clients' network browsers. It doesn't directly affect the share's functionality, but providing a descriptive comment can help users find the shares they need. The path parameter tells Samba what directory to share. The default value is /tmp, but that's not usually very useful. A synonym for this parameter is directory. Finally, setting read only = No tells Samba that users may write to the share. The writeable, writable, and write ok parameters are antonyms for read only; that is, writeable = Yes is equivalent to read only = No. An important caveat about Samba's write permissions is that they still work within the constraints of Linux file permissions, as described in Chapter 2. Every user who accesses a Samba server does so as an ordinary user. If that user can't write to a directory or file, Samba won't permit the user to do so (at least, not without using more advanced parameters). Thus, you must ensure that permissions are set appropriately within file shares if you want your users to be able to write to them. In fact, permissions must be set to enable users to *read* files in shares that they should be able to read, as well. In most cases, 0644 (-rw-r--r--) permissions do nicely for files in read-only shares, but managing permissions in read/write shares can be complex.

An important special Samba share is the [homes] share. Unlike most shares, this one doesn't point to a single directory; it points to the user's home directory, as defined in /etc/passwd. If you want users to be able to store their personal files on a Samba server, a [homes] share can be just the thing you need. Most smb.conf sample files include a working [homes] share, so you might not need to do anything to add one. In operation, this share appears as the user's username—for instance, the user john sees a share called JOHN.

Samba is a very complex and powerful server, and this description barely presents the most basic Samba information. If you need to do more with Samba, you should consult its copious documentation or a book on the subject, such as my *Linux Samba Server Administration* (Sybex, 2001).

Delivering Files with NFS

Samba is primarily a tool for file sharing with Windows clients. Although it can be used for sharing files with Linux or Unix clients, SMB/CIFS wasn't designed with these systems in mind. Thus, SMB/CIFS lacks support for certain features, such as Unix-style ownership and permissions, that Linux and Unix clients need. (A set of Unix extensions to SMB/CIFS add these features, and both Samba and the Linux kernel support Unix extensions, but this support is still imperfect, at least as of Samba 3.0.7 and the 3.0.8.1 Linux kernel.) A better option for file sharing between Linux and Unix systems is the *Network File System (NFS)*, which was designed by Sun as a network file-sharing tool for Unix.

In Linux, NFS server configuration is handled through a file called `/etc/exports`. This file contains lines that begin with a directory that's to be shared followed by a list of hostnames or IP addresses that may access it, with their options in parentheses:

```
/home taurus(rw,async) littrow(ro)
/opt taurus(ro)
```

These examples share two directories: /home and /opt. Two computers (`taurus` and `littrow`) may access /home, but only `taurus` may write to that directory because only `taurus`'s definition includes the `rw` (read/write) option; the `littrow` definition includes the `ro` (read-only) specification. The /home description for `taurus` also includes the `async` option, which can improve performance but slightly increases the risk of data loss should a disk error occur. The /opt directory is shared only with `taurus`, and that system may not write to the directory.

In order to deliver NFS support, you must run an NFS server program. (Most NFS server programs for Linux rely on special kernel features as well, but they are almost always compiled into the kernel by default.) Typically, this program is run by a SysV startup script, often called `nfsserver` or something similar. Check for this startup script and, if necessary, start or restart it once you've made changes to the `/etc/exports` file.

Most servers use passwords or some other authentication tool to control access to files. NFS works differently; an NFS server trusts the client system to control access to files. Once a directory is exported via NFS, any client computer that's authorized to access the directory in `/etc/exports` may do so in any way it permits. The idea is that the client computer will have a user base that's compatible with the user base on the server, and that the client computer is trustworthy. These assumptions weren't unreasonable when NFS was created, but in today's computing environment, they're a bit risky. Somebody with a notebook computer and wireless networking hardware may be able to access your server and masquerade as another computer if you use a wireless network. Even with a wired network, a compromised system or physical access can enable an attacker to pretend to be a trusted system. An attacker can control the user database on the attacking computer, or use a custom NFS client program that doesn't play by the usual security rules, thus bypassing the intent of the NFS security scheme. Thus, you should be cautious about NFS security. Don't add a computer to `/etc/exports` unless it's really necessary and don't give clients read-write access unless they really need it. You might also want to use IP addresses rather than hostnames to specify computers in `/etc/exports`; this practice makes masquerading as a trusted system a little more difficult.

Setting Up a Remote Access Server

Remote access servers enable a user on one computer to run programs on another. One of the oldest remote access protocols around is Telnet, and all major Linux distributions ship with a Telnet server, which is typically called `telnetd` or `in.telnetd`. This file may be distributed in a package called `telnet`, `telnet-server`, or something else. Telnet servers are very simple and therefore require no configuration beyond basic installation. They're normally launched from `inetd` or `xinetd`, which are programs that start other servers on an as-needed basis. The "Super Server Configuration" section, earlier in this chapter, described how to configure these programs.

Unfortunately, Telnet suffers from the same problem as FTP—it sends passwords (and all other data) unencrypted across the network. Therefore, the SSH protocol has emerged as a more secure replacement for Telnet. Until late in 2000, there were various legal barriers to the distribution of SSH, but these barriers have largely evaporated. Because of this, SSH is now a standard part of most Linux distributions. The most popular SSH package in Linux is OpenSSH (`http://www.openssh.com`). SSH typically comes in at least two packages: a client and a server. There may also be a "common" package and support libraries.

Once all the required packages are installed and the server is running, the default SSH configuration tends to work well. If necessary, though, you can fine-tune it. The normal SSH server configuration file is `/etc/ssh/sshd_config`. (There's also an `/etc/ssh/ssh_config` file that controls the SSH client.)

Some SSH packages come configured to allow root to log in directly. Even with the password encryption provided by SSH, this is inadvisable because it makes it too easy for somebody who has obtained the root password through other means to break into your system. To plug this security hole, change the PermitRootLogin option in sshd_config to no. Users who need to perform superuser tasks remotely can still log in as ordinary users and then use su to obtain the necessary privileges. This requires an outsider to have *two* passwords in order to do serious damage to the system.

Configuring Mail Servers

E-mail is a critical part of the Internet today, and Linux can function as a mail server computer. In fact, even Linux computers that don't exist as mail server computers often run mail server software. The reason is that certain local tools sometimes assume that a local mail server program will be present; these tools use the local mail server to deliver notices about their activities to root or to some other user. For instance, cron (described in Chapter 5) e-mails the output of the programs it runs to the user who runs them. Thus, basic e-mail configuration is often important, even on Linux systems that aren't primarily mail servers. The next few pages describe two common Linux mail server programs, sendmail and Postfix, as well as some of the commands and tools you can use to manage a mail queue on Linux. These servers both handle *the Simple Mail Transfer Protocol (SMTP)*, which is a common *push mail protocol*, meaning that the data transfer is initiated by the mail's sender. This contrasts with a *pull mail protocol*, in which the recipient initiates the data transfer.

SMTP servers can be misconfigured to function as *open mail relays*. These will forward mail from any address to any other address, and are beloved by those who send *spam*—unsolicited bulk e-mail. All Linux distributions released since 1999 or so are configured to *not* be open mail relays by default. If you're running an older distribution, or if you attempt to change your mail server's configuration, you should ensure that you aren't running an open mail relay. Consult `http://mail-abuse.org/tsi/` for more information on this important topic.

This section can only scratch the surface of e-mail configuration, particularly for large mail server computers. For more information on mail server configuration, consult the server's own documentation or a book on the subject, such as Craig Hunt's *Linux Sendmail Administration* (Sybex, 2001) or Kyle D. Dent's *Postfix: The Definitive Guide* (O'Reilly, 2003). The upcoming section, "Using an E-Mail Client," describes the basics of e-mail from the client perspective.

Configuring Sendmail

The sendmail program (`http://www.sendmail.org`) has long been the most common mail server program on the Internet. Over the past decade, its popularity has declined somewhat, but even with this drop in popularity, sendmail remains a very important mail server. Several Linux distributions, such as Fedora, Red Hat, and Slackware, use sendmail as the default mail server program. Most Linux distributions that use it provide it in a package called `sendmail`, so you can check to see if that package is installed on your system.

The presence of a binary program called `sendmail` might not indicate the presence of the sendmail server. Many programs assume that the mail server executable is called `sendmail`, so other mail server packages usually provide a binary or link of that name for compatibility purposes.

The main sendmail configuration file is `sendmail.cf`, which is usually kept in `/etc/mail`. This file has a very complex and confusing structure, though. In practice, most administrators write their sendmail configurations in another file, which is converted to a `sendmail.cf` file via a special utility, called m4:

```
# m4 < myconfig.mc > sendmail.cf
```

If you issue this command in the same directory in which the original `sendmail.cf` file resides, the command copies over the existing `/etc/mail/sendmail.cf` file. For added safety, back up that file first. You can then restore it from the backup if something goes wrong.

This command converts the `myconfig.mc` file into the `sendmail.cf` file. Where do you start, though? That is, where can you find a file to modify into `myconfig.mc`? Distributions that use sendmail typically provide sample configurations called `sendmail.mc`, `linux.smtp.mc`, or something similar. These files may exist in the `/etc/mail` directory or elsewhere (Slackware stores its file in `/usr/share/sendmail/cf/cf`, for instance). This file may be installed as part of the main sendmail package or as part of a separate package, such as Fedora's `sendmail-cf` package. You may also need to install the m4 package, which holds the m4 utility used to convert the `.mc` file to a `.cf` file.

For the most part, a typical desktop Linux system needs few or no changes to its sendmail configuration; the default values should work acceptably. Most recent distributions, including recent versions of Fedora and Red Hat, ship with sendmail configurations that cause the server to accept mail only from the computer on which the server runs. If you want sendmail to accept mail from other computers, though, you'll need to modify the configuration. To do so, look for a line like this:

```
DAEMON_OPTIONS(`Port=smtp,Addr=127.0.0.1, Name=MTA')dnl
```

 The Character before `Port` in this line isn't an ordinary single quote mark; it's an *open* single-quote mark, which can be typed from the key to the left of the 1 key on most keyboards. In some fonts, the result looks like "curly" single quotes around the options within the parentheses.

This line tells sendmail to bind only to the 127.0.0.1 address—that is, the localhost interface. To have sendmail accept mail from other systems, you must comment this line out. The .mc file uses the string dnl as a comment indicator, so you should add that string to the start of the line:

```
dnl DAEMON_OPTIONS(`Port=smtp,Addr=127.0.0.1, Name=MTA')dnl
```

You can then create a new `sendmail.cf` file by using `m4`, as just described. After you restart sendmail by using its SysV startup script, the server should accept mail from other computers.

Configuring Postfix

Postfix (`http://www.postfix.org`) isn't as popular on the Internet at large as sendmail, but it's now the default mail server for several Linux distributions, such as Mandrake and SuSE. On the whole, Postfix is simpler to configure than is sendmail; Postfix uses a single configuration file, `/etc/postfix/main.cf`, for most options, and the Postfix options are named more intuitively than are most sendmail equivalents. The default `main.cf` file is also copiously commented, so you can learn a great deal about Postfix configuration by reading that file.

As with sendmail, a default Postfix configuration works reasonably well for a standalone workstation or a non-mail server system. Most default Postfix configurations accept mail directed at the server computer from other systems, so reconfiguring it as described for sendmail isn't likely to be necessary. If you can't seem to send to the Postfix server from another computer, though, or if you want to close it off so that it rejects such access attempts, look for the `inet_interfaces` option:

```
inet_interfaces = $myhostname, localhost
```

This setting tells Postfix to listen on the network interface associated with `$myhostname` (which is set earlier to the computer's hostname, or set via a system call if it's not set) and to the localhost interface. You can remove `$myhostname` to have Postfix listen only on the localhost interface, or add it if it's not present and you want the server to listen on that interface.

After you make changes to the Postfix configuration, you can tell the server to immediately implement the changes:

```
# postfix reload
```

This command begins an orderly rereading of configuration files, and the various processes associated with Postfix restart at their earliest convenience. Using the SysV startup script's `restart` or `reload` option should have a similar effect.

One of the differences between sendmail and Postfix is that sendmail uses a monolithic design—a single program handles almost everything that the server package does. Postfix, by contrast, uses a modular design—a master program calls several smaller programs, each of which handles a particular detail. This design helps security by enabling programs that don't need root privileges to run as a lesser user. At any given moment, though, more Postfix-related programs may be running, each handling a particular subtask in mail delivery.

Managing Mail Queues

The `sendmail` program functions both as a daemon and as a command that can accept mail for delivery and manage mail queues. In fact, some Linux programs send mail by calling the `sendmail` program, which is why Postfix and other Linux mail servers typically provide a program of the same name, and that accepts the same options as the original program.

One of the most basic ways to use the `sendmail` command is to use its `-bp` option, which lists the mail messages that are still waiting to be sent. An equivalent command is `mailq`. In either form, this command is useful if you're not sure whether the mail server is delivering mail. For instance, if your configuration is bad or if a network connection is down, typing **mailq** should reveal a backlog of old messages. Such a listing might even provide clues to the nature of a problem. For instance, if mail to some sites is being delivered but mail to other sites isn't getting out, it could be a problem with routers, overzealous anti-spam configurations on the remote site, or something about your own configuration that's tripping anti-spam alarms on the remote site.

Seeing messages in a `mailq` listing isn't necessarily a sign of trouble. If your system is processing very many or very large messages, they will appear in the queue for a time. Likewise, a slow network connection will cause messages to hang about for a while. If messages regularly stay in the queue for very long, though, it could be your network connection is unreliable or overloaded, or it could be something about your mail server software's configuration is suboptimal. Checking the mail log files (typically /var/log/mail) may provide you with more clues.

If mail has accumulated in the queue and you believe you've corrected the problem, it should eventually clear out on its own. To speed up the process, though, you can type **sendmail -q**. This command causes the mail server to immediately attempt delivery of all queued messages.

Configuring Web Servers

Web servers are another staple of the Internet; in fact, many people don't fully realize that the Internet consists of anything *but* Web servers. These servers handle the *Hypertext Transfer Protocol (HTTP)*, which is why most Web page addresses begin with the string `http://`. (A secure HTTP variant also exists; such pages are denoted by a leading `https://`.)

Just as sendmail is the most popular mail server, Apache (`http://httpd.apache.org`) is the most popular Web server. Some distributions install Apache by default, but many don't, so if you want to run Apache, you may need to install it; it usually comes in a package called `apache`.

 Other Web server packages also exist, but none is nearly as popular as Apache. Because Apache usually ships with Linux, and is sometimes installed by default, it's often a good choice, even though it provides more features than many sites need.

Once it's installed, Apache relies on a configuration file, which is likely to be called `httpd.conf` or `httpd2.conf` (the latter name most often applies to Apache 2.0 or later installations). This file usually appears in `/etc/apache`, `/etc/httpd`, or `/etc/httpd/conf`. In any event, the usual Apache configuration file consists of comment lines that begin with hash marks (#) and options lines that take the form

```
Directive Value
```

`Directive` is the name of an option you want to set, and `Value` is the value you want to assign to `Directive`. This file also contains blocks of options, which are denoted by codes in angle brackets:

```
<IfDefine APACHEPROXIED>
  Listen 8080
</IfDefine>
```

A default Apache configuration typically delivers Web pages from a central location, which is specified with the `DocumentRoot` directive. Chances are you don't want to look at your distribution's generic Web page, so you should look for this directive and either change it to point to your own home page or replace the files in the default location with those you've created.

In addition to the main site Web page, Apache can deliver user Web pages, which it reads from a directory specified with the `UserDir` directive. These pages normally reside in a subdirectory of each user's home directory. For instance, if `UserDir` points to `public_html`, the `public_html` subdirectory of each user's home directory holds that user's Web pages, which can then be accessed by appending a tilde (~) and the username in the Web address, as in `http://www.asmallisp.net/~john/` to access `john`'s home page.

Many sites run a Web server merely to deliver static content—that is, pages whose content doesn't change. Web servers can also run dynamic content, though, such as Common Gateway Interface (CGI) scripts, which are scripts or programs that run on the Web server at the request of a client. In Apache, you typically point to a special CGI directory using the `ScriptAlias` directive:

```
ScriptAlias /cgi-bin /usr/www/cgi-bin
```

This line tells Apache to look in `/usr/www/cgi-bin` for scripts. This directory may be a sub-directory of the parent of the `DocumentRoot` directory, but their locations can be quite different if you prefer.

WARNING   Enabling CGI features on a Web server can be tricky, because an incorrect configuration with buggy scripts can give an attacker a way to compromise the computer's security as a whole. Thus, I strongly recommend that you not attempt this unless you learn far more about Web servers and their CGI capabilities than I can present in this brief introduction to Web servers.

Another Web server feature that's handy on large systems is *virtual hosting*—one server that hosts multiple Web sites. Suppose two organizations with two domains (say, `example.com` and `pangaea.edu`) both want to host Web sites, but to reduce costs, they decide to share a single computer to do the job. Both point hostnames in their domains to this computer's IP address. Virtual hosting enables the computer with this IP address to respond differently depending on the hostname the user enters in a remote Web browser. Web hosting ISPs make heavy use of this feature, supporting many domains on a single computer. It can also be handy if you've changed your company name—you can run a single server that responds to both old and new domain names, with a notice about the change on the old name.

Implementing virtual hosting can be done in a couple of ways. One is to create a block with the `VirtualHost` directive:

```
<VirtualHost *>
  ServerName www.example.com
  DocumentRoot /usr/www/example/html
</VirtualHost>
```

Directives inside this block apply only when the client contacts the server using the hostname specified on the `ServerName` line. A second method involves the `VirtualDocumentRoot` directive, which specifies a document root directory that incorporates the hostname. This is specified with a special code that takes the form `%N.M`, where `N` is the hostname component and `M` is the number of characters (all characters, if it's omitted). A negative number counts from the final component. For instance, with a hostname of `www.sales.example.com`, `%-2` expands to `example` and `%4.2` expands to `co`. This code is incorporated into a directory specification:

```
VirtualDocumentRoot /usr/www/%-2.1/%-2
```

Ordinarily, the HTTP used by Web servers is unencrypted. A secure HTTP variant (HTTPS) is also available, and many Web servers, including Apache, can implement it. This variant uses the Secure Sockets Layer (SSL) to encrypt traffic. Web-based merchants, banks, and other sites that transfer sensitive financial or personal data are the most common users of HTTPS. If you need to implement it, you should consult more in-depth documentation, as using it requires setting various Web server options and, at least as importantly, obtaining an SSL certificate, which is a sort of token verifying your identity to the client.

If you make changes to the Apache configuration, you may need to restart the server, which you can do with the server's SysV startup script. Apache normally runs stand alone; it's a large enough server that running it from a super server isn't efficient. In fact, Apache 2.0 and later *cannot* be run from a super server, although earlier versions can be.

Apache is an extremely complex server; this section only presents the barest features of the server. To learn more, consult its documentation or a book on the subject, such as Charles Aulds' *Linux Apache Server Administration, 2nd Edition* (Sybex, 2002).

Using Network Clients

Although Linux is often deployed as a server platform, Linux also provides client programs for all of the most popular network protocols. This makes Linux a suitable network client OS; or you might just want to run a network client on a system that's otherwise a server as a means of testing the system in some way. The following pages describe a couple of important network client uses: running X programs remotely (this actually distorts the usual client/server relationship, as described shortly), and using mail clients.

Using X Programs Remotely

Linux's GUI environment, the X Window System (or X for short), is unusual in that it's fully network-enabled. Using nothing but the normal X software and Linux network configuration, it's possible to run an X program on one computer while sitting at another computer, using the second computer's monitor, keyboard, and mouse. In fact, it's possible for one of these systems to be running a Unix OS that's not Linux. It's even possible to run an X server on a Windows, OS/2, or other completely non-Unix system, or on a system with a different class of CPU than the Linux system.

 Although most people think of clients as running on the computers at which they sit and servers as running on remote systems, this isn't true of X. In X, the server runs on the system local to the user. To make sense of this, think of it from the program's point of view. To a word processor, the display and keyboard are services to be used, much like a network-accessible printer.

Suppose that your local network contains two machines. The computer called zeus is a powerful machine that hosts important programs, like a word processor and data analysis utilities. The computer called apollo is a much less powerful system, but it has an adequate monitor and keyboard. Therefore, you want to sit at `apollo` and run programs that are located on `zeus`. Both systems run Linux. To accomplish this task, follow these steps:

1. Log into `apollo` and, if it's not already running X, start it.

2. Open a terminal (such as an xterm) on `apollo`.

3. Type **xhost +zeus** in `apollo`'s terminal. This command tells `apollo` to accept for display in its X server data that originates on `zeus`.

4. Log into `zeus` from `apollo`. You might use Telnet or Secure Shell (SSH), for instance. (See the sections "Setting Up a Remote Access Server" and "Remote System Administration.") The result should be the ability to type commands in a shell on `zeus`.

5. On `zeus`, type **export DISPLAY=apollo:0.0**. (This assumes you're using bash; if you're using `tcsh`, the command would be **setenv DISPLAY apollo:0.0**.) This command tells `zeus` to use `apollo` for the display of X programs.

6. Type whatever you need to type to run programs at the `zeus` command prompt. For instance, you could type **soffice** to launch Star Office. You should see the programs open on `apollo`'s display, but they're running on `zeus`—their computations use `zeus`'s CPU, they can read files accessible on `zeus`, and so on.

7. After you're done, close the programs you've launched, log off `zeus`, and type **xhost -zeus** on `apollo`. This will tighten security so that a miscreant on `zeus` won't be able to modify your display on `apollo`.

Sometimes, you can skip some of these steps. For instance, depending on how it's configured, SSH can forward X connections, meaning that SSH intercepts attempts to display X information and passes those requests on to the system that initiated the connection. When this happens, you can skip steps 3 and 5, as well as the `xhost` command in step 7.

Another option for running X programs remotely is to use the Virtual Network Computing (VNC) system (`http://www.realvnc.com`). VNC runs a special X server on the computer that's to be used from a distance, and a special VNC client runs on the computer at which you sit. You use the client to directly contact the server. This reversal of client and server roles over the normal state of affairs with conventional X remote access is beneficial in some situations, such as when you are trying to access a distant system from behind certain types of firewall. VNC is also a cross-platform protocol; it's possible to control a Windows or Mac OS system from Linux using VNC, but this is not possible with X. (X servers for Windows and Mac OS are available, allowing you to control a Linux system from these non-Linux OSs.)

Using an E-Mail Client

Linux supports two main ways to read e-mail:

Read mail from the local mail queue.   If you give correspondents your Linux system's name and your username on that system, you can let the Linux system function as an SMTP server and read mail directly on the Linux computer. For instance, if your system is `apollo.luna.edu` and your username is `hschmidt`, mail from other systems addressed to `hschmidt@apollo.luna.edu` will reach your system and be stored there for you to read. This configuration requires that your system run an SMTP server, as described earlier, in "Configuring Mail Servers."

Read mail from a remote system. If you don't want mail to be addressed directly to your own computer, you can use a pull mail protocol, such as the *Post Office Protocol (POP)* or the *Internet Message Access Protocol (IMAP)*, in conjunction with a separate mail server system. For instance, you might give your e-mail address as `hschmidt@mail.luna.edu`, and then use your `apollo` workstation to retrieve mail from `mail.luna.edu`.

Each of these cases requires you to configure your mail reader appropriately, as described shortly. Using a local mail queue can make sense if the system has many users who don't have mail accounts on other systems. Reading mail from a separate mail server makes sense if your system's IP address changes frequently or if it's not online at all times, because SMTP mail delivery to your system will be unreliable in these cases.

Linux supports a wide variety of e-mail clients. These include KMail (`http://www.kde.org`), KDE's mail client; Ximian Evolution (`http://www.novell.com/linux/ximian.html`), a very powerful mail and contact management program; Mutt (`http://www.mutt.org`), an advanced text-based mail reader; `mail`, a very basic text-mode mail reader; and many others. As with Web browsers, you can launch mail clients by selecting them from desktop environment or window manager menus, or by typing the program's name at a shell prompt. You must usually configure the mail client to use either the local queue or a remote mail server. If the latter, you must enter the server's name, the protocols it uses, your username on that server (this may not be the same as your local username), and perhaps other information. Figure 6.8 shows the Add Account dialog box for KMail, in which most of this information is entered.

FIGURE 6.8 An e-mail client using a pull mail protocol employs your account on a mail server to retrieve e-mail.

You'll also have to choose how to send your mail. Because most Linux systems include a mail server, most mail programs give you the choice of using the local mail server to send outgoing mail or using an outside mail server. Chances are if you receive mail directly, you should send it using your local mail server; but if you receive mail through another mail server, you should send it in a similar manner.

 Many organizations maintain separate incoming and outgoing mail servers. Therefore, you might not enter the same mail server's address as the outgoing mail server as you used when specifying the incoming mail server. Consult your ISP or network administrator for details.

The details of day-to-day mail client operation vary from one program to another, but as a general rule, these programs include functions to permit reading new mail, replying to such mail, sending new mail, deleting old messages, and organizing messages into mail folders. Many also let you save messages to files, spell-check your outgoing messages, and so on. When you use a remote mail server, you must either explicitly check for new mail (by clicking a button or selecting a menu option) or configure the program to do this automatically every once in a while.

When you want to read or send mail from a text-mode logins, text-mode tools such as `mail` and Mutt are the tools of choice. The `mail` program is particularly handy on systems with limited resources, but it's rather alien to users who are more familiar with GUI tools such as KMail. To use `mail` to send mail, type the command name followed by the recipient's e-mail address. (The program also accepts various command-line options; consult its man page for details.) The `mail` program then prompts you for a subject, after which you type your message, which you terminate with a line that consists of a single dot (`.`). Once this is done, `mail` concludes by prompting for a `cc:` line. The full exchange looks something like this:

```
$ mail harrison@luna.edu
Subject: The fall semester enrollment report
Harrison,

Have you gotten around to finishing up the report? Thanks.
.
Cc:
```

Instead of typing a message into `mail`, you can compose it in a text editor and redirect it through `mail`, as in **mail harrison@luna.edu < seen-one-earth.txt**. (Chapter 2 describes redirection in more detail.) You can even set a subject for the message using the `-s` option, as in **mail -s "Famous quotes" harrison@luna.edu < seen-one-earth.txt**. Such uses of `mail` are particularly handy in scripts—you can write a script that generates a file you want to send to somebody and then send it with `mail`.

You can also use `mail` to check for and read existing mail. By default, the program checks your local mail queue; however, some versions of the program also support reading mail from a POP account. If you simply type **mail**, the program looks for new mail and, if any is present, displays a list of messages you can read. If no new mail is present, the program says so.

Somewhat more sophisticated text-mode mail programs include Pine (`http://www.washington.edu/pine/`) and Mutt (`http://www.mutt.org`). These programs present text-based mail interfaces that can be run in a text-mode login or in an xterm or similar GUI window. Of the two, Mutt is the more recent. It uses a file called `~/.muttrc` as a user configuration file, in which you can tell the program where to look for new mail (the local computer, a POP server, or an IMAP server, for instance), how to send mail, what external program to call when composing messages, and so on. Mutt is similar in overall power to popular GUI mail clients.

Configuring Routing

As explained earlier, routers pass traffic from one network to another. You configure your Linux system to directly contact systems on the local network. You also give the computer a router's address, which your system uses as a gateway to the Internet at large. Any traffic that's not destined for the local network is directed at this router, which passes it on to its destination. In practice, there are likely to be a dozen or more routers between you and most Internet sites. Each router has at least two network interfaces and keeps a table of rules concerning where to send data based on the destination IP address. Your own Linux computer has such a table, but it's likely to be very simple compared to those on major Internet routers.

Linux can function as a router, which means it can link two or more networks together, directing traffic between them on the basis of its routing table. This task is handled, in part, by the `route` command, which was introduced earlier, in "Static IP Address Configuration." This command can be used to do much more than just specify a single gateway system, though, as described in that section. A simplified version of the `route` syntax is

```
route {add | del} [-net | -host] target [netmask nm] [gateway gw]
➥[reject] [[dev] interface]
```

That is, you specify `add` or `del` along with a `target` (a computer or network address) and optionally other options. The `-net` and `-host` options force `route` to interpret the target as a network or computer address, respectively. The `netmask` option lets you set a netmask as you desire, and `gateway` lets you specify a router through which packets to the specified `target` should go. (Some versions of route use `gw` rather than `gateway`.) The `reject` keyword installs a blocking route, which refuses all traffic destined for the specified network. (This is *not* a firewall, though.) Finally, although `route` can usually figure out the interface device (for instance, `eth0`) on its own, you can force the issue with the `dev` option.

As an example, consider a network in which packets destined for the 172.20.0.0/16 subnet should be passed through the 172.21.1.1 router, which is not the default gateway system. You could set up this route with the following command:

```
# route add -net 172.20.0.0 netmask 255.255.0.0 gw 172.21.1.1
```

One more item you may need to adjust if you're setting up a router is enabling routing. Ordinarily, a Linux system will not forward packets it receives from one system that are directed at another system. If Linux is to act as a router, though, it must accept these packets and send them on to the destination network (or at least to an appropriate gateway). To enable this feature, you must modify a key file in the /proc filesystem:

```
# echo "1" > /proc/sys/net/ipv4/ip_forward
```

This command enables IP forwarding. Permanently setting this option requires modifying a configuration file. Some distributions set it in /etc/sysctl.conf:

```
net.ipv4.ip_forward = 1
```

Other distributions use other configuration files and options, such as /etc/sysconfig/ sysctl and its IP_FORWARD line. If you can't find it, try using grep to search for ip_forward or IP_FORWARD, or enter the command to perform the change manually in a local startup script.

Remote System Administration

Many different protocols can be used to provide administrative access to a Linux computer. Although using such protocols can pose a security risk, remote administration is often extremely convenient, or even necessary in some situations. You can use several types of tools to remotely administer your Linux system, including text-mode logins, GUI logins, file transfers, and dedicated remote administration protocols.

Text-Mode Logins

The earlier section "Setting Up a Remote Access Server" mentioned setting up a couple types of servers that accept text-mode logins from distant systems: Telnet and SSH. You can use either of these to administer one system from another—even from a computer running another OS, such as Windows or Mac OS. Typically, you log in using a regular user account, and then you use su to enter the root password to acquire superuser privileges. Thereafter, you can do almost anything you could do from a text-mode login at the console.

Telnet passes all data in an unencrypted form. This means that both your ordinary user's login password and the root password you enter in conjunction with su might be intercepted by an unscrupulous individual on the source, destination, or any intervening network. For this reason, it's best not to use Telnet for remote administration. For that matter, if it's possible, you should totally avoid using Telnet. SSH encrypts all the data that pass between two systems, and so it is a much better choice for remote administration.

To use Telnet from Linux, you type **telnet *hostname***, where *hostname* is the DNS hostname of the computer you wish to contact. You'll then see the remote system's login prompt. The entire procedure looks like this:

```
$ telnet apollo.luna.edu
Trying 192.168.1.1...
Connected to apollo.luna.edu.
Escape character is '^]'.

speaker login: ecernan
Password:
You have old mail in /var/mail/ecernan.
Last login: Tue Sep 30 10:43:37 from gemini.luna.edu
Have a lot of fun...
[ecernan@apollo]$
```

At this point, anything you type (aside from Ctrl+], which is an "escape" character to let you enter commands into your local Telnet program) is processed by the remote system. You can use su to acquire root privileges, read mail with mail or Mutt, edit files with Vi, Emacs, or any other text-based editor, and so on.

SSH works in a similar way, except that you don't see the login: prompt; SSH passes your current username to the server, which attempts to use the same username to authenticate you. If you want to use a different username on the server than on your current system, you should include the -1 *username* parameter on the command line, or prepend the username to the hostname with an at-sign (@), as in

```
$ ssh ecernan@apollo.luna.edu
ecernan@apollo.luna.edu's password:
Last login: Tue Sep 30 10:43:37 from gemini.luna.edu
[ecernan@apollo ecernan]$
```

The first time you make a connection to a given server, you may see a message informing you that the authenticity of the server can't be verified. The message goes on to display a code associated with the server. If you want to continue connecting, type **yes** in response to the query about this.

You may omit the username and at-sign if your username is the same on both systems. Once you've logged in with SSH, you can use the system much as you would from a Telnet login or from the console—by typing text-mode commands, editing files with text-mode editors, and so on. Because SSH encrypts all data, it's extremely unlikely that your original password, or the password you type when you use su, will be usable to anybody who intercepts the data stream.

Remote text-mode login tools other than Telnet and SSH are available. One formerly common tool is rlogin, which uses a trusted hosts security model, in which the server relies on the client to authenticate users. This feature makes `rlogin` a potential security vulnerability. Because of this, it's best to either completely eliminate the `rlogin` server (typically called `/usr/sbin/in.rlogind`) using your package management tools (as described in Chapter 5, "Package and Process Management") or stop the server from running (also described in Chapter 5).

The `rlogin` server is often included in a package along with other utilities that you may need. Don't remove the package to which this server belongs without first verifying that you don't need its other programs.

A variant on remote login tools is `rexec`, which enables you to run a single program remotely. Although `rexec` can be handy, SSH can do the same thing—simply type the command you want to run at the end of the `ssh` command line, as in **ssh apollo.luna.edu cat /etc/fstab** to view the contents of `/etc/fstab` on `apollo.luna.edu`.

GUI Logins

If you want to use GUI administration tools remotely, you can do so, but you'll need appropriate software on the system you're using to access the Linux computer. Normally, this is an X server, as described earlier in this chapter, in the section "Using X Programs Remotely." Because all major Linux distributions include X servers, it's usually possible to use one Linux computer as a terminal for GUI configuration of another. (The main exception to this is if you haven't installed X on the computer that you want to use to administer another.) Likewise, you can use a Windows system running an X server or VNC client (if you've installed the VNC server on Linux) to remotely control a Linux system with a GUI.

Once you've logged on, you can use the `su` command to acquire root privileges, just as you can when using a text-mode login. You can then run GUI administrative tools or run text-mode administrative commands inside an xterm or similar text shell window.

Neither X nor VNC encrypts most data transmitted over the network, although VNC encrypts its initial password. Therefore, when you issue the su command to acquire root privileges, you'll send the root password unencrypted. As a result, it's possible that it will be compromised. The simplest solution to this problem is generally to use SSH to make the initial connection. When properly configured, SSH will tunnel the X protocols through its own encrypted connection. This will slow down the display slightly, but it will protect the data (including passwords you type) from prying eyes.

File Transfers

Although generally not thought of as such, file transfer tools can be useful in remote administration. If you like, you can edit a configuration file on one system and transfer it to another system. You might want to do this if one system has more sophisticated editors or configuration checking tools than another system does. For instance, if you're administering a print server on which you have only bare-bones tools, you might want to modify the configuration files in a more comfortable environment on some other computer and then transfer the configuration files to the print server. (This would require the print server to be running some file-transfer server like FTP, NFS, or Samba, of course.)

When using file transfers in this way, it's generally not a good idea to give direct access to the target directory for the configuration files. For instance, you probably shouldn't share a system's /etc directory using NFS or Samba. Although doing so makes it easy to read and write configuration files, it also makes it that much easier for an intruder to modify these files, especially if there is a flaw in the server or its configuration. Instead, you should transfer files to and from an ordinary user account and then use a remote login protocol, such as SSH, to enable the copying of files from that account to their ultimate destinations.

Remote Administration Protocols

Several tools are designed to allow you to administer a computer remotely. To do so, you'll need to run the server version of one of these tools on the computer you plan to administer, and you'll need to run a client on the system you intend to use to do the administration. (Many of these tools use ordinary Web browsers as clients, so you can administer a Linux computer from any system that supports a Web browser, even if it's not a Linux computer itself.) Examples of these tools include the following:

SNMP   This protocol was designed as a remote administration protocol, but it requires fairly tedious configuration on the system that's to be administered. It also requires specialized client programs. For these reasons, it's never become a very popular Linux administration protocol.

RMON   The Remote Monitoring (RMON) protocol is designed to enable an administrator to monitor network devices. It's conceptually similar to SNMP. This protocol is typically used to manage standalone network devices, such as switches, rather than other Linux computers.

SWAT   The *Samba Web Administration Tool (SWAT)* is, as the name implies, a Web-based means of administering a Samba server. Once configured, SWAT can be accessed on port 901 using an ordinary Web browser, as shown in Figure 6.9. You specify the port number by adding a colon (:) and the number to the URL; so to administer apollo.luna.edu, you'd enter `http://apollo.luna.edu:901` in a Web browser. SWAT is limited to administering the Samba server functions of a computer, which limits the utility of this tool. SWAT provides unusually complete control of Samba, however.

Webmin   Webmin is an ambitious Web-based administration tool. Its ambitiousness derives from the fact that it aims to support Web-based administration of multiple Linux distributions (and other Unix-like systems) that use different configuration files. It accomplishes this goal by installing a series of configuration modules that are unique to each distribution. Once installed and running, Webmin binds to port 10000, so you'd enter `http://apollo.luna.edu:10000` in a Web browser to administer apollo.luna.edu. You can read more about Webmin on its Web page, `http://www.webmin.com`.

FIGURE 6.9   SWAT enables you to administer Samba using a Web browser's point-and-click tools.

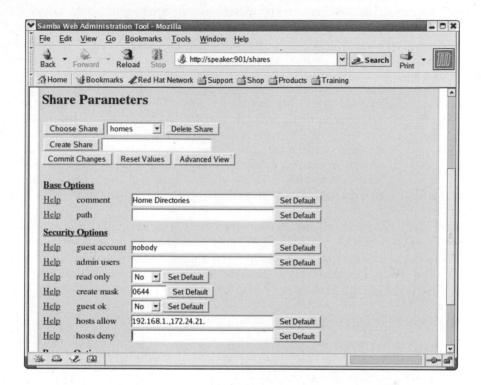

Web administration tools may be started using either standalone configurations or a super server.

WARNING   Remote administration tools frequently send passwords in an unencrypted form, so they're potentially dangerous tools to use except on well-protected local networks. Webmin supports using SSL to encrypt transmissions, which can greatly enhance its security. When using Webmin with SSL, you must use the `https://` lead-in to the URL rather than `http://`.

Using NIS

Network Information Service (NIS) is a protocol that's designed to simplify user authentication and related services on a network of multiple Unix or Linux systems. There are several variants of NIS, such as NIS+, NIS YP and Switch (NYS), and Name Switch Service (NSS). The original NIS was once called Yellow Pages (YP), but that's a registered trademark in some areas, so the name was changed. Nonetheless, most NIS utilities still include yp in their names.

Some distributions let you configure NIS during system installation. You may be required to enter the name of the NIS domain name (which may be different from your DNS domain name) and the address of the NIS server. If you want to use NIS after installing the OS, your task is a bit trickier. Your distribution might provide GUI tools to help the process, or you might need to configure the system manually. You should begin by installing the NIS packages. For an NIS client, the ypbind package is the most important one, but on most distributions it depends on other packages, such as yp-tools.

 NIS uses both clients and servers. The NIS server holds network account information, and the NIS clients use that information to authenticate users. This section describes the basics of NIS client configuration and the use of certain tools for NIS account maintenance. To learn about NIS server configuration, consult its documentation or a book on the subject, such as Hal Stern, Mike Eisler, and Ricardo Labiaga's *Managing NFS and NIS, 2nd Edition* (O'Reilly, 2001).

The ypbind NIS package's main configuration file is /etc/yp.conf. This file's main purpose is to point the NIS tools at an NIS server. The default file normally presents several possible ways to do this in comments. These methods differ in the amount of information you as an administrator have. For instance, if you know the name of your NIS domain and the name of the NIS server, you might use this format:

domain *NISDOMAIN* server *NISSERVER*

At the opposite extreme is a line that contains a single word: broadcast. This tells the tools to send out a broadcast query for a suitable NIS server. You should consult your network administrator to learn what option is best for your network.

Once you've told the NIS tools about your server, you must also configure Linux to use NIS. This can be accomplished by editing the /etc/nsswitch.conf file, which tells Linux what tools to use for name resolution, account information, and so on. A configuration that relies heavily on NIS is shown in Listing 6.4.

Listing 6.4: Sample /etc/nsswitch.conf File for NIS

```
passwd:      compat
group:       compat
# For libc5, you must use shadow: files nis
shadow:      compat

passwd_compat: nis
group_compat: nis
shadow_compat: nis

hosts:       nis files dns
```

```
services:     nis [NOTFOUND=return] files
networks:     nis [NOTFOUND=return] files
protocols:    nis [NOTFOUND=return] files
rpc:          nis [NOTFOUND=return] files
ethers:       nis [NOTFOUND=return] files
netmasks:     nis [NOTFOUND=return] files
netgroup:     nis
bootparams:   nis [NOTFOUND=return] files
publickey:    nis [NOTFOUND=return] files
automount:    files
aliases:      nis [NOTFOUND=return] files
```

Once this is set up, you should start or restart the ypbind daemon, which must be running at all times on the NIS client. Client-side tools contact this daemon for information that's normally stored in /etc/passwd and elsewhere, the ypbind daemon contacts the NIS server, and the NIS server delivers the requested information. Normally, you start ypbind via its SysV startup script.

Once NIS is up and running, you can manage the system with an assortment of commands whose names begin with yp. For instance, yppasswd changes a password much as passwd does, but yppasswd changes the password on the NIS server. On the server system, ypinit initializes the user account database.

Network Diagnostic Tools

Network configuration is a complex topic, and unfortunately, things don't always work as planned. Fortunately, there are a few commands you can use to help diagnose a problem. Three of these are ping, traceroute, and netstat. Each of these commands exercises the network in a particular way and provides information that can help you track down the source of a problem.

Testing Basic Connectivity

The most basic network test is the ping command, which sends a simple packet to the system you name (via IP address or hostname) and waits for a reply. In Linux, ping continues sending packets once every second or so until you interrupt it with a Ctrl+C keystroke. Here's an example of its output:

```
$ ping speaker
PING speaker.rodsbooks.com (192.168.1.1) from 192.168.1.3  : 56(84) bytes of data.
64 bytes from speaker.rodsbooks.com (192.168.1.1): icmp_ seq=0 ttl=255 time=149 usec
64 bytes from speaker.rodsbooks.com (192.168.1.1): icmp_ seq=1 ttl=255 time=136 usec
64 bytes from speaker.rodsbooks.com (192.168.1.1): icmp_ seq=2 ttl=255 time=147 usec
64 bytes from speaker.rodsbooks.com (192.168.1.1): icmp_ seq=3 ttl=255 time=128 usec
```

```
--- speaker.rodsbooks.com ping statistics ---
4 packets transmitted, 4 packets received, 0% packet loss
round-trip min/avg/max/mdev = 0.128/0.140/0.149/0.008 ms
```

This command sent four packets and waited for their return, which occurred quite quickly (in an average of 0.140ms) because the target system was on the local network. By pinging systems on both local and remote networks, you can isolate where a network problem occurs. For instance, if you can ping local systems but not remote systems, the problem is most probably in your router configuration. If you can ping by IP address but not by name, the problem is with your DNS configuration.

Tracing a Route

A step up from ping is the traceroute command, which sends a series of three test packets to each computer between your system and a specified target system. The result looks something like this:

```
$ traceroute -n 10.1.0.43
traceroute to 68.1.0.43 (68.1.0.43), 30 hops max, 52 byte packets
 1  192.168.1.254  1.021 ms   36.519 ms  0.971 ms
 2  10.10.88.1  17.250 ms   9.959 ms   9.637 ms
 3  10.9.8.173  8.799 ms   19.501 ms  10.884 ms
 4  10.9.8.133  21.059 ms   9.231 ms  103.068 ms
 5  10.9.14.9  8.554 ms   12.982 ms  10.029 ms
 6  10.1.0.44  10.273 ms   9.987 ms  11.215 ms
 7  10.1.0.43  16.360 ms  *  8.102 ms
```

The -n option to this command tells it to display target computers' IP addresses, rather than their hostnames. This can speed up the process a bit, and it can sometimes make the output easier to read—but you might want to know the hostnames of problem systems, because that can help you pinpoint who's responsible for a problem.

This sample output shows a great deal of variability in response times. The first hop, to 192.168.1.254, is purely local; this router responded in 1.021, 36.519, and 0.971 milliseconds (ms) to its three probes. (Presumably the second probe caught the system while it was busy with something else.) Probes of most subsequent systems are in the 8–20 ms range, although one is at 103.068 ms. The final system only has two times; the middle probe never returned, as the asterisk (*) on this line indicates.

Using traceroute, you can localize problems in network connectivity. Highly variable times and missing times can indicate a router that's overloaded or that has an unreliable link to the previous system on the list. If you see a dramatic jump in times, it typically means that the physical distance between two routers is great. This is common in intercontinental links. Such jumps don't necessarily signify a problem, though, unless the two systems are close enough that a huge jump isn't expected.

What can you do with the `traceroute` output? Most immediately, `traceroute` is helpful in determining whether a problem in network connectivity exists in a network for which you're responsible. For instance, the variability in the first hop of the preceding example could indicate a problem on the local network, but the lost packet associated with the final destination most likely is not a local problem. If the trouble link is within your jurisdiction, you can check the status of the problem system, nearby systems, and the network segment in general.

Checking Network Status

Another useful diagnostic tool is `netstat`. This is something of a Swiss Army knife of network tools because it can be used in place of several others, depending on the parameters it is passed. It can also return information that's not easily obtained in other ways. Some examples include the following:

Interface information   Pass `netstat` the `--interface` or `-i` parameter to obtain information on your network interfaces similar to what `ifconfig` returns. (Some versions of `netstat` return information in the same format, but others display the information differently.)

Routing information   You can use the `--route` or `-r` parameter to obtain a routing table listing similar to what the `route` command displays.

Masquerade information   Pass `netstat` the `--masquerade` or `-M` parameter to obtain information on connections mediated by Linux's NAT features, which often go by the name "IP masquerading." NAT enables a Linux router to "hide" a network behind a single IP address. This can be a good way to stretch limited IP addresses.

Program use   Some versions of `netstat` support the `--program` or `-p` parameters, which attempt to provide information on the programs that are using network connections. This attempt isn't always successful, but it often is, so you can see what programs are making outside connections.

Open ports   When used with various other parameters, or without any parameters at all, `netstat` returns information on open ports and the systems to which they connect.

Keep in mind that `netstat` is a very powerful tool, and its options and output aren't entirely consistent from one distribution to another. You may want to peruse its man page and experiment with it to learn what it can do.

Summary

Networking is very important to many modern Linux systems, which frequently function as servers or workstations on local networks. Networks operate by breaking data into individual packets in a manner that's dictated by the particular protocol stack in use by the system. Linux includes support for several protocol stacks, the most important of which is TCP/IP, the protocol stack on which the Internet is built. You can configure Linux for TCP/IP networking by using DHCP to automatically obtain an address, by entering the information manually, or by establishing a PPP link. You can do any of these things using text-mode or GUI tools, although the GUI tools aren't standardized across different distributions.

Once Linux is connected to a network, you can configure any of several server programs, making Linux available on the network. You can also use any of many client programs to access resources on the network (either the local network or the Internet). File transfer and sharing, Web browsing, e-mail, and remote access are just some of the applications of networking possible in Linux.

Exam Essentials

Determine appropriate network hardware for a Linux computer.   If the computer is to be used on an existing network, you must obtain a network card of a type that's compatible with that network, such as Ethernet or Token Ring. If you're building a new local network, Ethernet is the most common choice, although more exotic alternatives are also available and may be suitable in some specific situations.

Summarize how most network hardware is activated in Linux.   The `ifconfig` command brings up a network card, assigning it an IP address and performing other basic configuration tasks. Typically, this command is called in a SysV startup script, which may perform still more tasks as well, such as adding entries to the routing table.

Describe the information needed to configure a computer on a static IP network.   Four pieces of information are important: the IP address, the netmask (a.k.a. the network mask or subnet mask), the network's gateway address, and the address of at least one DNS server. The first two are required, but if you omit either or both of the latter two, you won't be able to connect to the Internet or use most DNS hostnames.

Determine when using /etc/hosts over DNS makes the most sense.   The `/etc/hosts` file provides a static mapping of hostnames to IP addresses on a single computer. As such, maintaining this file on a handful of computers for a small local network is fairly straightforward, but when the number of computers rises beyond a few or when IP addresses change frequently, running a DNS server to handle local name resolution makes more sense.

Summarize the function of PPP.   The Point-to-Point Protocol negotiates a TCP/IP connection, typically acquiring requisite information from the PPP server. It's used to connect computers via telephone lines, and is used in modified form for some broadband links.

Explain the nature of X clients and servers.   An X server controls a screen display and handles input from the user's mouse and keyboard. Therefore, the X server is used directly by the user, and X clients are the programs that rely on the X server's services.

Summarize the procedure for configuring sendmail.   Sendmail must be configured through its `/etc/mail/sendmail.cf` file, but this file's format is very tedious. Therefore, most administrators create another type of file that has a more manageable structure and create a `sendmail.cf` file using the `m4` utility.

Explain where Samba and NFS are best deployed.   Samba is an implementation of the SMB/CIFS protocol suite, which is most often used for file and printer sharing by Windows systems; thus, Samba is best used as a server for Windows clients. NFS, by contrast, was designed as a file sharing protocol for Unix systems, so it's best used for sharing files with Unix or Linux clients.

Describe how a Linux system may be administered remotely.   Remote administration may be achieved through text-mode login protocols like Telnet or SSH, through remote GUI sessions (X or VNC), or through specialized remote administration tools like SWAT or Webmin.

Describe the function of NIS.   The Network Information Service is a way to centralize Linux account, hostname, and other local system and network information on a single server. Using NIS enables you to maintain one account database rather than duplicate this information on many computers.

Explain what the `route` command accomplishes.   The `route` command displays or modifies the routing table, which tells Linux how to direct packets based on their destination IP addresses.

Summarize how `ping` and `traceroute` differ.   The `ping` command sends a simple packet to a target, waits for a reply, and reports on the total round-trip time. The `traceroute` command is similar, but it traces the route of a packet step-by-step, enabling you to track the source of a network connectivity problem.

Commands in This Chapter

Command	Description
ifconfig	Configures a network interface, or displays information on that configuration
ping	Sends a single packet to a target system, which should reply, confirming the existence of a basic connection
route	Configures a routing table entry, or displays information on the routing table
nslookup	Looks up an IP address from a hostname or vice versa
host	Looks up an IP address from a hostname or vice versa
dig	Looks up an IP address from a hostname or vice versa.
mail	Sends or reads mail from a command prompt
netstat	Displays information on a Linux computer's network configuration or the processes that use network resources
traceroute	Traces the route taken by packets between two computers, enabling you to isolate problems to specific areas of the trip

Review Questions

1.   Which types of network hardware does Linux support? (Choose all that apply.)

   A. Token Ring

   B. Ethernet

   C. DHCP

   D. Fibre Channel

2.   Which of the following is a valid IP address on a TCP/IP network?

   A. 202.9.257.33

   B. 63.63.63.63

   C. 107.29.5.3.2

   D. 98.7.104.0/24

3.   Which of the following is *not* a Linux DHCP client?

   A. pump

   B. dhcpcd

   C. dhcpd

   D. dhclient

4.   You try to set up a computer on a local network via a static TCP/IP configuration, but you lack a gateway address. Which of the following is true?

   A. Because the gateway address is necessary, no TCP/IP networking functions will work.

   B. TCP/IP networking will function, but you'll be unable to convert hostnames to IP addresses, or vice versa.

   C. You'll be able to communicate with machines on your local network segment but not with other systems.

   D. The computer won't be able to tell which other computers are local and which are remote.

5.   Which of the following types of information is returned by typing **ifconfig eth0**? (Choose all that apply.)

   A. The names of programs that are using eth0

   B. The IP address assigned to eth0

   C. The hardware address of eth0

   D. The hostname associated with eth0

6. In what way do GUI network configuration tools simplify the network configuration process?

   A. They're the only way to configure a computer using DHCP, which is an easier way to set networking options than static IP addresses.

   B. They provide the means to configure PPPoE or PPPoA, which are easier to configure than DHCP or static IP addresses.

   C. Once running, they provide easy-to-find labels for options, obviating the need to locate appropriate configuration files.

   D. They're consistent across distributions, making it easier to find appropriate options on an unfamiliar distribution.

7. Which of the following pieces of information are usually required to initiate a PPP connection over an analog telephone line? (Choose all that apply.)

   A. The ISP's telephone number

   B. The client IP address

   C. An account name (username)

   D. A password

8. You want to use an X server on an old Pentium computer to run X clients on a modern Alpha CPU system, with the goal of performing computationally intensive spreadsheet calculations. Which of the following is true?

   A. The spreadsheet will compute slowly because of the slow speed of the Pentium server.

   B. You won't be able to run the spreadsheet because the Alpha and Pentium CPUs need different executables.

   C. The computation will run swiftly, but graphics displays may be slowed by the Pentium's limited speed.

   D. Computations will run swiftly only if the Alpha computer makes its filesystem available via NFS.

9. How does an NFS server determine who may access files it's exporting?

   A. It uses the local file ownership and permission in conjunction with the client's user authentication and a list of trusted client computers.

   B. It uses a password that's sent in unencrypted form across the network.

   C. It uses a password that's sent in encrypted form across the network.

   D. It uses the contents of individual users' `.rlogin` files to determine which client computers may access a share.

10. Why might you configure a Linux computer to function as an NIS client?

   A. To mount remote filesystems as if they were local

   B. To defer to a network's central authority concerning user authentication

   C. To set the system's clock according to a central time server

   D. To automatically obtain IP address and other basic network configuration information

11. What function does SNMP fill?

    A. It enables remote systems to send mail to users of the computer.

    B. It enables remote monitoring and configuration of a computer.

    C. It monitors several network ports and runs other servers as required.

    D. It retrieves mail from a remote system using the POP protocol.

12. Why is it unwise to allow `root` to log on directly using SSH?

    A. Somebody with the `root` password but no other password could then break into the computer.

    B. The `root` password should never be sent over a network connection; allowing `root` logins in this way is inviting disaster.

    C. SSH stores all login information, including passwords, in a publicly readable file.

    D. When logged on using SSH, `root`'s commands can be easily intercepted and duplicated by undesirable elements.

13. How do you change the password used by `rlogin`?

    A. Use the `rpasswd` command.

    B. Change the normal user account password.

    C. Change the Samba encrypted password.

    D. You can't; `rlogin` doesn't use passwords.

14. Which of the following tools may you run on a Linux computer to allow you to administer it remotely? (Choose all that apply.)

    A. Netscape

    B. TCP Wrappers

    C. An SSH server

    D. Webmin

15. Which of the following programs can be used to perform a DNS lookup in interactive mode?

    A. `nslookup`

    B. `host`

    C. `pump`

    D. `ifconfig`

16. Which of the following entries are found in the `/etc/hosts` file?

    A. A list of hosts allowed to remotely access this one

    B. Mappings of IP addresses to hostnames

    C. A list of users allowed to remotely access this host

    D. Passwords for remote Web administration

17. Which of the following commands can you use to see if the mail service is functioning and view a backlog of old messages?

   A. `postfix`

   B. `traceroute`

   C. `sendmail`

   D. `mailq`

18. What is the default port used by the Simple Mail Transfer Protocol (SMTP)?

   A. 143

   B. 80

   C. 25

   D. 21

19. Which of the following commands should you use to add to host 192.168.0.10 a default gateway to 192.168.0.1?

   A. `route add default gw 192.168.0.10 192.168.0.1`

   B. `route add default gw 192.168.0.1`

   C. `route add 192.168.0.10 default 192.168.0.1`

   D. `route 192.168.0.10 gw 192.168.0.1`

20. You have just finished editing and changing the `inetd.conf` file. Which of the following commands will cause some Linux distributions to read the changed file?

   A. `/etc/inetd restart`

   B. `/etc/bin/inetd restart`

   C. `/etc/sbin/inetd restart`

   D. `/etc/rc.d/init.d/inetd restart`

Answers to Review Questions

1. Answers: A, B, D. Ethernet is currently the most common type of network hardware for local networks. Linux supports it very well, and Linux also includes support for Token Ring and Fibre Channel network hardware. DHCP is a protocol used to obtain a TCP/IP configuration over a TCP/IP network. It's not a type of network hardware, but it can be used over hardware that supports TCP/IP.

2. B. IP addresses consist of four 1-byte numbers (0–255). They're normally expressed in base 10 and separated by periods. 63.63.63.63 meets these criteria. 202.9.257.33 includes one value (257) that's not a 1-byte number. 107.29.5.3.2 includes five 1-byte numbers. 98.7.104.0/24 is a network address—the trailing /24 indicates that the final byte is a machine identifier, and the first 3 bytes specify the network.

3. C. Option C, dhcpd, is the Linux DHCP *server*. The others are all DHCP clients. Most distributions ship with just one or two of the DHCP clients.

4. C. The gateway computer is a router that transfers data between two or more network segments. As such, if a computer isn't configured to use a gateway, it won't be able to communicate beyond its local network segment. (If your DNS server is on a different network segment, name resolution via DNS won't work, although other types of name resolution, such as /etc/hosts file entries, will still work.)

5. Answers: B, C. When used to display information on an interface, ifconfig shows the hardware and IP addresses of the interface, the protocols (such as TCP/IP) bound to the interface, and statistics on transmitted and received packets. This command does *not* return information on programs using the interface or the hostname associated with the interface.

6. C. Once you know what tool to run in a distribution, it's usually not difficult to find the label for any given network configuration option in a GUI tool. You can configure DHCP, PPPoA, and PPPoE in text mode (and the latter two are arguably more complex than DHCP). GUI configuration tools, although they provide similar functionality, are not entirely consistent from one distribution to another.

7. Answers: A, C, D. You need a telephone number to dial the call (although this is *not* needed for a PPPoE or PPPoA broadband connection). Most ISPs use a username and password to authenticate access. Although you can specify an IP address, this option is only used in specialized circumstances.

8. C. The X server handles the display and user input only, so its speed will influence graphics displays. Computations occur on the fast Alpha-based X client system.

9. A. NFS uses a "trusted host" policy to let clients police their own users, including access to the NFS server's files. NFS does not use a password, nor does it use the .rlogin file in users' home directories.

10. B. NIS functions as a means of distributing database information across a network, most notably including user authentication information. It's not used for file sharing, clock setting, or distributing basic TCP/IP configuration information.

11. B. SNMP is a network management protocol. Option A describes SMTP. Option C describes the function of `inetd` or `xinetd`. Option D describes a program called fetchmail, which isn't a server at all.

12. A. Allowing only normal users to log in via SSH effectively requires two passwords for any remote `root` maintenance, improving security. SSH encrypts all connections, so it's unlikely that the password, or commands issued during an SSH session, will be intercepted. (Nonetheless, some administrators prefer not to take even this small risk.) SSH doesn't store passwords in a file.

13. D. The `rlogin` server relies on the client system to authenticate users. To control access, you specify trusted clients in the user's `.rhosts` file.

14. Answers: C, D. An SSH server enables you to log in and use normal text-based configuration utilities to administer a system. Webmin is a specialized remote administration tool that lets you administer a system from any computer with a Web browser. Although Netscape is such a Web browser, its installation on the computer you intend to administer remotely won't enable remote administration, because it's only a client. TCP Wrappers can be an important security tool in preventing unauthorized administrative access, but it doesn't enable remote administration by itself.

15. A. The `nslookup` program, though being phased out, offers an interactive mode that can be used for DNS lookups. The `host` program, though a replacement for `nslookup`, does not offer an interactive mode. `pump` is a DHCP client, while `ifconfig` is used for configuration of networking parameters and cards.

16. B. The `/etc/hosts` file holds mappings of IP addresses to hostnames, on a one-line-per-mapping basis. It does not list the users or other hosts allowed to remotely access this one, or affect remote administration through a Web browser.

17. D. The `mailq` utility can display a backlog of old messages and show you if the mail service is functioning. Postfix and sendmail are both mail server programs, while `traceroute` is an enhanced version of `ping` that shows the route data takes to reach a target.

18. C. The SMTP service by default uses port 25. Port 143 is used by IMAP, while port 80 is used for WWW, and port 21 is used by FTP.

19. B. To add a default gateway of 192.168.0.1, the command would be: **route add default gw 192.168.0.1**. Specifying the IP address of the host system is not necessary, and in fact will confuse the `route` command.

20. D. The `inetd` SysV startup script is usually located in `/etc/rc.d/init.d`, `/etc/init.d`, or `/etc/rc.d`. After changing the `inetd.conf` file, you can run this startup scriptwith the `restart` or `reload` option to tell the `inetd` super server to implement the changes you've made. The other options all refer to the `inetd` SysV startup script in locations in which it never resides.

Chapter

7

Security

THE FOLLOWING COMPTIA OBJECTIVES ARE COVERED IN THIS CHAPTER:

✓ **4.4 Detect symptoms that indicate a machine's security has been compromised (e.g., review logfiles for irregularities or intrusion attempts).**

✓ **4.7 Identify different Linux Intrusion Detection Systems (IDS) (e.g., Snort, PortSentry).**

✓ **4.8 Given security requirements, implement basic IP tables/ chains (note: requires knowledge of common ports).**

✓ **4.9 Implement security auditing for files and authentication.**

✓ **4.10 Identify whether a package or file has been corrupted/ altered (e.g., checksum, Tripwire).**

✓ **4.12 Identify security vulnerabilities within Linux services.**

✓ **4.13 Set up user-level security (i.e., limits on logins, memory usage and processes).**

Sadly, security is a very important topic. Sloppy configuration, program bugs, user error, and other problems can result in a system compromise. Such a compromise can result in confidential data falling into the wrong hands, data loss, abuse of your resources (such as network connectivity) to malicious or even criminal ends, and so on. For these reasons, you should pay careful attention to security, configuring your system in as secure a way as possible.

Security isn't an all-or-nothing matter. No computer can be absolutely 100 percent secure—if nothing else, somebody might physically break in and steal the system. Rather, security comes in degrees, from very poor security up to very good security. You must decide where you want your system to fall on this continuum, trading off the benefits of improved security against the effort it takes to maintain that security, for both you and the system's users.

This chapter begins with a rundown of the types of security vulnerabilities that exist. Understanding these will enable you to address each of the issues. Next up is physical security, which is the most fundamental type, and applies even to non-networked computers. Super servers are programs that can run other servers, and they provide special security tools, so this chapter describes their security features. Next up is firewalls, which provide another type of barrier against unwanted network access. Even if you employ these methods, you should be alert to the possibility of successful intrusions, so several intrusion-detection methods and tools are described next. You may also want to test your system for susceptibility to several possible methods of attack, so this chapter describes several tools you can use in this endeavor. Finally, this chapter looks at user-level security—that is, placing limits on how and when users may log into the computer.

Sources of Security Vulnerability

Threats to system security are many and varied, and they're changing all the time. That is, bugs or other problems in specific programs are likely to be fixed soon after they're found, but new bugs or problems may be discovered the next day. Thus, a program-by-program listing of security problems is impractical, although Web sites such as the Computer Emergency Response Team (CERT; http://www.cert.org) site do track known vulnerabilities. Instead of attempting to list all known problems, I describe security vulnerabilities in broad categories. These include physical access, stolen passwords, bugs in local (nonserver) programs, bugs in server programs, denial-of-service attacks, encryption issues, and humans.

Physical Access Problems

The first broad category of security problem relates to physical access to the computer. In fact, this category is important enough that it's covered in more detail shortly, in its own section, "Physical Security." In brief, if a miscreant has physical access to your computer, that person can do almost anything to it. Thus, controlling physical access to the computer is extremely important.

Stolen Passwords

Passwords are an integral part of Linux user accounts, and so if a password (with username) falls into the wrong hands, the password can give the intruder access to the computer. At first glance, this might not seem to be a huge problem—after all, ordinary user accounts have limited access. Unfortunately, if this access is combined with other problems (such as those described shortly, in "Local Program Bugs"), it can translate into a more severe **root** compromise. Even without this access, unauthorized use of local user accounts can be abused to send spam, to access other systems, to steal CPU time or other local resources, and to access whatever sensitive documents the user might be able to read.

Chapter 3, "User Management," describes password security in greater detail. Key points include selecting good user passwords, changing passwords frequently, disabling unused accounts, and educating users about the risks of divulging their passwords to others (both directly and indirectly). Be sure that your users know to *never* give their passwords to others or to write them down. Attackers sometimes masquerade as system administrators or others in authority in an attempt to collect passwords, and they've even been known to go rummaging through trash to locate discarded passwords or other sensitive data.

 The root password is particularly sensitive. Thus, you should be particularly **WARNING** diligent in selecting a root password and in protecting it from compromise.

Local Program Bugs

Perfection is very difficult—perhaps impossible—to attain. This is true in all fields of endeavor, and writing computer software is no exception to this rule. For the most part, bugs in computer programs are considered annoyances. When a spreadsheet program crashes, you may sigh in frustration or scream in rage, but chances are the computer on which the program is running won't be damaged or compromised by this crash. Some program bugs, though, are more serious, because they can be abused to give an attacker increased access to the computer.

Most programs have limited access to truly sensitive files, data, and hardware. Thus, most local program bugs are unlikely to be useful to attackers. The main risk comes from local programs that run with enhanced privileges—that is, those that enable a set user ID (SUID) or set group ID (SGID) bit. These features enable a program to run with the privileges associated with the program's owner or group, respectively. As described in Chapter 5, "Package and Process Management," SUID and SGID bits are risky, in part because bugs in these programs can turn into accesses by another user. As the other user is often root, bugs in SUID programs in particular might be abused to alter other files, including configuration files such as /etc/passwd. Thus, a clever attacker (or a not-so-clever attacker who uses attack scripts created by others) can, at least in principle, abuse local program bugs to acquire root privileges, effectively taking over the computer.

 When an attacker gains root privileges on a computer, that system is sometimes said to have been *rooted*.

Because of the security implications of SUID and SGID programs, you may want to check your system to learn what programs set these bits. You can do so with the find command, which is described in more detail in Chapter 2, "Text-Mode Commands."

```
# find / -perm +6000 -type f
```

This command finds all of the files on the computer (including any mounted removable media or network filesystems) that have their SUID or SGID bits set. To search for SUID files alone, change +6000 to +4000; to search for SGID bits alone, change +6000 to +2000. The -type f parameter is important to keep certain directories from showing up in the output; this parameter restricts the search to normal files. I've shown this example using the root prompt (#) because only root is likely to be able to read all the files and directories on the computer. Although this command can be run as an ordinary user, it will return several permission denied errors and might miss some files as a result.

Local program bugs can be exploited only by people who have access to local programs. Thus, they might at first seem to be of little interest if the computer has no local users aside from administrative staff, or if you're certain local users can be trusted. Unfortunately, these bugs can sometimes be exploited should an ordinary account be compromised (say, through a stolen password). Thus, you should be concerned with such bugs even on servers with no local users.

The main defense against local program bugs is keeping your system up to date. You should use the Advanced Package Tools (APT), Update Agent, YaST2, or any other tools available to you to keep your packages up to date—or at least, those that have been updated to fix security bugs.

Server Bugs

Server programs, like local user programs, can contain bugs. Like local user programs, these bugs are most serious when the program is run as root. Most servers don't use SUID bits to run as root, though; they're launched via SysV startup scripts or a super server. Thus, there's no find command to locate server programs that will run as root. Instead, you must review your SysV and super server configurations (as described in Chapter 5). Auditing your system to locate running servers can also be helpful, as described later, in "Checking for Open Ports." As with local programs, you should also be sure to keep all your server programs up to date, or at least update them when you hear of security issues that have been fixed.

Unlike local user program bugs, bugs in servers can cause security breaches even when the system has no local user accounts. For instance, a bug in a Web server could, at least theoretically, enable a cracker to run arbitrary code as root. That code could create a root-equivalent account and launch a Telnet server, enabling the cracker to gain full root-level shell access to the computer.

Denial-of-Service Attacks

A *denial of service (DoS)* attack is unusual because it needn't involve an actual security breach on your system (although it might). The term applies to any type of attack that denies you the use of your equipment. One common type of DoS attack is a *distributed denial of service (DDoS)* attack, in which the attacker uses many computers (typically hijacked in one way or another long before) to flood the victim's computer with useless data packets. The result is that the victim's computer cannot send or receive real data over the network. For a Web server, mail server, or other computer that's used mainly as a network server, the effect is as devastating as if the attacker had broken into the computer and shut it down.

Other types of DoS attack do exist. For instance, if a server program crashes upon receiving certain input, an attacker could simply send that input to the server, thus causing it to crash. The attacker hasn't broken into the computer, much less rooted it, but the disruption can be quite severe. Particularly to large Internet service providers (ISPs), spam can look a lot like a DoS attack—by consuming network resources, a spike in spam can cause disruption of the ISP's normal operation.

Some DoS attacks can be guarded against by keeping your system up to date. In particular, DoS attacks that target bugs in software can be thwarted by fixing those bugs. Other DoS attacks, though, require coordination between you and your ISP. If you find that a server is under a DDoS attack, for instance, you might not be able to do much about it on your server; you must work with your ISP to identify the sources of the attack or some other way to "fingerprint" the relevant packets and drop them before they're sent to your system. That said, some types of firewall configuration can mitigate the effects of a DDoS attack, either by keeping the traffic off of your local network or by causing the server computer to ignore the packets rather than reply to them. (The upcoming section, "Firewall Configuration," describes methods of configuring a firewall.)

Encryption Issues

Another type of vulnerability relates to encryption—or more precisely, the lack thereof. Many network protocols send data in unencrypted form. The Simple Mail Transfer Protocol (SMTP), the Hypertext Transfer Protocol (HTTP), Telnet, the File Transfer Protocol (FTP), and many others do not encrypt data. In some cases, users can encrypt data to be sent via these protocols. For instance, e-mail users can employ the GNU Privacy Guard (GPG; http://www.gnupg.org) to encrypt their e-mail messages, but the protocols themselves are unencrypted and often carry unencrypted data. This fact can become a threat because unencrypted data can be intercepted and read on any intervening system, and sometimes on computers on the same network as the source or destination. If sensitive data, such as passwords or credit card numbers, are passed over these unencrypted protocols, the result is a risk that the sensitive information will fall into the wrong hands.

The solution to this problem is to use encrypted protocols or to add encryption whenever possible. For instance, you can retire a Telnet or FTP server program in favor of the Secure Shell (SSH), which can do the same job as both Telnet and FTP, but using encryption. Some protocols have encrypted variants, such as the secure HTTP variant, HTTPS, which uses Secure Sockets Layer (SSL) encryption. (Most Web pages that ask for credit card numbers or other sensitive data use HTTPS, as indicated by the `https://` in the URL. Most browsers also display a closed padlock or other security icon when accessing a site that employs encryption.)

Not all encryption is equal, though. Encryption methods vary in many ways, one of the most important being the length of encryption keys. These are numbers that are used to mathematically scramble the data being sent. Without the original key or a key that's matched to it, the data can't be unscrambled. All other things being equal, longer keys are superior to shorter ones. Precisely how long your key should be depends on the protocol, the type of data you're transmitting, and how time sensitive the information is. Breaking a key might take a few minutes, a few months, or decades. As computers speed up, the time to break encryption goes down. Currently, most encryption tools support 128-bit (16-byte) or larger keys.

The Human Element

People can render even the best security plans useless, either through malice or through ignorance. One scenario involves *social engineering*—an attacker simply asks a legitimate user for a password or to otherwise bypass a security measure. Of course, the attacker refrains from twirling a long mustache while making the request. Typically, the social engineer poses as a system administrator or some other authority figure and asks for the information in a way that seems plausible. The attacker may claim that a password database must be reinitialized, for instance.

 A particular type of social engineering known as *phishing* has become quite common on the Internet at large. Phishing involves sending bogus e-mail or setting up fake Web sites that lure unsuspecting individuals into divulging sensitive financial or other information.

Users can also create security problems by leaving sensitive doors unlocked, by running poorly designed scripts on servers, by installing unnecessary server programs, and so on. Note that this list of activities includes some that are likely to be done by system administrators, as well as by ordinary users. Indeed, configuration errors are a major source of security breaches—for whatever reason, too many administrators don't take the necessary steps to secure their computers.

The main way to guard against human errors that lead to compromise is education. Reading this chapter, as well as other security advice in this book, is a good start for a Linux system administrator. Keeping up to date by reading security newsgroups and Web sites (such as the CERT site, `http://www.cert.org`) is another big way to help. Educate your users about the presence of social engineers and phishing.

Physical Security

Although a lot of attention is focused on network and other electronic forms of security, computer security begins with *physical* security. If your computer isn't properly protected against physical tampering or theft, it becomes an easy target for abuse. You can take several steps to minimize the damage should an intruder gain physical access to your computer, so for any critical system, you should create and follow a plan to secure your computer, starting with such mundane tools as locks on the door.

What an Intruder Can Do with Physical Access

Linux systems provide various software safeguards against abuse and unauthorized access, such as passwords, file permissions, and system logs. These mechanisms can be effective against remote attacks when used properly, but they're next to useless if an intruder can touch the computer hardware. Two obvious methods of attack, when given such access, are to steal the hard disk and to boot the system with the intruder's own boot medium.

If a thief takes your hard disk, that thief has access to all the data on the disk. Linux's password-protection mechanisms are under the control of the OS, so all the burglar needs to do is install the disk in a system the burglar controls to gain access to your computer's files. Indeed, a spy could conceivably copy your hard disk's contents and you'd be none the wiser.

Even short of stealing a hard disk, if a computer can boot from a floppy disk, CD-ROM, or other removable medium, an intruder can gain access to your system. The miscreant only has to bring a Linux emergency boot disk and boot that. The end result is full access to your files. If the goal is destruction, the intruder need not even be versed in Linux—a DOS boot floppy with a few disk utilities can quite effectively wipe out your data.

Theft of the entire computer is also a possibility, of course. Such a theft might not even be motivated by a desire to steal your data or do you harm personally—the burglar might be after the hardware.

Steps for Mitigating Damage from Physical Attacks

You aren't completely powerless against the threat of physical attacks on your computer. You can take several steps to protect yourself:

Remove removable media.   If a computer has no floppy drive, no Zip drive, no CD-ROM drive, no tape backup drive, and so on, it will be difficult for an intruder to either boot the computer from anything other than its hard disk or walk out with data on a removable disk. Of course, an intruder could bring a hard disk for booting, but on most *x86* systems, that would require opening the computer's case, thus slowing down the operation. Short of removing the drives, you can buy special locks that make them accessible only when the user has a key.

Restrict BIOS boot options.   Most BIOSs include options that enable and disable particular boot media. If your computer must have removable media, you can set the BIOS to boot only from the hard disk. This will slow down an intruder, but these settings can be easily changed;

therefore, this measure has a noticeable security impact only if used in conjunction with BIOS passwords (which are described next). This measure may still be worthwhile as a protection against viruses, however, some of which are transmitted on floppies. Although these viruses can't infect Linux, a few can damage LILO or GRUB and render a system unbootable.

Use BIOS passwords.   Most BIOSs have an option for setting a password that must be entered before the system will boot or before BIOS settings can be changed. Setting this password can go a long way toward preventing tampering, but it's not perfect. Motherboard BIOSs can be reset by modifying a jumper setting, so an intruder who can open the case can overcome this measure.

Use a LILO or GRUB password.   If a LILO boot image includes the option `password = pass`, LILO will boot that image only if the user enters the password (`pass`). If the boot image also includes the `restricted` keyword, LILO applies this password rule only if the user tries to issue any boot parameters, such as `single`, which normally boots the system into a single-user mode. GRUB offers similar functionality if you specify the `password pass` option.

Secure the computer.   To prevent tampering with the insides of a computer, you can replace the normal screws used on most computer cases with screws that require special tools. Check with a locksmith or hardware store for such screws. You can also buy a hinge with a lock, if you need heavy-duty case security. Many computer shops sell kits that consist of chains and additional hardware to secure a computer to a desk or wall in order to deter outright theft of the entire computer.

Secure the room.   Locks on the doors can go a long way toward keeping a computer secure. If an intruder can't touch the computer, he or she can't do any of the other nasty things I've been describing. You may need to secure windows as well—or better yet, place the computer in a room that doesn't *have* windows. Don't just install the locks—be sure to *use* them, too.

Use data encryption.   Assuming that an intruder can gain physical access to the computer, the best protection may not be a lock or a BIOS setting; it may be data encryption. Many applications provide some way to encrypt data. Some of these schemes are good, but some aren't. There are also separate programs that can encrypt any data file. No standard Linux filesystem currently supports automatic data encryption, but this feature may arrive in the future. There's also a tool that lets you add automatic encryption to files through a loopback device. Check `http://tldp.org/HOWTO/Loopback-Encrypted-Filesystem-HOWTO.html` for details.

The bottom line is that no security is perfect. You'll have to judge just *how much* security you need. In some environments, with some systems, you might be content to lock the door. In others, you may need to take extreme measures, up to and including routinely encrypting your data files.

Firewall Configuration

The first line of defense in network security is a *firewall*. This is a computer that restricts access to other computers, or software that runs on a single computer to protect it alone. Broadly speaking, two types of firewalls exist: *packet-filter firewalls*, which work by blocking or permitting access based on low-level information in individual data packets, such as source and destination IP addresses and ports, and *proxy filters*, which partially process a transaction, such as a Web page access, and block or deny access based on high-level features in this transaction, such as the filename of an image in the Web page. This chapter describes Linux's packet-filter firewall tools, which can be very effective at protecting a single computer or an entire network against certain types of attack.

Where a Firewall Fits in a Network

Traditionally, firewalls have been routers that block undesired network transfers between two networks. Typically, one network is a small network under one management, and the other network is much larger, such as the Internet. Figure 7.1 illustrates this arrangement. (More complex firewalls that use multiple computers are also possible.) Dedicated external firewalls are available, and can be good investments in many cases. In fact, it's possible to turn an ordinary computer into such a device by using Linux—either with a special-purpose distribution like the Linux Embedded Appliance Firewall (`http://leaf.sourceforge.net`) or by using an ordinary distribution and configuring it as a router with firewall features.

As described in more detail shortly, servers operate by associating themselves with particular network ports. Likewise, client programs bind to ports, but client port bindings aren't standardized. Packet filter firewalls block access by examining individual network packets and determining whether to let them pass based on the source and destination port number, the source and destination IP address, and possibly other low-level criteria, such as the network interface in a computer with more than one. For instance, in Figure 7.1, you might run a Samba file server internally, but outside computers have no business accessing that server. Therefore, you'd configure the firewall to block external packets directed at the ports used by Samba.

In addition to running a firewall on a router that serves an entire network, it's possible to run a firewall on an individual system. This approach can provide added protection to a sensitive computer, even if an external firewall protects that computer. It's also useful on computers that don't have the protection of a separate firewall, such as many broadband-connected systems.

FIGURE 7.1   Firewalls can selectively pass some packets but not others, using assorted criteria.

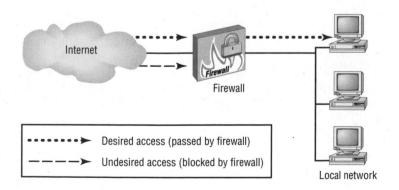

Linux Firewall Software

Linux uses the `ipfwadm`, `ipchains`, and `iptables` tools to configure firewall functions. These tools are designed for the 2.0.*x*, 2.2.*x*, and 2.4.*x* kernels, respectively. The 2.6.*x* kernels continue to use the `iptables` tool as well. (The 2.4.*x* and later kernel series include the ability to use the older tools, but only as a compile-time option.) You can configure a firewall in any of several ways:

Manually You can read up on the syntax of the tool used to configure your kernel and write your own script. This approach is described in the upcoming section, "Using `iptables`."

For more information on this approach, consult a book on the subject, such as Robert L. Ziegler's *Linux Firewalls, 2nd Edition* (New Riders, 2001).

With the help of a GUI configuration tool A few GUI configuration tools are available for Linux firewall configuration, such as Firestarter (`http://firestarter.sourceforge.net`) and Guarddog (`http://www.simonzone.com/software/guarddog`). Linux distributions often incorporate such tools as well, although the distribution-provided tools are often very simple. These tools let you specify certain basic information, such as the network port and the client and server protocols you wish to allow, and they generate firewall scripts that can run automatically when the system boots.

With the help of a Web site Robert Ziegler, the author of *Linux Firewalls*, has made a Web site available that functions rather like the GUI configuration tools but via the Web. You enter information on your system, and the Web site generates a firewall script. This tool is available at `http://linux-firewall-tools.com/linux/`.

If you use a GUI tool or Web site, be sure it supports the firewall tool your kernel requires. Most tools support `iptables`, and some support older tools or tools used in non-Linux OSs. Also, you shouldn't consider a firewall to be perfect protection. You might create a configuration that actually contains flaws, or flaws might exist in the Linux kernel code that actually implements the firewall rules.

One of the advantages of a firewall, even to protect just one computer, is that it can block access attempts to *any* server. Most other measures are more limited. For instance, TCP Wrappers (described later, in "Super Server Security") protects only servers configured to be run via TCP Wrappers from `inetd`, and passwords are good only to protect the servers that are coded to require them.

Common Server Ports

Most packet filter firewalls use the server program's port number as a key feature. For instance, a firewall might block outside access to the SMB/CIFS ports used by Samba but let through traffic to the SMTP mail server port. In order to configure a firewall in this way, of course, you must know the port numbers. Linux systems contain a file, /etc/services, that lists service names and the ports with which they're associated. Lines in this file look something like this:

```
ssh              22/tcp      # SSH Remote Login Protocol
ssh              22/udp      # SSH Remote Login Protocol
telnet           23/tcp
# 24 - private
smtp             25/tcp
```

The first column contains a service name (ssh, telnet, or smtp in this example). The second column contains the port number and protocol (such as 22/tcp, meaning TCP port 22). Anything following a hash mark (#) is a comment and is ignored. The /etc/services file lists port numbers for both TCP and UDP ports. Typically, a single service is assigned use of the same TCP and UDP port numbers (as in the ssh service in this example), although most protocols use just one or the other. When configuring a firewall, it's generally best to block both TCP and UDP ports; this ensures you won't accidentally block the wrong port type.

Table 7.1 summarizes the port numbers used by the most important protocols run on Linux systems. This list is, however, incomplete; it only hits some of the most common protocols. In fact, even /etc/services is incomplete and may need to be expanded for certain obscure servers. (Their documentation describes how to do so, if necessary.)

TABLE 7.1   Port Numbers Used by Some Common Protocols

Port Number	TCP/UDP	Protocol	Example Server Programs
20 & 21	TCP	FTP	ProFTPd, WU FTPd
22	TCP	SSH	OpenSSH, lsh
23	TCP	Telnet	in.telnetd
25	TCP	SMTP	sendmail, Postfix, Exim, qmail
53	TCP and UDP	DNS	BIND
67	UDP	DHCP	DHCP
69	UDP	TFTP	in.tftpd
80	TCP	HTTP	Apache, thttpd
88	TCP	Kerberos	MIT Kerberos, Heimdal
109 and 110	TCP	POP (versions 2 & 3)	UW IMAP

TABLE 7.1   Port Numbers Used by Some Common Protocols *(continued)*

Port Number	TCP/UDP	Protocol	Example Server Programs
111	TCP and UDP	Portmapper	NFS, NIS, other RPC-based services
113	TCP	auth/ident	identd
119	TCP	NNTP	INN, Leafnode
123	UDP	NTP	NTP
137	UDP	NetBIOS Name Service	Samba
138	UDP	NetBIOS Datagram	Samba
139	TCP	NetBIOS Session	Samba
143	TCP	IMAP 2	UW IMAP
177	UDP	XDMCP	XDM, KDM, GDM
220	TCP	IMAP 3	UW IMAP
389	TCP	LDAP	OpenLDAP
443	TCP	HTTPS	Apache
445	TCP	Microsoft DS	Samba
514	UDP	Syslog	syslogd
515	TCP	Spooler	BSD LPD, LPRng, cups-lpd
636	TCP	LDAPS	OpenLDAP
749	TCP	Kerberos Admin	MIT Kerberos, Heimdal
5800–5899	TCP	VNC via HTTP	RealVNC, TightVNC
5900–5999	TCP	VNC	RealVNC, TightVNC
6000–6099	TCP	X	X.org-X11, XFree86

Table 7.1 shows the ports used by the *servers* for the specified protocols. In most cases, clients can and do use other port numbers to initiate connections. For instance, a mail client might use port 43411 on client.pangaea.edu to connect to port 143 on mail.pangaea.edu. Client port numbers are assigned by the kernel on an as-needed basis, so they aren't fixed. (Clients can request specific port numbers, but this practice is rare.)

One key distinction in TCP/IP ports is that between *privileged ports* and *unprivileged ports*. The former have numbers below 1024. Unix and Linux systems restrict access to privileged ports to root. The idea is that a client can connect to a privileged port and be confident that the server running on that port was configured by the system administrator, and can therefore be trusted. Unfortunately, on today's Internet, this trust would be unjustified based solely on the port number, so this distinction isn't very useful. Port numbers above 1024 may be accessed by ordinary users.

Using *iptables*

The iptables program is the utility that manages firewalls on recent Linux kernels (from 2.4.*x* through at least 2.6.*x*). Although these kernels can also use the older ipchains tool when so configured using kernel compile-time options, iptables is the more flexible tool, and is therefore the preferred way of creating and managing packet-filter firewalls.

When using iptables, you should first understand how Linux's packet filter architecture works—you can create several types of rules, which have differing effects, so understanding how they interact is necessary before you begin creating rules. Actually creating the rules requires understanding the iptables command syntax and options. Finally, it's helpful to look at a sample firewall script and to know how it's installed and called by the system.

The Linux Packet Filter Architecture

In the 2.4.*x* and later kernels, Linux uses a series of "tables" to process all network packets it generates or receives. Each table consists several "chains," which are series of pattern-matching rules—when a packet matches a rule, the rule can discard the packet, forward it to another chain, or accept the packet for local delivery. Figure 7.2 illustrates the filter table, which is the one you normally modify when creating a firewall. Other tables include the nat table, which implements network address translation (NAT) rules, and the mangle table, which modifies packets in specialized ways.

As shown in Figure 7.2, the filter table consists of three chains: INPUT, OUTPUT, and FORWARD. These chains process traffic destined to local programs, generated by local programs, and forwarded through a computer that's configured as a router, respectively. You can create rules independently for each chain. For instance, consider a rule that blocks all access directed at port 80 (the HTTP port, used by Web servers) on any IP address. Applied to the INPUT chain, this rule blocks all access to a Web server running on the local computer, but doesn't affect outgoing traffic or traffic that's forwarded by a router. Applied to the OUTPUT chain, this rule blocks all outgoing traffic directed at Web servers, effectively rendering Web browsers useless, but it doesn't affect incoming traffic directed at a local Web server or traffic forwarded by a router. Applied to the FORWARD chain, this rule blocks HTTP requests that might otherwise be forwarded by a computer that functions as a router, but doesn't affect traffic from local Web browsers or to local Web servers.

Much of the task of creating a firewall involves deciding which chains to modify. Generally speaking, when you want to create a separate firewall computer (as illustrated in Figure 7.1), you modify the FORWARD chain (to protect the computers behind the firewall) and the INPUT chain (to protect the firewall system itself). When implementing a firewall to protect a server or workstation, you modify the INPUT chain and perhaps the OUTPUT chain. Blocking output packets can have the effect of preventing abuse of other systems or use of protocols you don't want being used. For instance, you might block outgoing traffic directed to a remote system's port 23, effectively disallowing use of Telnet clients on the system you're configuring.

All of the chains implement a default policy. This policy determines what happens to a packet if no rule explicitly matches it. The default for a default policy is ACCEPT, which causes packets to be accepted. This policy is sensible in low-security situations, but for a more secure configuration, you should change the default policy to DROP or REJECT. The former causes packets to be ignored. To the sender, it looks as if a network link was down. The REJECT policy causes the system to actively refuse the packet, which looks to the sender as if no server is running on the targeted port. This option requires explicit kernel support. Both DROP and REJECT have their advantages. DROP reduces network bandwidth use and reduces the system's visibility on the network, whereas REJECT can improve performance for some protocols, such as auth/ident, which may retry a connection in the event a packet is lost. Using either DROP or REJECT as a default policy means that you must explicitly open ports you want to use. This is more secure than using a default policy of ACCEPT and explicitly closing ports, because you're less likely to accidentally leave a port open when it should be closed. Setting a default policy is described in the next section.

FIGURE 7.2   Linux uses a series of rules, which are defined in chains that are called at various points during processing, to determine the fate of network packets.

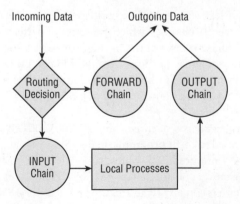

Creating Firewall Rules

To create firewall rules, you use the `iptables` command. You should probably start with the `-L` option, which lists the current configuration:

```
# iptables -L -t filter
Chain INPUT (policy ACCEPT)
target     prot opt source              destination

Chain FORWARD (policy ACCEPT)
target     prot opt source              destination

Chain OUTPUT (policy ACCEPT)
target     prot opt source              destination
```

The `-t filter` part of this command specifies that you want to view the `filter` table. This is actually the default table, so you can omit this part of the command, if you like. In any event, the result is a list of the rules that are defined for the specified (or default) table. In this case, no rules are defined, and the default policy is set to ACCEPT for all three chains in the table. This is a typical starting point, although depending on your distribution and your installation options, it's possible yours will have rules already defined. If so, you should track down the script that sets these rules and change or disable it. Alternatively, or if you just want to experiment, you can begin by flushing the table of all rules by passing `-F CHAIN` to `iptables`, where *CHAIN* is the name of the chain. You can also use `-P CHAIN POLICY` to set the default policy:

```
# iptables -t filter -F FORWARD
# iptables -t filter -P FORWARD DROP
```

These two commands flush all rules from the FORWARD chain and change the default policy for that chain to DROP. Generally speaking, this is a good starting point when configuring a firewall, although using REJECT rather than DROP has its advantages, as described earlier. You can then add rules to the chain, each of which matches some selection criterion. To do so, you use an `iptables` command of the form:

```
iptables [-t table] -A CHAIN selection-criteria -j TARGET
```

When modifying the `filter` table, you can omit the `-t table` option. The *TARGET* is the policy target, which can take the same values as the default policy (typically ACCEPT, REJECT, or DROP). In most cases, you'll use ACCEPT when the default policy is REJECT or DROP and REJECT or DROP when the default policy is ACCEPT. The *CHAIN* is, as you might expect, the chain to be modified (INPUT, OUTPUT, or FORWARD for the `filter` table). Finally, the *selection-criteria* can be one or more of several options that enable you to match packets by various rules:

Protocol   The `--protocol` or `-p` option lets you specify the low-level protocol used. You pass the protocol name (`tcp`, `udp`, `icmp`, or `all`) to match packets of the specified protocol type. The `all` name matches all protocol types, though.

Source port The `--source-port` or `--sport` option matches packets that originate from the port number that you specify. (You can also provide a list of port numbers by separating them with colons, as in `1024:2048` to specify ports from 1024 to 2048, inclusive.) Note that the originating port number is the port number for the server program for packets that come from the server system, but it's the port number used by the client program for packets that come from the client system.

Destination port The `--destination-port` or `--dport` option works much like the `--source-port` option, but it applies to the destination of the packet.

Source IP address The `--source` or `-s` option filters on the source IP address. You can specify either a single IP address or an entire subnet by appending the netmask as a number of bits, as in `-s 172.24.1.0/24`.

Destination IP address The `--destination` or `-d` option works just like the `--source` option, but it filters based on a packet's destination address.

Input hardware interface You can use the interface on which the packet arrives with the `--in-interface` or `-I` option, which accepts an interface name as an argument. For instance, `-I eth0` matches packets that arrive on the `eth0` interface. This option works with the INPUT and FORWARD chains, but not with the OUTPUT chain.

Output hardware interface The `--out-interface` or `-o` option works much like the `--in-interface` option, but it applies to the interface on which packets will leave the computer. As such, it works with the FORWARD and OUTPUT chains, but not with the INPUT chain.

State Network connections have states—they can be used to initiate a new connection, continue an existing connection, be related to an existing connection (such as an error message), or be potentially forged. The `--state` option can match based on these states, using codes of NEW, ESTABLISHED, RELATED, or INVALID. You must precede this option with the `-m state` option on the same `iptables` command line. This feature implements *stateful packet inspection*, which enables you to block connection attempts to certain ports while enabling you to initiate connections from those same ports. This feature is most useful in blocking connection attempts to unprivileged ports, thus denying miscreants the ability to run unauthorized servers on those ports.

You can combine multiple items to filter based on several criteria. For instance, in a default-deny configuration, you can open traffic to TCP port 445 from the 172.24.1.0/24 network with a single command:

```
# iptables -A INPUT -p tcp --dport 445 -s 172.24.1.0/24 -j ACCEPT
```

In this case, the `selection-criteria` consist of three rules. Packets that match *all* of these rules will be accepted; those that fail to match even a single rule will be denied (assuming this is the default configuration), unless they match some other rule in the chain.

A complete chain is created by issuing multiple `iptables` commands, each of which defines a single rule. You can then view the result by typing **iptables -L**, as described earlier.

A Sample *iptables* Configuration

Because `iptables` creates a complete firewall configuration only through the use of multiple calls to the utility, Linux packet-filter firewalls are frequently created via shell scripts that repeatedly call `iptables`. (Chapter 2 introduces shell scripts, so review it if you need more information on the basics of creating a script.) These scripts may be called as SysV startup scripts or in some other way as part of the startup procedure. For learning purposes, you may want to create a script that's not called in this way, though. Listing 7.1 shows a sample script that demonstrates the key points of firewall creation.

Listing 7.1: Sample Linux Firewall Script

```
#!/bin/bash

iptables -F INPUT
iptables -F FORWARD
iptables -F OUTPUT

iptables -P INPUT DROP
iptables -P FORWARD DROP
iptables -P OUTPUT DROP

# Let traffic on the loopback interface pass
iptables -A OUTPUT -d 127.0.0.1 -o lo -j ACCEPT
iptables -A INPUT -s 127.0.0.1 -i lo -j ACCEPT

# Let DNS traffic pass
iptables -A OUTPUT -p udp --dport 53 -j ACCEPT
iptables -A INPUT -p udp --sport 53 -j ACCEPT

# Let clients' TCP traffic pass
iptables -A OUTPUT -p tcp --sport 1024:65535 -m state \
        --state NEW,ESTABLISHED,RELATED -j ACCEPT
iptables -A INPUT -p tcp --dport 1024:65535 -m state \
        --state ESTABLISHED,RELATED -j ACCEPT

# Let local connections to local SSH server pass
iptables -A OUTPUT -p tcp --sport 22 -d 172.24.1.0/24 -m state \
        --state ESTABLISHED,RELATED -j ACCEPT
iptables -A INPUT -p tcp --dport 22 -s 172.24.1.0/24 -m state \
        --state NEW,ESTABLISHED,RELATED -j ACCEPT
```

Listing 7.1 consists of three broad parts. The first three calls to `iptables` clear out all preexisting firewall rules. This is particularly important in a script that you're creating or debugging because you don't want to simply add new rules to existing ones, because the result would likely be a confusing mish-mash of old and new rules. The next three calls to `iptables` set the default policy to `DROP` on all three chains. This is a good basic starting point for a firewall. The remaining calls to `iptables` configure Linux to accept specific types of traffic:

Loopback traffic   The script sets the system to accept traffic to and from the loopback interface (that is, 127.0.0.1). Certain Linux tools expect to be able to use this interface, and because it's purely local, the security risk in accepting such traffic is very slim. Note that the lines that enable this access use both the IP address (via the `-d` and `-s` options) and the `lo` interface name (via the `-o` and `-i` options). This configuration protects against spoofing the loopback address—an attacker pretending to be 127.0.0.1 from another computer. This configuration, like most `iptables` configurations, requires two `iptables` rules: one to enable incoming traffic and one to enable outgoing traffic.

DNS traffic   The second block of rules enables UDP traffic to and from port 53, which handles DNS traffic. A configuration like this one is necessary on most systems to enable the computer to use its local DNS server. You could strengthen this configuration by specifying only your local DNS server's IP address. (If you have multiple DNS servers, you'd need one pair of rules for each one.)

Client traffic   Listing 7.1 enables TCP packets to be sent from unprivileged ports (those used by client programs) to any system. This configuration uses stateful inspection to enable new, established, or related outgoing traffic but to allow only established or related incoming traffic. This configuration effectively blocks the ability to run servers on unprivileged ports. Thus, an intruder or malicious authorized user won't be able to log into an unauthorized server that runs on such a port—at least, not without `root` access to change the configuration.

SSH server traffic   The final block of options enables access to the SSH server (TCP port 22). This access, though, is restricted to the 172.24.1.0/24 network (presumably the local network for the computer). This configuration uses stateful packet inspection to outgoing traffic from the SSH server for established and related data, but not for new or invalid packets. Incoming packets to the server are permitted for new, existing, or related traffic, but not for invalid packets.

A configuration such as the one in Listing 7.1 is suitable for a workstation that runs an SSH server for remote administration but that otherwise runs no servers. For a computer that runs many servers, you might need to add several additional blocks of rules similar to the SSH block, each one customized to a particular server. For a dedicated router with firewall features, the emphasis would be on the `FORWARD` chain rather than the `INPUT` and `OUTPUT` chains, although such a system would likely need to perform some `INPUT` and `OUTPUT` chain configuration to support its own administration and use.

Super Server Security

Beyond firewalls, the first layer of access controls for many servers lies in the super server that launches the server in question. Chapter 5 describes the basics of configuring the inetd and xinetd super servers. You can use a package called TCP Wrappers with either super server, but it's more commonly used with inetd. The xinetd super server includes functionality that's similar to TCP Wrappers in its basic feature set.

> Whenever possible, apply redundant access controls. For instance, you can use both a firewall and TCP Wrappers or xinetd to block unwanted access to particular servers. Doing this helps protect against bugs and misconfiguration—if a problem emerges in the firewall configuration, for instance, the secondary block will probably halt the intruder. If you configure the system carefully, such an access will also leave a log file message that you'll see, so you'll be alerted to the fact that the firewall didn't do its job.

Controlling Access via TCP Wrappers

One popular means of running servers is via inetd, a server that listens for network connections on behalf of other servers and then launches the target servers as required. This approach can reduce the RAM requirements on a server computer when the server programs are seldom in use because only inetd need be running at all times. Chapter 5 covers inetd in more detail.

> Not all Linux systems use inetd. Fedora, Mandrake, Red Hat, and SuSE have all switched to xinetd, which includes its own access control features. TCP Wrappers isn't normally used in conjunction with xinetd.

One further advantage of inetd is that it can be used in conjunction with another package, known as TCP Wrappers. This package uses a program known as tcpd. Instead of having inetd call a server directly, inetd calls tcpd, which does two things: It checks whether a client is authorized to access the server, and if the client has this authorization, tcpd calls the server program.

TCP Wrappers is configured through two files: /etc/hosts.allow and /etc/hosts.deny. The first of these specifies computers that are allowed access to the system in a particular way, the implication being that systems not listed are not allowed access. By contrast, hosts.deny lists computers that are not allowed access; all others are given permission to use the system. If a system is listed in both files, hosts.allow takes precedence.

Both files use the same basic format. The files consist of lines of the following form:

daemon-list : *client-list*

The *daemon-list* is a list of servers, using the names for the servers that appear in /etc/ services. Wildcards are also available, such as ALL for all servers.

The *client-list* is a list of computers to be granted or denied access to the specified daemons. You can specify computers by name or by IP address, and you can specify a network by using (respectively) a leading or trailing dot (.). For instance, .luna.edu blocks all computers in the luna.edu domain, and 192.168.7. blocks all computers in the 192.168.7.0/24 network. You can also use wildcards in the *client-list*, such as ALL (all computers). EXCEPT causes an exception. For instance, when placed in hosts.deny, 192.168.7. EXCEPT 192.168.7.105 blocks all computers in the 192.168.7.0/24 network except for 192.168.7.105.

The hosts.allow and hosts.deny man pages (they're actually the same document) provide additional information on more advanced features. You should consult them as you build TCP Wrappers rules.

WARNING   Remember that not all servers are protected by TCP Wrappers. Normally, only those servers that inetd runs via tcpd are so protected. Such servers typically include, but are not limited to, Telnet, FTP, TFTP, rlogin, finger, POP, and IMAP servers. A few servers can independently parse the TCP Wrappers configuration files, though; consult the server's documentation if in doubt.

Controlling Access via *xinetd*

In 2000 and 2001, the shift began to xinetd from inetd. Although xinetd *can* use TCP Wrappers, it normally doesn't because it incorporates similar functionality of its own. The distributions that use xinetd use a main configuration file called /etc/xinetd.conf, but this file is largely empty because it calls separate files in the /etc/xinetd.d directory to do the real work. This directory contains separate files for handling individual servers. Chapter 5 includes information on basic xinetd configuration. For now, know that security is handled on a server-by-server basis through the use of configuration parameters, some of which are similar to the function of hosts.allow and hosts.deny:

Network interface   The bind option tells xinetd to listen on only one network interface for the service. For instance, you might specify bind = 192.168.23.7 on a router to have it listen only on the Ethernet card associated with that address. This feature is extremely useful in routers, but it is not as useful in computers with just one network interface. (You can use this option to bind a server only to the loopback interface, 127.0.0.1, if a server should be available only locally. You might do this with a configuration tool like the Samba Web Administration Tool, or SWAT.) A synonym for this option is interface.

Allowed IP or network addresses   You can use the only_from option to specify IP addresses, networks (as in 192.168.78.0/24), or computer names on this line, separated by spaces. The result is that xinetd will accept connections only from these addresses, similar to TCP Wrappers' hosts.allow entries.

Disallowed IP or network addresses   The `no_access` option is the opposite of `only_from`; you list computers or networks here that you want to blacklist. This is similar to the `hosts.deny` file of TCP Wrappers.

Access times   The `access_times` option sets times during which users may access the server. The time range is specified in the form *hour:min-hour:min*, using a 24-hour clock. Note that this option only affects the times during which the service will *respond*. If the `xinetd access_times` option is set to `8:00-17:00` and somebody logs in at 4:59 p.m. (one minute before the end time), that user may continue using the system well beyond the 5:00 p.m. cutoff time.

You should enter these options into the files in `/etc/xinetd.d` that correspond to the servers you want to protect. Place the lines between the opening brace (`{`) and closing brace (`}`) for the service. If you want to restrict *all* your `xinetd`-controlled servers, you can place the entries in the `defaults` section in `/etc/xinetd.conf`.

> Some servers provide access control mechanisms similar to those of TCP Wrappers or `xinetd` by themselves. For instance, Samba provides `hosts allow` and `hosts deny` options that work much like the TCP Wrappers file entries, and NIS includes similar configuration options. These options are most common on servers that are awkward or impossible to run via `inetd` or `xinetd`.

Intrusion Detection

Even the best-configured computer has vulnerabilities. With luck, these vulnerabilities won't be exploited, but you shouldn't make that assumption. Instead, you should actively search for evidence of intrusions on your systems. That way, you'll at least be alerted to an intrusion and be able to take appropriate steps soon after the intrusion occurs. ("Appropriate steps" are usually a complete reinstallation or restore from a clean backup, followed by tightening security around suspected points of entry. Once a system has been rooted, you can't completely trust *anything* on that system, and restoring everything from a known-clean source is usually easier than checking each and every file for signs of tampering.)

Several methods of detecting intruders exist. These range from being alert to suspicious activities to use of assorted programs that can monitor network activity or check for changes in critical files.

Symptoms of Intrusion

One way of detecting intrusion is to notice abnormalities in your system's operation. This approach is unreliable, but it's also the most general approach, and might therefore succeed even if the intruder has a way to defeat more specific monitoring tools you might employ. The basic approach sounds simple: Know how your system normally behaves, and be alert to changes in this behavior. Symptoms of intrusion can include:

System slowdown   Intruders might run programs on your computer that cause it to respond more slowly than usual to its normal workload.

Increased network activity   Just as intruders can consume CPU time, they can consume network resources. In fact, one reason crackers break into computers is to use your network connectivity. They may be using your system to launch a DDoS attack against others, to distribute files on an illegal FTP server, or for other purposes that consume a lot of network bandwidth.

Changed program behavior   Crackers often replace standard system tools with their own customized versions. These tools may behave slightly differently from the originals, so changes in the way common utilities behave (such as text that's output differently or a complaint that an option that worked yesterday is no longer working) can be a clue to a system compromise.

System or software crashes   If the computer, or just individual programs, begin crashing for no reason, it could be because they've been modified by an intruder. In some sense, this is just a corollary of the changed program behavior symptom, but it's more severe.

Mysteriously altered data files   If ordinary data files are changed without your having changed them, one possible explanation is an intrusion. In fact, depending on the nature of the change, it may be a flashing neon sign. For instance, intruders sometimes break in with the exclusive goal of defacing a Web site, so such a change is a virtual guarantee of system compromise.

Missing or corrupted log files   Intruders often try to cover their tracks by altering or deleting log files. (Chapter 8 covers log files in more detail.) Therefore, such changes should raise a red flag.

Off-site complaints   If the administrator of another site contacts you and complains of attacks from your site or other suspicious behavior, it may be that your computer has been compromised and is being used to attack another system.

Local user complaints   Local users can be alert to certain types of problems, such as system sluggishness and program behavior changes. Listen to their complaints and investigate them promptly.

The problem with using any of these symptoms is that they can all have causes other than an intrusion. A local program might be running out of control, consuming CPU time or network bandwidth; programs can behave differently or crash because of legitimate program upgrades, emerging hardware defects, or changed environment settings; data files and log files can be altered due to legitimate activities of other users or disk errors; off-site complaints can be generated in error or might be traced to rogue local users who haven't gained inappropriate local access; and local user complaints can reflect any of these or many other nonsecurity problems. Nonetheless, being alert to these clues can lead you to investigate the problem and fix it, whether it turns out to be a security problem or not.

Using Snort

Snort (http://www.snort.org) is a very powerful *packet sniffer* program—a program that monitors packets directed to its host computer (or to other computers on its local network segment).

Packet sniffers are very powerful network diagnostic tools because they enable you to dig into the "guts" of a network transaction. The knowledge you can gain from such investigations can help you diagnose problems of all sorts, but it requires extensive knowledge of the underlying protocols.

> **WARNING** Packet sniffers are also popular tools among crackers. Packet sniffers can help intruders discover users' passwords and other sensitive data. In fact, using a packet sniffer can be grounds for disciplinary actions in many organizations. Thus, although Snort is a very good and legitimate tool when used properly, you shouldn't install and use Snort unless you have authorization to do so.

In addition to functioning as a generic packet sniffer, Snort can function in a more sophisticated role as an *intrusion detection system (IDS)*. An IDS is a program that monitors network traffic for suspicious activity and alerts an appropriate administrator to warning signs. Put another way, an IDS is a packet sniffer with the ability to recognize activity patterns that indicate an attack is under way.

The first step when it comes to installing Snort is deciding where to place it. Figure 7.3 shows a couple of possible locations. Snort System #1 in this figure is able to monitor traffic to or from the Internet at large, while Snort System #2 is able to monitor local traffic. Both have a chance of catching outside attacks against specific local computers, but System #1 will be sensitive to attacks that are blocked by the firewall, while System #2 will be sensitive to purely local attacks. Also, System #2 requires either a hub rather than a switch locally or a switch that's programmed to echo all traffic to Snort System #2; a switch without such configuration will hide most traffic between the local computers from the Snort system, rendering it useless.

Most modern Linux distributions ship with Snort, so you should be able to install it in the usual way. Once installed, Snort is configured through the /etc/snort/snort.conf file. (Some distributions don't provide a file of this name, but do provide a file called snort.conf.distrib or some other variant. You can copy or rename this file and use it as a template that you can modify.) A default snort.conf file may work acceptably, but you may want to customize several variables, such as $HOME_NET, $SMTP_SERVERS, and $HTTP_SERVERS. The first of these specifies the IP addresses to be monitored. Others define the IP addresses of particular types of servers. The default values tell Snort to monitor all IP addresses, which may be fine, since you may want Snort to watch all traffic on its local network, which is all it will ordinarily be able to see.

Some distributions place a series of supplementary Snort configuration files, with names that end in .rules, in the /etc/snort directory. These rule files define the sorts of packets that Snort should consider suspicious. Most protocols have a single .rules file, such as smtp.rules for SMTP packets. These .rules files are referenced via include directives in the main snort.conf file, so be sure your main snort.conf file loads the appropriate rules for your network. If you don't see a .rules file for a protocol you want to monitor, check http://www.snort.org/snort-db/. This site hosts many Snort .rules files for less popular protocols.

To launch Snort, type its command name: **snort**. The program runs and logs its output in files located in /var/log/snort. These log files record information on suspicious packets. You should be sure to monitor these log files on a regular basis, as described in Chapter 4. To launch Snort on a permanent basis, you can run it from a startup script. In fact, many distributions provide SysV startup scripts to launch Snort.

FIGURE 7.3   A Snort system can be placed at any of several locations to monitor network activity.

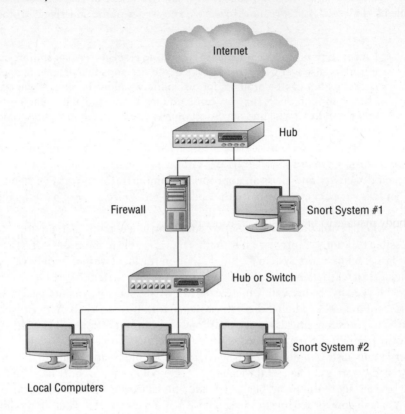

| | | |

Snort doesn't need an IP address to monitor network traffic. Thus, you can configure a dedicated Snort system with network drivers but without an IP address and use it to monitor network traffic. This configuration makes the Snort monitor very resistant to external attacks, because an attacker can't directly address the system. On the downside, you must use the Snort system's own console or an RS-232 serial link to it to monitor its activities.

Using PortSentry

Another IDS is PortSentry (http://sourceforge.net/projects/sentrytools/). The basic idea behind PortSentry is similar to that of Snort, in the sense that both are designed to alert you to suspicious network activity. One critical difference is that PortSentry runs on individual computers to monitor access attempts to their own ports, whereas Snort can monitor an entire network. Another difference is that PortSentry can actively block network scans. In fact, in some sense PortSentry is more like a firewall than an IDS.

After installing PortSentry (usually from a package called `portsentry`), you can configure it via its `portsentry.conf` file, which is generally found in `/etc` or `/etc/portsentry`. You specify ports you want PortSentry to monitor with the `TCP_PORTS` and `UDP_PORTS` options, which both specify comma-delimited lists of ports. PortSentry binds to these ports, logs attempts to access them, and can take various optional actions based on additional options in the PortSentry configuration file. These actions can include ignoring the access attempts, running external programs, dropping routes from the routing table, and so on.

Using Tripwire

Monitoring network traffic is a useful strategy for detecting undesirable activity, but it isn't guaranteed to detect an intruder. Perhaps the cracker is using an authorized protocol from an authorized location, for instance, and so the intrusion attempt doesn't trip any triggers in Snort or PortSentry. Should somebody manage to break into your computer, Tripwire (`http://www.tripwire.org`) may be your best bet to detect that fact. This utility records a set of information about all the important files on a computer, including various types of *checksums* and *hashes*—short digital "signatures" that enable you to quickly determine whether or not a file has been changed. (These can also be used in other ways; for instance, Linux uses hashes to store passwords.) With this database stored in a secure location, you can check your system periodically for alteration. If an intruder has modified any of your files, Tripwire will alert you to this fact. If you like, you can run a Tripwire verification on a regular basis—say, once a week in a cron job.

Many distributions ship with Tripwire, but it may not be installed by default. The utility is controlled through two configuration files: `tw.cfg` and `tw.pol`, which often reside in `/etc/tripwire`. The `tw.cfg` file controls overall configuration options, such as where `tw.pol` resides, how Tripwire sends reports to the system administrator, and so on. The `tw.pol` file includes information on the files it's to include in its database, among other things. Both files are binary files created from text-mode files called `twcfg.txt` and `twpol.txt`, respectively. You may need to edit `twpol.txt` to eliminate references to files you don't have on your system and to add information on files you do have but that the default file doesn't reference. Use the `twinstall.sh` program (which often resides in `/etc/tripwire`) to generate the binary configuration files and other critical database files. This utility will ask you to set a pair of pass phrases, which are like passwords but are typically longer, to control access to the Tripwire utilities. You'll then need to enter these pass phrases to have the utility do its encoding work.

Once you've generated the basic setup files, type **`tripwire --init`** to have it generate initial checksums and hashes on all the files it's configured to monitor. This process is likely to take a few minutes. Thereafter, typing **`tripwire --check`** will check the current state of the system against the database, and typing **`tripwire --update`** will update the database (say, in case you upgrade a package). The `--init` and `--update` operations require you to enter the pass phrase, but `--check` doesn't. Therefore, you can include an automated Tripwire check in a cron job. (Chapter 5 describes cron jobs in more detail.)

Tripwire is best installed and initialized on a completely fresh system, before connecting the computer to the Internet but after all programs have been configured. Although it's possible to install it on a system that's been up and running for some time, if that computer has already been compromised without your knowledge, Tripwire won't detect that fact.

Using *chkrootkit*

The chkrootkit program (http://www.chkrootkit.org) is something of a last-resort method of detecting intrusion, and is the closest thing in the Linux world to Windows virus scanners. (Linux virus scanning programs also exist, but they're intended mainly to check for Windows viruses on Samba shares. Linux viruses are not a problem in the real world, at least not as of late 2004.)

Many crackers use *root kits*, which are prepackaged intrusion tools. When an intruder runs a root kit against a target, the root kit software probes for known weaknesses (such as servers with known security bugs), breaks in, and installs software to enable simpler access by the intruder. The intruder can then log in using Telnet, SSH, or the like and gain full control of the system.

 Intruders who use root kits are often referred to as *script kiddies.* These miscreants have minimal skill; they rely on the root kit to do the real work of the intrusion. Some people prefer to reserve the term "cracker" for more skilled intruders, but others consider script kiddies to be crackers with minimal expertise.

Using chkrootkit is fairly straightforward: Type its name. The result is a series of lines summarizing checks that the software performs. These lines should all end with a not infected, no suspect files found, or similar reassuring message. If any message alerts you to an intrusion, you should take immediate corrective measures.

Using Package Manager Checksums

Package managers—most notably the RPM Package Manager (RPM)—maintain checksums on all their installed packages. As such, they can be used as intrusion detection tools. In particular, the -V (or --verify) option to rpm performs a package verification:

```
# rpm -V postfix
S.5....T c /etc/postfix/main.cf
S.5....T c /etc/postfix/sasl_passwd
S.5....T c /etc/postfix/sender_canonical
```

Each line of output reports files that have changed in some way. The first eight characters of the output lines report what's changed: the file size, the mode, the MD5 sum, device major or minor numbers (for device files), link path mismatch, user ownership, group ownership, or time. A dot (.) in a position indicates that a test passed; any other character denotes a change (the character used depends on the test and is intended to be mnemonic). Following the eight-character block may be another character that denotes the file type—c for configuration files, d for documentation, g for "ghost" files (those not included in the actual package), l for a license file, or r for a README file. Files that haven't changed are *not* displayed in the output.

In the preceding example, three files have changed: `main.cf`, `sasl_passwd`, and `sender_canonical`. All three files are marked as configuration files (the c characters preceding the filenames), and all three have changed file sizes, MD5 sums, and times. Because these are configuration files, these changes aren't particularly suspicious, but a similar pattern of changes in program executables would be cause for concern. Changes to the MD5 sum (the form of checksum used by RPM) are particularly likely to be the result of tampering; they indicate that the file's contents have changed compared to the file in the original package. Time stamp changes can sometimes be completely innocent. Ownership and permissions changes might be the result of unwanted tampering, or could be innocent in some cases (say, if you've deliberately removed world execute permission to improve security).

You can verify an individual package by providing a package name, as in the preceding example. You can also verify all the packages installed on a system by passing the -a option. The result is likely to be a very long list, though, because so many packages include configuration files and other ancillary files that are normally changed. You might want to pass the output to a file that you can peruse later, as in **rpm -Va > rpm-test.txt**.

WARNING   One major limitation of a package manager's checksums for detecting intruders is that it's very easily overcome. Unlike Tripwire's database, the RPM database isn't password-protected. In fact, intruders can easily mask their tracks by using RPM itself to install their modified tools. When you attempt to use RPM to verify the package, RPM will merrily report no problems.

Monitoring Log Files

Log files can provide clues to intrusions. Chapter 8 describes log files in detail, so you should consult it for basic information on where log files reside, how you can configure them, and how you can monitor them. You should be aware, though, that log files often contain clues about intrusions. Suspicious items that may appear in log files include:

Suspicious logins   A login might catch your eye for any number of reasons. Perhaps the user is on vacation with no network access, or perhaps the login is from a location to which the user has no access. If you notice such activity, you should investigate further.

Repeated login failures   Crackers sometimes attempt to log in by guessing passwords. This procedure is likely to leave a trace in log files in the form of a long series of login failures. Just one failure followed by a successful login isn't very suspicious, though; this sort of pattern is more likely the result of a mistyped or momentarily forgotten password.

Missing entries   Intruders often try to cover their tracks by deleting entries from log files. The result is suspicious gaps in the log files. For instance, if a system normally generates an average of one entry per minute, a gap of 20 minutes could signal that an intruder broke in and then deleted the log entries that would provide clues as to how this was done.

Entries for servers that shouldn't be running   If a cracker launches a new server to facilitate future logins or perform some other task, you may see log entries from this new server.

Unfortunately, monitoring log files for all of these things can be tedious. Log file monitoring tools, such as those described in Chapter 8, can help minimize this tedium, but some discoveries are still likely to be serendipitous unless you spend all your time watching your log files grow.

Security Auditing

From time to time, you should check your system for suspicious configurations. Such security auditing can detect intrusions that might have slipped past other detection tools and procedures. It can also catch sloppy configurations that might lead to trouble in the future. Examples of things you should check are scanning for open ports, reviewing your local accounts, and reviewing the installed files and packages.

Checking for Open Ports

Open ports are those that respond to connection attempts—that is, servers are running on the ports. Ideally, the only open ports on a system will be those associated with servers you intend to run. Sometimes, though, a port will be open because of an accidental misconfiguration or because a cracker has broken into your system. Thus, scanning for open ports is an important security precaution. Two methods of spotting unnecessary servers are to use local network activity tools and to use a network scanner.

Using Local Network Activity Tools

One tool that can be helpful in spotting stray servers is netstat. This program is the Swiss Army knife of network status tools; it provides many different options and output formats to deliver information on routing tables, interface statistics, and so on. For purposes of spotting unnecessary servers, you can use netstat with its -a and -p options, as shown here:

```
# netstat -ap
Active Internet connections (servers and established)
Proto Recv-Q Send-Q Local Address           Foreign Address         State
➥PID/Program name
tcp       0      0 *:ftp                   *:*                     LISTEN
➥690/inetd
tcp       0      0 teela.rodsbooks.com:ssh nessus.rodsbooks.:39361 ESTABLISHED
➥787/sshd
```

I've trimmed most of the entries from this output to make it manageable as an example.

The `Local Address` and `Foreign Address` columns specify the local and remote addresses, including both the hostname or IP address and the port number or associated name from `/etc/services`. The first of the two entries shown here isn't actively connected, so the local address and the foreign address and port number are all listed as asterisks (*). This entry does specify the local port, though—`ftp`. This line indicates that a server is running on the `ftp` port (TCP port 21). The `State` column specifies that the server is listening for a connection. The final column in this output, under the `PID/Program name` heading, indicates that the process with a process ID (PID) of 690 is using this port. In this case, it's `inetd`.

The second output line indicates that a connection has been established between `teela.rodsbooks.com` and `nessus.rodsbooks.com` (the second hostname is truncated). The local system (`teela`) is using the `ssh` port (TCP port 22), and the client (`nessus`) is using port 39361 on the client system. The process that's handling this connection on the local system is `sshd`, running as PID 787.

It may take some time to peruse the output of `netstat`, but doing so will leave you with a much improved understanding of your system's network connections. If you spot servers listening for connections that you didn't realize were active, you should investigate the matter further. Some servers may be innocent or even necessary. Others may be pointless security risks.

When you use the -p option to obtain the name and PID of the process using a port, the netstat output is wider than 80 columns. You may want to open an extra-wide xterm window to handle this output, or redirect it to a file that you can study in a text editor capable of displaying more than 80 columns. To quickly spot servers listening for connections, pipe the output through a grep LISTEN command to filter on the listening state. The result will show all servers that are listening for connections, omitting client connections and specific server instances that are already connected to clients.

Using Remote Network Scanners

Network scanners, such as Nmap (`http://www.insecure.org/nmap/`) or Nessus (`http://www.nessus.org`), can scan for open ports on the local computer or on other computers. The more sophisticated scanners, including Nessus, will check for known vulnerabilities, so they can tell you if a server might be compromised should you decide to leave it running.

Network scanners are used by crackers for locating likely target systems, as well as by network administrators for legitimate purposes. Many organizations have policies forbidding the use of network scanners except under specific conditions. Therefore, you should check these policies and obtain explicit permission, signed and in writing, to perform a network scan. Failure to do so could cost you your job or even result in criminal charges, even if your intentions are honorable.

Nmap is capable of performing a basic check for open ports. Pass the -sT parameter and the name of the target system to it, as shown here:

```
$ nmap -sT teela.rodsbooks.com

Starting nmap V. 3.55 ( www.insecure.org/nmap/ ) at 2004-12-21 12:11 EDT
Interesting ports on teela.rodsbooks.com (192.168.1.2):
(The 1581 ports scanned but not shown below are in state: closed)
Port      State      Service
21/tcp    open       ftp
22/tcp    open       ssh
```

> **NOTE** As with the output of netstat shown in "Using Local Network Activity Tools," this output has been trimmed for brevity's sake.

This output shows two open ports—21 and 22, used by ftp and ssh, respectively. If you weren't aware that these ports were active, you should log into the scanned system and investigate further, using netstat or ps to locate the programs using these ports and, if desired, shut them down. The -sT option specifies a scan of TCP ports. A few servers, though, run on UDP ports, so you need to scan them by typing **nmap -sU *hostname***. (This usage requires root privileges, unlike scanning TCP ports.)

Nmap is capable of more sophisticated scans, including "stealth" scans that aren't likely to be noticed by most types of firewalls, ping scans to detect which hosts are active, and more. The Nmap man page provides details. Nessus, which is built atop Nmap, provides a GUI and a means of performing automated and still more sophisticated tests. Nessus comes as separate client and server components; the client enables you to control the server, which does the actual work.

When you use a network scanner, you should consider the fact that the ports you see from your test system may not be the same as those that might be visible to an attacker. This issue is particularly important if you're testing a system that resides behind a firewall from another system that's behind the same firewall. Your test system is likely to reveal accessible ports that would not be accessible from the outside world. On the other hand, a cracker on your local network would most likely have access similar to your own, so you shouldn't be complacent because you use a firewall. Nonetheless, firewalls can be important tools for hiding servers without shutting them down.

Reviewing Accounts

Your computer's accounts are a potential source of vulnerability. If accounts go unused but remain active, an intruder could conceivably obtain a password and break in. Even system accounts (those used by Linux itself to run servers or for other purposes other than managing ordinary users) can pose a threat. An unused system account could be converted into a login account and used by an intruder, possibly escaping notice.

From time to time, you should study your local accounts by perusing the /etc/passwd and /etc/shadow files. These files and their contents are described in more detail in Chapter 3. Pay particular attention to security issues:

Unknown accounts   Most Linux systems have many system accounts, and you might not remember them all, so don't jump to conclusions, but if you see an account you don't recognize, you should investigate it. Check its characteristics for any suspicious features, compare your current file with a backup made after system installation, and check log files for activity involving the account.

Accounts with a UID of 0   Linux uses a UID of 0 to represent root, so any account with a UID of 0 other than root is *highly* suspicious. Attackers sometimes create such accounts, or change the UID of an existing account to 0 in order to give themselves root privileges on a system.

System accounts with passwords   System accounts, such as daemon and cron, are frequently used by Linux to run servers or other tools without root privileges. Ordinarily, these accounts don't need passwords, so if you see a password for such an account in /etc/shadow, it's very likely to be an indication of an intrusion. If you use shadow passwords, all accounts have an x in the /etc/passwd file's password field, so you must check the /etc/shadow file. Accounts without passwords are indicated by an exclamation mark or an asterisk in the password field, which is the second field in this file.

Login shells   The login shell is the final field in the /etc/passwd file. Most system accounts use /bin/false or /dev/null as a login shell, although there are a few exceptions. Most notably, the shutdown account uses /sbin/shutdown, the halt account uses /sbin/halt, and root uses a normal shell (typically /bin/bash). A few server packages create accounts with normal shells as login programs, too, although most don't. This practice varies with the server program and distribution. As a general rule, though, you should be suspicious of system accounts with login shells other than /bin/false or /dev/null.

One of the best ways to review your accounts is to keep backups of /etc/passwd and /etc/shadow on a write-protected removable medium, such as a write-protected floppy disk. You can then mount that disk and compare the backup to your on-disk file using diff:

```
# diff /etc/passwd /mnt/floppy/passwd
# diff /etc/shadow /mnt/floppy/shadow
```

If you haven't added, deleted, or modified accounts, these commands should return no output lines. If accounts have been changed, diff will summarize the changes. Note that changes to /etc/shadow include password changes, so this comparison is likely to turn up many changes on a multiuser system, particularly if users are diligent about changing their passwords on a regular basis.

WARNING   Password files stored on floppy disks pose a security threat themselves. They should be kept under lock and key—ideally in a safe that can be accessed only by system administrators who can ordinarily read the original files.

Verifying Installed Files and Packages

A final method of security auditing is verifying installed files and packages. One approach to doing this is to use a package tool such as RPM, as described earlier, in "Using Package Manager Checksums." This procedure will help look for sloppily replaced program files. It won't help you spot changes to files in programs you didn't install via your package manager, though. It's also overly sensitive to changes to configuration files, which you often alter yourself after installing the package. Tripwire (described earlier, in "Using Tripwire") is another tool that can be used in this way. It's more helpful in spotting changes to key configuration files, but it's more of a hassle to use.

Another approach you can take is to keep backups of known-good configuration files on read-only media. You can then compare your current configuration files to the backups from time to time. Using `diff`, as described in "Reviewing Accounts," can be an effective way to do this.

Of course, as with Tripwire, this approach is useful only if you make backups of your configuration files before your system is exposed to the Internet. Once the system has been online, the possibility exists that it's been compromised, so you can't trust the configuration files you back up—at least, not without careful examination.

Imposing User Resource Limits

Sometimes you may want to impose limits on how many times users may log in, how much CPU time they can consume, how much memory they can use, and so on. Imposing such limits is best done through a Pluggable Authentication Module (PAM) module called `pam_limits`. Most major Linux distributions use this module as part of their standard PAM configuration, so chances are you won't need to add it; however, you will still need to configure `pam_limits`. This is done by editing its configuration file, `/etc/security/limits.conf`. This file contains comments (denoted by a hash mark, #) and limit lines that consist of four fields:

domain type item value

Each of these fields specifies a particular type of information:

The domain   The *domain* describes the entity to which the limit applies. It can be a username; a group name, which takes the form *@groupname*; or an asterisk (*) wildcard, which matches everybody.

Hard or soft limits   The *type* field specifies the limit as `hard` or `soft`. A `hard` limit is imposed by the system administrator and cannot be exceeded under any circumstances, whereas a `soft` limit may be temporarily exceeded by a user. You can also use a dash (-) to signify a limit is both `hard` and `soft`.

The limited item   The *item* field specifies what type of item is being limited. Examples include `core` (the size of core files), `data` (the size of a program's data area), `fsize` (the size of files created by the user), `nofile` (the number of open data files), `rss` (the resident set size), `stack` (the stack size), `cpu` (the CPU time of a single process in minutes), `nproc` (the number of concurrent processes), `maxlogins` (the number of simultaneous logins), and `priority` (the process priority). The `data`, `rss`, and `stack` items all relate to memory consumed by a program. These and other measures of data capacity are measured in kilobytes.

The value   The final field specifies the value that's to be applied to the limit.

As an example, consider a system on which certain users should be able to log in and perform a limited number of actions, but not stay logged in indefinitely and consume vast amounts of CPU time. You might use a configuration like this one:

```
@limited   hard   cpu   2
```

This configuration applies a hard CPU limit of two minutes to the `limited` group. Members of this group will be able to log in and run programs, but if one of those programs consumes more than two minutes of CPU time, it will be terminated.

CPU time and total system access time are two entirely different things. CPU time is calculated based on the amount of time that the CPU is actively processing a user's data. Idle time (for instance, when a user's shell is active but no CPU-intensive tasks are running) doesn't count. Thus, a user can log in and remain logged in for hours even with a very low hard CPU time limit. This limit is intended to prevent problems caused by users who run very CPU-intensive programs on systems that should not be used for such purposes.

Summary

Linux's security mechanisms can help you keep your system from falling under the control of those who want to do you harm, or who simply want to abuse your system for their own ends. Like any OS's security measures, though, Linux's tools are only as good as their configurations. Although the default security of Linux systems has improved greatly since the late 1990s, maintaining a Linux system still requires that you understand the security tools available to you, and that you be able to configure those tools to suit your needs.

Security begins with physical measures. With direct access to your computer, a miscreant can do anything at all, from changing configuration files to stealing your data to stealing the hardware. Many physical security measures are common sense, but others are very computer-specific.

Beyond physical security, firewalls and super server configurations can help protect the servers running on your computer. These options enable you to block access to your servers from undesired sources, or to otherwise limit access to the computer.

Even the best configurations sometimes fail, so you should attend to the possibility by monitoring your system for intrusion. Various intrusion detection tools, such as Snort and Tripwire, will help you to do this. Don't neglect basic vigilance, though—if you notice something odd about how your system is behaving, that may be a sign of intrusion. You should also periodically review your security measures and look for weaknesses. Again, various tools, such as `netstat` and `nmap`, can help you in this task

Exam Essentials

Summarize important physical security measures.   Whenever possible, computers should be stored behind locked doors, or possibly chained in place. Depending on your needs and environment, you may want to eliminate removable media, set the computer to boot only from the hard disk, lock the case shut, set a BIOS password, set a LILO or GRUB password, or encrypt files on the hard disk.

Explain common access control mechanisms.   Firewalls, TCP Wrappers, and `xinetd` can all control access to particular ports, either by blocking them entirely or by controlling access to the servers that run on those ports. Passwords and file permissions can control access to individuals, by requiring authentication or restricting access to specific files once a user has gained entry to the system.

Identify some common symptoms of a compromised computer.   Intruders often make mistakes when invading a system. These mistakes can manifest themselves as a sluggish system, a system that suddenly consumes more network bandwidth than usual, programs that suddenly begin crashing, programs that don't behave as they normally do, or other strange changes in the system's operation.

Describe the differences between Snort and PortSentry.   Snort is able to monitor network activity directed at multiple computers, given appropriate network infrastructure, thus providing an early alert system for the network as a whole. PortSentry, by contrast, is a tool that's designed to monitor and restrict access to a single computer.

Describe the Linux packet filter firewall architecture.   The `iptables` tool organizes firewall rules into chains of rules, which in turn are organized into tables. Each chain can contain many pattern-matching rules that direct packets to be accepted, denied, or rejected, and the chains are linked together to direct the flow of traffic from input, through local programs, and to output.

Summarize the tools that can be used for locating open ports.   Local open ports can be found with the `netstat` program, which uses local system calls to locate ports that are currently open. The `nmap` program can locate open ports on the local computer or on other computers by sending network probes to all or a subset of the ports on the target computer.

Explain how corrupted files may be located.   Several tools can locate corrupt files, typically by using checksums to determine whether files on disk have been changed. These tools include Tripwire and the RPM system. Manually performing such comparisons using `diff` and backup files can also be effective.

Summarize the process for limiting users' access to CPU time, memory, and other system resources   The PAM system includes the means to limit users' access to system resources. This is configured via the /etc/security/limits.conf file, which provides the means to specify limits by username and the resource that's being limited.

Commands in This Chapter

Command	Description
tcpd	Implements access restrictions in conjunction with a super server; also known as TCP Wrappers.
ipfwadm	Linux firewall command for 2.0.*x* kernels.
ipchains	Linux firewall command for 2.2.*x* kernels.
iptables	Linux firewall command for 2.4.*x* and later kernels.
snort	Program that provides intrusion detection features for a network.
portsentry	Program that can block access to individual ports and report on activity directed at that port.
tripwire	Program that can monitor files for suspicious changes, based on stored checksum values for the protected files.
chkrootkit	Program that scans the computer for known root kits—intrusion software employed by script kiddies.
netstat	General-purpose network information tool. May be used to check for open ports.
nmap	Network probing tool. May be used to check for open ports.

Review Questions

1. A server/computer combination appears in both `hosts.allow` and `hosts.deny`. What's the result of this configuration when TCP Wrappers runs?

    A. TCP Wrappers refuses to run and logs an error in `/var/log/messages`.

    B. The system's administrator is paged to decide whether to allow access.

    C. `hosts.deny` takes precedence; the client is denied access to the server.

    D. `hosts.allow` takes precedence; the client is granted access to the server.

2. When is the `bind` option of `xinetd` most useful?

    A. When you want to run two servers on one port

    B. When you want to specify computers by name rather than IP address

    C. When `xinetd` is running on a system with two network interfaces

    D. When resolving conflicts between different servers

3. At what point during system installation should you configure Tripwire?

    A. Prior to installing major servers like Apache

    B. After installing major servers but before configuring them

    C. After installing and configuring major servers but before connecting the computer to the Internet

    D. After connecting the computer to the Internet and running it for 1–4 weeks

4. Which of the following ports are known as *unprivileged ports*?

    A. Those that have numbers above 1024

    B. Those that have numbers between 512 and 1024

    C. Those that have numbers between 1 and 100

    D. Those that have numbers below 1024

5. Which of the following measures should you take to secure your servers? (Choose all that apply.)

    A. Locate them behind locked doors.

    B. Eliminate removable media.

    C. Set a BIOS password.

    D. Set a LILO/GRUB password.

6. Which of the following tools is best suited for monitoring activity directed at multiple computers?

    A. LILO

    B. PortSentry

    C. Snort

    D. SWAT

7. Which port, by default, is commonly used by OpenSSH?

   A. 20

   B. 21

   C. 22

   D. 23

8. Which of the following programs uses local system calls to locate local ports that are currently open?

   A. `netstat`

   B. `nmap`

   C. `chkrootkit`

   D. `nessus`

9. Your access server is using PAM and you want to limit users' access to system resources. Which configuration file will you need to edit?

   A. `/etc/limits.conf`

   B. `/etc/pam/limits.conf`

   C. `/etc/security/limits.conf`

   D. `/etc/security/pam/limits.conf`

10. Which of the following programs scans the computer for known root kits?

    A. `hackroot`

    B. `rootmaster`

    C. `rootfind`

    D. `chkrootkit`

11. Which organization tracks known vulnerabilities in operating systems?

    A. FSF

    B. CERT

    C. OSI

    D. SourceForge

12. Which of the following is a tool that's designed to monitor and restrict access to a single computer?

    A. Snort

    B. PortSentry

    C. Telnet

    D. BIND

13. Which port, by default, is commonly used by HTTPS?

    A. 111

    B. 143

    C. 389

    D. 443

14. Which of the following programs can locate open ports on the local computer or on other computers by sending network probes to ports on target computers? (Choose all that apply.)

    A. `netstat`

    B. `nmap`

    C. `chkrootkit`

    D. `nessus`

15. What is the term used to describe a system when an attacker has gained `root` privileges?

    A. Sourced

    B. Embedded

    C. Rooted

    D. Cored

16. What files will be found when the command `find / -perm +2000 -type f` is executed?

    A. Files that have their SGID bit set

    B. Files that have their SUID bit set

    C. Files that have their SUID or SGID bit set

    D. Files or directories that have their SUID or SGID bit set

17. You suspect an attacker is using many computers to flood your Web server with useless data packets. What type of attack is this?

    A. Root kit

    B. DDoS

    C. Ping

    D. NetPing

18. Which of the following is the best definition of a checksum?

    A. An encrypted hash of the data

    B. A mathematical inverse of the ASCII value of all the characters added together

    C. A 56-bit encryption key used to protect the contents of a packet

    D. A digital signature that enables you to determine whether or not a file has been changed

19. You suspect that the `/etc/passwd` file may have been altered over the course of the evening. You want to compare the current file with an offline backup made last night. Which utility should you use to compare the two versions of the file?

    A. `tar`

    B. `cpio`

    C. `diff`

    D. `check`

20. Which of the following types of attacks involves sending bogus e-mail to lure unsuspecting individuals into divulging sensitive financial or other information?

    A. Phishing

    B. Script kiddies

    C. Spoofing

    D. Ensnaring

Answers to Review Questions

1. D. TCP Wrappers uses this feature to allow you to override broad denials by adding more specific explicit access permissions to hosts.allow, as when setting a default deny policy (ALL : ALL) in hosts.deny.

2. C. The bind option of xinetd lets you tie a server to just one network interface, rather than link to them all. It has nothing to do with running multiple servers on one port, specifying computers by hostname, or resolving conflicts between servers.

3. C. Tripwire records checksums and hashes of major files, including server executables and configuration files. Thus, these files should be in place and properly configured before you configure Tripwire. Once the system has been running on the Internet, there's a chance that it's been compromised; you should install Tripwire prior to connecting the computer to the Internet in order to reduce the risk that its database reflects an already-compromised system.

4. A. *Unprivileged ports* are those that have numbers above 1024. *Privileged ports* are those that have numbers below 1024. The idea is that a client can connect to a privileged port and be confident that the server running on that port was configured by the system administrator.

5. Answers: A, B, C, D. Whenever possible, computers should be stored behind locked doors, or possibly chained in place. Depending on your needs and environment, you may want to eliminate removable media, set the computer to boot only from the hard disk, lock the case shut, set a BIOS password, set a LILO or GRUB password, or encrypt files on the hard disk.

6. C. Snort is able to monitor network activity directed at multiple computers, given appropriate network infrastructure, thus providing an early alert system for the network as a whole. LILO is a boot loader, while PortSentry is designed to monitor and restrict access to a single computer. SWAT is the Samba Web Administration Tool.

7. C. The default port for OpenSSH is 22. FTP uses ports 20 and 21, while Telnet uses port 23.

8. A. Local open ports can be found with the netstat program, which uses local system calls to locate ports that are currently open. The nmap and nessus programs can locate open ports on the local computer or on other computers by sending network probes to all or a subset of the ports on the target computer. chkrootkit is something of a last-resort method of detecting intrusion, and is the closest thing in the Linux world to Windows virus scanners.

9. C. The /etc/security/limits.conf holds the configuration settings that will allow you to limit users' access. The other options listed do not give the correct path to this file.

10. D. The chkrootkit program scans the computer for root kit "signatures." It's similar in principle to a Windows virus scanner, although it looks for root kits rather than viruses because the former exist on Linux but not the latter. The other options listed are not valid programs.

11. B. The Computer Emergency Response Team (CERT) tracks known vulnerabilities. The Free Software Foundation (FSF), the Open Source Initiative (OSI), and the SourceForge Web site all contribute greatly to the Linux operating system, but are not focused on vulnerabilities within the operating system.

12. B. PortSentry is a tool that's designed to monitor and restrict access to a single computer. Snort is able to monitor network activity directed at multiple computers. Telnet is a remote login protocol and BIND is used to provide name resolution.

13. D. The default port for HTTPS is 443. PortMapper uses port 111, while the default port for IMAP 2 is 143. The default port for LDAP is 389.

14. Answers: B, D. The nmap and nessus programs can locate open ports on the local computer or on other computers by sending network probes to all or a subset of the ports on the target computer. Local open ports can be found with the netstat program. chkrootkit detects intrusions on a Linux system.

15. C. When an attacker gains root privileges on a computer, that system is sometimes said to have been rooted.

16. A. The list of files displayed will be those that have their SGID bit set. The -type f option limits the search to files only and not directories. To search for files with their SUID bit set, the 2000 needs to be 4000. To find files that have either SUID or SGID bits set, the numerical value needs to be 6000.

17. B. A distributed denial of service (DDoS) attack occurs when an attacker uses many computers (typically hijacked in one way or another long before) to flood your sever computer with useless data packets. A root kit is a tool used to break into a computer. A ping is a simple test for connectivity and NetPing is not a standard utility or type of attack.

18. D. A checksum is a short digital "signature" that enables you to quickly determine whether or not a file has been changed.

19. C. The diff utility can be used to check two files for differences. Both tar and cpio are used for backing up files, but they will not compare them, and check is not a standard utility.

20. A. Phishing involves sending bogus e-mail or setting up fake Web sites that lure unsuspecting individuals into divulging sensitive financial or other information. Script kiddies are intruders who use root kits. Spoofing involves pretending data is coming from one computer when it is coming from another. Ensnaring is not a type of attack.

Chapter

8

System Documentation

THE FOLLOWING COMPTIA OBJECTIVES ARE COVERED IN THIS CHAPTER:

✓ **3.10 Configure log files (e.g., syslog, remote log file storage)**

✓ **5.1 Establish system performance baseline**

✓ **5.2 Create written procedures for installation, configuration, security and management**

✓ **5.3 Document installed configuration (e.g., installed packages, package options, TCP/IP assignment list, changes—configuration and maintenance)**

✓ **5.4 Troubleshoot errors using system logs (e.g.,** `tail`, `head`, `grep`**)**

✓ **5.5 Troubleshoot application errors using application logs (e.g.,** `tail`, `head`, `grep`**)**

✓ **5.6 Access system documentation and help files (e.g.,** `man`, `info`, `readme`, **Web)**

Much of this book describes how to configure and use Linux to accomplish particular goals. In doing so, though, you're likely to need documentation of various sorts, and some of this documentation *you* must create. In particular, you must understand how your system normally operates. This means you should take notes on how you installed Linux and how you reconfigured it after installation. Documenting official policies on configuration and use can also be helpful, particularly in a large organization that employs multiple system administrators or as a tool to ease the transition when personnel leave the organization or are transferred to new duties. Another type of documentation you should record is baseline information on the system's performance. This information can be handy if the system begins behaving sluggishly or strangely, because you'll have some idea of its original performance levels.

In addition to these types of system documentation, which you must keep yourself, Linux keeps its own documentation in the form of *log files*, which maintain information on critical system events, such as system reboots and user logins. Log files can be important in debugging problems or in checking overall system performance. Knowing how to configure Linux's log file options and use those log files is an important skill for any system administrator.

Finally, you should know something about the documentation that comes with all Linux systems, in the form of man pages, info pages, other program documentation files, and Web resources. These tools can provide invaluable information on normal program operation, command options, and so on.

Documenting System Configuration

One very important system administration task that's easy to overlook is that of documenting your configuration. Even a lightly used Linux system is likely to collect dozens of changes to configuration files, program installations, and other modifications over the course of its lifetime. It's easy to forget these changes, which can cause problems down the line. For instance, if you alter a system startup script to launch a new server but then replace or upgrade that server, a failure to modify that startup script can cause error messages or result in the updated server not starting. Also, if the system is seriously damaged or if you need to reproduce the system's configuration on another computer, a good set of notes on the first system's configuration can be invaluable. The ultimate in administrative logs is arguably a backup of all the system's configuration files. Keeping such backups is fairly simple insurance, so you should be sure to keep such backups. Another type of documentation is recording policies and procedures—who may receive accounts on a system, what procedures to follow when installing or upgrading software, and so on. Such documentation can be very helpful when a system has multiple administrators, either simultaneously or over time. Explicit policies can help administrators avoid blunders such as creating accounts they shouldn't create.

Documenting the Installation

You should begin your documentation efforts with information on the core system installation. This information can help if you ever need to reinstall the OS from scratch or want to reproduce the configuration of an existing system on a new one. Information you may want to document includes:

Linux distribution and version   The Linux distribution may be obvious in some environments, particularly if you've standardized on one distribution on many computers. If you deviate from this choice, though, recording it may be necessary. The same is true if few systems at the site run Linux. In such cases, a new administrator brought on in the future might not know what distribution the system is running, but this knowledge can be important. Likewise, knowledge of the version number of the distribution as a whole can be valuable.

Hardware selections   In some cases, your hardware selections can be obvious by physical examination of the computer. Sometimes, though, it's not obvious, because the device might be generic or embedded within a larger device, such as a disk controller on a motherboard. Keeping all the manuals for the hardware is quite prudent—you never know when you'll need to look up a monitor's acceptable refresh rates or a hard disk's internal transfer rate, for instance. Likewise, you should keep any floppy disks or CD-ROMs with drivers and documentation, even if these contain no Linux-specific information. Hardware documentation can be particularly important when the system changes—for instance, if you reinstall after changing a video card, this fact may be important so that you can make appropriate adjustments.

Disk partitions   Your hard disk partitioning scheme can be quite important. You should note the start and end points of all partitions. Such information can be vital if your partition table becomes corrupted—with this information, you may be able to recover your partitions intact. After installing Linux, type **fdisk -l /dev/hda > file.txt** to store information on /dev/hda's partition table in file.txt. Repeat this command or change the device identifier and output filename as appropriate if you have multiple disks or SCSI disks. You can also record information on the disk filesystems. This information usually appears in /etc/fstab. Printing out these files and keeping them in a binder can be an immense help down the line.

Installed software   You should take notes on what software is installed in your system. If you install Linux from scratch, record what software packages you select during installation. After installation, you may be able to use a package management tool to do this job. For instance, on an RPM-based distribution, type **rpm -qa > packages.txt** to store information on the installed packages in packages.txt. On a Debian-based system, typing **dpkg -l > packages.txt** produces a similar list. Print out this file or store it on a removable disk for future reference. Make notes on package upgrades as you make them. You should record such upgrades as changes to the initial install set; this will let you track back to a change if you discover that it causes problems. You might want to periodically record a fresh installed package list, though.

Install-time configuration options   During installation, you make various choices, which vary from one distribution to another. Common examples include the X video driver, display size, mouse and keyboard options, TCP/IP options, firewall settings, time zone, and which servers to run. Although you can track down this information from various files in /etc, recording them at install time is the easiest course, if your goal is to be able to reproduce an installation at a later date.

Ideally, you should document these choices during installation or as soon after installation as possible. Some options, such as exact package versions, are likely to change as you use and upgrade a computer, and knowing its pristine original state can be a useful debugging tool. For instance, if the system worked properly after installation but a server breaks sometime later, knowing whether the package or any on which it depends have changed versions may help point you to a solution.

Maintaining an Administrator's Log

Many administrators keep a written log of all system maintenance. By *written*, I mean just that: recorded in a paper notebook. This format has an advantage in that it's not susceptible to many of the problems that can plague an electronic notebook. For instance, if you keep a log on the computer, that log will most probably be lost if your hard disk dies. A paper notebook is also easily transported to another system, even one without network connectivity, so that you can use your notes to reproduce a configuration on another system.

What should you write in this computer diary? Important information to record includes the following:

Initial configuration The information described earlier, in "Documenting the Installation," should lead your administrator's log book. (Depending on the format of your book, you might keep a few loose-leaf printouts with it or punch holes in printouts to put them in a binder.)

Package installations When you install a software package, as described in Chapter 5, "Package and Process Management," record this information. This is particularly important if you compile a package yourself or install it from a tarball since these installation methods leave no record in a package management database, as RPM and Debian package installations do.

Configuration file edits Whenever you edit a configuration file, summarize your changes in the notebook. For small changes, you may want to include precise descriptions of the change—for instance, give the exact environment variable settings you add. For larger changes, you may want to give an overview and leave the details to a backup file.

Filesystem changes Sometimes you must move programs around, or resize your filesystems. When this happens, record what changes you made. Again, when resizing partitions, record the precise sizes of the new partitions.

Kernel recompilations If you recompile or upgrade your Linux kernel, record the details of the changes, including the kernel version number, the major features you added or omitted, and the name of the new kernel.

The /usr/src/linux/.config file holds the precise kernel configuration options. You might want to print this file out or copy it to a floppy disk and store it along with your administrator's log book.

Hardware changes   When adding, deleting, or reconfiguring hardware, make note of those changes. Some of these will also be reflected in configuration file changes. For instance, adding a hard disk will almost certainly entail changing the /etc/fstab file.

Correcting earlier entries   If you make a change that invalidates information in earlier entries, you may want to track them down and note the change so that you don't accidentally use the wrong information if you ever need it in an emergency.

Ideally, the log book should be stored somewhere that's readily available whenever you administer the computer. A desk drawer next to the computer may work well, for instance. The log won't normally contain sensitive information, but if it does, keep it locked away from prying eyes when it's not in use.

Do not record any passwords in the log book, and *especially* not the root password. Only authorized administrators should know the root password, and writing it or any other password down is an invitation to disaster. There's no need for any system administrator to know other users' passwords because root can do anything to other users' accounts, or even assume other users' identities.

Backing Up Important Configuration Files

One way to document your system's configuration is to back up important configuration files. The easiest way to do this is to back up the entire /etc directory. This can be done with the tar command, described more fully in Chapter 5:

```
# mount /dev/fd0 /mnt/floppy
# tar cvfz /mnt/floppy/etc.tgz /etc
```

These commands create a compressed backup of the entire /etc directory's contents on a floppy disk mounted to /mnt/floppy. Some distributions, unfortunately, place more data in /etc than will fit on a single floppy disk, even with compression, so you may need to use multiple floppies or store the information on a higher-capacity disk like a Zip or LS-120 disk.

Backups sometimes fail. This problem is particularly common for floppy disks. You should ensure that you can read your backup as soon as you make it, and check it periodically thereafter.

Of course, you should perform regular full backups of your computer, which will store all your configuration files along with everything else. Keeping a separate backup of /etc is most useful when you've made some extensive change that's causing problems; this way, you can recover a single file from a smallish tarball on disk, which is usually much faster and safer than recovering that file from a tape backup.

The /etc directory contains some data that should not be made readily available. In particular, the /etc/shadow file (or /etc/passwd on systems that don't use shadow passwords) contains encrypted passwords. Although these passwords are encrypted, weak passwords can be extracted via brute-force attacks. Therefore, you should keep your /etc directory backups in a secure location.

Backups of the /etc directory tree are *not* a substitute for a written administrator's log. The administrator's log includes information on what files you've altered, which can help lead you directly to a change, rather than fumble around in various files looking for a change. Likewise, a log isn't a substitute for configuration file backups; a log isn't likely to contain the entire contents of all the configuration files, any one of which might be necessary on short notice in an emergency.

Documenting Official Policies and Procedures

When two or more people administer a single computer, either concurrently or sequentially, confusion can arise. Each individual can have a particular administrative style, favoring configuration files formatted in particular ways, use of specific utilities, and so on. Coordinating your efforts can be very important, lest you undo each other's changes or create incompatible configurations. Similarly, general site policies should be well understood by all administrators. For these reasons, you should document official policies and procedures for administration and use of your systems.

Documenting official policies and procedures can be important even if a system has a single administrator. If that administrator is promoted to a new position or leaves the company, the documentation can help the next administrator. In rare cases, written policy documents might be important from a legal perspective as well, as evidence that some action was or was not officially sanctioned. For this reason, some policy and procedure documents may need to be approved by, or even created in conjunction with, higher-ups in your organization.

As a general rule, your policies and procedures should be part of a document (or multiple documents) separate from your administrator's log book. These policies may apply to multiple computers, so they shouldn't be tied to any one computer. That said, you might want to have different policies for different computers—for instance, a router or time server might not need any user accounts beyond those needed by the administrators, whereas a file server might need many user accounts. Issues you should consider when deciding on your policies and procedures include the following:

Who may use a computer, and in what ways?   A critical issue is who may use a computer. Most obviously, this is a question of who may have accounts on the computer. For instance, a system might be restricted to use by particular employees of a company, or by faculty at a university. *How* these users may use the system is another question. For instance, some systems might be intended solely as file servers, so users might be permitted to use the system in that way but not via remote text-mode or GUI logins. Some servers, such as Domain Name System (DNS) servers, are meant to be used by anybody, so if you want to restrict its users, you must typically do so via a firewall, either on the server computer itself or on a router that controls access to the server system.

Who may administer a computer?   At a large site, you might want to carefully consider who should be authorized to administer particular systems. Perhaps some servers are more sensitive than others, and so should be entrusted to a smaller group of administrators. Advanced users of desktop systems might request `root` access for various reasons, so you need to consider whether or not to grant such requests.

Who is responsible for each system in the event of an emergency?   If a system crashes or otherwise misbehaves, who should be contacted? Perhaps your site has enough administrators to handle the systems in person 24 hours a day, 7 days a week. Perhaps your staff needs pagers or cell phones, with somebody on call at all times.

What servers may run on specific computers?   Every server program is a potential security risk. As a general rule, you should run as few servers as possible on any given computer, but the decision of which servers to run can be informed by a view of the network as a whole. For instance, you might want to set aside a single computer to run the Network Time Protocol (NTP) server (described briefly in Chapter 6, "Networking"), leaving others to run NTP clients, or at least to refuse NTP server access.

Who decides what software to install?   Even aside from the security implications of running unnecessary servers, not all software is desirable. Software can contain bugs that can give ordinary local users `root` privileges, or software might consume inordinate CPU time or other system resources. Thus, somebody should have final say on what software should and should not be installed on a computer, and you may need a detailed list of the types of software that may be installed. For instance, an organization might want a policy on whether distributed computing clients such as SETI@Home (`http://setiathome.ssl.berkeley.edu`) or Folding@Home (`http://folding.stanford.edu`) may be run, and if so on what computers.

What system administration tools may be used?   Different administrators have different preferences concerning their tools. Some like GUI tools; others prefer text-based interfaces. Some prefer specific GUI or text-based tools. Usually these choices are compatible, so one administrator can use one tool while another uses another. Unfortunately, sometimes conflicts arise if tools are mixed and matched. For instance, the Samba administration module for Linuxconf (a GUI and text-mode tool that was once popular with Red Hat and some other distributions, but has become less popular lately) is very fussy. If manual changes are made to the Samba configuration, they might cause Linuxconf to fail. Thus, you might want to standardize on a set of tools and procedures for managing your system.

What administrative procedures should be followed?   In addition to tool choice, administrative procedures can be important. The most vital of these is maintaining the administrative log book. Knowing what other administrators have done can greatly simplify administration. You might also want to have a formal procedure for maintaining backups of configuration files—say, a naming convention or location for storing old versions of configuration files.

How should you communicate with users?   Another matter is how to deal with changes that might impact users. If you need to reboot a computer (to begin using a new kernel, say), you might want to have a standard procedure to notify users so that they aren't unexpectedly cut off from the system. Precisely what this procedure might be will depend on the number of users and how they use the system. For instance, the shutdown command can notify text-mode login users of an impending shutdown, but you might need to notify Samba users in some other way.

What security policies should be followed?   Chapter 7, "Security," describes security issues in detail. Many of these issues require deciding how to configure a system, and you may want to consider such issues on a network-wide basis and create policies and procedures describing your desired configurations.

These issues have no clear and simple "best" solutions. For instance, granting advanced desktop users root access might be acceptable or even desirable in some situations (for instance, student-owned computers in college dorm rooms), whereas it might be completely unacceptable in others (such as systems on highly secure subnets). You'll have to evaluate your policies and procedures yourself, quite possibly in conjunction with your superiors and subordinates.

Most of these policies and procedures impact your users, so including them in discussions on these matters is probably desirable. If you set policies and procedures that cause your users problems, chances are they'll try to find ways around what they perceive as obstacles. The result can be *reduced* security and stability, where the goal of these policies and procedures is to improve security and stability.

Establishing Normal Performance Measures

Determining a baseline for normal system performance can be very helpful when it comes time to evaluate your system's performance in the future. Knowing that your CPU load or disk space use is at a particular level isn't very helpful without knowledge of typical performance levels. Broadly speaking, three performance measures are important on most systems: CPU load, memory load, and disk use.

Documenting CPU Load

The CPU is the brain of the computer; it performs the most important computations, such as recalculating a spreadsheet or compressing data you want to store in an archive file. Ideally, when you run a program, the CPU will spring into action and perform the necessary computations immediately. Unfortunately, sometimes other programs that are running on the computer consume significant amounts of CPU time, thus interfering with whatever task you want done. On a major server or other multiuser system, CPU loads can easily rise to the point where no user is getting significant amounts of CPU time. Being able to track these matters will help you decide when to take action to reduce extraneous CPU use, upgrade your CPU, or split the computer's duties across multiple machines.

> Although the CPU is the most important computing chip in common desktop and server computers, other chips also perform computations. Typically, these chips perform dedicated computations in service of the CPU, such as computations to help transfer data to and from a hard disk. One of the most powerful additional computational chips in modern computers is the graphics processing unit (GPU), which is the core of a modern video card. Some experimental techniques exist to offload certain nonvideo computing tasks onto the GPU, but these have yet to be widely implemented. The floating point unit (FPU) is another computing chip; it performs floating point math operations. All CPUs used on modern desktop and server systems integrate FPU functionality; it's only a separate chip on rather old systems, such as 80386 and some 80486 computers.

You can determine the CPU load at any given moment by using `uptime`. This command is mainly intended to tell you how long the computer has been running, but it also reports three load average values:

```
$ uptime
 22:17:50 up  7:55,  1 user,  load average: 1.21, 1.13, 0.94
```

The three load average values correspond to CPU use over the past 1, 5, and 15 minutes, in that order. In this example, the system has had a load average of 1.21 over the past minute, 1.13 over the past 5 minutes, and 0.94 over the past 15 minutes. Another tool for monitoring load averages is `top`, which can display a continuously updated list of load averages and of the programs that are consuming the most CPU time. (Chapter 5 describes `top` in more detail, as well as how to deal with programs that are consuming too much CPU time.)

Because load averages can vary dramatically over just a few minutes, you should take several load average readings as the computer is used normally and record those values. Take these measures over the course of one or more normal days—you don't want to record the load averages when nobody's using the computer (except perhaps as a baseline for an unloaded system). Knowing the maximum likely values can be useful, though, so if you expect system use to peak at particular times or on particular days, you may want to include measures at those times or on those days. You can use this information in the future if users report that the system is behaving sluggishly—if you record typical load averages of between 0.5 and 1.5, and find that a computer is suddenly running with a load average of 3.0, it means you've got a problem. Chapter 5 describes how to further isolate and fix such problems.

Documenting Memory Load

Programs consume memory just as they consume CPU time. You can discover your system's total memory load with free:

```
$ free
             total     used     free   shared  buffers  cached
Mem:        513056   465080    47976        0    42492  101112
-/+ buffers/cache:   321476   191580
Swap:      1254156   255316   998840
```

The first line of output (labeled Mem) reports total memory use, but isn't very useful unless you want to monitor buffers and caches. The Linux kernel is designed to allocate memory that's not currently used for other things to disk caches and buffers, which improves overall system performance. Thus, most systems have very small amounts of free memory, at least as reported on the Mem line of the free output. The more helpful line is the -/+ buffers/cache line, which reports the amount of free memory plus the amount devoted to buffers and cache. Linux can devote this memory to programs you choose to launch without using additional swap space. The Swap line shows the amount of swap space you have, and the amount that's active. Lots of used swap space can indicate insufficient memory, or perhaps a temporary spike in memory use. (After such a spike, Linux won't pull data out of swap space until it's needed, so swap space can remain used even after lots of RAM is freed up.)

In this example, 321,476KB of 513,056KB is used, leaving 191,580KB free. In other words, about 63 percent of available RAM is in use. As for swap space, 255,316KB of 1,254,156KB (about 20 percent) is in use.

You may wonder why swap space is in use when free RAM is available. The usual reason is that memory demands increased, forcing Linux to dip into swap space, followed by a reduction in memory demands. Rather than immediately pull data out of swap space, Linux leaves data there until it's needed. This procedure reduces the need to dump data back to swap when the memory load increases again.

As with CPU load, you should take several measures of memory load once your system is up and running normally. Take these measures when the system is seeing typical use and when it's heavily loaded. Chapter 5 describes how to use ps and top to help track down programs that are gobbling up inordinate amounts of RAM, so you can use these tools to help diagnose problems, should they occur.

Documenting Disk Use

Disk use has two components: disk speed and disk space consumed. You can perform benchmarks on your disk speed using the hdparm -t command, as described in Chapter 9. Performing such a benchmark shortly after installation isn't a bad idea. Sometimes a software upgrade (particularly a new kernel) will effectively de-tune hardware drivers, leading to a drop in disk performance. Knowing what's normal for the system will help you evaluate this problem.

Another disk use issue is used disk space. The df command reports on the disk space used on a partition-by-partition basis:

```
$ df
Filesystem    1K-blocks      Used  Available Use% Mounted on
/dev/sdb10     5859784    4812064    1047720  83% /
/dev/sdb12     2086264     985772    1100492  48% /opt
/dev/hda13     2541468     289616    2251852  12% /usr/local
/dev/hda9     15361340   12184484    3176856  80% /home
/dev/hda6       101089      19908      77006  21% /boot
```

The Use% column provides a good estimate of how close the disk is to filling up, although the absolute numbers can also be important. For instance, in this example /dev/sdb10 and /dev/sdb12 (that is, / and /opt) have similar absolute amounts of available space, but their use percentages are very different because the partitions have such dissimilar sizes.

As a very general rule of thumb, you should try to keep partition use to under 80%. At least as important, you should monitor disk use over time, starting from just after system installation. Check on disk space used every week or so (perhaps more or less frequently depending on how the system is used and how important it is). If you see that free space on a partition is falling too low, you can take steps to correct the problem, either by deleting unnecessary files or by creating new disk space. The latter can be accomplished by moving files across partitions and creating symbolic links in old locations to point to the new ones, by repartitioning the disk, or by adding a new hard disk (either to supplement or to replace the existing one). Chapter 4, "Disk Management," describes partition maintenance in more detail.

Collecting System Statistics

Although using separate utilities, such as uptime, df, and free, can provide you with baseline performance data, another tool for collecting a wide range of performance data is sar. This program isn't installed by default on many Linux systems. If you can't find it on your system, look for and install a package called sysstat. The sar program accepts a large number of options, but the key is to specify an interval in seconds and the number of samples you want to collect:

```
# sar 1 3
Linux 2.4.18-newpmac (teela.rodsbooks.com)        12/08/04

15:53:59        CPU     %user     %nice   %system     %idle
15:54:00        all      0.00     99.00      1.00      0.00
15:54:01        all      0.00     99.00      1.00      0.00
15:54:02        all      0.00    100.00      0.00      0.00
Average:        all      0.00     99.33      0.67      0.00
```

The default output shows the CPU use. In this example, three samples were taken at 1-second intervals. These show that user CPU use was low, with the exception of programs run with `nice`, which were consuming 99%–100% of CPU time. You can also pass options to `sar` to obtain similar reports on other system performance measures, such as:

Disk use   The `-b` option produces a report on disk input/output capacity used. (This is distinct from total disk *space* used; `sar`'s `-b` option tells you how much disk *bandwidth* is being consumed.)

Swap space use   You can learn about demand for swap space with the `-B` option. As with `-b`, this option provides information about the amount of data being transferred at the moment, rather than the total swap space being used. A related option is `-W`, which produces somewhat different measures of swap space use.

Process creation   On a heavily used system, processes may be created very frequently. The `-c` option to `sar` reports on this activity.

Hardware interrupts   Many hardware devices use interrupts to signal that they need attention—say, that an Ethernet card has received data that the kernel should process. You can monitor interrupts with the `-I` *number* option to `sar`, where *int* is the interrupt number.

Network activity   You can check on network activity by passing the `-n` *device* option to `sar`, where *device* is the network device, such as `eth0`. Passing `DEV` as the device creates a report on all network devices.

Memory demand   The `-r` option produces a report on total memory use. This report is likely to show very high memory demands (99% or thereabouts), much like the first line of `free` output. The `-R` option produces information on memory *activity*, in the sense of how many memory accesses are being performed.

CPU use   The `-u` option produces a CPU use table. This is the default option if no other option is specified.

Configuring Log Files

Linux maintains log files that record various key details about Linux operation. Using these log files is described later, in "Using Log Files." You may be able to begin using log files immediately, but knowing how to change the log file configuration can also be important. You do this by configuring the `syslogd` daemon, although some servers and other programs perform their own logging and so must be configured independently. You may even want to configure one computer to send its log files to another system as a security measure. You should also be aware of issues surrounding log file rotation; if your computer doesn't properly manage existing log files, they can grow to consume all your available disk space, at least on the partition on which they're stored.

Understanding *syslogd*

Most Linux systems employ a special daemon to handle log maintenance in a unified way. The traditional Linux system logger is syslogd, which is often installed from a package called sysklogd. The syslogd daemon handles messages from servers and other user-mode programs; it's usually paired with a daemon called klogd, which is usually installed from the same sysklogd package as syslogd.

 Other choices for system loggers exist. For instance, syslog-ng is a replacement that supports advanced filtering options, and metalog is another option. This chapter describes the traditional syslogd logger. Others are similar in principle, and even in some specific features, but differ in many details.

The basic idea behind a system logger is to provide a unified means of handling log files. The daemon runs in the background and accepts data delivered from servers and other programs that are configured to use the log daemon. The daemon can then use information provided by the server to classify the message and direct it to an appropriate log file. This configuration enables you to consolidate messages from various servers in a handful of standard log files, which can be much easier to use and manage than potentially dozens of log files from the various servers running on the system.

As described in the upcoming section, "Using a Remote Server for Log Files," another feature of log daemons is that they can pass the log information on to a log daemon running on another computer entirely. The advantage of this configuration is that it can help protect the logs from tampering—if a computer is compromised, the intruder can't eliminate evidence of the intrusion from the log file without first breaking into the computer that logs data for other systems. Administering a network on which all systems log to a single system can also be simpler in some ways, because you can monitor log files on one computer, rather than perform this task on many systems.

In order to work, of course, the log daemon must be configured. In the case of syslogd, this is done through the /etc/syslog.conf file. The next section describes this file's format in more detail.

Setting Logging Options

The format of the /etc/syslog.conf file is conceptually simple, but provides a great deal of power. Comment lines, as in many Linux configuration files, are denoted by a hash mark (#). Noncomment lines take the following form:

```
facility.priority    action
```

In this line, the *facility* is a code word for the type of program or tool that has generated the message to be logged; the *priority* is a code word for the importance of this message; and the *action* is a file, remote computer, or other location that's to accept the message. The facility and priority are often referred to collectively as the selector.

Valid codes for the *facility* are auth, authpriv, cron, daemon, kern, lpr, mail, mark, news, security, syslog, user, uucp, and local0 through local7. Many of these names refer to specific servers or program classes. For instance, mail servers and other mail-processing tools typically log using the mail facility. Most servers that aren't covered by more specific codes use the daemon facility. The security facility is identical to auth, but auth is the preferred name. The mark facility is reserved for internal use. An asterisk (*) refers to all facilities. You can specify multiple facilities in one selector by separating the facilities with commas (,).

Valid codes for the *priority* are debug, info, notice, warning, warn, error, err, crit, alert, emerg, and panic. The warning priority is identical to warn, error is identical to err, and emerg is identical to panic. The error, warn, and panic priority names are deprecated; you should use their equivalents instead. Other than these identical pairs, these priorities represent ascending levels of importance. The debug level logs the most information; it's intended, as the name implies, for debugging programs that are misbehaving. The emerg priority logs the most important messages, which indicate very serious problems. When a program sends a message to the system logger, it includes a priority code; the logger logs the message to a file if you've configured it to log messages of that level or higher. Thus, if you specify a *priority* code of alert, the system will log messages that are classified as alert or emerg, but not messages of crit or below. An exception to this rule is if you precede the priority code by an equal sign (=), as in =crit, which describes what to do with messages of crit priority *only*. An exclamation mark (!) reverses the meaning of a match. For instance, !crit causes messages *below* crit priority to be logged. A *priority* of * refers to all priorities.

You can specify multiple selectors for a single action by separating the selectors by a semicolon (;). Examples appear shortly.

Most commonly, the *action* is a filename, typically in the /var/log directory tree. Other possibilities include a device filename for a console (such as /dev/console) to display data on the screen, a remote machine name preceded by an at-sign (@), and a list of usernames who should see the message if they're logged in. For the last of these options, an asterisk (*) means all logged-in users.

Some examples should help clarify these rules. First is a fairly ordinary and simple entry:

```
mail.*          /var/log/mail
```

This line sends all log entries identified by the originating program as related to mail to the /var/log/mail file. Most of the entries in a default /etc/syslog.conf file resemble this one. Together, they typically cover all of the facilities mentioned earlier. Some messages may be handled by multiple rules. For instance, another rule might look like this one:

```
*.emerg         *
```

This line sends all emerg-level messages to the consoles of all users who are logged into the computer using text-mode tools. If this line and the earlier mail.* selector are both present, emerg-level messages related to mail will be logged to /var/log/mail *and* displayed on users' consoles.

A more complex example logs kernel messages in various ways, depending on their priorities:

```
kern.*              /var/log/kernel
kern.crit           @logger.pangaea.edu
kern.crit           /dev/console
kern.info;kern.!err /var/log/kernel-info
```

The first of these rules logs all kernel messages to `/var/log/kernel`. The next two lines relate to high-priority (`crit` or higher) messages from the kernel. The first of these lines sends such messages to `logger.pangaea.edu`. (The upcoming section, "Using a Remote Server for Log Files," describes remote logging in more detail.) The second of these lines sends a copy of these messages to `/dev/console`, which causes them to be displayed on the computer's main text-mode console display. Finally, the last line sends messages that are between `info` and `err` in priority to `/var/log/kernel-info`. Because `err` is the priority immediately above `crit`, and because `info` is the lowest priority, these four lines cause all kernel messages to be logged two or three times: once to `/var/log/kernel`, as well as to either the remote system and the console *or* to `/var/log/kernel-info`.

Most distributions ship with reasonable system logger settings, but you may want to examine these settings, and perhaps adjust them. If you change them, though, be aware that you may need to change some other tools. For instance, all major distributions ship with tools that help rotate log files. If you change the files to which `syslogd` logs messages, you may need to change your log file rotation scripts as well.

In addition to the system logger's options, you may be able to set logging options in individual programs. For instance, you might tell programs to record more or less information, or to log routine information at varying priorities. Some programs also provide the means to log via the system log daemon or via their own mechanisms. Details vary greatly from one program to another, so you should consult the program's documentation for details.

> Most programs that use the system log daemons are servers and other system tools. Programs that individuals run locally seldom log data via the system log daemon, although there are some exceptions to this rule, such as the Fetchmail program for retrieving e-mail from remote servers.

Rotating Log Files

Log files are intended to retain information on system activities for a reasonable period of time; however, system logging daemons provide no means to control the size of log files. Left unchecked, log files can therefore grow to consume all the available space on the partition on which they reside. To avoid this problem, Linux systems employ *log file rotation* tools. These tools rename and optionally compress the current log files, delete old log files, and force the logging system to begin using new log files.

The most common log rotation tool is a package called `logrotate`. This program is typically called on a regular basis via a cron job. (Cron jobs are described in Chapter 5.) The `logrotate` program consults a configuration file called `/etc/logrotate.conf`, which includes several default settings and typically refers to files in `/etc/logrotate.d` to handle specific log files. A typical `/etc/logrotate.conf` file includes several comment lines, denoted by hash marks (#), as well as lines to set various options, as illustrated by Listing 8.1.

Because log file rotation is handled by cron jobs that typically run late at night, it won't happen if a computer is routinely turned off at the end of the day. This practice is common with Windows workstations, but is uncommon with servers. Linux workstations should either be left running overnight as a general practice, or some explicit steps should be taken to ensure that log rotation occurs despite routine shutdowns. You might leave the system up overnight from time to time, for instance, or reschedule the log rotation to some time when the computer is likely to be powered on.

Listing 8.1: Sample /etc/logrotate.conf File

```
# Rotate logs weekly
weekly

# Keep 4 weeks of old logs
rotate 4

# Create new log files after rotation
create

# Compress old log files
compress

# Refer to files for individual packages
include /etc/logrotate.d

# Set miscellaneous options
notifempty
nomail
noolddir

# Rotate wtmp, which isn't handled by a specific program
/var/log/wtmp {
    monthly
    create 0664 root utmp
    rotate 1
}
```

Most of these lines set options that are fairly self-explanatory or that are well explained by the comments that typically immediately precede them—for instance, the weekly line sets the default log rotation interval to once a week. If you see an option in your file that you don't understand, consult the `logrotate` man page. (Man pages are described later in this chapter, in "Using Man Pages.")

The last few lines of Listing 8.1 demonstrate the format for the definition for a specific log file. These definitions begin with the filename for the file (multiple filenames may be listed, separated by spaces), followed by an open curly brace ({). They end in a close curly brace (}). Intervening lines set options that may override the defaults. For instance, the `/var/log/wtmp` definition in Listing 8.1 sets the `monthly` option, which tells the system to rotate this log file once a month, overriding the default `weekly` option. Such definitions are common in the individual files in `/etc/logrotate.d`, which are typically owned by the packages whose log files they rotate. Examples of features that are often set in these definitions include:

Rotated file naming   Ordinarily, rotated log files acquire numbers, such as `messages.1` for the first rotation of the `messages` log file. Using the `dateext` option causes the rotated log file to obtain a date code instead, as in `messages-20050205` for the rotation performed on February 5, 2005.

Compression options   As already noted, `compress` causes `logrotate` to compress log files to save space. This is done using `gzip` by default, but you can specify another program with the `compresscmd` keyword, as in `compresscmd bzip2` to use `bzip2`. The `compressoptions` option enables you to pass options to the compression command (say, to improve the compression ratio).

Creating new log files   The `create` option causes `logrotate` to create a new log file for use by the system logger or program. This option takes a file mode, owner, and group as additional options. Some programs don't work well with this option, though. Most of them use the `copytruncate` option instead, which tells `logrotate` to copy the old log file to a new name and then clear all the data out of the original file.

Time options   The `daily`, `weekly`, and `monthly` options tell the system to rotate the log files at the specified intervals. These options aren't always used, though; some configurations use a size threshold rather than a time threshold for when to rotate log files.

Size options   The `size` keyword sets a maximum size for a log file. It takes a size in bytes as an argument (adding k or M to the size changes it to kilobytes or megabytes). For instance, `size 100k` causes `logrotate` to rotate the file when it reaches 100KB in size.

Rotation options   The `rotate x` option causes x copies of old log files to be maintained. For instance, if you set `rotate 2` for the `/var/log/messages` file, `logrotate` will maintain `/var/log/messages.1` and `/var/log/messages.2`, in addition to the active `/var/log/messages` file. When that file is rotated, `/var/log/messages.2` is deleted, `/var/log/messages.1` is renamed to `/var/log/messages.2`, `/var/log/messages` becomes `/var/log/messages.1`, and a new `/var/log/messages` is created.

Mail options   If you use `mail` *address*, `logrotate` will e-mail a log file to the specified address when it's rotated out of existence. Using `nomail` causes the system to not send any e-mail; the log is quietly deleted.

Scripts   The `prerotate` and `postrotate` keywords both begin a series of lines that are treated as scripts to be run immediately before or after log file rotation, respectively. In both cases, these scripts end with the `endscript` keyword. These commands are frequently used to force `syslogd` or a server to begin using a new log file.

In most cases, servers and other programs that log data either do so via the system logging daemon or ship with a configuration file that goes in /etc/logrotate.d to handle the server's log files. These files usually do a reasonable job; however, you might want to double-check them. For instance, you might discover that your system is configured to keep too many or too few old log files for your taste, in which case adjusting the rotate option is in order. You should also check the /var/log directory and its subdirectories every now and then. If you see huge numbers of files accumulating, or if files are growing to unacceptable size, you may want to check the corresponding logrotate configuration files. If an appropriate file doesn't exist, create one. Use a working file as a template, modifying it for the new file. Pay particular attention to the prerotate or postrotate scripts; you may need to consult the documentation for the program that's creating the log file to learn how to force that program to begin using a new log file.

Using a Remote Server for Log Files

As noted earlier, in "Setting Logging Options," you can configure syslogd to send its logs to a remote computer instead of or in addition to logging data locally. This configuration is fairly straightforward on the system that's doing the logging; in /etc/syslog.conf, you provide a computer hostname preceded by an at-sign (@) rather than a local filename. For instance, this line causes all kernel messages to be logged to logger.pangaea.edu:

```
kern.*          @logger.pangaea.edu
```

You can use other selectors, of course, as described earlier, in "Setting Logging Options." Using this feature enables you to search log files for problems from a central location and provides an additional degree of tamper resistance, since an intruder would need to compromise the logging server as well as the primary target of a computer in order to erase evidence of an intrusion from log files.

Ordinarily, syslogd 1.3 and later doesn't accept logs sent to it from remote systems. Thus, if you have two computers and configure one computer to send some or all of its logs to the other computer, they won't appear in the logging server's logs by default. To have the logging system accept such submissions, you must launch syslogd with its -r option. Precisely how you do this varies from one distribution to another. This daemon is normally launched from a SysV startup script, such as /etc/init.d/syslog. You may be able to modify this script to pass the -r parameter to syslogd. Most syslogd SysV startup scripts, though, pass parameters to the daemon using a variable, such as SYSLOGD_PARAMS. This variable is most frequently set in another file, such as /etc/sysconfig/syslog (used by Fedora, Red Hat, and SuSE, among others). Some distributions set the variable in the startup script itself; for instance, Debian sets the SYSLOGD variable in its /etc/init.d/sysklogd startup script, enabling you to set this option in the startup script. If you need to change these features, do so and then restart the syslogd daemon using its own SysV startup script:

```
# /etc/rc.d/init.d/syslog restart
```

You must also restart the system logger on the system doing the logging after making changes to its `/etc/syslog.conf` file. Once this is done, the messages from all the computers configured to log to the logging system should appear in its logs. They should normally be identified by system name:

```
Feb 27 13:17:00 speaker /USR/SBIN/CRON[28223]: (rodsmith) CMD
➥(/usr/bin/fetchmail -f /home/rodsmith/.fetchmailrc-powweb > /dev/null)
Feb 27 13:18:04 halrloprillalar ntpd[2036]: kernel time sync enabled 0001
```

These lines indicate that the system `speaker` logged information about a run of `/usr/bin/fetchmail` on February 27 at 13:17:00 (that is, 1:17 p.m.). Soon thereafter, at 13:18:04, the system `halrloprillalar` recorded activity by the `ntpd` time server.

Using Log Files

Once you've configured logging on your system, the question arises: What can you *do* with log files? Log files are primarily tools in problem solving—debugging servers that don't behave as you expect, locating evidence of system intrusions, and so on. You should first know what log files to examine in any given situation. Understanding the problem-identification abilities of log files will help you use them effectively. Some tools can help in this task, too; these tools can help you scan log files for information, summarize the (sometimes overly verbose) log file information, and so on.

Which Log Files Are Important?

In using log files, you must first decide which ones are important. Unfortunately, the names of log files aren't completely standardized across distributions, so you may need to poke around in your `syslog` configuration files, and perhaps in the log files themselves, to discover which files are important.

Begin by looking over your existing `/etc/syslog.conf` file. Using the information presented earlier, in "Setting Logging Options," you should be able to learn which log files `syslogd` is using on your system, and for what these files are being used. This isn't the end of the story, though; some servers log data without the help of `syslogd`, so you may need to consult the configuration files and documentation for any programs you want to monitor. For instance, Samba frequently logs data independently of `syslogd`, storing files in `/var/log/samba` or a similar directory.

You may be able to get an idea of where to look by examining the names of files in `/var/log` and its subdirectories. Most Linux distributions use a log file called `messages` or `syslog` in this directory as a sort of catch-all log entry location. Some distributions split off another important file, often called `secure`, `warn`, or something similar, to hold security-related log messages or those that are considered important (that is, logged with high priority codes). All of these files are likely to be important for general-purpose log analysis. Other files that you may encounter include `mail` (for mail-related activities), `localmessages` (another catch-all file), `daemon.log` (a catch-all file for daemons), `boot.log` or `dmesg` (for boot-time logging), and auth.log (for messages related to authentication). You may also find log files named after specific servers or other programs, such as Xorg.0.log (for the X.org-X11 X server), cron (for the cron daemon), and xinetd.log (for xinetd).

If you're uncertain of the purpose or importance of a log file, feel free to examine it. The tools described shortly, in "Tools to Help Scan Log Files," can be useful in this task. For basic identification, less is likely to be very helpful, as in **less /var/log/messages**. This command displays the file screen by screen, which should give you some clue about the file's contents.

Using Log Files to Identify Problems

You can use log files to monitor system loads (for instance, to determine how many pages a Web server has served), to check for intrusion attempts, to verify the correct functioning of a system, and to note errors generated by certain types of programs. To one extent or another, all of these functions can be used to identify problems. Here are a few examples of information that can be useful when you are troubleshooting:

Verifying heavy loads   If a server is running sluggishly, log files may contain clues in the form of a large number of entries from the server. If a server has experienced a massive increase in the number of clients it handles or the size of the files it transfers, you may need to increase the server computer's capacity to restore good performance. Most nonserver programs don't log their activities, though, so you probably won't be able to diagnose similar load problems caused by increasing workstation demands in this way. You'll likely have an idea that workstation load has increased in a more direct way, though, because the workstation users should know that they're running more programs or more resource-intensive programs.

Sometimes the logging action itself can contribute substantially to a server's CPU and disk input/output requirements. If a server is behaving sluggishly, try reducing its logging level (so that it records less information).

Intrusion detection   Some system problems are related to the presence of an intruder. Crackers frequently modify your system files or utilities, thus affecting your system's performance or reliability. Their actions are sometimes reflected in log files. Even the *absence* of entries can sometimes be a clue—crackers often delete log files, or at least remove entries for a period. You might not notice such log file discrepancies unless you examine the log files soon after a break-in occurs, however.

Normal system functioning   If a system is misbehaving, the presence of and information in routine log file entries can sometimes help you pin down the problem, or at least eliminate possibilities. For instance, suppose your system is working as a Dynamic Host Configuration Protocol (DHCP) server for your network, dishing out IP addresses to other systems, as described in Chapter 6. If your clients aren't receiving IP addresses, you can check the log file on the server. If that file indicates that the DHCP server has received requests and given leases in response, you can focus your problem-solving efforts on the clients.

Missing entries   If you know that a program should be logging information but you can't locate it, this may be evidence that the program is misconfigured or is not starting properly. In some cases, missing entries may indicate problems outside the computer you're examining. For instance, suppose you configure Samba to log access attempts. If you can't access the Samba server from another system, you can check for Samba log file entries. If those entries aren't present, it could mean that Samba isn't running, that it's misconfigured, or that a network problem (such as a misconfigured router or firewall) is blocking access.

Error messages   The most direct evidence of a problem in a log file is usually an error message. A log file entry that reads `authentication failure` or `FAILED LOGIN` indicates an authentication failure, for instance, which should help you focus your troubleshooting efforts. (The user might or might not receive as informative a message as is recorded in the log file.) To improve this capacity, you can configure many servers and utilities to log more information than usual; consult the program's documentation for details. Be aware that different subsystems produce error messages that vary greatly in form, so one program's error messages will look quite different from another's.

Log files are most useful when you are diagnosing software problems with the kernel, servers, user login tools, and miscellaneous other low-level utilities. Information routinely recorded in log files includes kernel startup messages, kernel module operations, user logins, cron actions, filesystem mounting and unmounting, and actions performed by many servers. This information can reflect hardware, kernel, application, configuration, and even user problems.

Tools to Help Scan Log Files

Log files can sometimes be tricky to use because they often accumulate data at a rapid rate. This is particularly true when many programs' logs are sent to a single file or when you've increased the logging level in a program in an effort to help identify problems. Therefore, tools to help scan log files for important information are very helpful. You can think of these tools as falling into one of three categories: those that examine the starts of files, those that examine the ends of files, and those that can be used to search files. Some tools can be used for two or even all three of these tasks.

 Most log files are owned by root, and many can only be read by root. Thus, you may need to acquire root privileges before using any of these tools, although the tools themselves can be used by other users on non-log files.

 Most of the commands described here are covered in greater detail in Chapter 2, "Text-Mode Commands."

Tools to Check the Starts of Log Files

Sometimes, you know that information you need appears at the start of a log file. For instance, the kernel ring buffer file begins with information on the kernel version number, as well as when and how it was compiled:

```
Linux version 2.6.6 (rodsmith@speaker) (gcc version 3.3.3 (SuSE Linux))
➥#6 Wed Jun 9 23:39:40 EDT 2004
```

You can go about obtaining such information in any of several ways. One tool that's aimed specifically at displaying the beginning of a file is head. Used with only a filename as an argument, head displays the first ten lines of that file. You can change the number of lines with the -n argument, as in **head -n 20 file.txt** to display the first 20 lines of file.txt.

If you know the information you want to review is near the beginning of a log file but you're not sure of its exact location, you might prefer to use a pager program, such as more or less. The more program displays a file one screen at a time, whatever your screen size is. You can press the spacebar to move forward in the file a screen at a time. The less program's name is a bit of a joke, because less is intended to be a better more; it does basically the same thing, but supports more options within the program, such as searching (described shortly, in "Tools to Search Log Files"). Both programs enable you to quickly check the first few lines of a file, though.

Text editors can also be good ways to check the first few lines in a file. Most text editors open the file and display its first few lines when you pass a filename on the command line. Text editors do have some drawbacks, however. One is that you might accidentally alter the log file, which is undesirable. Another drawback is that opening a log file in a text editor is likely to take longer than using head or less to display the first few lines. This is particularly true if either the text editor or the log file is unusually large.

Tools to Check the Ends of Log Files

Information is added to the ends of log files. Thus, when you're performing some operation on a computer and you want to see if it happened as you intended, that information is likely to appear at the end of a log file, rather than at its start or somewhere in the middle. For instance, when you launch a new server, entries confirming the server's successful startup (or error messages relating to its failure to start) are likely to appear at the end of the file. The ability to check the end of a log file is therefore very helpful.

The tail program is noteworthy in this respect because it's designed to display the last few lines (ten by default) of a file. This program is very similar to head in most ways, except of course for the fact that it displays the end of a file rather than the beginning. The default action is sufficient for most purposes if you run the program on a log file immediately after some information has been logged. Sometimes, though, you might need to display a number of lines other than the default of ten. To do this, you use the -n option, as in **tail -n 15 /var/log/ messages** to display the last 15 lines of /var/log/messages.

Another feature of tail is realtime monitoring—you can use the program to keep an eye on additions to log files as they occur. You might want to do this just before performing some action that you want to monitor; you'll be able to see the relevant log entries as they're added to the log file. To do so, pass the `-f` or `--follow` option to `tail`, as in **tail -f /var/log/ messages**. The result is an initial display of the last few log entries, as usual; however, `tail` doesn't immediately terminate. Instead, it keeps monitoring the log file and echoes new entries to the screen. When you're done, press Ctrl+C to kill `tail` and regain control of your shell.

Although it's not quite as convenient as `tail` for displaying a fixed number of lines, the `less` pager can be useful for checking the end of a log file. Type **less *filename*** to display *filename*, then type **G** or press the Esc key followed by the greater-than symbol (>). This will bring you to the end of the file. If you want to scroll upwards in the file, type **b** or press Esc followed by V. You can scroll back down by typing **f**, pressing the spacebar, or pressing Ctrl+V. Using these commands, you can quickly examine the final lines of any file, including log files.

As with examining the start of a file, a text editor can be used to examine its end. Load a log file into a text editor and scroll to the end of the file in whatever way is appropriate. As with examining the start of a file, though, this approach has the drawback that it might result in accidental changes to the file being saved. It might also be slow, particularly on large log files or with large editors. On the other hand, some editors may notice when the log file changes and enable you to quickly load the changes. This feature can be handy if you want to monitor changes as they occur.

Tools to Search Log Files

Sometimes you need to search log files for information. For instance, you might want to see all entries created by Postfix or entries in which you know the string `eth0` appears. You can use any of several text searching tools to help out with such tasks. These tools can search one or more text files and display matching lines, or take you to matching lines in these files so that you can examine them in context.

The `grep` command is the most basic of the text-search tools. Type the command, a series of options (including the search string), and a file specification (which typically includes a wildcard) to have it search those files for the specified string. For instance, to find all log entries created by the Postfix mail server, you might type **grep postfix /var/log/***. The result is a series of output lines, each of which begins with the name of the file from which it's taken and concludes with the line in question. (If the string was found in a binary file, `grep` tells you so, but doesn't attempt to display the string in context.)

The `grep` command is most useful when searching for entries in multiple log files simultaneously—say, if you don't know to which file a server is logging information. It can also be useful if you want to display the log entries from a particular server or those that involve a single user, or by some other criterion you can easily express as a searchable string.

If you use grep to search for a string that's very common, the output is likely to scroll off the top of your screen, and possibly exceed the buffer of a scrollable xterm window. This may prevent you from taking a complete census of files in which the string occurs. You can pipe the output through `less`, as in **grep postfix /var/log/* | less**, to enable you to scan through the grep output in a more controlled way.

Another way to search log files is by using the less program. You can use this utility to view a single log file. Once you're viewing a file, press the slash key (/) followed by a search string, as in **/postfix** to locate the first occurrence of the string postfix in the log file. If that string is present in the file, less takes you to that point and highlights the string. Pressing the slash key again moves to the next line that contains the search string. This feature can be handy if you need to see the full context of the line in question. If you want to locate the *last* occurrence of a string, press Esc followed by the greater-than symbol (>) to move to the end of the buffer, then search backwards using a question mark (?; that is, the slash key with a shift modifier), as in **?postfix**. You can use a text editor to perform similar searches, but with the same caveats described earlier, in "Tools to Check the Starts of Log Files"—text editors can be slower than tools such as less, and you might accidentally alter the log file.

Additional Log File Analysis Tools

Manually examining log files with tail, less, and similar tools can be informative, but other tools exist to help you analyze your log files. One of these is Logcheck, which is part of the Sentry Tools package (http://sourceforge.net/projects/sentrytools/). This package comes with some distributions, such as Mandrake and Debian. Unfortunately, it requires a fair amount of customization for your own system, so it's most easily implemented if it comes with your distribution, preconfigured for its log file format. If you want to use it on another distribution, you must edit the logcheck.sh file that's at the heart of the package. This file calls the logtail utility that checks log file contents, so you must configure the script to check the log files you want monitored. You can also adjust features such as the user who's to receive violation reports and the locations of files that contain strings for which the utility should look in log files. Once it's configured, you call logcheck.sh in a cron job. Logcheck then e-mails a report concerning any suspicious system logs to the user defined in logcheck.sh (root, by default).

System Documentation and Help Resources

Nobody can know everything there is to know about Linux—the number of programs, each with its own set of options and features, is simply too great for anybody to fully understand everything about the OS. For this reason, documentation and help resources come with Linux and are available online. One of the oldest forms on help is the manual page system, referred to as *man pages* for short. A somewhat newer tool for accessing similar documentation is known as *info pages*. Both of these systems are designed to provide you with quick summary information about a program, such as the basic function of a program's options. Neither system is intended to provide comprehensive tutorial information; for that, you must typically turn to other documentation that ships with programs, or to third-party documentation. Some of these resources are available on the Internet, so knowing where to look for such help is critical.

Using Man Pages

Man pages provide succinct summaries of program functions. In the simplest case, they can be accessed by typing **man** followed by the name of a command, configuration file, system call, or other keyword. Each man page falls into one of nine categories, as summarized in Table 8.1. Some keywords lead to entries in multiple sections. In such instances, the man utility returns the entry for the lowest-numbered matching section by default. You can override this behavior by passing a section number before the keyword. For instance, typing **man passwd** returns information from manual section 1, on the passwd command, but typing **man 5 passwd** returns information from manual section 5, on the /etc/passwd file format. Some man pages have entries in sections with variant numbers that include the suffix p, as in section 1p. These refer to POSIX standard man pages, as opposed to the Linux man pages, which are, for the most part, written by the people who wrote the open source Linux programs the man pages describe.

TABLE 8.1 Manual Sections

Section Number	Description
1	Executable programs and shell commands
2	System calls provided by the kernel
3	Library calls provided by program libraries
4	Device files (usually stored in /dev)
5	File formats
6	Games
7	Miscellaneous (macro packages, conventions, etc.)
8	System administration commands (programs run mostly or exclusively by root)
9	Kernel routines

The convention for man pages is a succinct style that employs several sections. Common sections include the following:

Name   A man page begins with a statement of the command, call, or file that's described, along with a few words of explanation. For instance, the man page for man (section 1) has a Name section that reads man - an interface to the on-line reference manuals.

Synopsis   The synopsis provides a brief description of how a command is used. This synopsis uses a summary format similar to that used to present synopses in this book, showing optional parameters in square brackets ([]), for instance.

Description   The description is an English-language summary of what the command, file, or other element does. The description can vary from a very short summary to something many pages in length.

Options   This section summarizes the options outlined in the Synopsis section. Typically, each option appears in a list, with a one-paragraph explanation indented just below it.

Files   This section lists files that are associated with the man page's subject. These might be configuration files for a server or other program, related configuration files for a configuration file, or what have you.

See also   This section provides pointers to related information in the man system, typically with a section number appended. For instance, `less(1)` refers to the section 1 man page for `less`.

Bugs   Many man pages provide a Bugs section in which the author describes any known bugs, or states that no known bugs exist.

History   Some man pages provide a summary of the program's history, citing project start dates and major milestones between then and the current version. This history isn't nearly as comprehensive as the changes file that ships with most programs' source code.

Author   Most man pages end with an Author section, which tells you how to contact the author of the program.

Specific manual pages may contain fewer, more, or different sections than these. For instance, the Synopsis section is typically omitted from man pages on configuration files. Man pages with particularly verbose descriptions often split the Description section into several parts, each with its own title.

Man pages can be an extremely helpful resource, but you must understand their purpose and limitations. Unlike the help systems in some OSs, Linux man pages are not supposed to be either comprehensive or tutorial in nature; they're intended as quick references to help somebody who's already at least somewhat familiar with a command. They're most useful when you need to know the options to use with a command, the format of a configuration file, or similar summary information. If you need to learn a new program from scratch, other documentation is often a better choice. Man pages also vary greatly in quality; some are very good, but others are frustratingly terse, and even occasionally inaccurate. For the most part, they're written by the programmers who wrote the software in question, and programmers seldom place a high priority on user documentation.

Linux's man pages use the `less` pager to display information. This pager's operation is covered briefly earlier in this chapter, in "Using Log Files." The `less` pager is covered in more detail in Chapter 2. Of course, you can also consult the `less` man page by typing **man less**. The upshot of using `less` is that you can page forwards and backwards, perform searches, and use other `less` functions when reading man pages.

Although man is a text-mode command, GUI variants exist. The xman program, for instance, provides a point-and-click method of browsing through man pages. You can't type a subject on the command line to view it as you would with man, though—you must launch xman and then browse through the manual sections to a specific subject.

One of the problems with man pages is that it can be hard to locate help on a topic unless you know the name of the command, system call, or file you want to use. Fortunately, methods of searching the manual database exist, and can help lead you to an appropriate man page:

Summary search   The whatis command searches summary information contained in man pages for the keyword you specify. The command returns a one-line summary (the Name section of the man page, in fact) for every matching man page. You can then use this information to locate and read the man page you need. This command is most useful for locating all the man pages on a topic. For instance, typing **whatis man** returns lines confirming the existence of the man page entries for man, in sections 1, 7, and 1p.

Thorough search   The apropos command performs a more thorough search, of both the Name and Description sections of man pages. The result looks much like the results of a whatis search, except that it's likely to contain many more results. In fact, doing an apropos search on a very common word, such as **the,** is likely to return so many hits as to make the search useless. A search on a less common word is likely to be more useful. For instance, typing **apropos samba** returns fewer than a dozen entries, including those for cupsaddsmb, smbpasswd, and lmhosts—all tools related to the Samba file- and printer-sharing tool. (The exact number of hits returned by apropos will vary from system to system, depending on the packages installed.)

When you're done using the man page system, press the Q key. This breaks you out of the less browser and returns you to your shell prompt.

Using Info Pages

Linux's info page system is conceptually similar to its man page system, and info pages tend to be written in a similar terse style. The primary difference is that the info system uses a more sophisticated tool for presenting the documentation. Rather than a simple less browser on a linear file, the info command uses a more sophisticated hyperlinked format, conceptually similar to Web pages. The standard info browser, though, runs in text mode, so instead of clicking on help items with your mouse, you must select them with the cursor keys or move about using keyboard shortcuts.

Some tools for reading info pages support mouse operations. The Emacs editor, for instance, includes a mouse-aware info reading tool. The tkinfo program (http://math-www.uni-paderborn.de/~axel/tkinfo/) is a general-purpose X-based info browser.

Info pages are written in *nodes*, which are similar to the individual pages of Web sites. These nodes are arranged hierarchically. To move from one node to another in the standard text-based info browser, you use any of several commands or procedures:

Next page   Press the N key to move to the next node in a linked series of nodes on a single hierarchical level. This action may be required if the author intended several nodes to be read in a particular sequence.

Previous page   Pressing the P key moves back in a series of nodes on a single hierarchical level. This can be handy if you've moved forward in such a series but find you need to review earlier material.

Moving up   Pressing the U key moves you up in the node hierarchy.

Selecting a topic   To move down in the list of nodes, you select a topic and move into it. In the text-mode info browser, topics have asterisks (*) to the left of their names. You use your cursor keys to highlight the topic and press the Enter key to read that topic.

Last topic   Pressing the L key displays the last info page you read. This action can move you up, down, or sideways in the info tree hierarchy.

Top page   You can return to the top page for a topic (typically the one on which you entered the system) by pressing the T key.

Exiting   When you're done using the info system, press the Q key.

On the whole, info pages can be more difficult to navigate than man pages, at least for the uninitiated; however, the hierarchical organization of information in info pages can make them superior tools for presenting information—there's less need to scroll through many pages of potentially uninteresting information looking for some tidbit. If the info page hierarchy was constructed sensibly, you should be able to find the information you need very efficiently.

Broadly speaking, programs sponsored by the Free Software Foundation (FSF) are using info pages in preference to man pages. Many FSF programs now ship with minimal man pages that point the user to the programs' info pages. Non-FSF programmers have been slower to embrace info pages, though; many such programs don't ship with info pages at all, and instead rely on traditional man pages. The info browser, though, can read and display man pages, so using info exclusively can be an effective strategy for reading Linux's standard documentation.

Using Miscellaneous Program Documentation

Most Linux programs ship with their own documentation, even aside from man or info pages. In fact, some programs have so much documentation that it's installed as a separate package, typically with the word documentation or doc in the package name, such as samba-doc.

The most basic and traditional form of program documentation is a file called README, readme.txt, or something similar. Precisely what information this file contains varies greatly from one program to another. For some, the file is so terse it's nearly useless. For others, it's a treasure trove of help. These files are almost always plain text files, so you can read them with less or your favorite text editor.

If you downloaded the program as a source code tarball from the package maintainer's site, the README file typically appears in the main build directory extracted from the tarball. If you installed the program from a binary package file, though, the README file could be in any of several locations. The most likely places are /usr/doc/*packagename*, /usr/share/doc/*packagename*, and /usr/share/doc/packages/*packagename*, where *packagename* is the name of the package (sometimes including a version number, but more often not). If you can't find a README or similar file, use your distribution's package management system to locate documentation. For instance, on an RPM-based system, you might type **rpm -ql** *apackage* **| grep doc** to locate documentation for *apackage*. Using grep to search for the string doc in the file list is a good trick because documentation directories almost always contain the string doc. Chapter 5 describes rpm and other package-management commands in more detail.

README files often contain information on building the package or make assumptions about binary file locations that don't apply to binaries provided with a distribution. Distribution maintainers seldom change such information in their README files, though. You should be aware of this fact lest you become confused by it.

In addition to or instead of the README file, many programs provide other documentation files. These may include a file that documents the history of the program in fine detail, descriptions of compilation and installation procedures, information on configuration file formats, and so on. Check the source code's build directory or the directory in which you found the README file for other files.

Some of the larger programs ship with extensive documentation in PostScript, Portable Document Format (PDF), Hypertext Markup Language (HTML), or other formats. Depending on the format and package, you might find a single file or a large collection of files. As with the README files, these files are well worth consulting, particularly if you want to learn to use a package to its fullest.

Using Internet-Based Help Resources

In addition to the documentation you find on your computer, you can locate documentation on the Internet. Most packages have associated Internet Web sites, which may be referred to in man pages, info pages, README files, or other documentation. Check these pages to look up documentation. Frequently, online documentation ships with the software, so you might be able to find it on your local hard disk; however, sometimes the local documentation is old or sparse compared to what's available online. Of course, if your local documentation is old, your local software may be old, too—try not to use documentation for software that's substantially newer or older than what you're actually using!

Another online resource that's extremely helpful is the Linux Documentation Project (LDP; http://www.tldp.org). The LDP is dedicated to providing more tutorial information than is commonly available with most Linux programs. You'll find several types of information at this site:

HOWTOs Linux HOWTO documents are short and medium-length tutorial pieces intended to get you up to speed with a topic or technology. In the past, smaller HOWTOs were classified separately, as mini-HOWTOs; however, the distinction between the two types of document has diminished greatly in recent years. HOWTOs have varying focus—some describe particular programs, whereas others are more task-oriented and cover a variety of tools in service to the task. As the name implies, they're generally designed to tell you how to accomplish some goal.

Guides Guides are longer documents, often described as book-length. (In fact, some of them are available in printed form.) Guides are intended as thorough tutorial or reference works on large programs or general technologies, such as Linux networking as a whole.

FAQs A *Frequently Asked Question (FAQ)* is, as the name implies, a question that comes up often—or more precisely, in the sense of the LDP category, that question and an answer to it. LDP FAQs are organized into categories, such as the Ftape FAQ or the WordPerfect on Linux FAQ. Each contains multiple questions and their answers, often grouped in subcategories. If you have a specific question about a program or technology, looking for an appropriate FAQ can be a good place to look first for an answer.

LDP documents vary greatly in their thoroughness and quality. Some (particularly some of the Guides) are incomplete; you can click on a section heading and see an empty page or a comment that the text has yet to be written. Some LDP documents are very recent, but others are outdated, so be sure to check the date of any document before you begin reading—if you don't, you might end up doing something the hard way, or in a way that no longer works. Despite these flaws, the LDP can be an excellent resource for learning about specific programs or about Linux generally. The better LDP documents are excellent, and even those of marginal quality often present information that's not obvious from man pages, info pages, or official program documentation.

Most Linux distributions include the LDP documents in one or more special documentation package. Check your /usr/doc and /usr/share/doc directories for these files. If they're not present, look for likely packages on your installation media. If you have fast always-up Internet access, though, you might want to use the online versions of LDP documents because you can be sure they're the latest available. Those that ship with a distribution can be weeks or months out of date by the time you read them.

Summary

System documentation is important and easily overlooked. It begins with documenting your initial system installation—what distribution and version you used, what packages you installed, and so on. You should then back up configuration files and keep a physical log book of changes you make to this installation. These measures will help you recover or reproduce the system should the need arise. Keeping records on the system's performance (CPU load, disk use, and so on) can also be helpful in problem-solving situations. If your system is behaving sluggishly, such baseline measures will help you pinpoint the source of the problem, rather than guessing at it.

System log files represent another type of documentation, but log files are kept by the computer itself, rather than by you. You can configure the system log daemon, as well as the servers and other programs that create log files, to handle log files in the way you want. You can log more or less information from individual programs, and store the data in a variety of files. You can also send logs to another computer for storage, which can be a good way to keep them out of harm's way in the event the system that creates the logs is compromised.

A final type of documentation is information created by others that you read. All major Linux distributions include man pages and info pages to document common commands, configuration files, system calls, and so on. These tools can help you get the details right when using a program, but they aren't very good for tutorial information. For that, you must look elsewhere, such as README files that ship with a program or the Linux Documentation Project, which hosts a large number of documents on various Linux-related topics.

Exam Essentials

Describe methods of documenting system configuration and changes to it.   Keeping a paper log book in which you record important system configuration options and ongoing changes can help you recover and trace problems related to configuration changes. Backing up the entire /etc directory tree can help you recover a configuration should a file become seriously corrupted.

Summarize how system performance baseline information can be helpful.   Baseline information describes how your system performs under normal conditions. If your system develops problems, the baseline measures will help you identify the source and verify that a problem really is (or is not) in the subsystem you suspect it's in.

Describe the function of a system logger.   A system logger is a daemon that accepts information from servers and other programs that want to record information about their normal operation in standardized log files. The system logger creates and manages these files on behalf of the programs that generate the log entries.

Explain why using a remote system logger can be beneficial.   A remote system logger is a computer that accepts log entries for other systems. This practice improves overall network security because it protects logs from tampering by intruders—to change a log file, the intruder must compromise two computers rather than one. You can also search consolidated log files much more easily than you can search them on multiple computers.

Summarize how `tail` and `less` differ as tools for examining log files.   The `tail` command displays the final few lines of a file, which is handy if you know an entry you want to see is at the very end of a log file. The `less` command enables you to page through a file, search its contents, and so on. It's not as convenient as `tail` if you just want to see the last few lines of a file, but it's superior if you need to search for information or aren't sure precisely how many lines you need to examine.

Compare and contrast man pages and info pages.   Man pages and info pages both present summaries of commands, file formats, and so on, typically written in a similar terse style and useful for reference purposes. Man pages use a simple linear structure, one page per command. Info pages are structured hierarchically, much like Web pages, and provide links between levels in the document.

Describe the document types found at the Linux Documentation Project.   The LDP hosts three main classes of documents: HOWTOs, which are tutorial documents designed to help you learn how to use a program or perform a task; Guides, which are book-length tutorial and reference documents; and FAQs, which are collections of common questions and answers about Linux.

Commands in This Chapter

Command	Description
uptime	Displays the time the system has been running, as well as three load averages (for the past minute, the past 5 minutes, and the past 15 minutes).
free	Displays the amount of free memory (both RAM and swap space).
df	Displays the free disk space by partition.
logrotate	Performs log rotation.
sar	Displays a variety of system performance measures.
head	Displays the first few lines of a text file.
tail	Displays the last few lines of a text file.
more	Displays a text file a page at a time.
less	Displays a text file a page at a time. Provides more features than more.
logcheck.sh	Called from a cron job, this script checks your log files for suspicious or dangerous events and e-mails you a report.
man	Displays help information on a command, configuration file, or other system feature.
whatis	Searches the man page database for entries that match the specified keyword.
apropos	Searches the man page database for entries or descriptions that include the specified keyword.
info	Displays help information on a command, configuration file, or other system feature.

Review Questions

1. What types of information should you record in an administrator's log? (Choose all that apply.)

   A. The exact contents of all configuration files

   B. The locations of major utility programs, like `e2fsck`

   C. Major options selected during system installation

   D. Descriptions of changes to important configuration files

2. Which of the following methods is the best way to back up the `/etc` directory?

   A. Use `tar` to copy the contents to a floppy or other removable disk.

   B. Print each file and keep the printed record in a binder or notebook.

   C. Copy all the files to another system on the Internet.

   D. Use `diff` to record the differences between the current files and their original state.

3. Which of the following is an advantage of designating one well-protected computer to record log files for several other computers?

   A. Logging information in this way minimizes network use.

   B. The logging system can analyze the logs using Tripwire.

   C. Logs stored on a separate computer are less likely to be compromised by a cracker.

   D. You can log information to a separate computer that you can't log locally.

4. Why is a log file analysis tool like Logcheck useful?

   A. Logcheck translates log file entries from cryptic comments into plain English.

   B. Logcheck sifts through large log files and alerts you to the most suspicious entries.

   C. Logcheck compares patterns of activity across several days or weeks and spots anomalies.

   D. Logcheck uses information in log files to help identify a cracker.

5. Which of the following commands is an improved version of `more`?

   A. `grep`

   B. `tail`

   C. `cat`

   D. `less`

6. Which of the following statements is a fair comparison of man pages to HOWTO documents?

   A. Man pages require Internet access to read; HOWTOs do not.

   B. Man pages are a type of printed documentation; HOWTOs are electronic.

   C. Man pages describe software from a user's point of view; HOWTOs are programmers' documents.

   D. Man pages are brief reference documents; HOWTOs are more tutorial in nature.

7. Which of the following files holds the precise kernel configuration options?

   A. /etc/linux/.conf

   B. /etc/src/linux/.conf

   C. /usr/src/linux/.config

   D. /usr/src/conf/.linux

8. Which three of the following performance measures should be included in a baseline? (Choose all that apply.)

   A. CPU load

   B. Data retention policies

   C. Memory load

   D. Disk use

9. Which of the following commands can you use to determine the CPU load at any given moment?

   A. ps

   B. uptime

   C. du

   D. apropos

10. Which of the following commands can be used to discover your system's total memory load?

    A. time

    B. df

    C. mem

    D. free

11. Which of the following divisions does df utilize to show free disk space?

    A. Volume

    B. Partition

    C. Disk

    D. Sector

12. Which of the following configuration files does the logrotate program consult for its settings?

    A. /etc/logrotate.conf

    B. /usr/sbin/logrotate/logrotate.conf

    C. /usr/src/logrotate/logrotate.conf

    D. /etc/logrotate/.conf

13. Your manager has asked that you configure `logrotate` to run on a regular, unattended basis. What utility/feature should you configure to make this possible?

A. at

B. logrotate.d

C. cron

D. inittab

14. Your manager tells you that he wants statistics from the `sar` utility for all machines. You look on the web server, but `sar` is not there. What package should you install to make this utility available?

A. samba

B. sysklogd

C. sysstat

D. Sentry Tools

15. Which of the following commands searches the man page database for entries or descriptions that include a specified keyword?

A. info

B. apropos

C. grep

D. apackage

16. Info pages are written in sections that are arranged hierarchically. These sections are similar to the individual pages of Web sites, and are known as what?

A. Segments

B. Elements

C. Sectors

D. Nodes

17. The `man` utility displays help information for which of the following? (Choose all that apply.)

A. Commands

B. System features

C. Device chipsets

D. Configuration files

18. What are the three main classes of documents hosted by the Linux Documentation Project?

A. RFCs

B. HOWTOs

C. FAQs

D. Guides

19. Baseline information should describe how your system performs under which conditions?

A. Normal

B. Light

C. Heavy

D. Stressed

20. Your company is about to release a new application to the Linux market. You have been assigned the task of creating a file to accompany the application that will tell users how to install it. What format should this file take?

A. Autorun

B. FAQ

C. README

D. Make

Answers to Review Questions

1. Answers: C, D. The administrator's log should contain information to help you recover a nearly identical system should the need arise, or to help you back out of configuration changes that don't work. Options C and D are useful to one or both of these goals. On the other hand, the exact contents of all configuration files would be far too tedious to enter in a paper log, and the locations of major utility programs are standardized and easy to discover. (If you move a program from its standard location, though, recording this fact may be a good idea.)

2. A. Floppies are reasonably quick and can usually hold all of the /etc directory's contents when compressed. When floppies are too small, Zip disks or similar media do well. Printouts are impractical when you need to quickly recover an entire file. Some files in /etc are sensitive, and so should not be transferred over the Internet. Also, an Internet link could go down at an awkward time, preventing recovery of the data. Although diff could produce a compact file of changes, keeping this up-to-date could be difficult, and recovery after changes that were *not* recorded through diff could be impossible.

3. C. Crackers often try to doctor system logs to hide their presence. Placing logs on another computer makes it less likely that they'll be able to achieve this goal, so you're more likely to detect the intrusion. Logging to a separate computer actually *increases* network use. Tripwire doesn't do log analyses; that job is done by Logcheck, and Logcheck can run on any computer that stores logs. System loggers can record any information locally that can be logged remotely.

4. B. Logcheck uses pattern-matching rules to extract log file entries containing keywords associated with suspicious activity. Although the other options might be useful to have, Logcheck and other common log file analysis tools cannot perform these tasks.

5. D. The less program, like more, displays a text file a page at a time. The less utility also includes the ability to page backward in the text file, search its contents, and more.

6. D. Man pages are intended to give you quick information on commands, configuration files, or the like. HOWTOs are intended as introductions to packages or broad topics.

7. C. The /usr/src/linux/.config file holds the precise kernel configuration options.

8. Answers: A, C, D. Three performance measures are important on most systems and should be included in a baseline: CPU load, memory load, and disk use.

9. B. You can determine the CPU load at any given moment by using uptime. The ps command will show which processes are running, while du shows disk usage. The apropos utility helps locate man pages using a keyword that you specify.

10. D. You can discover your system's total memory load with free. While the display shows mem: as one of the headings, that is not the name of the command to use to see this information, and df is used to show the amount of disk space that is free.

11. B. The df utility displays the free disk space by partition.

12. A. The `logrotate` program consults a configuration file called `/etc/logrotate.conf`, which includes several default settings and typically refers to files in `/etc/logrotate.d` to handle specific log files.

13. C. The `logrotate` program can be started automatically—and unattended—on a regular basis by adding an entry for it in cron. The `at` utility would be used if you only wanted the program to run once, while `logrotate.d` defines how the program is to handle specific log files. The `inittab` table is used for services and startup and not for individual programs.

14. C. The `sar` program isn't installed by default on many Linux systems. If you can't find it on your system, look for and install a package called `sysstat`.

15. B. The `apropos` utility searches the man page database for entries or descriptions that include a specified keyword. The `info` utility simply returns help information on a utility, while `grep` is an all-purpose searching tool not focused on man pages. There is no standard utility called `apackage`.

16. D. Info pages are written in nodes, which are similar to the individual pages of Web sites. These nodes are arranged hierarchically.

17. Answers: A, B, D. The `man` utility displays help information on commands, configuration files, or other system feature. It doesn't provide information on low-level hardware device chipsets, although it does provide information on software interfaces to hardware devices.

18. Answers: B, C, D. The LDP hosts three main classes of documents: HOWTOs, which are tutorial documents designed to help you learn how to use a program or perform a task; FAQs, which are collections of common questions and answers about Linux; and Guides, which are book-length tutorial and reference documents. RFCs are Requests for Comments, which are networking standards documents that are not maintained by the LDP.

19. A. The baseline should contain information that describes how your system performs under normal conditions. (Understanding how the system works under heavy load can also be important, though.)

20. C. README files, which are plain-text files, are the most basic and traditional form of program documentation. They often contain information on building the package, may describe its basic purpose or use, and otherwise provide an introduction to the software, particularly for those who build it locally.

Chapter 9

Hardware

THE FOLLOWING COMPTIA OBJECTIVES ARE COVERED IN THIS CHAPTER:

- ✓ **1.12 Configure peripherals as necessary (e.g., printer, scanner, modem)**

- ✓ **2.16 Manage print jobs and print queues (e.g.,** `lpd`, `lprm`, `lpq`**)**

- ✓ **3.8 Configure Linux printing (e.g., cups, BSD LPD, SAMBA)**

- ✓ **3.9 Apply basic printer permissions**

- ✓ **6.1 Describe common hardware components and resources (e.g., connectors, IRQs, DMA, SCSI, memory addresses)**

- ✓ **6.2 Diagnose hardware issues using Linux tools (e.g.,** `/proc`, **disk utilities,** `ifconfig`, `/dev`, **knoppix, BBC,** `dmesg`**)**

- ✓ **6.3 Identify and configure removable system hardware (e.g., PCMCIA, USB, IEEE1394)**

- ✓ **6.4 Configure advanced power management and Advanced Configuration and Power Interface (ACPI)**

Most Linux distributions can detect and configure themselves to properly use your hardware at system installation. In fact, distributions increasingly include the facility to do this even after installation, through tools like Red Hat's Kudzu and Mandrake's HardDrake. Sometimes, though, you need to manually configure new hardware or tweak an automatic configuration.

This chapter covers this matter, with particular emphasis devoted to a few hardware issues that deserve extra attention: hardware configuration, diagnosis of hardware problems, power management, external hardware devices, and printing.

Another area that deserves special attention is configuring the X Window System, which was covered in Chapter 1, "Installation."

Checking Hardware Configuration

In the best of all possible worlds, you could simply plug in a computer and it would work. Unfortunately, that ideal world does not yet exist, either in the software realm or in the hardware realm. Many problems can plague hardware, but you can examine various settings to verify that your hardware is installed and working correctly—or at least to eliminate certain possible types of problems. You might want to perform such checks when you receive new hardware, prior to installing Linux on existing hardware, or if you're experiencing system reliability problems that you believe might be caused by hardware. Specific areas you should check include cabling, resource use settings, options for hard disks and related components, and the computer's basic motherboard settings.

Because most hardware is inside the computer's case, you must open that case to check the hardware's status. This poses three dangers. First, you might suffer an electrical shock if the computer is plugged into a wall outlet. Some power supplies have power switches independent of the computer's main switch; turning these off can reduce this risk. Second, static charges built up in your own body (say, from shuffling across a carpet in dry weather) can damage computer components. You can reduce this risk by grounding yourself frequently—for instance, by wearing a wrist strap designed for that purpose or by frequently touching a water faucet, radiator, or the computer's power supply if it's plugged into the wall. Finally, some computers (particularly notebooks and other small or specialized devices) aren't meant to be opened, so opening the case may void your warranty.

Checking Cabling

Several types of devices use cables, typically to link a device to the motherboard or to a controller card of some type. These cables can be entirely internal or external, depending on the device type. Particular types of cable have specific requirements, which are described in the following sections.

Power Cables

The most obvious power cable to most users is the one that stretches from a wall outlet, power strip, or uninterruptible power supply (UPS) to the computer. This cable is much like power cables on many other devices, and it should be fully inserted into the computer and its power source.

A second class of power cables resides inside the computer case. These cables stretch from the power supply (a rectangular metal box inside the computer to which the external power cable attaches) to the motherboard and various disk devices (hard disk, floppy disk, CD-ROM drive, and so on). Several types of internal power connectors are available. Most power supplies have about half a dozen connectors of various forms, each of which connects to just certain types of devices—the motherboard, hard disk devices, or floppy devices. You should check that power connectors are all inserted firmly in their respective devices because they sometimes work loose during shipping.

 WARNING So-called AT-style motherboards (used on many Pentium and earlier computers) used two motherboard power connectors, rather than the integrated connector used in later ATX systems. These AT connectors *must* be inserted side by side, with the black wires next to each other. These connectors can be inserted in each other's sockets, which will *destroy* the motherboard!

Some motherboards have connectors that supply power to fans—typically CPU fans, but sometimes extra case fans. Other systems rely on connectors direct from the case power supply to drive internal fans. In any event, be sure these power connectors are firmly attached to their appropriate supply points.

Internal Data Cables

Data cables are the second major form of internal cabling. These carry data between components—typically between a disk or tape device and a motherboard or controller. The most common form of data cable is a *ribbon cable*, so called because the cable resembles a ribbon. Ribbon cables differ in their widths and in the exact forms of their connectors. Some also have unique characteristics, such as a twisted portion on floppy cables. Common ribbon cables include 34-pin floppy, 40-pin ATA, 50-pin SCSI, and 68-pin Wide SCSI.

You should check that all cable connectors are inserted firmly and correctly. Most cables feature notches or asymmetrical connectors so that they cannot be inserted backward, but some cheap cables lack these safeguards. If some of your cables are so crippled, pay careful attention to the cable's orientation. Most cables include a colored stripe on one edge, which indicates the location of the first signal line. The matched connector on the device or board should indicate the location of pin #1, probably in tiny type by the connector. This pin also usually has a square (as opposed to a round) solder joint. Be sure to plug the cable in so that the stripe is next to pin #1.

Some types of ribbon cable can have more connectors than devices. For instance, it's possible to use a SCSI cable with four connectors when you have just two SCSI drives, leaving one connector unused (two connectors attach to the SCSI drives and one to the host adapter). For most types of cable, you should ensure that the end connectors are both used. Normally, one of these attaches to the motherboard or controller card, and the other end attaches to one of the devices.

Particularly on older systems, ribbon cables sometimes link internal to external connectors. For instance, a motherboard might have an internal connector for its parallel port, so a ribbon cable ties this to an external parallel-port connector. Such cables are rare on modern motherboards, which integrate the connector into the motherboard in a standard location so that it's directly accessible from outside the case. You might still find such cables on a few designs—for instance, if they are being used to link a USB port to a front-panel USB connector.

Ribbon cables aren't the only type of internal data cable. CD-ROM drives frequently sport three-wire cables to tie the CD-ROM drive's audio output to a sound card. There are also two-to-four-wire connectors that link the motherboard to front-panel computer components, such as the power button, the reset button, and the hard disk activity LEDs.

NOTE: LED cables must be connected in the correct orientation, but the cables aren't keyed, so you have a 50/50 chance of getting it wrong unless you pay careful attention to the positive and negative markings on the cables and motherboard. (Such an error doesn't damage the system, but it means the LED won't work.) This detail isn't important for the power or reset switches on modern computers.

External Cables

External cables connect the computer to its keyboard, mouse, and monitor. Printers, scanners, network connections, and so on also use external cables. (A few wireless devices exist, but even these often use short cables to link from a standard port to a radio or infrared transmitter.)

In all cases, for a device to function properly it's important that the associated cable be inserted firmly into its matching socket. Some cable types, such as Ethernet (RJ-45) cables, snap into place and cannot be removed unless you push a small lever or similar locking mechanism. Others, such as parallel, RS-232 serial, and some varieties of external SCSI connectors, have thumbscrews that can be tightened to ensure a snug connection (some of these require an actual screwdriver to tighten and loosen). Others, such as USB and keyboard connectors, have no locking or tightening mechanism, so you must be sure these connectors are fully and firmly inserted.

WARNING: Some cable types should not be routinely connected or disconnected when the computer is in operation. These include SCSI, RS-232 serial, and parallel connectors. When attaching or detaching such a cable, a short can damage the device or the computer. Other connectors, such as those for USB and Ethernet, are designed for *hot swapping*—attachment and detachment when the computer is in operation.

Because you'll be plugging external devices in yourself, you should be sure you do this job correctly. It's easy to mistakenly connect a device to the wrong port. This is particularly true for RS-232 serial devices since many computers have two such ports; for speakers, microphones, and audio inputs on sound cards; and for PS/2-style mice and keyboards. USB ports are interchangeable on most computers; it doesn't matter which one you use.

Some connectors are electrically compatible but come in different sizes or shapes. This is particularly true of RS-232 serial connectors (which come in 9- and 25-pin varieties), keyboard connectors (which come in large AT-style and small PS/2-style connectors), and external SCSI connectors (which come in several varieties, such as 25-pin, 50-pin Centronics-style, 50-pin miniature, and 68-pin miniature). Adapters for these are available, but be cautious with them—an adapter can add enough weight to the connector so that it's likely to fall out. This is particularly true of one-piece keyboard adapters and some types of SCSI adapters.

Figure 9.1 shows several common internal and external cable types. The 40- and 50-pin ribbon cables are hard to tell apart by sight except by width. (Floppy cables look like these, but have narrower connectors.) The external cables' connectors are more varied in appearance, although some can be easily confused at first glance. The ends of parallel printer cables that connect to printers look like slightly narrower versions of the 50-pin Centronics-style SCSI cable shown in Figure 9.1, for instance.

Checking IRQ, DMA, and I/O Settings

Most plug-in boards use various hardware resources that are in limited supply in the x86 architecture. Of particular interest are the board's *interrupt request (IRQ) number*, its *direct memory access (DMA)* channel, and its *input/output (I/O)* port. The x86 architecture supports just 15 interrupts (0–15, with IRQs 2 and 9 being the same), each of which permits a device to signal that it needs attention from the CPU. There are also just a handful of DMA channels, which enable devices to transfer blocks of data to and from memory with little CPU intervention. I/O ports are in less short supply, but still occasionally produce conflicts; these are memory areas that devices and CPUs use to exchange data. Boards use an interrupt to tell the CPU that something important is happening that requires the CPU's attention. DMA channels and I/O ports are used to transfer data from the board to the computer's memory or CPU.

FIGURE 9.1   Internal and external cables come in a wide variety of shapes and sizes, although some resemble each other.

Table 9.1 summarizes common IRQ, DMA, and I/O settings for some popular device types. Most of these settings can be changed, however, at least within limited ranges. Some devices, such as SCSI host adapters and Ethernet cards, don't have standardized resource settings. Also, not all devices use all of these resource types, so some cells in Table 9.1 are empty.

TABLE 9.1   Common Hardware Resource Settings

Device	Common IRQs	Common DMA Channels	Common I/O Ports (Hexadecimal)
System Timer	0		0040–005F
Keyboard Controller	1		0060–006F
Second Interrupt Controller (for IRQs 8–15)	2	4	
Real-Time Clock	8		
Math Coprocessor	13		00F0–00FF
PS/2 Mouse Port	12		
RS-232 Serial Port 1 (/dev/ttyS0)	4		03F8–03FF
RS-232 Serial Port 2 (/dev/ttyS1)	3		02F8–02FF
Parallel Port 1 (/dev/lp0)	7	3	0378–037F or 03BC–03BF or 0778–077F
Parallel Port 2 (/dev/lp1)	5		0278–027F or 0678–067F
USB Port	9 or 10		FF80–FF9F
SoundBlaster-Compatible Sound Card	5	1, 5	0220–0233, 0240–0253, or 0260–0263
Floppy Disk Controller	6	2	03F0–03F5
ATA Controller 1	14		01F0–01F7, 03F6, FFA0–FFA7
ATA Controller 2	15		0170–0177, 0376, FFA8–FFAF

Once Linux is booted, you can check on resource consumption by examining files in the /proc filesystem. In particular, /proc/interrupts holds IRQ use information, /proc/dma reveals the DMAs used by devices, and /proc/ioports enables you to check on I/O port use. You can view these files by sending them to your screen, as in **cat /proc/interrupts**. Some GUI tools also display this information. You should bear in mind, though, that these files only display information about devices that are *active*. If you haven't loaded a module for a device, evidence of its presence may not appear in the /proc filesystem. For instance, you might not see evidence that IRQ 6 is in use until after you've mounted a floppy disk.

With Industry Standard Architecture (ISA), it's important that two devices don't attempt to use the same IRQ, DMA channel, or I/O port. Doing so can result in one board being unavailable, and in extreme cases, it can crash the computer. Of particular interest, note that both SoundBlaster-compatible sound cards and second parallel ports use the same IRQ, which can cause problems with these devices. Fortunately, most modern sound cards are flexible in their IRQ use, and multiple parallel ports are becoming rare as USB becomes more popular. PCI boards may be able to share an IRQ with another PCI board, but even this sometimes causes the hardware to work slowly or behave strangely.

The motherboard uses several IRQs for its own devices. In fact, most of the devices specified in Table 9.1 reside on the motherboard on modern computers.

If you have any old ISA boards, you can check their IRQs by examining jumper settings on the boards themselves. Consult the board's documentation for details. Newer ISA boards use software configuration. PCI boards are auto-configured by the computer's BIOS or by the Linux kernel. In both of these latter cases, it's impossible to tell what hardware resources a board will use without booting the computer. Unfortunately, if the resources cause a conflict, the computer may not boot completely. If you suspect this may be happening, consult the upcoming section, "Diagnosing Hardware Problems," for hardware troubleshooting information.

Checking ATA Devices

Most *x*86 computers use *Advanced Technology Attachment (ATA)* for hard disks, CD-ROMs, and often other types of disk and tape devices. Several variants on ATA are available, ranging in speed from 8MB/s to 133MB/s, with faster speeds in the works. In early 2005, 66MB/s is considered very low end, 100MB/s is common, and 133MB/s is the interface of choice. These different interface types are referred to by various names, which usually include the speed, such as "UltraDMA/66" or "ATA/133," although the official names do not include these speeds. The more capable parallel ATA interfaces can communicate with less-capable devices, and vice versa, so you can mix and match if you need to—but each chain runs at just one speed, so you can seriously degrade a fast disk's performance by attaching it to the same cable as a slow CD-ROM or the like. Table 9.2 summarizes ATA hardware types.

Each *parallel ATA (PATA)* chain can support the controller and up to two devices. Traditionally, you must configure each device to be either the *master* or the *slave*. In Linux, the master device takes on a lower device letter in its /dev/hd*x* device filename, where *x* is the device letter. Configuring master/slave status is done through a switch or jumper on the device itself; consult your

TABLE 9.2 ATA Hardware Types

Official Name	Unofficial Names	Maximum Speed	Added PIO Modes	Added DMA Modes	Cable Type
ATA-1	IDE	8.3MB/s	0, 1, 2	0, 1, 2, Multiword 0	40-wire parallel
ATA-2	EIDE	16.6MB/s	3, 4	Multiword 1, Multiword 2	40-wire parallel
ATA-3		16.6MB/s			40-wire parallel
ATA-4	UltraDMA/33, ATA/33	33.3MB/s		UltraDMA 0, UltraDMA 1, UltraDMA 2	40-wire or 80-wire parallel
ATA-5	UltraDMA/66, ATA/66	66.6MB/s		UltraDMA 3, UltraDMA 4	80-wire parallel
ATA-6	UltraDMA/100, ATA/100	100MB/s		UltraDMA 5	80-wire parallel
ATA-7[1]	UltraDMA/133, ATA/133	133MB/s		UltraDMA 6	80-wire parallel
Serial ATA		150MB/s			7-wire serial

[1]ATA-7 has not been officially ratified as a standard, and most likely never will be, but many manufacturers produce hardware that complies with the draft ATA-7 specifications.

documentation for details. Most modern devices and controllers support an auto-configuration protocol, typically enabled by setting jumpers to a setting called Cable Select.

If you need more than two devices, or if you want to separate fast and slow devices, you must use multiple ATA chains, each of which corresponds to one physical ATA cable. Most motherboards support two chains (hence four devices total), and you can add more by adding plug-in ATA controller cards. You can use similar cards to upgrade to faster forms of ATA.

Normally, one ATA device will be the master on the first (or primary) chain. A second device might be the slave on the same chain or the master on a second chain. The former configuration preserves IRQs, which may be desirable if you have lots of other devices, but the second is likely to produce better performance.

Much of this description applies to traditional PATA devices, which use 40- or 80-pin cables. In 2003 and 2004, though, *serial ATA (SATA)* began making inroads into the marketplace. SATA overcomes certain engineering challenges of fast parallel devices, and so SATA and its descendents are likely to be the interfaces of choice in the future. SATA cables are much narrower than are PATA cables, and SATA supports just one device per cable, so SATA drives have no master/slave settings. SATA cables are more sensitive to being bent or crimped than are PATA cables, so you should be careful not to bend these cables too tightly or squeeze them into cramped spaces.

 Modern ATA controllers and drives all support both DMA-driven access and *Programmed Input/Output (PIO)* access. DMA access uses direct board-to-memory transfers, whereas PIO access uses the device's I/O ports and CPU to transfer data to memory. DMA access is therefore less CPU intensive than PIO access is. Table 9.2 lists the DMA and PIO modes used by each type of device, but you don't need to be concerned with this detail at this point; you can adjust the drive's DMA and PIO modes after you've installed and configured Linux.

In Linux, SATA drives can turn up as ordinary ATA devices (that is, under /dev/hdx device filenames) or as *Small Computer Systems Interface (SCSI)* devices (using device filenames of the form /dev/sdx). Which of these happens depends on the driver used. Some SATA controller drivers are classified in the Linux kernel as ATA drivers, but others appear as SCSI drivers. The reason is that SATA borrows a great deal from SCSI, and in fact plans are under way to merge the ATA and SCSI standards into one protocol in the future.

Checking SCSI Devices

SCSI is an unusually capable and complex interface bus. For this reason, SCSI busses can sometimes be difficult to configure correctly, particularly when they're loaded down with many devices. Factors you should consider when planning or checking a SCSI bus include the following:

SCSI variant   Many versions of SCSI are available, ranging from the original 5MB/s SCSI-1 to the 640MB/s Ultra640 SCSI. Most of these versions are compatible with one another, but adding a less-capable device to an otherwise more-capable SCSI chain can degrade performance. Also, the more different two devices are, the less likely they are to get along on one chain. Adding a SCSI-1 device to an Ultra3 SCSI chain, for instance, is likely to cause problems. Table 9.3 summarizes the features of current SCSI variants.

SCSI IDs   SCSI devices are differentiated by their ID numbers. Older SCSI variants (those that use a bus that's 8 bits wide) use ID numbers that range from 0 to 7, while Wide variants (which use 16-bit busses) have IDs that range from 0 to 15. The SCSI host adapter itself consumes one number, so this is the source of the 7- or 15-device limit on SCSI chains. SCSI IDs are generally set with jumpers on internal devices, or via some sort of switches or dial on external devices. Check your documentation for details. If two devices share an ID, it's likely that one will mask the other, or they'll both malfunction quite seriously. New devices can often use the SCSI Configured Automatically (SCAM) protocol, which allows devices to acquire IDs automatically.

Termination   A SCSI bus can be thought of as a one-dimensional chain of devices. The devices on both ends of the chain must be terminated, which keeps signals from bouncing back from the end of the chain. Several types of termination are associated with different SCSI variants, ranging from passive to active to low-voltage differential (LVD). Most SCSI devices include termination that can be activated by setting a jumper, or even automatically. Sometimes you need to add a separate SCSI terminator. Be sure this detail is set correctly because incorrect termination can lead to bizarre errors, which can crash a Linux system.

Cable quality SCSI—and especially high-speed SCSI—is quite susceptible to problems caused by low-quality cables. Particularly if your SCSI chain has many devices, it can be worthwhile to purchase high-quality cables. These are, unfortunately, likely to be expensive—often $50 or more.

Cable length Maximum SCSI cable lengths range from 1.5 to 12 meters (m), depending on the SCSI version. SCSI cable length limits apply to the *entire* SCSI chain. If you have two external SCSI devices, for instance, you sum the lengths of the external cables, along with any internal cables, to determine your SCSI chain's cable length.

Troubleshooting a SCSI chain is described in more detail later in this chapter, in the section "SCSI Problems."

As with ATA, SCSI is evolving from a parallel to a serial interface. The serial SCSI variant is known as *Serial Attached SCSI (SAS)*, but SAS has yet to become a major factor in the marketplace. If you do run into an SAS device, its cable will be physically much narrower than a conventional parallel SCSI cable. Plans are under way to merge SAS and SATA into a single specification.

TABLE 9.3 SCSI Hardware Types

SCSI Type	Speed	Termination	Cable Type	Maximum Cable Length
SCSI-1	5MB/s	Single-ended	25- or 50-pin	6m
SCSI-2	5MB/s	Single-ended	50-pin	6m
Fast SCSI-2	10MB/s	Single-ended	50-pin	3m
Fast/Wide SCSI-2	20MB/s	Single-ended	68-pin	3m
UltraSCSI	20MB/s	Single-ended	50-pin	3m or 1.5m[1]
UltraWide SCSI	40MB/s	Single-ended	68-pin	3m or 1.5m[1]
Ultra2 Wide SCSI	80MB/s	LVD	68-pin	12m
Ultra3 SCSI or Ultra160 SCSI	160MB/s	LVD	68-pin	12m
Ultra320 SCSI	320MB/s	LVD	68-pin	12m
Ultra640 SCSI	640MB/s	LVD	68-pin	12m

[1]Maximum cable length is 3m for four or fewer devices and 1.5m for five or more devices.

Checking BIOS Settings

The *Basic Input/Output System (BIOS)* is the lowest-level software component in a computer. The CPU runs BIOS code as part of its startup procedure. As a result, the BIOS configures many fundamental aspects of the computer before Linux has a chance to boot. The BIOS also provides tools that the computer uses to load the Linux kernel into memory.

Although the *x*86 BIOS provides some standard features, it's not entirely standardized. In particular, modern BIOSs provide a setup tool, often referred to as the *Complementary Metal Oxide Semiconductor (CMOS) setup utility*, which you can use to set various low-level options. The options available in a computer's CMOS setup utility differ from one computer to another, both because of differences in hardware and because of different BIOS designs.

Most computers display a prompt at boot time that tells you how to get into the CMOS setup utility. This is usually done by pressing a key, such as Delete or F2, at a critical point during the boot process. Once you've done this, you'll see a BIOS setup screen, such as the one shown in Figure 9.2. This screen allows you to select and set various options, typically by moving through menus by pressing the arrow keys on the keyboard.

SCSI host adapters often include their own BIOSs and setup utilities, which are separate from the motherboard BIOS. The SCSI setup utilities usually have setup options that you can adjust by pressing a key sequence at a particular point in the boot process. Watch your boot displays or consult your SCSI adapter's documentation for details.

FIGURE 9.2   CMOS setup utilities use menu-driven displays to let you adjust a computer's built-in hardware.

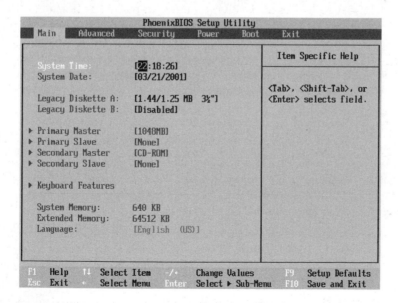

Most systems come with reasonable default BIOS settings, but you may want to check, and possibly adjust, a few. These include the following:

Disk settings   You may need to adjust two common hard disk settings. The first specifies the size of the disk. An auto-detection feature normally works well for this. The second setting determines how the BIOS interprets the disk's cylinder/head/sector (CHS) addresses. On most BIOSs, a linear block addressing (LBA) mode is the best choice. SATA disks may be detected separately from PATA disks. If you use SCSI hard disks, the main motherboard BIOS won't detect them. This is normal; the SCSI BIOS provides the necessary support.

On-board ports   Modern motherboards include RS-232 serial, parallel, USB, PATA, SATA, and frequently other types of ports. Some motherboards include video or audio hardware as well. You can enable or disable these ports or change their settings (for instance, you can change the IRQs used by the devices). Disabling unused ports can free up resources for other devices.

PCI settings   Some BIOSs enable you to specify how the system treats PCI devices. Most commonly, you can choose from two or more rules for how the BIOS assigns IRQs to PCI devices. Sometimes, one rule results in IRQ conflicts and another doesn't, so such a setting is worth investigating if you have problems booting and suspect IRQ conflicts.

Passwords   In a high-security environment, you may want to set a BIOS password. This prevents the system from booting unless the correct password is entered. It can slow down intruders who have physical access to the computer and boot with their own boot disk, but if intruders have physical access to the computer, they can bypass this feature in various ways. Setting a BIOS password also prevents automatic reboots in the event of a power failure. Nonetheless, slowing down an intruder may be worthwhile in some environments.

Memory settings   BIOSs can be configured to copy parts of themselves, or of BIOSs stored on other devices, to RAM. This practice, which is known as *shadowing*, speeds up access to the BIOS, and it is useful in DOS, which relies on the BIOS for input/output. Linux doesn't use the BIOS as much, so it's generally best to disable all shadowing in Linux, which can result in slightly more memory available in Linux. Some BIOSs also enable you to control one or more memory holes— regions of the CPU's memory map that are unusable. These sometimes cause Linux to incorrectly detect the amount of RAM installed in the computer, so you may want to experiment with different memory hole settings.

Boot devices   Modern BIOSs support booting from a wide variety of disk and disk-like devices, including floppy disks, ATA disks, SCSI disks, CD-ROM drives, and high-capacity removable disks like Zip or LS-120 disks. You can usually set the system to boot from some subset of these devices in any order you like. The BIOS tries each medium in turn, and if it's not present or isn't bootable, it tries the next one. For highest security, set the system to boot from your ATA or SCSI hard disk only; for convenient booting of installation or emergency media, set it to boot from a CD-ROM, floppy, or other removable media drive first.

In practice, you may need to experiment with a particular computer's CMOS settings to determine which work best. It's generally not a good idea to try random changes on a working system, though; experiment with these settings only if you're having trouble. Making changes without cause can produce an unbootable system, although if you remember what you changed, you can usually recover your system to a working state.

Most CMOS setup utilities include an option that restores the settings to the factory default values. These options may not always produce optimal results, but they'll usually work.

Configuring Power Management

Power management is an increasingly important part of computer use. Most laptop computer batteries can run for only a couple of hours, and power management tools can dramatically reduce the computer's need for power, thus extending battery life. On desktop systems and servers, power management can reduce a system's power draw, thus helping to control electricity bills. On both types of systems, power management tools can be used to fully power a computer down under software control. Two sets of system power management tools exist: *Advanced Power Management (APM)* and *Advanced Configuration and Power Interface (ACPI)*. Both require underlying support in the computer's BIOS. They fill similar roles, but their configuration and use are somewhat different. In the 2.4.*x* kernels, APM is mature, but ACPI is new and experimental. ACPI is more likely to be usable in late 2.4.*x* and 2.6.*x* kernels.

Both APM and ACPI are cross-OS power management protocols. These protocols are implemented by the computer's BIOS; Linux's support for these protocols therefore relies on the features being present in the computer's BIOS. Consult your computer hardware's documentation to learn if it supports either or both of these protocols. New hardware is likely to support both, but older hardware may support APM only or (for very old hardware) neither protocol.

Activating Kernel Support

Both APM and ACPI rely on kernel features to work. These features can be compiled into the kernel by activating appropriate options under the Power Management Options menu—both APM and ACPI have their own submenus with options to enable assorted specific features, such as support for fan control, or to enable basic support at system boot time. Generally speaking, enabling an option will do no harm, even if it doesn't apply to your system. You should read the description to see if it applies, though. A few APM options in particular can cause problems. The RTC Stores Time In GMT option can cause your system time to be set strangely after a suspend operation if it's set incorrectly, and a few other options can cause problems with some hardware, as detailed in their descriptions.

When you configure your kernel, keep in mind that Linux will use APM *or* ACPI, but not both. In practice, whichever kernel system loads first will control the system's memory management. The simplest way to deal with this situation is to compile support for one protocol or another, not both.

Another approach is to compile both as modules and load only the desired modules at boot time. In practice, if you try to use APM or ACPI features, as described in the next couple of sections, and they don't work, the cause could be the presence of support for the other system in the kernel.

If you're using your distribution's stock configuration, chances are it includes a reasonable default APM/ACPI configuration. It may try loading ACPI and then use APM as a fallback, for instance. In any event, you can try using one set of tools, and then the other if that doesn't work. You may need to consult distribution-specific documentation to learn the details of how it's configured on your system, though.

Hard disk power management is partially independent of APM and ACPI. Although these tools can put the entire system (including hard disks) into a low-power mode, hard disks have their own power management features that can be set independently of APM and ACPI and that do not rely on kernel support for these features. The upcoming section, "ATA Problems," describes the hdparm utility, which sets hard disk power management options, among other things.

Using APM

To use APM features effectively, you need some way to tell the computer when to enter power-conserving states. This task is accomplished with the apmd package, which ships with most Linux distributions and may be installed automatically. The main apmd program is a daemon, which means that it runs in the background waiting for some event to occur. Most daemons, including apmd, should be started when the computer boots. Once running, apmd monitors the system's battery status, and if the battery's charge gets too low, apmd kicks the system into a suspend mode in which most functions are shut down and only the system's RAM is maintained. The apmd program will also suspend the hard disk if it's gone unused for a long enough time. (You can also use the hdparm utility to control hard disk power management more directly.)

If you want to manually control APM features, you can do so with the apm utility. Typing this command manually presents basic power management information, such as how much battery power is left. The -s and -S parameters cause the system to go into suspend and standby modes, respectively. Suspend mode shuts off power to most devices, leaving only the CPU and memory operating, and those at minimum power. Standby mode leaves more devices powered up, so the system can recover more quickly; but there's less power savings in this mode. A fully charged laptop can usually last several hours in standby mode and a day or more in suspend mode. Many laptops include a key sequence that will force the system into suspend or standby mode. In most cases, apmd will detect such a keystroke and honor the request. Consult your laptop's documentation for details.

Using ACPI

Linux's ACPI handling is similar to its APM handling in broad strokes, but of course the details differ. In particular, an ACPI daemon runs instead of an APM daemon. The acpid program is a common ACPI daemon. This daemon is controlled through files in /etc/acpi/events. All the files in this directory whose names do not begin with a dot (.) are parsed and interpreted as sets of events and actions to be taken in response to the event. Each event line begins with the string event=, and each action line begins with action=. The actions point to scripts or Linux commands.

One simple ACPI configuration file contains nothing but comments and a very simple action/event pair, as seen here:

```
event=.*
action=/etc/acpi/default.sh %e
```

This configuration essentially passes all responsibility over to a shell script, /etc/acpi/default.sh. A shell script can be more complex than the simple default ACPI parser, but this approach may be overkill for you.

 Event names are not fully standardized. Thus, you may need to monitor your own system to determine what important event names are. Check the /proc/acpi/event file when you perform an ACPI-related event, such as closing the lid of a laptop computer. This file should change to display the event name, which you can then reference in your Linux ACPI configuration file.

You can use files in the /proc/acpi directory to monitor your system and to change defaults. Try using cat to view the contents of some of these files, as in **cat /proc/acpi/event** to view recent ACPI events. Various tools can link into these files to provide you with useful information, such as your CPU's temperature and battery status. The acpi program is one of these tools; type **acpi -V** to have the system display all the information it can.

Configuring External Hardware Devices

Many computer devices are internal to the computer itself; however, some are removable or entirely external. Three interfaces deserve special attention among external devices: *Personal Computer Memory Card International Association (PCMCIA)* devices; *Universal Serial Bus (USB)* devices; and IEEE-1394 (aka FireWire) devices. These devices have largely, but not completely, supplanted older interfaces for external hardware, such as the RS-232 serial and parallel printer ports.

Configuring PCMCIA Devices

Because laptops don't have ISA or PCI slots, manufacturers developed a standard for expansion cards that allows you to easily insert and remove many of the types of devices that would go in an ISA or PCI slot on a desktop computer. This standard was originally named after the industry group that developed the standard, the *Personal Computer Memory Card International Association (PCMCIA)*. To reduce the number of acronyms, though, this standard has since been renamed *PC Card*. More recently, a 32-bit variant (PC Card is 8- or 16-bits) called *Cardbus* has been released. Many Linux utilities still use the old PCMCIA name, and I use this term to refer to both PC Card and Cardbus devices.

Cardbus and PC Card adapters exist for desktop systems, so PCMCIA utilities sometimes find use on these systems. PCMCIA devices are much more common on laptops, though.

Several varieties of PCMCIA hardware are available. PCMCIA cards come in three sizes: Type I, Type II, and Type III, with each type being thicker than the preceding one. Type I cards are often used for memory expansion. Type II cards are the most common type, and they are used for Ethernet cards, modems, and the like. Type III cards are rare, and they are used for hard disks or other devices with internal moving components. Electronic standards include PCMCIA 1.0, PCMCIA 2.0, PCMCIA 2.1, and PC Card, with the last of these being the most advanced. As already noted, the bus width on these cards ranges from 8-bit to 32-bit, with 32-bit (Cardbus) devices providing the best performance.

You can learn more about all of these at the PC Card Web site, `http://www.pc-card.com`.

Unlike support for most hardware, PCMCIA support doesn't come with the Linux kernel. Instead, you must acquire and install an auxiliary driver package. This package is hosted at `http://pcmcia-cs.sourceforge.net`. Fortunately, most Linux distributions include these PCMCIA drivers, so there's no need to go looking for them unless you need support for a particularly new device or you upgrade your kernel by manually compiling it yourself.

PCMCIA cards are designed to be inserted and removed at will. Unfortunately, Linux's driver model doesn't work well with such hot swapping. Therefore, the PCMCIA driver set includes a feature known as *Card Services*, which helps you smoothly install and remove drivers from the kernel and also helps the kernel cope with potential problems (for instance, automatically starting or stopping network services when an Ethernet PCMCIA card is installed or removed). Card Services are controlled through configuration files in `/etc/pcmcia`. This directory contains scripts for different types of services, such as `network` and `ide`. If your distribution's maintainers paid proper attention to PCMCIA devices, these scripts should require no modifications to work correctly. In some cases, though, you'll need to edit these scripts to have them do the right thing. Details of doing this are very distribution- and device-specific. The "Basic Shell Scripting" section of Chapter 2, "Text-Mode Commands," may help you understand these scripts if you need to modify them.

Configuring USB Devices

Universal Serial Bus (USB) has risen from obscurity to an extremely popular interface in just a few years. Today, USB is commonly used for attaching keyboards, mice, printers, scanners, modems, digital cameras, removable disks, hard disks, speakers, and more. To support USB devices, Linux provides a set of drivers in the USB Support section of the kernel configuration.

You must compile the USB drivers for your particular device in order to use it. In many cases, though, you must also enable other drivers, because the kernel treats USB as a stand-in for other interfaces. For instance, USB disk devices are treated like SCSI disks, and USB speakers are treated like sound cards. Thus, you must enable basic SCSI support and support for SCSI disks to use USB disk devices, and you must enable basic sound support to use USB speakers. Fortunately, most Linux distributions include all of this necessary support in their default kernels, so chances are you won't need to deal with reconfiguring your kernel to use USB devices.

Some USB devices are supported through a special /proc filesystem directory, /proc/bus/usb. Software that accesses such devices typically only works if you've enabled the USB Device Filesystem kernel option. Such devices may not require explicit USB drivers for the device itself. For instance, some USB cameras are supported in this way, and don't need explicit USB camera support. As with devices that do need device-specific support, most distributions provide this support in their default kernel. Thus, you shouldn't need to reconfigure your kernel to use such devices. You might, though, need to change the permissions on certain files in /proc. Details vary greatly from one device and program to another, so consult your access program's documentation for information on what needs to be changed.

USB, like PCMCIA, is a hot-plug technology—in theory, you should be able to plug in a USB device that wasn't present when the system booted and begin to use it. Linux doesn't use Card Services with USB devices, though; instead, the kernel handles the task of registering the new devices. The driver must be built into the kernel or available and registered as a module. Most distributions' default configurations handle this task fine. If you recompile your kernel and find that you can't use a USB device, though, you may want to consider compiling the appropriate support directly into the kernel rather than as a module.

Broadly speaking, two speeds of USB device are available: USB 1.*x* and USB 2.0. USB 1.*x* tops out at 1.5MB/s (12Mbps), which is fast enough for mice, keyboards, low-end printers, and other low-bandwidth devices. This speed isn't enough for many potential USB applications, though—for instance, if you check Tables 9.2 and 9.3, you'll see that USB 1.*x* is very low in speed compared to even the oldest hard disk interfaces. For this reason, USB 2.0 increases the top speed of USB to 60MB/s (480Mbps). Although this speed still doesn't meet the best ATA and SCSI speeds available today, it is fast enough to handle disk devices, high-speed Ethernet, and other high-speed applications without causing undue frustration. (In fact, actual disk drives seldom tax the maximum transfer rates of the ATA and SCSI busses to which they're connected, so they may perform nearly as well on USB 2.0 as on a modern ATA or SCSI bus.) Linux supports both USB 1.*x* and 2.0, although different drivers are required. To support USB 1.*x*, you activate support for the Open Host Controller Interface (OHCI) or the Universal Host Controller Interface (UHCI); USB 2.0 requires support for the Enhanced Host Controller Interface (EHCI). Most distributions activate the necessary and appropriate drivers automatically at boot time, but you can compile one or more into the kernel if you recompile your kernel.

Configuring IEEE-1394 Devices

IEEE-1394, aka FireWire, is an external interface that competes with USB 2.0. At a theoretical maximum speed of 50MB/s (400Mbps), IEEE-1394 is in the same general range as USB 2.0. Traditionally, IEEE-1394 has been most commonly used for audio/visual devices, such as video cameras and external television tuner boxes, but it can be used for hard disks, scanners, and other tools, as well.

In broad strokes, IEEE-1394 is handled much like USB from a Linux perspective. The kernel support area for this interface is called IEEE 1394 (FireWire) Support, and it includes options for enabling the main IEEE-1394 subsystem and drivers for specific devices. Typically, you must enable either the OHCI-1394 Support option or the Texas Instruments PCILynx Support option; these provide drivers for the low-level IEEE-1394 chipset on your motherboard or IEEE-1394 card. Most external IEEE-1394 devices require the Raw IEEE-1394 I/O Support option, which provides a generic interface to IEEE-1394 devices via a /proc filesystem directory. Some devices, though (most notably hard disks and Ethernet adapters) require other IEEE-1394 drivers. As with USB devices, you may need to activate support in other kernel areas, such as the SCSI subsystem or the networking hardware subsystem, to use these features.

Most Linux distributions ship with IEEE-1394 support, so chances are you don't need to change your kernel configuration to use such hardware. If you recompile your kernel, though, you may need to be sure that appropriate IEEE-1394 support is compiled into your kernel or as a module.

Configuring Legacy External Devices

Prior to the development of USB and IEEE-1394, most external devices were connected via RS-232 serial ports and parallel ports. Most frequently, mice and modems used RS-232 serial ports, while printers were connected to parallel ports. Both ports have been used for other purposes, though— for instance, a few years ago, scanners and external Zip disks frequently connected to the parallel port. Most computers continue to ship with at least one RS-232 serial and at least one parallel port, although some computers (particularly Macintoshes) lack these features, and instead rely on USB and IEEE-1394 exclusively.

Naturally, Linux supports the older RS-232 serial and parallel ports. Kernel options appear in the Device Drivers ➤ Character Devices ➤ Serial Drivers area for RS-232, and in the Device Drivers ➤ Parallel Port Support area for the parallel port. Most distributions include the necessary kernel modules by default, so you shouldn't need to recompile your kernel just to use such devices.

RS-232 serial devices are accessed via the /dev/ttySx device files, where x is a number from 0 up representing the port number. When used to connect to a printer, the parallel port is accessed via /dev/lpx (again, x is a number from 0 up representing the port number). If you connect an old parallel-interfaced scanner or disk device, you may need to access it in some other way, typically as if it were a SCSI or some other type of device.

RS-232 serial ports are configured either through programs that access these ports, such as the Point-to-Point Protocol (PPP) dialing tools described in Chapter 6, "Networking," or through the setserial command. This command accepts a large number of parameters that enable you to set the RS-232 serial port speed, tell the system what subtype of RS-232 serial hardware is installed if it's misdetected it, and so on. These parameters are summarized in Table 9.4, and the syntax for the command is as follows:

```
setserial [options] /device/name [parameters]
```

TABLE 9.4   Common setserial Parameters

Parameter	Meaning
port *port_number*	The I/O port number of the device.
irq *irq_number*	The IRQ number of the device.
uart *type*	The model of the universal asynchronous receiver/transmitter (UART) used by the serial port. The *type* can be none, 8250, 16450, 16550, 16550A, 16650, 16650V2, 16654, 16750, 16850, 16950, or 16954. A *type* of none disables the port; the others tell the kernel to use the specified UART model.
autoconfig	Instruction to setserial to automatically configure the serial port.
baud_base *speed*	The speed of the serial port, in bits per second (bps). On most systems, the highest possible *speed* is 115200.

The options mainly affect the output of the program; for instance, -a produces a verbose report and –G produces output that can be fed back to setserial at a later date (say, in a configuration script). Additional options and parameters are available; consult the setserial man page for details. As an example of this program's use, though, consider a command to adjust the speed of an RS-232 serial port:

```
# setserial /dev/ttyS0 baud_base 57600
```

This command adjusts the speed of the first RS-232 serial port to 57,600 bps. You might issue this command before launching a program that accesses a modem but that can't set the speed itself.

Other external device interfaces exist as well. SCSI is both an internal and an external interface—SCSI scanners, disk drives, tape drives, and other devices are available in external form. Configuring and using external SCSI devices is just like configuring and using internal SCSI devices, except that the cables and connectors are different, and SCSI IDs are set using different mechanisms. Although ATA was never intended as an external interfaces, some companies have marketed kits that enable you to turn an ATA hard disk into an external device. (Today, such kits usually provide an ATA-to-IEEE-1394 or ATA-to-USB interface, but some older kits simply extend the ATA bus outside the computer's case.)

Dedicated keyboard and mouse interfaces are available, and these remain popular, particularly for keyboards. The keyboard interface is so standardized that it requires no special configuration in Linux; the keyboard should simply work, assuming it's plugged in and has no physical defects. (Recent kernels do provide options to support older XT-style keyboards as well as the more common AT-style keyboards.) In the late 1990s, the most common type of external mouse was the PS/2 mouse, which uses a connector known as the PS/2 mouse connector. This is supported by the kernel's Device Drivers ➤ Input Device Support ➤ Mice ➤ PS/2

Mouse option. Since 2000, though, USB mice have risen dramatically in popularity; most new computers now use USB mice. These require the support of the HID Input Layer Support option in the USB configuration area. Both of these drivers, and others, are provided by most major Linux distributions by default, and most distributions do a good job of auto-detecting your mouse interface during installation.

Configuring Basic Printing

Printing in Linux is a cooperative effort involving several tools. A system administrator must be familiar with what each of the tools in this collection does, as well as how they interact. As with many other programs that are part of Linux, some of these tools have several versions, which can lead to confusion or incompatibilities if you're not aware of how the system as a whole functions. The basic Linux printing architecture is the same in all cases. One key component of this architecture is the presence of PostScript printers or the use of a program called Ghostscript to convert PostScript into a format that the printer can understand. Whether you use PostScript or non-PostScript printers, one of two broad classes of printing systems is common in Linux: the traditional BSD Line Printer Daemon (LPD) system or one of its derivatives, or the newer Common Unix Printing System (CUPS) utility. In either case, the commands used to print files and to monitor print jobs are similar across all systems, which minimizes problems for end users moving between systems using different printing systems.

The Linux Printing Architecture

Linux printing is built around the concept of a *print queue*. This is a sort of holding area where files wait to be printed. A single computer can support many distinct print queues. These frequently correspond to different physical printers, but it's also possible to configure several queues to print in different ways to the same printer. For instance, you might use one queue to print single-sided and another queue for double-sided printing on a printer that supports duplexing.

Users submit print jobs by using a program called `lpr`. Users can call this program directly, or they may let another program call it. In either case, `lpr` sends the print job into a specified queue. This queue corresponds to a directory on the hard disk, typically in a subdirectory of the `/var/spool/lpd` or `/var/spool/cups` directory. The traditional Linux printing tool is called `lpd`; it runs in the background watching for print jobs to be submitted. A shift to use of another printing system, CUPS, is under way, but it works in a similar manner, at least when considered broadly. Whatever it's called, the printing system accepts print jobs from `lpr` or from remote computers, monitors print queues, and serves as a sort of "traffic cop," directing print jobs in an orderly fashion from print queues to printers.

One important and unusual characteristic of Linux printing is that it's highly network oriented. As just noted, Linux printing tools can accept print jobs that originate from remote systems as well as from local ones. In fact, even local print jobs are submitted via network protocols, although they don't normally use network hardware, so even a computer with no network connections can print. In addition to being a server for print jobs, `lpd` or CUPS can function as a client, passing print jobs on to other computers that run the same protocols.

One of the deficiencies of the traditional `lpd` printing system is that it's essentially unidirectional—print jobs originate in an application, which blindly produces PostScript (as described shortly) without knowing anything about the printer to which it's printing. The print queue takes this output and sends it on to the printer, which must deal with it as best it can. There's no way for a Linux application to directly query a printer concerning its capabilities, such as whether it supports multiple paper trays or wide forms. This is one of the deficiencies that CUPS aims to correct. Applications can query CUPS about a printer's capabilities—its paper sizes, whether it supports color, and so on. Support for these features is still rare, but this support is likely to become more common as CUPS takes over as the standard Linux printing software.

One confusing aspect of Linux printing is that Linux supports several competing printing systems. In the past, the two most popular have been the original Berkeley Standard Distribution (BSD) LPD printing system and the newer LPRng package. Both work according to the outline just presented, but they differ in some details, some of which are described in the upcoming sections. Between 2001 and 2003, most distributions switched to CUPS as their primary printing systems, although many distributions give a choice of which printing system to use. Even for those distributions that don't give you a choice at installation time, you can rip out one printing system and install another, if you like.

Understanding PostScript and Ghostscript

If you've configured printers under Windows, Mac OS, OS/2, or certain other OSs, you're probably familiar with the concept of a *printer driver*. In these OSs, the printer driver stands between the application and the printer queue. In Linux, the printer driver is part of Ghostscript (`http://www.cs.wisc.edu/~ghost/`), which exists as part of the printer queue, albeit a late part. This relationship can be confusing at times, particularly because not all applications or printers need Ghostscript. Ghostscript serves as a way to translate PostScript, a common printer language, into forms that can be understood by many different printers. Understanding Ghostscript's capabilities, and how it fits into a printer queue, can be important for configuring printers.

PostScript: The De Facto Linux Printer Language

Laser printers as we know them today began to become popular in the 1980s. The first laser printers were very expensive devices, and many of them supported what was at that time a new and powerful printer language: *PostScript*. PostScript printers became quite popular as accessories for the Unix systems of the day. Unix print queues were not designed with Windows-style printer drivers in mind, so Unix programs that took advantage of laser printer features were typically written to produce PostScript output directly. As a result, PostScript developed into the de facto printing standard for Unix and, by inheritance, Linux. Where programs on Windows systems were built to interface with the Windows printer driver, similar programs on Linux generate PostScript and send the result to the Linux printer queue.

A few programs violate this standard. Most commonly, many programs can produce raw text output. Such output seldom poses a major problem for modern printers, although some PostScript-only models choke on raw text. Some other programs can produce either PostScript or *Printer Control Language (PCL)* output for Hewlett-Packard laser printers or their many imitators. A very few programs can generate output that's directly accepted by other types of printers.

The problem with PostScript as a standard is that it's uncommon on the low- and mid-priced printers with which Linux is often paired. Therefore, to print to such printers using traditional Unix programs that generate PostScript output, you need a translator and a way to fit that translator into the print queue. This is where Ghostscript fits into the picture.

Ghostscript: A PostScript Translator

When it uses a traditional PostScript printer, a computer sends a PostScript file directly to the printer. PostScript is a programming language, albeit one that's oriented toward the goal of producing a printed page as output. As a result, a PostScript printer needs a fair amount of RAM and CPU power. In fact, in the 1980s it wasn't uncommon for PostScript printers to have more RAM and faster CPUs than the computers to which they were connected. Today, though, printers frequently have little RAM and anemic CPUs—particularly on inexpensive inkjet models.

Ghostscript is a PostScript interpreter that runs on a computer, offloading some of the need for RAM and CPU power. It takes PostScript input, parses it, and produces output in any of dozens of different bitmap formats, including formats that can be accepted by many non-PostScript printers. This makes Ghostscript a way to turn many inexpensive printers into Linux-compatible PostScript printers at very low cost. Ghostscript is available as open source software (GNU Ghostscript), with a more advanced variant (Aladdin Free Public License, or AFPL, Ghostscript) available for free. AFPL Ghostscript is not freely redistributable in any commercial package, though. Because all Linux distributions are available on CD-ROMs sold for a price, they ship with the older GNU Ghostscript, which works well enough for most users.

One of Ghostscript's drawbacks is that it produces large output files. A PostScript file that produces a page filled with text may be just a few kilobytes in size. If this page is to be printed on a 600 dots per inch (dpi) printer using Ghostscript, the resulting output file could be as large as 4MB—assuming it's black and white. If the page includes color, the size could be much larger. In some sense, this is unimportant because these big files will only be stored on your hard disk for brief periods of time. They do still have to get from the computer to the printer, though, and this process can be slow. Also, some printers (particularly laser printers) may require memory expansion to operate reliably under Linux.

Squeezing Ghostscript into the Queue

Printing to a non-PostScript printer in Linux requires fitting Ghostscript into the print queue. This is generally done through the use of a *smart filter*. This is a program that's called as part of the printing process. The smart filter examines the file that's being printed, determines its type, and passes the file through one or more additional programs before the printing software sends it on to the printer. The smart filter can be configured to call Ghostscript with whatever parameters are appropriate to produce output for the queue's printer.

When using BSD LPD or LPRng, the smart filter is specified with the `if` field in `/etc/printcap`, as described shortly, in "Configuring the /etc/printcap File." Several smart filter packages are available for Linux, including `rhs-printfilters` (used in older Red Hat distributions and some of its derivatives), Apsfilter (used in several other distributions), and magicfilter. CUPS ships with its own set of smart filters, which it calls automatically when you tell the system what model printer you're using.

> ### 🌐 Real World Scenario
>
> ## Choosing an Appropriate Printer for Linux
>
> If you want a speedy printer for Linux, choose a model with built-in PostScript. This is particularly true for textual and line-art output, which suffers the most in terms of size expansion going from PostScript to bitmap. In my experience, Ghostscript-driven printers work well enough for 600dpi black-and-white printers with speeds of up to about 6 pages per minute (ppm), although theoretically both the parallel port and USB 1.*x* port should be able to handle speeds of 3–5 times that value. If the printer's speed is greater than that, the parallel or USB 1.*x* port may not be able to deliver the necessary performance, although you may be able to tweak it to get somewhat better speed.
>
> Color inkjet printers are generally limited more by the speed of the print head than by the speed of the data coming over their ports. Few such printers directly support PostScript, either. Some models come with Windows-based PostScript engines that are conceptually similar to Ghostscript, but such software is useless under Linux. There are a few PostScript inkjets on the market, as well as color PostScript printers that use other printing technologies.
>
> For information on what printers are supported by Ghostscript, check the Ghostscript Web page or the GNU/Linux Printing Web page (`http://www.linuxprinting.org/printer_list.cgi`).

Configuration of the smart filter can be tricky, but most distributions include setup tools that help immensely. The upcoming section, "Using a Configuration Tool," describes the use of one such tool for BSD LPD or LPRng printing systems. CUPS uses its own Web-based configuration tool, as described in the upcoming section, "Using the Web-Based CUPS Utilities." I highly recommend that you use such programs when configuring your system to print.

The end result of a typical Linux printer queue configuration is the ability to treat any supported printer as if it were a PostScript printer. Applications that produce PostScript output can print directly to the queue. The smart filter detects that the output is PostScript and runs it through Ghostscript. The smart filter can also detect other file types, such as plain text and various graphics files, and it can send them through appropriate programs instead of or in addition to Ghostscript, in order to create a reasonable printout.

If you have a printer that can process PostScript itself, the smart filter is usually still involved, but it doesn't pass PostScript through Ghostscript. In this case, the smart filter passes PostScript directly to the printer, but it still sends other file types through whatever processing is necessary to turn them into PostScript.

Running a Printing System

Because Linux printing systems run as daemons, they must be started before they're useful. This task is normally handled automatically via startup scripts in `/etc/rc.d` or `/etc/rc?.d` (where *?* is a runlevel number). Look for startup scripts that contain the strings `lpd`, `lprng`, or `cups` in their names to learn what your system is running. If you're unsure if a printing system is currently active, use the ps utility to search for running processes by these names, as in:

```
$ ps ax | grep cups
3713 ?        S         0:00 cupsd
```

The ps command is covered in more detail in Chapter 5, "Package and Process Management." The grep command and pipes (used to link these two commands together) are covered in Chapter 2.

This example shows that cupsd, the CUPS daemon, is running, so the system is using CUPS for printing. If you can't find any running printing system, consult your distribution's documentation to learn what is available and check that the appropriate package is installed. All major distributions include startup scripts that should start the appropriate printing daemon when the computer boots.

Configuring BSD LPD and LPRng

Fortunately, basic printer configuration for both the original BSD printing tools and LPRng is similar. You can configure everything by hand by directly editing configuration files, but certain critical details—namely, how your smart filter is set up—differ from one distribution to another, and they can be tedious to locate. Therefore, direct file editing is best reserved for cases where you can forgo the smart filter or if you're willing to track down the documentation for whatever smart filter your system uses. In most cases, it's easier to use a configuration tool to do the initial printer configuration, and then you can tweak that configuration by hand, if necessary. Either way, the printing daemon runs in the background and accepts print jobs submitted via lpr.

Configuring the */etc/printcap* File

The /etc/printcap file is at the heart of both the BSD and LPRng printing systems. Listing 9.1 illustrates the format of /etc/printcap by showing an entry for a single printer. You can define multiple printers in /etc/printcap; just be sure to use different names.

Listing 9.1: A Sample */etc/printcap* File

```
lp|hp4000:\
        :lp=/dev/lp0:\
        :br#57600:\
        :rm=:\
        :rp=:\
        :sd=/var/spool/lpd/lp:\
        :mx#0:\
        :sh:\
        :if=/var/spool/lpd/lp/printfilter:
```

Technically, each printer definition is one line long. The /etc/printcap entries, however, traditionally make heavy use of the common Linux convention of using a backslash (\) to signal a line continuation. (Note that every line in Listing 9.1 *except* the last one ends in a backslash.) This makes the printer definitions easier to read. Each component within the /etc/printcap entry is separated from the others by colons (:). Common components of a print queue definition include the following:

Printer name   Each printer definition begins with one or more names for the printer. If the printer has multiple names, they're separated from each other by vertical bars (|). Traditionally, the default printer is called lp. Listing 9.1's example expands on this by adding the name hp4000. Users may print using either name with the same results.

Printer device filename   The lp=/dev/lp0 entry defines the device filename for the printer. In the case of Listing 9.1, the printer device is /dev/lp0, which corresponds to the first parallel port. Many modern printers support USB interfaces, which use the /dev/usb/lp*n* devices, where *n* is a number from 0 up. A few printers use the old RS-232 serial ports, which may be accessed as /dev/ttyS*n*. This entry may be omitted if the printer is shared from another computer.

Baud rate   The br parameter's name stands for "baud rate;" it defines the communications rate for RS-232 serial printers. This option is normally omitted for parallel-port, USB, and network printers. It doesn't do any harm to leave it in, however, as in Listing 9.1.

Remote machine   If you're defining a printer queue for a printer that's connected to another computer or that's connected directly to the network, you specify its machine name with the rm option. Like br, it can be omitted if not used.

Remote print queue   The rp option is used in conjunction with rm, but it specifies the name of the print queue on the remote system. For instance, your local epson queue might print to a queue called inkjet on a remote system. Your local users will use the name epson, and your lpd will pass the job on to the remote system's lpd, which will print to the remote inkjet queue. This option may be omitted if the printer is local, but leaving it blank in this case (as in Listing 9.1) does no harm.

Although you *can* use different local and remote names, using the same name for both will help avoid confusion.

Spool directory   The sd parameter name stands for *spool directory*. This is the location of the print queue on your hard disk. By convention, this is a subdirectory of the /var/spool/lpd directory, named after the print queue's primary name. If you create print queues by hand, you'll need to create this directory. It should normally have fairly restrictive permissions (such as rwx------ and ownership by root; see Chapter 2) so that people can't read or delete each other's print jobs.

Maximum print job size   The mx option sets the maximum size of a print job, in bytes. You can use this option to restrict abuses, but be aware that the print job size in bytes and its size in pages are poorly correlated. If it is set to 0, there's no limit on job size. This option uses a hash mark (#) rather than an equal sign (=) to set its value.

Suppress header The sh option takes no value. It stands for suppress header, and if it's present, Linux does *not* print a header page with information on the user who printed the job. This configuration makes sense for workstations, but on multiuser systems and print servers, omitting the sh option and using the resultant headers can help you organize printouts from multiple users.

Input filter This option sets the input filter filename, which is part of the smart filter associated with the queue. This is frequently a script located within the spool directory. The script sets various options (such as the name of the Ghostscript driver to be used) and calls the smart filter files located elsewhere on the disk.

The /etc/printcap file is fairly complex and supports many options. You can learn about more of them from the file's man page (type **man printcap**). The preceding options cover what you're likely to do with the queue, however, aside from smart filter configuration.

After reconfiguring your print queues, you may need to restart your printer daemon. On most systems, you can do this by passing the restart parameter to the LPRng or BSD LPD printing startup script (startup scripts are described in Chapter 5). The following is an example of how this might be done:

```
# /etc/rc.d/init.d/lpd restart
```

The exact name and location of this file will vary from one distribution to another. You should use this command only when your system isn't actively printing.

Using a Configuration Tool

Much of the challenge of printing in Linux doesn't come from the /etc/printcap file; it comes from telling the system about your printer—that is, smart filter and Ghostscript configuration. GNU Ghostscript comes standard with all major Linux distributions, and it is probably adequate for your system. In a few cases, though, you may need to upgrade to the more recent AFPL Ghostscript or obtain a version with some unusual drivers compiled into it. The GNU/Linux Printing Web page (http://www.linuxprinting.org/printer_list.cgi) can be an extremely useful resource in tracking down appropriate drivers.

In most cases, the easiest way to configure a print queue with a smart filter for a specific non-PostScript printer is to use a printer configuration tool. Most major Linux distributions come with these tools, although which ones come with which distribution vary substantially. This section describes the use of one popular printer configuration tool, Apsfilter (http://www.apsfilter.org).

Because most distributions now use CUPS as their primary printing system, distribution-specific tools frequently handle CUPS configuration, not BSD LPD or LPRng configuration. Apsfilter is distribution neutral but ships with many distributions to handle both BSD LPD and LPRng configuration. The package also includes a smart filter that it inserts into print queues to detect PostScript and other file types.

To use Apsfilter for printer configuration, you must first install the package. Look for it on your distribution's installation media or download and install it from the Apsfilter Web page. If Apsfilter doesn't ship with your distribution and you download it from the Web site, you'll need to compile and install the software; consult the Apsfilter documentation for details. You can then follow these steps:

1. Type **/usr/share/apsfilter/SETUP** as root from a bash shell, in either a text-mode login or an xterm window. (You may need to change the path to the SETUP program if it's installed in another location on your system.) The result is a license screen.

2. Accept the license terms. Apsfilter then presents a few more screens with summary information about your system and general information about the program. Check that the summary information is correct and read the general information, following the prompts to continue at each point. You should then reach the main Apsfilter menu, shown in Figure 9.3.

3. Type **1** to add a printer. Apsfilter displays a screen asking what type of printer you want to add. Options include a PostScript printer, a printer with native Ghostscript support, and assorted printers that rely on add-on Ghostscript drivers. Knowing which driver to select can be tricky; you may need to experiment to learn which option works with your printer. This example follows the native Ghostscript driver option (**3**).

4. Apsfilter shows a list of printer drivers available from your general selection option. This list may be several screens long, in which case you scroll through it using commands that Apsfilter summarizes before displaying the list. Figure 9.4 shows part of the list for the native Ghostscript selection. Scroll through this list until you find your printer or one with which it is compatible. For many printers, the list includes multiple entries that support different printer resolutions and other printing options. Note the number for the printer and options you want to use, such as 78 for the Epson Stylus 800 printer shown in Figure 9.4, then type **Q** to exit from the list.

FIGURE 9.3   The main Apsfilter menu provides options for creating and modifying printer queues.

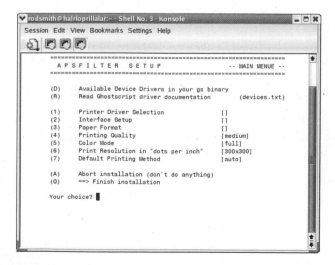

FIGURE 9.4 Apsfilter presents a potentially long list of printers and protocols from which you can select.

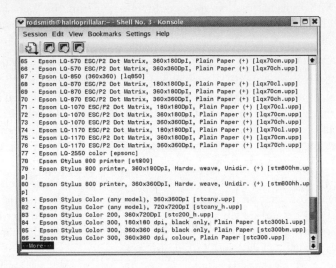

5. Apsfilter asks for the number associated with the driver you want to use. Type it, such as **78** to select the Epson Stylus 800 shown in Figure 9.4.

6. Apsfilter presents summary information and may ask additional questions. Confirm your selection and Apsfilter returns to its main menu (Figure 9.3), but the Printer Driver Selection line will show your driver selection rather than a blank.

7. Type **2** to tell Apsfilter how to connect to the printer. This action produces the interface setup screen shown in Figure 9.5.

FIGURE 9.5 Apsfilter knows how to configure a queue to use any of several interface methods.

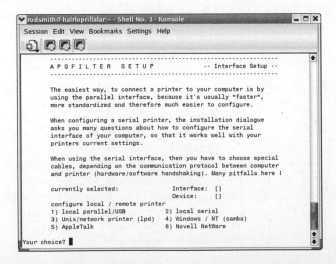

8. Type a digit between **1** and **6** to configure the system to use one of the six types of interfaces—a local parallel or USB port, a local RS-232 serial port, and so on. The precise questions you're asked next will depend on your selection. This example follows option 3, which enables you to print to a printer served via an LPD-style print server.

9. Apsfilter asks for information to further identify the printer interface. In the case of LPD networked printers, this information consists of the print server's hostname and the name of the remote queue. When you're done, Apsfilter returns you to its main menu (Figure 9.3), but the Interface Setup option should show the basic class of interface you selected in step 8.

10. Type **3** to set the paper size. When you've finished, Apsfilter returns to its main menu (Figure 9.3), but the Paper Format line should list your selection. A few additional options will appear near the bottom of the list, too.

11. If desired, adjust additional options (4–7). Some of these options will be meaningless with some printer drivers. For instance, the resolution information is useless for PostScript printers or if your driver included a resolution specification.

12. Type **T** to print test pages to be sure the configuration is working. Apsfilter will ask for confirmation several times before proceeding. If the test pages print correctly, then continue. If not, you'll need to go back and review your selections, making changes to the printer driver, printer location, or other options, as appropriate.

13. Type **I** to create an `/etc/printcap` entry for the printer. Apsfilter asks for a queue name, then returns you to its main menu (Figure 9.3).

14. Type **Q** to finish the installation. Apsfilter displays quite a few information screens, then exits.

You can create several print queues, even if you have just one printer. For instance, you might create one queue that prints at high resolution, and another that prints at a lower resolution. Your users can then pick the desired print resolution by choosing a different print queue, as described shortly—for instance, you might call one `epson360` and the other `epson720`. You can even create one queue that prints with the normal print filters and another that doesn't use a filter—that is, a raw queue. A raw print queue can be useful if you have programs that can print directly to the printer type you use. For instance, the GIMP includes drivers for many specific printer models, and so they can do without Ghostscript in many cases. To create a raw queue, type **7** (Default Printing Method) from the main menu and then type **3** (raw) from the resulting list of queue types.

Configuring CUPS

Although CUPS plays the same role in Linux as BSD LPD or LPRng, and uses Ghostscript in a conceptually similar way, CUPS configuration is quite different from BSD LPD or LPRng configuration. CUPS doesn't rely on an `/etc/printcap` file (although it generates a simple one on the fly for the benefit of programs that refer to it to learn what printers are available). Instead, it uses various configuration files in the `/etc/cups` directory and its subdirectories. You can edit these files directly, and may need to do so if you want to share printers or use printers shared by other CUPS systems. The simplest way to add printers to CUPS, though, is to use the tool's Web-based configuration utility.

Editing the CUPS Configuration Files

You can add or delete printers by editing the `/etc/cups/printers.conf` file, which consists of printer definitions. Each definition begins with the name of a printer, identified by the string `DefaultPrinter` (for the default printer) or `Printer` (for a nondefault printer) in angle brackets (`<>`), as in the following:

`<DefaultPrinter okidata>`

This line marks the beginning of a definition for a printer queue called `okidata`. The end of this definition is a line that reads `</Printer>`. Intervening lines set assorted printer options, such as identifying strings, the printer's location (its local hardware port or network location), its current status, and so on. Additional options are stored in a *PostScript Printer Definition (PPD)* file that's named after the queue and stored in the `/etc/cups/ppd` subdirectory. PPD files follow an industry-standard format. For PostScript printers, you can obtain a PPD file from the printer manufacturer, typically from a driver CD-ROM or from the manufacturer's Web site. CUPS and its add-on driver packs also ship with a large number of PPD files that are installed automatically when you use the Web-based configuration utilities.

As a general rule, you're better off using the CUPS Web-based configuration tools to add printers, rather than adding printers by directly editing the configuration files. If you like, though, you can study the underlying files and tweak the configurations using a text editor to avoid having to go through the full Web-based tool to make a minor change.

One exception to this rule relates to configuring the CUPS Web-based interface tool itself and CUPS's ability to interface with other CUPS systems. One of the great advantages of CUPS is that it uses a new network printing protocol, known as the *Internet Printing Protocol (IPP)*, in addition to the older LPD protocol used by BSD LPD and LPRng. IPP supports a feature it calls browsing, which enables computers on a network to automatically exchange printer lists. This feature can greatly simplify configuring network printing. You may need to change some settings in the main CUPS configuration file, `/etc/cups/cupsd.conf`, to enable this support.

The `/etc/cups/cupsd.conf` file contains a number of configuration blocks that specify which other systems should be able to access it. Each block controls access to a particular location on the server. These blocks look like this:

```
<Location /printers>
Order Deny,Allow
Deny from All
BrowseAllow from 127.0.0.1
BrowseAllow from 192.168.1.0/24
BrowseAllow from @LOCAL
Allow from 127.0.0.1
Allow from 192.168.1.0/24
Allow from @LOCAL
</Location>
```

If you're configuring a workstation with a local printer that you don't want to share, or if you want to configure a workstation to use printers shared via LPD or some other non-IPP printing protocol, you shouldn't need to adjust /etc/cups/cupsd.conf. If you want to access remote IPP printers, however, you should at least activate browsing by setting the directive Browsing On, as described shortly. You shouldn't have to modify your location definitions unless you want to share your local printers.

The /printers location, shown here, controls access to the printers themselves. Features of this example include:

Directive order   The Order Deny,Allow line tells CUPS in which order it should apply allow and deny directives—in this case, allow directives modify deny directives.

Default policy   The Deny from All line tells the system to refuse all connections except those that are explicitly permitted.

Browsing control lines   The BrowseAllow lines tell CUPS from which other systems it should accept browsing requests. In this case, it accepts connections from itself (127.0.0.1), from systems on the 192.168.1.0/24 network, and from systems connected to local subnets (@LOCAL).

Access control lines   The Allow lines give the specified systems non-browse access to printers—that is, those systems can print to local printers. In most cases, the Allow lines will be the same as the BrowseAllow lines.

You can also create a definition that uses Allow from All and then creates BrowseDeny and Deny lines to limit access. As a general rule, though, the approach shown in this example is safer. Locations other than the /printers location can also be important. For instance, there's a root (/) location that specifies default access permissions to all other locations and an /admin location that controls access to CUPS administrative functions.

Before the location definitions in cupsd.conf are a few parameters that enable or disable browsing and other network operations. You should look for the following options specifically:

Enabling browsing   The Browsing directive accepts On and Off values. The CUPS default is to enable browsing (Browsing On), but some Linux distributions disable it by default.

Browsing access control   The BrowseAddress directive specifies the broadcast address to which browsing information should be sent. For instance, to broadcast data on your printers to the 192.168.1.0/24 subnet, you'd specify BrowseAddress 192.168.1.255.

Once you've configured a CUPS server to give other systems access to its printers via appropriate location directions, and once you've configured the client systems to use browsing via Browsing On, all the systems on the network should auto-detect all the printers on the network. There's no need to configure the printer on any computer except the one to which it's directly connected. All printer characteristics, including their network locations and PPD files, are propagated automatically by CUPS. This feature is most important in configuring large networks with many printers or networks on which printers are frequently added and deleted.

Obtaining CUPS Printer Definitions

The basic version of CUPS ships with smart filter support for just a few printers, including raw queues that do no processing and a few models from Hewlett-Packard, Epson, and Okidata. If you use another printer, you should obtain extra CUPS printer definitions. These definitions may consist of PPD files, appropriate behind-the-scenes "glue" to tell CUPS how to use them, and possibly Ghostscript driver files. These printer definitions can be obtained from several sources:

Your Linux distribution   Many distributions ship extra printer definitions in a package called `cups-drivers` or something similar, so check your distribution for such a package. In truth, this package is likely to be the Foomatic or GIMP Print package under another name.

Foomatic   The Linux Printing Web site hosts a set of utilities and printer definitions known collectively as Foomatic (`http://www.linuxprinting.org/foomatic.html`). These provide many additional printer definitions for CUPS (as well as for other printing systems).

GIMP Print   The GNU Image Manipulation Program (GIMP) is a major Linux bitmap graphics program that supports its own printer drivers. These in turn have been spawned off into a package called GIMP Print, which can be integrated with CUPS to provide additional printer options. Check `http://gimp-print.sourceforge.net` for more information.

ESP Print Pro   Easy Software Products (ESP) is the company that first developed CUPS. Although CUPS is open source, ESP offers a variety of printer definitions for CUPS for a price. See `http://www.easysw.com/printpro/` for more details.

If you're printing to one of the basic printers supported by the standard CUPS definitions, you may not need to add anything else. You might also find that your distribution has installed a set of definitions as part of the main CUPS package or in an add-on package, such as `cups-drivers`, without explicit instruction. In either of these cases, you're set and need not do anything else. If you start configuring printers and can't find your model, though, you should look for an additional printer definition set from one of the preceding sources.

Using the Web-Based CUPS Utilities

The CUPS IPP printing system is closely related to the Hypertext Transfer Protocol (HTTP) used on the Web. The protocol is so similar, in fact, that you can access a CUPS daemon by using a Web browser. You need only specify that you want to access the server on port 631—the normal printer port. To do so, enter **`http://localhost:631`** in a Web browser on the computer running CUPS. (You may be able to substitute the hostname, or access CUPS from another computer by using the other computer's hostname, depending on your `cupsd.conf` settings.) This action brings up a list of administrative tasks you can perform. Click Manage Printers to open the printer management page, as shown in Figure 9.6.

If you're configuring a stand-alone computer or the only one on a network to use CUPS, the printer list will be empty, unlike the one shown in Figure 9.6. If other computers on your network use CUPS, you may see their printers in the printer list, depending on their security settings.

FIGURE 9.6   CUPS provides its own Web-based configuration tool.

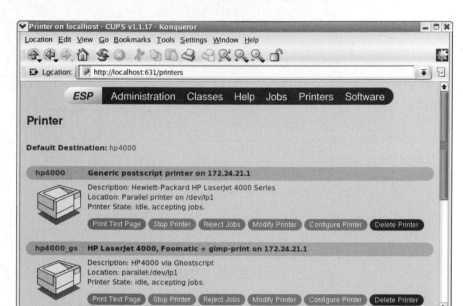

You can add, delete, or modify printer queues using the CUPS Web control system. To add a printer, follow these steps:

1. Scroll to the bottom of the page and click Add Printer. (This option isn't visible in Figure 9.6 because it's too far down the existing printer list.) You're likely to be asked for a username and password.

2. Type **root** as the username and the administrative password as the password, then click OK.

> **WARNING**   CUPS doesn't normally encrypt its data, so you shouldn't use it to administer printers remotely. Doing so would be a security risk, as the passwords would be exposed to sniffing.

3. The system displays a page asking for the printer's name, location, and description. Enter appropriate information in the Name, Location, and Description fields. These fields are all entirely descriptive, so enter anything you like. (Users will use your entry in the Name field to access the printer, though.) When you click Continue, CUPS asks for the printer device.

4. The printer device may be a local hardware port (such as a parallel printer port or a USB port), a remote LPD printer, a remote SMB/CIFS (Samba) printer, or other devices. The precise options available vary from one distribution to another. Select the appropriate one from the pop-up list and click Continue.

5. If you entered a network printer, the result is a page in which you enter the complete path to the device. Type the path, such as **lpd://printserv/brother** to print to the brother queue on the printserv computer. Click Continue when you're done.

6. If you entered a local device in step 4 or after you've entered the complete path in step 5, you'll see a list of driver classes, such as PostScript and HP. Select one and click Continue.

7. CUPS now displays a complete list of printer models within the class you selected in step 6. Select an appropriate model and click Continue.

8. CUPS informs you that the printer has been added.

If you click the Printers item at the top of the page, you should be returned to the printers list (Figure 9.6), but your new printer should be listed among the existing queues. You can print a test page by clicking Print Test Page. If all goes well, a test page will emerge from your printer. If it doesn't, go back and review your configuration by clicking Modify Printer. This action takes you through the steps for adding a printer but with your previous selections already entered as the defaults. Try changing some settings until you get the printer to work.

From the printer queue list, you can also click Configure Printer to set various printer options. What options are available depends on the printer, but common options include the resolution, color dithering options, the paper size, whether or not to enable double-sided printing, and the presence of banner pages.

Printing to Windows or Samba Printers

If your network hosts many Windows computers, you may use the Server Message Block/ Common Internet File System (SMB/CIFS) for file and printer sharing among Windows systems. Linux's Samba server also implements this protocol, and so can be used for sharing printers from Linux.

 Chapter 6 describes the basics of configuring a Linux Samba server, so consult it if you want to share an existing printer queue with Windows clients.

On the flip side, you can print to an SMB/CIFS printer queue from a Linux system. To do so, you select an SMB/CIFS queue in the printer configuration tool (such as Apsfilter or the CUPS configuration option). Figure 9.5 shows this option for Apsfilter as option 4, Windows / NT (samba). Under CUPS, it's called Windows Printer via SAMBA in step 4 in the preceding procedure.

Precisely how you proceed with configuration depends on the tool you're using. Most guide you through the process by asking for a hostname, share name, username, and password. Some servers enable you to omit the username or password, or to enter random values for these fields. Others require all four components to work. For CUPS, you must provide this information, but the format is not obvious from the Web-based configuration tool:

smb://*username*:*password*@SERVER/SHARE

This is a uniform resource identifier (URI) for an SMB/CIFS share. You must substitute appropriate values for *username*, *password*, *SERVER*, and *SHARE*, of course. Once this is done and you've finished the configuration, you should be able to submit print jobs to the SMB/CIFS share.

SMB/CIFS printers hosted by Windows systems are usually non-PostScript models, so you must select a local Linux smart filter and Ghostscript driver, just as you would for a local printer. Printers hosted by Linux systems running Samba, though, are frequently configured to act like PostScript printers, so you should select a PostScript driver when connecting to them.

In practice, you may be faced with a decision: Should you use LPD, IPP, or SMB/CIFS for submitting print jobs? To be sure, not all print servers support all three protocols, but a Linux server might support them all. As a general rule, IPP is the simplest to configure because it supports browsing, which means that CUPS clients shouldn't need explicit configuration to handle specific printers. This makes IPP the best choice for Linux-to-Linux printing, assuming both systems run CUPS. When CUPS isn't in use, LPD is generally easier to configure than SMB/CIFS, and it has the advantage of not requiring the use of a username or password to control access. Because SMB/CIFS security is password-oriented, clients typically store passwords in an unencrypted form on the hard disk. This fact can become a security liability, particularly if you use the same account for printing as for other tasks. On the other hand, sometimes use of a password on the server provides more of a security benefit than the risk of storing that password on the client. Generally speaking, if clients are few and well protected, while the server is exposed to the Internet at large, using passwords can be beneficial. If clients are numerous and exposed to the Internet while the print server is well protected, though, a password-free security system that relies on IP addresses may be preferable.

Monitoring and Controlling the Print Queue

Several utilities can be used to submit print jobs and to examine and manipulate a Linux print queue. These utilities are `lpr`, `lpq`, `lprm`, and `lpc`. All of these commands can take the `-P` parameter to specify that they operate on a specific print queue.

Printing Files with *lpr*

Once you've configured the system to print, you probably want to start printing. As mentioned earlier, Linux uses the `lpr` program to submit print jobs. This program accepts many options that you can use to modify the program's action:

Specify a queue name   The `-Pqueuename` option enables you to specify a print queue. This is useful if you have several printers or if you've defined several queues for one printer. If you omit this option, the default printer is used.

In the original BSD version of `lpr`, there should be no space between the `-P` and the *queuename*. LPRng and CUPS are more flexible in this respect; you can insert a space or omit it, as you see fit.

Delete original file   Normally, `lpr` sends a copy of the file you print into the queue, leaving the original unharmed. Specifying the `-r` option causes `lpr` to delete the original file after printing it.

Suppress banner   The `-h` option suppresses the banner for a single print job. It's not available in CUPS.

Job name specification   Print jobs have names to help identify them, both while they're in the queue and once printed (if the queue is configured to print banner pages). The name is normally the name of the first file in the print job, but you can change it by including the `-J` *jobname* option.

User e-mail notification   The `-m` *username* option causes `lpd` to send e-mail to *username* when the print job is complete. It's not available in CUPS.

Number of copies   You can specify the number of copies of a print job by including the number after a dash, as in `-3` to print three copies of a job.

Suppose you have a file called **report.txt** that you want to print to the printer attached to the `lexmark` queue. This queue is often quite busy, so you want the system to send e-mail to your account, `ljones`, when it's done so that you know when to pick up the printout. You could use the following command to accomplish this task, at least with the BSD LPD and LPRng versions of `lpr`:

```
$ lpr -Plexmark -m ljones report.txt
```

The `lpr` command is accessible to ordinary users as well as to `root`, so anybody may print using this command. It's also called from many programs that need to print directly, such as graphics programs and word processors. These programs typically give you some way to adjust the print command so that you can enter parameters such as the printer name. For instance, Figure 9.7 shows Konqueror's Print dialog box. Konqueror features a pop-up list button that lets you select the print queue. This is the Name field in Figure 9.7, but some programs call it something else. Some programs also provide a text entry field in which you type some or all of an `lpr` command, instead of selecting from a pop-up list of available queues. Consult the program's documentation if you're not sure how it works.

FIGURE 9.7   Most Linux programs that can print do so by using lpr, but many hide the details of the lpr command behind a dialog box.

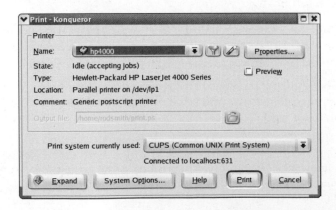

Displaying Print Queue Information with *lpq*

The lpq utility displays information on the print queue—how many files it contains, how large they are, who their owners are, and so on. By entering the user's name as an argument, you can also use this command to check on any print jobs owned by a particular user. To use lpq to examine a queue, you might issue a command like the following:

```
$ lpq -Plexmark
Printer: lexmark@speaker
 Queue: 1 printable job
 Server: pid 14817 active
 Unspooler: pid 14822 active
 Status: printing 'rodsmith@speaker+787', file 1 'Insight.ps', size 672386,
➡format '1' at 14:57:10
 Rank    Owner/ID          Class Job  Files        Size   Time
active   rodsmith@speaker+787  A  787  Insight.ps   672386  14:56:22
```

> This example shows the output of LPRng's lpq. Systems that use the original BSD LPD and CUPS display less information, but the most important information (such as the job number, job owner, job filename, and job size) are present in all cases.

Of particular interest is the job number—787 in this example. You can use this number to delete a job from the queue or reorder it so that it prints before other jobs. Any user may use the lpq command.

Removing Print Jobs with *lprm*

The lprm command removes one or more jobs from the print queue. There are several ways to issue this command:

- If it's issued with a number, that number is understood to be the job ID (as shown in lpq's output) that's to be deleted.

- If root runs lprm and passes a username to the program, it removes all the jobs belonging to that user.

- If a user runs the BSD lprm and passes a dash (-) to the program, it removes all the jobs belonging to the user. LPRng uses all instead of a dash for this purpose.

- If root runs the BSD lprm and passes a dash (-) to the program, it removes all print jobs belonging to all users. Again, LPRng uses all for this purpose.

This program may be run by root or by an ordinary user, but as just noted, its capabilities vary depending on who runs it. Ordinary users may remove only their own jobs from the queue, but root may remove anybody's print jobs.

Controlling the Print Queue with *lpc*

The lpc utility starts, stops, and reorders jobs within print queues. The lpc utility takes commands, some of which require additional parameters. You can pass the printer name with -P, as with other printer utilities, or you can pass this information *without* the -P parameter. In the latter case, the print queue name appears immediately after the command. The following are the most useful actions you can take with lpc:

Abort printing   The abort command stops printing the current job and any other jobs in the queue but leaves those jobs intact. Subsequently issuing the start command will resume printing.

Disable future printing   The disable command sets the queue to reject further print jobs but does *not* halt printing of jobs currently in the queue.

Disable all printing   The down command stops printing to the queue and sets the queue to reject further print jobs.

Enable future printing   You can enable the queue so that it begins accepting print jobs again by using the enable command. This is the opposite of disable.

Exit from the program   If lpc is started in interactive mode (described shortly), the exit command will terminate this mode, returning you to a shell prompt.

Start printing   The start command begins printing and starts an lpd process for the queue.

Stop printing   The stop command stops lpd so further printing is disabled after the current job completes.

Reorder print jobs   The topq *jobid* command moves the job whose ID is *jobid* to the start of the queue (after the currently printing document). Use this command to reprioritize your print queue.

Enable all printing   The up command enables the specified print queue; this is the opposite of down.

Obtain status information   You can display status information on all of the print queues, or on the one selected via -P, by using the status command.

 Although CUPS ships with an lpc command, its functionality is *very* limited; its only useful command is status. You can, though, disable a queue by clicking the Stop Printer link for the printer on the CUPS Web interface (Figure 9.6). When you do so, this link changes to read Start Printer, which reverses the effect. The Jobs link also provides a way to cancel and otherwise manage specific jobs.

You can run lpc in interactive mode, in which you issue one command after another, or you can have it execute a single command and then exit by specifying the command on the same command line you use to launch lpc. As an example, suppose you want to adjust the printing of job 945 on the brother queue (identified through a previous lpq command) so that it's next to print. You could issue the following command to do this:

```
# lpc topq brother 945
```

Although ordinary users may run `lpc`, for the most part, they can't do anything with it. Typical `lpc` operations require superuser privileges.

Using Scanners in Linux

A scanner is a device that converts a physical document to digital form. Scanners can be tricky to configure in Linux; many scanners are finicky in one way or another, and software support for scanners is weaker than for many other hardware devices. Nonetheless, Linux can handle scanners fairly well, assuming you've got supported hardware. Thus, you should begin a quest to get scanners working with a look at scanner hardware options. Once you've settled on the hardware, you can move on to the software side.

Understanding Scanner Hardware

Most scanners are designed to handle documents printed on paper or similar materials, but scanners for other media (such as film) also exist. The physical characteristics of scanners differ, depending on their designed purpose and prices. Several scanner types exist:

Flatbed scanners   These are the most common type of scanners. They're typically somewhat larger than a notebook, with a horizontal glass plate on which you place a document you want to scan. When you scan, a light source passes down the length of the document and a digitized version of the document is read by the scanning software. Some flatbed scanners are integrated into multifunction units that can print, fax, or function as photocopiers. Such units can be tricky to get working in Linux, because you need support for the scanning and other functions; you might find that one function is supported but another isn't. (Photocopying functions seldom require OS support, though.)

Hand scanners   A few years ago, small handheld scanners were common. Instead of having a scan head move along a document, these scanners used your hand to move the scan head along a document. The advantage of hand scanners was that they were less expensive than flatbed scanners. The drawback was that they were awkward to use and often produced poor results. Hand scanners are uncommon today, but some are still available as portable units.

Film scanners   This type of scanner is designed to scan film—that is, slides and negatives. They're typically smaller than flatbed scanners, but have very high resolutions. Because the needs of film scanning are somewhat different from the needs of other types of document scanning, film scanners are often paired with unique software packages.

Drum scanners   A drum scanner is a device that rotates the document to be scanned on a high-speed cylinder, which passes beneath the scan head. Drum scanners are very high in quality—and in price.

Digital cameras   Although not technically scanners, scanning software can sometimes interface to digital cameras as if they were scanners. If dedicated digital camera software, such as gPhoto, doesn't work with your camera, you might want to look into this option to recover digital photos from your camera.

Whatever the general class of scanner, it's likely to interface to the computer in any of a handful of ways. The most common interfaces for modern scanners are USB and IEEE-1394. Previous generations of high-end scanners typically used the SCSI bus, while older low-end scanners often used the parallel port. When connecting a scanner, you should ensure that you've compiled the appropriate support into the kernel. (For SCSI scanners, you must enable the SCSI generic device driver, which handles devices other than disks, tapes, or CD-ROMs, as well as the driver for your SCSI host adapter.)

Hardware compatibility is a big issue with scanners; some models are not supported in Linux, although many are supported. Check the documentation for the scanner software you intend to use to learn what works and what doesn't.

Choosing and Using Linux Scanner Software

Scanners, like other hardware devices, require explicit software support to be useful. In Linux, one scanner software package dominates the field, although a couple of others are available:

SANE   The Scanner Access Now Easy (SANE) package is the primary Linux scanner tool. SANE is a modular software package consisting of back-ends (scanner drivers), middleware "glue," and front-ends (SANE-aware scanning applications). SANE is described in more detail shortly. Consult its Web page, `http://www.sane-project.org`, for more information.

VueScan   This program, headquartered at `http://www.hamrick.com`, is a shareware scanner package intended for film scanning. It features a large number of options geared toward that purpose, such as a database of over 200 film types for optimal color correction based on the specific film you're scanning.

OCR Shop   This is a commercial program designed to perform optical character recognition (OCR) in Linux. Although open source OCR software that ties into SANE is available, the open source solutions lag behind commercial offerings, of which OCR Shop is the main Linux example. Check `http://www.vividata.com` for more details.

You should check the hardware compatibility list for whatever software you intend to use; each of these packages has its own unique set of scanners that it supports. Although there's some overlap, not all packages support all scanners.

For SANE, you may need to install two or more packages: one with the back-ends, one with the front-ends, and perhaps more. Furthermore, some SANE front-ends aren't part of the official SANE project. For instance, XSane (`http://www.xsane.org`) is a popular SANE front-end that provides better GUI controls than the minimal front-ends provided with the official SANE packages.

To configure SANE, you should look in `/etc/sane.d`. This directory holds many configuration files. You should pay particular attention to three of them:

The driver selection file   The `dll.conf` file contains a list of drivers. Depending on your distribution's defaults, most of these may be commented out by hash marks (#), or most may be available. Commenting out unused drivers can speed up certain SANE operations.

Your scanner configuration file   Your scanner should have a configuration file of its own, typically named after the scanner itself. For instance, the `umax1220u.conf` file handles the UMAX Astra 1220U scanner, while the `microtek.conf` file handles assorted Microtek scanners. For the most part, the default settings work; however, you should check the file, read its comments, and perhaps read further documentation on the SANE Web site to learn what the features in this file do.

The SANE network configuration file   An unusual feature of SANE is that it enables network scanning—one computer can host the scanner and a special server (`saned`) that interfaces with the scanner, while a SANE front-end runs on another computer. Although complete SANE network configuration is beyond the scope of this book, you should know that the `saned.conf` file handles the configuration of the `saned` server, which is typically launched via a super server (`inetd` or `xinetd`). On the SANE front-end computer, the `net.conf` file tells the SANE front-end software what servers to try to contact.

Once you've configured SANE, try typing **sane-find-scanner**. This command should return information on the scanners SANE has found. (Keep in mind that network scanners will not be detected.) Typing **scanimage -L** will perform a more complete verification of the scanner's presence. If this command reports that it's found the scanner, you should be able to use Linux scanning software. Although `scanimage` itself can do this job from a shell prompt, chances are you'll want a GUI tool. A good starting point for this is XSane, but other programs can also interface with SANE. The GIMP, for instance, can handle scanning (it uses a subset of XSane to do so). Kooka (`http://www.kde.org/apps/kooka/`) is a scanning package that's associated with KDE.

Diagnosing Hardware Problems

Sometimes, hardware doesn't work as you expect it to. There are many possible causes of such problems, ranging from defective hardware to errors when you load kernel modules. Diagnosing such problems is as much an art as a science, but the rest of this chapter provides some pointers to help you diagnose some common hardware problems.

Core System Problems

The motherboard (also known as the mainboard or system board), CPU, and RAM are the most critical hardware components on any computer. If these components act up, nothing else is likely to work reliably. Problems in RAM and the CPU are likely to affect many or even all programs. Motherboard problems might do the same, or they might be isolated to specific hardware devices on the motherboard, such as a USB or keyboard port.

Your first chance to spot core system problems comes during the system boot process. At this time, *x*86 BIOSs engage in a *power-on self-test (POST)*. This is a test of certain critical components, such as the RAM, the presence of a keyboard and video card, and so on. Most computers beep once if they pass the POST, and beep multiple times if they fail the POST. In fact, most BIOSs produce a different number of beeps depending on the exact nature of the problem. Unfortunately, these beep codes aren't standardized, so you'll have to check with your motherboard or BIOS manufacturer to learn what the codes mean for your particular system. If a system fails its POST, a good starting point is to reconnect all the devices that are connected to the computer, especially the keyboard, CPU, RAM, and all expansion cards. Sometimes a POST failure is accompanied by an on-screen indication of the problem. For instance, most systems display a progress indicator when they perform their memory tests. If that indicator stops partway through, there's a good chance that the BIOS has found defective RAM.

Sometimes you can detect internal components that have worked themselves loose by the reports during the POST. The RAM count, for instance, might tally a certain amount of RAM and then the boot process moves on. If the total RAM counted is incorrect, it's likely that some RAM has worked loose. Likewise, POST displays often summarize the installed PCI and ISA cards, and if you notice something missing, you can power down and take action. The problem with this approach is that the POST displays appear and disappear so quickly that you're not likely to be able to fully read and comprehend the display.

If you configure a computer to boot only from a floppy disk and then insert an unbootable floppy disk in the drive, the system will freeze on the last page of its POST display, enabling you to read it. This trick can be helpful if you're unsure whether the system is registering some critical new component you've added, such as a faster ATA controller. Of course, allowing Linux to boot and using Linux's tools to find the hardware is usually the superior approach, but deliberately halting the boot process can be handy if you're having problems in Linux and you want to be sure the BIOS has registered the device.

Other core system problems don't make themselves felt until Linux has begun booting, or even later. Defective CPUs and RAM often manifest in the form of kernel oopses, for instance. The Linux kernel includes code that displays a summary of low-level problems on the screen (and logs it, if the system still works well enough to do this). This summary includes the word oops, and it's usually the result of a hardware problem or a kernel bug. If you're running a release kernel (that is, one with an even second number, such as a 2.6.9 kernel), a kernel oops is almost always the result of a hardware problem, such as defective RAM, an overheating CPU, or a defective hard disk. Kernel oopses generally cause the system to crash or reboot.

If a problem occurs only in warm weather or after the computer's been running for a while after starting, you may need to get a better heat sink or fan for your CPU or improve the computer's internal case ventilation. The Lm_sensors package (http://secure.netroedge.com/~lm78/) is a good way to monitor your CPU's temperature, assuming your motherboard includes temperature-monitoring features, as most Pentium II, Athlon, or better motherboards do. The ACPI tools also provide a means to monitor your CPU's temperature.

One common type of problem relates to the activation of on-board devices. Modern motherboards include a plethora of such devices, including ATA controllers, RS-232 serial ports, USB ports, parallel ports, a floppy controller, and more. Many even include audio and video support. These devices can be enabled or disabled in the BIOS setup screens, which can usually be entered by hitting the Delete, F10, or some other key early in the boot process. (Watch the screen as the system boots; a message usually tells you how to activate the BIOS utility. If you don't see an obvious prompt, consult your motherboard's documentation.) Peruse the BIOS menus looking for options to enable or disable devices that are causing you problems. In some cases, you may want to deliberately disable devices simply so that they won't consume IRQs or other limited resources. If you're having problems you believe are related to the system running out of IRQs, try disabling any unused devices, even if they aren't showing up in the Linux `/proc/interrupts` output.

ATA Problems

Problems with ATA devices can be quite serious because they can prevent Linux from booting or can cause data corruption. One class of problem with these devices relates to what numbers Linux uses to access a particular sector on a disk. Large disks can usually be accessed using any of several incompatible disk geometries, and if Linux attempts to use one method when another was used to define partitions, Linux may fail to boot or cause data corruption if the OS does boot. In many cases, these problems result in an inability of the Linux Loader (LILO) or Grand Unified Boot Loader (GRUB) to boot Linux.

Another common type of ATA problem relates to bugs in ATA controllers. The Linux kernel source configuration procedures give you many options to enable workarounds and fixes for buggy ATA controllers. Most Linux distributions ship with all of these fixes enabled, so if you're using a common controller, you shouldn't have any problems. If your computer has a particularly new controller or if you've recompiled your kernel and not enabled a fix, you may experience bizarre filesystem errors. You might find that files you've written are corrupted or that your filesystem has errors that appear in routine `fsck` runs. In extreme cases, your computer might crash. You can overcome such problems by recompiling the kernel with appropriate bug workarounds enabled. Sometimes these problems occur because you're using a controller that's very new but that has bugs. In such cases, you may need to replace the controller or upgrade your Linux kernel to a newer version.

With the increasing popularity of SATA disks, a problem that's becoming more common is changes in disk device filenames. If you install Linux on an SATA disk and then recompile your kernel, you may find that Linux won't boot completely—it complains that it can't mount the root filesystem. This can happen because your distribution used an ATA driver but you compiled a SCSI driver, or vice versa. You can either compile your kernel again with the driver your distribution used, or you can change all references to your disk (most importantly in `/etc/fstab` and your boot loader configuration) to conform to the new driver. Sometimes it can be tricky telling precisely what device filename to use, particularly when switching to an ATA driver. Typically, SATA disks acquire letters above the usual PATA range (`/dev/hda` through `/dev/hdd`), and the name used depends on the SATA port to which the disk is attached. It's usually `/dev/hde` or `/dev/hdg`, although it could be something else.

Sometimes a hard disk just plain goes bad. The magnetic coating on the disk platters degrades, the drive electronics become flaky, or the drive hardware otherwise starts to fail. In extreme cases, this problem can cause the disk to become suddenly and completely unresponsive. In other cases, you may experience read/write errors, sluggish performance when accessing certain files, or other problems. All major drive manufacturers have DOS or Windows utilities that can query the drives about their reliability. Check with your drive manufacturer and run such a check if you think a drive is going bad. If it is, you'll need to buy a new drive and copy your Linux installation onto the new disk before the first one fails completely. In some cases you might not be able to recover everything from the first disk, in which case you may need to install Linux from scratch on the new disk or restore Linux from a backup.

Some Linux users experience very slow disk transfer speeds. These can be caused by several factors. For instance, although Linux's basic ATA drivers work with almost all ATA controllers, you must use specialized drivers to obtain the best possible performance from your drive. You can use hdparm both to test disk speed and to set various options that can improve the performance of a hard disk. The hdparm utility supports a large number of options, so you should read its man page for details. The more common features you can set include the following:

PIO or DMA operation   *x*86 ATA devices can be run in either Programmed Input/Output (PIO) mode or in Direct Memory Access (DMA) mode. In the former, the CPU directly supervises all data transfers, whereas in the latter, the CPU steps back and lets the controller transfer data directly to and from memory. Therefore, DMA mode produces lower CPU loads for disk accesses. Using -d0 enables PIO mode, and -d1 enables DMA mode. The -d1 option is generally used in conjunction with -X (described shortly). This option doesn't work on all systems; Linux requires explicit support for the DMA mode of a specific ATA chipset if you're to use this feature.

PIO mode   The -p *mode* parameter sets the PIO mode, which in most cases varies from 0 to 5. Higher PIO modes correspond to better performance.

Power-down timeout   The -S *timeout* option sets an energy-saving option: the time a drive will wait without any accesses before it enters a low-power state. It takes a few seconds for a drive to recover from such a state, so many desktops leave *timeout* at 0, which disables this feature. On laptops, though, you may want to set *timeout* to something else. Values between 1 and 240 are multiples of 5 seconds (for instance, 120 means a 600-second, or 10-minute, delay); 241–251 mean 1–11 units of 30 minutes; 252 is a 21-minute timeout; 253 is a drive-specific timeout; and 255 is a 21-minute and 15-second timeout.

Cached disk speed test   The -T parameter performs a test of cached disk reads. In effect, this is a measure of memory and other non-disk system performance because the disk isn't accessed.

Uncached disk speed test   The -t parameter performs a test of uncached disk reads. You can use it to see if your hard disk is performing as you expect it to. (New hard disks should return values of well over 10MB/s, and usually over 20MB/s; anything less than this indicates an old hard disk, an old ATA controller, or a suboptimal disk configuration.)

Display configuration   The -v option displays assorted disk settings.

DMA mode   The -X *transfermode* option sets the DMA transfer mode used by a disk. The *transfermode* is usually set to a value of sdmax, mdmax, or udmax. These values set simple DMA, multiword DMA, or Ultra DMA modes, respectively. In all cases, *x* represents the DMA mode value, which is a number. Table 9.2 summarizes some of the DMA mode types. On modern hardware, you should be able to use a fairly high Ultra DMA mode, such as -X udma5 or -X udma6.

WARNING Many hdparm parameters can cause serious filesystem corruption if used inappropriately. Precisely what's appropriate varies from one system to another. For instance, using -X udma6 may be fine on one system, but it could cause filesystem damage on another. You can use the -t parameter to test a disk's performance, and then you can try experimenting with hdparm settings only if your disk performance is poor.

Suppose that you suspect your hard disk is performing poorly. You could test it as follows:

```
# hdparm -t /dev/hda
```

```
/dev/hda:
 Timing buffered disk reads:  64 MB in 12.24 seconds =  5.23  MB/sec
```

Indeed, this test reveals a rather anemic disk performance by modern standards. You might be able to improve matters by enabling DMA mode transfers, using an appropriate transfer mode, and then retesting, thus:

```
# hdparm -d1 -X udma6 /dev/hda
```

```
/dev/hda:
 setting using_dma to 1 (on)
 setting xfermode to 70 (UltraDMA mode6)
 using_dma    =  1 (on)
# hdparm -t /dev/hda
```

```
/dev/hda:
  Timing buffered disk reads:  64 MB in 2.48 seconds = 25.81 MB/sec
```

Of course, this improvement, although substantial, still doesn't produce the best conceivable results. (This specific example was taken on a system with a four-year-old hard disk.) In most cases, such dangerous experiments won't be required, because most systems auto-configure themselves in a way that produces optimal (or at least reasonable) performance. It's best to perform such experiments *only* if an initial test with hdparm -t reveals poor performance. If you're still not satisfied, examine your Linux driver availability for your ATA controller and the capacity of the controller to handle the hard disk. (A speedy modern hard disk can outstrip a controller that's a few years old.)

NOTE You can check the specifications for your hard disk to determine how well it *should* be performing. Look at the *internal* data transfer rate, which should be buried on a specifications sheet for your drive. By real-world standards, this value will be optimistic. The hdparm utility should probably return a value of about 60–90 percent of the theoretical maximum.

SCSI Problems

There's an old joke that configuring a SCSI chain is nine parts science and one part voodoo. In reality, this isn't true, but SCSI configuration can be tricky once you get beyond two or three SCSI devices. Common sources of problems include the following:

Termination   Both ends of a SCSI chain must be terminated with a special resistor pack. Most SCSI devices have these built in, and adding or removing termination is a matter of setting a jumper or switch. To complicate matters, though, there are several *types* of termination, and different varieties of SCSI require different termination types. Using the wrong sort of terminator can produce data transfer errors and unreliable operation. Terminating devices that don't fall on either end of the chain can also cause unreliable operation. Remember that the SCSI host adapter itself is a SCSI device. If it's at the end of a chain, it should be terminated, but if it's in the middle of a chain, it should not be. Most host adapters include BIOS utilities that let you enable or disable termination.

SCSI IDs   SCSI devices are identified by ID numbers—0–7 for 8-bit (Narrow) SCSI, 0–15 for 16-bit (Wide) SCSI. If two devices share a single number, chances are that only one will show up, or one device may appear to occupy *all* the SCSI IDs. In either case, performance is likely to be slow and unreliable.

Cable lengths   Maximum SCSI cable lengths range from 1.5 to 12 meters, depending on the SCSI variety. Exceeding cable length limits typically results in data transfer errors, and hence filesystem corruption.

Cable quality   Cheap SCSI cables can cause data errors, just as can incorrect termination or cables that are too long. Unfortunately, good SCSI cables can be quite pricey—$50 or more is not uncommon.

Forked chains   Many modern SCSI host adapters include three connectors—typically one external connector and two internal connectors (for both Wide and Narrow internal devices). SCSI chains, however, should be one-dimensional—each device should be connected to the next one on the chain, with the SCSI host adapter itself counting as a SCSI device. Therefore, you should *not* use more than two connectors on a SCSI host adapter. Failing to heed this advice will produce data errors, much like other problems.

A few high-end SCSI host adapters actually support two independent chains. These host adapters frequently have four connectors, two for each of the chains.

Most SCSI problems can be traced to one of these issues, and especially to termination and cabling problems. Because of this, useful troubleshooting techniques involve simplifying the SCSI chain. For instance, suppose you've got a chain with two SCSI hard disks, a CD-ROM drive, and a tape drive. If you only need one hard disk to boot, you should try removing all of the other devices to make as short a chain as possible. If that works, swap in a longer cable and start adding devices back to the chain. By doing this, you may find that the problem is related to the length of the cable or to a particular device.

Linux doesn't include a driver that works with all SCSI host adapters, unlike the situation for ATA controllers. Therefore, your kernel *must* include support for your particular model SCSI host adapter. Most distributions ship with support for most SCSI host adapters, but you may find yourself unsupported if you've got a particularly exotic host adapter. In such a situation, you'll need to locate drivers or switch host adapters.

You can use the `hdparm` utility, described earlier, to test the performance of your SCSI drives. The `hdparm` program *cannot* be used, however, to adjust SCSI drive performance. In Linux, SCSI drives operate at maximum performance at all times; there are no configurable transfer modes or any way to switch between PIO and DMA modes. (All good SCSI host adapters use DMA mode exclusively, but some very cheap ones use PIO mode only.) This is also true of SATA drives that are driven by an SATA driver in the SCSI kernel subsection; as far as Linux is concerned, they're SCSI drives.

Peripherals Problems

In a computer context, a *peripheral* is a device that connects to and is controlled by a computer. Devices like keyboards, mice, monitors, and scanners are clear examples. Many devices that reside inside the computer's case are also peripherals, however. These include hard drives, CD-ROM drives, and tape backup devices. Most of these internal peripherals *could be* attached externally, given appropriate hardware.

In some sense, network problems can be considered problems with peripherals. Network problem diagnosis (including use of the `ifconfig` utility referenced in Objective 6.2) is covered in Chapter 6.

Because the realm of peripherals is so broad, diagnosing problems with them also covers a lot of territory. As a general rule, peripheral problems can be broken down into three general classes: problems with the peripheral device itself, problems with the cables connecting the peripheral to the computer, and problems with the computer interface for the peripheral.

Peripheral Device Problems

One of the first steps you should take when diagnosing problems with peripheral devices is to determine whether the problem is related to drivers for the device or to the device itself. The upcoming section, "Identifying Supported and Unsupported Hardware," should help you decide whether the device *should* work in Linux. Printers, scanners, cameras, and more exotic external devices are particularly likely to require special drivers that might or might not exist in Linux. Keyboards, mice, monitors, external RS-232 modems, and ATA and SCSI devices are almost always supported in Linux. (SATA controllers are less universally supported under Linux, although this situation is fast improving.)

One useful test to perform is to try the device under another OS. Because most peripherals come with Windows drivers, installing those drivers and trying the device in Windows should give you some clue to help you decide whether the source of the problem is defective hardware or drivers. If you dual-boot a computer into Windows and the device doesn't work, you can't be sure that the problem is in the device, though; it could be in the cable or computer interface to the device. If you move the peripheral to another computer and it does work, the problem could also be in the cable or interface on the Linux computer.

 WARNING   Coincidences happen, so you can't conclude much *with certainty* by moving a device to another computer or OS. For instance, if you move a malfunctioning device to another computer and it still doesn't work, it could be that the software configuration on *both* computers is in error.

Peripheral Cable Problems

Cable problems are usually fairly easy to test—you can replace a cable without too much difficulty in most cases. SCSI cables, though, can be quite expensive, so you may be reluctant to buy a new cable just for test purposes. A few devices, such as mice and most keyboards, come with built-in cables. Fortunately, this class of device is usually quite inexpensive, so if a problem develops in a cable, you can probably replace the entire affected device.

Most peripheral cables cannot be attached to the computer backward. Unfortunately, some particularly cheap ribbon cables (used for SCSI, PATA, and floppy devices inside the computer) lack the notch that serves to prevent backward installation. If you have such a cable, look for a colored stripe along one edge of the cable, and look for pin numbers printed on the connectors on the devices to which the cable attaches. Align the cable so that the colored stripe is associated with pin 1 on both ends, and it should work. If a cable is installed backward, the device will simply not work.

Floppy drive cables are unusual in that they include a twist—a section of cable that's cut and twisted to change the mapping of pins. You should attach your first floppy drive *after* this twist. If you attach your first drive before the twist, your drive identifiers will be confused. On a single-floppy system, your only floppy drive will be identified as `/dev/fd1` rather than `/dev/fd0`. Also, floppy cables normally include two types of connectors for the floppy drives. One form attaches to old 5.25-inch drives, and the other connects to 3.5-inch drives. You can't connect the drive to the wrong type of connector, but you should be aware of this difference so that you're not confused by it, or by the presence of five connectors on a typical floppy cable (one for the motherboard, two for the first floppy drive, and two for the second floppy drive). At most, three of these connectors will be used.

Peripheral Interface Problems

Most peripherals use one of a handful of interfaces. In addition to the ATA and SCSI interfaces described earlier in this chapter, common interfaces include the following:

Floppy   *x*86 computers include a floppy interface that can control up to two floppy drives. These interfaces are very mature, so the Linux drivers seldom cause problems. One configuration detail to which you may need to attend is enabling the port in your computer's BIOS setup screen. If this is not enabled, Linux might not detect the floppy. If the BIOS configuration is correct and Linux can't use the floppy, it may be that the floppy controller is defective. As a device that's built into a motherboard, a floppy controller can be difficult to replace, but old 486 and earlier systems often used floppy controllers on separate cards, so if you can find such an antique you may be able to make use of it. Another option may be to use an external USB floppy drive, although you might not be able to boot from it, depending on your BIOS options.

Monitor   The monitor port is part of the video card. Software problems with it usually relate to the X Window System (covered in Chapter 1). If the hardware is defective, there's a good chance that you won't even be able to see your BIOS startup messages.

Keyboard x86 computers have a keyboard port that uses either a large 8-pin DIN connector or a small mini-DIN connector. These are electrically compatible, so you can use an adapter if you have an incompatible keyboard. As with the floppy port, the keyboard port is highly standardized. In fact, there isn't even a kernel configuration option for it; the driver is always included in the kernel. A bad keyboard connector may turn up in the BIOS POST, but that isn't guaranteed. If the keyboard doesn't work in Linux, try booting a DOS floppy or using the BIOS setup utility to see if the keyboard works in a non-Linux environment.

PS/2 mouse   Most x86 computers sold in the mid- to late-1990s used mice that connect through the PS/2 port. (The USB port began taking over this role in 2000.) These mice are standardized, although there are variants for features like scroll wheels. The Linux drivers for PS/2 mice are mature and seldom pose problems, but they do need to be included in your kernel or compiled as modules. (All major distributions include these drivers in their standard kernels or module sets.) The PS/2 port can be disabled in the BIOS, so if you're having problems, you may want to check this detail. If a PS/2 port is physically bad, you may want to replace the mouse with a model that interfaces via the RS-232 serial or USB port.

Parallel   The parallel port is most commonly used for printers, but it can also handle some scanners, cameras, and external removable-media drives. Linux's parallel port support is mature, but it requires two drivers: one for the low-level parallel port hardware and one for the device being driven. These drivers are included in all major Linux distributions' standard driver sets. Like many other motherboard-based ports, most BIOSs enable you to disable the parallel port, so you may want to check this detail if you're having problems. If necessary, you can buy an ISA or PCI add-on parallel port to replace one that's gone bad on a motherboard. USB-to-parallel adapters can serve the same role, but they're likely to be a bit slower unless they're USB 2.0 devices.

RS-232 serial   Most x86 systems include two RS-232 serial ports, but some have just one. These ports are used to connect to older mice, external modems, and various other devices. These ports are highly standardized, and the Linux drivers for them are mature and reliable. You may want to check the BIOS if you can't seem to get an RS-232 serial device to work. Replacement or add-on ISA and PCI RS-232 ports are available, and USB-to-serial adapters can also fill this role.

USB   The Universal Serial Bus (USB) port is a high-speed serial port that's much more flexible than the old RS-232 serial port. Some computers use USB keyboards and mice, and many other devices can connect in this way. If you're using a kernel numbered 2.2.17 or earlier, its USB support is very limited. For better USB support, upgrade to a 2.2.18 or 2.4.x or later kernel. Linux requires support for both the underlying USB hardware (which comes in three varieties, OHCI, UHCI, and EHCI; the last of these is for the faster USB 2.0) and for each USB peripheral. Modern Linux distributions include USB drivers, but not all USB devices are supported. Many motherboards include the option to disable USB support, so be sure it's enabled in the BIOS.

IEEE-1394   The IEEE-1394 interface is much faster than USB 1.*x*, and it is considered both an alternative and a successor to SCSI for some purposes. Linux's IEEE-1394 support is limited, but it is likely to expand in the future. Check `http://www.linux1394.org` for more information. Older motherboards lack IEEE-1394 interfaces, so you may need to buy an appropriate PCI card to handle these devices.

Network   Network ports are handled by Linux's network drivers and a network stack, as described in Chapter 6. Network interface card drivers are far from standardized, but Linux includes support for the vast majority of Ethernet cards and many cards of other types. If you have a particularly new card, you may need to replace it to get a model with Linux support. Identifying defective hardware may require booting into another OS or moving the card to another computer.

Most of these interfaces, as noted, are highly standardized, so Linux drivers shouldn't be incompatible with your hardware. Network and IEEE-1394 interfaces are not so standardized, though, and so they sometimes cause problems. There's also the potential for driver incompatibility with many expansion card devices, like SCSI host adapters, sound cards, and video capture boards.

Identifying Supported and Unsupported Hardware

Over the years, Linux has acquired an extensive collection of drivers for a wide variety of hardware. Nonetheless, Linux doesn't support every device. Figuring out which devices are supported and which aren't can be a challenge at times because Linux drivers are usually written for a device's chipset, not for a specific device by brand and model number. For instance, it's not obvious from their names that the Linux Tulip driver works with the Linksys LNE100TX Ethernet card.

To identify what hardware is supported and what isn't, you may want to consult the hardware compatibility lists maintained by various distributions. For instance, `http://hardware.redhat.com` and `http://www.linux-mandrake.com/en/hardware.php3` are good resources. The Linux Hardware Compatibility HOWTO (`http://www.tldp.org/HOWTO/Hardware-HOWTO/`) can also be an excellent resource.

Hardware compatibility varies very little from one distribution to another. The only differences result from one distribution including a nonstandard driver that another doesn't include, or from peculiarities of configuration that result in conflicts between devices. Therefore, if a device is listed as supported in one distribution, that device will almost certainly work in any other distribution.

You should also check with the hardware's manufacturer if you can't find drivers or aren't sure which drivers to use. Some manufacturers include Linux drivers (usually just the standard kernel drivers) or links to information about Linux compatibility with their products on their Web pages.

WARNING Manufacturers sometimes change their products' design without changing their names. Therefore, the presence of a product on a compatibility database, or even compatibility information on the manufacturer's Web site, may not mean that the device will work. Pay careful attention to details like a board's revision number when you are searching for compatibility information.

Using an Emergency Boot Disk

An emergency boot disk can be a useful diagnostic tool, particularly if a problem is so severe that Linux won't boot at all. Once booted, you can use an emergency system to check a disk for errors, edit configuration files, probe your hardware, and so on. Examples of Linux emergency disk systems include:

Knoppix   This system, headquartered at `http://www.knoppix.org`, is derived from Debian GNU/Linux, but boots entirely from a CD-ROM. It can be used as a demo system, installed to a hard disk, or used for emergency recovery operations. It uses compression to fit about 2GB of programs on the disk, so it's a fairly complete Linux system in its own right.

LNX-BBC   This system, like Knoppix, is designed to run Linux from a CD-ROM boot. LNX-BBC's claim to fame, though, is that it can be burned on special CD-R blanks that are the size and shape of a business card, so you can easily fit it in your wallet. This practice greatly reduces the capacity of the media, though, so LNX-BBC isn't nearly as complete as Knoppix. Consult `http://www.lnx-bbc.org` for more information on this system.

SuSE Demo   SuSE (`http://www.suse.com` or `http://www.novell.com`) makes demo versions of its distribution available for download. You can burn these to CD-R, as with Knoppix or LNX-BBC. A still larger version is available that can be burned to recordable DVDs, as well.

ZipSlack   A condensed version of Slackware (`http://www.slackware.org`), ZipSlack is designed to fit on a 100MB Zip disk, but you can fit it on other small media, such as LS-120 disks. ZipSlack is decidedly bare-bones—for instance, it doesn't provide any GUI controls by default. Nonetheless, it can be handy if you have an appropriate drive, and the fact that Zip drives can be read/write media can be a big advantage over systems that boot from CD-ROMs.

Floppy-based distributions   A plethora of truly tiny Linux distributions that boot from floppy disk are available. Examples include muLinux (`http://mulinux.sunsite.dk`) and Tom's Root/Boot (aka tomsrtbt, `http://www.toms.net/rb/`). These distributions are truly minimalistic—after all, there's only so much you can fit on a 3.5-inch floppy disk!

Using *dmesg* for System Diagnosis

The `dmesg` command can be particularly useful for diagnosing certain types of hardware and kernel problems. This command displays the contents of the *kernel ring buffer*, which is a data structure that contains recent kernel messages. Many of these messages are logged to log files, but `dmesg` displays just the kernel messages. Immediately after you start the computer, you will see the messages in the kernel ring buffer scroll past on the screen at high speed as the computer boots. These messages contain potentially important information on your system's hardware and drivers—most of the information that drivers write to the kernel ring buffer concerns whether they are loading successfully, and what devices they're controlling (such as hard disks handled by ATA or SCSI controllers).

For instance, suppose your computer has two network cards but only one works. When you examine the output of `dmesg` just after booting (say, by typing **dmesg | less**), it should reveal information on the working card, and possibly on the one that's not working, as well. If there's no entry for the missing card, chances are Linux hasn't detected the card because the driver is missing. If there is an entry for the card, chances are some other aspect of network configuration is incorrect. You can search for specific information by using `grep`, as in **dmesg | grep eth0** to find lines that refer to `eth0`. This is most effective if you know that the entries for which you're looking contain certain strings.

The output of `dmesg` immediately after booting is so important that some distributions send the output of the command to a special log file (such as `/var/log/boot.messages`). If your distribution doesn't do this, you can do it yourself by putting a line like `dmesg > /var/log/boot.messages` in your `/etc/rc.d/rc.local`, `/etc/rc.d/boot.local`, or other late startup script. As the system operates normally, the kernel ring buffer will accumulate additional messages, which will eventually displace the boot messages, so storing them at bootup can be important.

Kernel messages may also be logged by your system log daemon or by a related utility, as described in Chapter 8, "System Documentation." The popular `sysklogd` package actually contains two daemons: `syslogd` and `klogd`. The former handles traditional logging from servers and other user-mode programs, while the latter handles the logging of kernel messages. Precisely where these messages are logged varies from one distribution to another.

Summary

Configuring hardware in Linux requires a wide range of skills. Some configurations are handled differently in Linux than in other OSs, but some issues, such as disconnected cables, will cause problems in any OS. Printer configuration is particularly unusual in Linux because it relies on the presence of either a PostScript printer or Ghostscript, a PostScript interpreter that runs under Linux. Scanners can also be tricky to install and use because hardware support for scanners is somewhat spottier than it is for many devices.

Sometimes, problems arise with new hardware. Common problems include defective or overheated motherboards, CPUs, and RAM; misconfigured or defective ATA devices; and misconfigured or defective SCSI devices. Other devices can also cause problems, especially if the hardware is exotic or uses a new design. One particularly tricky type of hardware is a laptop computer. Laptop displays, power management, and PCMCIA devices all pose challenges, but not insurmountable ones.

Exam Essentials

Describe the role of .1pd **and CUPS in Linux printing.**   The line printer daemon (1pd) and CUPS play similar roles. Both accept local and remote print jobs, maintain the local print queue, call smart filters, and pass data to the printer port in an orderly fashion. CUPS is rapidly taking over from 1pd as the standard Linux printing system.

Summarize how print jobs are submitted and managed under Linux.   You use 1pr to submit a print job for printing, or an application program may call 1pr itself or implement its functionality directly. The 1pq utility summarizes jobs in a queue, 1prm can remove print jobs from a queue, and 1pc can otherwise control a print queue.

Describe the symptoms of core system (CPU, RAM, motherboard, or plug-in card) failures.   The system might not boot at all, perhaps failing during the POST or during the boot process. The computer might perform erratically or crash, or individual hardware devices may be inaccessible.

Describe precautions to ensure your and your computer's safety when modifying hardware.   Be sure to ground yourself with a wrist strap, or at least by touching a radiator or other grounded object frequently. Don't work on a computer that's running.

Identify the tools that are used to troubleshoot ATA and SCSI drives.   The Linux hdparm utility can perform speed tests and, for ATA drives, adjust the drive parameters for optimum performance. Disk failures are best detected with DOS or Windows utilities from the drive manufacturer.

Summarize steps that you should take when diagnosing problems with peripherals.   Whenever possible, the peripheral should be tested under another OS and on another computer to help isolate the cause of the problem. If the device uses a cable, replace the cable to eliminate it as a cause. If appropriate, check for the presence of a Linux driver for the device.

Describe important configuration concerns when adding ATA components.   ATA supports up to two devices per chain, and each device must be configured as a master or a slave; only one of each type is permitted per chain.

Describe important configuration concerns when adding SCSI components.   SCSI devices are configured with unique SCSI ID numbers, which range from 0 to 7 or 15, depending on the SCSI variant. The devices on the end of each SCSI chain must be properly terminated, and those in between must *not* be terminated.

Explain the relationship between major power management tools.   The APM and ACPI protocols are both implemented partially in the BIOS and partially as OS-side software. They monitor for significant power-related events and enable you to reduce the power consumed by the system. You can also minimize power consumption by hard disks by configuring them directly with hdparm.

Summarize differences between USB 1.*x***, USB 2.0, and IEEE-1394 interfaces.**   USB 1.*x* is the slowest of these interfaces, making it suitable for relatively low-speed devices, such as mice, keyboards, and low-end printers. USB 2.0 and IEEE-1394 are both much faster—fast enough to handle disks and network interfaces, if necessary.

Describe the SANE architecture.   SANE provides layers of tools to support scanning: drivers (back-ends) that talk to the scanner, support libraries (middleware), and user programs (front-ends) that receive the scan data and save it in some convenient form.

Summarize how Linux emergency disk systems may be used.   These tools enable you to boot Linux from a floppy disk, Zip disk, CD-ROM disc, or other removable disk. You can then run standard Linux tools to study your hardware, edit files on a Linux system, and otherwise perform maintenance that might not be possible if Linux won't boot.

Commands in This Chapter

Command	Description
lpr	Submits a print job to a print queue.
lpq	Displays information on jobs in a print queue.
lprm	Deletes jobs from a print queue.
lpc	Monitors and controls a print queue.
hdparm	Sets disk driver parameters and tests disk performance.
apm	Controls APM features in Linux.
acpi	Controls ACPI features in Linux.
scanimage	Basic SANE front-end; used to test scanners and perform text-mode scans.
dmesg	Displays the contents of the kernel ring buffer.

Review Questions

1. Which of the following is generally true of Linux programs that print?

    A. They send data directly to the printer port.

    B. They produce PostScript output for printing.

    C. They include extensive collections of printer drivers.

    D. They can print only with the help of add-on commercial programs.

2. Which of the following describes the function of a smart filter?

    A. It detects the type of a file and passes it through programs to make it printable on a given model of printer.

    B. It detects information in print jobs that might be confidential, as a measure against industrial espionage.

    C. It sends e-mail to the person who submitted the print job, obviating the need to wait around the printer for a printout.

    D. It detects and deletes prank print jobs that are likely to have been created by miscreants trying to waste your paper and ink.

3. Which of the following is an advantage of printer configuration tools over manual configuration?

    A. Configuration tools allow you to enter options not possible with text-based tools.

    B. Configuration tools include the ability to detect ink cartridge capacity in inkjets.

    C. Configuration tools let you configure non-PostScript printers to accept PostScript output.

    D. Configuration tools hide the details of smart filter configuration, which can be tedious to set up manually.

4. What information about print jobs does the `lpq` command display? (Choose all that apply.)

    A. The name of the application that submitted the job

    B. A numerical job ID that can be used to manipulate the job

    C. The amount of ink or toner left in the printer

    D. The username of the person who submitted the job

5. What is the purpose of the POST?

    A. To shut off power after a system shutdown

    B. To perform basic hardware tests at power-up

    C. To hand off control from LILO to the kernel

    D. To test a printer's PostScript capabilities

6. Why should you be cautious when using `hdparm`?

   A. The `hdparm` tool can set hardware options that are not supported by some hardware, thus causing data corruption.

   B. Because `hdparm` modifies partition tables, an error can result in loss of one or more partitions and all their data.

   C. By changing hardware device file mappings, you can become confused about which drive is `/dev/hda` and which is `/dev/hdb`.

   D. The `hdparm` tool can cause Linux to treat an ext2fs partition as if it were FAT, resulting in serious data corruption.

7. A SCSI chain on a single-channel SCSI card is behaving unreliably, so you examine it. You find that devices are attached to all three connectors on the SCSI host adapter, for a total of five devices. The device at the end of each cable is terminated, the cables are of high quality, and no two devices share a SCSI ID number. Which of the following is the most likely cause of the problems?

   A. None of the devices should be terminated.

   B. Only one of the devices should be terminated.

   C. Only two of the host adapter's connectors should be used.

   D. There should be only four devices attached to the host adapter.

8. You're having problems with a digital camera under Linux. You move the camera (including its cable) to another computer that runs Windows, but the camera doesn't work under Windows, either, even when you install the Windows software that came with the camera. What can you conclude?

   A. The problem is almost certainly related to the Linux drivers or camera software.

   B. The problem is very likely related to the cable or the camera hardware.

   C. The problem probably resides in the computer's interface hardware.

   D. The problem is definitely *not* related to the camera's hardware.

9. Which of the following devices are highly standardized in $x86$ systems and so have mature Linux drivers that don't vary from one model to another? (Choose all that apply.)

   A. Parallel ports

   B. Floppy ports

   C. SCSI host adapters

   D. Ethernet adapters

10. Why is it best to unplug a computer from the wall or surge protector when performing work on it?

    A. If a computer is plugged in, you're more likely to damage it with an electrostatic discharge.

    B. Modern computers have live circuits even when turned off. The current in these circuits can injure you.

    C. Unplugging the computer reduces the chance that an electrostatic charge will build up in the system, thus damaging it.

    D. External surge protectors can damage equipment if that equipment is powered off.

11. What solution might you attempt if a computer routinely generates kernel oopses on warm days but not on cool days?

    A. Replace a 4500rpm hard disk with a 7200rpm model.

    B. Upgrade the heat sink and fan on the CPU.

    C. Upgrade to a more recent kernel.

    D. Nothing; kernel oopses are normal.

12. Which of the following is a challenge of PCMCIA devices, from a Linux point of view?

    A. PCMCIA devices draw more power than Linux can support, leading to unreliable operation if APM support isn't enabled.

    B. Linux wasn't designed to expect most devices to appear and disappear randomly, as they do when a user inserts or removes a PCMCIA device.

    C. Supporting PCMCIA devices requires adding a new type of device hierarchy, which conflicts with existing device types.

    D. The only way to support PCMCIA devices is to treat them like floppies, which makes using communication devices difficult.

13. When installing an ATA hard disk, what feature might you have to set by changing a jumper setting on the disk?

    A. The drive's bus speed (33, 66, 100, or 133MB/s)

    B. The drive's termination (on or off)

    C. The drive's master or slave status

    D. The drive's ID number (0–7 or 0–15)

14. Why might you want to check the motherboard BIOS settings on a computer before installing Linux?

    A. The BIOS lets you configure the partition to be booted by default.

    B. You can use the BIOS to disable built-in hardware you plan not to use in Linux.

    C. The motherboard BIOS lets you set the IDs of SCSI devices.

    D. You can set the screen resolution using the motherboard BIOS.

15. What is the most common form of data cable in use within the Linux computer?

    A. Ribbon cable

    B. Three-wire cable

    C. Two-to-four wire cable

    D. RJ45

16. Once Linux is booted, which file can you view to see which IRQs are in use on the Linux computer?

    A. `/etc/interrupts`

    B. `/boot/interrupts`

    C. `/root/interrupts`

    D. `/proc/interrupts`

17. What is the most common IRQ assigned to RS-232 Serial Port 1?

   A. 8

   B. 7

   C. 4

   D. 1

18. Your network consists solely of Linux workstations running the 2.4.*x* kernel and later. What two sets of power management tools are most likely in place within your environment? (Choose two.)

   A. PCMCIA

   B. APM

   C. ACPI

   D. DMA

19. You are having difficulty getting a USB camera to be recognized even though you know that the USB Device Filesystem has been enabled. After calling the vendor for support, they tell you that there is no need to reconfigure the kernel, but you may have to change permissions on some of the related files in order for the device to work properly. Under which directory should you attempt such permission changes?

   A. /etc/usb

   B. /proc/bus/usb

   C. /mnt/bus

   D. /tmp/bus/usb

20. You need to add a printer definition to a stand-alone workstation running LPRng. Which file should you edit to add the printer?

   A. /etc/cups/printers.conf

   B. /etc/printcap

   C. /etc/cups/cupsd.conf

   D. /etc/rc.d/init.d/lpd

Answers to Review Questions

1. B. PostScript is the de facto printing standard for Unix and Linux programs. Linux programs generally *do not* send data directly to the printer port; on a multitasking, multiuser system, this would produce chaos because of competing print jobs. Although a few programs include printer driver collections, most forgo this in favor of generating PostScript. Printing utilities come standard with Linux; add-on commercial utilities aren't required.

2. A. The smart filter makes a print queue "smart" in that it can accept different file types (plain text, PostScript, graphics, etc.) and print them all correctly. It does not detect confidential information or prank print jobs. The lpr program in the BSD, LPD, and LPRng printing systems can be given a parameter to e-mail a user when the job finishes, but the smart filter doesn't do this.

3. D. Linux smart filter configurations can be tedious to configure in various ways, and they vary from one smart filter package to another. Although configuration tools also differ, they're somewhat easier to figure out and have similar options to one another. Configuration tools are *not* more flexible than text-based tools; after all, the configuration tools simply manipulate the underlying textual configuration files. Both configuration tools and text-based configuration procedures can invoke smart filters to print PostScript on non-PostScript printers.

4. Answers: B, D. The job ID and job owner are both displayed by lpq. Unless the application embeds its own name in the filename, that information won't be present. Most printers lack Linux utilities to query ink or toner status; certainly lpq can't do this.

5. B. POST stands for "power-on self-test." It's a BIOS routine that checks for basic functionality of core system components, such as RAM integrity and the presence of a keyboard. Most computers provide an encoded beep if the POST fails.

6. A. The hdparm program manipulates low-level options in ATA hard disk controllers, such as the use of DMA or PIO modes. If a controller is buggy or doesn't support a specified mode, the result can be data corruption or lost access to hard disks. The utility has nothing to do with partition tables, device file mappings, or filesystems per se.

7. C. SCSI chains must be one-dimensional—each after the other along a straight line. By using all three connectors on a SCSI host adapter, the configuration described creates a Y-shaped fork in the SCSI chain, which is very likely to cause data transfer errors. The device at each end of the SCSI chain should be terminated.

8. B. Because the cable and camera are the only constants in both tests, they're the most likely source of the problem. This isn't absolutely certain, though; software or interface hardware problems could exist on both test systems, thus misleading you in your diagnosis.

9. Answers: A, B. Both parallel and floppy ports are standardized on $x86$ hardware. SCSI host adapters and Ethernet adapters both come in many incompatible varieties. Linux includes drivers for most models of both types of device, but you must match the driver to the chipset used on each device.

10. B. Modern computers use a motherboard-mediated power circuit, and so they carry some current even when you turn them off if they're still plugged in. You can get an electrical shock from certain circuits if you accidentally touch them even when the power's off.

11.   B. Temperature-related problems can often be overcome by improving ventilation within the computer. Because kernel oopses are often caused by overheating CPUs, upgrading the heat sink and fan can often improve matters. Although kernel oopses can sometimes be caused by kernel bugs, the temperature-sensitive nature of the problem suggests that option C won't have any effect. Kernel oopses definitely are *not* normal. Hard disks that spin faster are likely to generate more heat than those that spin slower, so option A will most likely have no positive effect on the problem, and may make it worse.

12.   B. Linux expects most devices, like Ethernet cards and hard disks, to remain available until Linux unloads the driver. PCMCIA cards can be physically ejected by the user. This requires an extra software layer (Card Services) that helps the kernel adjust to the sudden loss of a device or its reappearance.

13.   C. ATA drives can be configured for one of two positions on an ATA chain, master or slave. (Modern drives often support auto-configuration through a "cable select" or similar option, and sometimes a single-drive configuration, but these are just different ways of setting the same feature.) Termination and ID number are characteristics of SCSI devices, not ATA devices. The drive's bus speed adjusts automatically depending on the maximum of the drive and the ATA controller.

14.   B. Motherboards with built-in RS-232 serial, parallel, ATA, audio, and other devices generally allow you to disable these devices from the BIOS setup utility. The BIOS does *not* control the boot partition, although it *does* control the boot device (floppy, CD-ROM, hard disk, and so on). SCSI host adapters have their own BIOSs, with setup utilities that are separate from those of the motherboard BIOS. (They're usually accessed separately even when the SCSI adapter is built into the motherboard.) You set the screen resolution using X configuration tools, not the BIOS.

15.   A. The most common form of data cable is a *ribbon cable*. Common ribbon cables include 34-pin floppy, 40-pin ATA, 50-pin SCSI, and 68-pin Wide SCSI. CD-ROM drives frequently sport three-wire cables to tie the CD-ROM drive's audio output to a sound card. There are also two-to-four-wire connectors that link the motherboard to front-panel computer components. RJ45 cables are used for networking over Ethernet.

16.   D. Once Linux is booted, you can check on resource consumption by examining files in the /proc filesystem. In particular, /proc/interrupts holds IRQ use information. The other choices listed do not exist as standard, dynamically updated files within Linux.

17.   C. IRQ 4 is commonly assigned to the RS-232 serial port 1. IRQ 8 is used by the real-time clock, while IRQ 7 is commonly assigned to parallel port 1 (/dev/lp0) and IRQ 1 is used by the keyboard controller.

18.   Answers: B,C. Two sets of power management tools exist: Advanced Power Management (APM) and Advanced Configuration and Power Interface (ACPI). Both require underlying support in the computer's BIOS and they fill similar roles. In the 2.4.*x* kernels, APM is mature, but ACPI is new and experimental. ACPI is more likely to be usable in late 2.4.*x* and 2.6.*x* kernels. PCMCIA is a type of hardware interface common on laptop computers; it's not a power management tool. DMA is a method of transferring data between peripherals and memory; it's not a power management tool.

19. B. Some USB devices are supported through a special /proc filesystem directory, /proc/bus/usb. You can change the permissions on certain files in this directory to enable devices without needing to reconfigure the kernel. The other choices given are not valid entries.

20. B. You can add or delete printers by editing the /etc/printcap file, which consists of printer definitions for BSD LPD or LPRng. The /etc/cups/printers.conf file holds printer definitions for CUPS, and although you can directly edit this file to add a printer, doing so is tricky. /etc/cups/cupsd.conf is the main CUPS configuration file, /etc/rc.d/init.d/lpd is the BSD LPD printing startup script on some distributions.

Glossary

Numbers

1024-cylinder limit The *x*86 BIOS has traditionally been unable to read past the 1024th cylinder in a cylinder/head/sector (CHS) addressing scheme, which has limited the size of hard disks—first to 504MB (or about 528 million bytes, so some people refer to it as the 528MB limit), then to just under 8GB. On a computer with an old BIOS, the 1024-cylinder limit prevents the system from booting a kernel from higher than this limit, although Linux itself uses addressing schemes that aren't bothered by this limit. BIOSs made since the late 1990s also include ways around the limit, if the software understands those mechanisms. See also *cylinder/head/sector (CHS) addressing*.

3DES See *Triple Data Encryption Standard (3DES)*.

A

absolute directory name A directory name that begins with a slash (/), indicating that it's to be interpreted starting from the root (/) directory.

access control list (ACL) A security system that provides a list of usernames or groups and their permissions to access a resource. ACLs are expanding and supplementing traditional Unix-style permissions on new filesystems. Ext2fs, ext3fs, JFS, and XFS all support ACLs natively, and ACL extensions for ReiserFS are available.

account Stored information and a reserved directory that allows one individual to use a computer. The term is often used and thought of as if it were a distinct virtual component of a computer that a person can use, as in "Sam logged into his account," or "Miranda's account isn't working."

ACL See *access control list (ACL)*.

ACPI See *Advanced Configuration and Power Interface (ACPI)*.

Address Resolution Protocol (ARP) A protocol used to learn a network hardware address based on an IP address.

Advanced Configuration and Power Interface (ACPI) A power management protocol. Linux provides ACPI support.

Advanced Graphics Port (AGP) A type of bus for plug-in cards that's used by graphics cards. AGP provides better performance than common forms of PCI.

Advanced Power Management (APM) A power management protocol. Linux includes better APM support than ACPI support.

Advanced Technology Attachment (ATA) A type of interface for hard disks, CD-ROM drives, tape drives, and other mass storage devices. Also often referred to as *EIDE*.

AGP See *Advanced Graphics Port (AGP)*.

AMD64   A 64-bit extension to the *x*86 CPU architecture. This architecture was created by Advanced Micro Devices (AMD) and is used in its Opteron and Athlon 64 CPUs. In 2004, Intel adopted it as well, and began using it in some Xeon CPUs. Also referred to as *x86-64*.

APM   See *Advanced Power Management (APM)*.

AppleTalk   A network protocol stack used by Apple with its Macintosh computers. AppleTalk is used primarily on local networks for file and printer sharing.

ARP   See *Address Resolution Protocol (ARP)*.

ATA   See *Advanced Technology Attachment (ATA)*.

B

Basic Input/Output System (BIOS)   A low-level software component included on a computer's motherboard in read-only memory (ROM) form. The CPU runs BIOS code when it first starts up, and the BIOS is responsible for locating and booting an OS or OS loader.

baud rate   A measure of data transmission speed, commonly used over serial lines, corresponding to the number of signal elements transmitted per second. This term is often used as a synonym for "bits per second," but many modems encode more than one bit per signal element, so the two aren't always synonymous.

binary   1. The base-2 numbering system. 2. A program or file that contains data other than plain text, such as graphics or program data. 3. The version of a program that the computer runs, as opposed to the source code version of the program.

binary package   A file that contains a compiled and ready-to-run Linux program, including necessary configuration files, documentation, and other support files.

BIOS   See *Basic Input/Output System (BIOS)*.

bit   A binary digit (0 or 1).

blowfish   An encryption algorithm used by several important Linux security tools, such as SSL and SSH.

boot loader   A program that directs the boot process. The BIOS calls the boot loader, which loads the Linux kernel or redirects the boot process to another boot loader.

boot sector   The first sector of a disk or partition. The boot sector for a bootable disk or partition includes boot loader code, although this code may be absent from nonbootable disks or partitions. See also *boot loader*.

broadband   1. High-speed (greater than 200Kbps) Internet connections delivered to homes and small businesses. 2. Networking technologies that support simultaneous transmission of data, voice, and video.

broadcast A type of network access in which one computer sends a message to many computers (typically all the computers on the sender's local network segment).

build number A number identifying minor changes made to a binary package by its maintainer, rather than changes implemented by the program's author, which are reflected in the version number.

bus A data transfer mechanism within the computer, such as the SCSI bus or the memory bus.

byte An 8-bit number, typically represented as falling between 0 and 255.

C

C library (libc) Standard programming routines used by many programs written in the C programming language. The most common Linux C library is also referred to as GNU libc (glibc).

cache memory A fast form of memory that's used to temporarily hold a subset of a larger but slower memory store. When properly implemented, caches can improve system performance. Hard disks include RAM as cache for data on disk, and computers can implement their own disk caches. Modern CPUs include a form of cache for RAM, and some motherboards include the same.

Card Services A package that helps integrate PC Card or Cardbus (a.k.a. PCMCIA) devices into Linux.

Cardbus The high-speed version of PCMCIA; provides notebook computers with support for removable network adapters, modems, SCSI interfaces, and similar hardware. See also *Card Services* and *PC Card*.

cathode ray tube (CRT) A type of computer display that uses a glass screen with an electron gun that shoots charged particles at the screen to make images. CRTs are similar to conventional television sets, but they're declining in popularity in favor of LCD monitors.

central processing unit (CPU) The main chip on a computer, which handles the bulk of its computational tasks.

checksum A simple file integrity check in which the values of individual bits or bytes are summed up and compared to a stored value for a reference version of the file.

child process A relative term referring to a process that another one has created. For instance, when you launch a program from a bash shell, the program process is a child process of the bash shell process.

chipset One or more chips that implement the main features of a motherboard or add-in board for a computer. The chipset is *not* the CPU, though; the chipset provides more specialized functions, such as the ability to control a hard disk or produce a video display.

CHS addressing See *cylinder/head/sector (CHS) addressing*.

CHS mode   See *cylinder/head/sector (CHS) mode*.

CHS translation   See *cylinder/head/sector (CHS) translation*.

CIFS   See *Common Internet Filesystem (CIFS)*.

CLI   See *command-line interface (CLI)*.

client   1. A program that initiates data transfer requests using networking protocols. 2. A computer that runs one or more client programs.

command prompt   One or more characters displayed by a shell or other program to indicate that you should type a command. Many Linux distributions use a dollar sign ($) as a command prompt for ordinary users, or a hash mark (#) as a command prompt for root.

command-line interface (CLI)   A program that interacts with the user in text mode, accepting typed commands as input and displaying results textually. See also *shell*.

Common Internet Filesystem (CIFS)   Name for an updated version of the Server Message Block (SMB) file sharing protocols. CIFS is implemented in Linux via the Samba suite. It's often used to share files with Windows computers.

compiler   A program that converts human-readable source code for a program into a binary format that the computer runs.

Complementary Metal Oxide Semiconductor (CMOS) setup utility   A part of the BIOS that gives the user the ability to control key chipset features, such as enabling or disabling built-in ports.

conditional expression   A construct of computer programming and scripting languages used to express a condition, such as the equality of two variables or the presence of a file on a disk. Conditional expressions enable a program or script to take one action in one case and another action in the other case.

console   1. The monitor and keyboard attached directly to the computer. 2. Any command prompt, such as an xterm window.

Coordinated Universal Time (UTC)   See *Greenwich Mean Time (GMT)*.

CPU   See *central processing unit (CPU)*.

cracker   An individual who breaks into computers. Crackers may do this out of curiosity, malice, for profit, or for other reasons.

creating a filesystem   Writing low-level filesystem (meaning 1) data structures to a disk. This is sometimes also called high-level formatting. See also *filesystem*.

cron job   A program or script that's run at a regular interval by the cron daemon. See also *system cron job* and *user cron job*.

CRT   See *cathode ray tube (CRT)*.

cylinder/head/sector (CHS) addressing   A method of hard disk addressing in which a triplet of numbers (a cylinder, a head, and a sector) are used to identify a specific sector. CHS addressing contrasts with linear block addressing (LBA).

cylinder/head/sector (CHS) mode   See *cylinder/head/sector (CHS) addressing.*

cylinder/head/sector (CHS) translation   Modifying one CHS addressing scheme into another. CHS translation was commonly used by BIOSs in the mid-to-late 1990s to enable the systems to use hard disks between 504MB and 8GB in capacity.

D

daemon   A program that runs constantly, providing background services. Linux servers are typically implemented as daemons, although there are a few nonserver daemons.

Data Display Channel (DDC)   A protocol that enables a computer to query a monitor for its maximum horizontal and vertical refresh rates and other vital statistics.

DDC   See *Data Display Channel (DDC).*

DDoS attack   See *distributed denial of service (DDoS) attack.*

Debian package   A package file format that originated with the Debian distribution but is now used on several other distributions. Debian packages feature excellent dependency tracking and easy installation and removal procedures.

default route   The route that network packets take if a more specific route doesn't direct them in some other way. The default route typically involves a gateway or router system that can further redirect the packets.

denial of service (DoS) attack   A type of attack on a computer or network that prevents use of a computer for its intended function, typically without actually breaking into the computer. These attacks frequently involve flooding a network or computer with useless data packets that overload the target's network bandwidth. See also *distributed denial of service (DDoS) attack.*

dependency   A requirement of one software package that another one be installed. For instance, most Linux programs include a dependency on the C library.

desktop computer   A computer that sits on a desk and that's used by an individual for productivity tasks. A desktop computer is similar to a workstation, but some people use "desktop" to refer to somewhat lower-powered computers or those without network connections. See also *workstation.*

desktop environment   A set of programs that provide a friendly graphical environment for a Linux user.

development kernel   A kernel with an odd middle number, such as 2.5.67. These kernels incorporate experimental features and are not as stable as are release kernels. See also *release kernel.*

DHCP   See *Dynamic Host Configuration Protocol (DHCP)*.

DHCP lease   A temporary assignment of an IP address to a DHCP client by a DHCP server. Clients must periodically renew their DHCP leases or risk losing the right to use the address.

direct memory access (DMA)   A means of transferring data between devices (such as sound cards or SCSI host adapters) and memory without directly involving the CPU.

Disk Operating System (DOS)   An early 16-bit *x*86 operating system. This OS is the basis for Windows 9*x*/Me, but not for Windows NT/200*x*/XP. DOS is sometimes used as a platform for disk partitioning tools or as a way to boot a Linux kernel.

disk quota   A limit on the amount of disk space that an individual or group may use.

distributed denial of service (DDoS) attack   A type of *DoS attack* in which the attacker uses many hijacked computers to cripple a computer with much better network connectivity than any one of the hijacked computers.

distribution   A complete collection of a Linux kernel and programs necessary to do work with Linux. Dozens of different Linux distributions exist, each with its own unique characteristics, but they all work in a similar way and can run the same programs, assuming similar vintages of critical support libraries like libc.

DMA   See *direct memory access (DMA)*.

DNS   See *Domain Name System (DNS)*.

domain   A collection of related computers. See also *domain name*.

domain name   A name associated with an organization or set of computers. Individual computers are assigned names within a domain, and domains can be partitioned into subdomains.

Domain Name System (DNS)   A distributed set of computers that run servers to convert between computer names (such as ns.example.com) and IP addresses (such as 192.168.45.204). DNS servers are organized hierarchically and refer requests to systems responsible for successively more specific domains.

DOS   See *Disk Operating System (DOS)*.

DoS attack   See *denial of service (DoS) attack*.

dot file   A Linux or Unix file whose name begins with a dot (.). Most Linux shells and programs hide such files from the user, so user configuration files usually come in this form to be unobtrusive in directory listings.

DRAM   See *dynamic RAM (DRAM)*.

dual inline memory module (DIMM)   One of several types of small circuit boards on which memory chips are distributed, for ease of installation in computers. DIMMs are used on some Pentium-level and later computers.

Dynamic Host Configuration Protocol (DHCP)   A protocol used on local networks for dissemination of network configuration information. A single DHCP server can maintain information for many DHCP clients, reducing overall configuration effort.

dynamic RAM (DRAM)   One of several types of RAM. Plain DRAM is now largely obsolete in desktop computers.

E

effective user ID   The owner associated with a running process. This may or may not be the same as the user ID of the individual who ran the program.

EIDE   See *Enhanced Integrated Device Electronics (EIDE)* and *Advanced Technology Attachment (ATA)*.

Enhanced Integrated Device Electronics (EIDE)   Another name for the *Advanced Technology Attachment (ATA)* interface.

envelope   In networking, the portion of a data packet that directs the transmission and routing of the packet. The envelope includes such information as the source and destination addresses and other housekeeping information.

environment variable   A setting that's available to any program running in a session. Environment variables can define features such as the terminal type being used, the path to search for executable programs, and the location of an X server for GUI programs.

Ethernet   The most common form of wired local networking.

ext2   See *Second Extended Filesystem (ext2 or ext2fs)*.

ext2fs   See *Second Extended Filesystem (ext2 or ext2fs)*.

ext3   See *Third Extended Filesystem (ext3 or ext3fs)*.

ext3fs   See *Third Extended Filesystem (ext3 or ext3fs)*.

extended INT13   BIOS routines added in the late 1990s to enable x86 computers to boot from hard disks larger than 8GB.

extended partition   A type of disk partition used on x86 systems. Extended partitions are placeholders for one or more logical partitions.

Extent Filesystem (XFS)   One of several journaling filesystems for Linux. XFS was developed by Silicon Graphics (SGI) for its IRIX OS, and then ported to Linux.

external transfer rate   The data transfer rate between one device and another. The external transfer rate is frequently applied to disks and similar devices in reference to the speed of the ATA or SCSI interface, as opposed to the speed of the drive mechanism itself. In this context, the external transfer rate is almost always higher than the internal transfer rate.

F

failed dependency   A state in which a package's dependencies are not met when attempting to install it, or in which removing a package would cause other installed packages to have unmet dependencies.

FDDI   See *Fiber Distributed Data Interface (FDDI)*.

Fiber Distributed Data Interface (FDDI)   A type of network hardware that supports up to 100Mbps speeds over fiber-optic cables.

Fibre Channel   A type of network hardware that supports up to 1062Mbps speeds over fiber-optic cables.

file access permissions   Linux's file access control mechanism. Every file has an owner, a group, and permissions that define how the owner, group members, and all other users (the "world") may access the file. Permissions include read, write, and execute for the owner, group, and world.

file owner   The account with which a file is most strongly associated. The owner often has permission to do more with a file than other users can do.

file permissions   See *file access permissions*.

file sharing protocol   A network protocol that enables one computer to access files stored on a second computer as if the second computer's files were local to the first computer. Examples include SMB/CIFS (used on Windows-dominated networks), NFS (used on Unix-dominated networks), and AppleShare (used on Macintosh-dominated networks).

file type code   A special code that identifies the type of a file, such as a regular file, a directory, or a device file.

filename completion   A feature of some shells that enables them to complete a command or filename when you press the Tab key.

filesystem   1. The low-level data structures recorded on a disk in order to direct the placement of file data. The filesystem determines characteristics like the maximum partition size, the file-naming rules, and what extra data (time stamps, ownership, and so on) may be associated with a file. 2. The overall layout of files and directories on a computer. For instance, a Linux filesystem includes a root directory (/), several directories falling off this (/usr, /var, /boot, etc.), subdirectories of these, and so on.

firewall   1. A program or kernel configuration that blocks access to specific ports or network programs on a computer. 2. A computer that's configured as a router and that includes firewall software that can restrict access between the networks it manages.

FireWire   A name for IEEE-1394 that's favored by Apple.

font server   A program that provides font bitmaps to client programs on the same or (sometimes) other computers. The font server may work directly from font bitmaps, or it may generate the bitmaps from outline fonts such as PostScript Type 1 or TrueType fonts.

fork   The method by which one process creates another process.

forwarding-only DNS server   A DNS server that doesn't perform a *full recursive DNS lookup* for clients, but instead forwards the whole request to another DNS server. This configuration is common on small networks, and can improve overall DNS performance for a network.

fragmented   Adjective describing files whose contents are split across several parts of a disk, rather than placed contiguously. File fragmentation tends to degrade disk performance because it increases head movements when reading files.

frame   In networking, a data packet associated with network hardware (such as Ethernet), as opposed to the software (such as TCP/IP).

frame buffer   A low-level but standardized interface between software and video hardware. X uses a frame buffer interface on many non-*x*86 computers.

frequently asked question (FAQ)   1. A question that's asked frequently, particularly on Usenet newsgroups or other online discussion forums. 2. A document that collects many FAQs (meaning 1) and their answers.

full duplex   A mode of communication in which data can be transferred in two directions at the same time.

full recursive DNS lookup   A method of name resolution in which the DNS server queries a series of DNS servers, each of which has information on more and more specific networks, in order to locate the IP address associated with a hostname.

G

gateway   A computer that functions as a router between two networks.

GID   See *group ID (GID)*.

gigabit Ethernet   A variety of Ethernet that can transfer 1,000 megabits (1 gigabit) per second.

glibc   A specific type of C library used on Linux systems since the late 1990s.

GMT   See *Greenwich Mean Time (GMT)*.

GNU   Recursive acronym for GNU's Not Unix. GNU is a Free Software Foundation (FSF) project whose goal is to build an entirely open source OS that works like Unix. The term is also used by some non-FSF projects.

GNU/Linux   Generic term for a complete Linux OS to distinguish the complete OS from the kernel alone. This term is favored by Debian; most other distributions use "Linux" alone.

Grand Unified Boot Loader (GRUB)   A popular boot loader for Linux. Can boot a Linux kernel or redirect the boot process to another boot loader in a non-Linux partition, thus booting other OSs. Similar to the competing Linux Loader (LILO). See also *boot loader*.

graphical user interface (GUI)   A method of human/computer interaction characterized by a graphical display, a mouse to move a pointer around the screen, and the ability to perform actions by pointing at objects on the screen and clicking a mouse button.

Greenwich Mean Time (GMT)   The time in Greenwich, England, unadjusted for daylight savings. Linux systems use this time internally and adjust to local time by knowing the system's time zone.

group   A collection of users. Files are owned by a user and a group, and group members may be given access to files independent of the owner and all other users. This feature may be used to enhance collaborative abilities by giving members of a group read/write access to particular files, while still excluding those who aren't members of the group. It can also be used by system administrators to control access to system files and resources.

group administrator   A person with administrative authority over a group. A group administrator can add or delete members from a group and perform similar administrative tasks.

group ID (GID)   A number associated with a particular group. Similar to a user ID (UID).

group owner   The group with which a file is most strongly associated, after the file owner.

GRUB   See *Grand Unified Boot Loader (GRUB)*.

GUI   See *graphical user interface (GUI)*.

H

hacker   1. An individual who is skilled at using or programming computers and who enjoys using these skills in constructive ways. Many Linux programmers consider themselves hackers in this sense of the term. 2. A cracker (see also *cracker*). This use of the term is more prevalent in the mass media, but it is frowned upon in the Linux community.

half-duplex   A type of data transmission in which data can be sent in only one direction at a time.

hard link   A directory entry for a file that has another directory entry. All hard links are equally valid ways of accessing a file, and all must be deleted in order to delete a file. See also *soft link*.

hardware address   A code that uniquely identifies a single network interface. This address is built into the device itself rather than assigned in Linux.

hash   An encryption method in which a file or string is encoded in a manner that cannot be reversed. Hashes are commonly used for password storage and as a more secure variant on checksums, among other things. See also *checksum*.

header files   Files that contain interface definitions for software routines contained in a library. Program source code that uses a library must refer to the associated header files.

High-Performance Parallel Interface (HIPPI)   A type of network hardware that supports speeds of up to 1600Mbps over fiber-optic cabling.

HIPPI   See *High-Performance Parallel Interface (HIPPI)*.

home directory   A directory associated with an account, in which the user's files reside.

hostname   A computer's human-readable name, such as `persephone.example.com`.

hot standby   An optional feature of RAID arrays in which a spare drive may be automatically activated by the software if it detects that one of the main drives has failed.

hot swapping   Adding or removing hardware while the computer is turned on.

HOWTO documents   Linux documentation that describes how to accomplish some task or use a particular program. HOWTOs are usually tutorial in nature. They're archived at `http://tldp.org`, and all major distributions ship with them as well.

HTTP   See *Hypertext Transfer Protocol (HTTP)*.

hub   A type of network hardware that serves as a central exchange point in a network. Each computer has a cable that links to the hub, so all data pass through the hub. Hubs echo all data they receive to all the other computers to which they connect. See also *switch*.

hung   Term used to describe a program that's stopped responding to user input, network requests, or other types of input to which it should respond. Hung processes sometimes consume a great deal of CPU time.

Hypertext Transfer Protocol (HTTP)   A protocol used for transferring Web pages from a Web server to a Web browser.

I

IEEE-1394   An external bus technology that's used to connect high-speed external devices such as hard disks, scanners, and video equipment. IEEE-1394 is slowly gaining in popularity. Linux 2.4.*x* added limited IEEE-1394 support.

IMAP   See *Internet Message Access Protocol (IMAP)*.

incremental backup   A type of backup in which only files that have changed since the last backup are backed up. This is used to reduce the time required to back up a computer, at the cost of potentially greater restoration complexity.

Industry Standard Architecture (ISA)   The expansion bus used on the original IBM PC. Most manufacturers began dropping ISA from their motherboards around 2001. ISA is inferior to PCI in most respects, but it has a huge installed base.

info pages   A type of documentation similar to man pages (see *man pages*), but with a more complex hyperlinked structure within each document. The FSF and some other developers now favor info pages over man pages.

inode   A filesystem (meaning 1) data structure that contains critical information on the file, such as its size and location on the disk.

input/output (I/O)   A term that describes the acceptance of data from an external source or the sending of data to an external source. In some cases, the "external source" may be internal to the computer, as in I/O between a hard disk and the CPU or memory. In other cases, I/O is more clearly external, as in network I/O.

installed file database   A database of files installed via the computer's package manager (such as RPM or Debian), as well as associated information such as dependencies. Also called the package database.

internal transfer rate   The rate of data transfer within a device. This is typically applied to hard disks and similar devices to describe how quickly they can read or write data from their physical media.

internet   Any collection of networks linked together by routers. See also *Internet*.

Internet   The largest network on Earth, which connects computers from around the globe. When used in this way, the word is always capitalized. See also *internet*.

Internet Message Access Protocol (IMAP)   A protocol for exchanging mail messages. The recipient initiates an IMAP session. IMAP differs from POP in that IMAP enables the recipient to leave messages in organized folders on the server; POP requires that the recipient download the messages to organize them.

Internet Packet Exchange (IPX)   A protocol that underlies much of Novell's original networking protocols. Despite the name, this protocol is unrelated to the Internet.

Internet Printing Protocol (IPP)   A relatively new protocol for printing on a network.

interrupt request (IRQ)   A method by which peripherals (SCSI host adapters, sound cards, etc.) signal that they require attention from the CPU. An IRQ also refers to a specific interrupt signal line. The $x86$ architecture supports 16 IRQs, numbered 0–15, but IRQs 2 and 9 are linked, so in practice, there are only 15 IRQs, and many of these are used by basic hardware like floppy disks.

intrusion detection system (IDS)   Software that can detect suspicious activity on a computer or network and alert an operator to this activity.

I/O   See *input/output (I/O)*.

IP address   A computer's numeric TCP/IP address, such as 192.168.45.203.

IPP   See *Internet Printing Protocol (IPP)*.

IPv6   The "next-generation" Internet Protocol. This upgrade to TCP/IP allows for a theoretical maximum of approximately 3.4×10^{38} addresses, as opposed to the 4 billion addresses possible with the IPv4 that's in common use in 2005.

IPX   See *Internet Package Exchange (IPX)*.

IRQ   See *interrupt request (IRQ)*.

ISA   See *Industry Standard Architecture (ISA)*.

J

JFS   See *Journaled Filesystem (JFS)*.

Journaled Filesystem (JFS)   One of several journaling filesystems for Linux. JFS was developed by IBM for its AIX OS. A subsequent implementation was created for OS/2, and Linux's JFS is derived from this code.

journaling filesystem   A type of filesystem that maintains a record of its operations. Such filesystems can typically recover quickly after a power failure or system crash. Common Linux journaling filesystems are ext3fs, ReiserFS, JFS, and XFS. See also *filesystem*.

K

kernel   The core program of any OS. The kernel provides interfaces between the software and the hardware and controls the operation of all other programs. Technically, the Linux kernel is the *only* component that is Linux; everything else, such as shells, X, and libraries, is available on other Unix-like systems.

kernel module   A driver or other kernel-level program that may be loaded or unloaded as required.

kernel module autoloader   A utility that loads and unloads kernel modules as required by the kernel, obviating the need to manually load and unload kernel modules.

kernel ring buffer   A record of recent messages generated by the Linux kernel. Immediately after a Linux system boots, this buffer contains the bootup messages generated by drivers and major kernel subsystems. This buffer may be viewed with the `dmesg` command.

L

LBA   See *linear block addressing (LBA)*.

LCD   See *liquid crystal display (LCD)*.

libc   See *C library (libc)*.

library   A collection of code that's potentially useful to many programs. This code is stored in special files to save disk space and RAM when running programs that use the library.

LILO   See *Linux Loader (LILO)*.

linear block addressing (LBA)   A method of accessing data on a disk that uses a single sector number to retrieve data from that sector. LBA contrasts with cylinder/head/sector (CHS) addressing. Some sources refer to LBA as *logical* block addressing.

Linux   1. The open source kernel designed by Linus Torvalds as the core of a Unix-like operating system (OS). 2. A complete OS built around Linus Torvalds's kernel. See also *GNU/Linux*.

Linux Loader (LILO)   A popular Linux boot loader. Can boot a Linux kernel or redirect the boot process to another boot loader in a non-Linux partition, thus booting other OSs. Similar to the competing Grand Unified Boot Loader (GRUB). See also *boot loader*.

liquid crystal display (LCD)   A type of flat-panel display that's common on laptops and is becoming more common on desktop systems. LCDs are lightweight and consume little electricity, but they're more expensive to produce than are conventional monitors.

load average   A measure of the demands for CPU time by running programs. A load average of 0 means no demand for CPU time; 1 represents a single program placing constant demand on the CPU; and values higher than 1 represent multiple programs competing for CPU time. The `top` and `uptime` commands both provide load average information.

LocalTalk   A type of network hardware common on older Macintosh networks.

log file   A text file maintained by the system as a whole or an individual server, in which important system events are recorded. Log files typically include information on user logins, server access attempts, and automatic routine maintenance.

log file rotation   See *log rotation*.

log rotation   A routine maintenance process in which the computer suspends recording data in log files, renames them, and opens new log files. This process keeps log files available for a time, but ultimately it deletes them, preventing them from growing to consume all available disk space.

logical block addressing (LBA)   See *linear block addressing (LBA)*.

logical partition   A type of *x*86 hard disk partition that has no entry in the primary partition table. Instead, logical partitions are carried within an extended partition.

loop   A programming or scripting construct enabling multiple executions of a segment of code. Typically terminated through the use of a conditional expression.

M

MAC address   See *Media Access Control (MAC) address*.

machine name   The portion of a hostname that identifies a computer on a network, as opposed to the network as a whole (for instance, `gingko` is the machine name portion of `gingkgo.example.com`). The machine name is sometimes used in reference to the entire hostname.

main memory   The main type of RAM in a computer, as opposed to cache memory.

major version number   The first number in a program's version number. For instance, if a program's version number is 1.2.3, the major version number is 1.

man pages   An electronic "manual" for a program, configuration file, system call, or other feature of the system. Man pages are accessed by typing **man** followed by the program or other topic you want to learn about, as in **man man** to learn about the man pages system itself.

master   One of two ATA devices on a single ATA chain. The master device gets a lower Linux device letter than the slave device does.

Master Boot Record (MBR)   The first sector of a hard disk. The MBR contains code that the BIOS runs during the boot process, as well as the primary partition table.

MBR   See *Master Boot Record (MBR)*.

MD4 password   See *Message Digest 4 (MD4) password*.

MD5 password   See *Message Digest 5 (MD5) password*.

Media Access Control (MAC) address   A low-level address associated with a piece of network hardware. The MAC address is usually stored on the hardware itself, and it is used for local network addressing only. Addressing between networks (such as on the Internet) uses higher-level addresses, such as an IP address.

Message Digest 4 (MD4) password   A password stored using the Message Digest 4 (MD4) hash. MD4 passwords are common on Windows systems, and are also used by Samba's encrypted password system.

Message Digest 5 (MD5) password   A password that's stored using the Message Digest 5 (MD5) hash. Recent Linux systems generally use MD5 passwords.

mode   The permissions of a file. In conjunction with the file's owner and group, the mode determines who may access a file and in what ways.

mode lines   Definition of the timings required by particular video resolutions running at particular refresh rates.

modem   This word is short for "modulator/demodulator." It's a device for transferring digital data over an analog transmission medium. Traditionally, the analog transmission medium has been the normal telephone network, but the word "modem" is increasingly being applied to devices used for broadband Internet access as well.

module   A kernel driver or other kernel component that's stored in a separate file. Linux can load modules on demand or on command, saving RAM when modules aren't in use and reducing the size of the kernel.

motherboard   The main circuit board in a computer. The CPU, RAM, and add-on cards typically plug directly into the motherboard, although some designs place some of these components on extender cards. The motherboard is also sometimes referred to as the mainboard or the system board.

mount   1. The process of adding a filesystem (meaning 1) to a directory tree. 2. A command of the same name that performs this task.

mount point   A directory to which a new filesystem (meaning 1) is attached. Mount points are typically empty directories before their host filesystems are mounted.

N

NetBEUI   A network stack similar to AppleTalk or TCP/IP in broad outline, but used primarily on local networks.

NetBIOS   Networking protocols that are often used in conjunction with NetBEUI or TCP/IP. NetBIOS underlies the SMB/CIFS file sharing protocols used by Microsoft Windows and implemented in Linux by Samba.

netmask   See *network mask*.

Network Filesystem (NFS)   A file sharing protocol used among Linux and Unix computers.

Network Information Service (NIS)   A network protocol that enables computers to share simple database files. Commonly used to provide centralized login authentication and as a substitute for DNS on small networks.

network mask   A bit pattern that identifies the portion of an IP address that's an entire network and the part that identifies a computer on that network. The pattern may be expressed as 4 decimal bytes separated by dots (as in 255.255.255.0) or as the number of network bits following an IP address and a slash (as in 192.168.45.203/24). The network mask is also referred to as the netmask or subnet mask.

NFS   See *Network Filesystem (NFS)*.

NIS   See *Network Information Service (NIS)*.

node   An individual page in an info page (see *info pages*).

non-volatile RAM (NVRAM)   A type of memory that retains data even after power is cut off. NVRAM is commonly used to store BIOS settings.

O

open mail relay   An SMTP mail server that's configured to relay mail from anywhere to anywhere. Open mail relays are frequently abused by spammers to obfuscate their messages' true origins.

open port   A network port that's being used by a server program and that's accessible by outside systems. Ports that are open unnecessarily pose a security risk, and should be closed.

Open System Interconnection (OSI) model   A means of describing network stacks, such as TCP/IP, NetBEUI, or AppleTalk. In the OSI model, such stacks are broken down into several layers, each of which communicates directly with the layers above and below it.

OSI model   See *Open System Interconnection (OSI) model.*

P

package database   See *installed file database.*

packet   A limited amount of data collected together with an envelope and sent over a network. See also *envelope.*

packet filter firewall   A type of firewall that operates on individual network data packets, passing or rejecting packets based on information such as the source and destination addresses and ports.

packet sniffer   A program that monitors network traffic at a low level, enabling diagnosis of problems and capturing data. Packet sniffers can be used both for legitimate network diagnosis and for data theft.

parallel ATA (PATA)   The traditional form of ATA interface, in which several bits are transferred at once. See also *serial ATA (SATA).*

parameter   An option passed to a program on a command line, or occasionally as part of a configuration file.

parent process   A relative term referring to the process that started another. For instance, if you launch a program from a bash shell, the bash shell process is the new program's parent process.

partition   A contiguous part of a hard disk that's set aside to hold a single filesystem (meaning 1). Also used as a verb to describe the process of creating partitions on a hard disk.

partition table   The disk data structure that describes the layout of partitions on a hard disk.

PATA   See *parallel ATA (PATA).*

path   A colon-delimited list of directories in which program files may be found. (Similar lists define the locations of directories, fonts, and other file types.)

payload   The portion of a network data packet that contains the actual data to be transmitted, as opposed to the envelope.

PC Card   A type of expansion card that's common on laptop computers. This interface is commonly used for Ethernet cards, modems, and storage devices. Also known as PCMCIA. A higher-speed variant is Cardbus.

PCI   See *Peripheral Component Interconnect (PCI)*.

PCL   See *Printer Control Language (PCL)*.

PCMCIA   See *Personal Computer Memory Card International Association (PCMCIA)*.

peripheral   A device that connects to and is controlled by a computer. Many peripherals, such as Web cams and keyboards, are external to the computer's main box. Some definitions include devices that reside within the computer's main box, such as hard disks and CD-ROM drives.

Peripheral Component Interconnect (PCI)   An expansion bus capable of much higher speeds than the older ISA bus. Modern computers usually include several PCI slots.

permission bit   A single bit used to define whether a given user or class of users has a particular type of access to a file. For instance, the owner's execute permission bit determines whether the owner can run a file as a program. The permission bits together comprise the file's mode.

Personal Computer Memory Card International Association (PCMCIA)   1. An earlier name for PC Card and Cardbus (but one that's still used by many Linux utilities and documentation). 2. The trade group that developed the PC Card and Cardbus standards.

phishing   The process of sending bogus e-mail or putting up fake Web sites with the goal of collecting sensitive personal information (typically credit card numbers).

PIO   See *Programmed Input/Output (PIO)*.

pipe   A method of executing two programs so that one program's output serves as the second program's input. Piped programs are separated in a Linux shell by a vertical bar (|).

pipeline   See *pipe*.

Point-to-Point Protocol (PPP)   A method of initiating a TCP/IP connection between two computers over an RS-232 serial line or modem.

port number   A number that identifies the program from which a data packet comes or to which it's addressed. When a program initiates a network connection, it associates itself with one or more ports, enabling other computers to uniquely address the program.

Post Office Protocol (POP)   A mail server protocol in which the recipient initiates transfer of messages. POP differs from IMAP in that POP doesn't provide any means for the recipient to organize and store messages on the server.

PostScript   A programming language used on many high-end printers. PostScript is optimized for displaying text and graphics on the printed page. The Linux program Ghostscript converts from PostScript to bitmapped formats understood by many low-end and mid-range printers.

PostScript Printer Definition (PPD)   A configuration file that provides information on a printer's capabilities—its paper size, whether it prints in color, and so on.

PPD   See *PostScript Printer Definition (PPD)*.

PPP   See *Point-to-Point Protocol (PPP)*.

Preboot Execution Environment (PXE)   A system supported by most modern BIOSs, enabling them to boot from a network server via a supported network card. PXE is used by some Linux thin clients (see *thin client*).

primary boot loader   The first boot loader run by the BIOS.

primary partition   A type of *x*86 partition that's defined in a data structure contained in the hard disk's partition table in the MBR. An *x*86 computer can host only four primary partitions per hard disk.

print queue   A storage place for files waiting to be printed.

Printer Control Language (PCL)   A language developed by Hewlett-Packard for controlling printers. (Many of Hewlett-Packard's competitors now use PCL.) PCL is most commonly found on mid-range laser printers, but some inkjet printers also support the language. Several PCL variants exist, the most common ranging from PCL 3 to PCL 6.

printer driver   A software component that converts printable data generated by an application into a format that's suitable for a specific model of printer. In Linux, printer drivers usually reside in Ghostscript, but some applications include a selection of printer drivers to print directly to various printers.

privileged port   A port (see *port number*) that's numbered below 1024. Linux restricts access to such ports to root. In computing's early days, any program running on a privileged port could be considered trustworthy, because only programs configured by professional system administrators could be run on such ports. Today, that's no longer the case. See also *unprivileged port*.

process   A piece of code that's maintained and run by the Linux kernel separately from other pieces of code. Most processes correspond to programs that are running. One program can be run multiple times, resulting in several processes.

Programmed Input/Output (PIO)   A method of data transfer between memory and expansion cards in which the CPU actively performs the transfer. PIO tends to consume much more CPU time than DMA does.

protocol stack   A collection of drivers, kernel procedures, and other software that implements a standard means of communicating across a network. Two computers must support compatible protocol stacks to communicate. The most popular protocol stack today is TCP/IP.

pull mail protocol   A mail protocol in which the recipient initiates the transfer. Examples include POP and IMAP.

push mail protocol   A mail protocol in which the sender initiates the transfer. SMTP is the most common push mail protocol.

PXE   See *Preboot Execution Environment (PXE)*.

R

RAID   See *redundant array of independent disks (RAID)*.

RAMbus Dynamic RAM (RDRAM)   A type of RAM used in RIMMs.

random access   A method of access to a storage device (RAM, hard disk, etc.) in which information may be stored or retrieved in an arbitrary order with little or no speed penalty. See also *sequential access*.

RDRAM   See *RAMbus Dynamic RAM (RDRAM)*.

RDRAM Inline Memory Module (RIMM)   A small circuit board that holds memory chips configured as RDRAM. Used in some Pentium II and later computers.

redirection   A procedure in which a program's standard output is sent to a file rather than to the screen, or in which the program's standard input is obtained from a file rather than from the keyboard. See also *standard input* and *standard output*.

redundant array of independent disks (RAID)   A collection of two or more disks that are treated as a single physical hard disk. RAID can improve speed, reliability, or both, depending on precisely how it's configured. It can be implemented in special hardware RAID controllers or via special kernel options and Linux configuration.

regular expression   A method of matching textual information that may vary in important ways but that contains commonalities. The regular expression captures the commonalities and uses various types of wildcards to match variable information.

ReiserFS   One of several journaling filesystems for Linux. ReiserFS was developed from scratch for Linux.

relative directory name   A directory name that's specified relative to the current directory. Relative directory names often include the parent specification (..), which indicates the current directory's parent.

release kernel   A kernel with an even second number, such as 2.4.22 or 2.6.1. Release kernels should have few bugs, but they sometimes lack drivers for the latest hardware. See also *development kernel*.

release number   See *build number*.

remote login server   A type of server that enables individuals at distant locations to use a computer. Examples include Telnet, SSH, and XDM.

Request for Comments (RFC)   An Internet standards document. RFCs define how protocols like Telnet and SMTP operate, thus enabling tools developed by different companies or individuals to interoperate.

RFC   See *Request for Comments (RFC)*.

ribbon cable   A type of cable in which insulated wires are laid side by side, typically bound together by plastic. The result is a wide but thin multiconductor cable that resembles a ribbon.

RIMM   See *RDRAM Inline Memory Module (RIMM)*.

root directory   The directory that forms the base of a Linux filesystem (meaning 2). All other directories are accessible from the root directory, either directly or via intermediate directories.

root DNS servers   A set of DNS servers that deliver information to other DNS servers about top-level domains (`.com`, `.net`, `.us`, and so on). DNS servers consult the root DNS servers first when performing full recursive DNS lookups.

root filesystem   The filesystem (meaning 1) on a Linux system that corresponds to the root directory, and often several directories based on it.

root kit   A set of scripts and other software that enable script kiddies to break into computers.

root partition   The partition associated with the root filesystem.

rooted   An adjective describing a computer that's been compromised to the point where the intruder has full **root** access to the system.

router   A computer that transfers data between networks. See also *gateway*.

RPM   See *RPM Package Manager (RPM)*.

RPM Package Manager (RPM)   A package file format and associated utilities designed by Red Hat but now used on many other distributions as well. RPM features excellent dependency tracking and easy installation and removal procedures.

runlevel   A number associated with a particular set of services that are being run. Changing runlevels changes services or can shut down or restart the computer.

S

Samba Web Administration Tool (SWAT)   A server that allows administrators to configure Samba servers from another computer by using an ordinary Web browser.

SAS   See *Serial Attached SCSI (SAS)*.

SATA   See *Serial ATA (SATA)*.

script kiddies   Individuals with little knowledge or skill, who break into computers using scripts created by others. Such break-ins often leave obvious traces, and script kiddies frequently cause collateral damage that produces system instability.

scripting language   Interpreted computer programming language designed for writing small utilities to automate simple but repetitive tasks. Examples include Perl, Python, Tcl, and shell scripting languages like those used by bash and `tcsh`.

SCSI   See *Small Computer System Interface (SCSI)*.

Second Extended Filesystem (ext2 or ext2fs)   The most common filesystem (meaning 1) in Linux from the mid-1990s through approximately 2001.

secondary boot loader   A boot loader that's launched by another boot loader.

Secure Shell (SSH)   A remote login protocol and program that uses encryption to ensure that intercepted data packets cannot be used by an interloper. Generally regarded as the successor to Telnet on Linux systems.

Sequenced Packet Exchange (SPX)   Part of the Novell networking stack, along with IPX.

sequential access   A method of accessing a storage medium that requires reading or writing data in a specific order. The most common example is a tape; to read data at the end of a tape, you must wind past the interceding data. See also *random access*.

Serial ATA (SATA)   A type of ATA interface that uses serial data transfer rather than the parallel data transfers used in older forms of ATA. See also *parallel ATA (PATA)*.

Serial Attached SCSI (SAS)   A type of SCSI interface that uses serial data transfer rather than the parallel data transfers used in older forms of SCSI.

server   1. A program that responds to data transfer requests using networking protocols. 2. A computer that runs one or more server programs.

Server Message Block (SMB)   A file sharing protocol common on Windows-dominated networks. SMB is implemented in Linux via the Samba suite. Also known as the Common Internet Filesystem (CIFS).

server program   See *server*, meaning 1.

set group ID (SGID)   A special type of file permission used on program files to make the program run with the permissions of its group. (Normally, the user's group permissions are used.)

set user ID (SUID)   A special type of file permission used on program files to make the program run with the permissions of its owner, rather than those of the user who runs the program.

SGID   See *set group ID (SGID)*.

shadow password   A method of storing encrypted passwords separately from most other account information. This allows the passwords to reside in a file with tighter security options than the rest of the account information, which improves security when compared to storing all the account information in one file with looser permissions.

share   In file sharing protocols, and particularly in SMB/CIFS, a named network resource associated with a directory or printer that's being shared. May also be used as a verb to describe the process of making the share available.

shell   A program that provides users with the ability to run programs, manipulate files, and so on.

shell script   A program written in a language that's built into a shell.

signal   In reference to processes, a signal is a code that the kernel uses to control the termination of the process or to tell it to perform some task. Signals can be used to kill processes.

SIMM   See *Single Inline Memory Module (SIMM)*.

Simple Mail Transfer Protocol (SMTP)   The most common push mail protocol on the Internet. SMTP is implemented in Linux by servers such as sendmail, Postfix, Exim, and qmail.

Simple Network Management Protocol (SNMP)   A protocol for reporting on the status of a computer over a network, or adjusting a computer's settings remotely.

Single Inline Memory Module (SIMM)   A small circuit board that holds memory chips for easy installation in a computer. SIMMs come in 30- and 72-pin varieties. They were used on 80386, 80486, many Pentium-level, and a few Pentium II systems. They are still used in many peripherals such as printers.

slave   The second of two possible devices on a parallel ATA chain. The slave device has a higher Linux device letter than the master device does.

Small Computer System Interface (SCSI)   An interface standard for hard disks, CD-ROM drives, tape drives, scanners, and other devices.

Small Outline (SO) DIMM   A type of DIMM that's physically smaller than conventional DIMMs. Most commonly used to add RAM to notebook computers.

smart filter   A program, run as part of a print queue, that determines the type of a file and passes it through appropriate programs to convert it to a format that the printer can handle.

SMB   See *Server Message Block (SMB)*.

SMTP   See *Simple Mail Transfer Protocol (SMTP)*.

SNMP   See *Simple Network Management Protocol (SNMP)*.

SO DIMM   See *Small Outline (SO) DIMM*.

social engineering   The practice of convincing individuals to disclose sensitive information without arousing suspicion. Social engineers may pretend to be system administrators to ask for passwords, for instance. See also *phishing*.

soft link   A type of file that refers to another file on the computer. When a program tries to access a soft link, Linux passes the contents of the linked-to file to the program. If the linked-to program is deleted, the soft link stops working. Deleting the soft link doesn't affect the original file. Also referred to as a symbolic link. See also *hard link*.

software modem   Modems that implement key functionality in software that must be run by the host computer. These modems require special drivers, which are uncommon in Linux.

source package   A file that contains complete source code for a program. The package may be compiled into a binary package, which can then be installed on the computer.

source RPM   A type of source package that uses the RPM file format.

spam   Unsolicited bulk e-mail.

spawn   The action of one process starting another.

spool directory   A directory in which print jobs, mail, or other files wait to be processed. Spool directories are maintained by specific programs, such as the printing system or SMTP mail server.

SPX   See *Sequenced Packet Exchange (SPX)*.

SSH   See *Secure Shell (SSH)*.

stable kernel   See *release kernel*.

standard input   The default method of delivering input to a program. It normally corresponds to the keyboard at which you type.

standard output   The default method of delivering purely text-based information from a program to the user. It normally corresponds to a text-mode screen, xterm window, or the like.

startup script   A script that controls part of the Linux boot process.

stateful packet inspection   A firewall tool in which a packet's state (that is, whether it's marked to begin a transaction, to continue an existing exchange, and so on) is considered in the filtering process.

sticky bit   A special file permission bit that's most commonly used on directories. When set, only a file's owner may delete the file, even if the directory in which it resides can be modified by others.

subdomain   A subdivision of a domain. A subdomain may contain computers or subdomains of its own.

subnet mask   See *network mask*.

SUID   See *set user ID (SUID)*.

super server   A server that listens for network connections intended for other servers and launches those servers. Examples on Linux are `inetd` and `xinetd`.

superuser   A user with extraordinary rights to manipulate critical files on the computer. The superuser's username is normally `root`.

swap file   A disk file configured to be used as swap space.

swap partition   A disk partition configured to be used as swap space.

swap space   Disk space used as an extension to a computer's RAM. Swap space enables a system to run more programs or to process larger data sets than would otherwise be possible.

SWAT   See *Samba Web Administration Tool (SWAT)*.

switch   A type of network hardware that serves as a central exchange point in a network. Each computer has a cable that links to the switch, so all data pass through the switch. A switch usually sends data only to the computer to which it's addressed. See also *hub*.

symbolic link   See *soft link*.

system cron job   A cron job that handles system-wide maintenance tasks, like log rotation or deletion of unused files from /tmp. See also *user cron job*.

System V (SysV)   A form of AT&T Unix that defined many of the standards used on modern Unix systems and Unix clones, such as Linux.

SysV   See *System V (SysV)*.

SysV startup script   A type of startup script that follows the System V startup standards. Such a script starts one service or related set of services.

T

tarball   A package file format based on the tar utility. Tarballs are easy to create and are readable on any version of Linux, or most non-Linux systems. They contain no dependency information and the files they contain are not easy to remove once installed, however.

TCP/IP   See *Transmission Control Protocol/Internet Protocol (TCP/IP)*.

Telnet   A protocol used for performing remote text-based logins to a computer. Telnet is a poor choice for connections over the Internet because it passes all data, including passwords, in an unencrypted form, which is a security risk. See also *Secure Shell (SSH)*.

terminal program   A program that's used to initiate a simple text-mode connection between two computers, especially via a modem or RS-232 serial connection.

text editor   A program for editing text files on a computer.

TFTP   See *Trivial File Transfer Protocol (TFTP)*.

thin client   A very simple computer that provides a display, a keyboard, a mouse, and a network connection to another computer, which does most of the computational work. Using thin clients can be a way to cut costs compared to equipping every user with a modern desktop system.

Third Extended Filesystem (ext3 or ext3fs)   A variant of the *Second Extended Filesystem (ext2 or ext2fs)* that adds a journal to reduce startup times after a power failure or system crash. See also *journaling filesystem*.

Token Ring   A type of network hardware that supports speeds of up to 16Mbps or 100Mbps on twisted-pair cabling.

Transmission Control Protocol/Internet Protocol (TCP/IP)   A very popular network stack, and the one on which the Internet is built.

Triple Data Encryption Standard (3DES)   A data encryption standard.

Trivial File Transfer Protocol (TFTP)   A simple file transfer protocol that's most commonly used to provide files to computers, such as thin clients, that boot off of the network rather than from a local disk.

U

UID   See *user ID (UID)*.

umask   See *user mask (umask)*.

Universal Serial Bus (USB)   A type of interface for low- to medium-speed external devices, such as keyboards, mice, cameras, modems, scanners, and removable disk drives. Linux added USB support with the 2.2.18 and 2.4.*x* kernels. USB 2.0 increases the speed to the point that USB is useable for hard disks in less demanding applications.

unprivileged port   A port (see *port number*) that's numbered above 1024. Such ports may be accessed by any user, and so are commonly used by client programs and by a few servers that may legitimately be run by ordinary users. See also *privileged port*.

USB   See *Universal Serial Bus (USB)*.

user   An individual who has an account on a computer. This term is sometimes used as a synonym for *account*.

user cron job   A cron job created by an individual user to handle tasks for that user, such as running a CPU-intensive job late at night when other users won't be disturbed by the job's CPU demands. See also *system cron job*.

user ID (UID)   A number associated with a particular account. Linux uses the UID internally for most operations, and it converts to the associated username only when interacting with people.

user mask (umask)   A bit pattern representing the permission bits that are to be removed from files created from a process.

user private group   A group strategy in which every user is associated with a unique group. Users may then add other users to their groups in order to control access to files on an individual basis.

username   The name associated with an account, such as `theo` or `miranda`. Linux usernames are case-sensitive and may be from 1 to 32 characters in length, although they're usually entirely lowercase and no longer than 8 characters.

UTC   See *Coordinated Universal Time (UTC)* and *Greenwich Mean Time (GMT)*.

V

variable   In computer programming or scripting, a "placeholder" for data. Variables may change from one run of a program to another, or even during a single run of a program.

virtual filesystem   A filesystem that doesn't correspond to a real disk partition, removable disk, or network export. A common example is /proc, which provides access to information on the computer's hardware.

virtual hosting   A process by which a single computer can host servers (particularly Web servers) for multiple domains. For instance, one computer might respond to the names www.pangaea.edu, www.example.com, and www.littrow.luna.edu, delivering different content for each name.

virtual terminal (VT)   One of several independent text-mode or GUI screens maintained by Linux. You can log in multiple times and run different programs in each VT, then switch between them by pressing Ctrl+Alt+F*n*, where *n* is the terminal number (such as Ctrl+Alt+F4 to switch to VT 4).

VT   See *virtual terminal (VT)*.

W

wildcard   A character or group of characters that, when used in a shell as part of a filename, match more than one character. For instance, b??k matches book, back, and buck, among many other possibilities.

window manager   A program that provides decorative and functional additions to the plain windows provided by X. Linux supports dozens of window managers.

workstation   A type of computer that's used primarily by one individual at a time to perform productivity tasks, such as drafting, scientific or engineering simulations, or writing. See also *desktop computer*.

X

X   Shortened form of *X Window System*.

x86-64   See *AMD64*.

X.org-X11   A popular X server on Linux systems, starting in 2004. X.org-X11 6.7.0 forked from XFree86 4.3.99.

X client   A program that uses X to interact with the user.

X Display Manager (XDM)   A program that directly accepts either remote or local logins to a computer using X without involving a text-based login protocol like Telnet or SSH. Some Linux distributions use the original XDM program, but other distributions use variants such as the GNOME Display Manager (GDM) or KDE Display Manager (KDM), both of which provide additional features.

XDM   See *X Display Manager (XDM)*.

XFS   See *Extent Filesystem (XFS)*.

X server   A program that implements X for a computer; especially the component that interacts most directly with the video hardware.

X Window System   The GUI environment for Linux. The X Window System is a network-aware, cross-platform GUI that relies on several additional components (such as a window manager and widget sets) to provide a complete GUI experience.

XFree86   A set of X servers and related utilities for Linux and other OSs. Abandoned on most distributions in favor of X.org-X11.

xterm   A program that enables the running of text-mode programs in X. As used in this book, "xterm" refers both to the original xterm program and to various programs that provide similar functionality.

Index

Note to the reader: Throughout this index **boldfaced** page numbers indicate primary discussions of a topic. *Italicized* page numbers indicate illustrations.

Symbols and Numbers

& (ampersand), in command shell, 77
# (hash mark)
   in command prompt, 75
   for comments in /etc/ inetd.conf, 274
   for shell script comments, 113
$ (dollar sign), in command prompt, 75
* (asterisk), as wildcard, 80
? (question mark), as wildcard, 80
| (pipe), 90–91, 529
~ (tilde), for home directory, 81
10Base-2, 11
10Base-5, 11
10Base-T, 11
80x86 CPUs, 8
100Base-T, 11
802.11b (Wi-Fi), 308
1000Base-SX, 11
1000Base-T, 11
1024-cylinder limit, 43, 512

A

AbiWord, 19
absolute directory name, 81, 512
Accelerated-X, 12
access control lists (ACLs), 101–102, 512
accounts in Linux, 91–97, 512
   reviewing, 398–399
   script to create, 115–116
ACLs (access control lists), 101–102, 512
ACPI (Advanced Configuration and Power Interface), 461, 462–463, 512
acpi command, 502
Address Resolution Protocol (ARP), 315, 512

adduser command, 139
administrator. *See also* superuser account
   written log of, 414–415
Advanced Configuration and Power Interface (ACPI), 461, 462–463, 512
Advanced Graphics Port (AGP), 7, 512
Advanced Intelligent Tape (AIT), 215
Advanced Linux Sound Architecture (ALSA) driver, 14
Advanced Package Tool (APT) utilities, 250
Advanced Power Management (APM), 461, 462, 512
Advanced Technology Attachment (ATA) devices, 3, 181, 512
   configuring, 455–457
   problem diagnosis, 491–493
alien program, 254
Alpha, 9
AMANDA, 216
AMD processors, 8
AMD64, 513
ampersand (&), in command shell, 77
Apache web server, 21, 344
APM (Advanced Power Management), 461, 462, 512
apm command, 462, 502
apmd package, 462
appending text to file, 91
Apple/IBM/Motorola PowerPC, 9
Apple, LocalTalk, 307–308
AppleTalk, 313, 513
apropos command, 437, 442
apt-get tool, 250–253, 296
   commands, 251–252
ARKEIA, 216
Aspfilter, 474–477, 475, 476
asterisk (*), as wildcard, 80

at command, 282–283
AT power connectors, 451
ATA. *See* Advanced Technology Attachment (ATA) devices
audio CD-Rs, creating, 212
audio hardware, 7. *See also* sound cards
audio/visual programs, 20
auditing, 396–400
   check for open ports, 396–398
   verifying installed files and packages, 400
auto-mounter support, 197
awk command, 106–108, 120

B

background processes, 293–294
backups, 213–225
   common hardware, 214–216
   common programs, 216–221
      cpio program, 216–220
      mt command, 220–221
   partitions and, 29
   planning schedule, 222–223
   recovery, 223–225
   of system configuration, 415–416
baseline. *See* performance, normal measures
bash shell, 24, 74–75
   setting environment variables, 108–109
Basic Input/Output System (BIOS). *See* BIOS (Basic Input/Output System)
baud rate, 513
Berkeley Internet Name Domain (BIND), 23, 335
Berkeley Standard Distribution (BSD) LPD printing, 469, 472–477
   configuration tools, 474–477
   /etc/printcap file, 472–474
bg command, 294
binary, 513

binary package, 238, 513
BIND (Berkeley Internet Name
Domain), 23, 335
BIOS (Basic Input/Output
System), 40, 513
checking settings, **459–460**
restricting boot options,
375–376
bit, 513
blowfish, 513
BogoMIPS measure, 9
/boot/grub/menu.1st file, 47
boot loader, 27, **39–49**, 513
available options, **41–49**
GRUB configuration,
47–49
LILO configuration,
42–46
role, **40–41**
boot method, for Linux install,
34–35
/boot partition, 29
boot sector, 40, 513
bracketed values, for
wildcards, 81
broadband, 513
broadcast, 315, 514
BRU, 216
BSD. *See* Berkeley Standard
Distribution (BSD)
LPD printing
buffering disk accesses, 4
bugs
local program, 371–372
server, 372–373
build number, 241, 514
bus, 7, 514
byte, 514
bzip2 program, 254

C

C compiler, 24
C library (libc), 25, 514
cabling, **451–453**, *453*
problems with peripheral
devices, 496
for SCSI devices, 494
cache, for floppy disk writes, 200
cache memory, 10, 514
camera, 14
Card Services, 464, 514

Cardbus, 463–464, 514
carrier file, 236
case, changing in Vi, 105
case sensitivity
of parameters, 76
of passwords, 156
of usernames, 135
cat command, 76, **89–90**, 120
cathode ray tube (CRT), 3, 514
CD-based Linux system, 224
cd command, 76, 81–82, 120
CD-ROM drives, 13, 181
for Linux boot install, 34, 35
CD-ROM in book, xxiii
cdrecord command, 209, 227
cdrtools package, 209
central processing unit (CPU),
514. *See also* CPU (central
processing unit)
CERT (Computer Emergency
Response Team), 370
certification
exam objectives, xxiv–xxvii
process for, xx
reasons for, xx
chage command, **143–144**, 169
chains in filter table, 381, *382*
Challenge-Handshake
Authentication Protocol
(CHAP), 325
checksums, 514
from package managers,
394–395
from Tripwire, 393–394
chgroup command, 97
chgrp command, 120
child process, 285, 514
chipset, 514
on motherboard, 9
chkconfig utility, 271
chkrootkit program, 403
intrusion detection with, **394**
chmod command, **98–100**, 120
for script execute
permission, 113
chown command, **97**, 120
CHS address, 43
CHS translation schemes, 43
CIFS. *See* Common Internet
Filesystem (CIFS)
Cinelerra, 20
clients, 515
vs. servers, 319
Code Crusader, 24

color-coded file listing, 79
combining files, with cat
command, 89
command-line interface, 74, 515.
See also command shell
command mode for Vi, 103, 105
command prompt, 75, 515
command shell, **74–78**
retaining control, 77
shortcuts, **77–78**
starting, **74–75**
commands
external, in shell scripts,
113–115
scrolling previously used, 78
Common Gateway Interface
(CGI) scripts, 344–345
Common Internet Filesystem
(CIFS), 22, 515
Compact Flash card, 181
Compaq, 9
compiler, 24, 515
compiling source code, **258–262**
advantages and drawbacks,
239–240
Complementary Metal Oxide
Semiconductor (CMOS)
setup utility, 459, *459*, 515
compressed archives, 254
cpio or tar, 218
Computer Emergency Response
Team (CERT), 370
computers
evaluating requirements, 2–5
dedicated appliances, **4**
servers, **3–4**
special needs, **4–5**
workstations, **3**
hardware components,
6–14, *8*
CPU, **8–9**
hard disk drives, **10–11**
network hardware, **11–12**
RAM, **9–10**
video hardware, **12–13**
risks from opening case, 450
software needs, **15–26**
for any system, 23–25
Linux distributions, 15–18
server programs, **21–23**
validating requirements,
25–26
workstation programs,
18–21

Computing Technology Industry
    Association, certification
    exam, xix
concatenating files, **89–90**
conditional expressions, 515
    in shell scripts, **117–118**
Conectiva Linux, 16
configure script, 259–260
console, 515
Coordinated Universal Time
    (UTC), 38
copying files, 82
core system problems, 489–491
cp command, **82**, 120
cpio program, **216–220**, 227
    incremental backups
        with, 222
CPU (central processing unit), 6,
    8–9, 514
    limiting time for user, 401
    load as performance
        measure, 418–419
    problems, 489
    processes consuming,
        289–291, *290*
    restricting process use by,
        291–292
    temperature, 490
crackers, 155, 390, 515.
    See also security
    packet sniffer use by, 391
creating filesystem, 515
cron jobs, 280, 515
    creating system, 280–281
    creating user, **282**
    for distribution database
        update, 87
    for logrotate, 425–426
    for running Tripwire, 393
cron program, **280–283**
    role of, 280
crontab utility, 282, 296
cross-platform discs, creating,
    212–213
CUPS configuration, 469,
    477–482
    printer definitions, 480
    web-based utilities,
        480–482, *481*
current directory, finding and
    changing, **81–82**
cut command, in shell
    scripts, 114

cylinder/head/sector (CHS)
    addressing, 516
cylinder/head/sector (CHS)
    translation, 516

D

daemon, 516
daemon account, 158
daemon process permissions, 285
DAT (digital audio tape), 215
data cables, internal, 451–452
Data Display Channel (DDC),
    60, 516
data- plotting programs, 20
database, installed file, 237
date, Linux install settings, 38
dd command (Vi), 105
DDC (Data Display Channel), 60
Debian GNU/Linux, 16
Debian package tools, 236
    information about
        packages, 237
Debian packages, 15,
    247–254, 516
    apt-get tool, 250–253
    dpkg command set, 248–250
    vs. other package formats,
        253–254
    vs. RPM, 246–247
dedicated appliances, hardware
    requirements, **4**
default group, for new user
    account, 140
default permissions, 100–101
default route, 323, 516
default shell, for user accounts,
    131, 145
deleting
    directories, 85
    files
        with rm command, **83–84**
        sticky bit and, 97
    groups, **152**
    partitions, 186
    user accounts, **148**
denial-of-service (DoS) attacks,
    373, 516
dependencies, 238, **265–269**, 516
    failed, 25
    for RPM packages, 242
    tarballs and, 257–258

workarounds to problems,
    266–269
    forcing install, 266–267
    rebuilding packages,
        267–268
    upgrading or replacing
        package, 267
desktop computers, 3, 516. *See
    also* workstations
desktop environment, 18, 516
/dev/fd, 183
/dev/hd*x*, 182
/dev/nvram file, 184
/dev/sd*x*, 182
/dev/ttyS*x* device files, 466
/dev/zero file, 192
development kernel, 516
device drivers, 14–15
    identifying supported and
        unsupported, 498–499
    special procedures for
        compiling, 260–262
    for video card, 61
df command, 195, **202**, 226,
    421, 442
dhclient, 320
DHCP (Dynamic Host
    Configuration Protocol),
    320–321, 518
    configuring, 333–335
    servers, 23
DHCP lease, 320, 517
dhcpcd client, 320
diff command, 399
dig program, 317, 361
digital audio tape (DAT), 215
digital cameras, 487
digital linear tape (DLT), 215
digital signature, for Debian
    package, 253
digital video recorder
    software, 20
DIMM (dual inline memory
    module), 9, 517
direct memory access (DMA),
    457, 517
    configuring, 453–454
directories. *See also* home
    directory
    changing, 76, 81–82
    execute bit for, 96
    manipulating with
        commands, **85–86**
    moving, 83

order for backup, 219
in root partition, 28
viewing, **75–76**
disabling services, 333
disabling unused accounts, **158**
disaster recovery, backups for,
223–225
Disk Operating System
(DOS), 517
disk storage, 6
quotas, 166, 517
RAID, **204–208**
array design, 205–206
forms, 205
Linux configuration,
206–208
use as performance measure,
420–421
display devices. *See* monitor
DISPLAY environment
variable, 111
distributed denial-of-service
(DDoS) attack, 373, 517
distributions, 15–18, 517
mixing packages from
different, 242
DLT (digital linear tape), 215
dmesg command, **499–500**, 502
DNS (Domain Name Service)
for hostname delivery,
configuring, 335–336
iptables configuration for
traffic, 386
documentation
exam essentials, 441–442
help resources, **434–440**
info pages, **437–438**
Internet-based resources,
439–440
man pages, **435–437**
miscellaneous program
documentation,
438–439
log files, **422–429**
importance, 429–430
options, 423–425
for problem identification,
430–431
remote server for,
428–429
rotating, 425–428
syslogd for
maintaining, 423
tools for scanning,
431–434

normal performance
measures, **418–422**
CPU load, 418–419
disk use, 420–421
memory load, 420
system statistics
collection, 421–422
official policies and
procedures, 416–418
system configuration,
412–418
administrator's log,
414–415
backups, **415–416**
installation, **413–414**
dollar sign ($), in command
prompt, 75
domain, 517
Domain Name Service (DNS),
317–318, 517
configuring, 335–336
servers, 23
domain names, 316
dot file, 517
dpkg command set, **248–250**, 296
options, 249
primary actions, 248–249
drivers. *See* device drivers
drum scanners, 487
.dsc file, 253
dselect utility, 250
dual inline memory module
(DIMM), 9, 517
dump utility, 204, 218
DVD-ROM, 35, 181
Dynamic Host Configuration
Protocol (DHCP),
320–321, 518
for IP address delivery,
configuring, 333–335
servers, 23
dynamic RAM (DRAM), 10, 518
dynamic web content, 344–345

E

e-mail
network clients for, **347–350**
servers, 340–343
Postfix, **342–343**
sendmail, **341–342**
echo command, in shell
scripts, 114

ECLiPt Roaster, 209
Edit mode for Vi, 103, 105
EDITOR environment
variable, 111
edquota command, 167, 170
effective user ID, 518
EHCI (Enhanced Host
Controller Interface), 465
emergency boot disk, **499**
emergency system recovery, 224
encrypt passwords parameter, in
smb.conf file, 337
encryption, security and,
373–374, 376
end of log files, tools to check,
432–433
Enhanced Host Controller
Interface (EHCI), 465
Enhanced Integrated Device
Electronics (EIDE), 3, 518
env command, 110, 120
envelope, 309, 518
environment variables, 74,
108–112, 518
meanings of common,
110–112
and shell scripts, 117
user cron job to set, 282
where to set, **108–110**
error messages, in log files, 431
errors, checking filesystem for,
189–190
ESP Print Pro, 480
/etc/acpi/events directory,
462–463
/etc/apache directory, 344
/etc/apt/sources.list file, 251
/etc/cron.d directory, 280
/etc/crontab file, 280
/etc/csh.cshrc file, 109
/etc/csh.login file, 109
/etc/cups/cupsd.conf file, 478–479
/etc/cups/printers.conf file,
478–479
/etc/dhcpd.conf file, 333–334
/etc directory, backups, 415–416
/etc/exports file, 339
/etc/fstab file, 188, 203–204
for permanent partition
settings, 194
for permanent swap file, 192
/etc/ftpusers file, 162, 163
/etc/group file, 135–136, 149
editing, 151–152
/etc/gshadow file, 151

/etc/hosts file, 318
/etc/hosts.allow file, 387
/etc/hosts.deny file, 387
/etc/httpd directory, 344
/etc/ined.conf file, 273–274
/etc/inetd.conf file, 331–332
/etc/init.d directory, 271
/etc/inittab file, for permanent
    runlevel change, 279
/etc/lilo.conf file, 42–43
/etc/mtab file, 197
/etc/named.conf file, 335–336
/etc/nsswitch.conf file, 356–357
/etc/pam.d files, 147
/etc/pam.d/passwd file, 159
/etc/pam.d/system-auth file,
    159, 160
/etc/passwd file, 132, 136,
    158, 399
    modifying, **145–148**
/etc/pcmcia directory, 464
/etc/postfix/main.cf file, 342–343
/etc/ppp/chap-secrets file, 325
/etc/ppp/pap-secrets file, 325
/etc/printcap file, 470, 472–474
/etc/profile configuration file, 109
/etc/raidtab file, 207–208
/etc/rc.d/init.d directory, 271
/etc/rc.d/rc.local script, 276
/etc/rc.d/rcn.d directory, 271
/etc/samba/smbpasswd file, 337
/etc/securetty file, 165
/etc/security/access.conf file, 161
/etc/security/limits.conf file, 400
/etc/services file, 379
/etc/shadow file, 132, 148,
    157, 158
    modifying, **145–148**
/etc/snort directory, 391
/etc/ssh/sshd_config file, 162, 340
/etc/sudoers file, 171
/etc/syslog.conf file, 423–425, 429
/etc/xinetd.conf file, 275, 388
/etc/xinetd.d directory, 388–389
/etc/xinetd.d file, 275, 332–333
/etc/yp.conf file, 356
Ethernet, 307, 518
Ethernet card, 7, 11
    Linux support, 12
Evolution (Ximian), 19, 348
Ex mode for Vi, 103
execute permission, 96
Exim, 21
expired user accounts, **143–144**
    date for, 140

export command (bash), 120
    for environment variables,
        108–109
ext2 (Second Extended
    Filesystem), 30, 533
ext2fs, 30
ext3fs (third extended
    filesystem), 31, 536
extended INT 13, 518
extended INT13 calls, 43
extended partitions, 26, 518
    numbering in Linux, 183
Extent Filesystem (XFS), 31, 518
external cables, **452–453**
external commands, in shell
    scripts, **113–115**
external devices, **463–468**
    IEEE-1394 devices (FireWire),
        5, 465–466, 519
    legacy devices, 466–468
    PCMCIA cards, 463–464
    USB devices, 464–465
external transfer rate, 518

F

failed dependencies, 25, 519
FDDI (Fiber Distributed Data
    Interface), 307, 519
fdformat utility, 183
FDISK tool (DOS), 32
fdisk tool (Linux), 33, **184–186**,
    185, 227
    commands, 185
    for partition listing, 194–195
Fedora Linux, 16, 241
fg command, 294
Fiber Distributed Data Interface
    (FDDI), 307, 519
Fibre Channel, 308, 519
file access control string, **94–97**
file access permissions, 519
file access servers, **22–23**
File Allocation Table (FAT)
    filesystem, 32
file collections, 236–237
file owner, 92, 519
file permissions, **91–102**
    account and ownership
        basics, **91–97**
        file access components,
            92–93

        interpreting file access
            codes, 94–97
    ownership
        modification, 97
    permissions modification,
        98–100
    ACLs (access control lists),
        101–102
    default permissions, 100–101
file share definitions, in Samba,
    337–338
file-sharing protocols, 22, 519
file size, 93
    searching by, 86
File Transfer Protocol (FTP), 373
file transfers, in remote
    administration, 353–354
file type codes, 94, 519
filenames, 93
    completion, 519
    searching by, 86
files
    concatenating, **89–90**
    editing. *See* text editors; Vi
    examining contents, **88–90**
    listing for tarball, 257
    manipulating with
        commands, **78–91**
        copying, 82
        links, **84–85**
        locating, **86–88**
        moving, 83
        navigating, **79–81**
        removing, 83–84
        renaming, 83
    redirection and pipes, **90–91**
    Tab key for name
        completion, 77–78
    Tripwire to check for
        changes, 393–394
    viewing, **75–76**
    viewing last lines in, 90
filesystems, 180, 519
    checking for errors, **189–190**
    creating, **186–187**
    data structures, 93
    defining standard, **203–204**
    disk quotas, **166–167**
    exam essentials, 225–226
    network, **200–202**
        NFS shares, 201–202
        SMB/CIFS shares,
            200–201
    options for Linux, 30–32
    partitions and, 29

film scanners, 487
find command, **86–87**, 120
    to locate orphan files, 152
    to locate user-owned files, 148
    in shell scripts, 114
finding files, **86–88**
FIPS (First Nondestructive
    Interactive Partition
    Splitting) program, 33
Firestarter, 378
firewall, 519
firewall configuration, **376–386**
    common server ports,
        378–381
    iptables tool, **381–386**
    Linux software, 378
    location in network, 377, 377
FireWire (IEEE-1394), 5,
    465–466, 519
    interface problems, 498
flatbed scanners, 487
floating point unit (FPU), 419
floppy-based Linux
        distributions, 499
floppy drives, 13
    care in removing disks, 200
    identifier for, 183
    interface problems, 496–497
    for Linux install, 34, 36
    twisted cable, 496
folders. *See* directories
font server, 57, 520
fonts for X, path configuration, 57
Foomatic, 480
for loop, 118
foreground processes, 293–294
fork, 285, 520
FORWARD chain in filter table,
        381–382
forward-only DNS server,
        335–336, 520
fragmentation, of swap file, 193
fragmented, 520
frame buffer, 520
frame buffer drivers, 13
frames, 520
    in Ethernet, 309
free command, 190–191, 226,
        420, 442
Free Software Foundation
        (FSF), 438
free space bitmaps, 93
FreeCiv, 20
frequently asked question
        (FAQ), 520

Fresh RPMs, 247
fsck tool, **189–190**
    check order, 204
FTP (File Transfer Protocol), 373
    system access control, **162–163**
FTP clients, 19
full-duplex, 308, 520
full recursive DNS lookup,
        336, 520

G

gateways, 311, 520
gawk command, 106
gEdit, 23
Gentoo Linux, 16, 258
getfacl command, 102
gFTP, 19
Ghostscript, 468, 470–471
GIDs. *See* group IDs (GIDs)
gigabit Ethernet, 11, 307, 520
gigahertz, 9
GIMP, 20, 489
GIMP Print, 480
glibc, 25, 520
GNOME Toaster, 209
GNU (GNU's Not Unix), 520
GNU Compiler Collection,
        24, 259
GNU/Linux, 520
    Printing Web page, 474
GNU Network Object Model
        Environment, 19
GNU Parted, 33, 187–188
GNU plotutils package, 20
GNU Privacy Guard, 373
GnuCash, 20
Gnumeric, 19
gpasswd command,
        150–151, 170
    and user private groups, 153
Grand Unified Boot Loader
        (GRUB). *See* GRUB (Grand
        Unified Boot Loader)
graphical user interface
        (GUI), 521
graphics processing unit
        (GPU), 419
graphics viewers, 20
Greenwich Mean Time (GMT),
        38, 521
grep command, **88–89**, 120
    for log files, 433

in shell scripts, 114
group administrators,
        150–151, 521
group IDs (GIDs), 91, 92,
        131, 521
    coordinating across
        systems, 138
    mapping, **136–137**
    searching by, 86
group owner, 92, 521
groupadd command, 149, 169
groupdel command, 152, 170
groupmod command, 150, 170
groups, 92, **135–136**, 521
    adding, **149**
    deleting, **152**
    disk quotas, 166
    modifying information,
        149–151
    for new user account, 140
    user membership in
        multiple, **154**
groups command, 169
grpck command, 159
grpconv command, 158, 170
grpunconv command, 159, 170
GRUB (Grand Unified Boot
        Loader), 27, 41, 521
    configuring, **47–49**
        adding kernel or OS, 49
    passwords, 376
Guarddog, 378
GUI (graphical user
        interface), 521
GUI installations, **36–37**
GUI login server, shutting
        down, 55
GUI tools
    for firewall configuration, 378
    for network configuration,
        323–324, 324
    for package management,
        262–264, 263
    vs. command-line package
        management, 265
    for remote system login, 353
gzip program, 254

H

hackers, 155, 521.
    See also security
half-duplex, 308, 521

hand scanners, 487
hard disk drives, **10–11**, 181
    as backup media, 215
    documenting use, 420–421
    GRUB reference method, 47
    for Linux install, 35
    partition planning, **26–33**
        common options, 28–30
        Linux filesystem options,
            30–32
        Linux requirements,
            27–28
        for PCs, 26–27
    partitioning tools, **32–33**
    problems, 491–492
    statistics, 214
hard links, 84, 521
hardware. *See also* computers;
        printing configuration
    configuration, **450–460**
        ATA devices, **455–457**
        BIOS settings, **459–460**
        cabling, **451–453**, *453*
        IRQ, DMA and I/O
            settings, **453–454**
    documentation of, 413
    exam essentials, 501–502
    external devices, **463–468**
        IEEE-1394 devices
            (FireWire), 5,
            465–466, 519
        legacy devices, 466–468
        PCMCIA cards, 463–464
        USB devices, 5, 14,
            464–465, 536
    for networks
        basic functions, **306–307**
        configuration, 319–320
        types, **307–308**
    power management, **461–463**
    problem diagnosis, **489–500**
        ATA problems, 491–493
        core system problems,
            489–491
        dmesg for, **499–500**
        peripherals problems,
            495–498
        unsupported
            hardware, 498
        scanners, **487–489**
        SCSI devices
            configuring, **457–458**
            problem diagnosis, 494
hardware addresses,
        314–315, 521

hardware compatibility lists,
        498–499
hardware interrupts, statistics
        on, 422
hash mark (#), in command
        prompt, 75
hashes, 521
    from Tripwire, 393–394
hdparm command, 420–421,
        492–493, 502
    and SCSI device, 495
head command, 432, 442
header files, 522
    for compiling source code, 259
heat sink, for video card
        chipsets, 52
help resources, **434–440**
    info pages, 437–438
    Internet-based resources,
        439–440
    man pages, **435–437**
    miscellaneous program
        documentation,
        438–439
Hierarchical Filesystem (HFS), 32
High-Performance Filesystem
        (HPFS), 32
High-Performance Parallel
        Interface (HIPPI), 307, 522
home directory, 522
    importance, **138–139**
    for new user account, 140
    for system administrator, 28
    tilde (~) for, 81
    for user accounts, 131
HOME environment
        variable, 110
/home partition, 29
[homes] share, in Samba, 338
host program, 317, 361
HOSTNAME environment
        variable, 110
hostnames, 316–317, 522
    configuring DNS for
        delivery, 335–336
    resolution, **317–318**
hot standby, 205, 522
hot swapping, 452, 522
HOWTO documents, 522
HTTP (Hypertext Transfer
        Protocol), 21, 344, 373, 522
httpd.conf file, 344
HTTPS, 374
hub, 308, *309*, 522
human element, 374

hung processes, 291, 522
Hypertext Transfer Protocol
        (HTTP), 21, 344, 373, 522

I

i386 architecture code, 241
IA-64 CPUs, 9
IEEE-1394 devices (FireWire), 5,
        465–466, 519, 522
    interface problems, 498
if command, in shell scripts, 117
ifconfig command, 322–323, 361
i.LINK, 5
IMAP (Internet Message Access
        Protocol), 21
incremental backups, 222, 522
Industry Standard Architecture
        (ISA), 7, 455, 522
inetd server, 387
    configuring, **331–332**
inetd.conf file, **273–274**
info command, 442
info pages, 78, 434, **437–438**, 523
init program, 296
    to change runlevels, 277–279
initiating PPP connection,
        324–328
inode, 92, 523
    file permissions in, 100
INPUT chain in filter table,
        381–382
input devices, 7
input/output (I/O), 523
    port configuration, 453–454
input, redirecting, **90–91**
installed file database,
        237–238, 523
installing
    packages, **240–264**
        compiling source code,
            258–262
        Debian packages,
            247–254
        RPM packages, **240–247**
        tarballs, **254–258**
        X server, 53–54
installing Linux, **38–39**, *40*
    documentation for, **413–414**
    exam essentials, 63–64
    method selection, **34–37**
        boot method, **34–35**
        GUI installations, **36–37**

installation media, **35–36**
scripted installations, **37**
text-based installations, **37**
X configuration after, **50–63**
monitor options, **59–60**
screen options, **62–63**
selecting X server, **50–54**
video card options, **60–61**
integrated development
environment, 24
in.telnetd, 22
interactive mode, when copying
files, 82
internal data cables, 451–452
internal modem, 14
internal power connectors, 451
internal transfer rate, 523
internet, 311, 523
Internet , 311, 523
Internet-based help resources,
439–440
Internet Control Message
Protocol (ICMP), 312
Internet domains, 316
Internet Engineering Task
Force, 312
Internet Message Access
Protocol (IMAP), 21, 523
Internet Packet Exchange (IPX),
312, 523
Internet Printing Protocol (IPP),
478, 523
interpreted programming
languages, 24. *See also* shell
scripts
interrupt request (IRQ), 523
configuring, **453–454**
interrupts, statistics on, 422
intrusion detection, **389–396**
with chkrootkit, **394**
log monitoring, **395–396**, 430
with package manager
checksums, **394–395**
with PortSentry, **392–393**
with Snort, **390–391**, 392
symptoms, 389–390
with Tripwire, **393–394**
intrusion detection system (IDS),
391, 523
IP addresses, 315–316, 523
configuring DHCP for
delivery, 333–335
static, configuring, **321–323**
IP forwarding, enabling, 351

ipchains tool, 23, 116, 378, 403
ipfwadm tool, 378, 403
IPP (Internet Printing Protocol),
478, 523
iptables tool, 23, 378,
381–386, 403
creating firewall rules,
383–384
Linux packet filter
architecture, 381–382
sample configuration,
385–386
IPv6, 313, 524
IPX/SPX (Internet Packet
Exchange/Sequenced
Packet Exchange), 312
ISA (Industry Standard
Architecture), 455
ISO-9660 filesystem, 32
Itanium platform, 9

J

Java, 24
jed, 23
job numbers, for foreground and
background processes, 294
Joliet filesystem, 32
support, 213
Journaled Filesystem (JFS),
31, 524
journaling filesystems, 30–31,
32, 524

K

K Desktop Environment,
18–19
K3B program, 209
KDE PPP (KPPP) dialer, 326, 327
KDevelop, 24
Kedit, 24
kernel, 39, 524
adding to GRUB, 49
adding to LILO, **45–46**
naming files, 46
special procedures for
compiling, 260–262
kernel module, 524
kernel module autoloader, 524
kernel ring buffer, 499–500, 524

keyboard, 7, 13
interface, 467
interface problems, 497
Linux install options, 38
xorg.conf file for
configuring, 58
kill command, 276, 292–293, 296
for X server, 55
killall command, 293, 296
klogd daemon, 423
KMail, 19, 348
Add Account dialog box, *348*
Knoppix, 224, 499
ksysv utility, 272, 272
KWord, 19

L

language, for Linux install, 38
laptop computers, power
management, 462
LaTeX, 19
layout for keyboard, 58
LBA (linear block addressing),
43, 525
LD_LIBRARY_PATH
environment variable, 110
LED cables, 452
legacy devices, 466–468
less command, 76, 90, 442
to search log files, 434
for viewing log files, 432
for viewing man pages, 436
Libranet GNU/Linux, 16
Debian packages, 247
libraries, **25**
for compiling source code, 259
problems from missing or
incompatible, 265–266
software requirements, 26
library, 525
LILO (Linux Loader), 27, 41, 525
configuring, **42–46**
adding new kernel, **45–46**
adding new OS, 46
passwords, 376
linear block addressing (LBA),
43, 525
links for files, 84–85
Linspire, 16
Linux, 525
benefits of learning, xix
what it is, xix

Linux distributions, **15–18**
Linux Documentation Project, 439–440
Linux Embedded Appliance Firewall, 377
Linux Hardware Compatibility HOWTO, 498
Linux kernel, video drivers, 13
Linux Lab Project, 5
Linux Loader (LILO). *See* LILO (Linux Loader)
Linux packet filter architecture, 381–382
Linux Video Studio, 20
LinuxPPC, 241
liquid crystal display (LCD) monitor, 3, 525
Lm_sensors package, 490
ln command, **84–85**, 120
LNX-BBC, 499
load average for CPU, 291, 525
LOADLIN, 41–42
local program bugs, 371–372
LocalTalk, 307–308, 525
locate command, **87**, 120
locking user accounts, 142
log files, 412, **422–429**, 525
    for dmesg output, 500
    importance, 429–430
    monitoring for intrusion detection, **395–396**
    options, 423–425
    for problem identification, 430–431
    remote server for, 428–429
    rotating, 425–428
    syslogd for maintaining, 423
    tools for scanning, 431–434
log rotation, 525
Logcheck, 434
logcheck.sh script, 442
logging in, and starting shell, 75
logical partitions, 26, 525
    numbering in Linux, 27, 183
login access, system access control, **162**
login privileges, 131
login shells, 399
logrotate package, 425, 442
logs, administrator's, **414–415**
loopback traffic, iptables configuration for, 386
loops, 525
    in scripts, 117–118

lp account, 158
lpc command, **486**, 502
lpd tool, 468
    deficiencics, 469
lpq command, **485**, 502
lpr command, 468, **483–484**, 502
    dialog box, *484*
lprm command, **485**, 502
LPRng package, 469, **472–477**
    configuration tools, 474–477
    /etc/printcap file, 472–474
ls command, **75–76**, **79–80**, 119
    wildcards in, **80–81**
Lycoris, 16
LyX, 19

M

machine names, 316, 526
magnetic disks, removable, 181
magnetic tape, 181
    access devices for, 183–184
mail program (client), 348, 349, 361
mail servers, **21–22**
    configuring, 340–343
    Postfix, **342–343**
    sendmail, **341–342**
mail spool, for user accounts, 132
mailq command, 343
main memory, 10, 526
mainboard, 6. *See also* motherboard
major version number, 526
make utility, 259, 260
Makefile file, 260
man pages, 78, 434, **435–437**, 442, 526
    less command to display, 90
Mandrake Linux, 17
mangle table, 381
mapping UIDs and GIDs, **136–137**
markup languages, 19
Master Boot Record (MBR), 27, 526
master in PATA chain, 455, 526
Maxwell, 20
mdadm command, 206, 227
Media Access Control (MAC) addresses, 314, 526
/media partition, 30

megahertz, 9
memory, 6
memory load, as performance measure, 420
memory stick, 181
Message Digest 4 (MD4) password, 526
Message Digest 5 (MD5) hash, 159
Message Digest 5 (MD5) password, 526
Metrowerks CodeWarrior, 24
Microsoft Office documents, import/export filters, 19
mirroring, 205
mkdir command, 85, 120
mkdosfs utility, 187
mkfs command, 184, **186–187**, 227
mkfs.ext3 utility, 187
mkinitrd command, 261
mkisofs command, 208–209, 227
    for backup to optical media, 220
mkraid command, 208, 227
mkreiserfs utility, 187
mkswap command, 192, 194, 227
/mnt partition, 30
mode, 526
mode lines, 526
    for monitor resolution, 60
modems, 7, 14, 526
    network connections with, 324–325
module, 527
monitor, 7, 14
    CRT vs. LCD, 3
    interface problems, 497
    X server configuration, **59–60**
more command, 76, 90, 442
    for viewing log files, 432
motherboard, 6, 527
    chipset, 9
    problems, 489
mount, 527
mount command, **195–197**, 226
    options, **197–199**
    for SMB/CIFS shares, 201
mount points, 28, 195, 527
    in /etc/fstab file, 203
mounting partitions, **195–197**
mouse, 3, 7, 13–14
    3-button, 59
    interface, 467–468

interface problems, 497
Linux install options, 38
xorg.conf file for
   configuring, 58–59
moving files, 83
Mozilla, 19
MP3 players, 20
msisofs command, 212
mt command, 220–221, 227
multiple group membership, **154**
multitasking system, user
   accounts in, **132–133**
multiuser system, user accounts
   in, **131–132**
Mutt, 19, 348, 349, 350
mv command, 83, 120
MythTV, 20

N

names
   of files
      changing, 83
      problems from
         mismatched, 266
   for kernel files, 46
   for RPM packages, 241
navigating filesystems, **79–81**
Nedit, 23
Nessus, 397
Netatalk, 313
NetBEUI, 312, 527
NetBIOS, 312, 527
netconfig tool, 323
netmask, 315
Netscape, 19
netstat tool, 359, 361, 403
   to check for open ports,
      396–397
network account databases, 147
network addressing, **314–319**
   hostname resolution,
      317–318
   network ports, **318–319**
   types, **314–317**
      hardware addresses,
         314–315
      hostnames, 316–317
      IP addresses, 315–316
network clients, 19, **346–350**
   e-mail, 347–350
   remote use of X programs,
      346–347

Network Configuration, 323,
   324
network devices, 7
Network Filesystem (NFS),
   338–339, 527
network filesystems, **200–202**
   NFS shares, 201–202
      system access control,
         163
   SMB/CIFS shares, 200–201
network hardware, **11–12**
Network Information Service
   (NIS), **355–357**, 527
network mask, 315, 527
network scanners, **397–398**
networks
   configuration, **319–328**
      DHCP, 320–321
      with GUI tools, 323–324,
         324
      hardware, 319–320
      initiating PPP connection,
         324–328
      static IP addresses,
         321–323
   diagnostic tools, **357–359**
      network status check,
         359
      testing basic connectivity,
         357–358
      tracing route, 358–359
   exam essentials, 360–361
   hardware
      basic functions, **306–307**
      types, **307–308**
   interface problems, 498
   for Linux install, 35
   Linux install options, 38
   packets, **309**
   protocol stacks, **309–313**
      OSI model, 310, *311*
      TCP/IP, 311–312
      TCP/IP alternatives,
         312–313
   remote system
      administration,
         351–355
      file transfers, 353–354
      GUI logins, 353
      protocols, 354–355
      text-mode logins,
         351–353
   routing, 350–351

server configuration,
   329–346
   DHCP for IP address
      delivery, 333–335
   DNS for hostname
      delivery, 335–336
   mail servers, **340–343**
   NFS for file delivery,
      338–339
   remote access server
      setup, 339–340
   Samba for file delivery,
      336–338
   super servers, **329–333**
   web servers, **344–346**
New Technology Filesystem
   (NTFS), 32
newgrp command, 136, 154, 169
NFS. *See* Network Filesystem
   (NFS)
NFS shares
   accessing, 201–202
   system access control, **163**
nice command, 291–292, 296
NIS (Network Information
   Service), **355–357**
Nmap, 397, 398, 403
nmbd server, 336
NNTPSERVER environment
   variable, 111
nobody account, 158
nodes, 527
   for info pages, 438
nonvolatile RAM (NVRAM),
   182, 527
   access devices for, 184
nslookup program, 317, 361
ntsysv utility, 272
NVRAM (nonvolatile RAM), 182
   access devices for, 184

O

OCR Shop, 488
office tools, **19**
official policies and procedures,
   416–418
Open Host Controller Interface
   (OHCI), 465
open mail relays, 340, 528
open ports, 359, 528
   check for, 396–398

Open Sound System (OSS)
 drivers, 14
Open System Interconnection
 (OSI) model, 310, *311*, 528
opening computer cases, risk
 from, 450
OpenOffice.org, 19
OpenSSH, 22, 340
Opera, 19
operating systems
 adding to GRUB, 49
 adding to LILO, 46
/opt partition, 29
optical media, 181
 access devices for, 183
 as backup media, 215, 220
 statistics, 214
 writing to, **208–213**
  cross-platform discs,
   212–213
  example, 210–212
  tools for, 208–210
OS Loader, 41
OSI model. *See* Open System
 Interconnection (OSI) model
OUTPUT chain in filter table,
 381–382
overwriting files
 with redirection and pipes, 91
 when copying, 82
ownership of files
 modification, **97**
 when copying, 82

P

p command (Vi), 105
Package Management program,
 262–264, *263*
package manager checksums,
 intrusion detection with,
 394–395
packages
 basics, **236–240**
  file collections, 236–237
  installed file database,
   237–238
  rebuilding packages,
   238–240
 dependencies and conflicts,
  265–269
 exam essentials, 295–296

GUI package management
 tools, **262–264**, *263*
installing and removing,
 240–264
 compiling source code,
  258–262
 Debian packages,
  247–254
 RPM packages, **240–247**
 tarballs, **254–258**
 selecting for install, 38
packaging methods, 15
packet, 528
packet-filter firewalls, 376, 528
packet sniffer, 390–391, 528
packets, **309**
paging through files, 90
pam_access.so module, 161
pam_limits module, 400
PAP (Password Authentication
 Protocol), 325
parallel ATA (PATA), 528
parallel ATA (PATA) chain, 455
Parallel Line Interface Protocol
 (PLIP), 306
parallel port, 14, 466
 interface problems, 497
parameters, 528
 passing to program, 76
 in shell scripts, 115
parent directories, creating, 85
parent process, 285, 528
parity bit, 10
partial restores, 223
partition table, 27, 528
partitioning tools, **32–33**
PartitionMagic (PowerQuest),
 33, 188
partitions, **184–194**, 528. *See
 also* filesystems
 adding swap space, **190–194**
 creating during Linux
  install, 38
 df command for
  information, **202**
 documentation of, 413
 exam essentials, 225–226
 fdisk to create, **184–186**, *185*
 filesystem creation on,
  186–187
 identifier for, 183
 managing, **194–208**
  identification, **194–195**

mounting and
 unmounting,
 195–200
network filesystems, **200–202**
 NFS shares, 201–202
 SMB/CIFS shares,
  200–201
planning, **26–33**
 common options, 28–30
 Linux filesystem options,
  30–32
 Linux requirements,
  27–28
 for PCs, 26–27
 real world scenario, 31
 type codes, 193
passwd command, 141–142, 169
password requirements, 155
Password Authentication
 Protocol (PAP), 325
password cracking programs, 156
passwords, 131
 BIOS, 376, 460
 chage command for
  parameters, 144
 encrypted for Samba, 337
 enforcement, **155–157**
 on floppy disks, 399
 for groups, 150–151
 risk reduction for
  compromised, **157**
 security, 415
 stolen, 371
patch files, Debian support
 for, 253
path, 528
PATH environment variable, 76,
 109, 110, 111
payload, 309, 529
PC Card, 463–464, 529
PCL (Printer Control Language),
 469, 530
PCMCIA cards, 463–464
performance
 of CPU, 9
 normal measures, **418–422**
  CPU load, 418–419
  disk use, 420–421
  memory load, 420
  system statistics
   collection, 421–422
Peripheral Component
 Interconnect (PCI), 7, 529

peripheral devices, 529
    problem diagnosis, 495–498
Perl, 24
permission bits, 95–96, 529
permission string, 92
permissions. *See also* file
    permissions
    daemon process, 285
    process, **283–285**
    searching by, 86
    when copying files, 82
Person VUE, xx
Personal Computer Memory
    Card International
    Association (PCMCIA)
    cards, 463–464, 529
personal productivity tools, **20**
phishing, 374, 529
physical access, as security issue,
    371, **375–376**
pico, 23
Pine, 350
ping command, 357–358, 361
pipe (|), **90–91**, 529
pkgtool utility (Slackware),
    254, 258
Pluggable Authentication
    Module (PAM)
    configuration files, 147
    for controlling system access,
    160–162
Point-to-Point Protocol (PPP), 529
    GUI dialer for connecting,
    326–328, *327*
    initiating connection,
    324–328
    text-based utilities, 325–326
policies and procedures,
    documenting, **416–418**
POP (Post Office Protocol), 21
port number, 529
ports, 318–319
    common on servers, **378–381**
    open, 359, 396–398
PortSentry, 403
    intrusion detection with,
    392–393
Post Office Protocol (POP),
    21, 529
Postfix, 21, **342–343**
PostScript, 12, 469–470, 529
PostScript Printer Definition
    (PPD), 478, 530

POV-Ray, 20
power cables, 451
power management, **461–463**
    ACPI, 461, 462–463, 512
    activating kernel support,
    461–462
    APM, 461, 462, 512
    power-on self-test (POST),
    489–490
PowerPC distributions, 241
PowerQuest, PartitionMagic, 33
ppc architecture code, 241
PPP connection, initiating,
    324–328
ppp-off script, 325–326
ppp-on dialer script, 325–326
ppp-on script, 325–326
PPP Over Ethernet (PPPoE), 325
pppd utility, 325
Preboot Execution Environment
    (PXE), 5, 530
precompiled package, 238
primary boot loader, 40, 530
primary partitions, 26, 530
    identifier for, 183
    numbering in Linux, 27
print queue, 468, 530
    Ghostscript in, 470–471
    monitoring and control,
    483–486
    information display with
    lpq, 485
    lpc for control, 486
    lprm to remove jobs, 485
    using multiple, 477
Printer Control Language (PCL),
    469, 530
printer driver, 469, 530
printers, selecting for Linux, 471
printing configuration, **468–486**
    BSD LPD and LPRng,
    472–477
    configuration tools,
    474–477
    /etc/printcap file, 472–474
    configuring CUPS, **477–482**
    printer definitions, 480
    web-based utilities,
    480–482, *481*
    Ghostscript, 470–471
    Linux printing architecture,
    468–469
    PostScript, 469–470

print queue monitoring and
    control, **483–486**
    information display with
    lpq, 485
    lpc for control, 486
    lprm to remove jobs, 485
    printing to Windows or
    Samba printers,
    482–483
    running printing system,
    471–472
priority for process, 288, 290
privileged ports, 381, 530
problem diagnosis, **489–500**
    ATA problems, 491–493
    core system problems,
    489–491
    peripherals, 495–498
    SCSI devices, 494
    unsupported hardware, 498
/proc/dma file, 455
/proc/interrupts file, 455
/proc/ioports file, 455
process permissions, **283–285**
processes, **285–295**, 530
    CPU use restriction, 291–292
    foreground and background,
    293–294
    kill command, 292–293
    ps to examine process lists,
    286–291
    statistics on, 422
    top, 289–291
processor. *See* CPU (central
    processing unit)
Programmed Input/Output
    (PIO), 457, 530
programming tools, **24**
programs
    documentation, **438–439**
    launching, **76–77**
project groups, **153–154**
protocol stacks, **309–313**, 530
    OSI model, 310, *311*
    TCP/IP, 311–312
    TCP/IP alternatives, 312–313
protocols, ports used by, 379–380
proxy filters, 377
proxy servers, 23
ps command, 276, **286–291**, 296
    interpreting output, 287–289
    options, 286–287
PS1 environment variable, 111

PS_PERSONALITY
    environment variable, 287
pull mail protocol, 340, 530
pump DHCP client, 320
push mail protocol, 340, 531
pwck command, 159
pwconv command, 158, 170
pwd command, 81, 120
PWD environment variable, 110
pwunconv command, 159, 170
Python, 24

Q

QTParted, *188*, 188
question mark (?), as wildcard, 80
queue for mail, 343
quotacheck command, 167, 170

R

RAID (redundant array of
    independent disks), 28,
    204–208, 531
    array design, 205–206
    forms, 205
    Linux configuration, 206–208
raidtools package, 206
RAMbus dynamic RAM
    (RDRAM), 9, 531
random access, 531
random access devices for
    backups, 214
random access memory (RAM),
    6, **9–10**
    evaluating use, 191
    problems, 489
    vs. swap space, 191
ray tracing programs, 20
rc-update utility, 272
RDRAM inline memory
    modules (RIMMs), 9, 531
read-only memory (ROM), 6
README files, 438–439
rebuilding packages, 238–240
recovery, with backups, **223–225**
recursive copy, 82
recursive file listing, 80
Red Hat Linux, 17, 241. *See also*
    RPM packages

user private group, **153**
redirection, **90–91**, 531
redundant array of independent
    disks (RAID). *See* RAID
    (redundant array of
    independent disks)
refresh rate, X server
    configuration for monitor,
    59–60
regular expressions, 531
    in grep command, 89
ReiserFS, 31, 531
relative directory name, 81, 531
release kernel, 531
release number (build number),
    241, 514
remote access server setup,
    configuring, 339–340
remote configuration tools, 23
remote login access, 162
    by root user, 165
remote login servers, **22**, 531
remote server, for log files,
    428–429
remote system administration,
    351–355
    file transfers, 353–354
    GUI logins, 353
    protocols, 354–355
    text-mode logins, 351–353
remote use of X programs,
    346–347
removable magnetic disks, 181
    as backup media, 215
    statistics, 214
removing files, 83–84
renice command, 292, 296
repquota command, 167, 170
Requests for Comments (RFCs),
    312, 532
restart startup script
    command, 271
rexec tool, 353
ribbon cable, 451–452, 532
rlogin tool, 352–353
rm command, **83–84**, 120
rmdir command, 85–86, 120
RMON (Remote Monitoring)
    protocol, 354
Rock Ridge support, 213
root (/) directory, 28, 532
/root directory, 28
root DNS servers, 336, 532

root filesystem, 532
root kits, 394, 532
root partition, 28, 532
    for GRUB, 48
root password, 39
    security and, 371
root user, 170. *See also*
    superuser account
    dangers, 171
    and passwd command, 142
    system access control,
        165–166
rooted, 532
rotating log files, **425–428**
route command, 350, 361
router, 532
routing, **350–351**
    information about, 359
Roxen, 21
rpm command set, **243–246**, 296
    common operations, 243–244
    common options, 244–245
    query output, 246
RPM Package Manager, 15,
    236, 532
    checksums, **394–395**
    information about
        packages, 237
    vs. other package formats,
        246–247
    upgrades, 243
RPM packages, **240–247**
    compatibility issues, 242
    distributions and
        conventions, 240–242
RPMFind web site, 247
RS-232 serial ports, 466
    interface problems, 497
.rules files, for Snort, 391
runlevels, 54, 269, **277–279**, 532
    init or telinit to change,
        277–279
    permanent change, 279
    role, 277

S

Samba
    for file delivery, configuring,
        336–338
    printers, **482–483**

system access control,
163–164
user lists, 148
Samba Web Administration Tool
(SWAT), 354, *355*, 532
SANE (Scanner Access Now
Easy), **488–489**
sar program, 421–422, 442
saving changes in Vi, 106
/sbin/halt, 399
/sbin/shutdown, 399
scanimage command, 502
scanners, **487–489**
Linux software for, **488–489**
scheduling jobs, **280–283**
with at, 282–283
creating system cron jobs,
280–281
creating user cron jobs, 282
cron role, 280
scientific data acquisition, 5
scientific programs, **20–21**
SciGraphic, 21
script kiddies, 394, 532
scripted installations, **37**
scripting languages, 24, 533
scripts. *See also* shell scripts;
SysV scripts
Common Gateway Interface
(CGI), 344–345
for firewall, 378
for network connections,
325–326
scrolling previously used
commands, 78
SCSI (Small Computer System
Interface) devices, 3, 181,
457–458, 534
performance, 11
problem diagnosis, 494
searching
log files, **433–434**
in Vi, 105
Second Extended Filesystem
(ext2), 30, 533
secondary boot loader, 40, 533
Secure Shell (SSH), 22, 533
security
auditing, **396–400**
check for open ports,
396–398
verifying installed files
and packages, 400
exam essentials, 402–403

firewall configuration,
376–386
common server ports,
378–381
iptables tool, 381–386
Linux software, 378
location in network,
377, *377*
imposing user resource
limits, **400–401**
intrusion detection, **389–396**
with chkrootkit, 394
log monitoring, 395–396
with package manager
checksums, 394–395
with PortSentry, 392–393
with Snort, **390–391**, 392
symptoms, 389–390
with Tripwire, **393–394**
partitions and, 28
physical access, **375–376**
root account and, 171
super servers, **387–389**
access control via TCP
Wrappers, 387–388
access control via xinetd,
388–389
for system cron job
directories, 281
Telnet and, 22
with user accounts, **154–160**
disabling unused
accounts, **158**
risk reduction for
compromised
passwords, **157**
shadow passwords,
158–160
user password
enforcement,
155–157
user accounts with 0 UID, 137
vulnerability sources,
370–374
denial-of-service
attacks, 373
encryption issues,
373–374
human element, 374
local program bugs,
371–372
physical access, 371
server bugs, 372–373
stolen passwords, 371

sed command, **106–108**, 120
in shell scripts, 114
sendmail, 21, **341–342**
queue management, 343
Sentry Tools package, 434
Sequenced Packet Exchange
(SPX), 312, 533
sequential access, 533
for backup devices, 214
Serial ATA (SATA), 11,
456–457, 533
problems, 491
Serial Attached SCSI (SAS), 11,
458, 533
serial port, 14
server bugs, 372–373
Server Message Block/Common
Internet File System
(SMB/CIFS) protocol suite
accessing shares, **200–201**
Samba for, 163–164, 336
Server Message Block (SMB),
22, 533
servers, 533
vs. clients, 319
common ports, **378–381**
configuration, **329–346**
DHCP for IP address
delivery, 333–335
DNS for hostname
delivery, 335–336
mail servers, **340–343**
NFS for file delivery,
338–339
remote access server
setup, 339–340
Samba for file delivery,
336–338
super servers, **329–333**
web servers, 344–346
hardware requirements, **3–4**
programming tools on, 24
software needs, **21–23**
user lists, 148
services
ports used by, 379
removing from computer, 273
starting and stopping,
269–277
custom startup files,
276–277
editing inetd.conf file,
273–274

editing xinetd.conf or
xinetd.d files,
275–276
with SysV scripts,
269–273
set group ID (SGID) option, 97,
283, 533
bugs in programs, 371–372
finding programs using,
284–285
risk from, 284
set user ID (SUID) option, 96,
283, 533
bugs in programs, 371–372
finding programs using,
284–285
risk from, 284
setenv command (tsch), 109, 120
setfacl command, 101–102
setserial command, 466–467
shadow passwords, 132, 157,
158–160, 533
/etc/gshadow file to store, 151
shadowing, 460
share, 533
shell, 534. *See also* command shell
SHELL environment variable, 110
shell scripts, **112–118**, 534
beginning, **113**
conditional expressions,
117–118
external commands, **113–115**
variables, **115–117**
shell shortcuts, **77–78**
"shoulder surfing," 157
shutdown command,
278–279, 296
signal, 534
SIGTERM signal, 278
Simple Mail Transfer Protocol
(SMTP), 21, 340, 373, 534
Simple Network Management
Protocol (SNMP), 534
Single Inline Memory Module
(SIMM), 9, 534
Slackware Linux, 17
file database, 254
tarballs for distribution, 255
slave in PATA chain, 455, 534
slocate command, 87
Small Computer System
Interface (SCSI) devices, 3,
181, **457–458**, 534
performance, 11

problem diagnosis, 494
Small Outline (SO) DIMM, 9, 534
smart filter, 470–471, 534
SMB/CIFS (Server Message
Block/Common Internet
File System), 336
printer queue, 482–483
shares, 200–201
SMB (Server Message Block), 22
smbclient program (Samba), 200
smb.conf file, 336–337
smbd server, 336
smbmount program (Samba),
200, 226
smbpasswd utility, 337
smbumount command, 226
SMTP (Simple Mail Transfer
Protocol), 21, 340, 373, 534
SNMP protocol, 354
Snort, 403
intrusion detection with,
390–391, *392*
social engineering, 374, 534
soft links, 84–85, 534
software, **15–26**
server programs, **21–23**
validating requirements,
25–26
workstation programs, **18–21**
software modem, 14, 534
solid-state storage,
removable, 181
sound cards, 14
SoundBlaster-compatible sound
cards, 455
source code
available formats, 239
compiling, **258–262**
procedures for, 259–260
source package, 238, 535
source RPMs, 239, 535
spam, 373, 535
open mail relays and, 340
SPARC CPU, 9
spawn, 535
specialty accounts, deleting, 158
speed of drive interface vs.
device, 10
splash image, for boot process, 48
spool directory, 535
spreadsheet software, 19
Squid, 23
src architecture code, 241
SSH protocol, 352

iptables configuration for
traffic, 386
vs. Telnet, 340
SSH server, login access, 162
stable kernel, 535
standard input, 90, 535
standard output, 535
standby mode, 462
StarOffice, 19
start command, 271
start of log files, tools to
check, 432
starting services
custom startup files, 276–277
with SysV scripts, **269–273**
startup scripts, 112, 535
problems, 269
state, for network
connections, 384
stateful packet inspection,
384, 535
static IP addresses, configuring,
321–323
sticky bit, 96, 97, 535
stolen passwords, 371
stop command, 271
stopping services, with SysV
scripts, **269–273**
storage devices. *See also*
backups; partitions
hardware configuration,
182–184
types, **180–182**
Storm Package Manager, 262
string replacement, in Vi, 105
striping, 205
su command, 169, 170–171, 284
subdomains, 316, 535
subnet mask, 315, 535
sudo command, 169, 171
Super DLT, 215
super servers, 273, **387–389**, 535
access control via TCP
Wrappers, 387–388
access control via xinetd,
388–389
configuring, **329–333**
role, 329–330, *330*
superuser account, **133–134**, 535
SuSE Demo, 499
SuSE Linux, 17
demo version as CD, 224
suspend mode, 462
swap file, **192–193**, *535*

swap partition, 29, 31, **193–194**, *535*
swap space, 184, 420, 535
　adding, **190–194**
　real world scenario, 191
　statistics on, 422
swapoff command, 192–193, 227
swapon command, 192, 227
SWAT (Samba Web Administration Tool), 354, *355*
switch for network, 308, *309*, 536
symbolic links, 84–85, 534
　permissions, 96
symbolic modes, 98–99
sync command, 200
syslogd daemon, **423**
system access control, 160–167
　FTP access, **162–163**
　login access, **162**
　NFS access, **163**
　root access, **165–166**
　Samba access, **163–164**
　via PAM, **160–162**
system administrator, home directory, 28
System Commander, 41
system-config-packages command, 296
system configuration
　documentation, **412–418**
　administrator's log, **414–415**
　backups, **415–416**
　installation, **413–414**
system cron jobs, 280, 536
　creating, 280–281
system resources, for compiling source code, 259
system statistics collection, as performance measure, 421–422
System V (SysV), 536
syststat package, 421–422
SysV scripts
　for DHCP server startup, 333
　problems, 269
　starting and stopping services with, **269–273**
　startup, 536

T

Tab key, for filename completion, 77–78
tail command, **90**, 432–433, 442
tape drives, 13
　as backup media, 214, 215
　mt command for, 220–221
　statistics, 214
tar command, 216, **218–220**, 227, 296
　for configuration file backup, 415
tar command set, **255–257**
　qualifiers, 256–257
tarballs, 15, 237, **254–258**, 536
　compiling vs. packaging, 239
　file list for, 257
　and installed file database, 238
　vs. other package formats, 257–258
　vs. RPM, 247
.tar.bz2 file extension, 254
.tar.gz file extension, 254
.tbz file extension, 254
TCP/IP, 311–312, 537
　alternatives, 312–313
TCP Wrappers, 275, 378
　access control via, **387–388**
tcpd program, 387, 403
tcsh shell, 24, 75
telinit program, 54, 296
　to change runlevels, 277–279
Telnet, 22, 339, 536
　security issues, 162, 351
telnetd, 22
TERM environment variable, 111
terminal program, 324, 536
termination of SCSI chain, 457, 494
testing network connections, 357–358
TeX, 19
text-based installations, **37**
text editors, **23–24**, 536.
　See also Vi
　for composing mail, 349
　for viewing log files, 432
text-mode commands, 74
　exam essentials, 119
.tgz file extension, 254
theft of hardware, 375
thin clients, 5, 536

Third Extended Filesystem (ext3), 31, 536
Thomson Prometric, xx
thttpd, 21
tilde (~), for home directory, 81
time
　indicators for cron jobs, 280–281
　Linux install settings, 38
timeout, for booting default OS, 48
/tmp partition, 30
Token Ring, 307, 536
Tom's Root/Boot disk, 36
top-level domains, 316
top tool, **289–291**, *290*, 296, 419
traceroute command, **358–359**, 361
Transmeta, 8
Transmission Control Protocol/ Internet Protocol (TCP/IP), 311–312, 537
　alternatives, 312–313
Travan tape drives, 215, 216
Triple Data Encryption Standard (3DES), 159, 537
Tripwire, 403
　intrusion detection with, **393–394**
Trivial File Transfer Protocol (TFTP), 537
　server, 5
troubleshooting.
　See problem diagnosis
tsch shell, setting environment variables, 109
TurboLinux, 17
Tux Racer, 20
tw.cfg file, 393
twinstall.sh program, 393
tw.pol file, 393

U

UHCI (Universal Host Controller Interface), 465
UIDs. *See* user IDs (UIDs)
umask command, 100–101, 120
umount command, **199–200**, 226
Universal Disk Format (UDF), 32, 213
Universal Host Controller Interface (UHCI), 465

Universal Serial Bus (USB), 537. *See also* USB (Universal Serial Bus) devices
Unix, killall command, 293
Unix Filesystem, 32
unlocking user accounts, 142
unmounting partitions, **199–200**
unprivileged ports, 381, 537
unsupported hardware, 498
unused accounts, disabling, **158**
Update Agent (Red Hat), 264
upgrades of Debian packages, 250–253
uptime command, 291, 419, 442
USB (Universal Serial Bus) devices, 5, 14, **464–465**, 537
    interface problems, 497
user accounts, 39, **130–135**
    adding, **139–141**
    deleting, **148**
    disk quotas, 166
    modifying, **141–147**
    in multitasking system, 132–133
    in multiuser system, 131–132
    superuser account, **133–134**
    usernames, **135**
user cron jobs, 280, 537
    creating, **282**
User Datagram Protocol (UDP), 312
USER environment variable, 110
user IDs (UIDs), 91, 131, 537
    coordinating across systems, 138
    mapping, **136–137**
    searching by, 86
user management, 537
    account security, **154–160**
        disabling unused accounts, **158**
        risk reduction for compromised passwords, **157**
        shadow passwords, **158–160**
        user password enforcement, **155–157**
    common strategies, **152–154**
        multiple group membership, **154**
        project groups, **153–154**
        user private group, **153**

exam essentials, 168–169
filesystem quotas, **166–167**
groups, **135–136**
    adding, **149**
    deleting, **152**
    modifying information, **149–151**
home directory, importance, **138–139**
mapping UIDs and GIDs, **136–137**
system access control, **160–167**
    FTP access, **162–163**
    login access, **162**
    NFS access, **163**
    root access, **165–166**
    Samba access, **163–164**
    via PAM, **160–162**
user accounts, **130–135**
    adding, **139–141**
    deleting, **148**
    modifying, **141–147**
    in multitasking system, 132–133
    in multiuser system, 131–132
    superuser account, 133–134
    usernames, **135**
user mask (umask), 100, 537
user private group, **153**, 537
user resources, imposing limits, **400–401**
useradd command, **139–141**, 169
userdel command, 148, 169
usermod command, **142–143**, 169
    for groups, 150
usernames, 92, 131, **135**, 537
users, educating about passwords, 156
/usr/local partition, 29
/usr partition, 29
/usr/src/linux/.config file, 414

/var/spool/cron directory, 280
variables, 538. *See also* environment variables
    in shell scripts, **115–117**
verifying installed files and packages, 400
Vi, 23, **102–106**, *104*
    basic text-editing procedures, **103–105**
    launching and loading file, 104
    modes, **103**
    saving changes, **106**
video hardware, 7, **12–13**
    video acquisition boards, 14
    video card chipset, *51*
        determining, **50–52**
    video card option settings, **60–61**
video input, 4
Video4Linux project, 4, 14
viewing files and directories, **75–76**
Vim, 103
virtual filesystem, 538
virtual hosting, 345, 538
Virtual Networking Computing (VNC), 347
virtual terminals (VTs), 133, 538
VirtualDocumentRoot directory, 345
virus scanning, 394
visudo command, 171
VNC (Virtual Networking Computing), 347
VueScan, 488

W

web browsers, 19
web resources
    CUPS utilities, 480–482, *481*
    desktop environments, 19
    on Ghostscript, 471
    GNU/Linux Printing Web page, 474
    for GRUB, 47
    hardware compatibility lists, 498–499
    as help resources, 439–440
    on IPv6, 313
    Linux distributions, 16, 17, 18
    Linux Printing web site, 480

V

validating requirements for software, **25–26**
/var/lib/dpkg directory, 237
/var/lib/rpm directory, 237
/var partition, 30

office tools, 19
on PC cards, 464
for RPMs, 247
scanner software, 488
on security issues, 370
on X servers, 52
web servers, **21**
    configuring, **344–346**
Webmin, 23, 354
whatis command, 437, 442
whereis command, **88**, 120
Wi-Fi (802.11b), 308
wildcards, 538
    in ls command, **80–81**
window managers, 18, 538
Windows
    report on video card chipset,
        50, *51*
    sharing Linux files and
        printers. *See* Samba
Windows printers, **482–483**
wireless protocols, 308
word processors, 19
WordPerfect, 19
workgroup parameter, in
    smb.conf file, 337
workstations, 538
    hardware requirements, **3**
    software needs, **18–21**
write permission
    for directories, 96
    in Samba, 338

X

X-based program, launching, 77
X-CD-Roast, 209, *210*, **210–212**

X client, *50*, 538
X configuration, 39
    after installing Linux, **50–63**
        monitor options, **59–60**
        screen options, **62–63**
        selecting X server, **50–54**
        video card options,
            60–61
X Display Manager (XDM), 538
X Multimedia System, 20
X server, 538
    installing, **53–54**
    starting, 55
X sessions
    tunneling, 22
    virtual terminals (VTs)
        and, 133
X Window System, 12,
    18–19, 538
    remote use of programs,
        346–347
x86 CPUs, 8
Xandros Linux, 17
    Debian packages, 247
XAnim, 20
Xconfigurator command, 55, 65
XEmacs, 23
xf86cfg command, 56, 61, 65
XFree86, 12, 13, *52–53*, 65, 538
    font directory, 57
Xi Graphics, 53
Ximian Evolution, 19, 348
xinetd program, **275–276**, 387
    configuring, **332–333**
    super server access control
        via, **388–389**
xman program, 437
Xorg command, 53, 65

X.org-X11, 12, 13, *52–53*, 538
    font directory, 57
xorg.conf file
    Device section, 61
    keyboard configuration, 58
    manually editing, **56–57**
    Monitor section, 59
    mouse configuration, **58–59**
    path configuration, 57
    Screen section, 62
    ServerLayout section, **62–63**
XSane, 489
xterm, 538
    and starting shell, 75
XV (graphic viewer/editor), 20

Y

yanking text in Vi, **104–105**
YaST (SuSE), 264, 323
Yellow Dog Linux, 17, 241
Yellow Pages (YP), 355
yp-tools package, 356
ypbind package, 356
yy comand (Vi), 105

Z

Zeus, 21
Ziegler, Robert, 378
zip utilities, vs. tar, 254
ZipSlack distribution, 36, 499
    for emergency recovery, 224